W9-ADP-906

A COMPANION TO GREEK TRAGEDY

THIS BOOK IS PUBLISHED WITH THE ASSISTANCE OF THE
Dan Danciger Publication Fund

A
COMPANION
TO
GREEK
TRAGEDY

By John Ferguson

UNIVERSITY OF TEXAS PRESS, AUSTIN & LONDON

Library of Congress Cataloging in Publication Data

Ferguson, John, 1921–
    A companion to Greek tragedy

    Bibliography: p.
    1. Greek drama (Tragedy)—History and criticism.
2. Greek drama (Satyr play)— History and criticism.
I.   Title.
PA3131.F4   882'.01'09   74–38380
ISBN 0–292–71000–3

1-19-73

Composition and Printing by The University of Texas Printing Division, Austin
Binding by Universal Bookbindery, Inc., San Antonio

IN PIAM MEMORIAM

G. M.

QVI ME EVRIPIDIS AMORE INFLAMMAVIT

CONTENTS

V. AN ANONYMOUS TRAGEDY

VI. SATYRIC AND PRO-SATYRIC PLAYS

ILLUSTRATIONS

PREFACE

After a long period of only incidental contact with Greek tragedy, save in the theater, I found myself giving a course of lectures to nonclassical specialists in literature and drama at the University of Minnesota in 1966–1967. The following year, at the request of the graduate students in classics, I conducted a two-term seminar in Greek tragedy with an extended discussion of a different play each week. Much of what appears here is the fruit of those papers and discussions, and it is impossible to record my gratitude adequately for the detailed insights and general stimulus of those periods.

There is a wide interest in Greek tragedy, perhaps wider than ever before: witness the outstanding success of John Lewin's adaptation *The House of Atreus* at the Guthrie Theatre in Minneapolis, or the sensation caused by one of the lesser-known plays, *Iphigeneia at Aulis*, on Broadway. Further, since H. D. K. Kitto's seminal *Greek Tragedy*, much work has been done, especially in the United States, by Arrowsmith, Goheen, Knox, and Segal, to name the outstanding critics, and others. My debt to predecessors is marked and obvious, to Kitto on *The Oresteia*, to Knox on *King Oedipus*, to Murray on *The Women of Troy*, for instance. If in following their interpretation I have followed their language too closely, I apologize; vivid interpretation stays in the mind. I have avoided footnotes: the object of this Companion is to introduce readers to the plays, not to detail who said what about them. There is an extensive bibliography for scholars; it contains all the work I have found helpful, and a good deal of work that others have found helpful even though I have not. Quotations and references in the text are readily identifiable through the bibliography *ad loc*. It will not be difficult to find other commentaries that I might have known, ought to have known, and perhaps did know. Of books in English on the individual dramatists I regard Bowra's as the soundest guide to Sophocles and Grube's to Euripides. A book of comparable quality on Aeschylus is sadly lacking.

This Companion then tries to bring (a) a detailed awareness of the language, assonance, rhythms, and imagery of the plays (I have sought to present this meaningfully both to classicists and to Greekless readers); (b) a sense of the theater, reinforced by my own essays as actor and producer and by visits to Greek plays, in the original or in translation, and their modern adaptations, on all possible occasions, whether in England, Greece, Nigeria, or the United States; and (c) the social and political context of the plays, vital for an Athenian audience. Some of my own interpretations are inevitably controversial: I make no apology for this. I do not start from any preconceived theory of tragedy; the plays are scrutinized in their own light. As students may consult individual chapters, I have allowed slight, though not, I hope, excessive repetitiveness from one chapter to another.

After considerable thought I have decided to use my own translations of the Greek, with only one or two exceptions. I scrutinized other available versions, but different translators may try to bring out different points, and I needed versions that served my immediate purpose. I have tried to keep as close to the Greek as is compatible with a poetical version. I have borrowed occasional felicitous phrases from other translators (e.g. a master touch from William Arrowsmith at Eur. *Bacch.* 969). Anyone wishing to read the plays complete—and this book will have utterly failed if this does not happen—is recommended to the University of Chicago Press version edited by David Grene and Richmond Lattimore.

The basis of the Greek text is the Oxford Classical Text of each author, though I have occasionally diverged from this; for Sophocles's *The Trackers* I have used D. L. Page's text in the Loeb *Greek Literary Papyri*. Textual problems cannot be evaded, but I have not let them obtrude.

I have avoided Greek fonts and transliterated where necessary. Such transliterations cannot be satisfactory. Long vowels I have represented by the extension of the short vowel, which is what they were: o͡o or e͡e. It is nearly impossible and probably undesirable to be consistent in representing proper names in English. I hope the result is acceptable; it should perhaps be made clear that Hecabe is more familiarly Hecuba, Iocaste Jocasta, and Heracles Hercules.

I owe thanks to those who have read this work at different stages; they are not to be blamed for my eccentricities and errors: Miss Deborah Downing, Dr. Nesta Ferguson, Prof. Dennis Hurrell, Prof. Robert Sonkowsky, Miss Shirley Stewart. Special gratitude is due to Miss Connie Moss for the imagination to discern what lies behind my hieroglyphics and the skill to reduce them to a clarity of typescript, to Miss Lesley Roff for helping with the proofreading, and to my wife for her encouragement, her insights in discussion, and, not least, for undertaking the index.

JOHN FERGUSON

I

BACKGROUND

1. ORIGINS

The origins of Greek tragedy remain a matter of considerable controversy, and interpretations of the evidence are bound to be largely
speculative.

As a sophisticated art form it had its origin in or near the year 534
B.C. at Athens, when Thespis, of whom little is known, is said to have
won the prize of a goat in a competition. His originality lay in introducing an actor or "answerer" (*hypocrites*) who introduced the "play"
in a prologue, and delivered set speeches, either in the iambic or trochaic meter, which was felt to represent more reasonably speech
rhythms (Arist. *Poet.* 1449a25). Clearly it was the introduction of an
actor that made possible the invention of real drama. Equally clearly,
what went before was choral lyric and dancing, though that in itself
may have contained a strong dramatic element. Nietzsche, a shrewd
and original critic in his day, wrote in *The Birth of Tragedy* (p. 56):
"Thus we have come to interpret Greek tragedy as a Dionysiac chorus
which again and again discharges itself in Apollonian images. Those

choric portions with which the tragedy is interlaced constitute, as it were, the matrix of the *dialogue,* that is to say, of the entire stage-world of the actual drama." The general picture is confirmed by the strong lyric element in the early tragedian Phrynichus.

Tragedies were presented at the spring festival of Dionysus, and it is natural to look first at the choruses of Dionysus. These were called dithyrambs, and Aristotle explicitly says that tragedy developed out of them (*Poet.* 1449a10). Furthermore, the dithyrambic chorus numbered fifty, and there is some reason to believe that this was the original number in the tragic chorus, though it was later divided between the four plays that were presented together. On the other hand, there were differences. In all our notices dithyramb and tragedy appear as distinct from one another; if the one evolved from the other, one would expect a period of blurring; further, the arrangement of the dithyrambic chorus was circular, that of the tragic chorus rectangular, though, it is to be noticed, within a circular space. The authority of Sir Arthur Pickard-Cambridge has been weightily applied to reject a derivation from dithyramb. That tragedy was not exclusively derived from dithyramb seems certain; but it is equally certain that a development of choral lyric associated with Dionysus could not fail to be affected by dithyramb, and the rejection has been too decisive.

The issue has been complicated by Aristotle's apparent equation of the dithyramb with an early form of the satyr play, which in the early fifth century rounded off the performance of tragedy. Tragedy means "goat-song," and it has been suggested that it originated in a chorus of goat-tailed satyrs singing dithyrambs in honor of Dionysus. Aristotle has here blurred two elements in the tradition. There is no evidence that dithyrambs were ever performed by dancers in satyr costume, and a deal of evidence that they generally were not. But there were un-doubtedly mummers wearing different animal costumes in different parts of Greece. In Attica we know of horse costumes, but the evidence is not completely clear, as on the Pronomos vase we seem to have goat costumes with horse tails, and the dramatists refer to their satyr choruses as "goats" (Aesch. *fr.* 207; Soph. *Ichn.* 358).

But there is more than one possible interpretation of "goat song." The goat has ceased to be relevant to our economy. In West Africa

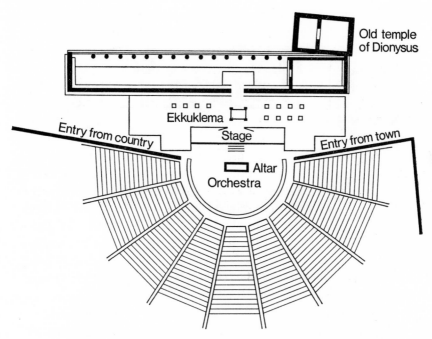

Figure 1. Ground plan of the theater of Dionysus at Athens

today, as in ancient Greece, the goat plays a far more important role. It is a scavenger and so helps, with the vulture, in the reduction of disease. It provides milk; it is, with the cock, the commonest animal for sacrifice; in classical times it was particularly sacrificed to Dionysus, as we know from several epigrams in the Greek Anthology that comment on the irony of the goat nibbling at the vine and being sacrificed to the god of the vine. It is also eaten; in fact the regular diet of the West African, like that of the ancient Greek, is largely vegetarian, and a sacrifice means a banquet including meat. In such an economy the goat is neither contemptible nor comic, and John Pepper Clark, a young Nigerian poet of great promise, centered his first play upon the sacrifice of a goat and actually entitled it *Song of a Goat*. Admittedly, Clark is sophisticated; he knows the literal meaning of "tragedy," and chose his title accordingly, but it spoke to his situation as it spoke to the Greeks.

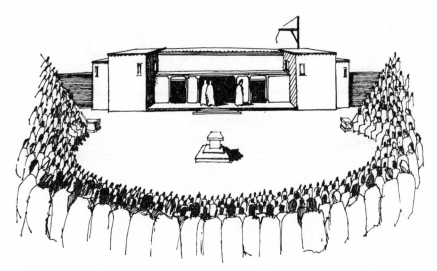

Figure 2. Possible reconstruction of the theater of Dionysus at Athens,
showing an opening scene before the entry of the chorus

The association of the goat with Dionysus is important. Dionysus is
the power that throbs through animal life, through all life, the power
of nature in the raw. He shows himself through wine, which liberates
the spirit from its inhibitions. In *The Bacchants* he appears in the form
of a bull, and it is a calf that his worshippers rend limb from limb and
devour, consuming the god in a sacred meal. Often their victim would
be a hare or deer. The goat is another, tamer, more controlled manifestation. It is natural then to find acolytes dressed as animals; but it is
also natural that a goat should be the prize for the victor in the *agon*
or contest at a festival of Dionysus, and that the goat should be sacrificed and eaten. In other words the goat may appear at more than one
point in the worship of Dionysus, and the name "tragedy" does not
compel us to postulate the origin of Attic tragedy in the broad buffoonery of goat-costumed mummers. We are in fact explicitly told in
the *Suda* that the satyr play was introduced by Pratinas, a man from
Phlius, about 500 B.C. It belongs to another strand of development,
and was added as a tail-piece to a set of three tragedies. The attempt to
derive tragedy from the satyr play is the most illusory of all theories.

In Jane Harrison's *Themis*, Gilbert Murray worked out a theory of origin on the assumption that Dionysus was a Year Spirit (*eniautos daemon*), a vegetation god like Adonis or Osiris, who represents the cyclic death and rebirth of the Earth and the World. Murray would thus make the origins of comedy and tragedy parallel aspects of the drama of the Year Spirit, comedy leading to the marriage feast and its associated reveling, tragedy to the death and its associated lamentation. The general pattern of thought is that the Spirit of the Old Year is killed by usurping Winter and resurrected in the Spirit of the New Year, which comes as an avenger; it underlies the myths of Orestes and Hamlet alike. The theory has considerable merits. Tragedy was performed at a spring festival, and it is easy for an urban society to forget what that means to a people whose roots lie deep in the unpaved soil. Further, allusions to fertility ritual do from time to time leap from the scene. There is a particularly striking example in *Agamemnon*, when Clytemnestra describes how she killed him:

> He fell, and gasped out his life,
> panted out a sharp jet of blood,
> spattered me with dark drops of crimson rain,
> while I exulted as the sown field rejoices
> in the heaven-sent shower at the birthtime of the buds. (1388)

The theory also helps to explain the parts of tragedy: the contest (*agon*), the sacrificial death, the messenger's speech, the lamentation, the recognition scene, the theophany. But as a comprehensive theory it will not do and it has not won acceptance. Orestes is not Dionysus, and, whether or not he was in origin a New Year Spirit, he was not that in the late sixth or fifth century. Still, we must not dismiss this pattern of thought altogether; it was inescapable at a spring festival. It remains one strand in the pattern.

Another key lies in the masks. In West Africa today there is a living tradition of masked dance-drama. The masks represent ancestors, not so much individuals, as the undifferentiated power of the ancestors. The masquerader must be covered from head to foot; no part of his body must show through to break the spell. Sometimes the masks are totemic. Such masquerades are a commonplace of ancestral festivals over most of the world. Yet there is no record of a masquerade in association with the spring festival of the ancestors at Athens, the Anthesteria. It is hard to believe that none existed. The most plausible explanation is that it has become transferred to the festival of Dionysus. There is an exceptionally interesting parallel in Herodotus (5.67), who tells us that at Sicyon there used to be "tragic dances" in honor of the hero Adrastus, but the dictator Cleisthenes transferred these to the service of Dionysus. The tragedies range widely over the field of mythology but they are usually linked with the ancestors, with the semidivine legendary figures of the heroic age. These heroic figures are however by no means exclusive to Athens, though in some of the tragedies we know the legendary kings, Aegeus and Theseus especially, and Demophon, play an important role as a unifying factor. But we are dealing with streams from all over Greece. The concept of the ancestors is important in another way, as West Africa may again remind us. The ancestors are buried in the soil, and the fertility of the soil is their special care. Sir William Ridgeway went further and derived tragedy from rites at the tombs of heroes. For this there is little evidence; this is another view which has not found acceptance. But the use of masks and elaborate costumes are ineluctably linked to the ancestors. Even the word *hypokrinesthai* (from which *hypocrites* "actor" is derived) in its earliest usage is connected with the spirit world and means to "interpret" dreams and other signs from beyond (e.g., Hom. *Od.* 19.535).

A further factor should not be neglected. Sometime during the seventh century, Athens had taken over responsibility for the Mysteries at Eleusis. It seems certain that in the celebration of the Mysteries there was a pageant of the sacred drama, the rape of Persephone or Kore ("the Maiden") by Pluto, the god of the underworld, of death and also of wealth, the lamentation of Demeter, the Earth-Mother or Corn-Mother, for her lost daughter, and the tale of her wanderings, and the final reunion of the goddesses. It should be noted that this story too contains lamentation and recognition. It is a fertility myth, apparently connected with the burial of the seed corn. It is also a message of life beyond death for the initiate. The Mysteries were a secret not to be revealed. But an initiate, seeking to develop public drama, could not fail to recall the principal drama he knew, and devise something parallel. It is significant that Aeschylus, who came from Eleusis, was actually accused of profaning the Mysteries. Furthermore the worship at Eleusis was linked to Dionysus through the mystic child Iacchus, who was identified with the god.

There is another point of some importance. It has often been noticed that women play a much more prominent part in Athenian tragedy than in Athenian society, and the usual explanation is, rightly, that the tragedies reflect the heroic age of legend, not the fifth century. But there is another possible explanation; writers used to the drama of Eleusis with Demeter and Persephone would be likely to give to women a prominent part in their plays. Eleusis does not explain the origin of Greek tragedy. But once lyric had moved in the direction of drama it helped to shape it.

There are other factors outside Attica; the language of tragedy, with its many Doric forms, especially though not solely in lyric passages, suggests that developments outside Athens were important in the formative stages. Important names, though they are little more, are Arion of Corinth and Epigenes of Sicyon. Arion was evidently responsible for some of the musical developments associated with tragedy; what Solon meant by describing him as the first composer of tragic drama is a matter for speculation. Epigenes, according to the *Suda*, introduced into the worship of Dionysus matters that had nothing to do with the god. This suggests a flexibility of myth for song and dance (an important innovation) but in itself nothing dramatic. At the same time the polymath Pollux (4.123) suggests that Thespis was not wholly original in introducing an actor, referring to performances before the time of Thespis when someone climbed onto a table and "answered" the chorus. Thespis was perhaps systematizing earlier improvisations.

No single explanation fits all the facts. We may imagine in the seventh and sixth centuries choruses engaging in song and dance on different occasions in different parts of Greece. At ancestral festivals they were probably masked *cap-à-pie*. Others were dressed as animals or mumming in different veins. Some were associated with the god Dionysus; some of these wore animal costumes, some did not. There was a strong fertility element in their ritual. Sometimes their song was linked with the epic stories, but the sing-song recitative of the bard was replaced by full song, and his rhetorical gestures by full mime. Gradually Dionysus's spring festival increased in popularity so that he began to usurp some of the other performances. In some such way the stage was set for Thespis.

Fascinating as these speculations on origins undoubtedly are, it is the end product that matters. As Max Pohlenz put it, tribal rites occur elsewhere, but tragic drama is found only in ancient Greece; he might have been more specific and said "only in ancient Athens." In other words, after all the religious ritual, the traditions of song and dance, come certain social conditions that encourage something new and great to develop. In this development there are three key dates. The first is 534, the original prize performance by Thespis; the second is 501 or 500, when the pattern of the tetralogy (three tragedies followed by a satyr play) was established; the third is 458, the date of *The Oresteia*, the culmination of fifteen years which saw all Aeschylus's surviving plays except the slightly later *Prometheus*. All take their place along-side important political events. In the middle of the sixth century the dictator Pisistratus, who, though himself a baron, was something of a popular champion against the other barons, put Athens on the map, modernized her, and made her a cultural center; the inauguration of tragedy was part of that process. The second date, 501, lies close to the constitutional reforms of Cleisthenes, which established democracy (meaning direct government by adult male citizens) at Athens. The third belongs to the great period of Athenian upsurge, when she had taken the initiative in liberating the Greek cities of coastal Asia from the Persians and her ships were scouring the Mediterranean and far into the Black Sea, the period too of the final breaking of the power of the barons when the old aristocratic council of the Areopagus was stripped of its political power and left with honorific and religio-legal functions only. In other words, we are dealing with an age of expansion, of experiment, of readiness for things new.

But there is another side to this. Tragedy deals with conflict, and experiment means conflict; the soaring certainties often overlie a deep spiritual uncertainty. The old culture was tribal, shamanistic, firmly structured; you knew where you were. The new democracy was ex-perimental, exciting, challenging, and nobody knew what would hap-pen next; it is exactly this which troubles the critics of the democracy. Alongside this process and associated with it, though already incipient somewhat earlier, is the change from a shame culture to a guilt culture, with its greater degree of introspection and introversion, its disposition to wrestle with moral problems, and its replacement of sympathy by empathy. Without some such social change tragedy could not arise, for there would be no audience for it. Yet the social change itself would not be enough were it not that there were some geniuses ready to seize the moment. When all honor has been paid to Thespis for his innovations, to the shadowy figures of Choerilus and Pratinas, to the evident lyrical talents of Phrynichus, that genius was found in Aeschy-lus. And when all has been said about the later poets whose work has not survived—and how much would we give for a winning play by Ion of Chios or Agathon—the verdict of posterity is probably just, and Aeschylus, Sophocles, and Euripides tower above their contemporaries. That one small city—the population of Attica could hardly have ex-ceeded 350,000—should have produced three such playwrights within a century remains one of the more breathtaking facts of history.

2. THE AUDIENCE AND THE THEATER

People meeting in hilly country will seek an open space where the slope allows some terracing of the seats and the curve of the hill draws the people round a focal point. The political assembly at Athens was of this kind, toward the top of the hill called Pnyx, on a lightly sloping expanse of rock exposed to the north. At some point the bitter winds led to a reversal of direction; earth was dumped in to provide an elevation at the northern end and thus some shelter, and a slope downward to where the speaker's platform (*bema*) was cut out of a rocky terrace. The pattern is closely similar to that of a theater, and it should not be forgotten that in democratic Athens the audience in the theater was the members of the political assembly met together, though for this occasion women were also present. Still, the political atmosphere was inescapable; politics for this audience was not a remote professionalism, but their breath of life, and we are right to seek the political context of any play, whether tragedy or comedy.

As the political assembly was volatile, so the audience in the theater was volatile, and emotional participation was enormous. We must not imagine a staid northern audience politely clapping, but a swift readiness for tears and laughter, approbation and disapproval. Approval was expressed by shouts, clapping and cries of encore (*authis*), disapproval by hissing, kicking the benches, and throwing fruit at the performers; spectators who were merely bored ate their fruit more vigorously, as Aristotle tells us (*NE* 1175 b). The audience was exceedingly knowledgeable, as the parodies by Aristophanes remind us; they were unpredictable, and Phrynichus got into trouble for reminding them of political disaster. They were highly critical, and an actor who mispronounced a word was howled down. Those who claim that there is no humor in Greek tragedy have not appreciated the nature of the audience; there are many scenes where they would have been roaring with laughter, since for such an audience laughter is a relief from tension far beyond what we normally understand by comic relief. Admission was open at a small fee, which was paid out of public funds for those who could not afford it; the disc that served as a ticket gave admission to a particular block of seats. The front seats were reserved for particular dignitaries, the seat of honor being assigned to the priest of Dionysus, at whose festival the plays were performed.

The theater of Dionysus at Athens stands on the south side of the Acropolis. Before that, plays were performed in the *agora* or city center, but the wooden benches collapsed during a play by Pratinas, and it seems likely that this was the reason for the new theater, which was inaugurated early in the fifth century B.C. All the plays of which we have any detailed knowledge were presented in this theater. The center of the theater was the *orchestra*, a great dancing floor sixty feet in diameter with the altar of Dionysus in the center. At the south end stood the stage building, which served as backcloth and greenroom. To north, west, and east of the orchestra rose the stone tiers of seats, holding in all some fourteen thousand people. It was thus some sixty feet from the stage building to the front row of spectators, three hundred to the back. There was no difficulty about audibility; even today in the absence of the stage building, the acoustics of Greek theaters are miraculous.

Of the theater as it was first erected we know little. Shortly after the middle of the fifth century alterations were made on which archaeology permits us to comment. There is evidence from this period of a stage building with some degree of permanence, with wings framing the stage area, and it is reasonable so to imagine the theater that saw the later plays of Sophocles and most of those of Euripides. The evidence about an actual stage is controversial. A high stage is out of the question; that came later when the chorus had become wholly divorced from the action. The archaeological evidence is negative; there is no trace of a stage from this period. In fact the overwhelming weight of evidence points to a low stage, and it will be useful to outline this:

1. "The only surviving picture of audience and actor in Attic comedy shows a low stage reached by a flight of four steps." (T. B. L. Webster *Greek Theatre Production*, p. 7). It is most unlikely that this was inserted for a particular play, or for comedy and not tragedy. The date is about 420 B.C.

2. Certain scenes seem to require the appearance of a ghost from the underworld; at the end of *Prometheus* it seems that the actor disappears into the ground.

3. Some admittedly late statements say that Aeschylus had a platform, though others contradict this.

4. Without a stage, entries from the stage building would be obscured for the reserved seats by the chorus.

5. The psychology of the chorus is important. It does seem as if there is a symbolic barrier that holds them away from the stage building; only rarely do they enter from it (*Libation Bearers*) or go into it (*Helen*), and the scene in *Medea* when they hammer at the barred doors is more effective because it is unusual. In *Oedipus at Colonus* they are decidedly apart from the action; in *Hippolytus*, when Phaedra listens at the door, the chorus do not, because they are at a lower level.

6. Actors seem to go *up* into the stage area (e.g. Eur. *Ion* 727; *El.* 489).

7. There are certain scenes of which it is not extravagant to say that if there were no stage it would be necessary to invent one. Notable is the entry of Agamemnon in *Agamemnon*, where Clytemnestra must appear at a higher level than Agamemnon's chariot, and the power of

Agamemnon's entry on the purple carpet would certainly be enhanced if it involved climbing even a few steps.

8. In early times it seems that the actor stood on a table or cart, and it is likely that some elevation of the actors would continue in a permanent theater.

The evidence is to me fully persuasive. In the theater of the last part of the fifth century there were forty-five feet between the wings; this was later increased to sixty. On the basis of the foundations, however, it has been suggested that there may have been a stage about twenty-six feet long and nine feet deep. It should be stressed that we are not to think of the stage as in the proscenium-arch theater, as a kind of isolated sanctum. The actors regularly entered on the level of the orchestra, by convention from stage-left, meaning from the city, and from stage-right, from the country. Some processional entries no doubt marched round the orchestra, and in studying individual plays I shall suggest that in certain scenes the actors were in the orchestra.

The stage building seems to have been about twelve feet deep, and to have consisted of two stories. On the top, divinities appeared; in later times there was certainly a platform for these appearances, called *theologeion*; I see no reason to doubt that this went back to the fifth century. A particularly dramatic example took place in Aeschylus's lost *The Weighing of the Souls*. There are examples of humans appearing at some elevated level, like the watchman in *Agamemnon* or the old man and Antigone in *The Women of Phoenicia*. There is some evidence that this took place at the level of the upper story, where there may have been a balcony, called *distegia*, which was used for comically unexpected effect in *The Acharnians*. It is possible that the watchman may have appeared on the roof of the older theater building; this would accord with his words. But the effect may have been contrived by a painted backcloth above the *distegia*, as suggested later. It should be remembered that the large majority of the audience was looking down on the roof of the stage building, and those who were below that level were far enough away to have a good view of an actor standing forward. All movements on the roof would be visible to the audience unless concealed by a parapet and an overhang.

Another device associated with the roof was a powerful crane (*mechane*, Latin *machina*). This was used to present divine or semi-divine beings in motion through the sky. The familiar *deus ex machina* is in fact often a misnomer for *deus ex theologeio*. The visibility of the roof to the audience makes it certain that the actor was lifted from behind the stage building to the appropriate height before being swung round to the front, and sometimes lowered onto the stage. The movement took a little time, and is invariably covered by a few lines of dialogue. The carriage might be variously represented. Oceanus in *Prometheus* is riding on a griffin; in Aristophanes's *The Clouds* Socrates enters in a basket rather like the car of a balloon; Medea leaves in a golden car drawn by winged horses; in the lost *Bellerophon* the hero was riding on Pegasus; in *Andromeda* Perseus was flying free, Peter Pan. One of the most spectacular uses of the crane was in *The Weighing of the Souls* when Dawn used it to transport the body of her son Memnon in her arms to the sky. The entry of the chorus in *Prometheus* and its parody in *The Clouds* are more controversial, but I am firmly convinced that the engineering equipment of the men who lowered the blocks of the Propylaea into place was fully up to the control of a car with several people in it, and that the entry of the chorus in these plays was from the crane, and spectacularly brilliant too.

One other device associated with the stage building must be mentioned. This is the *ekkuklema* or moving platform. The stage building had central doors perhaps twelve feet wide; tragedy requires no other doors, though comedy may. These central doors might open to display the spectacle within. Some scholars have argued that the device of the moving platform belongs to the Hellenistic age, others have seen in it a kind of revolving stage. It is most likely that it was a platform on wheels, perhaps running in grooves to bring a tableau from inside the building out into the light and view of the spectators, and though there is no firm evidence of its use in fifth-century tragedy, the scene in *The Acharnians* where Euripides is rolled out seems to be a parody of Euripides's own experimental uses of stage devices, and the visibility and audibility of the actors would certainly be greatly enhanced; it is needed in *Ajax* and *Heracles*, to name but two examples.

Scenery was on the whole simple. The stage building represented a palace or temple, sometimes a hut or tent. It is difficult to see how this can have been seriously altered from one play to the next, so details must have been conveyed by simple accoutrements, statues or altars. We may perhaps imagine some straw strewn on the stage for the peasant's hut in Euripides's *Electra*, and leather flaps over the doorway when it represents a tent. We are told by Aristotle that Sophocles introduced the science of scene painting, by Vitruvius that Agatharchus of Samos made a scene for a production of Aeschylus's. The careers of Aeschylus and Sophocles overlapped, so that the two statements are not contradictory, but Agatharchus's treatment of perspective, from what we know of it, does not appear in art before the late fifth century, and it is better to associate his work with a posthumous revival of Aeschylus. It does not seem likely that Aeschylus, a master of spectacle, was without scenic effects altogether, and the scene painting that Sophocles introduced may have been the prospect of distant views. Such a backcloth could perhaps be hung over the top of the stage building. In this way the *distegia* would be the roof of the stage building as represented for dramatic purposes, while the gods would appear in the sky. It should be remembered that the majority of the audience would be looking down, and a distant prospect above the palace or house would not seem unnatural. Painted screens at the sides are also possible; they could easily be changed. Later, revolving triangular structures at the sides were used to denote changes of scene, but there is no evidence for these *periaktoi* in the fifth century.

Much of the scenery must have been imagined; the word pictures are not descriptive of what the audience was actually seeing but conjuring up a scene for them to see with the mind's eye. Some scenic effects there must have been, a great rock in *Prometheus*, some bushes in *Ajax*, as well as tombs, statues, and altars, but on the whole we are to think (so to say) in Elizabethan rather than Victorian terms. The audience accepted the convention of scene shifting between two plays of a sequence. There is no evidence of scene shifting during a single play. Only three extant tragedies require a definite change of scene; in others, like *The Persians* or *The Libation Bearers*, there is rather a foreshortening of space than an actual change. The three are *The Kindly Goddesses*, *Ajax*, and *Hecabe*; in the first two I have suggested in treating each play how the change of scene was produced. In *Hecabe* the actual setting is vague, but a voyage from the Troad to Thrace is covered by a choral song.

Some highly spectacular effects there were; to an audience not used to dramatic realism, simple devices would be sufficiently startling. A thunder machine creates no problem; it would be used to herald certain divine apparitions, and was essential to the end of *Prometheus.* Some scenes call for fire; it seems probable that this was visibly suggested by the provision of smoke. The four most spectacular plays are *Prometheus*, with a variety of exotic effects and a conclusion that would be obviously enhanced by noise and smoke; *The Women of Troy*, where the last scene needs to be played against the crash of falling buildings and the smoke of the burning city; *Heracles*, where the visible appearance of Iris and Madness was accompanied by an earthquake, though the effect here might be audible rather than visible; *The Bacchants*, with its "palace miracle," in which again noise and smoke are needed. To deny such spectacular effects is perverse; it is to treat the plays as texts to be conned in the study, not presentations in the theater. Even Aristotle isolated visual effects as one of the six ingredients of tragedy (1449b32).

Even in broad daylight torches might be magnificently powerful. A splendid effect is created in *The Women of Troy* when the gleam of fire is seen within the stage building, and Cassandra emerges with lighted torches; the scene suggests that it must have been deep shadow inside and is a small added pointer to the use of the moving platform in the fifth century to bring tableaux into view. The torch procession at the end of *The Kindly Goddesses* is another fine spectacle. In general, there were no lighting effects, and it was impossible to produce any realistic representation of night. But the plays began early enough on a spring morning for the first scene of the first play to represent the transition from night to day without difficulty. This is well used in *Agamemnon*; other plays which we may reasonably suppose were for this reason first of their sequence include *Antigone*, Euripides's *Electra*, and *Iphigeneia at Aulis*. In the last play a lighted lamp emphasized the point. In *Rhesus* the whole play is set at night; this was emphasized by the use of lighted torches.

The Greek word for actor, *hypocrites* (which gives the word "hypocrite"), means "answerer"; his original function is thus seen in dialogue with the chorus. Aeschylus raised the number from one to two, Sophocles from two to three, and *Oedipus at Colonus* requires four. Even when three actors were the rule, the dramatists preferred to present their scenes as a series of confrontations between two characters. *Prometheus*, *King Oedipus*, and *Hippolytus* make effective use of the temporary silence of the third. The rôles were not however limited to the number of actors, one actor might double in several rôles. This was made easier by the fact that the actors were masked, and a quick change of rôle was readily possible.

The mask was assuredly a relic of the representation of the divine ancestor in the ritual dances that preceded drama proper. Such masks, as we have seen, were often undifferentiated, and the statement that Choerilus (or Thespis) invented or introduced the mask will simply mean that he invented the type of character mask familiar in the fifth century. The size of the theater did not allow facial expression to communicate itself to the audience, and a mask with exaggerated features had the merit of distinctive visibility. The actors were all men—with the social position of women at Athens it could hardly be otherwise—and the mask made characterization easier. Some of the masks were startling: Aeschylus in particular liked broad effects, and the swarthy chorus of *The Suppliant Women* was almost as shocking as the grotesque masks of the Furies in *The Kindly Goddesses*. Occasionally an actor changed his mask in the course of a single rôle; this must have happened with the blinding of Oedipus and of Polymestor, not to mention the Cyclops. Those who have watched masked productions swiftly accept the absence of varied facial expression; the added hieratic quality is more appropriate to Aeschylus and Sophocles than to Euripides. The masks were crowned with high wigs giving the actor added stature. It is a common illusion that the boot did the same, but this was not true till later. The fifth-century actor wore a loose-fitting, thick-soled buskin that fastened high up on the leg; the boot could be worn on either foot, and a cross-carpeting politician was nicknamed "Buskin." Robes were long, flowing, and colorful; tradition said that their cut was based on the priests' robes at Eleusis (yet another indication that the origin of tragedy was complex and not to be divorced

from fertility ritual). Some characters were instantly identifiable by
their costume and equipment, as Heracles by his lion skin and club,
or Athene by her helmet and aegis. Aeschylus was noted for vivid
costumes. Later, dress became more realistic, and Euripides was twitted
for his beggars in rags.

Acting was a skilled profession, and the actor was expected to be at
the peak of physical fitness. Gestures would have been broad and
sweeping; the Noel Coward creation of character by knocking off the
ash of a cigarette was impossible in the Greek theater. The actor had
to be a singer and dancer; he also had to be a master of oratory; in
Greek tragedy the characters generally either engage in brisk backchat
(*stichomythia*) or deliver elaborate speeches. The Greek stage had its
male prima donnas; we read of petty jealousies, of an actor (Theodorus) always wanting the first words of a play, of another complain-
ing that he had too few attendants in his rôle of king. The chief actor,
or protagonist, was chosen first, and he chose his colleagues. In addition to the main actors, extras were introduced for nonspeaking
parts; Aeschylus exploits this powerfully in *The Libation Bearers*,
when the apparently unspeaking Pylades suddenly speaks. In Sophocles's *Ajax* an extra takes over the part of Tecmessa, who does not
speak in the final scene, to release the actor for Menelaus or Agamemnon. There are many plays that require attendants, soldiers, and the
like; one or two demand a whole crowd of extras, as in the opening
spectacle of *King Oedipus*.

The center of the play was originally the chorus, and in Aeschylus's
archaizing *The Suppliant Women* we can see the type of plot this involved. But in Aeschylus attention was already diverted from chorus to
actors in the main plot of the play. It is a curious aberration which, on
the basis of a statement by Aristotle (1456a26), blames this on Euripides. Nietzsche pointed out that Sophocles does not venture to make
the chorus central to the action but assigns to it the rôle of detached
spectator, and indeed the chorus is a far more integral part of the drama
in *Medea*, *The Women of Troy*, and *The Bacchants*, to name but three,
than in most of Sophocles. Once the chorus enters, it is on the scene all
the time, with rare exceptions. In *The Kindly Goddesses* and *Ajax*
its absence marks a change of scene, and in the latter it makes possible

Ajax's soliloquy; in *Helen* the chorus is also briefly absent. Its presence on the scene inevitably seems artificial, and some of its conventional comments are little short of fatuous; there is a glaring example in *Antigone* (724). Horace (*A.P.* 193) summarizes the duties of the chorus: it must make relevant comments, support the "good guys," praise moderation and justice, and keep secrets. This last is dramatically most difficult, and oaths of secrecy have sometimes to be applied.

More important is the music and dancing. It must never be forgotten that Greek tragedy is much more closely akin to opera and ballet than it is to modern plays, but we lack the music and choreography. We do not evaluate the libretto of *The Magic Flute*, or, for that matter, *Iolanthe*, by the critical standards apposite to Shakespeare; yet much of Greek tragedy is libretto without music. The music was simple. The singing was in unison or solo, and the accompaniment was provided by a single recorder. We do not hear of percussive instruments, which are the natural accompaniment to dancing, save for a special effect such as the tambourines in *The Bacchants*, but the words used of the playing of the pipe (e.g. *otobos*) suggest a staccato, percussive, rhythmical use. There was also occasionally a small harp or lyre. The chorus was, as we have seen, originally fifty in number, then the fifty was divided between the four plays, twelve to each, and this number was later raised by Sophocles to fifteen. It will be observed that this gives dance patterns of 3x4 and 3x5. I have argued that in *The Suppliant Women* Aeschylus reverted, because of the myth, to a chorus of fifty and correspondingly archaic treatment. The chorus wore identical masks and costumes, though the leader and spokesman (*coryphaeus*) may have been marked out.

Of the actual dancing little is known for certain. The members of the chorus had each a definite position in the orchestra; the terms defining these were borrowed from military strategy, and one movement was a marching movement in rectangular formation. Choral lyric is patterned in a strophe followed by an antistrophe in identical rhythm (though not, in view of the pitch accent of Greek, with identical melody). In view of the explicit statement of a scholiast on Euripides's *Hecabe* (647), we may take it as certain, despite the scepticism of some scholars, that during the strophe the chorus moved round the circular orchestra to the right, during the antistrophe to the left, and during the epode stood still. We know from Hesychius of lines on the floor of the orchestra, like our chalk marks, to guide position and movement. There is a puzzling account of dance in Plutarch (*Mor.* 747B), written in his study centuries after the event. He identifies *phora*, movement and step, *schema*, pose and gesture, and *deixis*, interpretation. We have some miscellaneous evidence about these. We know for example of movements such as "walking past the four," perhaps with five rows of three dancers moving so that those from the front now pass to the back or vice versa, and "the double dance" no doubt with two half-choruses facing and matching one another. We know of gestures such as "the flat hand," a slapping movement to indicate joy, sorrow or anger, and "the snub-nosed hand," tensed and bent away and used in many different connotations. We know of dancing with staffs, which I have seen used with great power in *Oedipus at Colonus* at Bradfield School. We know of the energetic "fire-tongs" with leaps involving the quick crossing of the feet just as a modern ballet dancer does; of the miming of ball games; of acrobatic dances; of spectacular splits; of rhythms associated with rowing and (almost certainly) with flying; we know of dances of joy and sorrow, victory and defeat; we know of processional dances, usually in the anapaestic rhythm (i.e. 4/4 time). *The Bacchants* is in many ways unique; *ionicus a minore* (♩♩♩♩) predominates in many passages. The dances were wild and authentically Bacchic, miming the joys of the chase; the tambourine was used in accompaniment; and there was a superb solo dance for Agave.

The Bacchants reminds us that the plays were presented as part of a religious festival in honor of Dionysus. This was the Great Dionysia or City Dionysia. It fell in the month of Elaphebolion, overlapping our March and April, and lasted from the 9th to the 13th, with a day of preparation before. This was a spring festival, and the old wooden statue of the god was ceremonially carried round to celebrate the release from winter; the fertility element was strong, and phalluses were carried in the procession. There was sacrifice offered in the temple, and after the theater was established, the statue was carried in by torchlight so that the god might be present at the plays. We must think of a holiday that has not wholly lost its sense of holy day; yet we must not think of the atmosphere of a church, for that type of solemnity was alien.

Dramatists wishing to present plays at this festival applied to the magistrate for a chorus. The magistrate selected the three he deemed most meritorious. The chorus was paid for by a wealthy citizen who took the title of *choregus*, as a public duty or "liturgy"; he could nominate an alternate if he could prove that the other could afford it better. Prestige attached to success in the festival, and many citizens were generous in their outlay and proud of the outcome. By the end of the fifth century, war taxes were weighing on the rich, and the liturgy was shared. The actors were paid out of state funds.

Each dramatist submitted a set of four plays, generally called a "tetralogy." Three of these were tragedies; the fourth a rollicking farce with a strong fertility element and a chorus of satyrs with horses' tails and prominent phalluses. Euripides perhaps invented the substitution of a melodrama without satyrs for the fourth play. The dramatic festival lasted for three days. In early times the three tragedies were connected episodes in a single myth, and where they are so connected, they are usually termed a "trilogy." Only one trilogy survives complete, Aeschylus's *Oresteia*, but we know of many others. We are told that Sophocles abandoned the trilogy for a group of individual plays treating different myths. What we cannot discern for sure is whether there was any other principle of unity between the plays that were presented together. Euripides's plays of 415 all belong to the Trojan cycle; they also seem to show in different contexts sympathy with the underdog. It is tempting to suppose that *Heracles* and *Ion*, both with the theme of divine parentage, were presented together, and that Euripides may in 413 have presented a series of plays that depend on recognition.

The relation of the satyr play to its tragedies is likewise a matter of some dispute. It appears likely that the satyr play may have offered a comic treatment of some episode or episodes connected with the main series of plays. Thus the Orestes trilogy was completed by a satyr play, *Proteus*, which dealt with the return of Agamemnon's brother "eagle" Menelaus; the Oedipus trilogy of Aeschylus was completed by *The Sphinx*. It is tempting to associate Sophocles's satyr play *The Trackers* with *Ajax*, where cattle are likewise tracked, and Euripides's *The Cyclops* with his *Hecabe*, though it would also fit with *Iphigeneia among the Taurians*.

The plots were in general familiar to the audience, and the comic dramatist Antiphanes complains how inventive he has to be compared with writers of tragedy:

> Lucky in every way, the tragic poet!
> Take first the plot. The audience already know it
> before a line's declaimed. Just a reminding,
> that's all. Say "Oedipus-" and they know the lot,
> dad, mum and the kids, the killing and blinding.
> "Alcmaeon," and the schoolboys on the spot
> recite "Killed his mother. Crazy in the brain.
> Adrastus will be in, and off again." (*fr.* 191)

This familiarity meant that originality lay in interpretations and treatment, and the variation possible is readily seen by comparing the three plays on the killing of Clytemnestra and Aegisthus by Orestes and Electra, or reading Dio of Prusa's lecture-essay (52) on the three Philoctetes plays, or even contrasting what we know of Euripides's two essays on *Hippolytus*. It also allowed for vastly enhanced possibilities of dramatic irony. Of course there was at all times plenty of scope for invention among the incidents and the minor characters. Euripides in particular allowed invention to play an increasing role in his tragedies, thereby creating a new kind of romantic melodrama, but even he never invented his central characters, and it was left to Agathon to invent both plot and characters, like a modern novelist, in his *Antheus*.

The prize was awarded by a panel of ten judges chosen by lot. We are told that the verdict was given by selecting five of the verdicts at random. It is not clear how adjustment was made if the voting was two for A, two for B, and one for C: presumably by drawing another verdict, and a seventh if need be. Nor is it clear how the second place was awarded. It is often said that *King Oedipus*, for example, or *Medea* did not receive first prize, and this has been used to point the moral of the fallibility of human judges. The statement is misleading; what did not receive first prize was the set of plays by Sophocles which included *King Oedipus*, as presented at Athens on a given date. No doubt the quality of acting, stage direction, music, choreography, and dancing all influenced the judges' verdict. It is likely too that the satyr play, being the last of the sequence, influenced the decision disproportionately. Aeschylus was a noted writer of satyr plays. It is however just to say that Sophocles, who was not, is recorded as winning twenty-four prizes.

II

THE TRAGEDIES OF AESCHYLUS

3. AESCHYLUS

At the beginning of the sixth century Athens had shown little promise of her coming greatness. Attica was, it seems, something of a backwater, and the comings and goings of tribes elsewhere in Greece passed them by. Apart from the glorious geometric pottery of the ninth and eighth century there is little to record. Monarchy had been replaced by aristocracy, and the barons retained their political power intact into the sixth century. In addition, they held the country in an economic half-nelson. The gap between the haves and the have-nots grew; the peasants were reduced to serfdom or even slavery. Troubles stirred and exploded. The early years of the sixth century saw the reforms of Solon. Economically their effects were lasting. He ended serfdom and laid the foundations of commercial and industrial prosperity at Athens. Politically he left room for the breakthrough toward democracy by replacing an oligarchy of birth with an oligarchy of wealth. It could have made little immediate difference; it was pregnant with the future.

For the time the political troubles continued till Pisistratus finally established his position as tyrant or dictator about 545. Pisistratus, although an aristocrat himself, in attaining and maintaining his own power broke the power of the aristocrats. He had the support of the small rural landowners and of the new urban proletariat, whom he encouraged by public works; he also adroitly kept them apart. Of equal importance to his political and economic settlement was his success in developing Athens as a center of art and literature.

Now came the great flowering of genius in black-figure vase painting, and, about the time of his death, the experimental transition to red-figure. The emergence of tragedy as an art form coincided with a period of supreme skill in painting; and this reminds us that drama is always to be visually conceived. Now too came the recension of the Homeric poems and the building of a literary court that was to attract men like Simonides and Anacreon.

Two years after the death of Pisistratus, in 525, Aeschylus was born. He grew up among fresh troubles. Pisistratus's sons, Hippias and Hipparchus, lacked their father's political skill, though they continued his policy of fostering literature and music, painting, sculpture, and architecture. Aeschylus was eleven when Hipparchus was assassinated for private reasons by men who later achieved an unmerited reputation as liberators and revolutionaries. Hippias tightened his security measures, but four years later he was driven out. Athens was now prey to party politics. Out of conflict an aristocrat named Cleisthenes, a political genius of the first order, emerged dominant and established a constitution in which he broke the power of the clan or extended family, placed ultimate authority in the Assembly of the citizens (which consisted of all adult males except aliens, who included the slaves), and greatly extended the principle of representative government. The result was a radical democracy, though for the moment the leadership in the senior magistracies, the armed forces, and the initiative in the Assembly might be expected to remain with the upper classes. Aeschylus was too young to touch these events, but old enough to be absorbed in them.

The excitement of internal politics was soon replaced by external peril. At the very period when Pisistratus was establishing his power at Athens, Cyrus was establishing his power in Persia and extending the power of Persia to include Asia Minor and Mesopotamia. By 521, after a period of anarchy, Darius was on the throne, and two years later was able to begin his administrative reforms. An expedition into Europe in 512 may have caused some trepidation in Greece, but for the moment his ambitions were confined to Thrace. Then in 499 Miletus and some of the other Greek cities of Asia Minor, dissatisfied with a paternalism, however benevolent, which denied them their autonomy, revolted. They applied for help to mainland Greece. Athens and Eretria alone sent support. The rebellion was unexpected; Sardis was sacked and burnt, and a Phoenician squadron defeated at sea. But disunity weakened the ranks of the rebels, and, after five years of bitter fighting, the revolt was crushed. A punitive expedition was now mounted against Eretria and Athens. Eretria was sacked, but the Athenians won an unexpected victory against the odds at Marathon in 490 and saved their city. It was, in the eyes of later generations, who came to revere the Marathon fighters, the crowning deliverance. Aeschylus fought in the battle; in the epitaph he wrote for himself more than thirty years later it is his only boast:

> Aeschylus the Athenian, Euphorion's son, is dead;
>   his body lies beneath the grave in Gela's fields of corn.
> The holy ground of Marathon could tell his glorious bravery,
>   and one long-haired Persian came to know it.

War in Aeschylus's plays is never romanticized; his portrayal is realistic and authentic.

He had, it seems, already in his mid-twenties begun to write and to have his plays performed, but it was not till 484 that he won his first prize. The years after Marathon were evidently not idle; he was developing his dramatic technique. But the threat from Persia was scotched only. In 480 Darius's successor Xerxes mounted a new offensive. This was not punitive; it was a serious attempt at subjugation. Athens was abandoned and sacked, but the "wooden walls," in the form of ships, secured by the brilliant statesmanship of Themistocles, stood firm, and the Persian navy was defeated at Salamis in 480. In the following year the Spartan skill on land routed the invading army at Plataea. Aeschylus, still of military age, would have taken part in these battles. The victory was a victory of Greek unity, but the Greeks were not wholly united. Thessaly, Boeotia, and Argos followed a policy of appeasement, and the Delphic Oracle was gravely compromised in the minds of many. The victory at Plataea permitted a Greek counteroffensive across the Aegean. Sparta, obsessed with security at home, soon dropped out, and initiative passed to the Athenians with their navy in forming the liberated states into the Confederacy of Delos.

Meantime the Greek settlements in Sicily were facing a similar challenge from the mercantile imperialism of Carthage. The Sicilian states had not yet passed beyond the period of dictatorship, and an alliance of two dictators, Theron of Acragas and his son-in-law Gelon of Syracuse, defeated the Carthaginians at Himera in the same year as Salamis. Gelon died in 478 and was succeeded by his brother Hiero. Like so many of the dictators (including Theron) Hiero was a distinguished patron of the arts, and attracted to his court the lyric poets Pindar, Bacchylides, and Simonides, as well as representatives of the New Learning, which the freedom of the seas and renewed contact with Ionia helped to foster in the Greek world. There too in 476 or thereabouts came Aeschylus to present a play, *The Women of Aetna*, celebrating Hiero's new city of that name. It was an interesting commission, as Aeschylus had only just reached the top, though he was now about 50. Sicily had evolved its own dramatic idiom, and its outstanding exponent, Epicharmus, was in Syracuse at the time. One may suspect that Aeschylus's subsequent mastery in the satyr play was developed through contact with Epicharmus's farcical mimes. Furthermore, Epicharmus's plays, though containing a lyrical element and musical accompaniment, had no chorus, and were essentially for actors. It is a reasonable deduction that his experience in Sicily led Aeschylus to turn the emphasis of his drama from chorus and lyric to actors and action.

The surviving plays of Aeschylus cover a span of no more than fifteen or sixteen years, and he was over fifty when he wrote *The Men of Persia* in 472. Yet it is possible that the earlier plays would be of largely antiquarian interest. The supreme genius of Aeschylus flowered late. The years of his success were the years of emergence of Pericles as leader of the radical democrats; Pericles was *choregus* at the presentation of *The Men of Persia.* The dominant political figure was the conservative Cimon. Tradition tells that Cimon favored Sophocles over Aeschylus in 468; if it is true, the decision may have been more than half political. By 461 Pericles and his associate Ephialtes had destroyed the power of the Areopagus, which was by now perhaps a symbolic rather than an actual barrier to full democracy, and ousted Cimon. These events lie in the background of *The Oresteia* of 458; the impression is that Aeschylus supported the reforms. Nonetheless, he was not wholly happy at Athens. He is said to have been attacked for revealing the Eleusinian Mysteries in one of his plays; it looks like an early example of the sort of covertly political attacks to which the rationalist Pericles was later liable. Whether for this reason or for others he left Athens to return to Sicily, and it seems probable that there he composed and wrote his final masterpiece *The Prometheia.* He died in 456 in an unusual way: an eagle with a tortoise in its talons mistook his bald head for a rock, and dropped the tortoise on it. He was in his seventieth year. The people of Athens honored his memory by permitting the reproduction of his works after his death in competition with those of living authors. This became common practice in the fourth century; it was at the time unique.

Aeschylus's themes are found in the great moral problems at the heart of the universe: in destiny and fatality, working through human will and human passion; in the heredity of crime, both in that it provokes vengeance and in the solidity of a family under a common curse as a *massa peccatrix*; in the vengeance of the gods on *hybris*, a term that includes both arrogant pride and immoral violence; in the raveled mystery of suffering and the antagonism that permeates the world. The Athenians thought of him, and he may have thought of himself, as a moral teacher; "children are taught by schoolmasters, adults by poets." He often reminds us of the Hebrew prophets; in his plays the fathers eat sour grapes and the children's teeth are set on edge. One passage of *Prometheus* (447) is an echo of Isaiah, and it is not impossible that among the Phoenician community in Sicily Aeschylus encountered someone who shared with him the poetry of Palestine, as he was in turn to influence the author of the Book of Job. The trilogy or tetralogy, the series of connected plays, was ideal for working out his tragic concept.

To this he brought a magniloquence unique among the Greeks; in
English the only comparable poets are Shakespeare in *King Lear,* with
his

> sulphurous and thought-executing fires,
> Vaunt-couriers of oak-cleaving thunderbolts,

Milton, and, at his best, Francis Thompson with his "filigree petal" or
"clay-shuttered doors" or "Babylonian heart." *The Men of Persia*
throbs with sonorous proper names. Euripides in Aristophanes's comedy *The Frogs* attacks him for "sound and fury signifying nothing,"
but when their verses are tried in the balance, those of Aeschylus are
plainly weightier. Metaphor was his natural speech. Haigh says of the
beacon in *Agamemnon*: "The flame is conceived as some mighty spirit.
. . . It vaults over the back of the sea with joy; it hands its message to
the heights of Macistus; it leaps across the plains of Asopus, and urges
on the watchman; its mighty beard of fire streams across the Saronic
Gulf, as it rushes along from peak to peak, until finally it swoops down
upon the palace of the Atridae." Aristophanes, even in parody, speaks
of Aeschylus's adjectives as "fresh torrent-swept timbers, blown free
by a giant at war." Imagery is pervasive in his writing.

To these literary values he added a vivid sense of the theater and a
readiness for innovation that belies his later reputation as a traditional-
ist. His characters as a whole are not naturalistic because he is not writing naturalistic drama, but they are not stock figures such as New
Comedy later produced, and there is remarkable development even
in the plays we possess. Atossa, Danaus and Pelasgus, and Eteocles are
representative figures. But already in *Seven against Thebes* the chorus
are, realistically, women in panic, and the elders in *Agamemnon* are
well portrayed, anxious, cautious, yet at the last having no truck with
usurpation and tyranny. Clytemnestra is an astonishing portrait, and
Prometheus little less so, blending as he does in his person the professor of the New Learning (an impressive testimony to Aeschylus's
alertness to his contemporaries) and the revolutionary against a tyrannical regime (such as Aeschylus may have encountered in opposition
at Syracuse). It was in fact Aeschylus's introduction of the second ac-

tor that made possible real drama and the more flexible handling of character, and he was swift to see the possibilities of the third actor whom Sophocles employed. So too he introduced alongside his heroic characters homelier figures with touches of down-to-earth humor, like the watchman in *Agamemnon* and the nurse in *The Libation Bearers.*

He had a superlative sense of spectacle and liked exotic masks and costumes. Aristophanes in *The Frogs* comments on this. Few plays are without some touches of this kind. *The Men of Persia* is exotic from start to finish; so is *The Suppliant Women*; so is *Prometheus. Seven against Thebes* depends for its dramatic effect upon the central spectacle of the warriors with their shields. *The Oresteia* ends with a chorus of hell-hounds, three gods, and a torchlight procession. A different sort of spectacle was offered in *The Cabeiri,* which had a daring drunk scene; this was probably a satyr play, but the innovation was nonetheless bold for that. In pursuit of spectacle he invented or developed new mechanical devices for the theater. In the lost play *The Weighing of the Souls* there was a remarkable scene on the *theologeion* involving three gods and two souls. In the same play a daring use of the crane produced a beautiful moving tableau as the goddess Dawn swept the dead body of her son Memnon to the sky. Athene's arrival in *The Kindly Goddesses* must have been similarly spectacular. In *Prometheus* it seems that he actually used the crane for the entry of the chorus. At the beginning of *Agamemnon* he uses the *distegia* to create a striking opening; at the end the moving platform presents the bodies of Agamemnon and Cassandra and is used in the next play with deadly effect to show their murderers.

Gerald Else has well identified some of the less tangible qualities that Aeschylus brought to drama. Such are a bold speculative spirit that enabled him to reinterpret myth and challenge established belief, for though Aeschylus was profoundly religious he was certainly not orthodox; the broadening of the scene to include past actions, as in *Agamemnon* where the sacrifice of Iphigeneia and the Trojan War, as well as the remoter curse, are with us throughout the play, or in *Prometheus* where the gift of fire to man is a central theme; the more incisive presentation of contrast and conflict; the better organization of the episodes leading to and from the pathos; the increasing focus on the tragic choice that leads to the pathos; and his faith in the ultimate resolution.

> May the desire of Zeus be truly
> of Zeus; he is hard to track down.
> 　　On every road he shines,
> even in darkness, when fortune is black,
> 　　for mortal men.

> It falls firm, it does not trip,
> when by Zeus's will an act is brought to fulfilment,
> 　　Dark are the devices
> of his mind, shadowy their path,
> 　　beyond thought, indiscernible. (*Supl.,* 86)

Rightly did Gilbert Murray entitle his study *Aeschylus: The Creator of Tragedy.*

4. THE MEN OF PERSIA

The oldest surviving Greek play raises a number of acute problems. In the first place it is the only surviving play with a historical theme. The contrast with Shakesperian tragedy is obvious. It implies a difference of origin; Greek tragedy springs from ancestral and fertility powers, Renaissance drama from a sophisticated tradition of letters. It implies a difference of religious attitude; Greek religious values were more easily expressed through legend and myth, Renaissance values in their strange combination of Christianity and humanism, through history. It implies a difference of dramatic technique; Greek tragedy was not adapted to handling the flexibility of action demanded by most historical themes and did not have the naturalism to portray familiar human figures seriously, which is one reason why Phrynichus and Aeschylus alike set their plays on Salamis in Persia. In fact we know of only three tragedies of the fifth century with historical themes, and none is later than 472, the date of *The Men of Persia*. All deal with the Persian Wars. The first, by Phrynichus, was *The Capture of Miletus*; we are told that the audience burst into tears and fined the poet for reminding them of those unhappy events. He made amends with *The Women of Phoenicia,* an immensely popular play on the Salamis theme.

It was bold of Aeschylus to emulate his rival on the same subject, but he did, and his play was a success. Pericles, not yet established as the dominant figure in Athenian politics, was *choregus.* We can discount Murray's suggestion that for a while this was a prescribed theme for the dramatists. We can readily understand that no one else felt like tackling it after Aeschylus, that the technique of these two plays was not easily applied to other themes, and that other approaches to historical subjects proved intractable. It is, however, slightly odd that no dramatist essayed the theme of Marathon. A papyrus fragment of a play on Gyges, king of Lydia, is an important but indeterminate addition to our knowledge of Greek historical drama, indeterminate because we cannot date it (it may well belong to the fourth century), and because Gyges, though historical, passed into the realm of myth, as Herodotus, Plato, and Cicero may remind us.

In the second place *The Men of Persia* is the second play of a trilogy. Aeschylus used the trilogy form to work out his theme in a sequence of connected plays. Of the seven surviving plays, three form a single trilogy. One (*Seven against Thebes*) is the last of a trilogy; two (*The Suppliants* and *Prometheus Bound*) stood as the first plays of their series. In either case we can see how a play might be detached from its sequence and stand on its own. But the middle play depends upon its context; if you detach the props from both sides it must surely fall. Yet we are told that Aeschylus assented to the performance of *The Men of Persia,* detached from its trilogy, in Sicily. *The Men of Persia* thus stands with *The Libation Bearers,* and we have no other real comparison to make.

Unfortunately we know little about the remaining plays of the trilogy. The first, *Phineus,* dealt with a seer who was blinded for revealing Zeus's plans, and whose story is associated with the Argonauts. We know that the play told of the killing of the tormenting Harpies by the sons of Boreas. It is reasonable to see in the Argo expedition, as Herodotus saw, the invasion of Asia by Europe, to which the invasion of Europe by Asia was a counterblast; reasonable too to suppose that the seer prophesied the coming conflict. The third play was, we are told, *Glaucus of Potniae*. It is tempting to emend this to *Glaucus of the Sea* (*Pontios* for *Potnieus*), especially as some of our manuscripts omit the adjective, for Glaucus of the Sea was the craftsman who built the Argo, piloted her, and became a sea god. The temptation must be resisted. The reversion to the Argo would be without precedent. The other Glaucus was a fertility spirit, a hero who was torn to death by his own mares; more important, Potniae lies close to the battleground of Plataea where the finally decisive confrontation of the Persian Wars took place in the year after Salamis. If we wish to speculate, we can imagine the appearance of the hero at some decisive moment in the battle, like Castor and Pollux at Lake Regillus, or the Angels of Mons. The satyr play that completed the tetralogy was *Prometheus, Bringer of Fire*. It has been supposed that this dealt with a torch race in a festival of joy at victory, or with the purification of Athens by fire from Delphi after the Persian occupation. It is perhaps more likely that *Glaucus of Potniae* ended with such a ritual and that the satyr play took up the theme to parody it.

Thirdly, *The Men of Persia* is not a play as plays have generally been understood. Nothing happens. In this it is not unlike *Waiting for Godot,* but it is not "Waiting for Xerxes." Xerxes arrives, though his arrival changes nothing. This is a play of situation. Most tragedies lead up to and away from a moment of pathos. Here, pathos is inherent throughout, and we as audience and the participants on the stage pass through (a) foreboding, (b) confirmation, (c) explication, and (d) emotional response.

Fourthly, we must realize that *The Men of Persia* belongs to a comparatively early stage in the development of tragedy and that the techniques are still experimental. The spectacle is superb, and the scope for fine music and dancing boundless. We note that Aeschylus is not interested in the mythical unities that later criticism forced on the Greek playwrights. Unity of place is at best general; the scene begins in a council chamber and shifts to the tomb of Darius, who was presumably not buried in the council chamber. In fact he was buried in Persepolis, not Susa at all, but we need not suppose that Aeschylus or his audience knew or cared about this. The change is less startling than the change from Delphi to Athens in *The Kindly Goddesses,* but it is there. Nor is there unity of time. The express messenger is followed within half an hour by Xerxes, still implausibly wearing the clothes from Salamis. There is a similar time-lag in *Agamemnon.* To criticize these changes as defects would be study criticism of the most irrelevant kind. It is more important to note that Aeschylus was not interested in such academic unities, and he was right, for the breaks do not obtrude in the theater. The handling of the actors, however, is a little awkward. Aeschylus has made one advance on Phrynichus. By making his chorus one of elders, he has deprived himself of the more spectacular effects of lamentation and dancing that a women's chorus might be expected to provide. But he has made the impact of Salamis on the chorus more direct. This is implicit in the theme of trust applied to them by themselves (2), Atossa (171), and Darius (681). And he has released an actor. The play needs two actors; one for the messenger and Darius's ghost, the other for Atossa and Xerxes, and Atossa's exit to enable her to play the part of Xerxes is undeniably clumsy. Here alone the machinery creaks.

The play opens with a ceremonial procession in the traditional anapaestic rhythm for the entry of the Persian Council of Regents, who then engage in a solemn dance. There is plenty of opportunity for spectacular costume and movement, and it is not merely flippant to make comparison with the entry of the Peers in Gilbert's *Iolanthe.* In addition to the visual grandeur, Aeschylus makes play with the unfamiliar splendor of Persian names, Amistres and Artaphrenes, Megabates and Astaspes, Artembares and Masistres, Imaios and Pharadaces. Sonority of language extends far beyond the names; words of four, five, and six syllables, richly compounded adjectives, and lines of two words abound. From his first mention the titles pile up for Xerxes. But there is also a note of foreboding, which is characteristically Aeschylean. There is a masterful touch in the very first line. Phrynichus had begun his play with the iambic words:

This belongs to the Persians who have long gone away.

Aeschylus with a courtesy salute adapts the words for his choral procession, but in adapting them charges them with prescient irony:

> This belongs to the *departed* Persians. (1)

Phrynichus, a specialist in lyrical song, had begun his play with the announcement of the disaster and had developed the play as a cantata of lamentation, no doubt brilliant with its music and tedious without. Aeschylus, far more sensitive to strictly dramatic values, holds up the announcement and can thus produce the magnificent foreboding of his prologue, from its first mention of "prophecies of doom" (10).

> So from the land of Persia
> the flower of manhood is departed,
> and the whole land of Asia which nursed them
> grieves with unbearable longing,
> parents and wives count the days
> and tremble at the long-drawn time. (59)

The note of foreboding passes into the dance, whose accompanying song opens with Xerxes's act in bridging the Hellespont. The language is ambivalent; to the elders the act shows the monarch's divine vigor, to the Greeks it is a sign of his *hybris,* the pride that comes before a fall. The Persians have prospered on land; they have seemed to encroach successfully on the sea. But the divine power is subtle to deceive (93).

> These are the fearful thoughts
> which tear my black-cloaked heart—
> Oh! the Persian army! (115)

From the first line Aeschylus builds up a series of key words or concepts. We have already noted the ambiguous "departed" (*oichomenon*). The word recurs at 1, 13, 60, 178; then with immense power in the fourth line of the messenger's speech. The chorus has sung, "The flower of the land of Persia has departed" (60); the messenger reports, "The flower of the Persians has departed, fallen" (252). The same word recurs in a chorus (546) and finally in the mouth of Xerxes (916). Another key word appears in the third line. This is *polychryson,* literally "much-golden." It reappears a line or two later of the Persian army (9, cf. 45, 53); in the mouth of the elders it represents the glory of the host, but to the Greeks it would savor of pride and effeminacy, for you cannot forge fighting weapons of gold. (We may note the contrast at 147 between the arrows of the Persians and the more manly spears of the Greeks). Each half of the word is significant; the gold throughout the play symbolizes the society that depends on wealth; the word for "much" appears in one form or another 125 times in the play, and it represents the proliferating extravagance of the affluent society. Another three lines bring us to the first appearance of the word "all" (12, cf. 53, 62, 126), like "much" a simple word, but important for the total involvement of the Persian host.

Meanwhile another key concept has emerged. This is the theme of time. It starts with the regents who are there as elders (4). A sense of age and antiquity pervades the whole (e.g., 17, 102). This partly represents the apparent permanence of Persian dominion, partly the sense of protracted absence. Toward the end of the processional song the chorus declares the purpose of Persian arms to place the yoke of slavery on Greece (50). The metaphor was not the cliché it is today. As the ceremonial dance starts it takes on a sinister aspect; now it is the neck of the sea that Xerxes succeeded momentarily in yoking (72, cf. 130). The same word reappears of the Persian wives, who in the absence of their husbands are left "alone-in-the-yoke" (139); it is hard to say whether the poet intends a comment on Persian marriage. All this prepares us for Atossa's dream. Alongside the yoke is the net, less important here than in *Agamemnon,* but not unimportant:

> Who is the lord of the leap
> with light and nimble foot?
> Destruction with a smile
>   benign at first entices
> mortals into her net. (95)

One other key concept is the sea. The yoking of the sea is the great act of Persian sin. The Persian troops are compared with the flood of the sea (87), but, even in the Mediterranean a flood will ebb. The first words of the queen after the narration of Salamis are:

> Alas! an ocean of disaster has crashed
> upon the Persians and all the peoples of Asia. (433)

When she returns it is to speak of "a surge of disasters" (599). The last words of the chorus before Xerxes's entry are:

The crashing waves of war have overcome us by their power. (909)

This is an amply recurrent theme, and it would be possible to illustrate it more widely. In general we may say that no other play of Aeschylus is so richly furnished with these leitmotifs, and part of the function of this opening sequence is to introduce them. One would like to know whether their appearance was also indicated by the repetition of musical themes.

The first character now appears. This is the queen mother, Atossa. The chorus fall prostrate at her feet, no doubt among the jeers of the volatile audience, whose responsive participation would have been far greater than that of the colder audiences of Britain or America, and call her the wife and mother of a god (157). Her opening words bring back the theme of gold, and her opening speech is a warning against a society based on the accumulation of money. Poverty is debilitating, but human qualities matter more than wealth; and wealth leads to *hybris*, which leads to disaster. She comes to consult the chorus, "old and trusted friends" (171). Both epithets (adjective and noun in the Greek) are significant, and revert to the first introduction of the chorus; the one is the leitmotif of time, the other identifies the elders with the coming disaster. The speech that follows tells of a dream and omen which cause Atossa's anxiety. The dream is Freudian; Atossa may be feminine but Aeschylus is masculine, and this is a male dream. In it the theme of the yoke finds its culmination. Xerxes yokes two women, representing Persia and Greece. Persia submits proudly, Greece struggles, snaps the yokes and upsets Xerxes from his chariot. Aeschylus with skilled hand anticipates later scenes as he records how

> My son fell, and his father Darius stood there
> with pity for him. When Xerxes saw him
> he rent his robes. (197)

The affirmed clarity of the vision is noteworthy, and it is reaffirmed later (518–519). In Aeschylus those who are granted dreams or visions see distinctly; those who try to see without illumination have their verb shrouded in compound form and their vision clouded. The dream is followed by an omen of a falcon clawing an eagle; it points the way to the first omen of *Agamemnon,* and we are reminded of the similar omen in *Macbeth.* The point is not merely the weaker assailing the stronger, but the implied contempt, for the falcon normally uses its beak to fight. The eagle is the symbol of the Persian, as of other empires; the falcon is the representative of the sun god, also honored in Persia. Implicit is the fact that the very god of Persia has deserted them. This is important; it is no battle of tribal gods. Persian pride is judged by universal Heaven. The eagle is said to seek refuge at Apollo's hearth, taking refuge at the sun god's shrine from the sun god's bird; there is a topical political reference to the pro-Persian behavior of the Delphic priests.

Atossa ends, and the chorus comforts her in a dramatically effective scene; again Darius's name appears. But now the political theme comes uttermost. Atossa's last words have asserted that Xerxes is not answerable to any state; the Persians are his slaves. The chorus tells Atossa that Athens, built ominously "far to the west, where the lord Sun drops and sinks" (232), has citizen-soldiers who are no man's slaves or subjects. Athenians never never never shall be slaves. This mild jingoism no doubt met its expected applause.

Enter the messenger, who without delay announces the disaster. The might of Persia (the word "much" comes twice in successive lines) has been destroyed, destroyed in one blow. We have seen the power with which he takes up, in a different sense, the very words of the chorus, that the flower of the Persians is departed. He must unfold *all* the story, for *all* the army is lost (254–255); again the theme of total involvement. The chorus breaks into a song of grief. Atossa for the moment is silent. When she speaks it is with dignity, obliquely, to ask who survives. Her relief at Xerxes's safety is more than personal; we are again reminded that Xerxes is identified with Persia while Athens is identified with democracy.

MESSENGER: The gods guard the city of the goddess.
ATOSSA: What? Is the city of Athens still unsacked?
MESSENGER: While she has men, she has secure ramparts. (347)

Athens—the buildings—was ravaged, but the words stand. As Nicias says in the pages of Thucydides, "It is men who make a city, not walls and ships without men." This is the essential Greek *polis*, and, apart from its dramatic power, *The Men of Persia* is a revealing political document.

We need not examine the description of the battle in detail. It was grandly evocative for the Athenians. Aeschylus undoubtedly saw it and probably took part in it. It is our earliest account, and in some ways our most illuminating. It is filled out with majestically sonorous Persian names. Through the whole scene there is a fresh key concept. This is the theme of weight, power or strength, and the scales of fortune. We read it in the messenger's words that the gods weighed down the scale (346) or that the disasters of the second part of his story outweigh the first (437). This takes its place alongside the theme of the sea and its revenge. Another important aspect is the divine dimension and the offense of *hybris*. It was a divine power that destroyed the army (345). Xerxes was boastful in the mass of his ships (352). He did not think of the jealousy of the gods (362). He did not understand that the future lay with the gods (373). The Persians lost their rational faculty (392). Even on the retreat some god stirred up winter unseasonably (495). So the first word of the choral song that follows is an invocation to Zeus, and the song is a lyric of the battle, full of splendid Aeschylean phrases, as when fish are called "the voiceless children of the undefiled." The theme of totality is sounded, and Xerxes is unfavorably contrasted with Darius. At the end the political note rings out, with the commonplaces of Athenian democratic propaganda:

> No longer is the tongue of men
> gagged. The commons are loosed
> to speak in freedom.
> The yoke of power has slackened.
> The seaswept isle of Ajax,
> its fields stained with blood,
>   holds all that is left of Persia. (591)

There follows a touch characteristic of the new dramatic mastery that Aeschylus brought to Greek tragedy. Atossa on leaving told the chorus to welcome and console Xerxes, should he arrive. We expect Xerxes; instead Atossa reappears, bringing offerings for the shade of the dead king, Darius. In a spell that makes splendid drama the chorus evokes him, and his ghost emerges. The scene that follows does not advance the plot, for the sufficient reason that there is no plot to advance. But it is dramatically effective, and it is useful to analyze why.

1. It is good theater in itself. Ghost scenes are usually good theater—witness Shakespeare—and we need not be scornful of an injection of melodrama. Here the appearance is combined with spectacle, as in the renewed prostration of the elders.

2. The scene is excellently written; we may instance especially the superb iambics of Darius's speech at 759.

3. It increases the suspense; we are still waiting for Xerxes.

4. Alongside this, we are presented with the contrast between Darius in his wisdom and the unwise Xerxes.

5. At 739 Darius speaks of prophecies of doom, not before mentioned in this play. The prophetic power fascinated Aeschylus, and presumably his audience. But it may be regarded as certain that this is a tie with *Phineus,* where the prophecies were uttered.

6. This scene in fact is the king post of the trilogy. It holds all together. As it looks back, so it looks forward. Darius explicitly foretells the defeat at Plataea (817), and we may legitimately assume this as a link with *Glaucus of Potniae.*

7. The theme of power and wealth, and their capacity to mislead (754–756) reechoes more persuasively in the context of the spirit world. "Wealth is no use to the dead" (842).

8. The theme of totality sounds again. Darius asks, "Is the whole of our army wholly destroyed?" And Atossa answers, "The whole city of Susa mourns the loss of its men" (729–730).

9. The "much" words come again and again. We may note especially Darius's statement that much disaster comes by sea and much by land (707), or that in binding the Hellespont Xerxes made much of a road for much of an army (748).

10. Aeschylus is too skillful to overplay the theme of the yoke. He uses it once again (722) but replaces it by the image of fetters, manacles, and enslavement (745–747).

11. The time theme is used excellently. The permanence of Persian power has passed into the permanence of Persian defeat, always to be remembered (760). What is more, the scene is notable for its generalized statements (706–708, 742, 821ff., 842). These are important for they remind us that the drama is played out *sub specie aeternitatis,* and the particular lessons of its particular situation take on the aspect of eternal moral truths.

12. The most important feature of the scene is its foursquare assertion of the divine dimension. This is present in the very appearance of Darius. It is spelled out in the dialogue. It was a divine power who robbed Xerxes of his wits (724–725). It was Zeus who fulfilled the prophecies (740). It was mad folly in Xerxes, a mortal, to try and fetter the immortal god of the sea (749). The Persians had shown their *hybris* further in ravaging temples and shrines (809). But "Zeus appears to punish arrogant minds, a stern inquisitor" (827).

13. The scene ends on a slightly odd note. Atossa is distressed at what has happened to Xerxes's clothes. Attempts to see subtle feminine psychology here are misguided. But the effect is probably not deliberately comic, as Aeschylus has prepared for it. More probably it is an attempt at symbolism, such as a painter or film maker might use with power, but which does not come off in words, and it is likely that he would draw a laugh from some of his audience. Aeschylus, as well as Homer, can nod. It is a clumsy device to get Atossa offstage so that the actor can play Xerxes.

The chorus sings briefly but evocatively of those former Persian possessions now liberated; there is a further implicit contrast of Darius and Xerxes. Then at last Xerxes limps home, and the last scene is genuine old drama, a lamentation between actor and chorus. It is tedious to read, though there are resonant names, and one powerful moment when Xerxes identifies himself with his people in disaster (1008); we have an operatic libretto without music and choreography. Filled out with this, it is a magnificently spectacular ending to our oldest surviving European drama.

Patriotic themes seldom make for good drama or great poetry. The strength of *The Men of Persia* lies in the fact that Aeschylus transcends his theme. In the first place, Aeschylus looks at the events from a Persian standpoint, and he has taken care for authenticity. Of fifty-five Persian names, forty-two are utterly authentic, ten appear in their familiar Greek form, and the other three are unknown. The language includes Persian forms such as Darian (663), cries of grief, and technical terms such as *ballen* for a sovereign (657–658) or *baris* for a boat (553, 1076). The very Greek is at times that of Asia Minor, not of Attica. No Persian, except Xerxes, is other than noble, dignified, heroic. Especially is this true of Darius. Broadhead, the latest English editor, writes, "This imposing, dignified and majestic figure, more than any other in the play, shows how far Aeschylus has risen above the level of a narrow nationalism." The same is true of Atossa and the elders. By contrast no Greek general, not even Themistocles, is mentioned by name, and of the gods, in reference to the Greek victory, only Zeus, and, once, Athene. The contrast with the Old Testament or Livy or modern propaganda is painful. Kranz wrote of this play, "On the Greek side stood the God of justice, yet the poet draws tears for the lot of the Persians." In this sense *The Men of Persia* can be mentioned in the same breath as an even greater play, *The Women of Troy*.

Alongside this is the divine dimension. It is this, after all, that enables a play on a historical theme to take its place among the Greek tragedies. It is the note of Herodotus (8, 109): "It is not we who have done these things. It is the gods and heroes who judged that the sovereignty of Asia and Europe should be in the hands of a proud and impious man." Critics have often compared Henry V:

> O God, thy arm was here,
> And not to us, but to thy arm alone,
> Ascribe we all! When, without stratagem,
> But in plain shock and even play of battle,
> Was ever known so great and little loss
> On one part and on th' other? Take it, God,
> For it is none but thine! (4.8)

There is no comparison. That is the veriest jingoism. To Aeschylus, God is not *for* Athens; men are for Athens. God is *against* pride.

The Men of Persia is not a great play, but we can see a great dramatist behind it in the depth with which he treats his theme, and not least in language, spectacle, and dramatic effect.

5. SEVEN AGAINST THEBES

In Aristophanes's comedy *The Frogs* Aeschylus is made to put forward *Seven against Thebes* as the exemplar of tragedy that enshrined moral values. It is "a play filled with the war-god." Aeschylus claims that it made everyone in the audience yearn to be in the front line (Ar. *Frogs* 1022). The justification is more closely related to Athens in 405 than Athens in 467 when *Seven against Thebes* was produced, and if the play was valued for such reasons, it is a clear example of misinterpretation and misrepresentation. The play spoke to the audience of its own day, now sailing on a tide of political optimism, in recalling the emotions of the world from which they had escaped when Athens fell to the Persians under siege thirteen years before. This is clear in the choral imagination of a conquered city (338); it is also clear in the reference to the Argive host as speaking a foreign language (170, cf. 72) and in the exotic blazons on the shields of the assailants, which are more appropriate to Persian invaders than to fellow-Greeks; even the horses make a snort that sounds *barbaros* (463).

There are two other important background points to *Seven against Thebes*. The first is that it is the final play of a trilogy. This trilogy dealt with the curse on the house of Laius. The first play *Laius* and the second *Oedipus* dealt with earlier layers in the history of the house, but our knowledge of the plays is almost entirely speculative, though the broad outlines of the plot are familiar. The satyr play, *The Sphinx,* took up part of the legend also, though in a very different mood. Laius, the rightful king of Thebes, while in exile had found a supporter in Pelops, the unscrupulous father of Atreus and Thyestes. But he fell in love with Pelops's son Chrysippus and kidnapped the boy, thereby exposing himself and his house to a curse from Pelops.

The first outworking of this curse was covered by an oracular warning; if he had a son that son would kill him. So the saga of Laius became the saga of Oedipus, which we shall examine more fully in the plays of Sophocles. The curse extended to Oedipus's sons, who were doomed to fight for the kingdom and alike to die childless, thus fulfilling the curse. They agreed to reign for alternate periods of a year at a time. Polyneices abdicated after his year, but Eteocles refused to do so. Polyneices, with right on his side, raised an army from allies in Argos, thus putting himself in the wrong. Such is the situation at the beginning of the third play. The curse is always in the background, brooding over the drama, and must never be forgotten. The shadow of the first two plays falls on the third. For this very reason Aeschylus does not have continually to make mention of the curse and does not do so. The curse is already before the minds of his audience and he can interweave with it the sheer realism of a city under siege.

The other important point is that at a casual reading this appears an exceptionally static play even among Greek tragedies. To all intents and purposes there is only one character, Eteocles, and there is no significant interplay of personality between two characters on stage. Aeschylus may have invented the second actor, but in this play he uses him exclusively as a spotlight for the protagonist. Two factors offset this. The first is the element of spectacle in the scene with the champions and their gigantic emblazoned shields. The other is the chorus. If the rest of the play is conceived in a static convention, the chorus of frightened women is portrayed with a daring and active realism. Further, we are told that in the original performance Telestes, who must have been the chorus leader, danced with such superlative verve and skill that he induced the audience "to see the things that were going on" (Ath. 22). Once again we are reminded of the importance of filling out the choral lyric with music and mime.

Right at the outset we are confronted with a situation of public concern. The scene is sanctified by primitive statues of gods. A crowd of extras gradually assembles, talking excitedly. To them comes the present king, Eteocles. He silences them, addressing them as "citizens of Cadmus"; Aeschylus in fact, perhaps for political reasons, never uses the name Thebes in this play. His first sentence sets the play's principal image, the nautical metaphor.

> The man who stands on the bridge,
> holding the helm of state, watching events,
> sleepless, must speak what occasion demands. (1)

The thought of the ship of state was as old as Alcaeus, but not yet a complete cliché, not new coin, but not yet defaced. The image recurs as he tells the citizens in ambiguous language to man the parapets (or gunwales) and take their posts at the floors (or benches) of the towers (32). Eteocles stands as the bridge between what is happening inside the city and what is happening outside; there is a sense in which he is crushed between the two forces. For the moment he appears as the sane and devout leader, conscious of his responsibility. He lives up to his name, "the man of true glory." He tells them to guard city, altars, children, land (14); his gaze falls from high to low through the sequence, but his sense of value rises from high to highest. He brings news through the augurs that a major attack is now expected. He has sent out scouts, and one now returns. The scout describes what he has seen: seven champions sacrificing a bull, catching the blood in a black-rimmed shield (an evocative detail), dipping their fingers in it, and swearing by the Powers of War and by bloodthirsty Terror to crush the city or die in the attempt. The motif of the Seven is thus established but not yet developed. The sea metaphor returns:

> So be a skilled captain of your ship,
> make your city secure, before the storm of war bursts on us
> and blasts us. An armored wave is roaring on the land. (62)

The scout goes, and Eteocles calls on Zeus, Earth, and the gods who guard the town—and his father's curse, which he describes in another important image, as a Fury, mighty in strength (70). Eteocles does not know how, or even that, the curse will strike him. It is important to see that the attackers are referred to as "Achaeans" (28), "horde of foreigners" (34), "the army" (36, 40), "the entire force of Argos" (59); there is no mention of Polyneices.

And now Aeschylus, the poet of archaic grandeur, does an interesting and exciting thing. He clears the scene completely, and brings on a realistic chorus of hysterical women. There are no processional anapaests; they rush on to the rhythm of frantic dochmiacs. Myth is swallowed up in reality, and the curse is forgotten in the terror of the enemy's advance. Their words are full of sounds of war, and it seems likely that Aeschylus, who liked large effects, used all the resources of the theater to accompany their panic with appropriate noise.

> The clatter of hoofs on the soil of my country rings in my ears.
> The sound draws near,
> it takes wings, it crashes down
> with the irresistible thunder of a mountain-torrent. (83)

(The exact reading is speculative.)

> Do you hear the clang of shields? Do you not hear it? (100)
>
> I shudder at the clang. It is the sound of a host of spears. (103)
>
> I hear the rattle of chariots circling the city.
>   Queen Hera!
> The wheels are weighted, the axles groaning.
>   Artemis, have mercy!
> The very air is mad with the shimmer of spears. (151)
>
> A shower of stones on top of the battlements!
>   Apollo, have mercy!
> The thrumming of bronze-bound shields at our gates! (158)

In all the din the sea image returns:

> A surge of crested soldiers is seething
> round our city, whipped up by the winds of war. (112)

In their distress they call upon god after god by name: first Ares
(105), then in general the gods who guard the city (109), then Zeus
(116), Pallas (127), Poseidon (130), Ares again (135), Cyprian
Aphrodite (139), Apollo (145, 159), Artemis (147, 154), Hera
(152), Onca (an old goddess identified with Pallas Athene [164]),
and then all the gods en masse. And their prayer is to save "the city of
seven gates" (165).

Eteocles, always where he is needed, calms them with sharp words
against women in general, and the chorus in particular. Panic is treason
and will be punished by death. The chorus, though calmer, is still excited; he speaks to them, but they continue to sing, though clinging to
sanctuary and no longer flitting round the orchestra:

> Dear son of Oedipus, I was frightened
> to hear the rattle, rattle of the chariots,
> the whine of the axles as the wheels turn,
> the ringing noises of the bits in the horses' mouths,
>   rudders forged in the flame. (203)

The appellation "son of Oedipus" reminds us momentarily of the
curse, but it is immediately covered again by the chorus's fear. Their
description of the bits brings back the sea image, and Eteocles answers
in kind,

> Well? Does the helmsman rush from bridge
> to prow to find a means of safety
> when his ship is hard pressed in a swelling sea? (208)

and, a line or two later, with a pun that can be adapted in English,

> Pray that our walls remain watertight against the
>   enemy bows. (216)

In what follows there are three elements: religiosity from the chorus;
Eteocles pleading for common sense; and the continued accompani-

ment of noises outside, the drumming of stones (213), the confused clash of war (239), the neighing of horses (245), the very fortress groaning (247), the crashing at the gates (249). Effective is the way in which the chorus, when it breaks into speech rhythms and line-for-line dialogue, is utterly preoccupied with the sounds of battle (245, 247, 289) as they cling fervently to the archaic statues before the palace. Eteocles finally quiets them and tells them his plan.

> I will pick out six men, with myself as seventh,
> I will go and post them at the city's seven gates,
> rowing majestically against the enemy. (283)

He is reason; they are emotion. Again, he stands between them and the attackers represented by the noise.

He goes out where he is needed next, and they return to the orchestra to sing and mime in dance the fate of a conquered city. For they are still afraid,

> As a timorous dove
> fears for its nestling
> young the snake,
>   unwanted bedfellow. (292)

It is a doubly powerful image, for the snake, the dragon, is the emblem of Thebes, and we are reminded, without explicit statement, that Polyneices is the real attacker. War was never far from the Greek world, and Aeschylus knew it at first hand. There is a dread authenticity, and a kind of grim beauty, as the chorus sings:

> When a city falls, many
>   disasters ensue.
> There is captivity, murder,
> there is conflagration, the whole
> city is stained with smoke.
>   The god of war breathes fury,
>   slays the masses, defiles holiness.
>
>   There is tumult in the town, the network
>   of towers rises against it.
>   One man faces another

and falls by the spear.
Cries stream with blood
from breast-fed babies,
fresh-nursed cries resound.
Pillage and pursuit, blood-sisters, are there,
one plunderer passes another,
plunderless plead with plunderless,
willing to have a partner,
longing for the like or more.
What comes of it all?
The evidence is there! (346)

(The meaning of the last phrase is quite uncertain.) Rosenmeyer has spoken of this chorus as "impressionistic, not to say pointillistic." "This," as he says, "is the quintessence of war, its terror and its incalculability, and also its inhuman nonchalance."

There follows the central scene, which lasts for almost a third of the play. It is static, spectacular, and brilliantly planned. Simultaneously there enter from stage-right the scout at the double, and from stage-left Eteocles with his six champions, each with a huge emblazoned shield. Eteocles is again called "the son of Oedipus" (372); again we are covertly reminded of the curse. The scene is shaped so that a pattern repeats itself with growing intensity till it breaks. Six times the scout identifies one of the attacking champions, six times Eteocles sends a champion to the defense, six times the chorus sings its response, till we grow nearer and nearer to the final, inevitable confrontation of the two brothers before the seventh gate.

With each of the first five attackers the scout concentrates upon the hybristic boasting and the blazon on the shield, and the audible silence of the defenders (who no doubt pay devotion to the gods of the city as they leave for their task), and the visible blazons on their own shields provide a solid answer. The first attacker is Tydeus; in the tradition he was the sort of man who drank the brains from his fallen enemy's skull, and without the detail the characterization is maintained. He roars like a dragon and snorts like a war horse. Night is on his blazon, and Eteocles prophesies the night of death for him. He sends out Melanippus. Tydeus may roar like a dragon, but Melanippus

is a child of the land (413), a real dragon's offspring, for the Thebans
were born of the dragon's teeth. Melanippus perhaps had a figure of
Modesty (*Aischune,* 409) on his shield, a fit answer to the boaster.
The second attacker, Capaneus, adds blasphemy to boastfulness: "He'll
sack the city, whether God wills it or no" (427). He was in the tradition struck down by a thunderbolt from Zeus, and Eteocles and the
chorus look toward this. The sea image breaks through as the blasphemer's words "swell like waves" (443). His blazon is a flaming
torch with the motto "I'll burn this town." His opponent, Polyphontes,
is a man of few words but fiery action (448). He bore, it seems, the
image of Artemis on his shield. The third attacker is Eteoclus, and the
very name may represent a confusion in the myth. For a moment we
think that Eteocles may appropriately oppose him, but it is not to be.
Eteoclus has fierce mares, neighing in a foreign sound. His device is an
armed man scaling a city wall; he too boasts and blasphemes; but the
individuality of the man has disappeared behind the bestial energy of
his horses. It is, in a sense, a repetition of the bestiality of Tydeus.
Megareus, who is sent against him, carries on his shield Tyche, the
power of fortune; he will be a match for the man, and for the man and
fortress of the shield, and Eteocles engages in grimly jesting arithmetic
to say so (478). Fourth comes Hippomedon with shield as big as a
threshing floor, and on it the fiery monster Typhon. He is attacking
the gate near the temple of Onca Pallas, and she will protest. But for
human defender there is Hyperbius, and his blazon is Zeus with his
thunderbolt; and Zeus is mightier than Typhon.

Three things have marked the attackers so far. First, they are associated with images of fire. Tydeus shows the night sky aflame with stars
(388), Capaneus bears a blazing torch (433), Hippomedon has
Typhon breathing fire (493). Second, they are all associated with
horses. Tydeus's voice is like a war horse snorting (393); Capaneus
means "charioteer"; Eteoclus almost fades from sight behind his
mares; and Hippomedon means "horse lord." The horse is a symbol of
aggressiveness. Third, they are all blasphemers. The fifth attacker is
another blasphemer, but the other images fall away, since Aeschylus is
preparing us for the transition to Amphiaraus. Instead the ship image
returns; he is described as "fair-prowed" (533); he has, so to say, a

fine figurehead. But the blasphemy is there; he will destroy the city in despite of Zeus (531). His emblem is the Sphinx, the creature that wasted Thebes, with a Theban in its claws. He is the son of a mountain mother, Atalanta in fact, and with his profuse hair we have something of the image of a mountain lion. Aeschylus varies the pattern slightly by holding up the name till almost the end; it is Parthenopaeus. Eteocles's counter is Hyperbius's brother Actor; his emblem evidently a hammer with which the Sphinx may find herself knocked inside out. And now the mood changes, for the sixth attacker is the upright prophet Amphiaraus. At the first performance, when the scout spoke the words,

> He seeks to be noblest in reality not reputation,
> reaping harvest in his mind from a deep-ploughed furrow,
> from which good counsel springs, (592)

the audience turned and looked at Aristides the Just (Plut. *Arist.* 3). Amphiaraus rebuked the bloody blasphemy of Tydeus, whose words would wake an avenging Fury—so, subtly, Aeschylus brings us back to the curse, and follows it immediately with Amphiaraus's rebuke to Polyneices, whose very name means "steeped in strife," and who is here first mentioned. His shield bears no boastful blazon, no blazon at all. The scout says, with a reversion to the ship metaphor,

> To row against him I counsel you to send
> men of wisdom and courage. (595)

There is an obvious candidate, Eteocles himself. But Eteocles, though respecting Amphiaraus, does not fear for the city from him. He continues the metaphor:

> A religious man may board a ship
> with a crew of cutthroat villains
> and share their God-forsaken fate. (602)

He knows that Amphiaraus is doomed by an oracle, and disdains to go against him. He sends instead Lasthenes, whose shield perhaps depicted a large eye, such as we know from vase paintings that shields authentically bore (623). The chorus repeats its central thought, that Zeus with his thunderbolt will destroy the attackers. There is irony here, since Amphiaraus will be saved from death by the thunderbolt of Zeus.

And now Eteocles is left alone. He will, he must, defend the seventh gate, no matter who the attacker. Without delay the scout announces that it is his own brother. Again the omen of the name of strife is stressed; again there are boasts and blasphemy. Polyneices is set on revenge. He is willing to die if he can kill his brother, or else he prays to see Eteocles banished as he was banished. His shield bears a figure of Justice leading him back. The scout gives Eteocles the chance to appoint someone else to the gate.

> You take the decisions; you're the city's captain. (652)

But now wisdom in Eteocles gives way to hatred before the overpowering mastery of the curse (655). What does Eteocles bear on his shield? It cannot be blank, for that would match him with Amphiaraus. There is in fact only one emblem he can bear. It is another figure of Justice; and this is in fact what his words imply. Justice will confront Justice. In fact there is justice on neither side of the encounter between the brothers; neither shield will save. All the previous champions had been greeted by a sung prayer from the chorus. Now the chorus breaks into speech rhythm as they try to dissuade Eteocles; but even as they address him as "son of Oedipus" we know that their plea will be unheeded. Eteocles replies with a grim allusion to the "glory" in his own name (685), but when he says,

> If disaster must come, let it be without
> dishonor, (683)

his words are ambiguous, for the shame he is repudiating is the modesty with which his first champion set out to repel *hybris*. The chorus, after the initial protest, reverts to song. Eteocles recalls the curse, and joins it to the nautical metaphor.

> The event moves fast; it is the will of God.
> Let the whole house of Laius, with Phoebus's hate,
> heirs to the flood of death, speed on downwind. (689)

The chorus tries to answer in kind. If he is not hasty the black-cloaked Fury may depart (700).

> Yield while the danger presses. The spirit
> veers and backs belatedly. The god
> may change and come with gentler
>   breath, though now he rages. (705)

Eteocles answers, "The imprecations of Oedipus surge up" (709); the
sea-image and the curse come together. The chorus turns back to speech
rhythms, but Eteocles is intransigent. Some critics have seen his insistence as part of an *Opfertod*, a sacrificial giving of himself for the city.
There is no sign of this, only of hatred and the curse, and after it is
over the chorus's anxiety is not wholly allayed.

There follows a fine choral song. Its theme is the curse; its first word
is "I tremble" (720) and its final word "the Fury" (791). They re-
capitulate the first plays of the trilogy, Laius's defiance of the oracle
and the story of how Oedipus killed his father, married his mother,
blinded himself, and cursed his sons. Through their music two motifs
pulsate. The first is the familiar nautical imagery; but now we are
obsessed not with the skill of the pilot but with the fury of the sea
(758, cf. 769). The other is the image of the steel through which the
curse will be worked out and the inheritance divided; the thought
comes toward the beginning of their song (727) and again at the very
end (788); Eteocles has previously said that the chorus cannot blunt
his resolve (715). Another image that Aeschylus applies with some
skill is that of dust. In the opening chorus it was the dust in the sky
that warned them of the enemy's approach and set them in a panic
(81), but here the dust drains down the brothers' blood (730).

The scout returns. We expect a cry of sorrow that Eteocles is dead;
instead we have a shout of joy that the city is safe.

> Our city has reached a calm lagoon. The waves
> battered her hull; she shipped no water. (795)

At six gates all went well, but at the seventh Apollo took over as Commander of Seven (perhaps a naval title maintaining the metaphor).
The order of lines is uncertain here, but it looks as if the chorus interrupts and holds up the news. Eventually it is out; the sons of Oedipus
are dead; they have divided their inheritance with steel. In death they
are united. A choral lamentation follows, in which the death of the

brothers is treated as a single tragedy. Both are all too well named, both are steeped in strife, and both have achieved true glory (830). The thought of the curse rings through the dirge, as Oedipus and Laius are in turn named. The bodies are ceremonially brought in, and now Aeschylus brilliantly produces the culmination of the nautical image.

> Now, friends, row down the wind
> of your tears, beating hands on your head,
> with a stroke which speeds past the river of Death
> the sacred ship with black sails, the ship of grief,
> which Apollo may not board, or the sun lighten,
> to the unseen shore which awaits us all. (854)

The lamentation continues, but the end of the play has been transmitted to us in a later form, rewritten to link up with Sophocles's *Antigone*, and the lines from 1005 to the end are undoubtedly spurious. For the rest it is perhaps most likely that we have an adjustment of the original choral lyric, but it is not wholly impossible that Aeschylus introduced the dead men's sisters for the final dirge. The curse, the Fury, and the steel through which the curse was fulfilled are the keynotes. The sea makes one last bitter appearance:

> Their feud had a sharp arbitrator, a stranger
> from the Sea, sped from the fire-
> tempered iron. (941)

The general thought comes well from the chorus.

> O Fate, grievous giver of sorrow,
> O holy shade of Oedipus,
> O dark Fury, mighty in power. (986)

The extended threnody is an impressive conclusion, not merely to the play but to the trilogy.

Seven against Thebes is a play of unexpected power. It does not show us Aeschylus at his very greatest; for that we have to wait for *Agamemnon* and *Prometheus*. The restriction on the actors, both in number and treatment, causes a certain stiffness. Yet within the medium, it is masterly. The title, whether Aeschylus's or not, tells us something about the play. As in that skillful but ephemeral comedy *George and Margaret,* the main characters do not appear. They are brought to our imagination partly by sounds off stage, partly by the scout who acts as a go-between, partly by the hysteria of the chorus, partly by the solid, ominously silent departure of the six champions, partly by Eteocles. The chorus is magnificently handled, with a combination of musical lyricism and dramatic realism found in no other play. Eteocles too is realistic; perhaps for the first time we feel we are encountering a full human being on the Attic stage. But at the last the theme of this play, considered in isolation from the rest of the trilogy, is war, and it is the dramatist's success in evoking the emotions of the beleaguered city, whether in terror or reasoned defiance, that arouses our fear and our pity.

6. THE SUPPLIANT WOMEN

The Suppliant Women in form represents Greek tragedy of the earliest period, and for that reason it was assumed to be by far our oldest surviving Greek play by all except the most perceptive of critics. It has generally, and with reason, been assumed that the trilogy was completed by *The Men of Egypt*, which may be the same as the otherwise unknown *The Marriage Makers*, and *The Daughters of Danaus*. The appropriate satyr play would seem to have been *Amymone*; she was one of the girls who was rescued from a satyr by Poseidon, who then took her for himself. A fragmentary papyrus from Oxyrhynchus shows that when Aeschylus presented the tetralogy containing *The Daughters of Danaus* and *Amymone* he won the first prize from Sophocles. Sophocles first contested in 468, and in 467 Aeschylus presented his Theban trilogy. The probable deduction is that the Danaid trilogy did not appear before 466; two letters of what may be the archon's name point to 463. The conclusion that *The Suppliant Women* is to be dated to that year is not completely secure. It is possible that it belongs to a different tetralogy; it is possible that the performance recorded in the papyrus was a revival; it is possible that the plays were written in 493, proved inopportune in the political situation, and were shelved and pulled out again thirty years later. All these views have been propounded, but it remains probable that we are dealing with a fresh play of 463.

The conclusion is reinforced when we consider the trilogy as a whole. The legend was familiar. Aegyptus and Danaus (whose names represent eponymous ancestors of the Egyptians and Argive Greeks) were brothers. They quarreled. Aegyptus sought a solution in marrying his fifty sons to his brother's fifty daughters. Danaus and the girls objected, and, being weaker, escaped to Argos, taking sanctuary with King Pelasgus. In the ensuing war, Pelasgus was killed and Danaus succeeded. Danaus eventually agreed to the wedding, but instructed the girls to kill their husbands on the wedding night. All complied except one, Hypermnestra, who disobeyed her father and spared her husband Lynceus. For this offense she was acquitted by Aphrodite, the goddess of love. If we look for a dramatic parallel to this last, we shall think of the trial of Orestes in *The Kindly Goddesses* most readily. This is the issue of individual responsibility in a world where the divine voices sound conflictingly. The argument of some older critics that such a trial scene was unthinkable in a two-actor play is additional confirmation that the trilogy belongs to a three-actor period.

Why then did Aeschylus cast the first play of the trilogy in an archaic mold? The question is relatively simple to answer. Aeschylus had lived through, had indeed been the protagonist in, the transformation of tragedy from choral response to a situation of drama with well-marked characters interacting. One aspect of this transformation lay in the reduction of the sheer size of the chorus from fifty for each play to fifty for all four, twelve for each and two supernumerary. Any dramatist taking as his theme the Danaus myth is almost bound to center his attention on the fate of the chorus, and as there were notoriously fifty girls, he must be sorely tempted to revert to a chorus of fifty. The use of an archaic idiom, handled with the resources of developed drama, is a likely response. The use of fifty in the chorus cannot be regarded as certain; if it be accepted it points to a period when

Aeschylus had an established reputation and could command what resources he wished—perhaps also to a period of economic prosperity. It is just to add that the hypothesis of a full rather than a representative chorus raises certain problems for the third play of the trilogy, when Hypermnestra must have been set apart from the others. I do not regard it as beyond Aeschylus's restless experimentalism to contrast a chorus of 5X10 with one of 7X7; to an audience used to uneven dispositions it would be startling to see an even pattern.

One more important piece of background evidence relates to the political overtones. With an audience as politically involved as the Athenians these are inescapable. The play must have been presented at a time when Athens was in active relations both with Argos and with Egypt. On the face of it the play is favorable to Argos and unfavorable to Egypt. It is true that the Danaids are themselves Egyptians and were given swarthy masks and exotic clothes; true too that the word which it is tempting to render "Egyptians" really means "Sons of Aegyptus." But to press this is to overrate the sophistication of the Athenian audience. The late 460s or early 450s suits such a situation. Official Athenian policy favored an alliance that would draw Egypt away from Persia, but this is not to say that Aeschylus supported the official policy. Certainly an alliance with Argos was important at that period; it was achieved in 461.

The play itself has obvious spectacular qualities. The stage building is not used for dramatic purposes here, though it is important later in the trilogy. I think however that it must have stood as a shrine associated with the Altar of All the Gods where the suppliants take refuge. The altar with its attendant statues is likely to have been at the back of the orchestra. This creates stage effects unusual to a Greek audience— a tableau of the chorus in the stage area and the actors entering from the wings only and confronting the chorus from the orchestra. Aeschylus liked trying out such effects, as in *The Libation Bearers*, where the chorus enters from the palace. The masks and costumes were exciting, and the bizarre appearance of the chorus draws comment from the king; their suppliant boughs add to the spectacle. The Egyptian herald must also have looked striking.

By any standards the play required a large number of extras. The

daughters call on their maids (977). Some interpreters take these as
a secondary chorus. I think it more likely that they were used to provide a decorative back-cloth. They would have been the same in number as the chorus, marked off by different costumes, and on the scene
throughout the play. When Pelasgus enters he is certainly attended by
a bodyguard (500–503), even if they are not as many as the army
Danaus hears approach (180). We need not, however, be afraid of
attributing to Aeschylus crowd scenes comparable, if not with the
effects of Cecil B. DeMille, at least with *Aida* in the Baths of Caracalla.
Danaus sees chariots (183), and it is possible that the king so enters.
Whether the herald, when he arrives, is similarly attended, is more
controversial. Some interpreters bring him on with the full chorus of
Aegyptus's sons, others with a small but powerful bodyguard. He is,
however, always addressed in the singular, and it is possible that the
dramatic effect here is the fear his single person inspires in the chorus;
it creates a powerful contrast with their eventual capacity to deal with
their fifty suitors.

The scene is an open space near the sea, not far from Argos. The
chorus enters to the characteristic anapaestic rhythm. Their first word
is "Zeus"; they invoke him as Zeus Suppliant. Zeus is traditionally the
protector of suppliants, but this is a new and daring title, identifying
Zeus with them. They explain who they are and why they have come,
evading a union that they call "unholy." They then speak in significant
words of Danaus; we must remember that at Athens all marriages were
arranged by parents, and a father's will over his daughters was absolute. So they describe him in three words: father, initiator-of-decision,
initiator-of-uprising. Then, brilliantly, they say that he organizes the
situation like a "chess" player (12). The phrase is masterly. The
Greek form of chess was an old man's game, and a champion player
was known as a Libyan. But the word itself, *pessos,* is doubly ambiguous, for it also means both a ticket to the political assembly (which in
a sense is what Danaus is securing in Argos) and a vaginal plug to
prevent conception.

The chorus now turns to the primary image of the whole play, Io.
Io was loved by Zeus, made pregnant by the touch of his breath, transformed into a cow, driven by a tormenting gadfly half round the world,

and eventually gave birth to the divine Epaphus, "child of a touch."
Through him she is ancestress of the Danaids and their link with
Argos. We shall see the importance of the theme as the play proceeds.
A line or two later comes another brilliant ambiguity. They speak of
the boughs they carry as *encheiridia*. This means anything carried in
the hand, but particularly a small dagger, and reminds us of the way
they will dispose of their husbands: "bearing in our hand the suppliant's means of defense" (21). They call on Zeus again, now under
his cult title of Savior (26), and speak for the first but by no means
the last time of the *hybris* of their suitors (30). They pray, in an important image, for the breath of Zeus (which, be it remembered, made
Io conceive) to be for them a gentle breeze, and for their pursuers, a
storm wind.

They break into a song and dance in complex and varied rhythms,
and revert immediately to the story of Io and Epaphus, whom they
invoke as their protector, the calf of Zeus. Two other key images
follow, the bird and the flower. The chorus compares itself to the
nightingale chased by the hawk (60). Then, "I gather flowers of
grief" (72). Both images recur. Now they invoke their ancestral gods,
Zeus and Epaphus, we presume, to let justice triumph and check
hybris. Then, in strange and difficult words:

> May the desire of Zeus be truly
> of Zeus; he is hard to track down. (86)

There are many sentiments in Aeschylus that could be mistaken for
Euripides by the unwary. They invoke Zeus by yet another cult title,
the Fulfiller (92), and again pray for the punishment of *hybris* (104).
As they become increasingly excited the very language falls apart; the
metaphors are mixed, as rarely in Aeschylus, till a blossoming shoot
wields the ineluctable whip of a crazed intent (106); a double pun
bursts out in the description of a bull called Apias, now Argos, as "an
Apian brae" where Apis is the cow god of Egypt and brae, a dialect
word, would convey the precise effect if cows made the same noise as
donkeys (117). The chorus uses rare words (118), and short syllables
tumble breathlessly over one another till all sense of rhythm is lost

(112–124). The image of the storm returns. They have had a storm-free passage (136) but,

> O Zeus! Io—anger,
> vengeance is coming from the gods.
> I know the doom brought
> by heaven's victorious queen.
> When the wind blows
> fierce, the storm will come. (162)

There is a bold metaphor from an Athenian official whose duty was to exact the assets of public debtors. Again they invoke Zeus as the all-seeing father (139); there is an implicit contrast with Danaus, whose will they accept blindly as if it were the will of Zeus, but who is not all-seeing. They invoke Artemis, goddess of chastity, calling her not by name but as Zeus's daughter, to preserve their chastity. They call to Zeus the ruler of the dead "who welcomes guests without number," threatening suicide if the gods above do not listen. They call on Zeus compulsively, as father of Epaphus, claiming that their desire must be his will.

Enter Danaus "a wise captain, old and trustworthy." He has seen an army approaching, and advises them to take refuge at the altar. They do so, and in a scene of splendid spectacle move from statue to statue invoking Zeus (as their ancestral god), Apollo, Poseidon, and Hermes in turn. Danaus makes clear that the impiety of the marriage is that it is against their will and their father's will, and uses again the image of doves pursued by hawks (223).

No sooner have they taken up their position than Pelasgus, king of Argos, arrives with his bodyguard, expresses his surprise at their appearance, and introduces himself and his kingdom in a lengthy geographical and mythological excursus. He ends abruptly asking their business, with words that can hardly have failed to raise a laugh: "A self-governing state does not like long speeches" (273). The chorus takes the hint; they claim Argive blood, and a passage of *stichomythia* draws out the legend of Io. They explain their trouble—"On trouble's wing you could not find two feathers the same" (329)—stressing now not the *hybris* of the suitors but their dislike of marriage within the family. They stand as suppliants, and "Zeus, god of suppliants, shows oppressive anger" (347). Now they make their plea in song, turning appropriately from the bird image to that of a heifer harried by wolves (351).

What follows is full of political overtones. Right must be backed by law, and though the foreigners claim that the king is the state, the king himself sees that he must consult his people. He holds the fear of war; the chorus lays on him the fear of Zeus. Their real fears come out; it is now the violence they stress (393), the *hybris* (426). They sing in cretics, a rare meter used for extreme agitation. Fear in fact rules, and when the chorus forces the king's hand by threatening to commit suicide by hanging themselves on the sacred images he gives way with the words, "Fear is supreme among men" (479).

Meantime fresh images have made themselves felt, of Zeus poised with his scales (403), of the king searching the depths of his mind as a diver reaches the ocean bed (408), of a rejected suppliant led like a horse (431). Then comes the storm again, elaborately, vividly. The king is speaking:

> I have taken thought, and here's the reef which wrecks me.
> With one side or the other war must come;
> it's not to be avoided. My ship is wedged
> as if drawn tight by cables.
> There is no untroubled anchorage.
> When wealth is pillaged from a house,
> more goods than those lost may come by grace
> of Zeus the giver of good, and the cargo be replaced. (438)

Zeus is invoked under yet another cult title, the Guardian of Wealth. Then the thought of war leads to the picture of the tongue as an archer (446). The threat of suicide is like a whip on Pelasgus's mind (466). He is overwhelmed as by a river in flood (469) and returns yet again to the image of the storm:

> I am launched on a soundless sea of doom.
> There is no crossing, no harbor of refuge. (470)

This is the turning point of the play. Forebodingly, he bows to Zeus,

Protector of Suppliants, rejects the *hybris* of the men (487), accepts the suppliants, and promises to put their case to the people. He invites them to enter a sacred grove, represented by the orchestra with its altar. They reply in a startling oxymoron; a grove is essentially unapproachable; what protection is there in an approachable unapproachable place? (509). "I will not cast you out as prey to carrion birds," replies the king, taking up the bird image, and the chorus replies, "What then? As prey to men more dangerous than poisonous snakes?" (510–511). Once again it is clear that fear rules (513–514).

The chorus, in the grove of the orchestra, sings and dances. Their song starts from Zeus, king of kings, Zeus the Fulfiller, and prays him to avert *hybris* and drown in the sea the malignant power that presses on them. Their thoughts turn to Io, her suffering and deliverance. The poetry is exquisite:

> The lord of endless time,
> Zeus, held her in his hand,
> and by his gentle strength,
> and by the breath of godhead,
> her hurt was healed, and tears
> of shame and grief flowed free.
> She took Zeus's burden upon her in truth
> and bore a spotless child. (574)

Zeus is omnipotent; he wills, and it is done.

Danaus, who left with the king, returns and brings the news that the Argives have accepted the suppliants. The decision was unanimous; the king used persuasive political oratory; Zeus brought the issue to fulfillment (624). The girls break into a song and dance of thanks and benediction. It is another beautiful ode, subtly patterned. It begins with a long prayer that Argos may be free from war and plague, passes to prayers for piety and fruitfulness, reverts to the theme of freedom from war and plague, and passes again to prayers for fruitfulness and piety, inverting the order to end on the strong note of the gods. Zeus appears especially as Protector of Suppliants and Protector of Strangers. The bird image is not far from their minds; the Divine Avenger perches on the rooftop (686), and their own words take wings (657).

The flower is also there in the prayer, "Let the flower of her youth pass unplucked" (663). A vivid phrase pictures diseases as a swarm of insects (684). But there is irony in this ode. For the decision the girls have taken to reject their suitors means war. Their killing of their husbands under Argive protection will bring pollution on Argos, manifested in plague and sterility. It is itself an offense against Zeus Protector of Strangers. It is an offense against the piety and the fruitfulness they invoke.

Danaus has been watching. Without abruptness he tells them that he has seen the ships of Egypt. Let them remain in sanctuary, he will go for help. They try to dissuade him. Fear again rules (734–738). The ships have come swift-winged (734); we think of the hawks pursuing the doves; a few lines later the men are compared to carrion crows (751). They are pariah dogs, but the wolves of Argos will prove their match. They are weedy papyrus, no match for the sturdy wheat of Argos. So Danaus, to strengthen the girls' resolve as he goes.

The girls sing and dance in panic, an excellent opening for fine ballet. They start now not from Zeus, but from the "Apian braes." They make fantasies of escaping like smoke, of being blown away like dust, invisibly, winglessly. Even the dream of bird flight is useless; the hawk is about to pounce. They would rather be dead, a prey to real pariah dogs and carrion crows than married to these human predators. They invoke Zeus the Fulfiller who holds the scales of destiny (822). The Egyptian herald breaks in on their dance, and tries to drive them to the ships; Aeschylus, with characteristic imagination, uses the precisely correct Egyptian word (836, 873). Our text in this scene is obscure and contorted. The herald is excited; he repeats his words as Euripides liked to do in song (859–865). The girls are hysterical. They harp on the storm that did not prevent the Egyptians from coming. The herald is a spider with his prey, a black nightmare. In their frenzy they invoke the primeval goddess Mother Earth, Ma Ga, and Zeus only secondly as Father God. In the Eleusinian mysteries there was a moment when the congregation called on the sky to rain and the earth to conceive. Aeschylus was accused somehow, somewhere, of betraying the mysteries. One wonders whether here he gave the frantic girls the gestures appropriate to that moment.

At the last moment the king arrives to the rescue; it is excellent melodrama. To the herald the law of Argos is nothing; might is right and Ares the arbiter. But the king speaks firmly of the rule of law; the unanimous verdict of the assembly is binding. A free tongue speaking plain truth has a cogency beyond the written word. The herald leaves, darkling, and the king promises the girls the protection of Argos; his words imply a siege in the next play. Danaus arrives with an Argive bodyguard, and speaks more words of advice. He has taken all the decisions; he has molded their lives and characters. His last words emphasize this:

> Simply stand firmly by your father's advice,
> and value obedience more than you value life. (1012)

The girls dance after him to Argos. The final chorus raises an acute problem. There is evidently an antiphonal effect between the claims of chastity and love. As the girls are divided on this, 49 to 1, some in-terpreters make the maidservants the advocates of love. It seems to me more likely that the antiphonal was divided between two solo voices, one of whom would represent Hypermnestra, while the rest of the chorus danced (6X8). Aphrodite is pictured with her attendants, Desire, Persuasion, Music, and the Loves. But Zeus is central at the end as he was at the beginning. The question, asked in fear,

> Why has their voyage prospered
> in swiftness of pursuit? (1045)

is pertinent to the rightness of their own course. The purpose of Zeus is indeed a strong frontier that none can overstep. As they recess they return to the theme of Io:

> May the lord Zeus save us
> from harsh marriage to a hateful
>   husband—Zeus who freed
> Io from her affliction,
> restoring her with healing hand
> and use of gentle force.
>
> May he give strength to women.
> I am content with the least of evils,

> two shares if one be good,
> and judgment follow Justice,
> and through my prayers salvation
> comes from God. (1062)

Our prayers are not always answered as we will. To Aeschylus the women's cause was Hypermnestra's, and that received final victory.

This is a religious play. The conflict between Artemis and Aphrodite is as explicit as it is in Euripides's *Hippolytus,* except that there they are autonomous powers and here they are both under the ultimate power of Zeus. It is important to stress this conflict. Different interpretations have been given of the refusal of the girls to marry their cousins. According to one version of the myth, Danaus was given an oracle that Aegyptus intended to kill the girls once they were in his power; but Aeschylus would have assuredly alluded to this had he intended it. One brilliant analysis, by George Thomson, sees the theme of the trilogy as the conflict between endogamy and exogamy, and its conclusion in favor of the endogamy with which Aeschylus was familiar at Athens. There is no trace in our play that Danaus intended the girls to wed elsewhere, and the fear of marrying within the family is only a respectable argument for the Argives.

There are three elements in the play as presented. The first is the will of Danaus. That will is unexplained, and the lack of explanation must be deliberate. The father's will is enough for the daughter's obedience. I cannot understand those critics who complain about the characterization of Danaus; the portrait is not colorless, it is ambiguous and subtle. Pelasgus and the herald are sketched in broad outline, but Danaus is a character study. The theme of obedience is his last word, and it leads inexorably to the murders. Secondly, the suitors themselves are undesirable husbands; their violent *hybris* is stressed time and again. Thirdly, because of this the girls have persuaded themselves that every marriage is a rape. The counterclaims of chastity and love are openly and clearly stated, and the fact that one of the few fragments of *The Daughters of Danaus* shows Aphrodite speaking for Hypermnestra proves that this became the real issue, not the desirability of any particular husband.

For the whole thing is in the hands of Zeus, who holds the balance of destiny. I have counted over fifty direct references to Zeus in the play. He is the ultimate power, and he is ultimately beneficent. But the chorus takes too facile a view of this beneficence. From time to time a warning note is sounded. The ways of Zeus are inscrutable. The same gentle breath that brought Io to bliss may burst out into a storm wind; yet no storm wind but a following breeze escorted the pursuers. The girls do not merely misunderstand the will of Zeus; they seek to impose their will on Zeus. The appeal from Zeus of the living to Zeus of the dead comes near to blasphemy; *flectere si nequeo superos, Acheronta movebo.* The threat to commit suicide in a holy place is impiety. The girls are not interested in the will of Zeus; they know their father's will and project that onto the father of gods and men.

It is just here that what Robert Duff Murray called "the Danaids' atavistic obsession that they are in some sense a reincarnation of Io" is essential to our understanding of the play. Io ran away from union because of an oracle to Inachus; she was caught up and blessed. So the Danaids run away, and their blessing will only be in acceptance. There is a double parallel: the Danaids run from their suitors as Io ran from Zeus; Hypermnestra is blessed by union with Lynceus as Io was blessed by union with Zeus. This is the marvellous irony of the final prayer. There is a double entendre, in Greek as in English, within the word "force." To pray to be freed from sex to the Zeus who healed Io from her affliction by the touch of sex is a contradiction in terms. Hypermnestra alone will be truly identified with Io; the rest choose the path of war, murder, and pollution. For the breath that blesses is also the storm that destroys. But Hypermnestra's path lies through disobedience to her father. She has her own *agon.* For the path to bliss lies through suffering.

7. AGAMEMNON

Swinburne called *The Oresteia* "the greatest achievement of the human mind." Apart altogether from its intrinsic merit, it is of peculiar interest as the only surviving trilogy. Even so we cannot fully evaluate its impact, as we lack the satyr play that completed the tetralogy. This was *Proteus*, as we know from the scholiast to Aristophanes's *The Frogs*; it seems to have dealt with the shipwreck of Menelaus and his encounter with Proteus, the old man of the sea, but the sparse fragments do not allow us to begin a reconstruction. In *The Odyssey* (4.512) Proteus tells Menelaus something of the trap laid by Aegisthus for Agamemnon. Aeschylus would have taken this as his starting point, used his own storm sequence in *Agamemnon*, and perhaps made fun of the Helen theme that stands grimly in the background of *Agamemnon*.

The plot of the trilogy is said to have been derived from Stesichorus proximately, and we need not doubt this. More remotely, there are passages in *The Odyssey* that tell of the killing of Agamemnon by

Aegisthus and his avenging by Orestes (3.256ff.; 4.512ff.); and Clytemnestra is named as one who killed her husband (11.439). Apart
from the two surviving Homeric epics there were other bardic traditions, and the lost *Nostoi* or *Returns* ascribed to Agias dealt with Agamemnon's fate and Orestes's vengeance. But Aeschylus made the story
his own.

One other aspect of the trilogy is of some importance. As we have
seen, one theory of the origin of Greek tragedy, associated particularly
with the name of Gilbert Murray, is that it reenacts the Death and
Rebirth of the Year Spirit. We have seen that this is an oversimplifica-
tion, and most modern scholars reject it out of hand. We have, however, suggested that there may be a partial truth here, and that this may
be one of several strands woven into the fabric of Greek tragedy. Gilbert Murray, in a classic essay, took two types of this theme in Orestes
and Hamlet. In essence both stories tell of an old king killed by a
usurper and avenged by his son, and this is the same pattern as the
death of the Old Year before the assassin Winter and the restoration of
the New Year in spring. Such fertility festivals would have been
familiar in the countryside, and we may reasonably assume a response
to this pattern from some at least of the audience. Nonetheless, if this
was the origin, it is not the conclusion, and if this is the explanation of
the myth, Aeschylus has turned it to his own purposes.

His plot then would be familiar to the audience. In the background,
the rivalry of Atreus, Agamemnon's father, and Thyestes, Aegisthus's
father and the "Thyestean banquet" where Atreus served up Thyestes's other sons to him; the marriage of the brothers Agamemnon
and Menelaus to the sisters Clytemnestra and Helen; the rape of Helen
by Paris of Troy; the Greek expedition against Troy; Agamemnon's
sacrifice of his daughter Iphigeneia to procure a favorable wind in
face of the disfavor of Artemis; the war itself; the sack of Troy and the
impious rape of the virgin priestess and Princess Cassandra by Agamemnon. In the foreground the assassination of Agamemnon by
Clytemnestra and Aegisthus, the vengeance of Agamemnon's son
Orestes upon the murderers, and the moral, religious, and social problems created by the story.

It is in stressing this last dimension that the poet shows his originality. To bring out this aspect of his theme he points to Agamemnon's guilt; he is a guilty victim, not an innocent one, and Shirley J. Stewart has suggested that Aeschylus's special contribution to the moral development of the myth lies in the insertion into it of the idea of personal responsibility. The theme is reflected in the imagery. "All characters in *The Oresteia*," she writes, "are affected with a moral sickness which is brought to light by medical terminology, all, that is, except Orestes, who seems to be an exception to almost all the patterns of imagery, just as he will be a break in the chain of crimes. The most obvious imagery is seen, of course, in the light which is to prove no joy in the *Agamemnon*, but which will be a sign of the triumphal procession in the *Eumenides*." It follows in the nature of the case that the first play of the sequence, *Agamemnon*, is "one which illustrates men groping their way about, with their vision clouded, their hearing poor, their cries and actions like those of animals." It is, in short, in Stewart's pungent phrase "a play of distortion."

The opening is certainly startling enough. A figure appears on the palace roof—not right on top of the stage building, which is reserved for gods, but on the platform halfway up. It is no king or general, but a down-to-earth watchman. He yawns, stretches himself, then cries,

> I pray the gods: release me from this duty,
> release me from this year-round watch. (1)

His words betray an underlying mood of foreboding; they set a spirit of tension. The very cry for release, in words twice repeated (20), anticipates the net image that enfolds the play later. The structure of his sentences seems distorted. Clytemnestra is mentioned, though not by name, as a woman with a man's heart (11). And the note of fear is sounded (14). The watchman is waiting for a beacon to proclaim victory at Troy. As he watches, suddenly he sees the beacon; he raises a cry of joy, and calls on Clytemnestra, again not by name, but as Agamemnon's wife. Her shadow is already over the play. His words go on to a somber note. All is not well within the palace. Its very walls could tell the story. He cannot. He says, in picturesque language (36), "There's an ox on my tongue." He means, as the Greek commentator Zenobius tells us, that, as money talks, so also money (stamped with the image of the ox that represented wealth, as the Latin *pecunia*) can buy silence.

Clytemnestra does not come yet. The chorus, twelve elders too old for the army ten years before, file in to the characteristic anapaestic rhythm. The long opening choral sequence, over two hundred lines in all, is vital to our understanding of the whole *Oresteia*. It is perhaps the profoundest thing Aeschylus ever wrote. They begin factually and relevantly. Ten years ago Agamemnon and Menelaus set out for Troy. Their opening words contain a legal metaphor. Menelaus, with Agamemnon, is plaintiff (or defendant)—the word is ambiguous (41). Our minds are subtly prepared for the rule of law at the trilogy's end. Now comes first poetry, which images the brothers as eagles whose nest has been robbed—of children (50). This is a miraculous touch. Helen was wife, not child, and the word is not elsewhere used of the young of animals. A child has been killed—by one of the eagles. The eagles cry to the gods, and Zeus, protector of the rights of hospitality, hears. Pan hears. Apollo hears. And they send a Fury (59). As that word rings out, the palace doors open and Clytemnestra appears. The chorus does not yet see her; they continue with their chant. Zeus sent the sons of Atreus over a promiscuous woman (62). They do not name her; they mean Helen; but there were two brothers, and their wives were two sisters, and one is before our eyes. In the providence of God, crime brings disaster. The prayers of Troy cannot avert this, though the Greeks too suffer. As they meditate on old age, which kept them at home, Clytemnestra is offering sacrifice—to what god, with what prayer? We are not intended to know. She does not speak; her silent passage over the stage is tremendously impressive. They address her, first as "Daughter of Tyndareus," which could be Helen, and then, only then, for the first time as Clytemnestra. She does not answer. Their words are full of expectation, but also of dread.

They turn back to the audience and tell of a portent from ten years ago. Two eagles tore a pregnant hare. The eagles, we know, symbolize Agamemnon and Menelaus. But what of the pregnant hare? A pregnant animal contains unborn innocent young. In one sense the hare is Troy and the embryos the innocents who have suffered in an expedition that Zeus ordained against Paris (61); in another the rending is the

whole work of the expedition, and the unborn leverets represent the
innocent Iphigeneia. The repeated refrain rings out, "Cry sorrow,
sorrow—yet let good prevail!" The seer Calchas proclaimed the anger
of Artemis against Agamemnon and Menelaus, not because Agamemnon killed her sacred stag—Aeschylus deliberately leaves out this part
of the legend—but just because they tear the innocent. Cry sorrow,
sorrow—yet let good prevail!

There follows a passage of marvelous theology:

> Zeus, whoever he is, if this
>   name pleases him to hear,
> I use it to address him.
> I have weighed each choice,
> I cannot guess the means,
> but Zeus, to throw for once and all this load
>   of ignorance from my mind.
>
> No he who of old was lord,
>   bursting with pride in war,
>   shall have his being unknown.
> His successor met
>   his master, and is gone.
> Zeus is victor; proclaim it with understanding,
>   and win understanding in all.
>
>   He guided men to wisdom.
>   He laid down the law:
>   Learning comes from suffering.
> Sleepless we hear in our hearts the drip
>   of memoried pain; good sense
>   comes to us against our will.
> The blessing of the gods is brought with violence
>   as they sit on their lofty thrones. (160)

Zeus, whoever he is (160). There is a divine power in the universe,
call it what we will, and he has ordained that we learn through suffering. But in between these two thoughts Aeschylus puts a passage of
traditional mythology—with a purpose: Ouranos ruled the gods by
violence and was overthrown by violence. Cronos ruled by violence
and was overthrown by violence. Zeus now rules. Is there no end to the

cycle of violence, among gods or men? Aeschylus will work this out more fully in his *Prometheia.* Zeus has used violence, it is true, but violence affects its user too; and his rule is marked not merely by force, but by wisdom as well.

What then of man? Artemis opposes the expedition. The winds will not change unless Agamemnon sacrifices Iphigeneia—blasphemous, unnatural cruelty. This is not a sacrifice of Isaac demanded as a somewhat dubious test of faith. This is a barrier to the expedition. Agamemnon has to choose between this blasphemous crime and the censure of men. He chooses the crime. "May good prevail, and justify my deed"— that is not possible. He has not had the courage to break the cycle of violence. His violence breeds violence against him. For this is a law of life. When, in Nigeria, the Sardauna of Sokoto and Chief Akintola tried to impose tyranny by violence, they raised against themselves a group of Ibo soldiers who killed them. But this violence in turn provoked its reaction six months later in the killing of the Ibo commander-in-chief and the massacre of Ibos in the north. That in turn stirred up violence against northerners in the east, and armed secession, which led inevitably to the invasion of the east from the north. Violence breeds violence until someone breaks the cycle, or until all is brought under the rule of law.

So comes the exquisite description of Iphigeneia, powerfully echoed by Lucretius in his tirade against the crimes of religion, and beautifully evoked in paint by an artist in Pompeii. And when the tale is told the chorus returns to their first insight. Calchas had his way. "But Justice tilts the scale to give learning to those who suffer" (250). And all through the account of the sacrifice of the daughter, the mother has been in the background sacrificing in preparation for a bloodier sacrifice. She has not learned the lesson.

As they finish their song she comes forward, one of the most dominating figures in any play ever written. She gives them the news that Troy has fallen and explains that the news was brought by the fire god himself. She speaks in superb poetry with resounding and evocative names, full of the New Learning and the excitement of exploring the world that the defeat of the Persians had made familiar. Then comes an imaginative description of the fall of Troy—death, desolation, and destruction—but with a warning against sacrilege for fear that the Greeks impair their homecoming. At first hearing, this might be a typically sententious reflection of the chorus; yet it is given to the terrible, magisterial queen. Why? Because vengeance is hers; she will repay. The scene ends, and as it ends Clytemnestra speaks words overtly pious, underly grim: "May good prevail." This is the prayer we have heard from the chorus; in her mouth it means something very different. As she says this, she covers her prayer for the safety of the fleet under the pretense that it arose from feminine sentimentalism (348). She will say "many things to suit the time" (1372). The chorus, perhaps out of politeness, speaking more wisely than they know, perhaps with an instinctive grasp of the truth, says, "My lady, you speak like a man..." (351).

> Bring forth men-children only,
> For thy undaunted courage should compose
> Nothing but males,

cried Macbeth to his wife, and it has been shown that Shakespeare's Lady Macbeth derives, through Holinshed, Hector Boece, Livy, and Accius, ultimately from Clytemnestra in Aeschylus.

The long ode that follows has often been taken as a flood of joy on which fear supervenes. It is not. Its mood would be set by the music and choreography; in the absence of these we have the meter. This shows no change of mood. It is not excited, save for a moment at the beginning; it is almost in speech rhythm. It goes on with no change and little break for nearly 150 lines, thudding out its repeated pattern with sinister intensity. The chorus says the right things, but they say them in a spirit of cold, black fear. More, the rhythm picks up their song about the crime at Aulis. We carry on where we left off; we left off with Justice tilting the scale. Throughout this song the words that the chorus uses innocently of Troy point to the coming doom. A net, a hunter's net, was cast over Troy by Zeus (358); we shall meet this net again, for it will be cast over Agamemnon by Clytemnestra. Zeus's arrow was aimed at Paris and did not fall short of the mark or beyond the stars; nor will Clytemnestra's with Agamemnon. They fared as Zeus decreed (369); so will Agamemnon. Paris trampled in the dust beauty of in-

violable things (371); Agamemnon will trample a crimson carpet to
his doom. But more:

> The gods are not blind to those
> who kill by the mass. (461)

Agamemnon is Zeus's minister of justice on Paris, but in the indis-
criminacy of his killing he invites justice on himself. Aeschylus was no
pacifist; he fought the Persians. But he knew also that war breeds war,
and in one of the most memorable among his many memorable metaphors he wrote, "War's a money-changer, giving dust for flesh"
(438). So the Furies, whom we shall see before the three plays are
over, here for the second time, are on the prowl (463). Paris sinned:
Zeus struck him down:: Agamemnon has sinned: .... but the
chorus, in its masculine scorn of women, does not perceive the danger.

During this song, calculating in the coolness of the study, we may
reckon that we skip several days, since Agamemnon's ship, however
heroic, could not travel as fast as a beacon fire. The point scarcely matters in the theater—which is all that does matter—and the action is
presented as continuous. A herald from the Greek fleet arrives; we are
awaiting the Messiah and John the Baptist appears. This dramatic
suspense remains through a scene of two hundred lines and a chorus of
a hundred. Yet the scene holds us by its intrinsic merit and carries our
horrendous foreboding to a more inescapable depth. The herald's first
speech seems innocuous enough; he is not the watchman; he has no
forebodings. But what of us who watch and listen? He falls and grasps
his native soil, as Agamemnon will fall in death. He stretches his arms
to the sun, which Agamemnon will not see again. He invokes Zeus;
but what is Zeus's will? He invokes Apollo, as Savior and Healer; the
titles remind us of the damnable disease infecting the palace. He invokes Hermes, the god of heralds—but also the god who escorts the
dead. He invokes, in an ambiguous phrase, *agonioi theoi,* perhaps the
gods who preside over the great games, perhaps the gods of the assembly, perhaps the gods in their own assembly, perhaps all three, but conveying to us also the thought of the *agon* that stands at the center of
tragedy. He invokes the demigods, the ancestors, and a chill creeps
from his joyous words, for they remind us of the curse on the house of

Atreus. And now he speaks of Agamemnon's coming. Clytemnestra
has prayed for a safe return provided that the Greeks do not commit
sacrilege. The herald, the good, casual, worthy, unimaginative herald
says (and some foolish editors omit the key line):

> Give him a royal welcome, as is right
> for one who used Zeus the Avenger's pick
> to flatten Troy and work over her land,
> *exterminate the altars, the dwellings of the gods—*

and then,

> and extirpate the seed from all her soil. (524)

The seed—as the eagles extirpated the seed of the hare, as Agamemnon
extirpated the seed that was his own daughter. So Troy's deed was not
greater than its punishment, its suffering. At the very end of the speech
the herald throws in another of the legal metaphors that Aeschylus
deliberately uses in this trilogy. In Attic law the offender paid full restitution and, in addition, a fine. In Agamemnon's court the city of Paris
paid full restitution and, in addition, total destruction. Is that justice?

The herald cries, "Thank God I'm through!" No one can again so
speak till the very end of the play. They can only pray that "this is the
end." But it never is. Blood calls for blood, and somber but unexplained words from the chorus balance the herald's cheerful prattle.
He now launches us on a description of what war means, even to the
victors. Aeschylus was a soldier and knew war; he doesn't romanticize.

> We slept alongside the enemy's walls.
> From above and from the meadows under us,
> the damp seeped in, our clothes
> rotted, our hair was thick with lice. (559)

This is the realism of Passchendaele or the Mekong Delta.

Suddenly Clytemnestra is there. She speaks briefly. First, words of
triumph over the chorus who had said of her news, "Typical of a
woman to believe gossip"; they had not in fact done so in her presence
(cf. 485); it reasserts the theme that Clytemnestra is no woman in her
control of the situation. Then a terrible two-edged message to Agamemnon (604). His wife can be trusted (to go through with her
plan; and a skilled actor by a slight change of inflection can produce

an ambiguity with "cannot be trusted," *gunaika pisten* and *gunaik'
apisten*). She is as he left her (Helen's sister); a watchdog at his door
(but the words can mean "a bitch in the home"); loyal to *him*
(whom?); implacable to enemies (such as Agamemnon); in all else
the same (and the word can mean either consistent or the same as him,
a man of blood). And then, "I know no more delight in any other man
than I know how to dip a blade" (ostensibly to temper it, but also to
dip it in blood). Yet we call Sophocles the master of dramatic irony!
And she is gone.

There follows a further passage of magnificent rhetoric describing
how the fleet was scattered and shattered. The equation, as Kitto puts
it, is extended. Paris sinned: Zeus struck him down:: the Greek army
sinned: the gods struck them down:: Agamemnon sinned . . . .
and we have seen the Avenger, the Fury, waiting.

The chorus sings again of Helen, whose very name is hell, ship's
hell, man's hell, city's hell (there is a similar pun in the Greek) and of
the parable of the lion cub, which overtly applies to Helen in Troy but
also to her sister Clytemnestra at Argos; both came from Sparta where
they prided themselves on being lions. Helen became for Troy a Fury,
sent by Zeus the god of hospitality. Then the meter, music, and dance
all change, back to the sinister leitmotif of sin and punishment. The
chorus claims to be asserting something new. It is not true that prosperity excites the envy of the gods. Rather, crime begets crime, *hybris* fathers *hybris*. Says Duncan of a thane who betrayed him, "He was a
gentleman on whom I built an absolute trust." *Enter Macbeth.* So here
the chorus sings of Justice honoring the upright home, whether rich or
poor, and passing by the palace when wealth and sin go together. "She
directs all to their destiny" (781). *Enter Agamemnon.*

Agamemnon enters in a chariot, and in the chariot is a woman who
sits as a slave. She says nothing. Greek drama had introduced a third
actor, but there remained a strong tendency for the dramatic encounter
to be an I-thou between two people only. The third actor permitted
more subtle effects. Aeschylus is not writing a drawing-room comedy
with a seemingly eternal triangle. Cassandra, for it is she, sits through
Agamemnon's triumphs as a silent reminder of sacrilege and a crowning insult to Clytemnestra. The chorus greets Agamemnon in ana-

paests, which suggests a spectacular processional entry; one suspects that the chariot went all around the orchestra followed by an army of extras. As the chorus accompanies him their words are meaningful. They reveal that they thought Agamemnon wrong in taking the expedition. The text is uncertain, but there is almost certainly a reference to Iphigeneia's sacrifice and perhaps to Helen's wantonness (and we remember the wantonness of Clytemnestra, for throughout this play mention of Helen recalls her sister). But Agamemnon succeeded; they now approve his act. In less than an hour we shall see that he has not succeeded. Furthermore, their words contain a warning, discreet but clear to us, about how some harsh embittered faces will be forced into a seemly smile to welcome him.

Agamemnon is on the stage for less than two hundred lines of the play that bears his name, yet few scenes in all literature contain such intense drama. He is sketched with a sure brush. "Ambitious, proud, weak of will, self-confident, self-duped," writes Stewart, "he sees himself, his greatness, his authority, as always in the public eye. . . . He dwells throughout in unsuspicious security, even though his very life is in the balance. His monstrous egotism prevents him from penetrating the insincerity of his wife, whose words of affection mask her bloody purpose. An unconscious hypocrite himself, he is fooled by a hypocrite."

For the moment he ignores the chorus. He rightly addresses the gods who were his partners in sacking Troy; his words may perhaps seem more arrogant in English than they would to a Greek. But they contain the heart of the problem. Zeus and Agamemnon *were* partners in bringing justice on Troy, and yet on the human plane that act of justice calls for another counterstroke of justice, which will in its turn call out another counterstroke of justice. Agamemnon's lusty enjoyment in describing the destruction intensifies our awareness of this. Then he turns—without addressing the chorus—to their warning. Healing is needed; it is the image of disease again. Fire or the knife will cleanse the body politic. It will indeed.

He is about to come down from the chariot when the palace doors open and Clytemnestra appears. Brilliantly, she speaks not to Agamemnon but to the chorus. Her first words to Agamemnon refer to their son Orestes, "Your and my true love's pledge" (878). His absence at this point is vital to what happens later; it is given powerful dramatic force by being her first words to him. She then piles on the metaphors as she calls him "watchdog of his home"—the same word she earlier used of herself with the same innuendo "wolf of the barracks," especially as her sweeping gesture toward him cannot fail to take in Cassandra:

> our ship's protecting forestay, firm-fixed support
> of the towering roof, a father's only son—

the Orestes theme again—

> land in sight at sea when hope was gone,
> day brilliantly breaking after storm,
> a spring of water to a thirsty traveler. (896)

Then she prays that Heaven's jealousy may acquit them. And now the servants unroll a crimson carpet, and she invites him to trample underfoot the beauty of holy things.

If he sets foot on it, he is doomed. This will be the visible symbolical moment when his *hybris* challenges heaven. He is not an utter fool; he is flattered but deprecating. He addresses Clytemnestra, with a wealth of suggestion, as "Leda's daughter" (914). In elaborate words that should probably be transposed from 958 to follow 929 she piles on somber imagery—the inexhaustible sea, the shadow of the vine, and the vintage of bitter grapes. She presses her point. What would Priam have done? Exactly. Agamemnon cannot break the vicious circle. He makes the crimes of Troy his own. She presses again.

AGAMEMNON: Delight in battle does not suit a woman.
CLYTEMNESTRA: In triumph there is grace in giving way.
AGAMEMNON: Do you count so much on victory in this conflict?
CLYTEMNESTRA: Yield. You have the power. Let me have my way. (940)

If he yields, she will indeed have her way. A slave unties his shoes. He is about to step out; then he checks himself. Will he at the last minute be saved? No! It is to give orders about Cassandra; it rubs in his sin. This is superlative drama. He stalks in to death.

Clytemnestra utters a piercing cry of triumph—not in our manuscripts but almost certainly to be restored here (cf. 1236)—and follows it with a prayer to Zeus the Fulfiller. Zeus will fulfill, but the end is not yet.

The fourth chorus is difficult Greek and uncertain. It reinforces the chorus's foreboding. In climax they seem to say, "The universe is an order, a cosmos, in which action and reaction are equal and opposite" —an idea of contemporary philosophy. "If this were not so, I would be easy in my mind, but because it is so, I am afraid." Here philosophy and religion come together in complete relevance to drama. Further, the brooding song that the chorus instinctively sings they themselves describe as "a Fury's dirge" (992).

Now comes another master stroke. Cassandra has throughout been sitting, unmoving, unspeaking. Suddenly Clytemnestra is back. Has the plot succeeded? Has it failed? Not yet. Clytemnestra orders Cassandra into the house. Cassandra sits stock-still. The chorus speaks kindly words; she does not respond. Perhaps she does not understand Greek—an excellent touch of realism; someone tries using gestures. She ignores him; then suddenly rises, writhing in ecstasy. For the first time Clytemnestra is baffled and retires defeated. Who has defeated her? The god Apollo, by whose oracle she herself will be killed. For Cassandra had received Apollo's love. He bribed her with the gift of prophecy; then, when she withheld her body, he turned the gift into a curse: she should not be believed. But she remained a virgin, wedded to the god, and her violation by Agamemnon was an offense against the gods.

Suddenly Cassandra breaks her silence with a wild cry "Otototototoi popoi da. O Apollo! O Apollo!" It is the most tremendous cry in Greek tragedy. Then, a grim pun on the god's name: "Apollo my destroyer" (1081). She looks at the palace and sees it dripping with blood. The color of *Macbeth* is black, black as the thick and seeling night, black as the raven, black as the filthy, black, and midnight hags, black as Macbeth's soul. The color of *Agamemnon* is red, red as the beacon fires, red as the fires that burn Troy, red as the flame of sacrifice, red as the fire that will purge the state, red as the crimson carpet, red as the fire that burns within Cassandra, red as the tawny lioness, red as blood. Cassandra sees in her vision the dead children of Thyestes;

she sees new deaths; she sees a cleansing ritual in a bath; she sees a hunting net; she sees a cow goring a bull.

A moment before, the chorus thought that she needed an interpreter; it is they who need the interpreter. But they see (1119) that she is calling a Fury upon the house—to bay at it like a hellhound, yes, but also to set it right, for the word is ambiguous. The rushing, breathless short syllables grow quieter, and she speaks in ordinary speech rhythms, stripping the veil off her prophecies (1178). Her words are still spiced with visionary insight. She sees a reveling company of Furies, drunk with human blood, settled in the house (1190). Animal imagery is intensified: the cowardly lion, the bitch, the basilisk, Scylla, or shark (1224 ff.). She tells her own story, her offense against Apollo, and at one moment she speaks the stark prophetic fact, "I say that you shall see Agamemnon lying dead" (1246). The chorus is horrified, but Cassandra presses on, relentlessly sane. She understands; she speaks good Greek, as good as Apollo. A fire is blazing within her (1256). She strips off her prophetic robes and garlands, or rather she feels Apollo strip her of them (1269). Slowly, inexorably, she moves toward the palace door. Then, as she is about to move in, she reels away, choked with the reek of blood that her prophetic sense detects. She prophesies the vengeance that will overtake her murderers and passes inside.

And what is this scene about? Of course it is splendid drama, and Cassandra a vividly fascinating character to bring in, the ample justification of the third actor. But she is not the theme of this episode. The Greek audience liked scenes *à deux,* and this is a scene between Cassandra and the as yet unseen Apollo. This is the point: the presence, the introduction of Apollo. Her repeated cry is "Apollo! Apollo!" And when she cries "Apollo is stripping me of my robes," we must sense the invisible hands pulling at her dress, leaving her helpless for the rape that is death. She has no word against Agamemnon or Clytemnestra for her own fate, no word, for that matter, *against* Apollo. She has offended against Apollo. Apollo has brought her to this pass. So be it. Clytemnestra will offend against the gods, and Apollo will bring her to the same pass, the selfsame pass in the selfsame position within the selfsame tableau. And, for the first time explicitly, we have had the curse on the house of Atreus, the unending cycle: "Blood will have blood."

And now Aeschylus is too wise to prolong the agony. The next choral anapaests are brief, and a ringing cry from within the house cuts across their song. It is Agamemnon's death cry. It was the practice of Greek tragedy to report events too appalling to see. Here murder is heard, and the effect is devastating. The chorus is in consternation; they are politicians not soldiers, old not young. The twelve give their opinion of the situation in turn with the formality of a committee meeting. Then the doors of the palace open and on the mobile platform we see in tableau the bodies of Agamemnon, entangled in a great net-like robe, and Cassandra; Clytemnestra with blood-bespattered sword stands exultant over them. Now at last Clytemnestra reveals her true feelings, her cold savage hatred for Agamemnon that stabbed his dead body and rejoiced as the blood spurted to fall upon her, as the sown cornfield rejoices in rain from Zeus (the old fertility ritual behind the drama peers through for a moment) (1392). She reveals her masculinity in a barrage of military metaphors; she reveals what she really thought of the killing of Iphigeneia, the killing of her own birth pangs (1418); she reveals her biting jealousy of Cassandra and her view of Agamemnon as the wolf of the barracks. Here at least, she says, is a just journey to the dead (1396). A just death, perhaps—but a just killing?

What follows is technically a lament. These are rhythms of song and dance. The chorus sings and dances its grief, but Clytemnestra sings and dances her triumph. The image of the net, the spider's web, recurs. Clytemnestra repeats the equation between Agamemnon's killing of Iphigeneia and her own killing of Agamemnon, and bitterly pictures Iphigeneia running to greet her father in the land of the dead. That is the only mourning he shall have. She appears in her true light as the Avenger, the Avenger on the house of Atreus. And this reminds us that the equation is not simple: the account is not balanced. There are Avengers and Furies to come. For through the song of the chorus once again throbs the ineluctable rhythm we have met before, the rhythm of sin and retribution, as they cry:

> All through Zeus,
> cause of all, doer of all.
> What fulfillment can humans find except through Zeus?
> What here is not ordained of heaven? (1485)

So at the end of the song the chorus goes back to its first insight. The doer suffers. The sinner dies. Yes, says Clytemnestra, he has, but she does not see the pointing finger: "Thou too art the one." She believes she has freed the house of the chain of murder (1577). She has not.

Aegisthus comes, Thyestes's son and Clytemnestra's paramour, a cock strutting before his hen, and vaunts over his enemy:

> Day of vengeance! Light of joy!
> Now I assert that the gods on high look down
> on earth's sorrows, and avenge men.
> I have seen this man lying
> in the Furies' entangling net, atoning
> his father's crimes—I have seen and laughed. (1577)

The avenging Furies are still waiting. The chorus taunts him with cowardice, and calls him "Woman." There is a too obvious contrast with the masculine strength of Clytemnestra. Aegisthus appears and is called the typical dictator. The elders will not accept his authority. The name of Orestes is bandied among them. Aegisthus is ready to use violence, a weak man's bluster. Clytemnestra is ominously quiet; she has committed the decisive act and has no more use for violence; she knows that the elders' yapping has no bite to it. With proud sarcasm she uses what she calls a woman's wisdom to plead for peace. The elders file out taunting Aegisthus; they do not dare to taunt her. She gets down to the business of ruling.

So this mighty play ends in disaster and helplessness. The last scene has pointed forward to the coming of Orestes. But this will be only one more link in the seemingly unending chain. Yet we *have* had the assurance that Zeus, the very power behind the universe, who has decreed that crime shall meet retribution, which in its turn becomes crime, has decreed also that through suffering there lies a road to wisdom. Will man but take it.

THE LIBATION BEARERS

Years have passed. The second play opens upon a tomb standing in the middle of the orchestra; in the background is the palace. A young man enters with an unspeaking friend. He looks around; the scene is half-familiar, half-strange. Unfortunately the first page of the play is lost, but we quickly find that the tomb is Agamemnon's and the young man is his son Orestes. He has come to avenge his father. He prays to Hermes (son of Zeus the Deliverer and guide of the spirits of the dead) and to his dead father to support him, and offers on the tomb locks of his hair, one in thanks and symbol of his manhood, and one in grief for his father. As he stands there he sees a procession of mourners approaching and recognizes his sister Electra. With a final prayer to Zeus he and his friend Pylades withdraw to the shadows, where they can watch without being seen.

The processional entry of the chorus, led by Electra and loaded with offerings for the dead, is effective spectacle and good theater, the more so as they are slaves whom Agamemnon brought from Troy and no doubt reveal their exotic character through their mourning. Their entry is startling, for they come, exceptionally for the chorus, through the great doors of the palace. As mourners they do not chant in the familiar anapaests of choral entry. They walk on with checked step to a solemn melody, clapping their hands, and then burst into excited lamentation. We learn that they come with sincere grief for the dead, but that they come sent by Clytemnestra, who had had a nightmare ominous of evil from the dead for those who have killed. But the very attempt at propitiation is blasphemy. Politics is controlled by fear not respect, and success has become a god and higher than the gods. But the scale of justice brings darkness upon those who sit bathed in light, and turns to light the darkness of others: the exact words are uncertain, but their purport is clear (61). We have met this scale before, in the first chorus of *Agamemnon* (250), as in the first chorus here, and there it was explicitly said, "Justice tilts the scale to give learning to those who suffer." It is this that morally holds the three plays together.

Electra speaks, maturely and sensibly. She is uncertain how to act—reluctant to offer the gifts of a murderess, tempted to throw them away, and spill them as her father's blood was spilt. The chorus tells her to pray on her own behalf, and on theirs, and on Orestes's, and on behalf of all who hate Aegisthus—Aegisthus, be it noted, not Clytemnestra—and to invoke on the murderers (plural) some divine or human power. . . . Here Electra cuts in, for this is true dialogue: "As a judge or bringer of retribution" (120). We know about retribution; it breeds retribution in its turn. Agamemnon brought retribution on Troy. Clytemnestra brought retribution on Agamemnon. Orestes, if he brings retribution, will provoke retribution. But the word "judge" points to the court scene, which is the climax of the trilogy; it belongs to the legal and political imagery we have already noticed in *Agamemnon.* The chorus is not interested in this distinctly: "Simply pray for one to shed blood for blood." But Electra presses this new spirit of hers: "Can this be pious for me in the gods' eyes?" It is an astounding question, fifty years and more before *Euthyphro.* "Why not?" asks the chorus with the sturdy common sense that for two thousand years has rejected the uncommon sense of the Sermon on the Mount. "It's only meeting evil with evil" (121–123). Electra leaves the subject, but we

have not been far from "render to no man evil for evil." The scene
ends with Electra echoing Orestes's prayer to Hermes and to her father,
a prayer for victory (a key word), a prayer in which the fertile and
fostering power of Earth the Mother of All is set against Clytemnestra's
unmotherly conduct (though her name is not spoken), a prayer in
which Aegisthus's complicity in the guilt of the murder is again significantly stressed, a prayer that ends with words about a paean for the
dead, reminding us again of the theme of disease and the part Apollo
will play in the events that follow, for Paean was his cult title as
Healer, a prayer for herself to be "far purer of thought and holier of
hand than my mother" (140). Again the new spirit breaks through.

The choral dirge that follows is short and direct. Electra pours out
the libation and suddenly stops short. She has seen the locks of hair.
The recognition scene that follows was very famous in antiquity, but
nothing can absolve it from the charge of fatuousness, and the information from a papyrus that it was culled from Stesichorus adds to the
reputation of neither poet. The hair of a brother and sister is seldom
indistinguishable, and not even in Sparta did they breed girls with
feet as large as their brothers'. One can get away in the theater with
improbabilities that leap from the printed page, but not this, and
Euripides was ruthless in pillorying the scene. Orestes discloses himself, and by an excellent touch of realism Electra, who a moment before has been clutching at straws so fragile that some critics have
thought that their very fragility is designed to point to Electra's state
of mind, now is reluctant to believe the truth, till, more plausibly, she
recognizes her own weaving, which he is wearing. Then she believes
and flings herself into his arms with all the emotionalism of a Mediterranean reunion. Orestes is four in one to her; her father is dead, her
mother is hateful, her sister cruelly killed, and he is himself her faithful brother. It is Electra who speaks of Iphigeneia as cruelly killed; in
this play Clytemnestra never mentions her; yet she was killed by the
very father they are avenging. The reference must be deliberate;
Aeschylus is preparing for the final solution, in which the killing of a
woman by a man is less heinous than the killing of a man by a woman.
At the same time it does remind us that we are dealing with a cycle of
crime: Agamemnon was not innocent, and his avengers are aware of

this. "Faithful" (243) is the word Clytemnestra used of herself (*Ag.* 606); perhaps we should not press this, as it is a common word, but it forms another small link in the chain.

Electra prays for Might, Right, and Zeus to be with them. Orestes too calls on Zeus. Agamemnon was liberal in sacrifice: the words seem innocent but take us back again to Iphigeneia. The children are the eagle's brood—this takes us back to the imagery at the beginning of the play before—and the eagle has been caught in the twining, knotted, netted (recalling *Agamemnon* again) coils of a viper and killed. This vital figure identifies Orestes first as the eagle in inheritance from his father; but, as we shall see, he is also the viper in inheritance from his mother. The identification with Agamemnon is pursued: Cassandra saw Agamemnon as the bull gored by the cow (*Ag.* 1125); Orestes describes himself as "turned to a bull" in his vengeful purpose (275). Turned to a bull in anger and in power—but will he too be gored? Will he become the proud destroyer who is in turn destroyed—the slayer who shall himself be slain, as they called the priest-king in the fertility cult at Nemi?

In a long speech Orestes proclaims Apollo's oracles. This is linked with the theme of death for death, the requital philosophy of the *Agamemnon* chorus, the outlook that Electra has recently questioned, but now accepts in silence. If he does not avenge his father the Furies of bloodguiltiness will assail him (283); at the end of the play they assail him because he does avenge his father. For a moment he hesitates. Can he believe such oracles? Then he reasserts himself. Even without the oracles, family piety and his own disinheritance and patriotism would direct him to revenge. The conquest of Troy is now seen as glorious, not only because we see it through Orestes's eyes, but because in the last play our eyes were focused on Agamemnon's crimes and they are now directed to Clytemnestra and Aegisthus. "The land," says Orestes, "is enslaved to a pair of women" (304). But he is wrong. Aegisthus may be a woman; Clytemnestra is not.

Now we see why the dirge was so short. The true dirge follows, and lasts for a hundred and fifty and more lines. As we read the play it holds up the action. This is less evident in the theater, where all the resources of opera and ballet are brought to a magnificent swirling dance round the tomb with vocal accompaniment; in Guthrie's famous Minneapolis production of the trilogy this was in many ways the high point of the sequence of plays. Of course it does in the strict sense hold up the action, and a skillful dramatist in a play of swift action such as this is at the end, does just this, for purposes of contrast. So far as the advancement of the plot is concerned, the first half of this play is relatively static, the second half relatively dynamic. But there are other factors too in this scene. Our sense of family solidarity is weak, and we do not feel the power of the ancestors watching us, or even the community of parent and child, as the Greeks did. Any African understands this scene immediately; we have lost something. A couplet from the chorus, stark in its symmetry, expresses the power of the dead:

> The man who dies is mourned,
> The man who kills revealed. (327–328)

It is a power which supports Orestes, but which will also turn against him. Furthermore, there are key motifs that recur in this scene. Zeus, Justice, and the law that the doer must suffer come in the first stanza of the chorus, and Orestes and Electra call on Zeus again and again. They are a she-wolf's brood with all her ferocity. The theme of Agamemnon's glory at Troy is sounded. So is the theme of the inexorable dialectic of history, "War must match with War and Justice with Justice" (461), linked with the unending chain of disaster, and the chorus ends with the key word "victory" (478).

In the words that follow as the music dies away and the dancing is checked, the children pray for their natural fulfillment, Orestes as king, Electra as bride. We know that it will not be. Orestes will be exiled. Electra's very name means "unwed," and there is no trace here of the marriage to Pylades that appears in some versions. Their prayer appeals to the deepest family instincts—they are the last survivors of the line that can live only through them—but, by calling us back to the ancestors, it reminds us that there is a curse upon the whole house. But whereas before (244) Electra called on Might, Right, and Zeus, and their song was filled with Zeus, in the colder language of reasoned dialogue they speak of Might and Right, but not of Zeus (490, 497).

Now we hear of Clytemnestra's nightmare. She dreamed that she gave birth to a snake, which she suckled, and which drew blood from her breasts. The snake portent is vital. For the snake is a chthonic power, coming from the world of the dead. It comes with poison, but like Apollo (destroyer and healer), it comes also with healing, the attendant of Asclepius, the healing god. But more. Clytemnestra was the viper that killed the eagle. Now Orestes is the viper that will kill her. Again the wheel spins. Just now they have claimed to be fierce like their mother the she-wolf. If she is a viper they must be vipers. Justice matches Justice, War War, and Viper Viper.

Orestes outlines his plan. He will be disguised as a foreigner, a guest, and will get into the palace that way. Here something very significant happens. Orestes ignores his mother. This is a feud between the house of Atreus and the house of Thyestes. Atreus killed Thyestes's sons. Thyestes's surviving son killed Atreus's son. Atreus's grandson will now kill Thyestes's son. The Furies will drink the third draught, a libation to Zeus the Deliverer, and be satisfied. Only they will not be satisfied, for Clytemnestra is involved.

The chorus has the scene to itself as the conspirators go to prepare their plot. They sing and dance; their opening words suggested to Sophocles the opening words of the most famous chorus in all Greek tragedy, the praise of Man in *Antigone*. They remember what Orestes has forgotten, and their whole song points to Clytemnestra. They sing of women of legend, first of Althaea, who quenched the life of her son, then of Scylla who brought death to her father, and lastly and climactically of the brides of Lemnos who killed their husbands. The burden of their refrain is the evil of such acts. Then come the leitmotifs again—Justice, Zeus, and, as the last terrifying word of the song, the Fury.

Greek plays do sometimes allow a change of scene; here we have not so much a change as a foreshortened scene. The tomb and palace are represented in unnatural proximity. So far the scene has been the tomb, but the palace has brooded in the background. Now our attention switches to the palace, but the tomb is still in the foreground as a reminder of Agamemnon. Orestes and Pylades enter, dressed as trav-

elers from Phocis. They knock at the door, invoking the hospitality of
Aegisthus; our breath catches as we remember that Zeus the god of
hospitality avenged the rape of Helen, and Orestes is invoking hospitality for purposes of treachery. A porter goes with the message—
and there, where we saw her last triumphant with blood-stained sword,
stands the Avenger of *Agamemnon*, the doomed victim of this play,
Clytemnestra. She is older now, every inch a queen, gentle and welcoming. They are taken aback. They think of Clytemnestra as a woman,
of Aegisthus as the danger; he must be killed first. They stick to the
plan, and Orestes invents a story of his own death to lull her suspicions. The invention is brilliant, and Sophocles, as we shall see, puts
it to still more brilliant use. Clytemnestra utters words of grief, and it
is not for us to doubt their sincerity. She steels herself and remains
courteous and hospitable. They go in.

The chorus sings a brief prayer for the success of the enterprise. And
now, as we wait for the climax, out bustles an old body, Orestes's
nurse. She provides comic relief, and it is preposterous to suggest
otherwise, though we may call it tragic relief if we wish. The scene has
the same function, if not of the porter in *Macbeth*, then certainly of the
gravediggers in *Hamlet*; the character is certainly the antecedent of
Juliet's nurse.

> But my darling Orestes—he quite wore me out.
> I took him from his mother's arms and brought him up.
> He broke my nights with screaming and calling for me.
> What a lot I had to do—and it's all gone
> for nothing. A baby's like an animal, knows no better.
> You've got to nurse it, of course you have, follow its whims.
> A baby in the cradle can't explain
> if it's hungry or thirsty or wants to make
> water. Its inside's young, a law to itself.
> You have to be a prophet, and sometimes
> I was wrong—and then all the washing there was to do!
> Nurse or laundrywoman—it was all one to me. (749)

But there is another element in this scene. The nurse gives us a detached look at Clytemnestra with laughter in her eyes behind a feigned

sadness. More, with subtle precision, she tells us that she received Orestes *from* his mother (750), but brought him up *for* his father (762). There is a bitter implication that Clytemnestra did not care. The nurse's first word is "Aegisthus"; for a moment we think that the act is done, but it is not so. She proceeds: "Aegisthus" (object) "my mistress" (subject) "the strangers" (indirect). All the chief characters (for Electra is insignificant in this play) are brought together in one line, and Clytemnestra is in control. But the nurse's words are a miracle of ambiguity: "My lady told me to fetch Aegisthus straight away *for the strangers*." Yes, indeed. And now, when the nurse's garrulity admits a flash of silence, Aeschylus does an unusual thing. By convention the Greek chorus did not intervene in the action. Here they do, and their intervention leaves no doubt about Aeschylus's sympathies. There is no cardinal reason why they should not intervene; after all the chorus was originally the center of the play, and Aristotle and Horace alike insist that the chorus should be treated as one of the actors. Still, it remains a surprise. The chorus intercepts the nurse and persuades her to change the message so that Aegisthus does not bring a bodyguard. All is in the hands of Zeus, but Zeus, we know, uses human agents, and Zeus, we also know, exacts further judgment yet.

There follows a long choral ode, wholly relevant, a prayer to Zeus, to Apollo (who is not named but is alluded to in his own oracular language); there is an appropriate reference to Cassandra in their words, "May light shine brilliant through the veil of darkness" (811), for in *Agamemnon* (1178) she prefaced her clearest and most deadly prophecy with similar words, and to Hermes, who in addition to being a god of the dead and a messenger is a popular god and a trickster. Through the chorus Aeschylus does not let us forget Clytemnestra. Their mind is on her confrontation with Orestes. When she calls him "child" he must keep his mind fixed on his father: the tomb no doubt continues to play a visual part in the drama. He must be like Perseus, who killed the monstrous Gorgon by turning his eyes away. So must Orestes turn his eyes from his monstrous mother and strike without ruth.

Aegisthus strides in, purposeful and unguarded. "Well, here I am, in answer to the message" (838). The message was deceitful; Hermes is on the side of the plotters.

> Well, is this the living truth? Shall I think so?
> Or rumor born of women's panic,
> springing high, dying fruitless. (844)

The chorus in *Agamemnon* (485) took the same view of Clytemnestra's reliability. They were wrong then, which makes doubly powerful the fact that the doubt is here dismissed—and justified. For the words are not true, but the truth is indeed living, and Aegisthus will die in the death of the rumor. He goes in, and again the chorus prays to Zeus. Again the key word comes and the prayer ends with a call for Victory. Suddenly there is a scream from inside the palace; the cry echoes not Agamemnon but Cassandra, and briefly reminds us of Apollo. The chorus has played its part. They dare not compromise themselves further till they are sure. Then out rushes a servant to tell of Aegisthus's death and to warn Clytemnestra. Her head, if we may so amend the text, is close to the executioner's block (883), the block Cassandra saw as her doom (*Ag.* 1277). Clytemnestra, ever active, is there. "What's the matter?" she asks. "I tell you, the dead are killing the living," he replies (886). The dead, plural. Orestes was thought to be dead, but it is more than that. O Agamemnon, thou art mighty yet. In five tremendous lines Clytemnestra asserts her authority. She sees the riddle immediately. She uses the language of balance, the historical dialectic: "We are to die by the craft we used for killing" (888). Then she calls for "a man-killing ax." She has not changed; she will be as merciless to her son as to her husband. Then the key word: "Let us now know whether Victory is ours or let us be vanquished." It is too late. Orestes, sword in hand, is before her. He speaks with terrible restraint: "Yes, I'm looking for you. So much for him." She commands him, her son—ten years old when she last saw him—to drop his sword. He stands unmoving. Then, with an imperious movement she bares her breasts, the breasts that suckled him, she says, the breasts that the viper bloodied in her dream. She does not kneel—Clytemnestra kneel! She stands before him. She calls him

"Son"; he will not call her "Mother." Her words, we know, are false; it was at the nurse's breasts that he lay. But he does not know this. The sword wavers, and without taking his eyes off her, Orestes speaks to Pylades at his side. We catch our breath, for Clytemnestra is only playing for time; the man-killing ax is on its way. Then Aeschylus does another unusual thing. A short time before, the chorus intervened. Throughout the play Pylades has been silent, and the convention may already have been established that his was a walk-on, nonspeaking rôle. The effect when he speaks must have been electric. "Where then are Apollo's oracles?" (900). It is like the voice of the god himself. Clytemnestra is now doomed. The exchange that follows only drives the spiritual sword home into Orestes. For Orestes now knows that he is confronted with the Furies of his mother's curse if he strikes, and his father's if he does not. Clytemnestra's last words recall her dream: "Here is the snake I bore and fed." Orestes accepts the rôle; the eagle's child has become a snake. "You killed wrongfully; die wrongfully" (930). There is no glory here; only the unending chain of crime and punishment, each link ugly and rusted.

To this the chorus is deaf. They drop a conventional tear for their sovereign, and then raise a song of triumph: Zeus, Justice, and Apollo have triumphed. A colossal oxymoron speaks of the guileless guile of Apollo. But is it? For guile is guilt, and Orestes is not innocent.

The moving platform emerges. The bodies of Aegisthus and Clytemnestra lie where Agamemnon and Cassandra lay. The netlike cloth that entangled Agamemnon hangs by them. Orestes stands where his mother stood and like her holds a bloodstained sword. For a while he speaks rationally but urgently of his mother's crime; the animal imagery piles up (994); at one moment he oddly speaks of the robe as dyed red by Aegisthus's sword (1011), revealing his preoccupation with the blood feud. To him his mother's death has been incidental; to his future it is central. The chorus cries that suffering, the suffering of the *Agamemnon* song, flowers for him who is left. Can he learn from suffering and break the chain? She did wrong and she suffered. The doer suffered—but no lesson was learned. Apollo said the act was right. To Apollo he will go as suppliant. And now the vision of his mother's Furies rises before his distracted mind and he rushes from the stage. One snake has killed another, and monsters with snakes in their hair pursue him. The drama is not yet played out, as the chorus well knows. Electra's new spirit has not prevailed.

> Where shall the fury of the curse end? Where
> shall it find sleep and rest? (1075)

9. THE KINDLY GODDESSES

From the bloodstained palace to the oracle at Delphi. Here all is light as the priestess tells us of the gods of the place. Apollo now rules; with him are Pallas (a link with the play's conclusion), the river Pleistos and his daughters the nymphs (symbols of cleansing), Dionysus Bromius (whose victim Pentheus reminds us by his name of the wrong way to learn through suffering) and Poseidon (another link with Athens); all is under the care of Zeus the Fulfiller. The priestess invites inside any enquirer from Greece, and passes within.

Suddenly the polarity of the play asserts itself by a powerful stroke of drama. It is as if the sun were eclipsed; day and night are side by side. She entered with dignity and grace; she scrambles out on all fours; her words stammer. There are four *k* sounds in one line: "I go on the ground; my legs give way" (37). Inside the sacred shrine, a suppliant with bloodstained hands is resting, and round him a company of black, hideous monsters lies asleep. The contrast between the attractive power of Apollo and the repulsive power of the Furies is graphically presented through the priestess. She leaves all in the hands of Apollo, prophetic healer, priestly seer and purifier (62–63). For Delphi that is well. But just as here we see Man pulled by two higher powers, so those two powers must themselves come under judgment.

The priestess leaves. The doors open, and the moving platform emerges. Here is another unexpected master stroke from Aeschylus. The platform was usually used for a tableau toward the play's end; here it appears at the very outset. The vision is unexpected, in the outcome breathtaking. For there is the conical stone believed to be the navel of the world, and, clinging to it as a suppliant, Orestes. There huddled together in a black and indistinguishable mass is the externalization of Orestes's seeming fantasy at the end of the previous play, Clytemnestra's Furies; there, on the stage, not remote on the rooftop, readily distinguishable by their characteristic emblems, stand the gods Apollo and Hermes. This is tableau at its finest. Apollo, his radiant gold contrasting with the grim black of the sleeping Furies, speaks. He promises to stand by Orestes and sends him in care of Hermes to Athens. Orestes responds in strange words:

> Lord Apollo, you know how to refrain from what is not right.
> Then, since you have understanding, learn to refrain from
> not helping. (85)

The contorted negatives express Orestes's uncertainties; the key word "right" is used negatively and suggests that he is no longer sure what is right, but trusts to be not wrong; and there is the suggestion, startling on reflection and important in context, that a god may learn.

The gods withdraw, Hermes, leading Orestes out, presumably stage-left, to Athens, Apollo into the temple. But Aeschylus has not done shocking us. Rising through a concealed entrance in the stage floor comes—Clytemnestra: the same mask that we have seen in the last play but now pallid and bloodless. The Furies are the externalization of Orestes's sense of guilt; she, as they dream, is the externalization of their purpose. As she stands by them they whine and growl like hounds in their sleep. She wakes them and vanishes. They see that Orestes is gone, and in a vivid and spectacular dance they tumble into the orchestra and mime hounds after their quarries, intoning as they go.

Hags they are, and old in years but ageless in power; they do not shamble; they pounce and pursue. This concept of the Furies as hounds fulfills the imagery of the first play. Their words show that the chain is not yet broken:

> Hide beneath the earth—he shall win no freedom.
> Blood-guilty, he shall find another
> avenger of his kindred on his head. (175)

Now Apollo comes out again and confronts the Furies. The power of the old matriarchal society and of the blood bond, and the power of culture and of Hellenic civilization and of the marriage bond face and reject one another. The Furies dash out on the trail and Apollo withdraws. It would be hard to exaggerate the effect of this opening on an Athenian audience, and we are told, though the story may be apocryphal, that this entry of the chorus was so terrifying that pregnant women miscarried. Our other choruses in this trilogy have comprised state elders and slave women. The audience was used to seeing gods in dramatic rôles, but there is nothing in Greek tragedy to match these horrible, monstrous Furies.

There follows the most startling change of scene in surviving Greek tragedy, from Delphi to Athens. The exit of the chorus has pointed to the change. It is identified by Orestes's entry from stage-right and his kneeling before Athene's statue. Where and what is this statue? We must not think of the Parthenon and its statue, which lie twenty years in the future. But Pheidias's earlier *Athene Promachus* is to be dated to about 460 B.C. It was new; it was sensational, visible to ships out to sea, awesome, adorable, protecting. Aeschylus could hardly use another image. *Athene Promachus* was freestanding. I suggest that Aeschylus had a replica standing in the center of the orchestra; in this way it is visible all along but is dissociated from the Delphi scene, which does not use the orchestra; it also enables the chorus on their reentry to use the orchestra to the full. Orestes prays to Athene; he is followed by the Furies grotesquely sniffing at the trail, catching the scent of blood, claiming their prey as he clings for sanctuary to Athene's statue. Orestes speaks. His first words tug at our memory:

> Schooled in evils, I know well
> the ways of absolution, and when it is lawful
> to speak and when say nothing. (276)

"Lawful"—here we are under the rule of law. "Schooled in evils"—it takes us back to the *Agamemnon* chorus. Learning comes from suffering. Zeus has ordained this. Has Orestes learned the lesson? A moment later he says,

> And now from pure lips with words of good omen
> I invoke Athene, queen of this country,
> to come to my help. (287)

Perhaps it is merely ritual purity of which he speaks. But his words echo Electra's insights, and they come within the context of a new divinity, Athene. Zeus is the presiding power. Yet Zeus prescribes the punishment, which is also the crime. Apollo is the god of healing. But Apollo sent Cassandra to her death; he is the Destroyer also. As Socrates put it later in the century, the doctor will be the most efficient murderer. What of Athene? We do not know, though, as an Athenian audience, we expect a favorable picture, we expect new wisdom. For the moment the chorus spurns Athene with Apollo. And now, as the suppliant clings to the statue, they weave a fantastic pattern of song and dance as they bind him with an incantation. The meaning hardly matters compared with the sound. The music is lost, but the Greek, intoned with a pitch accent, must convey something of the effect; the rhythm is cretic (♩♩♩) or rather its variant the paean (♩♩♩♩), followed by three trochaic lines (♩♩)

♩♩♩ ♩♩♩ | ♩♩♩♩   *epi de to͡-o-i | tethumeno͡-o-i*

♩♩♩ ♩ | ♩♩♩♩   *tode melos | parakopa͡-a*

♩♩♩ ♩ | ♩♩♩♩   *paraphora͡-a | phrenodale͡-es*

♩♩ | ♩♩ | ♩♩ | ♩   *humnos ex Eri͡-inuo͡-on*

♩♩ | ♩♩ | ♩♩♩ | ♩   *desmios phreno͡-on, aphor-*

♩♩ | ♩♩ | ♩♩ | ♩♩   *miktos, a͡uona brotois*

They sing of their part in life—to exercise a judgment just and true. The man whose hands are really open and pure has nothing to fear. They hound down the blood-guilty, who have shed blood within their own family. An obscure verse, easily misinterpreted, seems to mean that they exercise this function within the providence of Zeus, for Zeus repels the presence of the blood-guilty (363). Then the last pair of stanzas begins strikingly, "It lives" (381). What? The language is deliberately vague, but they plainly mean the pattern of sin and retribution. So they twice (382, 393) describe themselves and their work as "bringing to fulfillment," the title under which Zeus has been vainly invoked.

Aeschylus has still not done startling us with spectacle. At the very top of the stage building the glint of metal catches our eye. Are we seeing double? Before us in the center of the orchestra is the familiar statue of the city goddess—and there, high above the scene, is the same divine being, brilliant in the glory of her armor, but breathing, moving. All the emotions of patriotism thrill out as she swings lightly down on the "crane" that the stage crew used for this effect. How much of the scene was played at two levels we cannot be sure. Perhaps the first eight lines, which stand apart, were spoken from the upper platform, and the next words during her descent as the full scene comes more closely into her view. She is astonished at the spectacle but greets the monsters with courtesy. They address her—significantly—as "Daughter of Zeus" (415), and introduce themselves as curses and Children of Night, who drive out murderers. Athene demands to hear both sides of the case: if they deny that, they are seeking the form of justice rather than the reality. We are dealing here with the key concept of the whole trilogy. For the concept of Victory (432), the key word of *The Libation Bearers,* is made subordinate to judgment, and justice itself is made subject to judgment.

Orestes speaks, and the war with Troy again appears as an approved subject. Aegisthus, who dominated his view in *The Libation Bearers,* has now dropped out of the picture altogether. Orestes admits killing his mother, but claims that it was an act of legitimate punishment and that it was sponsored by divine sanction. In other words he pleads guilty to manslaughter but not to murder, and pleads extenuating circumstances. He submits to Athene's judgment. But the spiritual powers of Apollo and the Furies make it difficult for Athene to produce a verdict, and the case is too grave for an individual human. She therefore grants sanctuary and establishes a court of jurors; it is implied that this is something new.

Orestes goes out under law of sanctuary, presumably into the temple, and Athene either accompanies him or goes out stage-left to the city to gather her jurors. The chorus now sings. If the murderer is acquitted, there will be a change to new laws (490). There will indeed, but not as they imagine. For in the past, justice has been equated with the power of the Furies, the power of the blood feud, blood always calling for blood in endless succession. A fine stanza has important political implications:

> Reject
> the life of anarchy,
> the rule of tyranny.
> Power is God's gift to those who take the middle way,
>   to each in different measure. (526)

This is not cheap Athenian propaganda. It expresses a truth, that man finds his fulfillment only in ordered society, or, as Aristotle puts it, "Man is a city-state animal," a truth that is not far from the center of the trilogy.

Court scenes are always good theater, and this is no exception. Unfortunately the rules of the court are not quite clear. The normal assumption, well based on ancient evidence, points to twelve jurors; the suggestion then is that as the votes are equal Athene casts the deciding vote for acquittal (on her understanding of the merits of the case), and establishes the precedent that when the votes are equal, the defendant shall always be acquitted. Kitto has argued with some force that there are eleven human jurors and Athene herself makes the twelfth. After the pleading is complete (710) there is an interchange between the Furies and Apollo that covers the vote. This interchange lasts for ten couplets and a triplet. After the triplet Athene speaks. If the act of casting a vote occupies a couplet there is no room for twelve votes; there is room only for eleven full votes and for the twelfth juror,

Athene, to move to the urn in readiness for voting. The Furies have spoken six times, Apollo five; there are six votes for condemnation, five for acquittal. If this is so, then Athene actually belongs to the jury, a tremendous thought for Athenian justice. Whatever our interpretation of the voting, we have had Zeus acting with Agamemnon, the Furies are with Clytemnestra, Apollo stands by Orestes, and it is left to Athene to make the decisive move in breaking the chain.

We must return to the case. Athene presides (the Court of the Areopagus did not have the modern distinction between jury and judge —another pointer in favor of Kitto's view), the Furies prosecute, and Apollo is advocate and witness for the defense, in the strict sense (though he does not use the word) Orestes's paraclete. In Guthrie's production nothing was visually more impressive than the frail figure of Orestes standing in the protecting embrace of the great golden god. The Furies show themselves to be able lawyers. They begin by challenging Apollo's presence in the court. Thwarted here, they proceed to cross-examine Orestes skillfully and ruthlessly. They make no attempt to disown the weakness in their own general position, that they are interested only in murder of kin (it is legally wise to admit such weaknesses rather than let opposing counsel seem to drag them to light), but they claim that it is irrelevant to Orestes's guilt in the particular circumstances of this case. Apollo speaks for the defense, but his words are not fully persuasive. He is too conscious of his own dignity. He stresses the authority of Zeus behind him, but the issue is one of justice not authority. He pleads Clytemnestra's treachery, playing on the emotions with the freedom permitted in ancient courts, but the point is strictly irrelevant and the Furies are quick to cut across him.

Their spokeswoman makes brilliant use of myth. Apollo claims that Zeus values the father more than the mother, yet he imprisoned his own father. They gauge their opponent well. Incensed with the interruption, Apollo loses his temper: "Yes, you hags, but prison is not death. Death is irremediable" (644). The Fury, like a skillful lawyer or politician, has goaded out the response she wanted. She is unruffled: "Precisely. Clytemnestra's death is irremediable." Apollo controls himself with an effort, and after this marvellous stroke of drama the play falls apart. For now Apollo argues from a curious physiology that the substance of a child comes entirely from the father and that the mother is purely a receptacle, incubator, and nurse.

Athene, with careful equity, makes no attempt to sway the vote, but establishes the Court of the Areopagus to hear homicide cases in perpetuity (there is politics here, for only three years before the democrats had shorn away its other powers) and urges pure and upright judgment. Two urns have been brought in. Each juror has two pebbles, white for acquittal, black for condemnation. They come forward in turn and drop their vote into the first urn, discarding the unused pebbles into the second. Then Athene comes forward and speaks. She was born, without mother, from the head of Zeus. Therefore fathers matter and mothers do not. Therefore she votes for acquittal. The votes are equal; Orestes is acquitted and leaves unconstrained. Well, well!

The rest of the play, more than a quarter of the whole, speaks less forcibly to us than to the original audience. The Furies are outraged at the judgment. Against a dance of baleful anger, in repeated words they invoke justice and call vengeance on Athens. Athene replies in the calm words of ordinary conversation. She relies on Zeus (826). Then she offers them a place in her city as spirits of blessing, checking crime, under the new dispensation. The Furies at first persist with their dance and song of protest, but are gradually wooed by her patient persuasion (881). They accept. So the dread Furies become the Eumenides, the Kindly Goddesses; and they have learned this transformation through suffering (837, 870). This is the title of the play, and this, at the last, is what the play is about. For Athens has learned the sound judgment and wise moderation that was the burden of Electra's prayer (1000). So, except for a brief speech of welcome from Athene (1021), the play and the trilogy end in a great operatic finale of which we have only the libretto, as the Kindly Goddesses call down blessings on their new home and are escorted in ceremonially spectacular procession out stage-left to the city of Athens. The torches flare out, and the light that shone balefully in *Agamemnon* now shines gloriously.

Let us go back. The play cycle is about the blood feud coming under the rule of law, and the people caught up in this process. Hence *The Eumenides*. The individual requital of crime always becomes itself criminal. This is a theme of immense power, and up to a point Aeschylus has treated it with immense power. But the breakthrough comes at the point of Orestes's acquittal, and the reason for that acquittal is the higher status of man than woman. This is in the first place irrelevant; Clytemnestra's femininity is an accident, for she is in many ways more masculine than Aegisthus. The sequence Iphigeneia-Agamemnon-Clytemnestra-Orestes is superimposed upon the hostility of the houses of Atreus and Thyestes, and the two are blurred in the process: Clytemnestra's femininity is not relevant to the introduction of the rule of law. In the second place it is immoral; it would make the Oedipus complex evil and the Orestes complex good; we may not say that it is venial to kill a woman, however guilty, but grievous to kill a man, however guilty. In the third place it is trivially grounded, being based on a physiology and mythology that the best minds in Greece were already questioning.

Why then did Aeschylus base his solution to a mighty problem upon such an inadequate support? Partly because of the very different position of women in Athenian society from the part they played in the myths; Aeschylus was blinkered by his own environment as Euripides was not, and the position of women at Athens was very Victorian. Partly because Aeschylus, for this reason, sees the movement from arbitrary authority to the rule of law as identical with the change from a matriarchal to a patriarchal society. This last is not, as has been sometimes said, the theme of *The Oresteia,* but it is necessary to the understanding of that theme as presented by Aeschylus. But when we have made, as we must, the imaginative effort to understand why Aeschylus reaches this conclusion in this way, it remains true that *The Oresteia* is like the Book of Job in presenting a profound problem in marvellous poetry and superb drama, and then emerging into an utterly unworthy solution.

Yet there is something more to be said, and it may be discerned by looking at the divine dimension. The Furies are outvoted; they are in measure wrong, and they change. Apollo on the other hand is not wholly in the right; he destroys Cassandra, and his defense of Orestes does not stand unscathed; the Athenians could not forget, though we may, that Apollo's Delphi compromised with the Persians in the year of their attack on Greece little over twenty years before; Apollo is not infallible. Athene alone is not wrong and does not change, and she is the pure child of Zeus and represents the unsullied will of Zeus.

What then of Zeus—"Zeus whoever he is" (*Ag.* 160)? He broods over the whole action of the trilogy from the first to last. In the first chorus Zeus Protector of Strangers sends Agamemnon on his criminal vengeance. The last words of all show Zeus the All-Seeing as protecting Athens. All the characters in this last play, the priestess, Apollo, Orestes, the Furies, and Athene, acknowledge him. As Zeus Savior he is the object of prayer, and Orestes thanks him (760). Right at the end of the play, at a key point, Athene sings that Zeus Agoraeus has triumphed (973). Zeus Agoraeus is the god of the political assembly. We have passed from Zeus Protector of Strangers in an arbitrary society to Zeus the god of the political assembly. We have seen the politicizing of Zeus. We have passed from individual action to democracy and the rule of law, and the last word is of Zeus as guardian of Athens precisely because Athens stands for political democracy and the rule of law. The divine dimension reflects the human. At the least we must say that man's understanding of the ultimate power has changed. Has the ultimate power itself changed? Has Zeus the Fulfiller fulfilled himself? Aeschylus does not answer this question here. But it was an insistent question. It had to be answered. It led him beyond *The Oresteia* to the Prometheus trilogy.

10. *PROMETHEUS BOUND*

It can be confidently stated, despite some sceptics, that *Prometheus Bound* is an authentic work of Aeschylus. It is a work of towering genius; we could not begin to guess at an alternative attribution. It is Aeschylean in its magniloquence, and in its boldly spectacular staging, Aeschylean too in the nature of the problems it presents. Stylistic tests place it late, and a number of factors suggest that it may have been written in Sicily: the description of Etna in eruption; traces of Orphic language; an interest in the doctrine of the four elements and the identity of the founder of the Sicilian school of medicine. Probably we should attribute the play to 457 or 456, during Aeschylus's last stay in Sicily. One other more tenuous link with Sicily may be noted. At one point Prometheus tells how mankind at first "in seeing saw vainly, in hearing did not apprehend" (447). This is so close to Isaiah's "Hear ye indeed but understand not; and see ye indeed but perceive not" (6.9) that it is difficult to argue accidental coincidence. It is possible that the Phoenician trading communities from the Near

East had brought Jewish businessmen with them, and that Aeschylus had had contact with the thought. If so, the apparent parallel with Genesis, where man in his disobedience eats of the fruit of the tree of the knowledge of good and evil, may not be coincidental either.

In the background of *The Oresteia* is Zeus; we saw man's awareness of him change from the god who sent Agamemnon to destroy Paris to the god who presides over the rule of law. Man's awareness—but what of Zeus himself? Aeschylus brooded on the theme, and took it up in his final trilogy, linking it to the theme of Prometheus.

Prometheus was a fire spirit. The name seems to mean "fore-thought," but it may have its origin in the Sanskrit *pramantha*, fire-stick; one of the primitive ways of making fire is to twirl a hard stick inside a soft one. According to the myth Zeus hid away fire, but Prometheus stole it in a reed (the soft stick) and gave it to man. Because fire is the necessary instrument of technology, Prometheus became the master inventor; in some versions he was responsible for the creation of man. Another famous story told how he deceived Zeus over sacrifice by offering him the choice of two packages, a large one with fat and bones, and a small one with the good meat. Zeus naturally chose the large one.

The story is a typical etiological myth to explain why men keep the best parts of the sacrificial offerings. It displays Prometheus as the typical trickster, like Spider or Tortoise in West Africa or Coyote among the American Indians. In punishment Zeus bound Prometheus to (perhaps originally inside) a stake, with an eagle to torment him by eternally pecking his liver. But Prometheus had a secret: Thetis, the sea nymph, was fated to bear a child stronger than his father. In his foreknowledge Prometheus knew that Zeus would fall in love with Thetis. If Zeus took her he would be doomed. However, Prometheus revealed the secret, and Zeus was saved. Prometheus was released by Heracles, who killed the eagle. Chiron, the centaur, who tutored Thetis's son Achilles (in one version Chiron appears as the boy's father) gave Prometheus his immortality so that he could himself escape through death from an incurable wound.

Unfortunately, we cannot be quite certain whether the surviving play is the first or second of the trilogy. It would seem at first sight that the first play should be *Prometheus, Bringer of Fire* and that the trilogy would be rounded off by *The Unbinding of Prometheus*; supporters of this view have drawn useful parallels between our play and *The Libation Bearers*. The release of Prometheus, it is argued, is the natural culmination and conclusion, and it would be impossible to find material for another play after that. This would be true only if Prometheus had revealed his secret before his release, and in some ways the parallel of situation is closer between *The Libation Bearers* and *The Unbinding of Prometheus*.

Prometheus Bound is scrupulous in expounding the events that have brought Prometheus to his pass; such exposition would be needless if the events had already been dramatically presented. The theft of fire, in this case, plays the part that the Trojan War plays in *The Oresteia*. It is not directly presented, but it is the catalyst of all that follows. It is not possible to be dogmatic, but it seems most likely that our play is the first of the series. It introduces Oceanus, and the chorus consists of the sea nymphs who are his daughters; the central character after Prometheus is Io. The second play, *The Unbinding of Prometheus,* then, must have dealt with the release of Prometheus by Heracles, descendant of Io. We know that it introduced Ge, the Earth Mother, and that the chorus consisted of her sons, the Titans. The third play, *Prometheus, Bringer of Fire*, would have incorporated the reconciliation between Zeus and Prometheus. Zeus may have appeared in person, as he did in *The Weighing of Souls.*

It is likely that Io in the first play was balanced by Thetis, reaching the Caucasus in her escape from Zeus. If so, Aeschylus is following the device he used in the Danaid trilogy, whereby a member of the chorus in the first play becomes a significant character later. We know that Ouranos was introduced, and he may have been the instrument of reconciliation and Zeus's advocate. With his presence the personification of the elements is complete. It has been reasonably conjectured that the chorus consisted of men. There would have been the prophetic vision of Achilles, and perhaps of Prometheus's immortality through Chiron, and the play would have ended, somewhat as *The Kindly*

Goddesses, with the institution of a festival in honor of Prometheus, Bringer of Fire. Of the satyr play we know nothing.

As in *The Oresteia* Aeschylus used the third actor, though he keeps his conversations between two only. He also used all the resources of spectacle that were beginning to emerge. He chose to begin with a colossal scene of the crucifixion among the mountains of Caucasus. Under the guidance of the god Hephaestus, Strength, helped by Violence (who does not speak), drags in Prometheus and rivets him to a gigantic rock at the back of the stage. The riveting would have been realistically done with great hammer blows, and there are echoed sounds in the Greek to suggest the blows (e.g., 39–43). It is a mistake to think that Prometheus was represented by a dummy; Aeschylus's technique with the third actor enabled him to keep the scene a dialogue while maintaining Prometheus in an obstinate silence: the Cassandra scene is a perfect parallel. The scene is set by Strength in clear, decisive language. This is Scythia. Here is Prometheus, who has stolen fire, to be chained by the Father's authority. Strength ends with a sentence structured in cross-rhythms. Prometheus has given fire to *mortals*, and must make amends to *gods* till he learns to accept the dictatorship of *Zeus* and to lay aside his love of *man*. The structure stresses the importance of the words. Zeus's rule is described by an ugly word; alongside it, to describe Prometheus, is the first appearance of a key word of later politics and theology, *philanthropos*, "man-loving"; it will be used of gods from Hermes, Peace, and Love to the god of the Christians, and of monarchs till it becomes a formal title of forgotten meaning, and as a political catchword all through the fourth century B.C. Strength is brutal and ruthless, a political thing, the typical manifestation of Zeus's new regime. Hephaestus is reluctant. He is the god of fire, but he shows no anger at the theft; the anger is Zeus's, and it is anger because Prometheus would not submit; in speaking of it Hephaestus again uses the word *philanthropos* (28). *O felix culpa!*

It is notable that he calls Prometheus "Son of Themis." Themis is a title of Earth as an oracular goddess. This reminds us of Prometheus's foresight. But Themis is also Law and Right, and we begin to link Prometheus with Right (cf. 209, 874). The language used as they fetter Prometheus is language used of harnessing a horse (54, 61, 71,

74, 76, cf. 108, 323, 562, 931, 1009–1010). This is important for two reasons. In the first place it is an example of Aeschylus's dramatic irony. Prometheus will tell us (462–466) that he taught man to bring animals under control, and he is himself harnessed in the same way. Second, it is the verbal demonstration that Zeus's rule treats people as animals, and Io with her cow mask provides visual evidence of the same point. It is the technology Prometheus supplied that enabled man to rise above the animals; before, men lived like ants (453). We may note the recurrence of the word *thoüssein*, literally "bark," in the play as part of this motif; Aeschylus uses it only once elsewhere (73, 279, 395, 1041). Strength, as he flings insults at Prometheus, calls him a sophist (62); the word is not essentially opprobrious, and the sophists, lecturing for money, were barely if at all established, but it conveys all the scorn a young Nazi might have put into the word "intellectual." He goes out with a bitter pun on the foresight implied in the name Prometheus.

Only when they have gone does Prometheus break his silence in a resounding cry:

> Divinity of air, swift-winged winds,
> river-springs, and sea-waves'
> uncountable laughter, earth, mother of all,
> all-seeing orb of the sun—I call on you.
> See what a god suffers at hands of gods. (88)

Here, not oversystematized, are Empedocles's four elements. But in the cosmology of Empedocles there are six elements not four. The others are the forces of Love and Strife. Is it too much to suggest that these are represented by Prometheus, with his love of mankind, and Zeus? It is pertinent to add that in Empedocles's scheme the sort of world in which we live cannot exist where Love is absolute and all is in an undifferentiated whole, or where Strife is absolute and all is utterly discrete, but only where both forces are at play.

Suddenly, with a cry of alarm, Prometheus hears the whirr of wings. Here is a dramatic master stroke. We know what to expect—the eagle. Instead we have a chorus of flighty nymphs. Prometheus explicitly says that he hears them in the upper air, and we need not doubt the capacity of the engineers who built the Propylaea and the Parthenon to lower the chorus, perhaps in two groups of six, spectacularly from the stage building; it is this entry that Aristophanes parodies in *The Clouds*. Certainly the chorus does not enter in processional anapaests; they drop immediately into a lyrical dialogue with Prometheus. Furthermore they do not leave their "rising seat" and "the air which is the holy highway for birds" till the very end of the scene (278–280); the reason is no doubt that they have been poised in the air, which would have provided a striking visual effect. They have heard the sound of hammering and come through the air to see. They sing of pity while he sings of defiance and alludes to the secret, which is his last power. Then the song dies away, and he narrates his services to Zeus in winning power, advised by his mother Themis, and to mankind. In his words and the words in which the chorus questions him there are three important features. The first is a phrase let drop by Prometheus:

> I dared. I rescued mankind, saving them
> from utter destruction, from Hades. (235)

We cannot be certain, but it is possible that this was an element in the final dénouement, that Zeus had intended to destroy mankind and create something finer, and that Prometheus had thwarted his intent. The second feature is the introduction of a number of terms that are important to the play. Chief among these is the imagery of disease and healing, which we have already noted in *Agamemnon*. It was touched in the opening sequence (27, 43), here it is explicit. According to Prometheus, Zeus is diseased:

> To suspect all friends seems to be
> an endemic disease with dictators. (224)

The chorus says that Prometheus saved man from disease: "What remedy did you discover for their disease" (249)?

But underlying all the words of Prometheus's pain is the suspicion that he is himself diseased and needs the injunction: "Physician, heal thyself." Associated with this thought is a comparatively rare series of words (*aïstos, aïstoun,* etc.), of which Aeschylus is fond, with a root meaning of making unseen, and so destroying. Zeus aimed to destroy previous authority (151), to destroy mankind (232). Linked again is the thought of mankind as creatures of a day (253, cf. 83, 547, 945). Thirdly, here and elsewhere in this play the chorus has a marked tendency to speak in groups of four lines (193ff., 242ff., 259ff., 472ff., 507ff., 631ff., 782ff., 819ff., 1036ff.). This has not been finally explained; it may have something to do with the technique of Sicilian mime.

As the chorus leaves the airship and enters the orchestra, there swings down from the sky after them their father Oceanus, a slightly comic character, riding a fantastic four-footed winged griffin. Their conversation merely serves to make Prometheus's firmness more obdurate. Oceanus is a typical trimmer, a politician of the type the Greeks called "buskin," who likes to be in with all parties. Prometheus's response is tinged with sarcasm. Oceanus offers to intercede with Zeus if Prometheus will be reasonable. Prometheus replies, "Don't stick your neck out for me!" The scene contains a long, vivid description of Etna in eruption, irrelevant to the play except in anticipating the final cataclysm, but justified on its own merits. The medical imagery returns:

PROMETHEUS:	I'll drain my present cup of sorrow
	till Zeus recovers from his attack of bile.
OCEANUS:	Prometheus, don't you realize that anger
	is a disease which words can cure?
PROMETHEUS:	Yes, if you treat the spirit at the moment of crisis,
	not roughly diet a swelling rage.
OCEANUS:	Tell me, do you see any danger
	in my risking support of you like this?
PROMETHEUS:	Superfluous effort and simple silliness.
OCEANUS:	Then let me suffer from that disease. (375)

Oceanus, like others of us, prefers giving advice to receiving it, and goes off in a huff. Prometheus has treated him cavalierly. The Titan's intransigence is a sign of *hybris*.

The chorus now sings explicitly of Zeus's tyranny; their light flutterings round the orchestra contrast powerfully with the immobile giant. Prometheus gives them a splendid account of his services to man: the New Learning is seen in the wide-ranging geography and the theory of the emergence of civilization, to which we must return. He seems to despair, but returns to his secret. Zeus "cannot escape his fate" (518). Again the chorus sings and dances. They sound a note of warning; they will not offend against Zeus; Prometheus has too little fear of Zeus and too much respect for mortals. Men are creatures of a day (547)—the word recurs—feeble as a dream.

> Never
> shall human plans transgress Zeus's order. (550)

These are striking words; there is more here than an acceptance of *force majeure*. Zeus's reign is seen not as arbitrarily despotic but as ordered.

Suddenly there is a cry, and another fantastic character bursts onto the scene. This is Io, victim of Zeus's outrages, wearing a cow mask. Her dance, as she mimes the stinging of the gadfly that pursues her, must have been wonderful ballet. "His treatment of Io," wrote Gilbert Murray, "is like the last infamy of a licentious tyrant. For the traditional tyrant in Greek poetry behaves like the traditional wicked baronet of the English stage." It is sometimes said that she is pregnant, but this is not so; she will be made pregnant by the touch of Zeus at the end of her wanderings. She is seeking to escape from Zeus, as Zeus must seek to escape from Thetis; this is the point. We hear of her past; in her eagerness to tell she provides a fine example of the Greek tendency to alliterate positive assertions on the letter *p*: "perceive the perfect purport of your question in plain speech" (641). We hear of her visions of Zeus's love, of the oracle that forced her father to turn her out, of her transformation and torment.

We hear also from Prometheus of her future in words again full of the new geography: she will pass along the northern boundary of the world eastward, turn south, cross the strait between Europe and Asia (an allusion to the name Bosporus, precisely Oxford, though it is placed further east), then to India where the Ethiopians or "burnt-faced," a general term for the black and brown peoples, live, and so into the Ganges-Nile complex (for the ancients believed that any great river must be a part of the Nile, and thought that India must link with Africa to the south). As he reaches the climax of his story even

Prometheus shows excitement, and the *s* sound occurs nineteen times in three lines (840–842). For the journey is not fruitless. At the last the hand of the Almighty shall overshadow her, and she shall bear a son to Zeus, to be called Epaphus, "child of a touch." From him in generations will come a link with Greece through the Danaids. They will kill their suitors—and in an outburst of ironical bitterness Prometheus's mind turns to Zeus and he digresses to cry: "May such love fall upon my enemies!" (864). But one will spare her husband; from her will come a line of kings and from that line will come Prometheus's rescuer. It is Heracles, as we know, though he is not named. In the next play he must have appeared, and Prometheus would have prophesied his journeying along the western edge of the world to the Pillars of Heracles, balancing and completing the picture already given. Prometheus concludes with yet another reference to the source of his oracular foreknowledge, his mother, calling her unequivocally by the name Themis.

As he finishes, Io gives a great cry and bursts into a song and ballet of frenzy, rushing from the stage. When she has gone the chorus sings a brief lament. In the final scene, Prometheus, in a spirit of some arrogance, defies Zeus: the word "headstrong" (*authades*), which was used of him at the beginning (64, 79, 436), but not at all during the Io scene, where he is portrayed in relation to Io not to Zeus, returns intensively (907, 940, 1017, 1034, 1077). Hermes, the "lackey of the gods," says Prometheus (954), confronts him in a scene that echoes passages from the opening of the play (955 with 149–151; 985ff. with 173ff.). There is a bitter little pun:

PROMETHEUS: Alas!
HERMES: Alas? That is a word Zeus does not *know*.
PROMETHEUS: Time, as it ages, teaches everything.
HERMES: You don't *know* discretion—yet. (980)

The play on words points to something important. Time is going to bring change. For the moment the play ends in a tremendous earthquake, which must have strained all the resources of the stage management, as Prometheus sinks from sight to torment with the cry of injustice on his lips.

What are we to make of this awesome play that has behind it—apparently—a devil-god?

Theater must come first. Of drama as we normally understand it there is little; the play represents a situation, and within this play the situation does not change. But there is magnificent poetry, particularly in Prometheus's opening words, and splendid rhetoric. There is taut structure, the scenes with Zeus's lackeys flanking the central scenes with Oceanus and Io. There is spectacle unequaled in any surviving Greek play, from the opening scene where the giant is hauled in, physically helpless, mentally alert, grimly silent, through the entries of the chorus, Oceanus and Io, and the dances of Io and the chorus, to the final cataclysm as Prometheus and his rock sink below the ground while the chorus flees from the scene.

The second dimension may be called intellectual. Havelock went so far as to describe *Prometheus Bound* as "a full-scale dramatization of the doctrines of scientific anthropology" and to entitle his study of the play *The Crucifixion of Intellectual Man*. We have already noted the emphasis on *philanthropia*, love of mankind. According to this view, the key to the play lies in its humanism. Aeschylus rejects the traditions of Homer and Hesiod. Homer is fundamentally a pessimist; man's life may not be solitary, but it is poor, nasty, brutish, and short; he lives and dies as the leaves of a tree. According to Hesiod there was a Golden Age in the days of Cronos. The Age of Zeus brought degeneration, first to silver, which he himself destroyed in anger, then to bronze, then after the interlude of the Heroic Age (invented by Hesiod to intensify the sense of modern degeneracy), to iron, which Zeus will again destroy. It is a "historically regressive and morally cynical" picture. Man is at best a fallen creature, and at worst a costly mistake. One recalls Josh Billings: "Mankind wuz made a little lower than the angels, and has bin gittin a little lower ever since."

By contrast, Prometheus takes the view that man is worth preserving and worth loving, and Aeschylus presents us with a doctrine of progress, by contrasting man at the pre-Promethean stage with man's development. That development is carefully analyzed: consciousness, language, architecture, woodworking, the calendar, numerals, writing, the domestication of animals, the use of horses for transport, navigation, medicine, divination and augury (regarded with a rationalist touch as the science of propitiation), mining and metallurgy. *Homo sapiens*, has had, so to speak, an origin of species. Prometheus is thus an ambivalent figure. On the one hand he is a god, conferring "gifts," a "benefactor." On the other he describes himself as teaching, expounding, explaining, and initiating:

> I tracked down, hidden in fennel-stalk,
> the secret source of fire, fire the teacher
> of every science to men, their great resource. (109)

Again (noting the Homeric and perhaps Orphic image at the beginning):

CHORUS: Do men whose life is but a day possess fire?
PROMETHEUS: Yes, and with it they shall master many skills. (253)

So Prometheus is twice described as a sophist.

There is much truth in this, but it will not do to overstate it. It is dangerous to read too much into the word "sophist." If the group of intellectual freethinkers and educators we call the sophists had already started their careers, which is doubtful, they had only just started them. Aeschylus is not defending the liberal tradition in Greek politics against Plato, who was not born for another thirty years. The intellectual element is there in the play, and it is strong, but Aeschylus's sympathies are not unequivocally on the side of intellectual revolt. There is *hybris* in man, and there is *hybris* in Prometheus, and, since 1945, we may more easily understand Aeschylus, for in New Mexico we came to a new power of fire, which may exalt us but may also crucify us.

So we come to the theological dimension. Aeschylus's presentation of conflict has helped to mold a mood of theological protestantism. Three examples: *The Book of Job* (probably, though not quite certainly, influenced by Aeschylus); the figure of Satan in *Paradise Lost*; Shelley's *Prometheus Unbound*. But what of Aeschylus's resolution of conflict? Here the key figure is Io. In *The Suppliant Women*, which we now know to be a comparatively late play, Io's ordeal is seen as preparing her for bliss:

> The lord of endless time,
>   Zeus, held her in his hand,
> and by his gentle strength,
>   and by the breath of godhead,
> her hurt was healed, and tears
>   of shame, and grief flowed free.
> She took Zeus's burden upon her in truth
>   and bore a spotless child. (*Suppl.*, 574)

That child, we must remember, is the ancestor of Prometheus's savior. The mood and language are closely similar to those of Prometheus here in describing the same events (844ff.)—except for his curse on his enemies. That curse is significant. Before the trilogy is ended Prometheus must change. It reveals the tragic flaw: the pride, the intransigence—a flaw that does not make his service of mankind wrong in itself, but, as Aristotle might put it, alienates us fractionally from him so that our sympathies are not all on one side, and there is, in a real sense, tragic conflict. There is reconciliation between him and Zeus; he does reveal his secret. The question, almost the whole question, is "What makes him change?" It cannot have been torture; the defiant Titan cannot have been transformed into the brainwashed victim of tyranny, loving Big Brother. Yet the secret was revealed, freely, and, one suspects, by a Prometheus freed and standing on his own feet. Can he have learned that he was wrong about Zeus, that the hound of heaven is a faithful watchdog?

> All which I took from thee I did but take,
>   Not for thy harms,
> But just that thou might'st seek it in My arms.
>   All which thy child's mistake
> Fancies as lost, I have stored for thee at home:
>   Rise, clasp My hand, and come!

There may be truth in this, though the Christian emotion will be misleading.

But what of Zeus? It is Heracles, son of Zeus, who releases Prometheus. Does Zeus not change? Here we may rightly turn back to *The Oresteia*; dare we apply the insights of that first chorus to Zeus himself? There does seem to be a progression from Zeus as protector of hospitality, but arbitrary in his will, to Zeus the god of the Assembly. The Fulfiller fulfills himself. And here in *The Prometheia* we seem to have a picture of a god who learns. Von Hartmann said, "To work with God is to redeem God." Shelley's play gives us the perfectibility of man; dare we think here more profoundly of the perfectibility of God?

Of course we are not to think of a God who is Love. Zeus is Power, and Prometheus is Intelligence, and they clash. For Power, however tyrannical, means order, and Intelligence is revolutionary. Aeschylus's lesson is the reconciliation of Power to Intelligence, each at the last needing the other. This much is reasonably certain. But reconciliation through what? Dare we catch at the *Agamemnon* chorus and answer "through suffering"? If so, Aeschylus is on the way to being one of the world's most elemental thinkers. The *élan vital,* from being a blind striving, becomes first intelligent and then spiritual. Meantime our play gives us the agony. And in compassion and in sympathy the daughters of Ocean share the agony. Here the Christian assertion is not irrelevant or misleading. "The whole creation groaneth and travaileth waiting for the glorious manifestation of the sons of God."

III

THE TRAGEDIES OF SOPHOCLES

11. SOPHOCLES

Sophocles was born some thirty years later than Aeschylus, in about 496; he was of wealthy family, and his father owned an armaments factory. He never knew the period of dictatorship or the reforms of Cleisthemes. The Persian Wars found him too young to participate, though as an athletic teenager he played a prominent part in the Victory Games after Salamis. But war, which is in the foreground for Aeschylus, a generation older, and for Euripides, half a generation younger, is for Sophocles only a background. Of politics he was acutely aware. He watched the establishment of full democracy by Pericles and Ephialtes, and watched too how the very nature of that democracy made possible the dominance of a single individual of strong personality and powerful eloquence, so that the theory of the authority of the masses led in practice to one-man rule.

Ehrenberg has argued that Pericles, the rationalist, who combined the official position of legal ruler or *strategos* with the actuality of an autocratic dictatorship or tyranny, underlies the portrayal of Creon in

Antigone and Oedipus in *King Oedipus*. Underlies, no doubt; but Sophocles also saw the Confederacy of Delos transformed into an Athenian empire, and his portrayal of the autocrat in politics seems rather representative of Athens as a whole than a mirror held to one individual. In the pages of Thucydides (1. 68–71) the Corinthians describe the typical Athenian: a restless modernist, enterprising, here, there, and everywhere, expending physique and intellect for his country, resilient in defeat, inordinately ambitious in success, decisive in action, self-confident, incapable of either leading a quiet life or allowing anyone else to do so. This was the character that Sophocles saw around him. He saw its dynamic authority; he saw also its dangers.

He himself was quieter, more genial and congenial. He played his part in public affairs. He was elected to office in 441, because, it is said, of the political impact of *Antigone*. When war broke out in 431 with Sparta, suspicious of Athenian power and urged on by Corinthian economic rivalry with Athens, Sophocles was already well over military age. Yet he was to live twenty-five more years, through wars hot, cold, and hot again, and die at the age of 90 just too soon for the final defeat. He was now an elder, and his reputation for wisdom was enhanced by his general aloofness from the hurly-burly of partisan politics. They turned to him at special times.

In the early years of the war Athens was cruelly struck by plague; *King Oedipus* contains a grimly realistic evocation of this. In 421 an uneasy peace was patched up out of war-weariness, and in the following year Sophocles, now in his mid-seventies, was chosen by the state to go to Epidaurus and bring the healing-god Asclepius to purify Athens from the years of plague. Sophocles was evidently known for his piety, as we find him also dedicating a chapel to Heracles. Again, after Athens overreached herself and lost two armies in Sicily in 413, Sophocles, in his eighties, was chosen as one of the administrators to see the state through the immediate crisis.

But it was not for these public offices he was remembered so much as for his rich humanity. He enchanted Ion by his skill at getting a kiss from a handsome young waiter. When he was in office in 441 Pericles had to speak sharply to him for watching an attractive boy instead of the plan of campaign. Plato has a story of a friend meeting

Sophocles in extreme old age, and asking whether he kept up his love affairs. "Hush!" said the old man, "It's like escaping from a brutal dictator." One doubts it. He retained his faculties to the end. His sons, eager for their inheritance, charged him with incapacity to manage his own affairs; he sang or recited the Colonus chorus from *Oedipus at Colonus,* which he was then writing, and the jury did not doubt his competence. Aristophanes in *The Frogs* described him as the Athenians remembered him "amiable in death as in life"; another writer of comedies, Phrynichus, said of him: "Blessed is Sophocles. He had a long life, enjoyed happiness and talent, wrote many excellent tragedies, and ended his life well without suffering any misfortune."

Sophocles saw in the formative period of his life the achievement of perfect mastery by the Athenian sculptors and architects led by Pheidias and Ictinus. The stiff formalism of the sculptural representations of the age of Aeschylus melted into a mellow naturalism, yet a naturalism that remained somehow aloof. Symbolic of this aloofness is the female figure, seldom or never portrayed in the nude, by contrast with the warm sensuality of Praxiteles's females in the following century. It is not merely epigramatic to say that Pheidias's humans bear a divinity about them, Praxiteles's divinities wear human flesh. There is an interesting comparison with the familiar words of Sophocles that he portrayed men as they ought to be, Euripides portrayed them as they are.

Architecture too achieved a new flexibility. The Parthenon is the supreme architectural monument of the period as its frieze is the supreme sculptural achievement. The Parthenon stands above all for two principles. The first is the use of illusion in the service of art: a convex base line to counter the optical illusion of sagging; swelling columns to counter the illusion of tapering; columns leaning inward to counter the illusion of disclination; the end columns thicker to counter the illusion that they are thinner. That, after all, is what the skilled dramatist practises in his own medium. Sophocles applied similar effects visually when he adapted the recent advances in the study of perspective to theatrical scenery; more subtly he devotes his dramatic skill to creating illusions and counter-illusions in the structure of his plays. The other principle behind the Parthenon is the principle of a single unit of

structure produced by the careful fitting together of parts into a balanced whole. The Parthenon is integral not trilogic, and Sophocles
rejected the trilogic structure favored by Aeschylus and used the single
play as a unit, with meticulous care for an effective and harmonious
structure. What Kitto has called the "cross-rhythms" of the revelation
scene in *King Oedipus,* where Oedipus passes from fear to assurance
while Iocaste passes from assurance to fear is but one example.

As with Aeschylus, we have no play from Sophocles's early period.
Some 120 plays are recorded, with no less than eighteen prizes. This
is astonishing, for even if all the plays were performed at the City
Dionysia this would represent a victory three times in every five presentations. His first victory was in 468, and there was some complaint
of political jobbery against the conservative Cimon for preferring
Sophocles to Aeschylus. The first surviving play, *Ajax,* dates from some
twenty years later; Sophocles was nearly if not quite fifty when he
wrote it. Of the seven surviving tragedies, *Ajax, Antigone,* and *The
Women of Trachis* stand apart from the others stylistically; he was all
but seventy when he wrote *King Oedipus,* all but eighty for *Electra,*
and all but ninety for *Philoctetes* and *Oedipus at Colonus.* It is doubtful
whether there has ever been work of comparable quality from a man
of such an age.

Part of his secret lay in his flexibility. He built on Aeschylus but was
also critical of him, saying that when he did compose correctly he did
not understand what he was doing (Ath. 1. 22b). The anonymous
author who sketched his life says that he learned expertise in tragic
drama from Aeschylus and was a great innovator himself. This was
typical of the man, original in his own thought but ready to learn from
others. By the end of his career, even in old age, he was still ready to
learn from Euripides, and *Electra, Philoctetes,* and *Oedipus at Colonus*
are considerably influenced by the younger poet. He himself recognized
that his early style (of which no examples survive) was grandiloquent
and derivative from Aeschylus, and only after a transitional period of
painful ingenuity, exemplified by *Ajax, Niobe, Polyxene,* and *Tereus,*
was he able to perfect his style to make it expressive of character as he
sought; the words may date from 441, and, if so, cover only the first
three surviving plays (Plut. *Mor.* 79b). His innovations were all di-

rected toward making the drama more effective. Thus he made his unit the individual play rather than the trilogy, because an episodic drama is as artistically bad as an episodic building. He drastically reduced the lyrical element, and centered his plays firmly on the actors; his choruses are far less involved in the action than those of either Aeschylus or Euripides, though he links his choral songs closely to the plot. At the same time he raised the number of the chorus from twelve to fifteen, thus increasing the spectacular and dramatic effect of their dances.

His introduction of the third actor (accepted by Aeschylus, who was similarly ready to learn from others, as in *The Oresteia*) was his most important single innovation. By the end of his life he was, it seems, using four. The use of three actors made the drama far more mobile. It is not so much that it made possible scenes for three; these are in effect rare, though there are often three actors on stage at once. It is rather that it opened up within a single scene a variety of contrasting confrontations. Sophocles found the tradition that the dramatist should act in his own plays a hampering one, and dropped it; he regarded acting as a skilled profession for the expert. He was bold in introducing action onto the stage, such as the suicide of Ajax or the agony of Philoctetes. He indulged less in spectacular costumes than Aeschylus, but made practical innovations in this field. More important, he introduced scene painting, apparently in the form of a backcloth depicting the distant scene.

With Sophocles the play's the thing. His virtuosity in the handling of plot and the use of dramatic irony and similar devices is unsurpassed. In *King Oedipus* the details of the plot are contrived, but what a contrivance! In *Electra* Sophocles (though this has been disputed), unlike Aeschylus before him or Euripides after him, pushes the moral problem to one side, and concentrates on the dramatic possibilities, first of the false story of Orestes's death, and then of Aegisthus arriving to triumph over Orestes dead and finding Clytemnestra's body in his place. The choice of this apparently in place of a satyr play shows a movement away from the tragic implications.

With plot goes character. The two are interlocked, and Aristotle's dictum that plot is the more important because you can have plot without character but not character without plot is trivial. Sophocles is interested in character, in breed (*physis*), in dominant personalities. He likes to set off character contrasts in pairs: Antigone-Ismene, Antigone-Creon, Creon-Haemon, Oedipus-Creon, Oedipus-Teiresias, Oedipus-Iocaste. His characters, as Aristotle approves, are good but not perfect; they have their tragic flaw. Sophocles is particularly brilliant in the way in which he shows this flaw as the defect of a quality, and links energy with violence, firmness with culpable obstinacy, principle with arrogance, and idealism with folly. His characters are almost a textbook in Aristotelian ethics. In one point he differs from a modern dramatist. On the whole the figures who people his plays display their character without development. But Sophocles comes nearer than any other ancient dramatist to portraying development of character, from Ajax to Neoptolemus.

His characters are set in a divine dimension. Simone Weil, in a decidedly odd book, said that Sophocles is the Greek poet whose inspiration is most visibly and perhaps most finely Christian, a decidedly odd judgment. E. M. Forster's *caveat* is useful: "Boys will regard Sophocles as a kind of enlightened bishop, and something tells me that they are wrong." But their wrongness, and Weil's wrongness, consists not in recognizing this dimension in Sophocles's thought, but in an unhistorical identification of Sophocles's attitude to it with their own. Victor Ehrenberg wrote well in *Sophocles and Pericles* (p. 24):

The notion of tragic guilt . . . is . . . alien to his tragedies. His heroes are not guiltless, for they are human; but their fate does not depend on their moral or unmoral conduct. Their tragedy is that, in spite of their faults and misdeeds, they are "innocent" or perhaps better put, outside the standards of guilt and innocence. Their tragedy is the tragedy of man, of the very fact of being a human being. Man is a toy in the hands of superhuman forces. It is the gods' role over man that is called "fate," and man's reactions against it, which make human life great as well as tragic. Man is born into a world which is the work of the gods, in its good as well as its evil things. It is this world which man has to free, in which and with which he has to live, and in which he has to prove his worth. His fate is bound up with the divine order of the world, and tragedy occurs by the clash between that divine order and human disorder.

The last words are the key to Sophocles's thought-world. He is not a theologian like Aeschylus or an exponent of the New Theology like Euripides. He is concerned with men, in action and in passion. But the divine cosmos is his spiritual backcloth, and it is in breach of that divine order that the tragic situation arises.

12. *AJAX*

The burial of the dead was—if the paradox be permitted—a more vital issue to the Greeks than it is to most of us. Even recognizing this, it is a surprise to find that two of the seven surviving plays of Sophocles turn upon it. We need to remember that, in the war that was shortly to break out, the Thebans were castigated because after Delium they did not permit the Athenians to bury their dead, and that in 406, after a notable sea victory, the Athenian commanders were actually condemned to death because in their exuberance in following up their success they were overtaken by a storm and failed to rescue the bodies for burial. In fact the unburied dead were left haunting this side of the fatal river, as various passages in Plato, Horace, and Vergil may remind us.

Ajax is a strange figure in the Homeric saga, the champion who comes off worst. He is a superbly heroic figure. He and Achilles hold the key positions at either end of the camp, a fact which Sophocles uses effectively in his play (4); he fights with devastating courage in defense of the ships and again over the body of Patroclus; he more than holds his own in single combat with Hector, the Trojan champion. Yet there is something curiously negative about the way he is depicted. He is associated with defense, not attack. His characteristic weapon is the shield, not the spear. In the games in honor of Patroclus he suffers defeat three times. First, in the wrestling, he is thrown by the smaller but cunning Odysseus. Then, in the duel with spears, the Greeks intervene before Diomedes can damage him. Finally, in the weight throwing, he is ousted by the insignificant Polypoetes. Furthermore, the other Ajax, son of Oileus, competes in the footrace and takes the lead, but loses to Odysseus when Athene makes him slip in some cow dung, so that all the spectators laugh at him. This looks very like a story of Telamon's son that has been transferred. There is already in *The Iliad* an ambiguity about Ajax. In *The Odyssey* Odysseus speaks to him in the underworld with compliments; Ajax turns on his heel and walks away. The author of *On the Sublime* saw this silence as more sublime than speech. Vergil paid it the homage of imitation when he portrayed his Dido. Sophocles undoubtedly had it in mind, but could not use it in the theater. Elsewhere in the epic tradition appeared tales of the quarrel between Ajax and Odysseus over Achilles's armor, of Ajax's madness and suicide. In *The Little Iliad* came the attempt to kill the Greek commanders, which Sophocles also used. In addition we must remember that Ajax was a cult hero at Athens, and one of the ten tribes was named after him; he was naturally especially associated with the victory at Salamis. This too is important in the emphasis on burial; a cult hero may be expected to have a tomb. A formidable, daemonic hero.

Ajax is almost certainly the earliest surviving play by Sophocles. Numerous stylistic tests have been used and point to the priority of *Ajax, The Women of Trachis*, and *Antigone* over the other plays. On the whole *Ajax* is likely to be the earliest of the three, and a date in the middle 440s is not likely to be far from wrong. Kamerbeek argued for a date after the death of Cimon in 449 and before the political events of 446. We have no play of Sophocles written before he was nearly fifty, a fact that may make us pause before thinking that we can make anything like a definitive evaluation of his work. We know nothing of the plays with which *Ajax* was presented. Two other plays of Sophocles, *Teucer* and *Eurysaces*, dealt with the same group of legends. *Teucer* was evidently a powerful play, much admired by Cicero; about *Eurysaces* we know next to nothing. But even if we knew enough to say that they might have made a coherent trilogy, we could not claim that they did so, since we know that Sophocles abandoned the connected trilogy for a discrete sequence; the Theban plays form an excellent example of this. It is however tempting to suggest that if there was a parodic link between the satyr plays and the tragedies, the satyr play to *Ajax* may have been *The Trackers. Ajax* is a diptych; it falls sharply into two halves, and critics have been much exercised about the unity of these two halves. Waldock has shown that the diptych structure is commoner than we might expect in Sophocles and Euripides. Such a structure is likely to arise from the abandonment of the trilogy, though it is just to remark that when Aeschylus wrote his trilogy, *The Award of Arms, The Thracians, The People of Salamis,* the events of our play were confined to the middle play of the three. There must have been many themes that fell readily into two plays and were padded to provide a third. When Sophocles opted for the single play he must have found himself tending to compress the material of at least a dilogy into his single unit. It is to be expected that the earlier plays show this, and not surprising if it continues to appear.

Not that there is any uncertainty of handling in other ways. The opening is powerful. A crouching figure enters the scene closely examining the ground for spoor; this and the suppliant procession in *King Oedipus* are arguably the most genuinely *dramatic* openings in Greek tragedy. As he crouches near to the door of the stage building, the unmistakable figure of Athene appears on the top of the building in full view of the audience, but unseen by him. She speaks and identifies him as Odysseus, and the building as the tent of Ajax. The relations of goddess and mortal are as in Homer. We learn that in the night, Ajax, angered because the armor of Achilles was awarded to Odysseus not to himself, set out to kill Agamemnon, Menelaus, and Odysseus, but Athene checked him and turned his fury against the flocks of sheep and herds of cattle that lay as spoil. The scene is excellent, the narrative direct, skillfully unfolded and exciting. We are introduced to seven important images or themes. All are vital to the whole play. One is the sword, a second the shield. The sword (16) is the weapon which has destroyed the animals, which will destroy Ajax, and which, we learn, was a gift from Hector. The shield (19) is traditional in Ajax's armory and representative of his vast powers as a defender of others; himself he could not defend. The third image, here first introduced, is the yoke (24). Ajax has so treated the animals; he himself comes under the yoke; here in the first appearance Ajax thinks he has yoked Odysseus, but Odysseus has freely yoked himself to the task of tracking. The fourth image is the hunt. It is ambivalent and ironical. Ajax, the hunter, has become the hunted. Pentheus in *The Bacchants* is in like case. Fifth, there is the image of light and darkness which starts with the passage from night to day. Sixth, there is the thought of time, of transitoriness and permanence. The first word of the play is "Always" and it comes time and again (117, 320, 342, 379, 570, 599, 676, 682, 765, 835–836, 1036). Finally there is the obsessive image of disease.

The scene is not yet over. It bursts out into strong drama as Athene calls Ajax out of the tent. He emerges with the bloody whip with which he has been torturing the animals; the play took its popular title *Ajax with the Whip* from this spectacle, which must have been frightening. Odysseus, in view of his association with Athene is a curiously unattractive figure to the Attic dramatists. He quails with a cowardice which is comical. But by the end of the scene he is showing pity, for Ajax is not his real heroic self any more than Odysseus in quailing is all that he can and should be (124); he is yoked to doom (123). For men, in the cliché which ultimately goes back to Homer, are shadows. Athene shows no pity. Ajax offended by refusing her support in battle, as we are later explicitly reminded. There is fearful bitterness in the opening exchange:

> ATHENE: You there! Ajax! Must I call you more than once?
> Such slight respect for your ally?
> AJAX: Welcome, Athene! Welcome, Zeus's daughter!
> How well you have stood by me! (88)

She is offended, and utterly inflexible. And this is the goddess of

Athens, and the poet Sophocles not Euripides! The play might well be subitled "The Wrath of Athene."

There is another aspect of the opening scene that permeates the whole play. This is the note of ambiguity. Slight ambiguities of language pile upon one another more thickly in *Ajax* than any other Greek play. There are at least a dozen in this opening scene (2, 9–10, 15, 21, 24, 40, 51, 52, 53, 81, 90, 98, 100, 117, 123), some of them with several levels of meaning. Sophocles later, in *King Oedipus* and *Electra*, showed himself the master of dramatic irony. There is dramatic irony here too. Ajax asserts that the commanders will not again dishonor him (98); it is true, not because, as he thinks, they are dead, but because Odysseus feels pity. "Now let them take away *my* arms," he cries (100). The only arms he can really call his own is Hector's sword, on which he dies. But irony only explains a very small proportion of the ambiguities. One example of many will suffice. Athene checks Ajax (51), setting on his eyes *dusphorous gnomas*. *Gnomai* are recognitions, or opinions, or purposes; *dusphorous* means "hard to bear" or "leading astray." She checks him from—or the *gnomai* are of (or both)—a joy that is incurable and also damaging beyond cure. All these levels of meaning are present in the Greek. These ambiguities of language are deliberate, for ambiguity is the theme of the play. We are introduced in this first scene to Athene, the ally who is no ally, Odysseus, the hero who is a coward and the enemy who shows pity, and Ajax the victor who is no victor but who in degradation finds glory. So among the central images are the shield which does not save, and the sword, the gift which is no gift. Sophocles is inviting us to look below the surface, alike with language, things, and people.

The chorus enters to the familiar anapaests; they are the sailors who have come with Ajax. As they file in they chant anxiously of the rumors Odysseus is spreading about Ajax. "I tremble," says their spokesman, "like the eye of a winged dove" (140). The image of the eye, *omma*, with its other layers of meaning, face, light and glory will return (167, 192, 462, 977, 1004). The chorus themselves revert finely to the bird image as they call to Ajax:

> Turn your eyes away—
> they chatter like a flock of starlings.

Appear again, in a flash
they cower before the eagle's strength,
silent, quivering, voiceless. (167)

Another powerful ambiguity speaks of Ajax "the horse-mad plain traversing" (143). It is a powerful picture, made more powerful by the inevitable tendency of the listener to think at first that it is Ajax who is horse-mad; for he is horse-mad, alike in treating men as horses and horses as men, and in himself becoming irrational like an animal. The chorus breaks into song as they ask what god has sent his sickness—Artemis or Ares? They do not think of Athene. Their lament ends poignantly: "For me grief stands firm" (200).

Tecmessa, captive and consort of Ajax, joins them in their anxiety; she combines two images as she speaks of him as "lying diseased in a turbulent storm" (205). She depicts a masterful, awesome man who yet inspires affection. It is important to see that the madness has exaggerated elements in the real Ajax. The chorus describes him as "blazing" (221, *aithon*). This may be partly descriptive: a mask with red hair would be wholly appropriate. But, more it recalls the Homeric simile of the "tawny" lion (*Il.* 11.548), and means at one and the same time fierce and yet, in a less repellent and more warming way, ardent. But also there are more sinister overtones of "feverish" and "ready for the pyre." The sailors think of escape; they would rather have the yoke of the oars (249); the sons of Atreus are "plying" threats (251). Tecmessa assures them in vivid language that the storm is past (257). Now Ajax is seeing what he has done with no one else —and ambiguity sets in again—"helping" or "going beyond their proper function" (261, *parapraxantos*). Athene has helped, but *she* has not gone beyond *her* proper function.

The song and dance die away for the moment, and Tecmessa, rich in compassion, tells the story of bloodshed and a diseased mind. Then comes a great cry of anguish from within, and the sound of Ajax's voice as he calls first for his son Eurysaces and then for his brother Teucer. The sound wails eerily; at one point Ajax has four circumflex accents, with their rising and falling pitch, in six syllables, three actually consecutively (342). The effect must have resembled the howling of banshees. Then the doors open, and the moving platform emerges with a dramatic tableau of Ajax among the slaughtered cattle. The effect was tremendous, and an artist named Timomachus later painted it in a picture world-famous in its day. The song of lament bursts out afresh, but this time it comes from Ajax alone, and the prevalent dochmiacs show his state of mind. Tecmessa and the chorus turn from their own outburst and speak calming words in sober iambics; the contrast between their prosaic interventions and the wild lyrical out-pourings of Ajax is magnificent drama. His words are infested with ambiguity. The sailors turned the oar blade in the sea, but also to no effect (359, *halion*). He calls for death and curses Odysseus, a dra-matically powerful stroke in view of what is to come. Then:

> O
> darkness, my only light,
> o blackness of death, a brilliant beam to me,
> take me, take me into your house,
> take me. (394)

Then, with another masterly ambiguity, he cries that he has no hope from gods or from men, children of (a) day (399). He is divided from men who are children of light where he is a child of darkness, but they are united in weakness and all ephemeral. In addi-tion there is a pun on the word for "tame" or "civilized"; Ajax has behaved like a beast of prey and a barbarian. He says goodbye to the land of Troy, not as the home of his Trojan enemies, but as the shore that gave sustenance to the Greeks.

Ajax now grows calmer, and with a play on his name and the Greek cry of grief (430), comparable to Shakespeare's "Old Gaunt indeed; and gaunt in being old" (*R. II* 2.1.74), he breaks into iam-bics. He has no penitence. He should have received Achilles's armor, and if Athene had not struck him down with the disease of madness, his enemies among the Greeks would now be dead.

> What am I now to do? Plainly the gods
> abominate me, the Greek soldiers loathe me,
> Troy and the soil beneath my feet hate me. (457)

Here he introduces a new theme of some importance, that of true birth. His father Telamon was a hero; in disgrace he cannot face him. It must be death.

> Honor in life or honor in death—there is no other way
> for one of noble birth. (479)

"Ajax" says the chorus leader, "no one can say that your words are bastard" (481). Tecmessa's reply is one of the most moving things in the play, and Sophocles has heightened the effect by echoes designed to remind us of the parting of Hector from Andromache in *The Iliad* (6.407). Tecmessa is a slave (489) but free born (the theme recurs; cf. 524). She has accepted her changed standing, let him accept his. She appeals to him to think of her, of his parents, of his son, and then again of her; it is a marvelous attempt to recall him from himself to others. According to the old story, Ajax had killed Tecmessa's parents; Sophocles eases that away by changing the myth. At one point a more sinister note sounds through. She is speaking of being a slave:

> It was the will of heaven,
> yes and of your hand. (489)

We cannot forget that Ajax's offense was to scorn Athene's help. Ajax replies gently, but does not answer her plea. He calls for her obedience. "I will obey in all things," she responds, but the words can mean "I will suffer all things" (529). He calls for his young son Eurysaces—the name means "him of the broad shield." Again the scene recalls the parting of Hector and Astyanax, and the comparison is the more poignant because Hector was in glory and Ajax is in disgrace. Again the note of breed is sounded:

> Bring him. Bring him here. There'll be no drawing back
> at the sight of new-spilled blood,
> not if he's my true son.
> The time's come to break in the colt, to train him
> like his father in a tough school.
> Lad, may you be all your father was—
> but less unfortunate. (545)

He gives the boy his shield, and declares that the rest of his armor

shall be buried in his grave, then sends him off with the weeping
Tecmessa:

> Lock the door, move; no sensible doctor
> sings spells for a wound that needs the knife. (581)

His words are harsh, cold and detached, and when she protests, his
temper flares. The platform is wheeled in and the doors clang shut.

The chorus sings a song of grief. They invoke Salamis, and contrast their own plight on a foreign shore awaiting an unexpected death,
dark and destructive (609; the language is ambiguous). Then they
turn to Ajax, and in a few brief lines play on the thought of disease,
the motif of breed, and the image of the bird, here the nightingale,
as the type of lamentation that Ajax's mother will surpass; the syntax
is contorted and the exact meaning uncertain.

The next scene is the crux of the play. Ajax emerges with a sword
in his hand, and speaks in strangely contemplative mood and with
unfamiliar gentleness. His words are throughout ambiguous.

> All is subject to time's unmeasured passing.
> It brings them from dark to light, hides them from light in
>   dark. (646)

A straightforward philosophical reflection, but with strong overtones
of the exaltation of the unworthy Odysseus and degradation of the
worthy Ajax, with an allusion to his own passage to death. "There is
nothing for which a man may not look" (648). Nothing is impossible
or unexpected, but we remember that Ajax in a more positive sense is
looking for death. His edge is blunted (651), but the words also
mean "I have grown womanish in my speech," with a possible emphasis on "speech." "I feel pity at the thought of leaving her and my son"
(652), with the double meaning "Out of pity I revoke my decision to
leave them" and "I intend to leave them in pity." He will find purification by the sea (indeed, in death). He will bury the sword (yes,
in his own body), a gift from Hector that was no gift. At this point
alliteration adds biting quality to his words (661). He has learned
his lesson for the future (a short future except beyond the grave), to
yield to the gods and reverence the sons of Atreus (we expect the

verbs to be reversed). They are in authority; he must yield ("they" is ambiguous, but Ajax means "the gods"). Then more philosophical reflection about the seasons, leading to Sleep, the jailer who "at last releases his prisoners" (676)—but what of the sleep of death? "Must I not learn to discipline myself?" (677, *sophronein*). Enemies may become friends (indeed) and friends enemies. For the commons a caucus is a dangerous harbor (a line with strongly political overtones, but also a reminder that Ajax is seeking the harbor of Death, which is secure).

> Do as I tell you, and you yet may hear
> that these present ills are past, and I am at peace. (691)

Throughout there is a contrast between the mood of firm resignation and the word for things that cause fear (648, 650, 669, 674, *deinos*).

In this speech lies the play's central ambiguity. It has been termed *Trugrede*, but is Ajax deceiving himself or others? Does he believe himself to have abandoned suicide, or is he set on suicide? If the latter, does he intend to hide his purpose, and if so are his words deliberately ambiguous? So the questions are asked; they pay Sophocles the tribute of treating Ajax as a real person. For the one thing of which we may be certain is that the words and their intention are deliberately ambiguous on the part of Sophocles. Nonetheless there has been a change in Ajax. There is compassion for Tecmessa (the scene is made more powerful by her unspeaking presence), even if it is only to spare her the anticipation of his death. There is also self-discipline, even if it is obedience to the gods, who drive him to death in defense of his honor, rather than to the sons of Atreus.

He goes out stage-right, and the chorus, which has taken his words to indicate a change of purpose, sings in unrestrained joy. The cloud of distress has lifted (the storm image). Their song is radiant with light. Yet when they take up Ajax's philosophical mood, "The power of time withers all things" (714), referring to Ajax's quarrelsome mood, they use the word that Io, in Aeschylus's *Prometheus*, used of the disease afflicting her (Aesch. *P.V.* 597) and there are grim overtones; their words are as ambiguous as his own.

A messenger enters; we expect news of Ajax's death, but are held in suspense. The messenger tells first of Teucer's return from campaign and of his hostile reception by the Greeks. He calls for Ajax, but the chorus answers with terrible irony that he is "gone" (743). The messenger, with an excitement marked by alliteration (745), then tells that Calchas the seer had revealed that Ajax by his hybristic refusal of Athene's help had earned her wrath, but that the wrath would die away if Ajax could be kept safe that day. Kamerbeek has shrewdly remarked that in Sophocles the warnings of seers take their dramatic effect from the fact that they come too late. They call Tecmessa and tell her the news, and all go off in different directions in search of Ajax, leaving the scene bare.

The exit of the chorus marks a change of scene, as in *The Kindly Goddesses*, and we are now in an isolated spot among bushes near the sea. It is hard to be certain how the next scene was staged. The simplest device might have been to open the doors, revealing an inner set with Ajax among bushes; it might have been effective to use the moving platform and bring it slightly out from the doors. Ajax rises from planting the sword, blade uppermost in the soil and delivers what is all in all perhaps the finest monologue in Greek tragedy. The sword will be "most cutting" (815), practically because it is newly sharpened and firmly fixed, psychologically because it is Hector's gift, fixed in the soil of Troy. He describes it in a remarkable line with two freshly minted compounds as "new-sharpened on the iron-eating whetstone" (820). His words bring together his enemies, the soil of Troy, Hector, who gave him the sword ("most hated of my friends" as he says in powerful oxymoron; 817), the sons of Atreus, and the Greeks.

He speaks five prayers, one to Zeus to bring news to Teucer, one to Hermes for gentle sleep, one to the Furies for vengeance on the sons of Atreus, one to the Sun God to bring the news to Ajax's parents in his westward passage, and one to Death to be his medical attendant. Then he turns back to the Sun, greeting him for the last time, and recalling the Light-Darkness imagery, invokes Salamis and Athens and the forces of nature around him, and leaps on his sword: the actor Timotheus was renowned for his performance in this scene. Either the death scene is withdrawn from our eyes, or, while our attention is distracted by the entry of the chorus, a dummy is substituted for the actor (who has to return to the stage as Teucer).

The chorus, searching, enters from both sides. The words of the first group begin startlingly with seven successive words beginning with *p,* and then an equally startling repetition of the sound *dou,* somewhat with the effect of "Oi! Noise!" (870). Would that some divinity from Olympus would give them news (881); they mean the nymphs of Mysian Olympus, but there is an Olympian goddess who knows Ajax's fate. A cry from Tecmessa within a thicket (that is, within the stage building) shows that she has found the body. The chorus's first thought is of their own journey home (900), but Tecmessa's thoughts are wholly of Ajax, and she takes off her own cloak and lays it over the body. Then she throws in cries of sorrow, but whereas the chorus sings, she speaks of the yoke of slavery awaiting her child and herself (944), but also defiantly, for she knows that the Greeks who have scorned Ajax will come to miss him. The chorus imagines Odysseus exulting; they describe him as "much-enduring" (956); it is a stock epithet of Odysseus, but it in fact identifies him with Ajax, and though the chorus in using it is thinking of his effrontery, it points forward to his boldness in contradicting the commanders.

Teucer (Ajax without his daemonic authority) joins the scene of sorrow and acts decisively in sending Tecmessa to bring Eurysaces for protection; this incidentally enables the actor playing Tecmessa to play Odysseus, for when Tecmessa returns she does not speak and the mask was transferred to an extra. Teucer speaks, as appears later (1263), with a strong accent. He has heard a rumor, as from some god, that Ajax was dead. This is a vital line; it tells us that Zeus answered Ajax's prayer, and thus that in his death Ajax was accepted by the gods. As Teucer confronts the dead body of his half-brother, Sophocles, as Kamerbeek puts it, pulls out all the organ stops of pathos, as superlative piles on superlative (992). Then, as he takes the cloak off and looks at the body, a strange thing happens. Teucer utters one exclamation rich in ambiguous meaning: "O eye not to be seen! O cruel courage!" (1004) and, like the chorus, thinks first of the effect of the death on himself. And now we have a very different picture of Tela-

mon, their common father, and see him as an unsmiling, sarcastic, bitter, quarrelsome man, and, because Sophocles is a great artist and because Ajax has insisted that he is his father's true son, we learn something about Ajax, who was no plaster saint gone momentarily astray.
Teucer knows that he will be rejected at home. He tries to move Ajax's
body, and in so doing recognizes the sword and meditates upon the
cross-stroke of fortune: Hector dragged at Achilles' chariot rail by
the belt Ajax gave him, Ajax committing suicide with the sword he
received from Hector, a sword sharp and piercing both literally and
metaphorically (1024).

Menelaus, a paltry figure with the typical villain's mask, comes on
to forbid the burial of Ajax. He addresses Teucer haughtily and Teucer
answers in a slow-moving line with no true caesura (1049). Menelaus
speaks with strong oligarchical bias, claiming that the commons should
obey (1071) and attacking the familiar democratic slogan about "living as you like" (1081), and points his sententious language with a
rhymed aphorism (1085–1086). In his politics, his cult of military
discipline, and his aphoristic speech he is the typical Spartan. Teucer,
the archer, says that Menelaus has missed his mark, and answers him
vigorously, disclaiming Menelaus's authority over Ajax or himself; his
speech is phrased to suggest the cross-examination of the law courts.
Menelaus can answer only with a mixture of cheap abuse and self-
righteous pomposity. They fling contradictions at one another, ending
with a rather weak exchange of allegorical stories about one another.

Menelaus stalks out, discomfited, to complain to his big brother.
Tecmessa comes back with Eurysaces, and Teucer begins defiantly to
prepare for the burial. I suspect that he carries the body out to the foot
of the altar in the middle of the orchestra. He brings Eurysaces to kneel
by the body, sitting back on his heels, and places in his hand three
locks of hair, theirs and Tecmessa's. Then the boy falls forward,
clutching and guarding as by sacred right his father's body. It is a splendid tableau, as Teucer goes to dig the grave, and the chorus dances solemnly around the altar. Their song is a curse on the inventor of war,
and on the way strife breeds strife, a thought that points back to the
theme of birth, and forward to the way Odysseus by his magnanimity
breaks the vicious circle. They go on to yearn to escape from this

wooded promontory to the wooded promontory of Sunium, which was the promise of home for the sailor returning from the east.

And now we move to the final confrontation. Teucer and Agamemnon arrive almost simultaneously. Agamemnon, entering in full panoply, speaks in powerful rebuke of Teucer's *hybris* and in effective defense of the decisions of authority. He bandies about the thought of Ajax as "nothing" (1231, cf. 1257). His words recall many of the play's motifs.

> A huge-bodied ox can be directed
> straight along the road by quite a small whip.
> I can see you enjoying a taste of the same
> medicine, if you don't get some sense in your head. (1253)

He demands self-discipline from Teucer, and recollection of his parentage (as a citizen on one side only, by a recent Attic law). Teucer answers angrily, first of the glorious heroism of Ajax when the other Greeks were "as nothing" (1275), then of Agamemnon's poor heritage from the murderous Atreus and loose-living Aerope, then of his own noble parentage. He flings a bitter taunt at Agamemnon. Better to die in defense of Ajax than in fighting for "that woman you claim, or your brother" (1312). This may be contemptuous of Helen, or refer to Briseis and Helen, or suggest that Menelaus is a woman, or, more likely, be a loose taunt to be interpreted in any of these ways.

The situation seems irreconcilable, for the quarrel is far beyond the point at issue when Odysseus comes in, and, with a change of front worthy of Restoration comedy, persuades Agamemnon to permit the burial. True that Sophocles has pointed forward by Odysseus's pity in the opening scene; true that he points back by making Odysseus self-centered in his reason for supporting the burial (1365); it remains unsatisfactory. But there is fine dramatic point. Ajax has won death through his enemy Hector, burial through his enemy Odysseus. Agamemnon goes out, still hating, and in one of those golden moments of the stage, Odysseus, without looking at Teucer, says:

> Now I have a message for Teucer. From now on
> I shall be as keen a friend as enemy in the past.
> And I would wish to help in burying this body,

> share in the labor, and omit no pains
> a man should give to a hero. (1376)

Then, and only then, does Teucer address him directly. He rejects the offer of help with the burial for fear of offending the shade of Ajax, but accepts his friendship. So, in ceremonial procession, the body, the body of a good man (1415), is carried out to burial.

Ajax is not a wholly satisfying play. It is easy intellectually to understand what Sophocles was driving at in the second part: the power of Ajax after his death ("O Julius Caesar, thou art mighty yet" comes in a play of similar structure), and what Reinhardt has called the contrast between the noble wrongness of Ajax and the ignoble rectitudes of smaller men. But, even when we have added the greater Athenian interest in the burial of the dead and the establishment of their cult hero, and in political and forensic debate, the climax of the play comes too early, and the second leaf of the diptych suffers by comparison with the first. For the first is superb. There is no question here, as there might be in *Antigone*, about the ultimate theme of the play. It is about Ajax, "a solitary shame-culture figure thrown up by a literature of guilt" (said John Jones), a figure of heroic stature caught in an antiheroic situation, no longer at ease, (as Eliot says of his Magi after their journey), and choosing suicide rather than ridicule in an alien climate. This was a topical theme, for this was happening in the fifth century. Thucydides reminds us how the sense of honor linked with an essentially simple view of life was laughed out of court and disappeared. This is the theme of Sophocles's play. He does not give a simplicist view of Ajax's simplicity; he portrays him "warts and all." As Kamerbeek put it: "The hero is a committer of *hybris* but his greatness is inconceivable detached from the *hybris*." It is part of what Knox calls his "heroic presumption." But though Ajax succumbs to the inevitable march of history, and though he has flagrant and obvious faults, he leaves lesser men behind. Further, whereas all the characters, with the exception of Tecmessa, are pointedly egocentric—the chorus and Teucer responding to Ajax's death with "What will happen to me?", Athene, Menelaus, and Agamemnon all concerned with the slight to themselves rather than with the fate of the Greeks lacking Ajax, and even Odysseus explicitly saying that he advocates the burial from selfish motives—Ajax attains compassion. For Tecmessa tries to move him by the thought of others, and her arguments fail, but inwardly he is moved by her attitude. For whatever view we take of the *Trugrede*, it arises from compassion for Tecmessa. The compassion is, so to say, Stoic; it affects his attitude not his decision to commit suicide: *mens immota manet, lacrimae volvuntur inanes.*

Vergil, himself compassionate, knew this well, and blended it with the epic tradition, so that his Aeneas, with some of the lineaments of Ajax, in the war books pities his victims even while killing them. Perhaps the closest parallel is Achilles in *The Iliad.* There, at the last, confronted with Priam, the cruel soldier learns to pity. So it is with Ajax here. *Ajax* is not at the last a great play, but Ajax is a great rôle for a great actor.

13. *THE WOMEN OF TRACHIS*

The Women of Trachis is the most neglected of the seven surviving plays of Sophocles. Dr. Johnson called it "puzzling." It is therefore startling to find Ezra Pound prefixing to his granite translation the words: "The *Trachiniae* presents the highest peak of Greek sensibility registered in any of the plays that have come down to us, and is, at the same time, nearest the original form of the God-Dance." Pound took pleasure in deliberately shocking, but in *Poesis* (p. 155) the sober Kitto asked, "Where, even in the work of Sophocles, shall we find a more moving tragedy than of this desolate wife who, at what is for her the supreme crisis, tries to win back her husband's love, but destroys him instead?" It is indeed a supreme *peripeteia* in Aristotle's sense, when a course of action designed to one end has as a result its diametrical tragic opposite.

The play has another point of particular interest. It is one of the few Greek tragedies, and the only surviving one by Sophocles, which centers upon love between woman and man. Indeed Bowra says that "the two chief characters, Heracles and Deianeira, are man and woman, husband and wife. They might be typical of any married pair, and their tragedy private and domestic." Murray states it even more forcibly: "You can see Heracles and Deianeira most Monday mornings in some police court or other, as you can see in Broadmoor asylum Medeas who have murdered their children." Bowra adds that Sophocles makes his play of universal interest by making his woman extremely womanly and his man extremely manly. Of course, in fifth-century Athenian society, as in African or Asian traditional society, falling in love was a process that took place after marriage rather than before, and relationships with members of the same sex were socially more significant. Sophocles here does something Euripidean. He unbolts the door of purdah, as Euripides does in *Medea*; it is likely (compare the motif of the poisoned dress) that *The Women of Trachis* gave Euripides his opening. The comparative rarity of the theme endows the play with peculiar appeal.

Deianeira, the wife of Heracles, begins the play. Critics sometimes speak of her almost as if she were a girl, but she has a full-grown son. She is in fact the aging wife, in her thirties, still full of desire, but anxious about her own desirability (25, 547). She comes out with her old nurse, and her opening words set a tone. They were a familiar saw, apposite to the end of a play, as Sophocles was to use them in *King Oedipus*. As an opening they are ominous.

> There's an old saying of men, a clear saying,
> that till a man's dead you never really know
> whether his life has turned out good or bad. (1)

Her words reveal an inhibited, emotional woman (7, 49). She tells the strange story of her wooing, first by the river god Achelous, who came to her in monstrous shapes as a bull, a snake, or a man "with bull's prow." The animal imagery is important; it prepares us for the horse-man Nessus. The story contrasts acutely with the realistic portrayal of Deianeira; it takes us into a dream world, and this is no doubt its function. Deianeira lives helpless in a strongly imagined world of powers too great for her. Heracles came as her fairy prince; she did not dare to look at the struggle between her suitors (another fact about her).

> Zeus, god of battles, saw that it ended right.
> Did it end right? (26)

Her marriage to Heracles brought her little joy and less tranquillity.

> One night brings anxiety,
> the next night takes it over and lets it go.
> We produced children. He only sees them
> like a farmer with a remote field,
> once at seed-time and at harvest. (29)

The familiar image of sowing for the act of sex is handled with exquisite delicacy. Now, she tells us, they are in exile in Trachis, and Heracles has been away for fifteen months. Her son Hyllus comes in with the news that his father, after a period of enslavement to Omphale, is campaigning in Euboea, and Deianeira recalls an oracle that he was destined "in this place" (as she says with startling ambiguity; 77) either to meet death, or success, and a life of happiness for the future. "His fate lies in the balance" (83). She sends Hyllus to find news. The moment is critical; they think the critical decision is "will Heracles return home?" But it is not.

The boy goes, and the chorus, women from the town of Trachis, dance in, singing an exquisite and plaintive song. First they call on the Sun whose all-seeing eye must know the fate of Heracles. They describe Deianeira as a bird sorrowing for its mate. In the third stanza they return to Heracles; they use the image of the sea round Crete for his troubled journey through life. That sea was notoriously stormy, but Crete had other associations; there Theseus, Heracles's ally in legend, had also overcome a bull-man; and Euripides's *Hippolytus* reminds us that Crete was mythologically associated with warped and destructive love. In the fourth stanza they address Deianeira directly and tell her to retain hope, for though life is never without pain, pain and joy circle round as surely as the Great Bear rotating in the sky. It is this thought which brings the philosophical conclusions of the final stanza.

> Nothing is firm. The twinkling
> night, disaster,
> riches pass
> away, another knows
> joy and desolation. (131)

This carefully, almost too carefully, patterned song ends with the thought that Zeus will not neglect any of his sons.

As they finish, Deianeira, becoming more confident in response to their sympathy, shares with them what is on her mind. She lets slip that after years of married life she is frightened by responsibility, and yearns to be back in the sheltered life an Athenian girl enjoyed before puberty led to marriage. She elaborates the moment of crisis. Heracles left a tablet; fifteen months from the day of his last departure would bring either his death or a life free from trouble.

> He declared that this was destined by the gods
> to be the final point of Heracles's labors. (169)

Yes, indeed. The prophecy was given from Dodona, a shrine of Zeus, by two dove priestesses, and we know that Deianeira, the shrinking bird, will bring its fulfillment. As she speaks a messenger arrives with the news that Heracles is alive, victorious, and coming home. The herald Lichas has been detained by the crowds in the town, so he has come on, as he says in words designed by Sophocles for a laugh at the moment of relief, "Hoping for your favor—and something for myself" (191). For the messenger it is news of triumph, for Deianeira sheer joy. But in her joy she calls on Zeus, god of Oeta's unharvested fields (200). We have had the agricultural metaphor; and it is Heracles's lust to harvest Iole that will win him a pyre on that same Mt. Oeta. For the moment Deianeira has a harvest of happiness (204), and the chorus, identified with her, expresses that joy in a vigorous dance in which the meter, based on the paean, contains some strikingly bold effects.

The herald, Lichas, has at last shaken off the crowds and comes with first-hand news; he has with him a group of prisoners, women. Deianeira's first question is of Heracles, and Lichas's answer is on the face of it reassuring:

> I left him full of energy
> and life and vigor, not crushed by disease. (234)

This is the first mention of disease, a key word later, and the words are ominous. He identifies the women as prisoners, as Deianeira reaches out to them in compassion. Then in a long speech he tells of Heracles's bondage to Omphale, and how he swore revenge on Eurytus of Euboea for the humiliation. Lichas, as we shall discover, does not tell the whole truth. Even so, his story, though apparently of success, is grim enough. A conventionally and sincerely religious man, Lichas lards his speech with the name of Zeus. Zeus punished Heracles for killing a man by treachery, for that was *hybris* (80) and the gods are intolerant of *hybris* as men are, as Heracles was. For though Heracles may give thanks to Zeus, it was Heracles not Zeus who sacked the city of Eurytus. That city is destroyed, the men killed, the women enslaved, and thudding through Lichas's smooth words is the inexorable question, "Who will pay?"

Deianeira's joy is tempered with pity for the prisoners (289), and she prays to Zeus that none of her children may suffer so. She is strangely drawn to one girl whose bearing is especially pathetic but who does not answer her questions. She asks Lichas about her, but he with gruff embarrassment brushes aside her questions, revealing only that the girl might be from the palace. The girl's tearfulness reveals her as Deianeira's double, and Deianeira will take up and echo her silence. The virile he-man evidently likes melting women. Lichas takes the girls into the house and the first messenger, who has been waiting vainly for his tip, thinks to earn it by additional information. He tells Deianeira that he heard from Lichas that it was love, lust, passion (354) which led Heracles to sack the city. He had fallen in love with Iole, the very girl Deianeira was addressing, and when her father wouldn't let him sleep with her, trumped up a grievance and sacked a city to get her. Lichas comes out again and Deianeira falteringly begins to tax him. Lichas takes evasive action, but the original messenger, with growing confidence, brusquely intervenes, and presses him to admit that the girl is Iole, Eurytus's daughter, that he called her "the wife of Heracles" (428), and that it was the passion for this girl that destroyed the city. Lichas tries to pretend that the man is diseased (435); it is not he whom disease is to destroy. Deianeira is now roused by his continual evasions and breaks in. Her first words are charged with irony:

> By Zeus who lets his fires fall on the forests
> of Oeta, stop stealing the truth away from me. (436)

On Oeta, Heracles, Zeus's son, will find his end in fire. She knows that Love is an irresistible boxer; it is folly to oppose him (441). In these words she seals her doom, for this is exactly what she seeks to do. She is overmastered by Love; it would be madness to blame either Iole or Heracles because they have succumbed *to this disease* (445). It is Lichas's deceitfulness that is reprehensible. She cannot be hurt by the truth. No one has loved more women than Heracles. She does not blame Iole; she is sorry for her and the destruction her beauty has caused. But "let wind and current carry these events along" (467). So Lichas tells the truth, that it was for love of Iole that Heracles sacked Oechalia, and Heracles had no intention of concealing it. He asks Deianeira to be patient with Iole.

> It's Heracles's nature—always victorious in battle,
> always surrendering to love. (488)

There is irony here too, and it is pointed when Deianeira asks him to wait to take to Heracles gifts in return for gifts. The only gift she has received is a girl to push her out of her bed; the gift she returns will kill her husband.

They go into the house, and the choral ode that follows is a masterpiece in a small compass. It starts from Aphrodite, goddess of love, and goes back to the battle between Heracles and Achelous for the love of Deianeira, with Aphrodite standing as umpire, and Deianeira seated on a hill apart.

> Thud of fist and twang
>   of bow,
> chaos of bull's horns,
>   close-knit
> grappling, deadly
>   fullface

> blows, both panting.
> The lovely gentle girl
> on the hill in the distance
> sitting, waiting for her husband ... (516)

We can imagine a powerful, evocative, mimetic dance, and there is poignancy at the end as Deianeira is compared, in an image of Lucretian tenderness, with a calf straying from its mother.

Deianeira slips out to share a secret with the chorus. She is unnaturally excited. She uses long words, one of seven syllables (*sunkatoiktioumene,* 535). She has a bitter little joke in which she describes Iole precisely as "baggage" (537). She imagines them, like the wives of Dai Bread in *Under Milk Wood,* sharing one bed. She is biting at the expense of Heracles "with his reputation for virtue and fidelity" (541). But she does not know how to be angry with him; he is always liable to suffer from this disease (544). But she will not tolerate the rivalry of a girl of ripening beauty while her own flowers are fading; she will not tolerate that Heracles might be called her husband but Iole's man. It is characteristic of Deianeira's unhappy nature that she has not the strength to stand up to Heracles directly. She uses a love charm. And the theme of monstrous animal life returns with power. She tells how the Centaur Nessus, half-horse half-man, ferrying her across a stream, pawed her with roving hands, and Heracles shot him with an arrow poisoned by black bile from the Lernaean hydra. The dying Centaur told her to preserve the blood from round the wound as a love charm if Heracles's fancy should ever stray; it would prevent him from loving another woman more than her. That was true, bitterly and tragically true. Poor, gullible Deianeira!

We can see through her words all her uncertainties, all her fairy-story dreams, and all the attractive but dangerous innocence that rebukes Lichas for telling a white lie and never doubts that the combination of the blood of one monster and the poison of another will produce a love charm. She has smeared a tunic with the salve and is sending it as a present to Heracles. Lichas, coming out impatient to be gone, promises to take it for her. He, the herald, claims to "make a sound show of Hermes's skills" (620). The words are doubly ironical. Their natural meaning is simply that Hermes is the god of heralds. But

Hermes was also a twister, a god of lies and deceit, and Lichas has already shown his obedience there. And Hermes escorted the dead to Hades.

Deianeira goes in, and the chorus sings a slight song of Heracles's long-delayed voyage home, notable only in the irony that starts from Oeta and ends with the Centaur; they speak ambiguously of his persuasive power, and the word, which has medical connotations linking it to the disease theme, also means a false argument or alleged motive; the last word is "beast" "creature" (602).

Deianeira comes out in a panic; she realizes with what foolish haste she has acted. The knot of wool she used to smear on the ointment became exposed to the sun, and crumbled into nothing, like sawdust; and where it lay, the earth bubbled like the juice of grapes at the vintage; in the last simile the death and deification of Heracles are momentarily linked to the old festival of Dionysus (704). Now she realizes that the Centaur, the wild beast (the word recurs: 680, 707) had no thoughts of kindness, and that the ointment must have been poison, which will kill Heracles. Deianeira has made one decisive act in her life, and it has killed the man she loves; she will make one more, and kill herself. The chorus speaks words of idle comfort, but Hyllus bursts in accusingly. She spars vaguely with him, then listens to his tale. Heracles was sacrificing, dedicating a precinct to Zeus in honor of his godless victory, killing oxen; he had won Deianeira by fighting a bull-god. Deianeira's gift came. He put on the tunic, and before the flame of sacrifice the poison began to do its work; it was like a snake's venom (771). In his agony he accused Lichas of treachery. The words of a man who is ready to lie as Lichas was ready to lie are not to be trusted. Lichas's protestations were thrust aside, and Heracles hurled him with superhuman strength into the sea. The people set up a great keening to see Heracles diseased and Lichas done for (784). With frantic cries he cursed Deianeira and called on Hyllus to take him away. So Hyllus put him in a boat, said that alive or dead Heracles would be there shortly, and solemnly called on the Furies, as he cursed his mother. She has listened to the narrative and this final tirade in silence, and now she shuffles in without a word. The poison was like a snake's venom and three times it is said that she crawls away, like a snake (813, 815, 819). Hyllus gives her time to be out of his way, and then follows in to prepare for his father's arrival.

The chorus sings a sad, moralizing little song. The boat theme returns. The oracle promised the end of labors to the son of Zeus.

> A fair wind speeds it
> safe and sound.
> When eyes close
> in death, a man
> is free from slavery. (826)

We may parallel this passing of Heracles with the passing of Arthur. They sing in extenuation of Deianeira; she acted deliberately, but neither knew nor willed the consequences—disease and tears. And all is the work of Aphrodite. They are interrupted by a cry of grief from inside the house. The nurse emerges with news of Deianeira's suicide, driven herself by a disease of the mind (882). The chorus chants excitedly in response

> This new bride has born
> has born to these halls
> a mighty child, a Fury. (893)

The Fury is the natural consequence of Heracles's behavior. The nurse tells of Deianeira's act of courage, her suicide with a sword, and Hyllus's swift regret of his hasty words. Hyllus is the child of the man who hurled Lichas into the sea impetuously and the woman who grasped at the first hope of winning her husband back and thought afterwards. The nurse ends with words which recall Deianeira's opening sentence:

> There is no tomorrow
> until today is safely past. (945)

A brief lamentation follows from the chorus. Brief it is, yet vital. It is the center of a succession of episodes involving Hyllus:

Hyllus attacks Deianeira and prepares Heracles's bed.

Old woman calls Hyllus to help his mother.

Hyllus, beside himself at thought of his mother's death.

Choral ode.

Hyllus, beside himself at thought of his father's death.

Old man calls Hyllus to help his father.

Hyllus defends Deianeira and prepares Heracles's pyre.

The choral verses are pointed by an astonishing succession of assonances, impossible to render in translation:

> *potera proteron episteno͡o*
> *potera telea peraitero͡o*
> *dyskrit' emoige dustá-ano͡oi*
>
> *tade men echomen horá-an domois*
> *tade de metomen' ep' elpisin*
> *koina d'echein te kai mellein.* (947)

The correspondence of sound between the first two lines in each stanza is remarkable, as is the recurrence of the syllable *te* in each of the first six words. The internal rhyme in the last line rounds it off. The chorus, says Hoey in an enlightened discussion, are "joiners of the plot," "treading cautiously over the point where the structure might come apart," and their words "having and waiting are the same" (952) are the key to this point in the play.

A brief lamentation follows from the chorus. They pray for the wind to sweep them away. Deianeria was compared to a bird: they, at one with her, think of themselves as of a nightingale singing sorrowfully, as they wait for the son of Zeus. And now he comes, sleeping on a litter, with an elder in attendance, and Hyllus comes out from the house with a great cry to see him. The noise awakens him, and he calls on Zeus and screams in torment at the pain. It is a bold scene; we know nothing like it in Greek tragedy before, and, after, only when Sophocles surpassed himself in daring in *Philoctetes*. Through this long scene the note of disease, pain, and anguish is primary; the word "disease" recurs (1030, 1115, 1121), and there are many words of reflected meaning, but the language is less important here because the thing is visually present. Second comes the Zeus-theme. Heracles in agony invokes god after god, but Zeus first (983) and continually. Zeus has laid the torment on him (990), Zeus alone can heal him (1003), and he calls on Zeus to blast him with his thunderbolt (1086). Third is the Deianeira-theme. Heracles seems almost to regret the fact, even the agony of death less than the ignominy of death at the hands of a woman. He tells Hyllus to bring her out so that he may make her suffer; when he hears of her suicide, he says that it has deprived him of the right of killing her; when he learns of her innocence he dismisses her from his mind without further thought. Fourth is the theme of bestiality. The very disease is wild, like a beast (1030). Heracles has fought with wild beasts and monsters, and recounts his exploits at some length. Now he has himself become sub-bestial, "incapable of crawling, incapable of anything" (1108). Hyllus reveals the truth about Nessus, and Heracles sees that the wild beast, the Centaur, has killed him (1162). Worse, he has been brought to death by a dead creature. He was promised that nothing living could kill him, rather as Macbeth was cozened with similar prophecies; but it is oddly clumsy of Sophocles to drag this in at the end when earlier it might have been used with powerful irony, but here its introduction is pointless. Two other themes are briefly touched, the theme of the Fury (1051) and the theme of death as the end of labor (1169). Both are of some importance; the one reminds us that death is the natural consequence, under a divine dispensation, of Heracles's earlier actions, but also shows by a verbal echo that in Heracles's mind Deianeira is a kind of Clytemnestra; the other points us to a quieter close and a willingness to accept the conclusion. But above all the scene is dominated by the personality of Heracles, as his shadow has dominated the first part of the play. Massive, violent, impetuous, selfish, and utterly without moral scruple, he seems on a different scale from those around him.

Now he calls on Hyllus to obey his words and makes him swear by Zeus. He wrings from the boy the promise to set him upon a pyre on Mt. Oeta; this alone will cure his troubles: the words are ambiguous (1209). Then he makes him promise to marry Iole. Hyllus finds it repugnant to think of marrying the woman who has caused his mother's death, but Heracles is inexorable. I can see here none of the tenderness that some interpreters find. He treats the girl as a possession; he has already raped her, and perhaps wants to keep a possible child in the family. There is arrogant will and any attempt to act otherwise meets not with a plea for Iole but with self-centered anger at being thwarted. Hyllus twice speaks of his father's diseased state (1230, 1241, cf. 1260); the implication is that his judgment is distraught but also that it must be humored. He gives in, and Heracles breaks into a chant of anapaests as they lift him up and he steels himself against the pain. The cortège moves off stage-right, followed by Hyllus, moralizing as he goes upon the lack of feeling shown by the gods, and man's incapacity to see the future. And now in the last moments of the play Sophocles does a strange thing. At some point, Iole emerges from the house, and the chorus, moving around the orchestra to follow the procession urge her to go before them. They have the last words:

> Girl, do not stay within the house.
> You have seen great deaths, strange deaths,
> sorrows numerous and new in suffering,
> and nothing of these that is not Zeus. (1275)

Wiliamowitz thought that Sophocles had probably seen Euripides's *Heracles*, and was, we might almost say, outdoing Euripides at his own game. The astonishing fact is that this play must be some twenty-five years before that of Euripides. It is the only surviving tragedy of Sophocles named after the chorus, though we know of several others by name and repute. The rôle of the chorus is relatively insignificant in the drama, but they represent the community that is going annually to reenact the immolation on Mt. Oeta. By their very womanhood they are closely linked to Deianeira.

It is clear that those who interpret the play so that either Deianeira or Heracles is central are wrong; they are focal, both of them. (The suggested title for an adaptation *The Wife of Heracles* is ingenious, because it links them and also brings in Iole, who is given the title). What we have is fearful. It is a child's fairy story gone wrong. We meet Deianeira, dreaming, idealistic, sentimental, wooed by the monstrous, bull-shaped river god. Prince Charming comes to the rescue. But he too is in the shape of a beast. For the key to the play is the central chorus (497), which describes the battle for Deianeira; and it is a battle between monsters. The beast that wins never takes the prince's shape.

From the first Deianeira makes it tearfully clear that marriage has

meant for her one fear after another (28). Heracles sacks a town for
Iole, rapes her and sends her home as one of a bunch of prisoners,
bowed with grief. When he appears we see him as he really is, arrogant
and egotistical, racked with self-pity, careless of others. This is the
creature whom Deianeira loves, still hoping that her kiss will provide
the magical transformation. But she passes from her dream world to
meddling with serious magic. Here her innocence ceases for a Greek
audience to be venial, and becomes dangerous folly, partly because
she, a woman, is trying to bend a man to her will, partly because magic
is notoriously unpredictable, partly because by the most coldly rationalistic standards she is unwise to trust Nessus. Yet she would not
be like this, had Heracles been less bestial.

The strange thing about Sophocles's treatment is that in his hands
the story is not crude and sordid. Deianeira's love, starry-eyed and im-
mature though it is even after years of marriage, is still a lovely thing.
Even Heracles, however unsympathetic, is impressive in his endurance,
in his sheer monumentality. For Sophocles knows life. He knows that
men are beasts; he knows that even a pure love may fail of its object.
Yet his mood is not that of Housman's "whatever brute and black-
guard made the world."

Somehow Zeus, who presides over the *agon* (26), has presided over
this *agon,* and the last word is with him. Sophocles's view of life is in
one sense pessimistic: this is a story of failure and suffering. But, *sub
specie aeternitatis,* the failure that springs from a good heart and the
suffering endured with power become transmuted, and, whatever has
gone before, through the pyre on Mt. Oeta benefaction will come to
men.

14. *ANTIGONE*

Antigone was among Sophocles's most popular plays in antiquity. It may have been revived in his lifetime; one story tells that he died of joy when he received the first prize after some performance or reading of it. It was certainly frequently revived in the fourth century, and we know from Demosthenes (*F.L.* 246) of the performances of the actors Theodorus and Aristodemus in the title rôle. There was another story to the effect that the impact of the play on first performance was so great that Sophocles was elected general for the war against Samos. The story is not impossible or even implausible; this would date the play to 441 B.C. Internal evidence suggests a relatively early date, and this would also accord reasonably with the statement that *Antigone* was the poet's thirty-second play, though one would have thought that his thirty-second ought to be a satyr play. We know nothing of the plays that accompanied it. Sophocles did not write a Theban cycle of the Aeschylean kind, but we do not know whether the plays were linked according to some other principle.

The theme was perhaps an invention of Sophocles; we cannot trace it back beyond this play. Neither Homer nor the bardic traditions of the Theban cycle know any children of the incest, and the daughters of Oedipus by one Euryganeia play no discernible part in the story. We begin to glimpse them in the seventh- and sixth-century poets, but there is no trace of Antigone's burial of Polyneices against the will of the sovereign, and, as we have seen, the end of Aeschylus's *Seven against Thebes* is a spurious introduction of later date, due entirely to the fame of Sophocles's play. If Sophocles did not invent the episode, it must represent a tradition, perhaps from the northern boundaries of Attica, which is not otherwise recorded.

Sophocles, using to the full his resources of three actors, opens his play with the two girls, Antigone and Ismene, daughters of Oedipus. They are, we must remember, teenagers in an adult world; they are also, to the Athenians, girls in a man's world. The time is daybreak. The prologue sets the scene. The Argive attack on Thebes, we learn, has been repulsed, the girls' brothers have both fallen, and Creon, the ruler, has given just and customary burial to Eteocles, and has decreed that Polyneices be left unburied. We have seen in *Ajax* the horror of this decree. Antigone is resolved to undertake the burial herself; she invites Ismene's help. But to Ismene this would be an act of *hybris* against their position as women and, as such, subjects; it would be an act of the same kind as destroyed their father, mother, and brothers, and would expose them to destruction. Antigone expresses her determination to go on and in a vivid oxymoron says that she will "commit a holy crime" (74); Ismene promises to keep her secret and to love her in her folly.

This is an excellent scene. First, it establishes the situation, clearly and concisely, and points to the plot. Second, Ismene and Antigone are both beautifully sketched. It was a brilliant idea of Sophocles, repeated in *Electra*, to produce a normal woman to offset his central character. Ismene shows herself gentle, loving, somewhat timid ("You're hot-headed for things which set a chill on me" 88), essentially obedient to her womanhood, the sort of woman the Athenians understood and admired. Antigone is brash and obstinate; it is important not to start with a predisposed sympathy toward her, which an Athenian audience would not feel. Ismene says that she is in love with the impossible (90). After her original greeting she is cold to Ismene and sarcastically defiant toward Creon (31); Haemon she does not even mention. Third, there is an important expressed contrast:

> ANTIGONE: All right!
> Desecrate the sacred ways of heaven!
> ISMENE: I desecrate nothing. Only I am
> powerless to act illegally. I can't do it. (76)

This introduces the religious dimension. Fourth, the scene introduces the animal imagery, which is one of the keynotes of the play, when Polyneices is described as "a treasure-store of food for birds" (29). The point, which will recur, is that Creon treats human beings as animals.

The sisters go off, Ismene back into the palace, Antigone stage-right to where the body lies, and the chorus of Theban elders files on from stage-left in a stately dance. They greet the rising sun in an exquisite song, which, characteristically of Sophocles, is tied up with the dramatic situation; they turn immediately to the attack on Thebes. The animal language rings out strongly without reference to Creon. Polyneices descended on Thebes like an eagle; an ironic comment since he has himself become a prey for birds. He was repelled by the dragon, the natural symbol of the Thebans who were sprung from the dragon's teeth sown by Cadmus. In this ode the dawning sun represents the lifting of the clouds of war, another ironic touch, since it in fact heralds a day of darkness and doom. Another important metaphor echoes through their song, the storm image. The eagle's wings are snow-white; this is more than a picturesque touch; he came as with a snow-storm (114), and his assault is described as the blast of a tornado (137).

While they are still singing, Creon approaches. His opening speech of almost fifty lines is longer than any other in the play except that of the messenger; we feel that he is enjoying his new-found power and his first speech from the throne that he, as uncle of the dead brothers, has now inherited. He begins with an expression of religious piety and takes up the storm image at once. He pays a compliment to the rule

of Oedipus (now dead); we must guard against the temptation to read
the later *King Oedipus* back into this play. He remarks with an irony
he does not realize:

> There is no means of learning all about a man—
> his personality, intelligence, judgment—until
> you see him actually taking political decisions. (175)

He then proceeds to his proclamation. Eteocles is to be honored,
Polyneices to be unmourned and unburied, a prey to birds and pariah
dogs. He calls upon Zeus (184) to bear witness to his principle "Seek
ye first the political kingdom and its righteousness"; the name of God
prefaces his godless decree. The chorus makes no protest, especially
when they learn that a watch is already set and the penalty for disobedience is death.

Across this display of pomposity cuts a bumbling sentry. He is a
frankly comic figure.

> My lord, I must say that I haven't been hurrying.
> If I'm out of breath it's not from moving at the double.
> As a matter of fact I kept stopping to think,
> going round in circles, half turning back.
> My mind had a great deal to say to me:
> "You fool! What's the use of going? You'll only pay for it.
> You idiot, stopping again? If Creon hears the news
> from someone else, then you *will* be in for it."
> I thought it all out, and here I am, hurrying slowly along.
> It made a mountain out of a molehill of a journey.
> What won? The decision to come here
> to you. I've nothing to tell—but I'll tell it.
> I've got my fingers on one shred of hope,
> a man can't suffer anything unless it's already coming to him. (223)

The details of his story are important. Someone had come and scattered dry dust over the body. It was so discovered by the sentry on the
first watch, and there was no sign of pick or shovel and no track of an
animal. After some mutual objurgation they decided to report to the
king, drew lots for the post and, as he ruefully remarks, the lot fell on
him. The chorus immediately comments:

My lord, if you ask my opinion, it's an act
of the gods. I suspected it from the first. (278)

Creon, swiftly incensed, will have nothing of this. How could the gods
care about a corpse? He sees the whole thing as a plot in which money
has been talking; the sentries themselves have been suborned. Creon
speaks in the only terms he understands. He swears by Zeus (304)
that the perpetrator is to be punished, and stalks out. We shall return
to the implications of this scene.

The chorus now sings the most famous song in Greek tragedy:

Many mysteries there are, none more mysterious than man—
a thing which crosses the gray sea in storms
of winter, passing through the echoing surf. (332)

The opening owes something to a song in *The Libation Bearers*
(585), much to the humanism of *Prometheus Bound* (441ff.) and
the New Learning. We note incidentally but significantly man's power
to ride the storm. The first part deals with *homo sapiens* and his
achievements—navigation, agriculture, hunting, domestication of animals, language, intellectual activity, community life, architecture, medicine, and law—and this has led the unwary to think that this is the
theme of the song, that it is a humanist paean "Glory to Man in the
Highest, for Man is the master of things," and hence to give it an irrelevance beyond that of any Euripidean chorus. It is not so. "What a
piece of work is a man! how noble in reason! how infinite in faculty!
in form and moving how express and admirable! in action how like an
angel! in apprehension how like a God! the beauty of the world! the
paragon of animals!—And yet to me, what is this quintessence of dust?
Man delights not me: no, nor woman neither." Hamlet's words are not
a hymn to Man; the sting is in the tail. So here; the last two stanzas
provide the key. In the third we have the words: "*Resourceful: resourceless* he faces nothing . . . except death" (360). In the last, at the
same point, we have: "When he obeys the laws of the land and the
gods, *high-citied. Cityless* the man who lives with dishonor." This is
the point. Man, for all his genius, is helpless before death and isolated
when he goes wrong. Man's achievements belong to community. Whatever is true elsewhere, here at least we may say with Schadewaldt

that Sophoclean tragedy presupposes a divine cosmos corresponding to the social one of the *polis*. It will be noted that this chorus, unwittingly, condemns Creon and Antigone alike. Antigone has not obeyed the laws of the land, Creon has not obeyed the laws of the gods.

As the song ends the sentry returns with Antigone under guard. He speaks again in character, in fear of the storm of Creon's anger (393), and tells how they swept the earth off the body and took up guard again upwind from the stench. Then in the middle of the day a dust storm (the dominant image returns), and suddenly Antigone, screeching like a bird that has lost its young (424), picking up dry earth and pouring a triple libation to the dead from a bronze bowl. They arrested her, charged her with the previous offense and this. She did not deny the charges (435). So the sentry is dismissed, much to his relief, and Antigone is left with Creon.

Why did Antigone, having achieved the burial safely, attempt it again? The question has dogged interpreters of the play. For by the ritual burial, the immutable laws of heaven have been satisfied, and the uncovering of the body does not undo the burial. Antigone is not merely protecting the body from animals at the second burial, she is fulfilling the ritual, with libations. The explanation is simple. Antigone did not perform the first burial, could not have performed it, did not know it had been performed and never admits to performing it. Creon proclaimed his ban on burial during the night and set a watch. The initial burial was discovered by the sentry of the first watch. When Antigone and Ismene meet it is daybreak, and the burial has already in fact been performed. But Antigone has not yet been near the body. The action that she plans with Ismene is the action she performs under cover of the noontide dust storm, as the bronze bowl for libation also proves. When the guards charge her with both acts, she does not admit it; what the guard says is that she does not deny the charges; the wording is careful and explicit. Who then performed the burial? Again the answer is explicit. The sentry says that there were no tracks round the body, no animal tracks, and *a fortiori* no human tracks. In fact no human was responsible, and the chorus gives the right answer when they attribute it to the gods (278). So we have the colossal irony of Creon swearing by Zeus that the perpetrator shall be punished (304), when the perpetrator is Zeus. The gods can look after their own. What this means to our understanding of the play we shall see later.

The long scene continues. Sophocles uses a third actor, but he organizes his play in a series of confrontations. Our next confrontation is between Creon and Antigone. It is notable for five things. First, and most important, is Antigone's affirmation of divine law:

> I did not think that your edicts had the power
> to override the unwritten, unchangeable laws
> of the gods—you are a mortal.
> Those laws are not of today or yesterday; they live
> for ever, and no one knows their origin.
> I do not intend, from fear of any man's
> authority, to offend against the gods
> in this. (453)

Second is the chorus's evaluation of Antigone's character—stubborn, her father's daughter (471); a thought which leads Creon to suppose that Ismene is tarred with the same brush. Third is Creon's continued propensity to treat humans as animals:

> It only needs a little halter to break in
> a horse's temper. (477)

Fourth, one line of Antigone's points to a way of life that Creon rejects but which Sophocles clearly views with sympathy.

CREON: Death cannot change hatred to love.
ANTIGONE: It is my nature to join in love, not join in hate.
CREON: Then join the dead, and if you must love, love them. (522)

Finally Creon snaps out a phrase that shows what is at issue in the scene. "No woman shall be my sovereign, as long as I'm alive" (525).

Ismene comes in and Creon promptly depersonalizes her too, calling her a "creeping viper" (531). She confronts first Antigone and then Creon. Courageously, she is willing to share Antigone's fate; this is important, for it shows that her original refusal to share in the burial did not spring from cowardice. Antigone shrugs her off proudly and harshly, and forces from her a curious little pun on her own name (558). Creon is resolved to execute Antigone. Ismene brings a new plea: "Do you mean to execute your own son's bride?" (568). Creon, still treating humans as things: "Oh there are other fields for him to plough." And now Ismene says, "Haemon darling, how your father dishonors you!" (572). This seems so odd to some editors that they give the line to Antigone. But this will not do; it would break across the duologue pattern and would be out of character for Antigone, who shows no enthusiasm or emotion except toward the dead and at no other point evinces an affection for or even an interest in Haemon.

There is profound psychology here. When Anouilh wrote his version of the story he showed Haemon spending all his time with Ismene and then suddenly proposing to Antigone, perhaps because Ismene has no hidden depths. In Sophocles, it is Ismene who takes on a new dimension as a person. She is in love with Haemon. Yet when Antigone is condemned her whole reaction is not "now I can have him" but "let me die with you." Antigone is a martyr and, in the strict sense, repulsive. Ismene has a streak of sainthood, and is thereby the more attractive. She should be strongly not weakly played, but her strength is different from Antigone's.

The girls are led out, and the chorus sings of the curse on the house of Labdacus; the culmination of their song is this wonderful stanza.

> Zeus, how can man's
> presumption check your power?
> It is not subject to sleep which makes all else old
> or to the gods' tireless
> months. Ageless, everlasting monarch,
> you live in Olympus's
> marble splendor.
> Now and in time to come,
> as in the past, this law
> is all: nothing passes
> into man's life with glory, without disaster. (604)

As the music dies down, Haemon, the king's son, Antigone's intended husband, comes in. He is only sketched, but the sketch has aroused the admiration of commentators. "A brief, masterly study," says Letters. He is important because he provides the emotional link between Creon and Antigone, and because he represents the voice of the ordinary citizen; in Athenian terms he speaks as democrat to auto-crat. After a brief exordium, Creon launches into lengthy self-justifi-cation, and Haemon into equally lengthy, though patient and con-trolled, criticism of his position. Creon's temper rises; they shout off a salvo of a couplet each, and then with the staccato of machine-gun fire a line-by-line interchange for nearly thirty lines, ended by a bitter quatrain apiece. Of the different dimensions of the scene the political is the most important:

CREON: Why should I take orders from the people?
HAEMON: Can't you see? You're behaving like an adolescent.
CREON: I am the only authority in this land.
HAEMON: A one-man state? A contradiction in terms!
CREON: Every state is its ruler's property.
HAEMON: You'd be a magnificent monarch—of a desert island. (734)

Alongside this is the dimension of family life and the authority of man over woman. Creon stresses that the man with sound authority at home will be a just political leader. He is determined not to be over-ruled by a woman (678, 680, cf. 740, 746, 756); the point receives such stress that it is plainly vital to the scene and to the play. It is natural that in this stormy scene the language of the storm shall recur. Creon says that the strong paterfamilias is the man you can trust in the storm of war (670), and Haemon turns the image neatly when he says that the trees that give way before a storm-swollen river and the sailor who slackens his sheets before a gale survive.

This is a powerful scene, yet even Sophocles nods, and twice his certainty of touch deserts him. Choruses in dialogue make many fat-uous comments, but the supreme fatuity is here, after Haemon has answered Creon's long speech at length:

My lord, you should learn from what he says—
and you from him. There is much to be said for both points of view. (724)

A little later, as tempers flare up, Haemon shouts, "If you weren't my father, I should call you a silly old fool." Creon answers, "It's no good trying to wheedle me, woman's slave" (755). It is possible to analyze what he means, but the touch is wrong. Still, these are minor defects, compensated by a superb touch at the end. Haemon rages off,

and Creon, with the words "monarch—of a desert island" still ringing and rankling in his mind, cries, "I'll have her taken to a desert
place" (773).

There follows one of the most marvelous songs in Greek literature.
It is only twenty lines, but of themselves they are perfect. Except in
Oedipus at Colonus, where the influence of Euripides is strong, Sophocles's choruses are usually too deeply embedded in their context to be
detached as separate poems; they are strangely unmemorable. The
choral lyrics in *Antigone* remain in the mind, but to detach them from
context is to misinterpret them, as we have seen in the ode on Man.
The ode to Love is entirely relevant after Haemon's display of devotion, but it can also stand on its own. Yet it is in context that we must
see it. Love of course is Eros not Agape, the divine power of Plato's
Symposium, not the divine power of Paul's letter to Corinth; at once
a passion and an aspiration. He seizes on men from without, over-
mastering, uncontrollable. Sappho, the peerless hymnodist of Love,
calls him "limb-loosening" (137.1). There is a slight problem about
the meaning of Sophocles's second line. "Love unconquered in battle"
is clear. Then, "Love who falls on possessions"? "Who falls on men
and makes slaves of them"? Or must we emend? Probably the second
is right.

There remains a deeper problem. This song is so familiar that we
miss its extraordinary content. *Antigone* is, at least in part, about those
unwritten laws of heaven that Antigone seeks to sustain and Creon,
wrongly, to ignore. Here Eros is put alongside those eternal laws
(796), enthroned among the gods. We continually hear the lesson
of self-control in Greek tragedy; now we find that Eros is more glorious, and assuredly more powerful, than self-control. And his power
is strictly amoral. This is no guide as to how men should live, except
in affirming that we ignore the power of Eros at our peril. And this is
not Euripides but Sophocles!

And now Antigone is led out, ready for execution, and the chorus
breaks off their dance to say that the sight makes them forget about
laws in pity: but they show that they have in their minds no clear
distinction between human and divine law, for the word for laws
(*thesmon*) is echoed from their previous song. The musicians and

choreographers take over the long dance of death that follows. The chorus joins in the lament, and even sings of Antigone's glory and praise (817). But they are not uncritical; they describe her as "a law to herself" (821), a victim of her own self-will (875) and sing:

> You've pushed to the limit of recklessness,
> encountered the high throne of justice,
> and ridden for a mighty fall, my girl. (853)

They go on to describe this as the expiation she must make for her father's offense, and she herself sees her fate in terms of the curse on the house. It is to be noticed that Antigone belongs to that house; Creon does not. At one point (823) Antigone makes an important comparison of herself with Niobe. This is at first sight very curious. Niobe was a presumptuous mortal who boasted that her children were finer than Leto's. Leto's children, Apollo and Artemis, shot Niobe's and Niobe's sorrow turned her to stone. It is true that there are certain superficial parallels that make the comparison apposite. Niobe's husband was Amphion of Thebes, and there is a grim similarity in that she and Antigone are both encased in rock. But there is a deeper reason for the comparison. Aristotle takes Niobe as an example of excessive good. She is not, in the obvious sense, morally blameworthy, but she has carried a good thing, love of her children, to excess. So Antigone has carried her love of her brother to excess—and similar ruin ensues. As the song ends Antigone describes herself as "unwept, unfriended, unwedded" (876); death is to be her groom (816). Yes, but unfriended, or unloved? What of Haemon?

The music stops as Creon comes in with biting words to speed her on her way, alone, deserted (887). She will not be killed, but left to die, so that her blood will technically not be on Creon's hands. She speaks her last words, echoing her own thought that the tomb will be her bridal bed (891), and thinks of the welcome she will receive from father and mother and Polyneices. Eteocles, the other brother, she does not mention.

The passage that follows (904) is a notorious crux. Antigone examines her action and says she would not have challenged the community for a husband or son, for she could get another, but now her parents were dead she could not get another brother. This is a characteristic piece of folklore. The Nigerians have a riddle: "If your wife and mother were drowning, which would you rescue?" Answer: "Mother, because I can get another wife but not another mother." A similar thought is found in a Scottish ballad quoted by Bowra:

> O hold your hand, Lord William! she said
> For your blows are wondrous sair:
> True lovers I can get many an ane,
> But a father I can never get mair.

Proximately, the passage is derived from Herodotus (3.119), where the wife of a Persian noble uses the argument to Darius to save her brother's life. This is not itself against its authenticity in the play, and the fact that it was in Aristotle's text makes it probably, though still not quite certainly, by Sophocles. The problem was well put by Goethe: "In the course of the piece, the heroine has given the most admirable reasons for her conduct, and has shown the noble courage of a stainless soul; but now, at the end, she puts forward a motive which is quite unworthy of her, and which almost borders on the comic."

Her absolute obedience to the divine law has suddenly become relative and conditional. The point, if point there be, is dramatic. Psychologically it is reasonable that Antigone, after her stand on absolute principle, might reexamine her action and reassert her position in terms which, though less profound, were more immediate and familiar. "A frigid sophism borrowed from Herodotus?" cries Kitto. "Yes, the finest borrowing in literature. This is the final tragedy of Antigone: *novissima hora est*—and she can cling to nothing but a frigid sophism." She echoes the oxymoron of the first scene, and claims that she has committed a reverent irreverence (924, cf. 74), the chorus sings of the storm in her soul (929), and with a final aria she is gone.

The chorus sings relevantly but discreetly. In a carefully structured ode they sing of three heroes of mythology who were immured: Danae, in whom the miseries of prison were the means of glories when she was visited by Zeus; Lycurgus, who insulted the god Dionysus and was imprisoned in penalty, a milder fate than that of Pentheus;

and Cleopatra, wife of Phineus, whose exact legend is uncertain, but who seems to have been an innocent victim. There may be a deliberate correspondence with the three victims here, Antigone, Haemon, and Eurydice. Certainly the song represents an ambivalence on the part of the chorus toward Antigone, but it also links her with heroic legend.

Generally the appearance of a new character is anticipated by the chorus. Teiresias enters unannounced. Instead, Sophocles has allowed the chorus an unconscious anticipation in their reference to the blinding of Cleopatra's sons. If Haemon represents *vox populi*, Teiresias represents *vox dei*. It was a fine dramatic stroke to bring in the blind seer; Bowra calls it well "the Device of the Warner"; the supreme example in drama is the Button-Moulder in *Peer Gynt*. Creon, says Teiresias in a phrase not yet utterly hackneyed, is poised on a razor's edge (996). Now we see the awesome consequences of Creon's treating men like beasts. The birds, at war with one another, uttering gibberish cries (1002), are behaving like men; the pariah dogs and vultures are licking up carrion. But it is not too late, if Creon will give in to the dead man and not try to kill him twice (1029). Creon will not heed; as with the guard, all he can think of is venality, and Sophocles leads brilliantly into this by letting Teiresias end with "if the words are profitable" (1032, cf. 1047). It is now too late. Teiresias indicts Creon of a double crime, against Antigone and Polyneices; he links them in describing Polyneices as "unburied, unhonored, unblest" (1071), a clear echo of Antigone's words about herself (876). Before the day is out, says Teiresias explicitly, Creon's son will be dead. But there are two crimes to requite; Haemon atones for Polyneices, and we are given the hint (no more) that Eurydice will atone for Antigone. As Teiresias ends his terrible proclamation, the animal theme recurs with pariahs, wild animals and birds, and the Furies, hounds of hell.

And by this Creon is at last shaken. The chorus presses on him. In the same order that Teiresias has used, they tell him to release Antigone and bury Polyneices, and Creon decides to act. His words are distraught but decisive: "On the road, slaves, you who are here and you who aren't" (1109). And he speaks solely of rescuing Antigone. As they go the chorus breaks into a glorious ode to Bacchus and his

delight in Thebes. If it had been written by Euripides the critics would
have called it irrelevant. It is in fact appropriate to the tragedy and to
Thebes, in exactly the way that Euripides's allegedly irrelevant lyrics
are appropriate. It is also very beautiful. At this point foreboding and
undiluted joy in the situation would have been alike inappropriate.
The irrelevant is appropriate.

The play moves swiftly to its end. A philosophical messenger arrives:

> I would not dare to honor or criticize
> the life of any man as final.
> Chance is always lifting a man from the dust,
> Chance is always dashing him from the height.
> No prophet can foretell certainty for us men.
> Creon was once an object of envy ... (1156)

He speaks of Haemon's death, and as he speaks the queen Eurydice
enters. She hears his report. They first cremated Polyneices and buried
the ashes, then made for Antigone's rocky prison. From inside they
heard Haemon's voice. They forced their way in, found that Antigone
had hanged herself with strips from her dress. Haemon, hopelessly
embracing her, spat in his father's face, drew sword on him, and, when
Creon fled, stabbed himself. In this scene Creon's capacity to turn men
to animals has its final effect on Haemon. As the king reached the
tomb he cried, "My son's voice wags its tail at me"—or something
very close to that (1214). When Haemon saw his father he rushed at
him "with the eyes of an animal" (1231), unspeaking; he had lost the
gift of speech, which marks men off from animals. The messenger's
speech is undistinguished by Sophocles's own standards. As he finishes
Eurydice moves out without a word; she too has lost the gift of speech.

Creon arrives with Haemon's body in his arms, and sings the first
stanza of a song of sorrow. He has learned his lesson in suffering—
Sophocles has had Aeschylus before him—but too late. And now he
sees himself as a driven beast and some god as the driver (1272). A
second messenger brings the news of Eurydice's suicide, cursing her
husband, and the second stanza of Creon's song meets this news. It
begins with a curiously ironical phrase that is the culmination of the
storm image: "Insatiable harbor of Death, why do you destroy me?"

(1284). Creon's bitter song alternates with the sober comments of messenger and chorus, and the chorus ends with some sententious anapaests representing the Greek equivalent of "the fear of the Lord is the beginning of wisdom."

Antigone is a problem play, and the problem is "is there a problem?" No one has done more to confuse the issue than Hegel. Hegel, finding a dialectical confrontation under every bush, saw the play in terms of the clash of two rights, which we may call state law and family law, represented by Creon and Antigone respectively. "In the view of eternal justice," wrote Hegel, "both were wrong because they were one-sided; but at the same time both were right."

Nothing is more certain than that this was not Sophocles's view. Creon is not right. He behaves as a tyrant, and the word slips out from the gentle Ismene at the beginning (60). He pays lip service to free speech (180) but pounces on anyone who provides it. He is suspicious of the power of money. He condemns Ismene unheard. He treats his subjects, even in his own family, as slaves (479). He demands obedience, right or wrong (667), and claims to be responsible only to himself (736). He appeals, like many politicians, to the divine powers to back his all-too-human policies, but in the scene with Teiresias he has no time for the seer's omens. He stresses the way he avoids the pollution of killing Antigone by leaving her to die, but Teiresias shows that by leaving Polyneices unburied he is responsible for polluting the state. Hegel is simply wrong in claiming that Creon's law is good for the state. It is not. It is disastrous for the state. What is ethically wrong cannot be politically right. Antigone claims that Creon is breaking the holiest laws of heaven, the unwritten commandments of Zeus, which are set above man-made laws. In this she is right, and the chorus at the last says to Creon, "Alas, too late you have seen justice" (1270). Creon himself admits that he acted from willful stubbornness and was in the wrong.

But what now has happened to our tragedy? If Antigone is right and Creon wrong, is not this melodrama? The innocent girl facing the conventional tyrant? And why is the play *Antigone* not *Creon*? Let us now look at Antigone. She is not wholly sympathetic. Bowra says of her, "Antigone is right but often seems to be wrong." Ismene describes her as "in love with the impossible" (90). After her first tender words she shows herself cold and harsh to Ismene, defiant and disrespectful to Creon, and as far as we can see indifferent to Haemon—indeed one wonders why he should want to marry her. The chorus sees her pride, which comes out in action in her refusal to let Ismene stand alongside her. They call her "a law to herself" (821); they see her as her father's daughter, and almost their last word to her is of her effrontery (853). We are liable to forget that she is only a teenage girl, and fail to realize what that meant in Athens. In West African traditional society, if a girl's father dies she will pass into the authority of her uncle, to whom she owes absolute obedience. If he ordered her to do something irreligious senior members of the family might remonstrate with him on her behalf, but her duty would lie in obedience. So in Athens. Little over ten years later Pericles was to say that the greatest glory of a woman was not to be spoken about by men *for good or bad*. "It is improper for a woman to show a man's courage," says Aristotle, and again, "A woman who talked as much as a man would talk too much." Antigone claims a man's courage and talks more than most men. Ismene puts the normal Athenian view:

> Don't forget that we were born
> women; we can't fight against men.
> We have to be obedient to our betters
> and give way in this, yes and in worse than this. (61)

This was the audience's view, and it was Sophocles's view, for Sophocles is not Euripides. Creon's refusal to be ruled by a woman is natural, and it is his tragedy that Antigone's view of the situation is the true one. Wilamowitz said perceptively, "The people approve of what she did, but they do not approve of the fact that *she* did it." The gods condemn the refusal of burial, but in making the burial their own concern condemn Antigone's disobedience. To the Athenians Antigone has *hybris*, and however good her case she cannot be justified. That is what the play is about, and why it is called Antigone. It is in Antigone not Creon that the curse on the house of Labdacus is fulfilled. Both, as we have seen, are judged by the ode to Man, and equally by the ode to Love. There is not right on both sides. There is wrong on both.

In fact the play is marvelous up to the Bacchus ode, but then it falls away. The messenger's speech is not Sophocles at his best; it does not compare with *Electra* for instance. The Eurydice episode is a sad aberration. She enters, speaks seven lines, hears the messenger, goes out and commits suicide. We cannot feel this as a tragedy, and as a means to Creon's downfall it creaks at the joints and puts the play off balance. Anouilh saw this, and by using her in the introduction and leaving her unspeaking but knitting improved the thing slightly, but only slightly. But there is a further point. In the scene with Teiresias, at the beginning Teiresias warns Creon to act before it is too late. At the end he tells him it is too late. Teiresias by implication and the chorus explicitly tell him to release Antigone and bury the body, in that order. If he does them in that order it is not too late. Why does he reverse the order? Plainly because of his psychological make-up. He has held out against the burial; when his resistance is broken down the burial is all important, and he carries it out with needless elaboration. The refusal of burial has caused the pollution; it must be undone. The state still comes first. Of course this makes for splendid melodrama—the arrival just too late. But it *is* melodrama, and will not stand up to reflection. And here, as with the dragging in of Eurydice, Sophocles has been diverted from Antigone to Creon.

The last reflection of the chorus is directed solely to Creon. It does not sum up the play. There is a lesson in the story, a lesson that Anouilh saw we had not learned, and drew for his own day. The state cannot override that which is just without ceasing to be a true state, and those in authority who seek to do so must learn wisdom. Sophocles is less concerned with the lesson than with the people caught up in the nexus of events—Creon, and above all Antigone.

15. *KING OEDIPUS*

The exact date and dramatic context of the most famous of all Greek plays are not known. It may be taken as almost certain that it dates from the early years of the great war between Athens and Sparta, between the outbreak of plague in 430 B.C. and a possible reference in *The Acharnians* in 425. Of the plays presented with it we know nothing. Sophocles was defeated in the contest by Philocles, a nephew of Aeschylus. The fact has sometimes been used as a text on the fallibility of human judges, but might equally point to the quality of the plays we have lost from other hands or the difficulty of sustaining quality through four plays, especially when disconnected or at best loosely connected. Since that time it has held its position as the most generally admired ancient tragedy. Aristotle mentions it more frequently than any other, and treats it as the typical masterpiece. Centuries later, D. H. Lawrence called it "the finest drama of all time."

The raw material of Sophocles's story goes back far into the legendary past. The myth belongs to Boeotia, and gold seals from that area, dating to about 1500 B.C., appear to show Oedipus encountering his father and Oedipus encountering the Sphinx. In *The Iliad* we learn that Oedipus died of violence at Thebes (23.679). *The Odyssey* is a little more explicit, and has the story of the incestuous marriage between the mother Epicaste and her son Oedipodes. More important were other bardic traditions: *The Oedipodeia*, where Oedipus had children from a second wife; *The Cypria*, where Nestor recounted the story of Oedipus; and *The Thebaid*, in which we know of a curse laid by Oedipus on his sons. These were the main source of myth for the Attic dramatists, though, as we have seen, the closeness of Athens to Boeotia allowed them access to local traditions. Aeschylus, as we have also seen, treated the myth in a tetralogy; the connected trilogy dealt with the curse on the house of Labdacus worked out through the generations.

Sophocles departed from the tradition in minor but important ways. For one thing he never mentions the curse on the whole house of Labdacus. In Aeschylus's version Laius, king of Thebes, was warned three times by Apollo not to have children, and disobeyed. For this disobedience Oedipus pays the price. Sophocles eliminates the command. Laius asked the oracle if he will have a son; the oracle answered, "Yes, and he will kill you." The child was born, and exposed at birth with an iron pin driven through his feet, leading to the name Oedipus or "Swellfoot." But the herdsman to whom the task was assigned passed the child on to a herdsman from Corinth. The Corinth theme is original with Sophocles, and enables his complex dénouement. Polybus, king of Corinth, and his wife Merope were childless and reared the baby as their own. Oedipus grew up in happiness, but in drunken brawling someone called him a bastard. He went to Delphi to find the truth, received no answer to this question, but was told that he was doomed to kill his father and commit incest with his mother. To escape his doom he resolved not to return to Corinth and departed through Phocis. Meantime Laius was again on the way to Delphi; they met at a crossroads, quarrelled, and Oedipus killed Laius without realizing his identity. This is geographically sound; the place is still wild and open to brigandage; in Aeschylus they met by a shrine of the Furies, but this did not suit Sophocles's treatment.

Oedipus journeyed on to Thebes where he found the country ravaged by the monstrous Sphinx. The creature propounded the riddle: "What goes on four legs and two legs and three legs, and when it has most legs is at its weakest?' Oedipus found the answer: "Man, who crawls as a baby, walks erect in the noon of life, and needs a stick in old age." In solving the riddle he freed the country and received in reward the kingdom, and the widowed queen in marriage. They had four children —Eteocles, Polyneices, Antigone, and Ismene. All this lies in the background to Sophocles's play; it is prologue and prelude. The play deals with the discovery. Iocaste kills herself, and Oedipus goes out a self-blinded exile. Sophocles has further innovations in the oracle which commands the banishment of Laius's murderer, and in the scenes with Teiresias and Creon.

The story is powerful in itself. Sophocles brings to it two dominant qualities, imagery and irony, linking the two closely together. The play is based upon irony. Oedipus is at once the savior and destroyer of his people; he is the hunter and the quarry; his success is his undoing; he knows everything except himself; he cannot see until he is blinded. Sophocles plays continually on his very name. With a very slight change of accent the name can be read *Oi-dipous* "Ah! two-foot," the answer to the Sphinx's riddle. The theme of the "foot" returns, as when Teiresias tells Oedipus that he will be driven out by his parents' fierce-footed (*deinopous*) curse (418), and the chorus in the next song describes the murderer as wandering with miserable foot (479). Later there is a terrible contrast between Oedipus and Iocaste's scorn of oracles and the true "highfooted" laws (866), and an image of Hybris treading with useless foot (878). Besides this the first part of the name can be punned on the Greek word for "know," and Sophocles repeatedly plays on this, as when Oedipus describes himself sarcastically as "know-nothing Oedipus" (397); still more in the astonishing words of the messenger (924–926) in which a line ending *Oidipou* is sandwiched between two lines ending with a verb of knowing followed by the relative adverb *hopou*; above all in the final revelation that begins with the imperative "know" (1181).

The imagery of the play has been carefully studied by Bernard Knox and others. Knox emphasizes three images of Oedipus—hunter, helmsman, and ploughman—and shows how this corresponds with the picture of man in his pride, *homo sapiens*, civilized man, given by the fifth-century anthropologists, by Aeschylus in *Prometheus*, and Sophocles himself in *Antigone*, with the warnings contained in both those plays. All three images are peculiarly apposite to Oedipus: the hunter because he is tracking the murderer, the helmsman of the ship of state, the ploughman and sower of his mother's womb.

Two other fields of imagery are of special importance. One is the field of medicine and disease. The plague from which the city is suffering is itself a symbol, and the opening scene is filled with technical medical terminology (23–24, 27, 44, 68, 87, 101); similar language recurs throughout the play. The other field is mathematics. It is used with great boldness. In the opening scene Oedipus is described as "not equated with the gods" (31), and the language of equality comes time and again (e.g. 53, 61, 408, 425, 544, 563, 579, 581, 627, 845, 937, 1018, 1019, 1187, 1507). There is other mathematical language of measurement (561, 795), commensuration (73, 84, 1113), calculation (461), approximation (1111), definition (723, 1083), and infinity (168, 179). Numbers are significant:

CREON: No, they were killed, all but one. He escaped in terror, and could not see to tell us what he'd seen—but for *one* thing.

OEDIPUS: What was that? *One* thing might lead the way to *many* if we but had a handle of hope to grasp.

CREON: His story was that they met with robbers who killed the king, not with *one* man's strength but with *many* hands. (118)

So again with the place where *three* roads meet (716), and the *five* in the king's party (752). Three passages seem especially powerful in these mathematical equations. In the first, Teiresias says to Oedipus, "You do not realize the plurality of other evils which will equate you with yourself and your children" (424). In the second, Oedipus has been told that Polybus is not his father, no more than the Messenger, but equally, and asks in reply, "How can my father be equal to Zero?" (1018). The third is a choral reflection:

> O generations of men,
> I count you and those
> whose life is nothing, as equal. (1186)

All three passages are charged with irony. In general it is true to say that the play is filled with the scientific language of the New Learning.

Athens had become increasingly the center of this New Learning. Protagoras had been a familiar figure on and off from the middle of the century; Parmenides and Zeno had visited the city; Gorgias stirred up a sensation there in 427, at much the time of this play; Socrates, the first native Athenian to make a name in the intellectual world, was engaged in physical speculation in his "Thinkery," and Sophocles uses the same word for thought, *phrontis*, three times (67, 170, 1390).

It is one outstanding merit of Bernard Knox's great study of *Oedipus at Thebes* to have shown that the play cannot be isolated from a political context, and that its political reference is not simply to Themistocles or Pericles, though parallels adduced between these staesmen and Oedipus are just, but to Athens as a whole.

The title by which we know the play, in which Oedipus is called *turannos*, king or dictator, is not Sophocles's title. But it is a good title, because the word comes many times in the play, sometimes noncommittally, but in one choral ode—"Pride breeds the dictator" (873)—with clearly pejorative purport. Oedipus is not the typical sixth-century dictator; this is not in issue. What is in issue is the dominance of Athens in Greece. Plutarch, reflecting anti-Periclean propaganda, says that the rest of Greece saw Athenian hegemony as dictatorship (*Per.* 12). Thucydides reports Pericles, no doubt authentically, as reminding the Athenians that their empire is a dictatorship (2.63); Cleon uses the same language (3.37), and so does Euphemus (6.85), as do the Corinthians in attacking Athenian power (1.122). In the opening scene the priest speaks of "strength in wall or ship" (56); this is inapposite to Thebes, which had no navy, but excellent for post-Themistoclean Athens. The vigor and decisiveness of Oedipus represent a typical Athenian trait, identified by the Corinthians in Thucydides (1.70): "They are swift to form plans and swift in the practical accomplishment of their plans. . . . With them as with no-one else, to hope for is to have, so swiftly do they put their intentions in hand." The self-confidence of Oedipus seems very Athenian; so does his adaptability; and when in the scene with Teiresias he describes himself as the amateur ("know-nothing," 397) who outstripped the professional, the gentleman who outplayed the player, we cannot help thinking of the closely similar claims made for Athens by Pericles in the Funeral Speech (2.39). "A constant will to action," wrote Knox (p. 77) "grounded in experience, inspired by courage, expressing itself in speed and impatience but informed by intelligent reflection, endowed with the self-confidence, optimism, and versatility of the brilliant amateur, and marred by oversuspicion and occasional outbursts of demonic anger—thus is the character of Athens and Oedipus alike. Both the virtues and the faults of Oedipus are those of Athenian democracy. . . . The audience which watched Oedipus in the theater of Dionysus was watching itself."

The play opens spectacularly. The backcloth represents the royal palace of Thebes. A cluster of citizens of all ages enter from stage-left, from the city. This is not the chorus; they do not sing as they enter, but move listlessly. They wear white tunics and cloaks, and white ribbons around their hair. They carry olive branches tied round with white wool. In front of the palace are altars and statues of the gods; here they lay the branches of supplication. The priest of Zeus, a venerable figure, stands facing the palace. Presently the doors open, and Oedipus, regal in all but his limping gait, stands before them. He asks their need—the state is carrying a cargo of incense offerings, prayers for healing, and sorrow (4)—and hears of a plague that is devastating the city; the Athenians would at once recognize their own experience. The priest ends his tale with an echo of Aeschylus:

A fortification is nothing, a ship is nothing
when empty, with no men to live in them. (56; cf. Aesch. *Pers.* 349)

One wonders whether it was Nicias or Thucydides who knew the play so well that he echoed it in the Syracusan disaster (7. 77). Oedipus is paternalistic; he speaks like a schoolmaster who knows all the answers already; we learn that he has already sent Creon to Delphi in search of the right measures. The scene is filled with the exaltation of

Oedipus, "whose power all acknowledge" (40). He is not equated with the gods (31) but he is first of men "in life's disasters and in special visitations of supernatural powers" (33)—ironic words since he will be confronted with both in plenty. We learn something also of his own self-satisfaction; he is known to all as the famous Oedipus (8), and has already acted in their need; he is in fact patronizing toward them.

At this point Creon returns and brings his news. His words and those of Oedipus are charged with meaning. Oedipus tells him to give his news publicly—"I care more for their plight than for my own life" (93). Creon brings the explicit instructions of Apollo. We have seen that the play is fraught with the power of number, and we know in effect that this is Apollo's third oracle.

> There is a pollution on this land, bred from this
> soil. We must drive it out, not keep it to corrupt us. (971)

We hear the story of Laius's death, at the hands, it is said, of robbers (122); vengeance is to be exacted from his murderers (indefinite but plural) (107). The helmsman motif is strong in this scene. The state is tossed in a storm of blood (100). Laius had been captain of the land (103)—there are political overtones of contrast with the *turannos*— till Oedipus set the state on a straight course. Oedipus promises vengeance. "Not for friends far off, but for my own interest I will dispel this pollution" (138)—but the words could grammatically mean "I will dispel this pollution from myself" or even "which is myself"— "for perhaps his murderer might wish to take vengeance on me."

This concludes the prologue. Oedipus goes into the palace with Creon. The crowd disperses, and as they go music is heard. The chorus of elders comes in to stately anapaests. Their chant is a prayer to the gods in time of pestilence. The description is vivid and reflects the experience of Athens; the unburied dead (180) are explicitly mentioned by Thucydides (2.50). Their prayer is instinct with the power of number: the infinitude of their disasters (168, 179) being countered by the power of Three (164), for their prayer is directed to Athene, Artemis and Phoebus Apollo.

Oedipus returns and in a long speech pronounces sentence of banishment and excommunication upon the murderer and his accomplices. The speech calls for little comment; its irony is repeated and obvious. He pronounces himself a foreigner to the story of Laius and to the act in question (219); we must remember that he believes himself a Corinthian. He forbids anyone to receive the murderer "no matter who he may be, in all this country where I exercise power and authority" (236), then, more intensely but still obviously:

> If with my knowledge he is within my house
> sharing my board, I call on my own head
> the curses I have just heaped on others. (249)

Then he turns to Laius. He possesses his power, as a fellow-sower (280) he possesses the wife who bore him children—offspring who, had they survived, might have proved a common tie between them both; so he will think of him as of his own father. The irony here is so patent as to be almost unbearable.

The chorus now suggests that he send for the seer Teiresias. The super-efficient Oedipus, who sees everything except the truth and provides for everything except the calamity that actually occurs, has already done so. There follows the most brilliant scene of the play. Teiresias is blind; Oedipus will blind himself. The interchange begins gently, though the irony that dominates the scene is there from the first. "Save yourself and the city," says Oedipus. "Save me and save the whole pollution of the dead man" (312); the strange phrase could mean all that is polluted or all that causes the pollution. "Me" and "the pollution" are set apart from "yourself and the city" for we know that both parts are not possible. There is in fact irony at two levels here. Teiresias knows the truth and is unwilling to speak; because he will not speak Oedipus accuses him of a share in the deed. This brilliant conceit means that when Teiresias does tell the truth, that Oedipus is the murderer, it sounds like a paltry *tu quoque*. Tempers are frayed. In a terrible phrase Teiresias says, "You blame my temper but do not see to what you yourself are wedded" (337). Oedipus abuses Teiresias in a line of rarely exaggerated alliteration, with nine *t*'s: "Shameless and brainless, sightless, senseless, sot" (371; trans. E. F. Watling). But more literally, since it is a key line, "You are blind in ears, mind, and eyes." There follows a much-misunderstood exchange, whose real sense runs:

> OEDIPUS: You live in perpetual night. I cannot harm you,
> nor can anyone who looks on the light.
> TEIRESIAS: It is not my doom to fall by your hand.
> Apollo is enough, and that's his business. (374)

The irony of Oedipus's words is plain, but Teiresias's words are ironical too, for "that" can refer to his own fall or to the general concept of making men fall. But more, these lines explain the sequence of the scene. Oedipus treats Teiresias with contempt, and because he does so, looks for someone else to attack, and in the very next line accuses Teiresias of being a tool of Creon. Two longer speeches follow. Each springs from Oedipus's autocratic power. Oedipus vaunts his achievement with the Sphinx: "You failed but I, know-nothing Oedipus, succeeded." Teiresias now speaks out:

> You mock my blindness. Very well, I will speak.
> You have eyes and do not see where you are in evil,
> do not see where you are living, or with whom you are housed.
> Do you know your parents? You are an enemy
> to your own, the living and the dead, and do not discern it.
> Two-edged, with your mother's and your father's power
> a fierce-footed curse shall drive you from this land,
> your now clear gaze fixed upon darkness. (412)

The scene ends with these fearful words:

> I am speaking to you. The man whom you so eagerly
> are searching for, indicting him with threats of punishment
> as Laius's murderer—that man is here.
> A seeming alien, he will soon be seen
> a native Theban, and will find no joy
> in that fortune. Sightless instead of seeing,
> beggared instead of rich, he'll go about his business,
> feeling his way with a stick, to an alien land.
> He shall be revealed a partner to his sons,
> brother and father at once, and to the woman
> who bore him, son and husband, and to his father

fellow in sowing and murderer. Go in,
use your reason on that. If you can prove me wrong,
then say my skill in prophecy is nothing. (449)

The sower theme is here especially dreadful, recalling as it does the very words of Oedipus (260).

The chorus has heard all this; it creates in them a sombre mood that presses forward later. Here they sing briefly but relevantly; the choral odes of this play are curiously unmemorable, though it is unfair to judge an operatic libretto without its music. Who, they ask, can be the murderer? They will not believe it to be Oedipus, without further evidence. But Oedipus has believed the worst of Creon without evidence, as we are reminded when Creon bursts on the scene.

The second episode falls into two clear parts, the scene with Creon and the scene between Oedipus and Iocaste, divided by the *kommos,* which Aristotle defines as a short lamentation with the actors on stage. Creon comes on full of indignation; the chorus tries to calm him down, but Oedipus bursts out with overbearing accusations and will not listen to reason. There is little that calls for detailed comment. In a beautiful piece of irony Creon asks leave to cross-question Oedipus. "I'll answer. I'll not be found guilty of murder," he replies (576), and Creon's apparently unrelated question is, "Are you my sister's husband?" The language of mathematics follows: Iocaste has equal power, and Creon is equal with the other two as third (581). As the third wave is greatest, Creon will in fact emerge with the power. A long speech from Creon gives a cynical, worldly wise view of autocracy (*turannis*) and emphasizes the political dimension; Creon is content with the actuality of autocratic power and does not seek the name; this is to him intelligent moderation (*sophronein,* 589). Oedipus will not listen. "What are you after? My banishment?" asks Creon, and he replies, "No, I want your death, not your banishment" (622). Here, in view of Oedipus's fate, is more irony. Creon's comment is more ironical yet: "I see (well) that you are not thinking (well)"; the word "well" is ambiguously placed (626).

Iocaste comes in and achieves a sullen reconciliation, as the chorus sings, cutting across the dialogue in support of her. In support of her—

yes, but Oedipus says they are asking for his death or banishment (659), and the chorus cries "No—in the name of the Sun, the first of gods." But the Sun is Apollo, by whose decree Oedipus has already pronounced his own banishment. At the end of the song they use the image of Oedipus as helmsman of the ship of state (694). Creon has now gone, and Iocaste turns to assure Oedipus that he need not fear accusations that he was guilty of Laius's death. An oracle came that Laius would be killed by his own child. But the oracle was not true. The child was exposed with feet pinned together, and Laius was killed by robbers where three roads meet. Iocaste is queenly and masterful; in authority, if in nothing else, she owes something to Aeschylus's Clytemnestra; and her scorn of oracles, Sophocles not being Euripides, is *hybris*. It is noteworthy that here she blames the priests (712) but before the scene is over she is blaming the god (853). Her reference to the place where three roads meet stirs a memory in Oedipus. He asks questions. "Tell me—this Laius, what was he like? What age was he?" "Tall—with silver newly sprinkled in his hair—not unlike you to look at" (741). Oedipus tells the story of the slander and his visit to Delphi, the doom proclaimed that he would kill his father and marry his mother, his escape and his encounter with Laius. Now it begins to look as though the hands that killed Laius have foully fondled his wife (821). The one hope is that the survivor from the encounter at the cross-roads spoke of robbers in the plural; it is a matter of arithmetic; one is not equal to many (945). He must be summoned.

The second episode has been marked by three features: the rising suspicion of Oedipus's bloodguiltlessness; the overbearing conduct of Oedipus toward Creon; the scorn of oracles voiced by Iocaste. The immensely skillful choral song that follows is marked by three corresponding features: an opening prayer for purity, a deprecation of *hybris,* and a prayer to Zeus to restore faith in the divine. "Pride breeds the tyrant" (873) they sing, and when we hear of Pride treading the precipice with useless foot (878), the picture of Oedipus with his lameness rises before us; in contrast are the "high-footed laws" (865). As the chorus prays for a return to religion, Iocaste enters with offerings to Apollo and the other gods. It is a spectacular diversion; it is also a clever swing of the pendulum, perhaps a shade too clever as her conversion has no clear cause. As she prays, the helmsman image comes uppermost; the master pilot is knocked off balance (923).

Now we move swiftly toward the doom. A messenger comes from Corinth to greet first Iocaste and then Oedipus with news of honor for Oedipus because Polybus is dead; we have already noted the extraordinary shape of his opening words; their "know-foot" pattern grimly takes up the choral song before. The news relieves Oedipus's fears of one-half of the oracle which oppresses him, and he follows his wife in her scorn of oracles; we today are inevitably reminded of the way Macbeth ("Come, seeling night") echoes Lady Macbeth ("Come, black night") and takes his lead from her. Iocaste is in the prime of life, perhaps in her late forties, at most her early fifties. He still fears marriage with his putative mother Merope. It happens that the messenger is the shepherd who found the baby on Cithaeron, and can free him from that fear. He tells how he discovered him with ankles pinned together. Here is the second masterstroke of the drama. Euripides had produced his *Hippolytus* in all probability either one or two years earlier. In it he had devised a powerful scene between Hippolytus and the nurse with Phaedra on stage, ignored by the other actors, but involved in and responding to their every word. Sophocles borrows the effect and makes it his own. Through nearly seventy lines of close dialogue between the messenger and Oedipus Iocaste is on stage but silent. They ignore her, and she says nothing; but the truth has dawned upon her. The scene in fact, as Kitto has put it, is a brilliant pattern of cross-rhythms. As Oedipus moves from fear to security, Iocaste moves from security to fear. At length Oedipus addresses her. She frantically tries to dissuade him from further enquiry. He thinks that she is afraid that he may prove to be of menial parentage and impatiently thrusts her aside. The theme of knowledge thrusts itself forward; he insists on finding out, she prays that he may never realize who he is. Then with a great cry:

> Poor lost soul—I have no other name
> for you—and shall never have another. (1071)

As in *Ajax* Sophocles substitutes a short joyous dance-song for the more elaborately meditative chorus we expect. Its brevity prevents it from holding up the action excessively, its gladness relieves the tension momentarily and drives home the final calamity. There is irony behind it. Oedipus is to be shown a Theban, perhaps even a son of the gods.

The one refugee from the slaughter at the crossroads turns out to be the very herdsman who was given the task of exposing the baby. He now arrives and is confronted with the messenger from Corinth. He was summoned to be questioned about the murder of Laius, but other questions supervene. The truth gradually emerges. Oedipus is Laius's son. Most cruel is the way in which he himself, eager to know the facts, presses on to his own ruin, and drags the words from the old man. The last twist of the knife comes when the herdsman, having revealed that the child came out of Laius's palace, adds, "It was his child, they said. Your lady within could say how these things are best" (1171). Every word is charged with meaning: "your," doubly true; "lady," noncommital; "within"—and why did she go within?; "could say," but her mouth is stopped; "how these things are"—the facts and their interpretation; and the supreme irony and ambiguity of "best." Oedipus in his turn rushes from the stage, and leaves the herdsmen to a long slow exit as the music begins.

The choral song that follows is the most brilliant of them all, direct, stark in its emotion, and utterly relevant. It begins with the mathematical theme, shooting at pride in learning:

> O generations of men,
> I count you and those
> whose lives are nothing, as equal.
>   Who—whoever was there
> whose share of happiness was more
> than a moment of illusion
> and an eternity of disillusion?
> Your fate is my example,
> your fate, yours,
> unblessed Oedipus. For mortals
>   happiness is—nothing. (1186)

At the end Sophocles uses one of his favorite devices. In words, apparently innocent, he anticipates what is to come in the scene that fol-

lows the song. The chorus end "To tell the truth, I received new life
from you, and now I have closed my eyes as in sleep" (1221). It is not
their eyes that are closed.

Another messenger, one of Oedipus's staff, emerges from the palace
and tells how Iocaste hanged herself and Oedipus put out his eyes.
Sophocles uses all the devices of the new science of rhetoric:

> Her dress was pinned with gold-worked
> brooches. He tore them off,
> lifted them high, thrust them into his eyeballs,
> crying "They shall not see
> my fate, my guilt.
> In darkness for all time they shall see forbidden
> faces, fail to recognize those they love."
> This was his chant. Not once, but time and again
> he struck his eyes with the brooches, bloody
> the eyeballs gushed out and stained his beard, the drops
> of blood never slackened, they gushed, a dark
> cascade, a torrent dyed scarlet. (1268)

Oedipus comes out with the blood still dripping from his sightless
eyes and joins the chorus in a long period of lamentation. The rushing
irregular anapaests drop into regular iambics and gradually into the
ordinary speech of tragedy (1367). We are moving toward a quieter
close. Oedipus makes a long speech. "Do not teach me," he says, "I
do not know" (1369). He has accused Teiresias of being blind in
ears, mind, and eyes (371). Now he has put out his own eyes, and
would, if he could, shut out his ears (1386), to wrap himself in silence
and darkness (1337). The mind remains (1347, 1487). Creon comes
in and behaves with notable magnanimity. He allows Oedipus to
fondle, though not to hold his daughters. His future is in the hands
of the gods, but the banishment proclaimed by the oracle and by
Oedipus himself is inescapable. For the moment the pathetic, broken
figure, leaning on a stick, passes into the palace, and the chorus closes
with words that are typically but not unworthily sententious:

> Sons and daughters of Thebes, look. This is Oedipus.
> He understood notable riddles. He was a man of power.

All citizens gazed with envy on his glory and his fortune.
Look how the high seas of disaster have broken over him.
We are all mortal. Keep your eyes fixed on a man's
last day, and call no one happy, until
he crosses the frontier of life unharassed by trouble. (1524)

It is, of course, a mighty play. Aristotle valued it highly for its structure. The *peripeteia*, by which action designed to one end leads to its diametrical opposite, is peculiarly impressive. In the first place, there is a double *peripeteia*; one in the background, where Oedipus in turning away from Corinth toward Thebes flees headlong into the jaws of the very destiny he is seeking to avoid; one in the foreground, where the Corinthian messenger, who comes with news of glory and security for Oedipus, brings degradation and disaster. Second, this second *peripeteia* coincides with the recognition of the truth about Oedipus and his identity, a coincidence Aristotle regards as endowed with special power. Third, the scene itself has been well analyzed by Jebb. The thread of evidence from the reported statement of the herdsman as to the place of the murder seems to show that Oedipus killed Laius, being presumably unrelated to him. The thread of evidence from Corinth shows that Oedipus is not the son of Polybus and Merope and relieves him of the fear of parricide and incest. In this scene the weaving together of the two threads shows that Laius's killer committed parricide and incest.

There are other structural points. In the central episodes the truth is revealed in reverse order—first the suspicion that Oedipus killed Laius, then Iocaste's account of exposing the child, and eventually the identification of its birth. In this way this play operates on a double time scale, the events on stage and the revelation of the past. The irony, perhaps more intense here than in any other play ever written and at times almost too intense, is part of the structural strength; so are the cross-rhythms we have noted in the third episode. The treatment has far greater certainty than Sophocles showed in *Antigone*; compare the two Teiresias scenes, or the handling of Eurydice and Iocaste.

Modern critics tend to add the extraordinary skill of Sophocles's portrait of Oedipus. To Aristotle Oedipus is an excellent subject for tragedy, because he is preeminently great and glorious without being preeminently just and virtuous, and because he falls through a fault but not a criminal fault. The modern critic admires Sophocles's instinctive psychology: whether or not we should take Oedipus as representative of the Oedipus complex, he is a study in repression. So, it is suggested, we should interpret his failure to see the truth, his temper, his projection of blame onto Creon, and his behavior, which is wrong but realistically portrayed. Again we are aware of the poet's increased mastery; there is something of both Antigone and the earlier Creon in Oedipus, but the touch is more certain and the portrait more persuasive.

Yet for all its merits *King Oedipus* has three grievous defects. The first is its intrusive improbabilities. Aristotle tries to suggest that they lie outside the plot. Even so it is hard to swallow Oedipus's ignorance of the story of Laius; hard to credit that Oedipus and Iocaste had never compared oracles; hard to think that with those oracles before him Oedipus would ever allow himself to marry a woman twenty years his senior; hard to suppose that the evidence of the pinned feet had never come out. But the improbabilities do not all lie outside the plot. Even if we allow Oedipus's extraordinary obtuseness to be a matter of repression, we have still the implausible coincidence that the messenger from Corinth and the survivor from the battle of the crossroads should be the very two herdsmen who alone could identify Oedipus. The second defect is the inevitability of Oedipus's destiny. It was this that Freud saw: "The *Oedipus Rex* is a tragedy of fate: its tragic effect depends on the conflict between the all-powerful will of the gods and the vain efforts of human beings threatened with disaster; resignation to the divine will and the perception of one's own impotence is the lesson which the deeply moved spectator is supposed to learn from the tragedy." Freud explains the play's continuing appeal because Oedipus's fate might have been our own, "because the oracle laid upon us before our birth the fate which rested upon him." Knox made a gallant attempt to rescue the play from the curse of inevitability. The play, he maintains, is not about Oedipus's murder of Laius and marriage with Iocaste, but about his discovery that he has done these things, and that is not inevitable. But we cannot think that the tragedy lies not in the acts of offense but in the fact that Oedipus found out. Dramatically we cannot in this way separate act from discovery. The play starts with the pollution caused by the act. The inevitability of Oedipus's destiny does detract from the power of the play.

The third defect is the brutal description of Oedipus's self-blinding, followed by his appearance with a new, eyeless, bloodsmeared mask for a scene of lamentation. Aristotle claims that the play excites pity and fear by what is heard rather than what is seen. But this is not true. As Oedipus appears at the end the chorus cries, "Disaster fearful for men to see" (1297). This scene abandons the traditional reticence and reserve of Greek art. It is close to Grand Guignol. It has been unfavorably compared with Herodotus's story of the tyrant who served up Harpagus's children to him for a meal and revealed what he had done. Harpagus controlled himself, and when the tyrant taunted him he replied that he was satisfied with whatever the king did. He then left the table, taking up the remains—I suppose, says Herodotus, to bury them. That self-control is lacking; we expect the lesson of *sophrosune,* and when the equation is worked out, it is missing from the solution.

The power remains. Waldock wrote well: "There is no meaning in the *Oedipus Tyrannus.* There is merely the terror of coincidence, and then, at the end of it all, our impression of man's power to suffer, and of his greatness because of this power." Yet even that is not the full truth. In another age of New Learning Thomas Fuller wrote, "Who hath sailed about the world of his own heart, sounded each creek, surveyed each corner, but that there still remains much *terra incognita* to himself?" Or, in the words of Sir John Davies:

> We seek to know the moving of each sphere,
> And the strange cause of th' ebb and flow of Nile;
> But of that clock within our breasts we bear,
> The subtle motions we forget the while.   ✳
>
> We that acquaint ourselves with every zone,
> And pass both tropics and behold the poles,
> When we come home, are to ourselves unknown,
> And unacquainted still with our own souls.

Oedipus is indeed, in words that Seneca used in another context, *notus nimis omnibus, ignotus sibi,* "too well known to the whole world, unknown to himself." For the riddle of the Sphinx, as De Quincey saw, is answered in the life of her destroyer—the weak infancy, the strong independent manhood, the blind man's stick. There *is* meaning in the play; it is meaning that we in yet another age of New Learning do well to take to heart; it is most simply in words that were themselves associated with Delphi—"Know yourself."

16. PHILOCTETES

In Homer's *Iliad* (2.716) we read of Philoctetes, an expert archer and commander of seven ships, who was bitten by a snake and left behind on the island of Lemnos. In *The Odyssey* it is evident that he went to Troy and returned (3.190, 8.219). The fuller account of his experiences lay in other songs of the epic cycle, *The Little Iliad*, *The Cypria*, and *The Sack of Troy*. According to a later reconstruction the seer Calchas told the Greeks that victory depended on their securing knowledge possessed by the Trojan Helenus. Odysseus captured Helenus and forced him to divulge that the Greeks had to bring Neoptolemus, Achilles's son, from Scyros and Philoctetes from Lemnos. Odysseus went for Neoptolemus, Diomedes for Philoctetes, who came to Troy, was healed by the surgeon Machaon, and killed Paris in single combat. Neoptolemus subsequently killed Priam. This is the raw material of the next to last of Sophocles's surviving plays.

The theme had already been treated by Aeschylus and Euripides. Their plays have not survived, but a lecture (52) in which Dio Chrysostom discusses the comparative merits of the three tells us something about them. We do not know at what stage of Aeschylus's career he wrote his *Philoctetes*, but perhaps the fact that the title names a single character implies a late date. Nor do we know its dramatic context, usually an important feature in evaluating his individual plays. The chorus consisted of Lemnians; this very fact, one would think, would reduce the impact of Philoctetes's desolation. However, although he had been nine years on the island, he has to tell them the story of his sufferings. In Aeschylus's play Odysseus undertook the embassy in person, though he with Agamemnon was the main object of Philoctetes's hatred. Odysseus however evaded recognition, and by some device of craft secured the bow; Neoptolemus played no part in these events. At the end of the play Philoctetes accompanied Odysseus to Troy, now knowing who he was, and we must assume some reconciliation between the two. It is clear that Dio valued the play for the sonorous splendor of its language, and the exalted dignity of its characters, even the crooked Odysseus being crooked on the grand scale; but the play creaked with improbabilities.

Euripides treated the theme in 431 in the same tetralogy as *Medea*. His *Philoctetes* was evidently a powerful play, though we are frustratingly uncertain of some of the details. There was overt criticism of Aeschylus, of the type he produced in *Electra* and elsewhere. The implausibility of Philoctetes's failure to recognize Odysseus was countered by putting Odysseus in disguise, and the chorus did at least acknowledge and apologize for their failure to visit Philoctetes. The prologue was spoken by Odysseus; he had Diomedes to help him in his enterprise. Odysseus won Philoctetes's confidence by pretending that he was an Argive harried by Odysseus, a situation allowing for rich irony, and offered to help Philoctetes escape. The chorus were again Lemnians, but a Lemnian named Actor was also a character, reducing Philoctetes's isolation. There was an embassy from Troy, seeking to win Philoctetes, and their presence created an opportunity for one of Euripides's celebrated set debates. Euripides certainly complicated his plot, and filled his stage. After this, during an attack of pain from Philoctetes's wound Odysseus secured the bow. We can only guess how the play ended. It is possible that Odysseus gave back the bow in order to give Philoctetes the confidence to come freely to Troy. If so Sophocles is varying a dramatic device already used by Euripides; but this is speculative. It is likely that Athene appeared as *deus ex machina.* Dio praises extravagantly Euripides's realism, his attention to detail, his skill in handling the plot, and the brilliance of his language, alike in dialogue and lyric.

Sophocles's play was, as we know, produced in 409; he was nearer ninety than eighty when he wrote it. We do not know what plays accompanied it, but between them they won the first prize.

The set must have had some suggestion of a wild countryside, with stylized rocks or bushes, and the great doors of the stage building were perhaps draped with skins to represent the entrance to a cave. Enter, from one of the side entrances, three men, one old, one young, the third, who does not speak, a sailor of subordinate rank. The older speaks; he identifies the scene as Lemnos, and his companion as Neoptolemus, Achilles's son; he links the scene with Philoctetes; and his words make us suspect that he is Odysseus, a suspicion immediately confirmed. His opening sentence, a long one, contains four concepts that are vital throughout the play. These are loneliness, nobility, disease, bestiality. The picture is drawn of the repulsive nature of Philoctetes's wound. Immediately Odysseus introduces a new theme, his own cleverness, and this leads us to distrust the words he has just spoken in saying that he marooned Philoctetes under orders from higher authority. We learn that he is afraid of Philoctetes; Odysseus in *Ajax* was similarly afraid of direct confrontation. The dialogue moves swiftly, yet with curious ambiguity, as they explore the purpose of their journey. At one moment Odysseus speaks with a plan to abduct Philoctetes (14,101); for this they must secure his bow with its "arrows that never miss, death's ambassadors" (105). At another moment, it is the bow and arrows that seem to be in question. The transition of thought is clear

NEOPTOLEMUS: What profit to my account to get him to Troy?
ODYSSEUS: Troy will not fall without those arrows of his.
NEOPTOLEMUS: I was under the impression that the sack of Troy
                      would be my doing.
ODYSSEUS: You need the arrows; they need you. (112)

There are three methods possible: persuasion, violence, and cunning. Odysseus rules out persuasion from his knowledge of Philoctetes, and violence because of the power of the bow. Neoptolemus is unwilling for deceit; he would rather miss the mark (an important metaphor) by fair means than win by foul (95). Odysseus's answer is also important:

> You're your father's son. What a man! When I was your age,
> my tongue was slow to move, my hand was swift.
> I now realize that when it comes to the point, with men
> actions go for nothing, words are in control. (96)

He succeeds in confusing for Neoptolemus cleverness, disguised as intellectual virtue, and excellence, which for the Homeric hero was prowess that led to military renown but for Neoptolemus includes ingenuous honesty (119). By this casuistry, a little flattery, and the promise of glory, he wins Achilles's son, in the short term. "Sophocles," says Rosenquist, "has coated the inherent nature of Neoptolemus over with the inherent nature of Odysseus." Odysseus goes, promising to send back the sailor (who has been keeping watch) disguised as a merchant skipper. As he goes he prays to Hermes, god of trickery, and Athene; it is noteworthy that it is neither of these who appears at the play's end. Odysseus does not control the action.

The chorus enters—Neoptolemus's crew. This is a sensible solution of a genuine difficulty, but it creates its own problem, since the chorus is bound to side with Neoptolemus. There is no formal anapaestic entry; indeed the song and movement are a little puzzling. The opening line appears to be in speech rhythm, yet to have been sung as part of a lyric; there is a lyrical exchange with Neoptolemus, which then changes to anapaests. Neoptolemus is on stage, exploring the cave, the chorus in the orchestra, watching. The notes of loneliness and disease re-echo.

> His loneliness and labor
> are sent him by some god;
> he may not bend that blessed bow
> in victory against Troy,
> before the time has come when it is fated
> that they shall fall before him. (195)

There is strong alliteration on *t*.

Neoptolemus assumes Philoctetes's presence at Troy. Suddenly there is a cry of pain offstage, and Philoctetes, in rags, with the bow in his hand, drags his way in. It is an effective entrance. He addresses the chorus, who move away in fear; Neoptolemus answers from the other side. He identifies himself as a Greek and as Achilles's son; each announcement brings from Philoctetes an emotional splutter of alliterative labials (234, 242). Philoctetes tells his story at length, with the notes of loneliness, disease, and bestiality sounding strongly, and the bow as sole compensation; sometimes sailors in need put in at the island, but no one offered to take him home. Neoptolemus begins to invent a story of his own indignities at the hands of Odysseus. He speaks of Achilles's death, and is momentarily brought up short.

PHILOCTETES: O no! Don't say more. I must know
              first, is it really true that Peleus's son is dead?
NEOPTOLEMUS: He is dead, shot down by god
              not man, laid low, they say, by Phoebus.
PHILOCTETES: A victor worthy of his victim.
              My son, I am at a loss. Shall I question you
              further, or show my sorrow for him?
NEOPTOLEMUS: Sir, you have enough sorrow
              of your own. No need to mourn for others. (332)

Pity is beginning to break through; the interchange is also important for establishing that Achilles fell to an arrow. Neoptolemus for the moment returns to his story. His words are filled with irony because of the half-truth that the fall of Troy depends on him. He tells how Odysseus brought him to Troy with that promise, how Achilles was dead when he arrived, and how Achilles's armor was awarded not to him, but to Odysseus. The effect is to establish a link with Ajax in the play Sophocles wrote some forty years before, and this may influence the softening of tone toward Odysseus and hardening toward the commanders at the end of Neoptolemus's speech; it is in any case a powerful dramatic touch for it shows Neoptolemus's natural warmth reaching out to Odysseus too honestly to make him an efficient partner in the deceit. In pique, he says, he sailed for home. Philoctetes learns more of his old associates, and between them they deplore the death of the worthy, Ajax (411), Antilochus (425), and Patroclus (434), and the survival of the unfittest, Diomedes (416), Odysseus (417, 429), and Thersites (442).

> War never willingly
> picks off a scoundrel—always the men who matter. (436)

There is excellent irony when Neoptolemus, speaking of Odysseus, says:

> He's clever in the ring, but, Philoctetes,
> clever minds are often thrown. (431)

He is not expecting the fulfillment of the words at his own hands within an hour. More obvious, but delightful, is Philoctetes's enquiry after "that worthless fellow, that slick, clever talker" (439). "Odysseus?" asks Neoptolemus, puzzled; but this time it is Thersites. During these exchanges a bond of sympathy is audibly growing between the two men. Neoptolemus realizes it. Abruptly he takes his leave. This drives Philoctetes to a frenzied plea that Neoptolemus will take him to some place from which he can reach home. He appeals to Neoptolemus's parents (the Achilles theme, 468), to his nobility (475) and his impulse to glory (476, 478), and falls before him and grasps his knees (485). Neoptolemus is silent, but his silence is eloquent. It is the chorus that speaks. They know Neoptolemus; he cannot refuse such a moving plea, nor does he do so. There is no indication that this is insincere on the part of the chorus or that they are playing Odysseus's game and seeking to shanghai Philoctetes; rather do we see a division growing in the mind of Neoptolemus.

They go to take a last look at Philoctetes's cave, when the sailor whom we have already met returns, played now by a different actor, disguised as a merchant. This episode oddly plays no part in Dio's summary of the plot. He brings an invented story that pursuers are following Neoptolemus, and Odysseus with Diomedes has gone after. . . . He pretends to spot Philoctetes and lowers his voice: this alarms Philoctetes, who imagines a process of barter with himself as merchandise, not without justification. It is, he says truthfully, Philoctetes whom Odysseus is pursuing; but we know that his associate is not

Diomedes. The agent tells of an oracle revealed by Helenus to the effect that Troy would not fall unless Philoctetes were *persuaded* to come to Troy (612). The effect of the bogus message is to determine Philoctetes to leave at once with Neoptolemus. This is according to plan; yet Neoptolemus stalls, even though Odysseus said he would send the pseudo-merchant only if things were moving too slowly. He protests contrary winds, asks Philoctetes if he has all he needs (we are reminded of his disease), and is led naturally to ask to handle the famous bow. His nervousness expresses itself in a line of curious assonance, something like: "And yet you—no! I'd like, you know, to hold the bow" (660). He speaks of it (with a slightly forced pun on the Greek word for "sight") as a divinity (657). Philoctetes promises that at some point in the future he will be able to hold it and give it back, and be proud that he was the only man worthy to do so; the words are packed with irony (667). For the moment he keeps the bow firmly in his own hands.

The chorus sings, and their song is of Philoctetes, and again their themes are loneliness, pain and disease, bestiality, and the bow as his one salvation. The last stanza raises a curious problem. The chorus turns to his journey home to Oeta. Some critics have supposed that this represents a change of mood; Philoctetes and Neoptolemus are coming out from the cave again, and the words are designed to deceive Philoctetes. There are no grounds for this, and it would be exceedingly difficult to convey such a contrast between the antistrophe and its corresponding strophe. The truth is that the chorus are not privy to Odysseus's plot, and have no reason to believe that Neoptolemus's offer to take Philoctetes home is other than sincere.

But now Odysseus's plan is held up by an attack of the disease. Philoctetes's cries are agonizing, and his writhing movements must have offered a startling visual effect. It is astonishing, without parallel in surviving Greek tragedy, unless in *The Women of Trachis*. For this is the scene that is traditionally portrayed in the powerful rhetoric of a messenger's speech. This play has no messenger's speech, and the dramatist casts off the traditional reserve of Greek art in his visual portrayal of pain; his aim is to shock. He goes beyond what he did in the last scene of *King Oedipus,* and, perhaps because the portrayal is uninhibited, he brings it off as a tour de force.

As the agony strikes, Philoctetes gives the bow to Neoptolemus, exacting a promise that he will not hand it over to anyone else, should the Greeks come during his pain or subsequent sleep. That he should freely hand over the bow like this is unexpected, and we can imagine Neoptolemus half-afraid to touch, half-clutching. He offers an ambiguous prayer:

> Gods, hear our prayers and bless us both, and grant us
> a safe voyage in fair weather to the port
> the gods direct us to, our journey's destination. (799)

He promises to stay by the sufferer; he may not go without him—the words are again ambiguous (812).

The chorus sings an invocation to sleep, and Philoctetes sinks into a coma. But Neoptolemus, half-meditating to himself, half-speaking to the chorus, breaks into dactylic hexameters:

> He hears nothing. I can see we have our prey,
> the bow—and it's useless unless he sails with us.
> He is to have the glory; the god said we were to fetch him.
> All our boasting and all our lies—if we fail—will be bitter and
>   shameful. (839)

"Leave that to heaven," sings the chorus, and its words are pointed, for heaven will intervene. The hexameters are unparalleled in the surviving plays, and paralleled only in fragments of Aeschylus's *Xantriae* and Euripides's *Aeolus.* The effect is twofold. First, they are a reminder of Homer, and a link back to Achilles. Second, they are oracular. The chorus, who do not seem to understand what is going on, tell Neoptolemus to go while the going is good. But now Philoctetes stirs and opens his eyes; the period of sleep, with Philoctetes on stage, must have seemed short even allowing for the free time-sequences of the Greek theater. But now Neoptolemus, wrung with pity, cannot go through with his deceit, yet cannot abandon the plan. Four magnificent lines point to the effect:

PHILOCTETES: My wound is disgusting. Is it this
              that makes you sail without me on board?
NEOPTOLEMUS: Everything is disgusting, when a man
              is false to himself and acts against his nature. (900)

He speaks out. Philoctetes must go to Troy. But the reasons, in order, are:

> To save you from this agony—that first—and then
> to be your ally in the sack of Troy. (919)

Philoctetes demands his bow back, and when Neoptolemus refuses, bursts out in a great vituperative repudiation of his treachery. He pleads again, but Neoptolemus turns away. He calls on the headlands that have masked him (936) and the wild animals that have companied him to witness what Achilles's son has done in breaking his oath; there is almost an oxymoron involved. He pleads again with Neoptolemus to be his true self; then calls upon his rock with its two openings; he has found Neoptolemus two-faced and hard as a rock. The theme of the beasts returns; if he has no bow to kill the animals he will become their prey. "Strange, I feel pity for him," says the boy (965) and is about to give back the bow when Odysseus bursts dramatically in, interrupting him in mid-line. Neoptolemus relapses into a silence, which, apart from these four and a half lines and six more as he goes out, lasts for three hundred lines.

Odysseus now takes charge. His men bind Philoctetes to prevent him from suicide. Philoctetes flings curses at him; his words stream out in tumbling tribrachs (1018,1029). Odysseus has made Philoctetes his prey, using the boy as his mask (1008); Philoctetes has had only the shore to mask him (936). But the boy is not Odysseus's sort, but Philoctetes's; and he is already sorry that he has missed the mark. He taunts Odysseus with the pollution he will bring to the ship. Odysseus's response is strange.

> I am all things to all, as need dictates.
> When justice and virtue are at stake,
> you could not find a more honorable man.
> My nature it is always to look for victory,
> except over you. In this case I gladly withdraw for you. (1048)

They have the bow, and Teucer can use it. The volte-face is unexpected. Does it arise from fear of pollution? From a half-pity? From a bitter contempt? From some deep plot to bring Philoctetes to come freely? From an indifference to the details of the oracle? We do not know. Odysseus goes out with Neoptolemus, but the boy again voices his pity and leaves his sailors to look after Philoctetes till the last moment.

A long song of lamentation follows from Philoctetes and the chorus. Some of its turns of phrase, such as the continual use of repeated words, seem almost Euripidean, and one wonders whether Sophocles tried his hand at modern music. The themes are familiar: the cave, the birds and beasts, the loneliness, the absence of the bow, the wings of birds and arrows, the prospect of being prey himself, but they are expressed with an eloquent lyricism; these are the play's freest lyrics. What is of special interest are the comments of the chorus. They first tell Philoctetes that he is there by his own choice; there is another way open to him. They tell him that all that is happening springs not from their treachery but from divine destiny. Finally they repeatedly reassure him of their friendship. Philoctetes will not listen. He asks for a weapon to kill himself, and when they do not respond, drags himself into his cave. "I am already nothing" (1217).

But now come raised voices. Neoptolemus comes back, hotly followed by an expostulating Odysseus. He is going to restore the bow. He had missed his mark (1224); in using the phrase, he identifies himself with Philoctetes. He has cleared his mind of the confusion between cleverness and excellence.

> NEOPTOLEMUS: You're clever, but you're talking like a fool.
> ODYSSEUS: You're talking and acting like a fool.
> NEOPTOLEMUS: Justice is more potent than cleverness. (1244)

The quarrel flares up, and they make to draw swords. The scene is slightly awkward since Neoptolemus is carrying the great bow, even if it is slung on his back. However, Odysseus, with a prudence or cowardice that would certainly bring jeers and cheers from the audience, thinks better of it and withdraws.

Neoptolemus calls Philoctetes from his cave. He comes reluctantly, expecting further mocking. The lad now tries to persuade him to come

freely. Philoctetes turns away with a curse; the boy has disgraced his
father. But Neoptolemus calls him back and hands him the bow.
Odysseus makes a last effort to prevent this, but Philoctetes threatens
him with the restored bow, and it is only Neoptolemus's intervention
that saves him. The scene is powerful, heady melodrama, but it serves
the subtle purpose of asserting Neoptolemus's independence of Philoctetes. Odysseus has gone. In the restoration of the bow Neoptolemus
has shown himself his father's true son. Now he speaks to Philoctetes
rationally, coolly, persuasively. Philoctetes, he says, is clinging to his
suffering. Rejected by society, he is afraid to lose hold of the rejection.
He has become an animal (1321). His disease came from the gods as
punishment for trespass, and the gods have offered healing if he will
come to Troy *of his own free will* (1332). There, then, he will be
cured and with the help of the bow and of Neoptolemus will sack Troy.

It is striking that Neoptolemus, son of the Homeric hero who made
glory his aim in life, gives to Philoctetes the chief place in the victory,
and himself the role of divinely appointed instrument, like the bow.
Philoctetes is torn, but his hatred of Agamemnon, Menelaus, and
Odysseus remains uppermost. Neoptolemus, genuinely concerned
about his sufferings, presses him, speaking now of that alone, not of
the glory. But Philoctetes, with mounting suspicion of fresh treachery,
becomes violent in his refusals, and Neoptolemus promises to take him
to his home. They burst out excitedly in fragmented trochaic tetrameters. The arrows of Heracles will protect them. The arrows of
Heracles—the two men are on the point of leaving by the side entrance
and Neoptolemus's sailors are forming up to follow, when they are
brought up short by a great chanted cry of "Not yet" (1409) from
above the stage building. They turn to see the very Heracles of whom
they have been speaking, gigantic, with club and lion skin. He reminds
them that he labored and through those labors found an excellence
that conquered death (1419). Philoctetes has suffered—to win glory
in life. Philoctetes is to go to Troy, be cured, kill Paris, sack Troy, and
return to his home. The demi-god now turns to Achilles's son. He can
do nothing without Philoctetes. They must be as lions hunting together. The image is significant. It is the theme of bestiality—Philoctetes is not miraculously transformed—without the loneliness. The

partners accept; Heracles withdraws. And now, led by Philoctetes and Neoptolemus, the chorus forms up for departure. They move round the orchestra as Philoctetes chants his farewell to different parts of the island, and as Philoctetes and Neoptolemus disappear to the ship the chorus follows with a prayer for a safe voyage.

Sophocles in this play has shown himself willing to learn from Euripides in old age as he learned from Aeschylus in his youth. The play is romantic melodrama of the type that Euripides popularized. The central character in rags is typically Euripidean. There are bold theatrical effects; even Euripides never essayed anything quite as bold as the portrayal of Philoctetes's agony on stage. There is something Euripidean in Philoctetes's criticisms of the gods (446), though by the end of the play Sophocles leads us to a very different conclusion. In his earlier plays Sophocles has either not been interested in the portrayal of young men, or is not particularly successful in his character drawing; here Neoptolemus is delightful, and if we seek a parallel we shall find it in Euripides's Ion. Odysseus is a Euripidean villain, though Dio thought him an improvement on Odysseus in Euripides's corresponding play. In general the characters are brought down to earth. There is humanity, realism. The *deus ex machina* is an effect that Sophocles did not in general espouse (he seems to have used it in *The Banqueters, Tyro,* and *Tereus*), but Euripides had again popularized it. Euripides is sometimes accused of introducing the final epiphany because his plot is so tangled that there is no other means of finishing the play. This is unjust, but at first sight it would be legitimate criticism of Sophocles's usage here. The point is so important that we shall have to return to it. We may add a speculative point. There is a strange emphasis on the fact that Philoctetes's cave has two entrances (16–19). This might have been used dramatically, but it is not. Euripides lived in just such a cave on Salamis. Can this be a deliberate allusion? It seems otherwise pointless. Euripides criticized his predecessors; is it impossible to suppose that Sophocles here hoists the younger man with his own petard?

The character drawing is excellent. Neoptolemus is an admirable invention, *ingenui vultus puer ingenuique pudoris.* On the one side he sets off Odysseus, an unsympathetic character whose very cleverness leads him astray; on the other Philoctetes, countering his rough rejection of society with a gentle acceptance of him as a person. Each in turn dominates him by appealing to an element in his father's character. Odysseus subtly and skillfully appeals to his yearning for glory; Philoctetes draws out his sense of compassion, and *The Iliad* is after all at the last the story of how Achilles learned to pity. There is delicate irony in the way in which the man who is cut off from society calls out Neoptolemus's social feelings. Yet each in a sense misleads him, Odysseus obviously, Philoctetes in turning him aside from the road of destiny. At the same time in being involved with both he asserts his independence of each. He repudiates Odysseus's plans because of his sympathy with Philoctetes; he lays a restraining hand on Philoctetes to prevent him from killing Odysseus. Yet this play is about Philoctetes, not about Neoptolemus.

Philoctetes is the human without a *polis*. Aristotle said that such a being could only be a god or a beast. Philoctetes has something of each about him, but more of the latter. He is not a god, yet he is awesome, numinous, touched by the gods and kept alive by the divine bow (657) of Heracles. Touches of the animal are everywhere. His food is fodder (43, 162, 706, 712, 1108); his movement is a crawling movement (207, 291, 294, 701–702, 730, 985, 1155, 1223). He is savage, wild (9, 173, 265). He lives "in loneliness with furry or dappled beasts" (183). The first news of his approach is an inarticulate cry. In the long years of isolation two emotions have built up inside him. One is hatred of those who have marooned him—Odysseus, Agamemnon, Menelaus. The other is his suffering that is his one contact with reality. He clings on to it, as Neoptolemus discerns (1318). Further the two are bound together. He uses his pain to feed his hatred. In this sense the wound is a vital symbol. With Philoctetes's departure for Troy the wound and the hatred will alike disappear.

Some have seen political allusions in the play. This is not impossible. The audience at the theater was, with some additions, composed of the people who made the political decisions. They would be swifter to pounce upon political allusions than even the scholar poring over his reference books. Alcibiades had been accused, like Philoctetes, of offenses against sacred things. He had been allowed to cut himself off from the community at Athens. Now he had shown his readiness to return. At Cyzicus he had won a startling victory: his men, says Plutarch, came to regard themselves as invincible, as was Philoctetes with his bow, and Aristophanes's picture of the attitude of the Athenians toward him is much the attitude of the Greek high command to Philoctetes.

> They miss him and hate him and yearn to have him back.

Such political involvement is the spice of Attic tragedy. But it is not the substance. Philoctetes is in no sense Alcibiades, he is Philoctetes; and attempts to find political equivalents for Neoptolemus and Odysseus are misconceived and misbegotten. The play stands on its own feet as drama.

It is powerful in its visual effects. Indeed it is unusual among Sophocles's plays in abjuring verbal irony for the visual irony of the bow. The bow is Philoctetes's only link with society, and he uses it as a protection against society. The one thing that will save the Greek community at Troy is outside that community, visibly, demonstratively rejected. But there is another aspect of the visual irony of the bow. It is identified with Philoctetes. The result is that, when Neoptolemus gets possession of it, it is as if he is holding a piece of Philoctetes, and the image of Philoctetes preys upon his mind with increasing strength.

The structure of the play depends on Helenus's oracle, and it is here that Sophocles in pursuit of excitement has muddied the waters. In the opening scene of the play the emphasis is upon securing the bow; at first it is not clear whether this is to disarm Philoctetes, or because the bow is needed at Troy, but before the scene is ended Odysseus announces that the bow with Neoptolemus will take Troy (113); it is also said, though not stressed, that Philoctetes's presence is needed (112). Of three means, persuasion and force are ruled out, and only trickery is left. There is no indication that Philoctetes's agreement must be freely given. In the scene that follows Neoptolemus seems to be playing for the abduction of Philoctetes. The bogus merchant announces Helenus's oracle; Philoctetes must be *persuaded* to go to Troy (612); there is now no mention of the bow. The sole effect of this announcement is to make Philoctetes more eager to leave with Neoptolemus. The merchant is Odysseus's man and we certainly cannot trust anything he says any more than we can trust Odysseus. When Odysseus has Philoctetes bound, while Neoptolemus has the bow, he suddenly gives orders to release him. "We do not need you" (1053). This is an extraordinary procedure. Are we to suppose with Bowra that Odysseus is blinded by his own cleverness to the exact words of the oracle? Or that he is aware of the true oracle and knows that it is no use taking Philoctetes by force and thinks he may well abandon him? Or that he is taking a very subtle line and hopes by releasing Philoctetes into destitution to persuade him freely to beg a passage to Troy? Or that he is deceiving us about the oracle all along?

We are given no answer; it is left in the air. After he has restored the bow Neoptolemus makes much of the importance of Philoctetes's voluntary move to Troy (1332). Yet even here the issues are blurred. The bogus merchant has said that Helenus gave his oracle publicly; but in the opening scene Odysseus has to explain to Neoptolemus the object of their visit, and it does not seem that Neoptolemus was present at the original revelation. If this is so, he has nothing to go on but the bogus merchant's words. Various solutions have been propounded; the very fact that this is so shows that none is right. For what matters here is what appears in the theater, and in the theater the issue is blurred. Sophocles has sacrificed clarity to excitement.

Humanly speaking, the play leads to an impasse. Neoptolemus will lose the glory we expect a son of Achilles to achieve. Philoctetes will remain uncured. Odysseus's reputation for cleverness will lie in shreds. The Trojan War will go on forever. It is this situation that the appearance of Heracles solves, and so put it seems an implausible miracle to save the appearances. Is there another possible explanation? Sophocles continually writes in terms of a divine cosmos and man's disharmony, part willful, part in ignorance. For Philoctetes the wound symbolizes the disharmony, the bow the promise that harmony may be restored.

Philoctetes is to be seen alongside *Oedipus at Colonus* in having as its theme this restoration of harmony. As far back as *Antigone* we saw that the gods laid down their law; Creon's offense was to resist, Antigone's to busy herself in ways that were not for her. Something similar happens here: Philoctetes resists, and Odysseus busies himself in ways that are not for him. It is just here that the choral lyrics are negatively illuminating; they throw darkness where we expect them to throw light. For the choral songs usually take up the play's theme and link it with myth and legend, transmute it, and display it *sub specie aeternitatis*. Here the chorus does not, with one exception (676), use myth, and they never sing of the divine origin of Philoctetes's wound. The divine dimension is absent. Bowra is here half-right. It is not so clear as he makes out that we have the authentic terms of the oracle, and in the early part of the play there is no attempt to elucidate them. But it is clear that Odysseus is an operator who does not care about them. In these terms the function of Heracles is not to provide a solution to an unsolvable problem as an intruder from the divine world. We might almost say that he represents the true world, and the muddling humans, Philoctetes with his obstinacy, Odysseus with his self-satisfied over-cleverness, and Neoptolemus with his human loyalties, are the intruders.

This is not one of the great plays. The theme itself was restrictive. On any interpretation there is some blurring of the issues, and the human and divine dimensions are not fully integrated. It remains, despite its faults, exciting theater.

17. *OEDIPUS AT COLONUS*

The end of *King Oedipus* was intolerable. In old age Sophocles returned to the theme in a play that was, it seems, produced only after his death. No other Greek dramatist took as his theme the passing of Oedipus. It is a play quite unlike any other Greek tragedy; perhaps the only remotely comparable play is *King Lear*. It is very long, 250 lines longer than any other of Sophocles's surviving plays. It is full of powerful action and glorious poetry. Above all it is instinct with the numinous, *das Heilige*, the quality in which Rudolf Otto has taught us to seek the essence of religion. It centers upon the daemonic personality of Oedipus.

The scene is the Grove of the Furies at Colonus on the outskirts of Athens, whose hills and towers are represented somewhere on backcloth or flats. A statute of a horseman stands in full view. The scene is set, and the opening of the play is startling. From stage-right a blind man, white-haired and in rags, gropes forward, his hand on the shoulder of a young girl. She, we learn is Antigone, he Oedipus. We

learn too that three masters—pain, time, and the royalty in the blood—
have taught him patience (7). The ragged figure shows us already that
Sophocles is not averse from learning a trick or two from Euripides;
but he leans still, as in the past, on Aeschylus also. Man must suffer to
be wise. This patience stressed in the opening lines is vital. When,
later in the play, Oedipus loses patience, it is not mortal weakness but
daemonic possession.

The opening sets the pattern of imagery that is retained throughout
the play. The primary symbolic theme is that of sight and blindness.
There is a contrast established between Oedipus's outward blindness
and his "in-sight," a contrast too between the blind man who "sees"
and the seeing men who are blind. The theme of blindness is established visually before Oedipus has spoken, by his mask and his entry,
and confirmed by the second word he speaks; the visual impact remains
throughout, reaching a powerful climax in his final departure. This
theme is subtly re-enforced as the play proceeds. Although Oedipus
cannot see with his eyes he knows by hearing (53, cf. 323, 1171) he
sees by speech (138, a proverbial phrase, as we might say "his ears are
his eyes"). It is the peal of thunder and the divine voice which at the
last bring him to his rest. Or he communicates by touch (173, 329,
1105). This lends poignancy to the countryman's description of the
grove as "untouchable" (39), for at first blow it seems that this must
put Oedipus in every sense out of touch with it. But in fact the word
is skillfully ironic, since at the last Oedipus applies it to himself as he
leads the way untouched by a guide (1521, cf. 1544).

Three other themes press forward in these opening lines. These are
the motifs of the wanderer or traveler seeking a home (there are ten
words appropriate to a journey in the first thirty-five lines), of time
and old age (established in the first line by his description of himself as an old man), and of learning and teaching (from the first
appearance in line 8, seven times within twenty lines). Furthermore,
all these themes are expertly blended. In his opening words Oedipus
asks Antigone,

> Antigone, I am old and blind. Where
> have we come? Who live in this land? (1)

so linking the themes of blindness, age and journeying, and in the opening scene there are other collocations: time as a teacher (7, 22), a journey toward knowledge (8, 26), a journey in time (22). This interwoven imagery continues throughout the play. We are already being prepared for the moment when the fullness of the time has come, when the blind man can dispense with the eyes of others, when the lesson of life is learned and passed on to Theseus, when the traveler finds home and the wanderer rests.

In the opening scene Oedipus asks Antigone where they are, and Antigone, for all her faculty of sight, can only use phrases like "so far as the eyes can tell" (15) or "to make a guess" (16). She looks to the wall and towers that are Athens, and then describes their immediate surroundings, overgrown with laurel, olive, vine; then, in an exquisite phrase painting the birds' swift fluttering, "many-winged nightingales are tuneful here" (17). Strangely, she does not mention the statue. Oedipus sits down on a rock within the precinct. A local enters and tells him to leave the seat; it is holy ground, the home of fearful goddesses, the Eumenides, the Kindly Goddesses. We are called back to Aeschylus. Oedipus, with a grim pun, hopes that they will be kindly to him. He feels that he has reached his goal. We learn that the place is Colonus, and the rider in the statue its eponymous hero. The city is Athens, and Theseus its king. Oedipus sends a message that he has a benefit for Theseus. Benefit from a blind man? "My words—my words will see sharply and clearly" (74).

This is not a trilogy, but we may—we must—look back at *King Oedipus*. Oedipus has here the rôle that Teiresias played there. The local goes, and we expect further conversation between Oedipus and Antigone. Instead we have a mighty prayer for grace and blessing. The theme of the journey is linked first with the theme of time (88), then with the theme of knowledge (96), then with the theme of sight (111), as Oedipus asserts that this is to be his resting place, and the image of the nightingales takes on a new dimension when he says that "a winged thing" (he means an omen) from the goddesses brought him to the grove, and he could rely on the omen (97). This is of its kind wonderful drama, in a muted key, but setting the scene for the whole.

Suddenly Antigone hushes him. Some of the local elders are coming to see him (111). Here the themes of age, journeying, and sight are linked again, though not for Oedipus. The entry of the chorus is intensely dramatic, as was amply demonstrated in the Bradfield production, where the simple dance movement of the old men with their staves, accompanied by their staccato questions, struck chill fear for the intruders. They have found out that a stranger has invaded the sacred grove. Their repeated "Look," using different words, but all within the language of sight (121), calls up the theme of blindness.

Oedipus comes out. His appearance arouses a mixture of horror and pity; he himself says that he sees with the voice, and the chorus cries that it is awesome to see and hear (141). They tell him that he must leave the grove, and Antigone escorts him a little way out where he sits on a ledge of rock, putting himself under the protection of the chorus. They now ask his name and country. This is still the first question asked of the traveler in Greece, and it shows the value structure of the play, since they do not turn to that question till the religious contamination of the grove has been withdrawn. Reluctantly, Oedipus reveals his identity. There is a cry of horror, and a moment of powerful visual drama as they avert their faces and order him away; he tricked them into promising their protection. And now Sophocles does a beautiful thing. Antigone moves toward them and pleads with them in words of great beauty, not spoken but sung.

> Sirs, you are kindly men,
>   yet will not brook my father's age,
>   because you know some rumor
> of his unpurposed acts.
>   Yet, sirs, I entreat you,
>   show pity on my sorrow.
>   For my father alone I plead,
>   plead with unblinded eyes
>   looking straight in yours—I might be
>   your own daughter—pleading for kindness
>   toward his wretchedness. We wait
>   on your compassion as on God's. Please—
>   we have no hope—be generous.

> By all you love I plead—
> your children, wives, possessions, by your god.
> Search: you will never see a mortal who
>   when God directs
>   can find escape. (236)

We can be certain that here, if anywhere, Sophocles would lavish all his melodic gift, as the themes of sight and blindness, and of the journey, come together with the motif of the gods. The chorus is gentle but still fears divine wrath. Now Oedipus speaks with powerful authority. He asks if this is the reputed godliness of Athens, their welcome to strangers. ("The gates of our city are flung open to the world," said Pericles.) Were they afraid of his *acts*? His only act was to suffer! *Quantum mutatus*; this is markedly different from the unwisely active Oedipus of *King Oedipus*; man must suffer to be wise. It is, he says, the mere name that scares them; his apparent offenses were unwitting, suffered not done. But,

> I am a holy man, touched by heaven. My journey
> brings blessings to this people. (287)

The chorus agrees to refer the matter to Theseus.

Antigone suddenly exclaims. A woman, well mounted on a colt imported from Sicily and wearing fashionable clothes, is riding down the road from Thebes. It is her sister Ismene, as she recognizes with her eyes, as does Oedipus from hearing her voice. Sophocles points a contrast between the sisters. The one has stayed in the luxury of the palace, the other has faced destitution and hardship; the one is well dressed, the other in rags; the one wears a broad-brimmed hat to keep off the sun, the other is exposed to the elements; the one is carried, the other trudges on her feet. The visual antithesis is powerfully effective. Yet Ismene is not in any way an unsympathetic character; the effect on the audience is to pity Antigone more, not to like Ismene less. Sophocles has his *Antigone* in mind, and the contrast there between the normal girl with a streak of sainthood and the abnormal girl with an obsession for martyrdom. He is showing something of what has gone before. There is a touching reunion. Then Oedipus asks, pregnantly, after "those young blood brothers." They are of course Ismene's blood brothers, but they are also blood brothers of Oedipus, whose sons are his half-brothers. Ismene replies, "They are—where they are. It is a dark moment for them" (336).

Oedipus, who has learned patience, bursts out in fury, and Sophocles uses Herodotus's picture of Egypt, where the women work and the men loll at home, to embellish his angry words. Oedipus draws out the contrast between the sisters: Antigone, vagrant, hungry, barefoot, unprotected, and Ismene, his one contact with palace life, yet facing danger to bring him news; but he does it in such a way that he draws them together in united contrast with the abominable brothers. Ismene brings two items of information. First, the brothers have quarreled, and Polyneices is banished to Argos, where he is raising an army. Second, the Delphic oracle has declared that Oedipus's body in life or death will give Thebes greatness. But to bring him back will pollute the land. Oedipus says bitterly,

> The bastards! They knew all this, yet put me
> out of their minds, and clung to their absolute power. (418)

The word for "absolute power" is *turannis,* tyranny, the word that was used in the earlier play of Oedipus's own rule. Again he bursts out; his rage is daemonic. He punished himself, all too severely, and they did nothing to help him. But alongside his rage against his sons is his tenderness toward the girls, and his eager desire to stand alongside the Eumenides as a blessing to Athens. As they came to terrorize and stayed to bless, so will he.

The old master shows his hand. In a beautiful scene, attractive to an audience already "in all things most religious," Oedipus is told how to appease the goddesses for his trespass: the drink offerings, the sprigs of lamb's wool, the ritual gestures, the use of water and honey without wine, the quiet prayer. Ismene goes to make the preparations. "Quickly —act," says Oedipus,

> Only do not
> leave me alone, I have not the physical strength
> to move on my own without a hand to guide me. (500)

Sophocles is anticipating a scene of vivid drama which is to follow.

Now, in a sung dialogue, the chorus drags from Oedipus the re-capitulation of his story of incest and murder. He tells it reluctantly, as he was reluctant to reveal his name at the first. Throughout he fervently asseverates his ignorance and innocence; it is almost as if Sophocles is asserting moral law against ritual uncleanness. The chorus seems to share this attitude, for they tell Oedipus to fetch sacred water, touching it (the word is significant) with holy hands (469). Some might have said that his hands were forever unholy; they do not. Waldock comments that we have now reached line 550, halfway through many plays, and a third of the way through this, and we have been moving steadily backward. This is plainly deliberate. If it were a mere matter of filling in the background, Antigone could have spoken a Euripidean prologue in thirty lines. Rather, we need this brilliantly contrived movement backward in time to set off the vigorous action that follows, to establish the principle of time and suffering as Oedipus's tutors, and, above all, to reveal the personality of Oedipus as daemonic. It is the gods who have cursed him, and the gods can use him for blessing.

Enter Theseus. His words immediately take up the opening imagery. He has *heard* in the *past* of Oedipus's self-*blinding*, and now he recognizes him (551). He comes with the compassion of a man who has himself been a homeless exile; the word "foreign" comes three times in two and a half lines.

> A stranger comes, as you do now, I could not
> turn my face away, refuse him help, since I
> know I am but a man; tomorrow brings
> to me the slice of life which now is yours. (565)

These are noble words. The motif of turning is important and is linked to the theme of the journey. Oedipus turns to Theseus (558), and Theseus will not turn away (566). Oedipus in response makes a strange offer—his pitiable broken body as a blessing. Theseus does not understand, but Oedipus replies, significantly coupling two of the themes "In time you will learn, but not at the present" (580). In return he asks for protection against his sons. The meaning of the gift remains obscure, but Theseus accepts and promises that "no one shall take you away without my leave" (656). In the course of their interchange Sophocles put a passage of golden pessimism into the mouth of Oedipus.

> Theseus, good friend, only the gods
> are free from age and death.
> Time, invincible Time, brings chaos everywhere else.
> Strength drains from the soil, strength drains from the body,
> trust dies, distrust blossoms,
> the spirit shifts and changes between a man
> and the one he loves, between country and country.
> For some men soon, for some men late
> joy turns to bitterness, and delight returns again.
> Today the sun is shining on you
> and Thebes. Good. But Time, uncounted Time,
> is fathering uncounted nights and days as he passes,
> and as they come the spear will shatter
> your present harmony for some casual word.
> Then my body, sleeping, buried,
> cold, will warm with drinking their blood—
> if Zeus is Zeus, if Phoebus's words are true. (607)

There are contemporary politics behind those words; within a very few years the Thebans were howling for the annihilation of Athens in her defeat as fiercely as Cato ever cried for the destruction of Carthage. But it is also closely involved with the theme of time in the context of this drama.

Theseus goes, Oedipus reluctantly releasing him, and as the two refugees wait for Ismene's return, the chorus sings the loveliest choral lyric that Sophocles ever wrote. It is addressed to Oedipus their "foreign guest" (*xenos*, 668) and is in praise of "white" Colonus, which was in fact the poet's own birthplace and home of his childhood, white with its whitewashed houses, standing out against the green countryside, like the houses on Mykonos today, white too in that two hills of light-colored soil contrast with the normal red clay of Attica.

> Stranger and guest, you have come in this land
> of fine horses to earth's loveliest home,
>   white Colonus. Here
>   the melodious nightingale,

> a constant visitor,
> trills in green thickets,
> camping in the ivy, dark
> as wine, and in the god's inviolable
> grove, with its clustered berries. No sun shines here,
> no wind blows, no storm
> breaks. Here Dionysus
> revels as he treads the ground
> among the nymphs, his childhood friends. (668)

The song is instinct with divinity, from Dionysus through Aphrodite and the Muses to Zeus and Athene and a perhaps older Athenian god Poseidon. More, Colonus's chief pride lay in its horses; the hero on his horse stands visibly before us; and the song begins from horses, centers on Aphrodite of the golden reins, and ends with Poseidon, horse tamer and tamer of the sea. The horse is a basic symbol of man's thrust and drive, in a sexual sense, but not merely in a sexual sense, of his libido and all the energy that comes from his libido. For Oedipus this includes his passion for Iocaste and the willful impetuosity and pride of his youth and prime. These are now tamed; love remains, as we shall see, but it is a very different mode of love; and it is right that he shall find his rest at Colonus. This chorus is carefully placed to form the play's first climax. The story is told that Sophocles's son Iophon, anxious to lay hands on the long-delayed inheritance built up from the family shield factory, brought a plea that the old man was no longer competent to handle his business. Sophocles appeared in court, and recited or sang this song, which he was at the time composing, and his competence was promptly proved.

We are waiting for Ismene's return; we have an expectation that one of the brothers may appear before the play's end. With an excellent surprise touch, almost a double twist, it is Creon who appears, an older man of course than Oedipus, but without his experience of suffering. He is attended by an escort. The chorus shows alarm. Creon addresses them with hypocritical courtesy; then follows a smooth invitation to Oedipus to return to Thebes. Oedipus knows that it is not genuine. His words are poignant. After his exposure, he yearned for exile, but Creon would not let him go. Then his passion died down,

and home became a comfort; Creon threw him out. Now he has found
his true home, and Creon is seeking to tear him from it. Now he rises
to his full daemonic power and curses his country. Sophocles does a
daring thing for this curse. In *King Oedipus*, Oedipus taunted Teiresias in two lines of fantastic alliteration (370), the first a spluttering
pattern of *s* and *t* sounds, the second a vicious, mordant explosion
of *t*. Now, as he faces Creon, Oedipus echoes the first of those lines so
closely that we are meant to recall the earlier taunt:

> *That* you shall not see, *this* you shall—

And then, as we wait for the explosion, he follows instead with one
of the most somberly majestic lines Sophocles ever wrote:

> my spirit of vengeance inhabiting your country!

And then these terrible words:

> My sons' inheritance in my land
> shall be enough to die in and no more. (787)

In this masterful strain he takes up the theme of sight and blindness
and knowledge through the other senses. His judgment of the state
of Thebes is sounder than Creon's, because he hears—hears the voice
of Phoebus and of Zeus. Does he mean the oracles of Delphi and
Dodona? Or is this an inward ear? Sophocles is deliberately ambiguous;
but it is Oedipus's willingness to listen that matters, and that is the
inward disposition he has learned.

Creon drops the mask. There are other ways.

> You have two daughters. One I have just
> kidnapped and removed. The other I shall now take. (818)

Now we see the dramatic purpose that led Sophocles to send Ismene
on the mission of cleansing. Creon is uneasy about touching Oedipus;
there is something numinous about him (830, cf. 863). His guards
drag Antigone away.

> You won't have these two staffs to lean on
> in your travels. (848)

He does not dare to take Oedipus, but taunts him that he will have
to learn in time that his temper is his ruin. Creon has misjudged the

situation; Oedipus has learned in time; the temper that was once his ruin is now no longer directed blindly, but with authority. Creon turns to go. The chorus interrupts him. Creon's response is illogical but human; he turns to seize Oedipus. Oedipus dares him to touch, then, standing on the verge of the sanctuary, calls on the Eumenides with a mighty curse. Creon is unmoved. The chorus cries "Sacrilege!" Creon with bitter cynicism answers, "Yes, and you must put up with it." And then this most action-packed scene in the whole of Greek tragedy comes to its climax as Theseus returns in the nick of time, at the eleventh hour, and with all the other clichés of melodrama in a situation that was not yet a cliché and was undeniably and superbly exciting. In *Antigone* Creon does things in the wrong order. Theseus, the Athenian hero, makes no such mistake. His first act is to send a rescue party for the girls, holding Creon as a hostage.

Action cannot continue at this pace, and we now have a set debate between Creon and Oedipus. Theseus begins by rebuking Creon. Athens is not a city of slaves; law rules here. This is a deliberate return to the theme from *The Kindly Goddesses*. Theseus carefully says that Creon's behavior was not typical of Thebes. Sophocles was no doubt concerned to be irenic in a dangerous political situation. Theseus suggests that Creon has failed to take time as his tutor; time has brought him to old age and indiscretion (930). Creon in this way is a direct foil to Oedipus. Creon too picks up *The Kindly Goddesses*; the Areopagus does not sanction parricide and incest. And Oedipus once more asserts his innocence and ignorance

> She bore me, she bore, me ahhh!
> She not knowing, I not knowing, and when she had born me
> produced me sons to her own shame. (982)

Creon shows his own character in recalling that shame. Theseus now takes Creon off till the girls are rescued. This part of the scene has marked time; this play has not the taut structure of *King Oedipus*, but its purpose is different. We have seen Oedipus in his helplessness dominating not merely the despicable Creon but the impeccable Theseus; we may perhaps think of the Hecabe-Helen debate in *The Women of Troy*. And again the assertion of innocence.

The chorus now, still in Oedipus's presence, sings a characteristical-ly Sophoclean song bridging the action, and scarcely to be excised from its context. They use their imagination to brood upon the pursuit and encounter; their theme is "I have a vision of victory" (1080). The theme of the horse returns, as the horsemen come into their own in pursuit of the abductors. At one moment they take a thought that Euripides loved to use for escape, and direct it toward involvement:

> O to be a dove, riding the storm, strong and swift,
> > to reach the towering
> > clouds, to cast
> my gaze upon this battle. (1081)

This chorus too is instinct with religion. As they imagine the pursuit they think of the temple of Apollo at Daphne, over the brow from Athens, or of the shrine of the goddesses at Eleusis. Ares, the god of war, is fighting with them, and the soldiers as they gallop in pursuit, call on Athene and Poseidon. The song ends with a beautiful prayer to Zeus the all-seeing and all-ruling, august Athene, Apollo the hunter, and his sister who companies with the swift-footed dappled deer.

The chorus, addressing Oedipus as "Wanderer" (1096), tells him what they *see*. It is the girls. Oedipus is overcome. "Where, where? What's that? What do you mean?" They come in with Theseus and there is another affecting scene of reunion. This recapitulation is de-liberate. The first reunion intensifies the sense of loss; in the context of this play it is union followed by reunion. The theme of love, that solid, affectionate, reciprocated love that the Greeks called *philia,* comes right to the front (1108). Further, there is the sheer theatrical effect open to a good producer, the blind old man embracing the air blindly and the girls perhaps tiptoeing round behind him and snug-gling into his arms from the rear (1107). And the reunion prepares us for the final parting; for the ultimate theme of the play is, after all, the passing of Oedipus. So Oedipus's own words—"Now I can die in happiness" (1110) and "Give me rest from my former lonely miser-able wandering" (1113)—point forward to the end. He asks their tale, and Antigone tells him to listen to Theseus. The language is the language of hearing, but Oedipus turns to Theseus. He uses twice the language of sight—his children have appeared to him, joy has appeared to him (1120, 1122)—and twice the language of knowledge as he acknowledges his debt to Theseus (1121, 1128). He blesses Theseus; he wishes to embrace him, then remembers that he is polluted and withdraws his hand; it is essential for Sophocles that we retain a certain awe of Oedipus.

Then, with the extraordinary skill with which in this play Sophocles links his scenes together, Theseus introduces the subject of Polyneices. Back at her first appearance Ismene told us of his banishment to Argos. Theseus has found at the altar of Poseidon a suppliant who wants to speak with Oedipus. He does not know his name, but he comes from Argos. Oedipus immediately realizes who it is and refuses to see him, but a gentle plea from Antigone persuades; this girl, strong but gracious, is a far cry from the earlier Antigone, for all the links that Sophocles seeks to forge, and is, with Euripides's Iphigeneia at Aulis, one of the loveliest characters in Greek drama; it is interesting that both belong to plays of old age.

And now the chorus sings again in a brooding beauty of pessimism.

> Not to be born—the thought masters
> all others. Next, from the light
> to return to the place out of which we emerged
> is best—and at that with all speed,
> since, once youth passes
> with all its empty follies,
> what trouble is beyond
> us, what agony lacking?—
> jealousy, conflict, strife, fighting,
> bloody death. And then the hated end,
> old age, strengthless, companionless,
> friendless, with all that is evil
> in all that is evil our mate. (1224)

We must remember the sheer pessimism of the Homeric picture of man, the urns from which Zeus dispenses evils and blessings (*Il.* 24. 527), the assertion that man is the feeblest of all the creatures nourished by earth (*Od.* 18.130), the comparison of men with leaves (*Il.* 6.146). We must remember Hesiod's picture of the degeneration of

man (*WD* 109), or of the evils released by Pandora, and man's de-
privation even of Hope (*WD* 109). We must remember the story of
Solon and Croesus (Hdt. 1.30–34). We must remember Alcman:

> There is a vengeance from gods.
> Happy is he who weaves
> a single day with cheerful mind
> without a tear.

We must remember Semonides:

> Wisdom is not for men; we live for a day.
> We live like animals in ignorance
> how god will lead each to his destined end.

We must remember Mimnermus, taking up Homer's comparison of
man with leaves, seeing the dark Fates offering an old age of misery
or death as their choice, depicting the prime of life as a brief beam
of sunlight, after which death is best, listing the evils that lay waste
to a man. We must remember Theognis, whom Sophocles has here
in mind:

> Not to be born at all is best of all things for mortals,
> never at all to see the rays of the piercing sun,
> or, once born, to journey straight to the gates of Hades
> and securely to lie under the heaped-up earth. (425)

We must remember Pindar: "We are creatures of a day. What is a
man? What is he not? Man is a dream of a shadow" (*P.* 8.95). We
must remember the Greek proverb that Menander canonized: "Whom
the gods love dies young." We must remember Sophocles himself. For
he had here in mind the end of *King Oedipus*:

> We are mortal. Let each man look carefully to the day
> of his ending. Call no man happy till the time
> when he reaches the goal of life without bitter suffering. (1528)

In one fragment a character cries, "There is no anguish like long
life" (*fr.* 569); in another, "Though you count over all men you will
not find one truly happy" (*fr.* 616). Sophocles had seen, lived through
disaster, and we can understand a mood of pessimism. It is a permanent
part of man's heritage. Witness Omar Khayyam:

> The Worldly Hope men set their Hearts upon
> Turns Ashes—or it prospers; and anon,
>   Like Snow upon the Desert's dusty Face
> Lighting a little Hour or two—is gone.

Or Housman:

> Dust's your wages, son of sorrow,
> But men may come to worse than dust.

Yet it is a part only, an aspect, a mood. There are other things too, a wind on the heath, a pink and gray cloud. Yeats had it:

> An aged man is but a paltry thing,
> A tattered coat upon a stick, unless
> Soul clap its hands and sing, and louder sing
> For every tatter in its mortal dress.

In this play the chorus may be drawn into momentary pessimism, but Oedipus's soul claps its hands and sings, and louder sings. And the chorus themselves recognize this, for in the last stanza they sing of Oedipus as a rock in the sea:

> So on him without respite
> Dread, like great billows breaking,
> Shocks fall upon him and shake him,
> Some from the side where the sun sinks,
> Some from its orient dawning,
> Some by the midday glow,
> Some from the Arctic night. (1242, tr. C. M. Bowra)

The waves may thunder and break, but the rock remains.

Enter Polyneices; we need not think that Sophocles was embittered by Iophon to write this scene. The young man pleads, first with apparent pity for his father. The themes return in full intensity. He sees Oedipus's age, exile, and eye-bereft face. He professes to admit his guilt; he has been late in learning. Oedipus turns away (1272); Antigone encourages him to go on, and he turns to Oedipus in entreaty (1309). The scene is an analogue of the earlier scene when Oedipus turned to Theseus and Theseus did not turn from him (558, 566), but there Oedipus's journey was coming to an end; his approach was

right and Theseus was right not to turn away. Here Polyneices's journey is doomed, his approach is wrong, and Oedipus is right to turn
away. Polyneices with growing confidence outlines his case, expelled
by Eteocles, seeking vengeance with his six allies, and needing only his
father's blessing. Oedipus says nothing; his very silence is awesome.
The chorus persuades him to speak, and he speaks in thundering curses.
His daughters showed themselves men; his sons drove him to a life of
wandering.

> Be off, damn you—you are no son of mine,
> you bloody bastard—and take my curse with you.
> I here pronounce it. May you never conquer
> your native land by arms. May you never return
> to Argos's valleys. With a brother's hand
> may you be doomed to death, and kill your banisher.
> This is my prayer, and I invoke the grim
> blackness of hell to be your father, take you home,
> I invoke the goddesses of this grove, I invoke War,
> who cast the curse of hatred upon the two of you.
> Begone, with these words in your ears, and take the news
> to all the men of Thebes and to all your
> trusty allies, about the inheritance
> Oedipus has willed his sons. (1383)

Polyneices is withered and broken; his journey has come to nothing
(1399), but he cannot now turn back (1403); he reminds us of the
earlier play by asking his sisters to give him burial. Then comes a remarkable brief scene. Antigone tells him to disband his army and withdraw. Polyneices does not do so, and, whether or not he was in the
right before, puts himself patently in the wrong. There was a lesson
here, directed to the politicians of Sophocles's own day, like Cleophon,
who refused opportunities of negotiation and committed the army
to a long and destructive war rather than risk losing face. Only, unlike
Polyneices, the politicians in the Assembly did not lead the army into
battle and lost only other people's lives. This play is steeped in *The
Kindly Goddesses,* and the lesson there was that the cycle of vengeance
must be broken by the rule of law.

The chorus begins a brief song in which helpless, blind Oedipus is seen as a divine power dispensing disaster, when suddenly a crash of thunder rings across the stage. It is the summons for Oedipus to enter the world of the dead. Where is Theseus? The chorus echoes their song as the thunder crashes louder, ever louder.

Theseus arrives. Oedipus will take him to his place of death. None but Theseus and his heirs shall know the secret; it will keep Athens safe from Theban aggression. He is now to be untouched; the holiness of the grave is his (1521, 1544, cf. 39). And now in a tremendously impressive scene the blind man calls his daughters not to lead but to follow, and he slowly but surely, deliberately, arms outstretched as if to an invisible guide, moves forward. Then he turns back, and raises his face and the palms of his hands to the sky:

> O lightless day! Once on a time I possessed you.
> Now my body for the last time feels your touch.
> At last I am slowly moving to bury my life's
> ending in the world below. (1549)

There is a final blessing on Theseus, and the procession passes.

The chorus sings a dark and fearsome song to the powers of the Underworld, the Unseen Goddess, and the Hound of Hell, and then a messenger comes to announce in a word the passing of Oedipus. There follows one of the most impressive messenger's speeches in Greek tragedy. In this mighty narration we may single out two features. The first is Oedipus's words to the girls that only love, their love for him and his for them, (*philein*, 1617) made life supportable for him. This is part of the answer to the pessimistic view of life; it is this that sustained the rock. The other is the tremendous, daemonic, awesome, numinous, holy power that invests the scene.

> We moved apart,
> then, after a moment turned round. We missed him.
> The man was nowhere to be seen—
> only the king, screening his eyes
> with his hands before his face as if at the appearance
> of something awesome, numinous, intolerable to gaze at.
> Then quickly with no passage of time
> we saw him reverently honor Earth
> and Heaven in a single act of prayer. (1647)

The girls return, and some critics have found the closing scene too long. But it is only a hundred short lines, and what can anyone now say except music? This is to be compared with the Siegfried funeral music, or the Good Friday music in *Parsifal*. Yet perhaps the last words of the chorus are meant in the fullness of their meaning: "Cease lamentation; these things are with authority" (1777).

This is in many ways a finer play than *King Oedipus*; certainly it has fewer faults. Of course it is drama of a different kind; it is properly less taut, there is less room for irony, less evocation of *Schadenfreude*. As the work of a man all but ninety, it is probably without parallel. The flexibility that is still open to learn from others is astonishing. There is a debt to his predecessors. This is in essence an old-type play, like *The Suppliant Women*, in which a refugee comes to a strange place and asks for help against his persecutors. There is a clear debt to Aeschylus in the references to *The Kindly Goddesses* and in the general use of spectacle. More impressive is his willingness to learn from Euripides: the characters in rags, the legitimate element of melodrama, the set debate, the antiwar mood of the Polyneices scene, the picture of Antigone, the introduction of choral songs (such as the praise of Colonus) that will stand on their own as poetry while remaining relevant to their context, even the desire of the chorus to be transformed to birds. Yet all this Sophocles has made distinctively his own, and all his skill in construction and his capacity to create characters larger than life are added. The play is immensely exciting; it is tender and moving; it is also in the most sacred sense mysterious.

Of course it depends wholly on Oedipus. The other characters, even Theseus, even Antigone, are either his appendages or his foils. Oedipus is a being of daemonic power. Throughout this play he asserts his innocence; yet he will not let Theseus touch him. For the power of the gods is on him, for ill or good, and to touch him might be dangerous. We may think of poor Uzzah reaching out to steady the ark as it jolted on the rough road, and being struck dead by the *mana*. Or we may think of Cleomedes of Astypalaea, who won the boxing at Olympia but was disqualified for a foul; he went to his home village, and, like Samson in the temple of Dagon, pulled down the pillars of the boys' school. Pursued by angry parents, he took refuge in a chest in the temple, and when they opened it he was not there; they consulted Delphi who told them that Cleomedes must be honored as a hero or demigod. There was, for good or ill, something superhuman about him. But combined with this heroic or semidivine dimension about Oedipus, there is another element. This is the self-projection of Sophocles into his own play, with candor for his faults, a humble intellectual ignorance about life, an acceptance of the deeper sensitivity that had come to him through suffering, a yearning for the divine dimension. It is not a self-portrait, any more than Prospero is a self-portrait of Shakespeare. We know that Sophocles was in his contact with his fellows amiable, clubbable. It is a projection of elements he knew to be in himself below the surface. The combined result is a marvelous rôle for a great actor; there is nothing else quite like it, save perhaps Lear.

Yet at the last the play is not without a message, and this is another debt Sophocles owes to both Aeschylus and Euripides. The message is in three parts. The first, "Man must suffer to be wise." The second, "Love." The third, "Cease lamentation; these things are with authority."

IV

THE TRAGEDIES OF EURIPIDES

18. EURIPIDES

In the early days of the Persian invasion, while the Spartan troops were fighting their brave defensive action at Thermopylae, the Greek fleet was similarly engaged off the coast of Euboea. The strait between Euboea and the mainland is called Euripus, and it was no doubt in honor of this not unsuccessful action that two Athenian parents called their son born at this time Euripides. Later legend placed his birth on the very day of Salamis, but that is too schematic to be true. There remains something ironic that the great antiwar propagandist should be named after a battle. The parents were named Mnesarchides and Clito; they seem to have been respectable tradespeople, perhaps owning a farm on the island of Salamis and selling the produce; there are continual references in the comic dramatists to Clito's operations as a greengrocer, which would be pointless without some basis in fact.

Euripides grew up in an age of intellectual ferment. Aeschylus and Sophocles also reflect this age, but as members of an older generation sensitive to contemporary trends of thought. For Euripides it was the air he breathed. It became a part of him, as it did not of them. Further, it was an age of intellectual change, in some ways of breakdown. The century-long investigations set off by Thales of Miletus, seeking a simple explanation of ultimate matter and a coherent account of its changes, had broken down. To Heraclitus the material world was in flux (a modern attempt to deny this is misguided), held in stability by a principle of balance or proportion or tension; this led Euripides's younger contemporary Cratylus to the view that we cannot name anything, since a name implies a degree of permanence, we can only point. Parmenides asserted on intellectual grounds that flux is impossible and nothing changes, and his disciple Zeno, ten years older than Euripides, argued with notable acumen that it is impossible to accept the evidence of the senses. It became clear that a simple explanation could not account for the facts, and Empedocles in Sicily and Anaxagoras, who came to Athens as a friend of Pericles, offered an explanation in terms of pluralism.

The basis of Ionian science, though there were residual pockets of superstition, was to explain the universe in terms of an analysis of physical force rather than a myth of divine action. The rational approach to medicine by Hippocrates and his school toward the end of the century is one of many results of the change. Epilepsy, "the sacred disease," was thought to be directly caused by divine visitation, but the Hippocratic treatise on the subject dismisses this view with good-humored raillery in favor of natural causes. Anaxagoras, the great rationalist of the middle of the century, was, we are told, a direct influence on Euripides's thinking. He it was who dared to assert that the sun was not a god, but a red-hot stone bigger than the Peloponnese, and to interpret the crumpled horn of a ram in terms of a rational malformation rather than a supernatural omen.

Alongside these were the sophists. Cicero said that Socrates brought philosophy down from heaven and planted her on earth, meaning that he diverted philosophy from cosmology to man. In fact the sophists, men like Protagoras and Prodicus, had done this long before Socrates turned from an inconclusive pursuit of natural philosophy to concentrate on ethics and politics. Aeschines called him "Socrates the sophist," and he was following where they had pioneered. They cashed in on the new situation in mid-century: leisure at least among the wealthy, prosperity, and extrovert optimism, the pushing back of the frontiers of knowledge, travel, and curiosity, and a form of government (whether democratic or oligarchic hardly mattered, save that democracy offered more clients) in which leadership depended on a combination of expertise and persuasive power. The sophists offered training in both, for a fee; Socrates differed from them in not claiming fees, and in using the question rather than the lecture as the means to education, *educere* not *educare*. The sophists shared and spread the scepticism of the age. Protagoras was an agnostic in religion, and a subjectivist in epistemology, and Gorgias, the great teacher of rhetoric, put the famous case that nothing exists; if it did, we could not know it; and if we could know it, we could not communicate our knowledge. Our sources tell us that Euripides studied not only with Anaxagoras, but also with Protagoras, the ablest of the sophists and one of the most versatile, and with Prodicus, an expert in the precise use of words, a trait which Plato delightfully parodies in his *Protagoras*. They also record him as an associate of Socrates, but this is impossible: Euripides was an established figure while Socrates was still a schoolboy. There were affinities between the two men in their challenge to conventional society, and the story that Socrates never missed a play by Euripides is a more likely truth.

It seems that there were problems in his education. His father wanted to make an athlete out of him, and Euripides combined considerable promise with a whole-hearted loathing of the cult of games, which came out later in a famous attack on athletes in his satyric *Autolycus*. He turned to painting as a profession, but by the age of eighteen was writing plays, and was only twenty-four when his plays were first accepted for performance in 455, though not surprisingly they only received third prize; one of these was *The Daughter of Pelias*. He had to wait fourteen years before he won first prize.

His plays were popular with the masses, but not with the judges. The number he wrote is uncertain. The records later give either 98 or 92, of which 78, 77 or 75 survived at that point, but some of these were not genuine. It has been suggested that the figure of 92 is based on official records and represents 23 tetralogies. The problem is that

we know of only seven satyr plays. There is however some indication
that he used romantic melodrama with a humorous twist in place of
the satyr play. *Alcestis* was certainly one such play, and *Orestes* probably another. Despite his great reputation he won the first prize only
five times, and one of those was posthumously with *Iphigeneia at
Aulis, Alcmaeon at Corinth, The Bacchants* and presumably one other
play. Of his major surviving plays only *Hippolytus* is known to have
belonged to a prize-winning sequence.

We are fortunate in that his popularity led to the survival of ten of
his plays in the general curriculum; one of these, *Rhesus*, is clearly
not authentic; in addition nine others survived by accident from some
library. It is a sobering thought that in the later Byzantine period the
selection was whittled down to three, *Hecabe, The Women of Phoenicia,* and *Orestes,* none of which many would today account among the
supreme masterpieces. It is important to realize that apart from the
pro-satyric *Alcestis,* all the surviving plays date from the last twenty-
five years of his life, and all were written under the shadow of war.
He was almost fifty when he wrote *Medea,* the earliest surviving
tragedy. He loved Athens but loathed her arrogant exclusiveness,
loathed her subjection of women, loathed her imperialist ambitions,
loathed war. All his plays must be seen against the backcloth and in
the context of war. His plays are plays of protest; we are told that his
vision of peace in the lost *Erechtheus* was instrumental in helping to
produce the willingness to negotiate the Peace of Nicias in 421.

Euripides is by far the most contemporary of the ancient dramatists;
he seems strangely akin to the crisis of conscience that took place in the
United States in the 1960s. He was a restless modernist, a propagandist
with a genius for poetry and drama. He has been compared with
Bernard Shaw; there is the same iconoclasm, the same dramatic genius,
the same dedicated revolt. But Euripides uses poetry where Shaw uses
wit, and time has not blunted his weapons.

He made considerable innovations in his approach to drama. The
most obviously influential of these was the diversion of tragedy along
the path of romantic melodrama, with a degree of invention in the
plot that the earlier dramatists do not seem to have permitted. He at
first felt that this mood, with its happy ending, fitted more closely the

satyr play than the tragedy, and in 438 substituted the romantic *Alcestis* for the satyr play. It seems likely that this was not a success, and it may have been some time before he repeated it, though the shortage of satyr plays in his recorded works suggests that he preferred pro-satyric to satyric plays. In the mid-410s he turned again to plays of this kind, now substituting them for tragedies. The most notable of those surviving is *Iphigeneia among the Taurians*; the lost *Andromeda* seems also to have been outstanding. In *Helen* he seems almost to be parodying himself. These plays of rescue are psychologically of great interest; they point forward to New Comedy and to much later European drama.

Of more immediate impact was his realism. This extended back to the early days of his career. *Telephus* in 438 introduced the hero as a beggar in rags. In *The Acharnians* Aristophanes girds at such low realism, and speaks of a whole succession of Euripidean beggar-heroes: Oeneus, Phoenix, Philoctetes, Bellerophon (lame as well, another feature of strong theatrical realism), Thyestes, and Ino; we may add from later plays Electra and Orestes. Euripides had a beggar for every myth. More important still was his psychological realism, his treatment of those who wear rags in their souls, like Jason, his reduction of heroes to human stature (which led Sophocles to say that he himself portrayed men as they ought to be, Euripides portrayed them as they are), his interest in the minds of women (Sophocles's Electra is fine, but Euripides's Electra is true), his awareness of abnormal or obsessional psychology (in Hippolytus, Phaedra, Heracles, Electra, or Pentheus), his good people who are naturally, humanly, unaffectedly good without being larger than life, priggish or namby-pamby (Alcestis, Macaria, Theseus, Peleus, and Iphigeneia at Aulis), his wide understanding of different kinds of weakness that are not wickedness (Creon in *Medea*, Menelaus in *Helen*, Agamemnon in *Iphigeneia at Aulis*, Cadmus in *The Bacchants*).

His characterization is superb: only Shakespeare and Ibsen stand beside him. The author of *On the Sublime* says that he excels at the representation of passion and madness, but he is no mere Scopas of the theater, his palette is much richer. Of particular human interest is his use of children. In five of the plays children are the central motif: *Medea, Heracles's Children, The Suppliant Women, Heracles,* and

Ion. In five more they are a strong factor in one or more scenes: *Alcestis, Andromache, Hecabe, The Women of Troy,* and *Iphigeneia at Aulis.*

He brought to the theater a splendid clarity of language. There is occasional bathos but there is also inescapable challenge. Apart altogether from his theatrical sense, he is magnificently readable. Norwood once said that the only Greek authors one would lay on a guest's bedroom table were Homer, Herodotus, Euripides, and Plutarch; I would add Sappho and Theophrastus, but the point is taken. He has been criticized for faulty construction without overmuch justification. He is not a dramatic architect like Sophocles, but who outside the study wants him to be? There is a revealing passage in Norwood. He gives a technical analysis of faulty construction in *Andromache,* and then asks rhetorically, "Who has ever read the play without zest for each brisk scene, without eagerness to know what comes next?"

Five aspects of Euripidean drama call for special assessment. The first is the prologue. It is used to set the scene; since Sophocles changed from the trilogy to the unit of the single play, some such introduction was needed. It offers a quiet start on which to build. Aristophanes in *The Frogs* accuses him of loose rhythms and casual falling into an easy formula, by fitting "lost his little oil bottle" onto each prologue Euripides quotes. If a dramatist uses the prologue, as Euripides does, to establish a situation, he is liable to write something like, "Hamlet, prince of Denmark, who is a young man of academic interests, in love with a girl named Ophelia, and inwardly disturbed about his father's unexpected death and his mother's subsequent behavior—lost his little oil bottle." This is exactly what Euripides is careful not to do, and Aristophanes picks almost the only plays where the formula works. In fact Euripides's prologues are by no means formulaic, or undramatic: witness *Alcestis, Medea, The Women of Troy,* the lost *Andromeda,* and *Iphigeneia at Aulis.*

Second, Euripides was famed for his rhetorical debates, and Aristophanes, though he does not choose to use these in *The Frogs,* except in that the whole confrontation of Aeschylus and Euripides is something such, has a capital parody in *The Clouds* where the Just Argument and the Unjust Argument meet in head-on collision with occasional quotations from *Telephus* to point the reference. It is not necessary to list such debates, from Jason and Medea in *Medea* through Hecabe and Helen in *The Women of Troy* to Menelaus and Helen in *Iphigeneia at Aulis.* They are dramatic, like the court scenes of modern drama, and they had an immediate appeal to an Athenian audience used to acting as arbiters in the law courts and the political assembly. They are also intellectually exciting; they reflect the intellectual excitement of the discovery that the gathered wisdom of the fathers is not the whole or only truth, the discovery that has a rather trivial outcome at the end of the century in the document called *Dissoi Logoi* or *Pros and Cons.* Euripides is not trivial. He may acknowledge that there are two sides to a question, and he does not give one an easy victory over the other, but he also believes passionately in the supremacy of truth. The scenes of debate sometimes pall in the reading, though not in the theater, and in them Euripides with his dialectical approach appears most modern.

Third, his messenger's speeches are the vehicles for brilliant rhetoric. They are carefully prepared. In Sophocles's *King Oedipus* the messenger simply comes out and speaks. In *Medea, Hippolytus,* and *Electra,* to name three outstanding examples, Euripides skillfully builds up the tension before letting the full flood of the narrative gush out. The messenger's speeches contain more consciously fine writing than the dialogue, but the rhetoric is seldom exaggerated or offensive, and the variety of pace comes from a master of the theater. Where so much is fine it is hard to single out any, but he never wrote anything finer than the messenger's speech in *The Bacchants,* with the unparalleled description of the god drawing the tree down, down, down, and the evocation of a numinous silence.

The fourth aspect is the song. The music is lost, but Euripides was famed for his marvellous avant-garde musical effects that Aristophanes parodied in *The Frogs.* One of his devices is the trilling of a syllable, and his use of repetition is probably for musical effect; in general his musical structure is much freer, more Wagnerian and less Handelian, so to say. Aristotle suggests that the chorus is less relevant in Euripides than in Sophocles. This is hard to sustain. It is true that choral odes in Euripides can be detached from the action and treated as songs in their own right to a far greater extent than those of Aeschylus or

Sophocles; they are not mere comments on the action as they sometimes are in Sophocles. But they are also relevant in context. In *The
Women of Troy, Ion, Helen,* and *Orestes* (where of all the plays the
choral lyric occupies the smallest proportion) the choral odes are
Sophoclean in their integration with the action. But, rightly understood, the escape odes of *Hippolytus* (732) and *Iphigeneia among
the Taurians* (1089) have full dramatic relevance. There are very few
odes in which the dramatic relevance is not clear, so few that we must
attribute their seeming irrelevance to our blindness or ignorance. In
Ion the handling of the chorus is particularly effective; in *The Suppliant Women* and *The Bacchants* they are in the center of things.
Apart from lyric, as these remind us, Euripides's choruses are involved
in the action; in *Medea, Heracles,* and perhaps *Helen,* they virtually
intervene. Furthermore, he is flexible in his effects, and produces on
occasion a second chorus, as in *Hippolytus* or *Iphigeneia at Aulis.* And
his solor arias are varied, exacting, superb. Decharme called him "the
master of monody."

Fifth, from various sources we have indications of an elaborate technique of presentation. Thus a scholiast tells us of the extraordinary
visual beauty of setting in *The Women of Phoenicia. Iphigeneia
among the Taurians* and *Helen* may well have had exotic scenery. In
Hippolytus and *Helen,* a pack of hounds is introduced on stage. Whatever happens in the Palace Miracle in *The Bacchants* there must be
some startling effect with fire on Semele's tomb. The appearance of
Euripides in *The Acharnians,* where he is rolled out on the moving-
platform (*ekkuklema*) at first-floor level on the *distegia,* suggests a
fondness for two-level scenes and an elaboration of mechanical devices.
Certainly the *distegia* is strikingly used in *The Suppliant Women* and
in *Orestes,* and there are some startling epiphanies as at the beginning
of *The Women of Troy,* in the middle of *Heracles,* and at the beginning and end of *Hippolytus* and *The Bacchants.* In the extant plays Euripides does not make great use of the *ekkuklema*; it is a powerful device in *Heracles.* But he was famed for his employment of the crane in
introducing a *deus ex machina,* though in some instances the appearance may be on the *theologeion.* The effect is especially bold in *Medea*

where the appearance is not even of a divinity. He has been criticized
for using the god to cut a hopelessly ravelled knot, and when Horace
wrote his *Science of Composition* centuries later he assumed that this
was the only reason for the *deus ex machina*. With Euripides the contrary is almost true. In *Iphigeneia among the Taurians* he ravels his
plot in order to introduce the goddess. The device had a number of advantages: the chief was spectacular and theatrical; Euripides was interested in contemporary cult and ritual and it enabled him propheti-
cally to link his story with these; it introduces a cosmic dimension, of
destruction in *Medea,* of beauty in *Hippolytus,* of judgment in *Electra,*
of power in *The Bacchants.*

This is important, for Euripides was a dramatist of ideas. His was
an age of scepticism, free-thinking, and the tumbling of the idols. He
rejects the established gods and their ministers; he rejects the legends
about anthropomorphic deities (*Hcld.* 1341, *I. T.* 386); in particular,
he rejects the Delphic Oracle, which time and again he attacks as
Apollo. Sometimes he seems overtly agnostic. "We are slaves of the
gods—whatever the gods are" (*Or.* 418). One of his characters suggests that perhaps chance rather than the gods holds sway (*Hec.* 488).
Sometimes he is speculative. There is a remarkable prayer in *The
Women of Troy* (884):

> Sustainer of the earth, throned on the earth,
> whoever you are, hard to discern,
> Zeus, whether natural law or human intellect,
> I call on you; for moving on a noiseless path
> you guide all things human along ways of justice.

Elsewhere he writes, "The mind within us—that is our god" (*fr.*
1018). Sometimes he speaks of the ether as god, the fiery upper air
that is the immanent appearance, within our universe, of the tran-
scendent divine mind-stuff (*fr.* 340, 941). He is certain that there
are powers at work in the universe, greater than man, powers that we
defy or ignore at our peril. These, for dramatic convenience he personifies as gods. We meet them in *Hippolytus,* they lurk in the background
of *Heracles,* and burst through in final glory in *The Bacchants.*

One of those powers, which he does not personify, is morality. Euripides is a moralist. *The Women of Troy* is a mighty antiwar play; but the same mood recurs in *The Suppliant Women,*

> But if death stood before our eyes, when votes
> were cast, war-maddened Greece would not have perished. (484)

in *Helen,* and in *Orestes.* This is but one aspect of his moralism. In *Electra* he is strong against the actions of Electra and Orestes. There is a revealing exchange in *Orestes*:

> MENELAUS: What's wrong with you? What illness is wearing you out?
> ORESTES: My conscience. I know what crimes I've committed. (395)

Orestes is here illuminating. In *Electra* Apollo is blamed, and the two humans are his weak and vicious instruments. In *Orestes* the whole blame is on human crookedness. Man is the cause:

> Heaven is not unjust, but evil men
> cause sickness and confusion. (fr. 606)

Euripides is full of a high moralism. He was attacked for immoralism on the strength of a line in *Hippolytus*: "My tongue swore—but not my mind" (612). The line is dramatic; Hippolytus in fact keeps his oath and dies for it. Euripides is in fact deeply concerned for righteousness.

Socially he is on the side of the underdog, and it is this that adds fervor to his plays. It is told of Socrates—or Plato—that on rising every morning he gave thanks that he was born a Greek and not a barbarian foreigner, a freeman and not a slave, a man and not a woman. It was exactly this intolerable attitude of superiority that Euripides set himself to attack. In *Medea* we see the foreigner's point of view; we also see the woman's. Euripides presents us with an unsurpassed constellation of strong women. Inevitably in tragedy some of them are criminal, like Medea and Electra; hence the accusations of misogyny. But what of Alcestis, Macaria, Andromache, Hecabe, Iphigeneia? Euripides presents us with a whole range of womanhood, loathsome and lovely, but always with power. He is on the side of the slaves. In the lost *Alexander* a slave is the hero; in *Ion* and *Helen* it is asserted that it is the name not the actuality of being a slave that is shameful; the relation between Alcestis and her slaves in the earliest surviving play is noteworthy. In *Electra* the only decent character is a peasant farmer. In *The Women of Troy* Euripides sides with the victims of war.

His life is in his plays. We know something of his appearance in old age, with a long beard and moles on his face. A portrait bust shows him sensitive, thoughtful, worried. He lived on Salamis in a cave with two openings and a beautiful view; it would have been more comfortable than many houses. There he sat, meditated, wrote, "all day long thinking to himself and writing, for he simply despised anything that was not great and high." He wrote slowly. An anecdote tells of him rebuking a facile writer: the speed of the other's production was matched by the durability of his own. His associates were few. "I have skill," says his Medea. "Some are jealous of me; others think me unsociable" (303). One of his associates was his father-in-law Mnesilochus, who is guyed in Aristophanes's *Festival of Women*, and who need not have been much older than the poet. Yet Euripides was not completely aloof. Timotheus was a musician of genius: his first performance was a failure. He was contemplating suicide when the old poet sought him out and told him to hold on, and those who hissed him now would cheer him. Euripides had been hissed, but Athenian prisoners-of-war from Sicily came home to say that they had been released because they could recite his plays.

Then in his seventies something broke inside him. We do not know what; there was hatred, jealousy, lawsuits, perhaps a good-humored allusion in *Philoctetes* misinterpreted, and he left Athens with the jeers of the people. He went first to Magnesia in Asia Minor; then to the court of Archelaus in Macedon. Timotheus was there and the dramatist Agathon, the painter Zeuxis, and the exiled historian Thucydides. It was a strange, wild country where someone who insulted Euripides was handed over to him by the king for flogging, where a man was not a man until he had killed a boar, where an old man out walking might be torn to death by hounds. Here for just over a year

he lived. Here in the winter of 407–406 he died, and among his papers
were found the fruits of his retirement, three great plays: *Iphigeneia
at Aulis,* unfinished but superb in power; *Alcmaeon at Corinth,* a romantic melodrama with a happy ending; and *The Bacchants,* which
some account the finest of all his plays. They were produced posthumously, as we have seen, and won one of his only five prizes. Thucydides—or Timotheus—wrote his epitaph:

> All Greece is headstone to Euripides,
> > His bones let Macedon his death-place claim,
> Athens his home—the very Greece of Greece,
> > The world his plays delighted owns his fame.

(tr. W. Leaf)

On Nov. 22, 1831, Goethe wrote, "Have all the nations of the world
since his time produced one dramatist who was worthy to hand him
his slippers?" Even more delicate is Browning's tribute in *Bishop
Bloughram's Apology*:

> Just when we're safest, there's a sunset-touch,
> A fancy from a flower-bell, someone's death,
> A chorus-ending from Euripides,—
> And that's enough for fifty hopes and fears
> As old and new at once as nature's self.

19. *MEDEA*

Medea is probably the earliest surviving tragedy by Euripides, and as such, even when we reflect that the poet was nearly fifty, it is an astonishing piece of work. We know that it was presented in 431 as the first play of a sequence that included *Philoctetes* (a strong play of which some account is preserved in an essay by Dio Chrysostom), *Dictys* (a play about Danae and Perseus, of no great repute), and the satyr play *The Reapers* (which is utterly forgotten). The four plays have no obvious common theme. Euripides was placed at the bottom by the judges. Later tradition attributed this to his transference of the guilt of child murder from the people of Corinth to Medea; at the start of the Peloponnesian War pro-Corinthian propaganda was not likely to be popular in Athens. The reason seems implausible; the play is not pro-Corinthian, and it is unlikely that the audience or judges would expect adherence to any one version of a highly fluid tradition. It is more probable that Euripides's failure lay in the fact that two of his four plays were nonentities. Nonetheless, *Medea,* one of the greatest of all plays, had in itself elements that were certain to offend the male and patriotic prejudices of Athenian citizens.

We are told that in this play Euripides plagiarized Neophron. The statement is found in the Argument to *Medea,* and Dicaearchus and Aristotle are cited in support. Neophron is a shadowy figure in early drama, who has disappeared leaving scarcely a wrack behind save a high reputation as an innovator. That Euripides's play is, in any sense that matters, plagiarized seems unlikely; it bears his characteristic stamp throughout. That the surviving fragments of Neophron's *Medea* were written in the first half of the fifth century is impossible; language, style, and meter belong to the fourth, and we must suppose either two Neophrons or a confusion between Neophron and Nearchus. That there was any play on the Medea theme before Euripides is not very likely; Aristophanes of Byzantium tells us that neither Aeschylus nor Sophocles wrote one, and mentions no other. Still, there is one curious feature of Euripides's play. The third actor had long been introduced, but *Medea* requires two only. It is not in other ways archaizing: on the contrary. It is thus possible that Euripides borrowed some elements in the structure of his play from an earlier play by Neophron, not necessarily about Medea; the *Suda* tells us that Neophron introduced tutors and the investigation of slaves, and it is certainly possible that the opening scene followed by a sequence of scenes *à deux* may have been suggested by the earlier writer.

The legend Euripides used had in the background one of the stories of epic heroism, itself perhaps a folk memory of the ancient journeys of the Minyans, the legendary voyage of Jason and the Argonauts from Greece to the Black Sea to secure the Golden Fleece—this last a memory of the way gold dust was caught on fleecy skins. In Colchis the witch-princess Medea fell in love with the adventurer and by her magic powers helped him to the object of his enterprise, much as Ariadne helped Theseus in Crete. She killed her brother Apsyrtus as a means of delaying pursuit, and escaped with Jason. The dowry she brought Jason was the Golden Fleece, the betrayal of her father and the murder of her brother. Arrived at Iolcus, where Jason was the rightful heir, she encompassed the death of his usurping uncle; as a result of this they were exiled from Iolcus and settled in Corinth. Here traditions diverge. According to Pausanias, Medea was the rightful queen of Corinth, and through her Jason became king of Corinth. Media, it seems, had rejected amorous approaches from Zeus, and in reward Hera had promised her children immortality. She left them in Hera's temple and they died. Evidently something went wrong. Perhaps it was Medea's own spells turning against her or perhaps she had offended by actually giving birth within the temple. Jason threw her off and Medea left.

In another version Creon was king of Corinth and offended Medea. She killed him and escaped to Athens. The people of Corinth took vengeance on her children and killed them within the sanctuary of Hera's temple, and in requital had to supply seven boys and seven girls as temple servants—an obvious etiological myth. Yet another story told of a princess named Glauke, who, to counteract Medea's poisons, jumped into a well that was later called by her name. In these stories we see something of the raw material with which Euripides had to work. It is important to note that though Jason undoubtedly depended on Medea for his success he never appears as a type of anti-hero before Euripides.

Euripides wrote most powerfully when he was stirred by a cause, and here he has two causes. The first is the status of woman. Let us again remind ourselves that this is the Athens in which Pericles proclaimed that the greatest glory of woman is not to be spoken of by men for good or bad. Euripides is out to attack this Victorianism; he would have enjoyed Philip Barry's definition of man as "the second strongest sex." Medea kneels three times, once to Creon, once to Aegeus, once to Jason, each time to win a victory. Well may the chorus sing:

> Currents of sacred rivers flow uphill;
> the order of nature, the whole world is turned upside down.
> Men's schemes are crooked, the gods'
> names are taken in vain.
> History will restore honor to my sex
> Glory is coming to womankind.
> Women will escape the grip of ugly rumor. (410)

The supreme example of Euripides's imaginative sensitivity to the woman's point of view is in Medea's opening speech. The words, not least at the beginning of a great war, must have seemed infuriatingly nonsensical to most, to a few revelatory:

> They say we live in security
> at home while they do battle in the field.
> Bloody nonsense! I would choose three times
> to stand in the front line rather than bear one child. (248)

The whole speech merits close examination. It contains an attack on dowry: "Why should *we* pay to let *them* handle *our* bodies?" It contains an attack on arranged marriages (the normal Athenian practice), which leave it to the mercy of chance whether a woman gets a good or bad husband. It contains an attack on double standards of morality, by which it is acceptable for a husband and infamous for a wife to break off. Nor is it merely here. Medea's very concern for her reputation is itself a rejection of the double standard; to Pericles women should have no reputation. Almost equally important is the first stasimon with its reassertion of the woman's standpoint (410), and the later anapaests that begin with praise of women (1081). By contrast Jason says that there would be no trouble in the world if men did not need women to produce children (574). It is precisely this male arrogance that Euripides is assailing. He is saying that as long as men treat women merely as incubators (or, we may add, in an age of simple contraceptives, as masturbation machines) and not as people in their own right, partners and fellows, so long there will be trouble.

Alongside this is the status of the foreigner, the non-Greek, in Greece. The non-Greek was called *barbaros,* from which we derive "barbarian," but which literally means one who is deaf to the lucidities of Greek and utters unintelligible noises like "bar-bar-bar." Aristotle was to declare that the *barbaros* is a slave by nature. The Athenians were particularly exclusive; in 450 they had passed a law limiting citizenship to those born of Athenian parents on both sides. Euripides is concerned to challenge the assumptions that underlie this haughty exclusiveness. Medea's opening words to the chorus (214) tell them that she has come out for fear of being thought standoffish; she is an alien and does not understand their ways. She describes herself as "picked up in a foreign country" (*barbarou*, 256). To Jason she bitingly styles herself "your foreign wife" (*barbaron*, 591). There is something more here: the failure of the majority of Greeks—Herodotus like Euripides was an outstanding exception—to reverse rôles in the imagination. For Jason had been a foreigner in Medea's land, and she did not treat him as he treats her. Euripides emphasizes his point by giving Medea all the traits that the Greeks associated with Eastern foreigners—unrestrained emotionalism, passionate love, magical power, sun worship, and horror of the broken promise. Jason is complacent about the privileges of Greek culture he has opened before her:

> In the first place, you're no longer in a foreign land.
> You're in Greece now. You've experienced justice—
> the rule of law instead of anarchic violence.
> All the Greeks acknowledge your cleverness.
> You've quite a reputation. If you were still living
> at the ends of the earth, no one would be talking about you. (536)

What more can she want? God help her, she wants him. She attributes her downfall to the fact that she trusted a Greek (801). "No Greek woman," says Jason at the last, "would have done such a thing" (1339). It sounds terribly British, and perhaps an Edwardian soldier of fortune returning to Britain with an African princess whom he has married by native law and custom is the closest parallel we can find. Of course no Greek woman would have done such a thing. No Greek woman ever loved like that.

Two images dominate the play. The first is the image of children linked with the curse of childlessness. Over much of the world we do not feel this, but any African would understand immediately. In the nurse's first speech Medea is living in Corinth with her husband *and children*. Jason has betrayed *his children* "and my mistress" and is going to marry Creon's *daughter*. Medea now hates her children. The children come in with their tutor from their play. The nurse and tutor talk of the fate of the children, and they are warned to keep away from their mother. From inside Medea screams, "You accursed sons of a

mother who knows nothing but hate, damn you, your father and your
whole house" (112). Attention is thus focused on the children from
the first. Creon comes and pronounces exile on Medea and her two
sons. She pleads with him for the sake of the children, appealing to
his own feelings as a father, those very feelings with which she will
do havoc (344). These feelings of Creon ring through the scene. "I
love you less than I love my own family," he says (327), and, "Apart
from my children, my country is my dearest love" (329). Jason is
quite happy that the children should go into exile (461), and Medea
rebukes him for it (516). The end of his long speech is full of the
children:

> You blame me for marrying a princess.
> On this point I shall demonstrate that it was (a) clever
> (b) natural (c) inspired by deep love for you
> and for my children.

He is an orator making points.

> Keep calm.
> I emigrated here from the land of Iolcus.
> The problems were enormous. There seemed no solution.
> I was an exile. What happier device
> could I devise than marriage with a princess?
> I hadn't fallen out of love with you (you're jealous)
> carried away by passion for another woman.
> I wasn't set on a competition in size of families.
> The children I have are enough.

—here we must see Medea's reaction—

> I've no complaints.
> My principal object was a good home for ourselves
> without having to scrape. I realized that
> when a man's poor his friends avoid him.
> I wanted to bring up my sons worthily of my ancestors,
> to produce brothers for your children,

—he has already contradicted himself, and again we must see Medea's
reaction—

> treat them the same, bring our families together,
> and all be happy. *You* don't need children, do you?
> It pays *me* to enrich my living children
> with more to come.

Strong irony!

> Is that such a bad scheme? (547)

His mind is on the children of both marriages, on Medea not at all. Then comes the Aegeus scene. The whole point of this is Aegeus's childlessness. It is a scene of cross-rhythms; Aegeus is promised a change from childlessness to parenthood, Jason from parenthood to childlessness. Medea is the pivot; during this scene she first forms the explicit plan to kill the children. She now summons Jason and asks him to intercede—for the children. The children are sent with gifts, and as the chorus, which knows Medea's plans, sings, the children are now doomed. In a wonderful speech Medea wrestles with her motherhood, wrestles with her love for the children. Then the chorus sings of parenthood, ending with the thought that the death of children is the crowning agony. The messenger brings the news of Medea's successful crime against the girl in the palace, and Medea steels herself and goes in. The cry of the children is heard and then silence. Jason speeds in to save the children, too late. These are his words (1325): "You had the heart to take the sword to your children, you their mother, *leaving me childless.*" Throughout the last scene, in Medea's taunts, in Jason's self-pity, the theme recurs. Jason's last words are, "I should never have fathered them, to see them dead at your hands" (1413).

The other theme is the Argo motif. This is the theme of high heroic endeavor, of Jason's achievement and Medea's happiness, and it lies behind the play as a kind of spiritual backcloth. The note is sounded in the nurse's opening words:

> If only the ship Argo had never winged its way
> through the dark Clashing Rocks to the land of Colchis!
> If only the pine tree was never felled and fallen
> in Pelion's forests! If only those heroes
> who went in search of the Golden Fleece for Pelias
> had never set hand to oar! (1)

She compares Medea with a rock or wave of the sea (28–29). Medea's entry is prefaced by a reference to the sea passage that brought her to Greece. (210). Medea herself in her opening speech says that she has no harbor (258, cf. 279) and the chorus sings that some god has piloted her into an impassable swell (362, cf. 441). The first stasimon refers to the passage through the Clashing Rocks. On Jason's first entry Medea hisses out how she saved him "as all know who embarked with you on Argo" (476). Jason's answer begins with a plethora of nautical metaphors:

> It looks as if I must show some skill in oratory.
> A strong hand at the helm!
> Reef the sails and ride
> the storm of your angry words! (522)

It rings false, as the others do not; we almost expect him to don a yachting cap and dance a hornpipe. Medea finds her harbor in Aegeus (769). At the moment of the murder the chorus most appositely recalls the passage through the Clashing Rocks. And oh! the nostalgia at the end as Jason talks of his lovely Argo (1335), and when Medea prophesies his death we know that he will be killed by a beam from the old ship falling on him.

Euripides is saved from being a mere pamphleteer, partly by his sense of drama, partly by this quality of his poetry, partly by his interest in the exploration of character. *Medea* is theatrically superb. It is arguably the most finely written of all Greek plays; the language is brilliant and flexible. But it depends upon its characters. The minor characters are without exception nicely sketched, but the play depends on Jason and Medea.

"Jason," wrote Norwood, "is a superb study—a compound of brilliant manner, stupidity and cynicism." He is one of the most difficult of all rôles to act, and it is good to pay tribute to a remarkable performance by Abraham Sofaer in the part. Jason is the young man of enormous promise that he has never quite fulfilled. It might have been he of whom the epigram was penned: "He has a splendid future behind him." He has the one achievement of the Argo behind him—and how much of that is really his is not wholly clear—and he is content to rest on it. He has gone to seed, and it is his true nature to go to seed. He wears rags in his soul. He is the adventurer seeking security, the romantic lover playing for a *mariage de covenance.* His love for the children is no redeeming feature; he is typical of all fathers who want sons rather than daughters so that they can mold them in their own wretched image. His patronizing way with his sons must have made some Athenian fathers, at least momentarily, wriggle in their seats. He is the complete egotist. He thinks that he is being kind and gentle when he is merely wallowing in the luxury of an emotional bubble bath. He is so self-centered that he is incapable of putting himself in anyone else's place: even at the last he finds it hard to believe that Medea could kill the children. He has lived with her, as man with wife, for years but has not begun to know her. Before we jeer, we do well to look at ourselves! For this is Euripides's point. Jason is detestable, and uncomfortably like us.

By contrast Medea, except that she is intensely a person in her own right, might be called Eros incarnate, and because Love and Hate are closely allied powers, she has become a living fiery ball of incarnate hate. Jason is the whole of her life. She says it twice:

> He is my all—he knows that well—
> yet he, my husband, has turned out utterly vile. (228)

> We women have to look to one man only. (247)

There is a flippant but relevant verse:

> Higgamus Hoggamus women are monogamous.
> Hoggamus Higgamus men are all polygamous.

She has given him everything, for him betrayed her parents, murdered her brother, exiled herself from her home, for him made every effort to come to terms with these self-satisfied Greeks; she is courteous to the chorus and popular at Corinth. The children she bears and loves for Jason. Her mother love is real but at the last secondary; and she uses them for his destruction. For her love must serve or destroy, and because no man is an island it brings down with it a royal house and two little children.

The prologues of Euripides came in for some criticism from Aristophanes and others. They serve to set the scene, and do it with considerable skill. First, Medea's old nurse comes out from the house, shortly to be joined by the children and their tutor. Both servants are delightfully sketched; they are not mere appendages to the action but exist in their own right. Throughout the play the minor characters are all real and none heroic. This is important: Medea operates in a real world of real people. The nurse is homely, loyal to her mistress without understanding her. The tutor is worldly wise and self-important, he talks in clichés, he listens at keyholes and pretends that he does not. The prologue, as we have noticed, brings the two main images before our eyes and ears. The nurse's first words are of the Argo, and their eloquence struck home to generation after generation of poets, Greek and Latin, who imitated them. The children appear before us, and the conversation is full of them. The prologue does indeed set the scene, but it is important to observe what scene it sets. The account of the past is minimal, but it gives us the death of Pelias and shows us Medea as a murderess. It gives us her love for Jason; it gives us her popularity at Corinth. It gives us a compassionate picture of her sorrow; it gives us at the same time the looks of hatred she shoots at Jason's children. Then, as the children and tutor disappear inside, with the scene set and our sympathies with—anxiously with—Medea, there comes without warning the roar of the lioness from within the house. It is brilliant.

Medea's first cry is of herself; in her second she damns the children, their father, and the whole house, calling them "children of a hateful mother" (113). The nurse keeps the thought of the children uppermost and ends also on the destruction of the house. The chorus, Corinthian women sympathetic to Medea, comes on moving rhythmically to anapaestic strains. They have heard the great cry, and listen with fascinated horror as again and again it comes. Medea calls on Zeus (144), the god of oaths, and Themis (160), the power who protects promises, for Jason has broken his word to her. She recollects how she killed her brother, and the nurse hastens to cover up her words (167–168). The latter relieves herself of a little homely philosophy about the uselessness of music; when you are happy, you are happy, and when you are in grief, music does not allay it—words that Plutarch knew well and cites once approvingly and once disapprovingly (*Mor.*143d, 710e). She goes in to fetch Medea and as she goes a really bloodcurdling scream echoes through the air.

Yet when Medea comes she is calm and courteous; she speaks the normal rhythms of dialogue. This is deliberate; Euripides wishes to show us a combination of exotic emotion and steely will. The speech is eloquent and imaginative; we have already noticed its attack on male presumption, and the references to herself as a foreigner. She stresses her homelessness. She asks the chorus for the complicity of their silence should she plan revenge; this she receives, and the chorus, unlike Jason, keeps its word. She ends with ominous words:

> A woman's generally timid,
> a coward in the face of cold steel.
> But wrong her in her marriage-rights,
> you won't find a more murderous disposition. (263)

Enter Creon. He is slightly but by no means inadequately drawn, an elderly man, a weak man who thinks that he is strong, who begins by playing the bully and ends by giving in. He has nothing but convention to fall back upon. His words and judgments are conventional. He wants to be popular; so he cannot bring himself to be greatly good or greatly bad. He has a goodness that lacks the courage of its convictions, lamentable anywhere, disastrous in politics. He knows his weakness: "I'm not naturally dictatorial; my kind heart is always getting me into trouble" (348). He has come to proclaim Medea's instant banishment; he fears her witchcraft. She feigns and fawns, clasps his knees, wins from him a day's respite by playing on his sentimental attitude to children, and when he has gone snarls her contempt for him. Her quick mind plots a revenge that must now be quick, through poison. Again she stresses her homelessness; she must secure some refuge. Again she reveals her magical power in the centrality of Hecate to her worship (397). Again she shows a masculine concern for reputation; no man is going to injure her and get away with it (398). She ends with words designed by the poet to shock his audience into reexamining the position of women, words that nonetheless led the average Athenian to see him as the assailant of the morals of "the sweet little woman" rather than the champion of their power:

> We have a woman's
> nature, incapable of good,
> skilled architects of wrong. (407)

The choral ode that follows is short, composed with sensitive care, and Sophoclean in its involvement with the action. The chorus are women, and they represent the woman's view. The sacred rivers are flowing backward; justice is subverted. *Men* are treacherous; honor is passing from them to *women.* If there were more women poets, we would hear some very different stories. Then they turn to Medea. It seems that she remains on stage through the central choral odes, a visual reminder of their point of reference. They sing of her voyage through the Clashing Rocks, her arrival in a foreign land, the breakup of her marriage, and her homelessness, and return to the thought of Jason's broken word and the fact that she is harborless.

The structure of the play is built around the three scenes of confrontation between Jason and Medea. The first follows the choral ode, and it is superlative. It is characteristic of Euripides that by Medea's bitter outburst at the end of the previous scene he has caused our sympathy to recede from her. Now we see Jason, cold, reasonable, not wanting to be thought a cad. "Even if you do hate me, I could never think badly of you" (463), he says—to the woman who loves him and whom he has taken! *Nec me meminisse pigebit Elissae.* Medea in contrast shows a passionate hatred that would revert to love at one sign from him. "I saved your life," she hisses in words where every other letter is an *s.* A little earlier the nurse described her as made wild like a bull (188). Now she reminds him that she helped him yoke the fire-breathing bulls (478). She is now the bull, and he will not have her help to establish control. The themes of promise breaking (492, 511) and Greek arrogance (509) throb through her outburst. And before her passion Jason reefs his sail and remains calm, reasonable and utterly despicable, ending with the brutal words that the world would be better without woman—a pleasant promise for his prospective bride. Jason offers Medea everything except the thing for which she yearns. She asks for nothing except the thing he will not give. "Love," wrote Murray perceptively, "to her is the whole world, to him it is a stale memory." The scene ends in defiance.

The chorus sings, again briefly, again eloquently, again relevantly. There is no greater joy than love in moderation. In excess it destroys reputation and moral principle. The women pray for that saving wisdom which is *sophrosune*, moderation or self-control; but they know that these things are beyond human power. Euripides has many great songs to love. Some are more powerful, none is more delicate. Then they pass from a theme that reflects the previous scene to one that anticipates the next. They deplore the thought of exile. No city, no friend pitied Medea in her suffering. Enter Aegeus.

The scene that follows was criticized by Aristotle as irrelevant, a clumsy device to give Medea a refuge, and Norwood talks about the utter futility of the scene. This is a misunderstanding. No one would worry if Medea escaped in the sun chariot without Athens as a destination, though once Euripides has conceived the scene he uses it pivotally, leading up to it and away from it. The function of the scene is first to provide relief. It is the one tranquil scene in the play, and in its historical context, to an Athenian audience, it is something more. It is the lull before the storm. It contrasts the brightness of Athens with the darkness of Corinth. Second, it shows us another Medea, a princess in her own right, courteous, genuinely—need we doubt it?—concerned about the troubles of others. Third, the scene is pivotal to the theme of childlessness. It is here that as Medea promises to turn Aegeus from childlessness to the possession of children, she resolves to turn Jason from the possession of children to childlessness. It is important at the same time to see the reverse side of this; there is an important emotional counterweight to her killing of the children in her gift of children to Aegeus. Fourth, Aegeus is beautifully delineated. He is not to be thought of as old; after all Theseus is to be his son, and is grown to manhood when he dies. He is full of his own troubles and thinks that everyone else wants to know about them. It is some time before he realizes that anything is wrong with Medea. Then he is sympathetic, though he needs a great deal of prodding before he offers help. Fifth,

Euripides is able to introduce the traditional riddling phallic response from Delphi (679). Oral societies love riddles, especially with a sexual slant—witness West Africa today—and ancient Greece was no exception. Sixth, in this pivotal scene, Medea kneels for the second time to a man (710), and for the second time she has her way. Finally, the theme of the promise returns with strength in the mighty oath that Medea exacts from Aegeus and that holds the stage for no less than twenty-five lines (731). After he has gone, Medea invokes Zeus, who is among other things god of oaths, Justice as daughter of Zeus, and the light of the Sun. She has found a harbor (769). She reveals her plan to the chorus, to speak softly to Jason, the use of the children as a trap, to send by them a poisoned dress to the girl, and then to kill them. She ends with the words:

> Let no one imagine I am poor, weak
> and peaceable. The opposite is true.
> I am cruel to my enemies and generous to my friends.
> That's the way to a life of glory. (807)

The chorus tries ineffectually to dissuade her, but she sends for Jason. It is noteworthy that Euripides, who is evidently here inventing his plot, at this stage of his career feels constrained to reveal it in advance, in accordance with the normal convention that the basic plot is known.

The choral ode that follows is of great beauty. It is a hymn in praise of Athens. But here too the first two stanzas look back to the scene with Aegeus, the next two forward to the murder of the children. As they try to persuade themselves that she will not bring herself to the act, Jason appears, and we see her justification. This is the second confrontation. Medea is hypocritically subservient, Jason complacently compliant; even in his egotism we pity his blindness.

We may note five points. First, when we hear her hypocritical words the way has been prepared by the scene with Creon. There we thought at first the emotion sincere; when Creon went out she revealed a savage exultation. Here from the first we discern the viper beneath the stone. Second, she tells the children to take their father's right hand (899). This is a deliberate echo of some words she has earlier spoken to Jason: "Ah, my hand, which you so often grasped" (496). As Jason deceived her, she deceives him. Action and reaction are equal and opposite. Third, in the middle of the scene Medea bursts into tears for the children. In the ancient world some insensitive critics blamed Euripides for inconsistency here. It is of course magnificent. Medea does love the children; how could she not? But her love and hatred for Jason is greater than her mother love. Euripides knows the human heart better than these ancient professors. Fourth, Medea tells Jason to command his wife (His wife! Did he ever command Medea?) to plead with her father to annul the children's banishment. The next two lines should both be given to Jason. He replies:

> Yes, and I reckon they will persuade her—
> if she's like the rest of women. (944)

The rest of women!—with Medea there, in Jason's blinkered eyes so pliable and easy. Finally, the last words to the children as she sends them off with poisoned gifts are terrible:

> Go quickly. Be successful. Bring
> your mother the good news she longs to hear. (974)

There follows a choral song of utter hopelessness, and the tutor and children are back. The tutor brings what he believes to be good news of the acceptance of the gifts and the reprieve of the children, and wrings a cry of momentary despair from Medea. The tutor thinks that it is the prospect of separation that disturbs her, and offers patronizing consolation in words of bitter irony to her:

> Tutor: Cheer up! Your children will bring you home.
> Medea: First I have others to bring home. (1015)

He goes, and what follows is possibly the finest speech in all Greek tragedy, as all Medea's mother love pours out to the children, only to be blotted out by her fury. She says goodbye as if she were leaving them, but we grimly know that they will leave her. Twice she stands on the verge of giving up her scheme. Once it is the thought of her enemies' mockery that moves her, once the realization that the other murder is committed and things cannot be the same. In all we see a true woman. It is a superb piece of artistry, backed by profound understanding of the human will.

The killing of the children is not yet. Euripides knows his Medea too well; she could not act until she knew that the rest of her revenge had succeeded. Euripides also knows his theater too well; a further period of suspense gives added power, and the murder of the children must come after the narrative of the girl's death, as the culminating horror. A choral chant follows. We wonder what more Euripides can say, yet he finds something fresh and appropriate—a processional-type song in anapaests that starts from the praise of women, and whose central theme is the blessing of not having children. Children are a delight, but they are also a worry; they need looking after, and may turn out badly or die. To our sophisticated society this is almost a cynical commonplace. To an ancient Greek, as to a modern African audience, the death of a son was deeply held, but the suggestion that it is better to be childless would appear a scandalous paradox.

The death of the children is the crowning agony. Enter the messenger. It is hard not to use superlatives in writing of *Medea*, and the messenger's speech is among the finest of its kind. It is a brilliantly vivid narrative. We see the joy of the servants in the reconciliation. The messenger speaks of "the mistress whom we now honor instead of you" (1144)—it has happened so swiftly that he does not realize that she is dead. We see her with eyes only for Jason, jealous of Medea's children, excited over the fine clothes—she was, after all, only a teenager. Then follows the dreadful account of the death agonies of the girl and her father—it is Creon not Jason who goes to the rescue—clinical in its observation, but with a bitterly excited identification with the scene. Where is the traditional reticence of Greek art? Nowhere. Euripides is not interested. The grandeur of Medea's passion brings destruction on a colossal scale. To minimize this would be to minimize his theme. He plays nothing down. He does not now seek our sympathy for Medea's suffering, only our fear at the power of her love. He speaks to each man in the audience: "You unfaithful husbands, suppose this power, which is in your wife, for that she like Medea is a woman—suppose it flared out."

The messenger goes, and the chorus comments that the divine power is fitting together a weight of disaster for Jason, as he deserves. Medea speaks directly. She is resolved to kill the children and escape. Still she half wavers, still she is their mother. Then she goes in. We hear the great bolts clang shut. The chorus, helpless, raise a prayer to Earth and the Sun to intervene, in a splendid tableau; then in an equally fine tableau turn their backs to the audience and sing to Medea in the house, appealing to her better nature, her mother love. Their song is cut off by a scream. What can they do? Another scream. And then they rush from the orchestra onto the stage and beat with bare hands at the barred door. So far from the chorus being, as some critics have alleged, detached and inactive, they are involved and active, power-fully, dramatically, unconventionally, boldly active. The screams continue—and then stop. It is over. Then and only then does the flute start again; with somber steps they return to the orchestra and sing a sad song about children killed in legend. The death of the children is transfigured by being seen as a part of timeless sorrow. To understand this is to understand the soul of Greek tragedy; to fail to understand it is to leave empty formalism and dead convention.

Jason rushes in with an armed guard and learns from the chorus of the children's death. He sends his men to burst open the doors. We are expecting the moving platform with the bodies. Suddenly at the top of the building there is Medea in a great golden-winged chariot; the bodies of the children are with her. It is a magnificent moment; we expect the *ekkuklema* and receive the *mechane*. So we have the final confrontation. Jason is a pricked balloon, a jelly of self-pity. His vaunted self-control broken, he curses Medea as Medea has cursed him, but the curses are empty words. He is incapable of action. Argo was his one action, as he nostalgically recalls, and that is past. In the present he can do nothing and is nothing. Medea, triumphant, exultant, has complete victory. In the first confrontation Jason has power, Medea apparently only words, and the end is defiance. In the second, there is apparent reconciliation. Jason seems to have control of the action, but we know that Medea has control in fact. In the third, Jason has only words, Medea power, and the end is defiance.

From Aristotle on, the final escape in the sun chariot has been criticized as irrational—a *machina* without even a *deus*. One thing is certain: it is deliberate on the part of Euripides. It was not beyond his inventive capacity to devise an escape by land or by sea. Why then did he choose this ending? For three reasons. First, it is superb spectacle, whether the chariot was riding freely in mid-air, hoisted from behind the stage buildings by the crane and swung round to the front, or whether it was a moving platform on top of the building, drawn from behind a protecting parapet (a scene of parody in *The Acharnians* suggests that Euripides used the moving platform at unexpected levels). Aristotle was an armchair critic, though a very good one. There were revivals in his day, but many of the plays he had read but not seen, though he may have seen this one, as he talks of the crane. We must never disparage the sheer force of theatrical effect. Second, a final confrontation between Jason and Medea was necessary to the structure of the play, and, apart from the theatrical power of a two-level confrontation it was essential in every way that they should be separate. But there is a third point, which Kitto has made well. Just before the murder the chorus prayed to Earth and Sun to avert the calamity. Jason now says:

> After this crime, can you gaze at the sun,
> at the earth, after this godless outrage?
> Damn you. (1327)

What Earth responds we do not know, but the Sun sends his chariot to rescue the murderess. "Is this illogical?" asks Kitto. "Could anything be finer, more imaginative?" In this universe there are powers that surround us. We cannot understand or control them, but we must come to terms with them for they are there. We shall meet them again in *Hippolytus* and in *The Bacchants*. The blazing, scorching, searing power of Love-Hate is one of these.

"The familiar tag," writes Grube, "which the chorus sing as they walk off the stage (it is found at the end of three other plays) brings no comfort. The play ends in violent discord; there is no peace here, only Violence and Hate." Only people.

20. HERACLES'S CHILDREN

Heracles's Children remains all in all the least attractive of Euripides's surviving plays; it is certainly one of the most neglected in the theater and can seldom have been performed in recent years. Yet its merits are considerable. Schlegel called it "very paltry" and found the end particularly weak, and the judgment itself shows misunderstanding. By contrast Zuntz sees it as "a gem of concentrated presentation." The false evaluations arise from a failure to relate Euripides's thought to the play's political context, and a consequent too-ready acceptance of the play as a glorification of Athens; even the normally judicious Grube falls into this error and fails to detect the almost satirical twist that the conclusion gives to the play. The praise of Athens is there; but what at the last does her glorious behavior achieve?

The approximate date is not in doubt; considerations of style and rhythm place the play close to *Medea* and *Hippolytus*. It is morally certain that its context is war, and that it is to be dated to the early years of the Peloponnesian War. At the end of the play Eurystheus prophesies that from his grave he will defend the land from invasion (1034). The first Spartan invasion of Attica took place in 431; in 430 they actually passed Eurystheus's tomb at Pellene, and the subsequent invasion was the most devastating of all. It might therefore seem best to date the play to the spring of 430, since otherwise the prophecy would have already been falsified by events.

The conclusion is not rigid. The promise of protection might refer to the area around Marathon called the tetrapolis, the traditional refuge of Heracles's family, which it seems the Peloponnesians did spare for their sake, unless there were inroads in 427 (D.S. 12.45; Schol. Soph. *O.C.* 701, but cf. Thuc. 3.26.3). Another likely reference is to the illegal execution of Peloponnesian envoys at Athens in the winter of 430–429 (Thuc. 2.67.4, cf. Hdt. 7.137.3). Argos was theoretically neutral at the time, but one of them came from Argos. This would explain Euripides's transformation of the legend so that Eurystheus is executed rather than killed in battle. This might accord with a date of 428; a play about Heracles's children could well appear with a play about Theseus's son. But 429 is not out of the question; Euripides's play must have been in draft at the time of the executions, but drafts can be altered. We may further note that Macaria's apology for her public appearance (474) is clearly related to Pericles's public statement about the place of women in society, delivered in the winter of 431–430 (Thuc. 2.45.2). It is hard to be certain, but probably 429 or 428 is the right date.

It is necessary to add a brief word on the integrity of the play. It is a short play—apart from the satyric *The Cyclops* and the spurious *Rhesus* the shortest in the Euripidean corpus—and this has led some scholars to posit omissions, especially as some passages not in our text are quoted as from this play by Byzantine anthologists. The arguments are not cogent; the attributions are almost certainly wrong; there are no obvious lacunae in our text; the play stands as a well-knit, compact whole.

One final introductory point relates to Euripides's originality. It happens that in the uncritical repository of myths, *The Library*, attributed to the polymath Apollodorus, but in its present form much later, we have an account of the adventures of Heracles's children:

After Heracles had been taken up to heaven his sons fled from the persecutions of Eurystheus to Ceyx, king of Trachis. Eurystheus demanded their surrender with threat of war; Heracles's family left Trachis in terror and wandered over Greece as refugees. Finally they reached Athens. There they took up position at the Altar of Pity, and asked for sanctuary. The Athenians, rather than give them up to Eurystheus, declared war. In the subsequent fighting Eurystheus's five sons were killed. The king took to his heels; Hyllus in pursuit caught up with him by the Rocks of Sciron and killed him there. His head was cut off and carried to Alcmene, who gouged out the eyes.

There is the outline of the story, but there is nothing of Euripides's drama except the hatred of Alcmene, nothing of the brutality of the herald, Demophon's refusal to be intimidated, the self-sacrifice of Macaria, the pathetic heroism of Iolaus, the surprising gentleness of Eurystheus. Whether or not Euripides's play is successful, it is certainly original.

The situation is dramatic. The scene is the temple of Zeus at Marathon, and may have been identifiable as such at sight. It is not named for thirty lines. An old man and a bevy of young boys take up their positions by the altar in front of the temple. They all wear the garlands of suppliants. These children, we must remember, are to remain on stage throughout the play, a mute reminder of the innocent victims of violence. The play is named after neither the chorus nor one of the speaking actors; it revolves round these mute onlookers. The old man speaks; if we expect a typical narration of scene and events we are mistaken. He is sententious, in character:

> I have long fixed upon the following view:
> one man is innately just towards his neighbors,
> another sets his whole energies on material gain,
> politically useless, difficult to deal with,
> putting Number One first. I'm speaking from experience. (1)

He still does not tell us his name. He is a friend of Heracles, who has taken the children under his wing (10), a protector in need of protection. He speaks of his own sense of honor (6) and the outrages they have suffered (18). Eurystheus is harrying them from city to city. Now they have reached Marathon. Alcmene and the girls are inside the temple, Hyllus and the older boys have gone for refuge elsewhere.

The scene explodes into swift movement. Eurystheus's herald, here unnamed, in Homer (and in the *dramatis personae*) called by the ugly name of Copreus, arrives, a stage villain and typical tough, who promptly proclaims the doctrine that might is right, throws the old man out of the way, and makes to break the children's sanctuary. The old man cries out at the violation of Zeus Agoraeus (70). This is a key moment. *The Oresteia* saw the movement from Zeus, protector of strangers, to Zeus Agoraeus, the god of the political assembly. It corresponded to the emergence of an ordered society out of an anarchic cycle of revenge. *Heracles's Children* starts from Zeus Agoraeus and the ordered society, and shows the reversion to anarchy, just as the ordered society of Greece was broken by the Peloponnesian War.

The old man's cries bring in the chorus of elders of Marathon. Here is no anapaestic procession; they rush in to excited dochmiacs. What is happening? The old man splutters, "He, friends, me, your . . ." (78), bringing the participants vocally as well as visibly together. They ask who the suppliants are, and only now does the old man identify himself as Iolaus (89). The herald remains truculent, but decides to deal with the king, Demophon, who opportunely arrives with his brother Acamas. He comments that the herald is behaving like a foreign savage (131).

A set debate before the king now follows this explosive action, but Euripides is too wise to spin it out; it is taut and to the point. Yet its course is not obvious. The herald asserts his legal right to the extradition of criminals; for the rest he lays before Athens the choice between alliance with the might of Argos, and war to the teeth, and warns the Athenians not to let their traditional sympathy with the underdog warp their judgment. The herald's personality is repulsive, and his character is excellently if obviously drawn. Iolaus's answer is poorly persuasive either in law or rhetoric. His claim that as refugees condemned by the Argives they were no longer Argive citizens is decidedly odd; Enahoro had much stronger claims for asylum than that. This is his only point of substance; he flatters the Athenians, draws up a family tree of kinship too complex to be verbally effective (though the production of two charts might be good theater and more persuasive), introduces the theme of *charis*, the mutual exchange of favor and gratitude (220, cf. 241), and relies on a final extravagant appeal to the emotions that might carry more weight with a Greek audience than with us.

The elders sympathize with the old man, and Demophon gives judgment for him. His reasons are first the religious claims of sanctuary, which Iolaus has not mentioned, second the ties of kin and friendship, third his own prestige, lest he be thought to have yielded to the herald's bullying. Euripides could have given Iolaus a far more eloquent speech had he chosen. That he did not do so is partly in the dramatic character of Iolaus, who is moved by sentiment more than reason, but more in the essential moral ambiguity of the play. Copreus is a loathsome creature, and we reject his case however reasonable. Iolaus is warm, and willing to suffer for others, and we are with him, however muddle-headed he may be. This anticipates the reversal at the play's end, when we have come to accept Alcmene's case and reject Eurystheus's, and find to our puzzlement Alcmene detestable and Eurystheus sympathetic.

The scene ends in a bitter exchange between the herald and Demophon. Copreus tries to grab the children. Demophon raises his staff of office, but the chorus intervenes. "For God's sake don't strike an envoy," they say (272), and the king growls, "The envoy had better learn to behave." Copreus goes out, threatening war, and Demophon asserts that Athenians never, never, never shall be slaves (287). Before the play is over a prisoner with promise of safety will be killed.

The chorus now sings with extreme brevity of the need for preparation and the unreliability of envoys' reports. Iolaus makes a dignified speech of gratitude; this has been rightly seen in the context of *charis*, the reciprocal ties of favor and response, especially when he educates the children in their obligations. "This land," say the elders, "always tries to help the helpless, when right is on their side" (329). The king goes to mobilize his troops and to consult the seers; Iolaus remains at the altar to pray. These last inventions save an awkward change of scene and prepare the way for Macaria's sacrifice.

The mood of the song that intervenes has been compared, unkindly but not unjustly, with "We don't want to fight, but, by jingo, if we do. . . ." This apart we need note only the description of Athens as rich in graces or favors (*charis*, 379). The song is relevant, but slight; clearly to lavish too eloquent a lyrical gift here would spoil the balance of the play. For the next scene must be Macaria's. Demophon comes back with hunched shoulders and bowed head. He is confident in his military dispositions, but all the signs point to Persephone demanding the sacrifice of a girl. This is obviously something the refugees can provide, yet Demophon is too chivalrous to suggest it; he is content to draw attention to his own dilemma. He is no dictator to force his people as foreigners do; there is an implicit contrast with the Argives (423, cf. 131, 361). "A just king has just subjects" (424).

Iolaus starts with an extended image from sailing; they were all but in port when the wind veered and blew them out to sea again. Still, he will not forget Demophon's gracious kindness (*charis*, 438, cf. 434). As he addresses the children he loses emotional control; his voice rises and falls; two of his lines begin with two circumflex accents followed by a third in a wave of keening (439, 449), and the second of these is associated with a concatenation of choking *k* sounds with sobbing aspirates.

At this point the door of the temple moves slightly ajar, and a girl looks out, wondering at the noise. Through all that follows she watches and listens, unseen by the men. Iolaus, with futile gallantry, suggests that if he surrenders himself, Eurystheus will call off the war; as Demophon remarks, the proposal is noble but impractical. But now Macaria, for it is she, Heracles's eldest daughter, intervenes. Her name, which means "blessed," is curiously not mentioned. She is one of Euripides's noblest creations, in the line of succession from Alcestis, predecessor of Polyxene, and Iphigeneia. We should not forget either that she stands between Medea and Phaedra. An innocent woman as well as a criminal woman can dominate the action in Euripides, and this is what, in 150 lines, she does. She apologizes for her presence; in that she is Periclean woman, though Euripides does not impose other Athenian prejudices on her as he does more than twenty years later with Iphigeneia.

Iolaus explains the situation to her, and without delay she volunteers to die. There are three elements in this decision. The first is, quite simply, her own free choice; with this she begins and ends (501, 531). She, like Polyxene in *Hecabe*, is an existentialist heroine; indeed she is under less constraint than Polyxene. The second is the debt of reciprocal gratitude they owe to Athens; she does not use the word *charis* here, but that is the framework of thought. The third is parentage; she is truly child of the heroic Heracles, and Iolaus stresses the fact (540). Wellmeaningly he suggests that she draw lots with her sisters. Indignantly she thrusts the suggestion aside:

> I won't be butchered at the beck of chance.
> There's no *charis* in that! (547)

Demophon admires her pluck and her sense of right and wrong. She says goodbye to Iolaus and her brothers. She is dying for her family:

> This is my treasure, not children,
> not virginity—if there is anything beneath the earth.
> May it not be so! If when we die
> we mortals have our troubles there too,
> I do not know where we can turn. (591)

It is Euripidean scepticism, not inapposite in the adolescent girl. She goes without a word to her grandmother inside the temple; we shall find her grandmother to be of very different mettle. Iolaus, a complex of contradictory strength and weakness, collapses in a faint, and the old men of the chorus sing, in words which recall Theognis, of the ups and downs of life, and of Macaria's glory with the haunting phrase "True goodness picks its way through pain" (625). There is no further mention of her in the play. It is obvious why: the play escapes from her.

The scene that follows is by any standards strange, but a dramatist may legitimately include a scene that does not bear too close a scrutiny, because of its place in the structure of the whole. In this scene there are three elements. First there is the arrival of an attendant with the news that Hyllus has appeared with an army. The news is unexpected; we were not even aware that he was seeking troops. The first part of the play concentrates upon a sacrificial willingness to suffer. Iolaus shows it, so does Demophon, and Macaria fulfills it. The second part is the other side of the coin, war and violence and vindictiveness. Second, Alcmene, Heracles's mother, is introduced. Iolaus calls her out to hear the news. She immediately assumes that the attendant is an enemy and flares up threateningly. In her aggressiveness, rooted in the strong sexuality that attracted Zeus and gave birth to Heracles (as Iolaus makes clear in summoning her, 644), we are prepared for her sadistically vengeful attitude later. More, if Alcmene is Heracles's mother, what of Heracles's son? Are we not meant to see Hyllus as glorying in war? There are more sides to Heracles than Macaria has shown. Finally, Iolaus becomes caught up in the general spirit of militarism, and arms himself for battle. The scene is ludicrous and is intended to be. Alcmene tells him soundly that he is crazy (709). Zeus will look after her, says Iolaus, and Alcmene replies

> Hm!
> I don't propose to criticize Zeus
> It's for him to say if he's treated me right. (718)

Euripides cannot resist a touch of rationalism. The old man's enthusiasm is pathetic but laughable.

IOLAUS: All right! Bring my armor. Keep it
             at the ready. Set a spear in my hand.
             Grip my left elbow to guide my steps.
ATTENDANT: Does a soldier really need a nursemaid?
IOLAUS: We must avoid bad luck—watch your step.
ATTENDANT: I wish you had as much strength as enthusiasm.
IOLAUS: Come along: I don't want to miss the battle.
ATTENDANT: You think I'm dawdling, it's you!
IOLAUS: Can't you see how fast I'm moving?
ATTENDANT: I can see you're not going as fast as you think.
IOLAUS: You'll change your tune, when you see me there.
ATTENDANT: Doing what? Enjoying luck—I hope!
IOLAUS: Smashing some enemy right through the shield.
ATTENDANT: If we ever arrive. Which I doubt. (726)

There must have been veterans of the Persian Wars behaving like Iolaus and Euripides drives home the point with a gratuitous reference to Sparta (742).

The choral song that follows is a prayer for victory. The chorus invokes in Homeric language the all-seeing Sun and Earth together with the Moon to witness before gods and men to the victory of Athens. In the second stanza Zeus is introduced, and with the mention of Zeus they pass from fear to confidence; in this context they introduce the theme of *charis*; here it is the favor of Zeus (767). So, climactically, to Athene, with an outburst of joy as they recall her festivals.

The attendant returns with news of victory and is promised his freedom by Alcmene, and we learn of the miraculous rejuvenation of Iolaus. There is here a slight problem: Alcmene's language suggests that he is present (*hode*, 793), but the narrative reveals that he is not, and we must accept textual corruption. The account of the battle is interesting enough, but ultimately unmemorable; it is not to be compared with Euripides's finest messenger speeches. First we hear how Hyllus challenged Eurystheus to single combat, and the king refused; to our image of Eurystheus's brutality is added cowardice. Then the seers sacrificed. Again there is a problem. Our text speaks of "human throats" (822): this can hardly be right, and it is better to read "animal throats" (*boteion* for *broteion*). Macaria is here not mentioned; she gave herself for the safety not the danger of others. So to the battle, tense, ding-dong, with the Athenians narrowly victorious. Then the pursuit with Iolaus in a chariot hard on the heels of Eurystheus, and the miraculous appearance of Heracles and Hebe, his heavenly wife and the goddess of youth, as stars above the chariot, till Iolaus regained his husky youth, caught Eurystheus and took him prisoner.

The element of fantasy here is important. It enlivens the narrative, and is dramatically economical; it also simplifies the change in the tradition. But miraculous interventions in Euripides are always suspicious. Sometimes they represent the dramatic expression of natural forces; sometimes, as here, a *reductio ad absurdum*. This is a *reductio ad absurdum* of the military spirit. Alcmene bursts into a spiteful tirade against Eurystheus. The attendant closes the scene with an earthy and slightly comic note of realism:

> Goodbye, madam. Don't forget what
> you promised me when I started my story—

freedom. In matters of this sort, you must
mean what you say. *Noblesse oblige.* (888)

The chorus sings a song of triumph, which includes a stout affirmation of the apotheosis of Heracles. Their last reflection begins with
ambiguous words: "Most things correspond with many others," or
perhaps "Most things work out well for many people" (919). The
meaning is obscure—perhaps deliberately.

And at this moment Euripides turns his play upside down. The attendant— Hyllus and Iolaus are too busy erecting a trophy to Zeus—
returns once again, with Eurystheus as a prisoner. The attendant speaks
with his characteristic down-to-earth humor: "Fate organized things
differently and turned the tables on him" (934). Alcmene assails her
enemy with bitter spitefulness and lacerates him with her tongue; we
should probably assume that she maltreats him physically, bound and
helpless as he is. But when she threatens to kill him the chorus intervenes. The attendant takes up the cudgels, and they wrangle for a
minute or two, but the chorus is adamant: "There is no one here who
can kill this man" (972). Then Alcmene breaks in again: "I can."
Suddenly Eurystheus speaks, calm, dignified, and courageous. The
feud with Heracles was foisted upon him. He did not seek it, and it
left him with a life of fear; it made him a kind of professor of torture
(993). Then Heracles died, and the others carried on the feud. He
persecuted them in self-defence:

> If you had been in my shoes, you'd
> have pressed hard on those blasted cubs
> of the lion who loathed you. (1005)

He does not seek nor fear death. Alcmene is determined to have
his life; she absolves the city of responsibility. Eurystheus takes his
leave of life with dignity and makes the promise of help against invasion by descendants of his enemies. The fury of Alcmene is implacable.

> Why the delay in killing the fellow
> since you can win security for your country
> and your descendants? You heard what he said.
> He points to the safest route.

> He's your enemy, and in his death becomes your friend.
> Slaves, take him away. Kill him and
> throw him to the dogs. You needn't expect
> to live and exile me from my fatherland again. (1045)

And the chorus weakly accepts. And that is all.

It is of course a shocking conclusion and is intended to be. For we realize that where there is conflict there is propaganda, distortion, lies, self-deception. Eurystheus has been built up as a monster of depravity and tyranny, and we find him gentle, troubled, and brave. Our picture of Heracles's family has been built up through the ineffective but warm personality of Iolaus and the unique glory of Macaria. We now find ourselves asking what sort of son did Alcmene really produce— and what sort of grandson. Hyllus is adept at raising an army. Has the wrong been all on one side?

Meantime the situation, which through Iolaus, Demophon, and Macaria seemed sacrificial, has broken into war, and that war has meant moral degradation. Neither Macaria nor Demophon can arrest this, noble as they are; Iolaus gets caught up in it. And all the praise of Athens, which critics have reasonably emphasized in the earlier part of the play, is designed to make the moral compromise of the chorus at the end the more devastating. Hence the abruptness. When war comes, the spirit of Alcmene triumphs.

Heracles's Children, of all Euripides's plays, cannot be divorced from its political context. It is his first protest against the war. He was to write stronger plays on the same theme, culminating in *The Women of Troy*, *Helen*, and *Orestes*, but in context it is not negligible. And it has Macaria.

21. *HIPPOLYTUS*

There were links between Trozen, thirty miles south of Athens in the Peloponnese, and Athens. Theseus, the heroic king of Athens, was born in Trozen of a Trozenian princess. Theseus had a legendary son, the hero Hippolytus, born according to later stories of the Amazon Hippolyta. Hippolytus was a cult figure at both Trozen and Athens. In both he was associated with the healing god Asclepius and the love goddess Aphrodite. At Trozen girls before marriage cut their hair and dedicated it to Hippolytus. There is no discernible association with Artemis. But Artemis in Asia Minor appears as the fertility goddess, and in other guises often has a young male attendant and consort, Attis with Cybele, Tammuz with Ishtar. Perhaps originally Hippolyta was a local fertility goddess of Trozen, and Hippolytus her young consort. It will be noticed that in the rending of Hippolytus by his horses we have one of the clearer year myths. But legends develop far beyond their origin and attached to Hippolytus became a folktale akin to that of Potiphar's wife. In this folktale Hippolytus appeared as a chaste athlete, a natural development for one whose sexual powers were dedicated to a goddess of hunting. His stepmother, Phaedra, fell in love with him, and when rebuffed accused him of rape. Theseus cursed his son, and Hippolytus was killed when his horses panicked before a monstrous bull sent by Poseidon, and Phaedra committed suicide.

Euripides had already treated this in the play popularly known as *Hippolytus Veiled*. The scene was set in Athens. Phaedra appeared as a shameless wanton who swore Hippolytus to secrecy and then tried to seduce him, at which Hippolytus veiled his head in horror; a reminiscence of the gesture remains when Theseus accuses him in the later play. Phaedra supported her charge to Theseus by faked evidence of violence. Theseus summoned Hippolytus, and there was a formal accusation and defense ending in the curse and sentence of exile. Hippolytus drove off to Trozen and was killed. The truth came out, perhaps through the nurse, and Phaedra killed herself. Finally a *deus ex machina* prophesied the cult of Hippolytus. The play was unsuccessful. Phaedra was portrayed as something of a sex maniac, and Euripides's interest in feminine psychology seems to have led him to extremes. The failure rankled.

Sophocles probably next took up the theme in *Phaedra*. This centered on Phaedra not Hippolytus, and caused no offense. Any reconstruction is controversial, but the following is reasonable. Theseus was depicted as absent for some years on an expedition to Hades and thought to be dead; Phaedra's approaches to Hippolytus were thus not adulterous in intention. She probably made those approaches through the nurse. Hippolytus rejected them, drove straight off to Trozen, and and did not appear again. On Theseus's unexpected return, Phaedra panicked and trumped up a false story for the sake of her reputation and her children. Theseus took Hippolytus's flight as proof of guilt, and cursed him in his absence. The curse took effect, and with the news of Hippolytus's death Phaedra experienced remorse, confessed, and committed suicide.

It was rare for a dramatist to write a second play on a theme he had used earlier, but Euripides was fascinated by the theme, dissatisfied with the rejection of his earlier play, challenged by Sophocles's success, and he did just that, and did it successfully with his new *Hip-*

polytus and the other plays, whatever they were, winning one of his few first prizes. The year was 428. It is important to see that Euripides swings back the balance of the play from that of Sophocles. His play is about Hippolytus not Phaedra. Hippolytus is the battlefield of the goddesses. Aphrodite says that he is her only concern and Phaedra does not matter; Artemis is interested only in Hippolytus. He is the first human character to appear, his part is the longest, and he is on stage at the end.

A dramatist often adumbrates in one play ideas that he elaborates in a later, and vice versa, and it is useful to see *Hippolytus* in the light of *Medea*. Thus each play centers on a character who is not, in Athenian terms, a citizen, being not born of citizen-parents on both sides: this is a side of Hippolytus's bastardy that is not always remembered. Each throbs with the power of love, in *Medea* incarnate in Medea herself, who takes the place of a divinity in the final scene, in *Hippolytus* manifest and personified in Aphrodite; each contains a choral song to Eros. In *Medea* one of Medea's characteristics is her insistence on promise-keeping; in *Hippolytus* this becomes a major dramatic point when Hippolytus threatens to break his oath though eventually keeping it. In both plays the chorus is sworn to silence. In *Medea*, Medea is on stage during the central chorus; in *Hippolytus* this device is more effectively handled with the bed-ridden Phaedra. In both places an unsympathetic male character puts a jaundiced view of women, but Jason's is mere bluster where Hippolytus's springs from his psychology. Both contain strong assertions about the rights of women; in *Medea* these are put overtly in Medea's mouth. In *Hippolytus* the theme is more subtly handled. The repudiation of a double standard of morals is put into the mouth of Theseus as part of his attack on Hippolytus. But there is a more important point. In *The Kindly Goddesses* Aeschylus maintained a view of physiology by which inherited traits come from the father and the mother is a mere receptacle and incubator. In *Hippolytus* Phaedra fears her inherited sexuality from Pasiphae, and Hippolytus's puritanism comes from his mother, Hippolyta, not from Theseus.

The play opens before the palace at Trozen. A statue of Aphrodite stands by the door (101), and somewhere else, asymmetrically placed if the stage manager knows his job, a statue of Artemis. As we wait for the play to begin we contemplate the two images confronting one another, durably, unmovingly, unshakably—the virgin athlete and the great power of sex. For this is what the play is about. In Homer gods are power; there is no moral norm to be seen among them. For a hundred years radicals had been criticizing the myths on moral grounds; so did Euripides attack Apollo again and again. But here we have amoral powers—Passion and Purity, Sex and Chastity. Both exist, and, as we shall learn, we ignore either at our peril. Euripides has made a profound psychological discovery. It is equally unhealthy to give one's libido a free rein, as the Phaedra of his first play did, and to repress one's sexual nature by pretending that it does not exist, as does Hippolytus here. Euripides, in revising his treatment, turns his emphasis from the first to the second, but he does not forget the first. But Phaedra is now no longer unleashed libido, for Euripides's treatment has become more subtle and complex. There is a sense in which the nurse represents this part of her nature. But it is in Aphrodite and Artemis that these aspects of human nature are externalized; Euripides is putting a mythical tradition and theatrical convention to profound dramatic and human use. We are not to suppose that he believed crudely in an anthropomorphic Aphrodite and Artemis. But he believed intensely in the powers they represent. Throughout the play the visual impact of the two statues reminds us of those powers.

On a high balcony appears a divine figure; she identifies herself as Aphrodite. Her opening words are carefully chosen. She has a name, and gives it as Cypris, not Aphrodite, and this continues with rare exceptions throughout the play; the effect is slightly to detach her appearance here from the accepted anthropomorphic deity. The effect is intensified by a deliberate ambiguity; her words may mean "I, a goddess, am called Cypris" or "I am called Cypris a goddess" (2). So later the nurse calls her "not a goddess, but something bigger" (359). This is what Euripides intends, and he intensifies the effect by linking her from the first with the sea, a recurrent image in this play, for Aphrodite is the foam-born, and the sea represents the illimitable subconscious powers of human nature—and Phaedra came across the sea from Crete as Aphrodite from Cyprus. For the moment Aphrodite's

function is to present the prologue. Euripides likes a prologue that sets
the scene; if we are to know all, a divinity must tell us, and Aphrodite
does; Euripides abjures the more obvious forms of surprise. Hippolytus has scorned her; Hippolytus must be punished. He enjoys the company (a key word) of Artemis. When he visited Athens, Theseus's
young wife fell helplessly in love with him. Theseus is spending a year
at Trozen to expiate an offense and with Hippolytus nearby her love
has become a wasting disease. It must be revealed. Theseus will curse
his son. Hippolytus will die. Phaedra will die too. Aphrodite is Power
without Mercy. "Today he looks his last upon the light" (57).

Enter from stage-right Hippolytus with a hunting song, attended by
a secondary chorus of his hunt. They ignore Aphrodite's statue and
gather before the statue of Artemis and sing a hymn in her honor, a
hymn that contrasts more frighteningly with Aphrodite's somber
words because it echoes them (cf. 2, 4, 15, 17). Hippolytus lays a
garland on the statue in one of the most exquisitely lovely speeches in
Greek tragedy:

> For you, my lady, I have wreathed this garland
> and brought it from a virgin meadow,
> where no shepherd thinks to feed his flocks,
> no steel comes, only the bee
> in spring passes through the virgin meadow,
> and Modesty waters the flowers from a running stream.
> Only those who, without instruction, show in their nature
> complete and utter self-discipline
> may gather flowers there. The impure are forbidden.
> O my beloved lady, receive this crown
> for your golden hair from a reverent hand.
> Alone among humans I enjoy this privilege,
> to be with you and converse with you,
> hearing your voice, though never seeing your face.
> So I have begun my life's race. So let me reach the finish. (73)

Innocent words to all appearance, yet charged with meaning for the
play. For the inland meadow is to be invaded by the sea. The word
"virgin" will be flung back tauntingly at Hippolytus by Theseus
(949). The bee will reappear as the very symbol of Aphrodite (564);

in some parts the great fertility goddess of the east had priestesses called "bees," and Sir William Ramsay argued that the protuberances on her statue are not a multiplicity of breasts but the ova of the bee. Modesty, *aidos*, the sense of shame is the dominant power in the mind of Phaedra (385); self-discipline, *sophronein, sophrosune*, dominates Hippolytus, and we shall see that each violates what he professes. "Untaught," he thinks he has nothing to learn, but Phaedra comes to see differently (731). And the end of Hippolytus's life, to come that day, will be as the beginning. Conceived in violence, he will end in violence.

An old retainer speaks, hesitantly: "Prince!—the title Lord is reserved for gods" (88). It is a brilliant touch. The correlative of *lord* is *slave*. The pious old man puts himself as slave in the gods' hands; yes, but the gods whom Euripides personifies do treat men as slaves, and we are in their absolute power. Hippolytus is reasonable, courteous. We are trained to hate pride, says the old man. Of course, says Hippolytus, a proud *man* is detestable. Then what of a proud goddess? He refers to Aphrodite; the effect of the words is slightly odd, and is meant to be, for Hippolytus in reality does hate Aphrodite.

Here he gives four answers. First, he keeps away from her because he is chaste. This is reasonable, but elements other than reason help to form our nature. Second, he says that different gods suit different men. This implies that he has chosen and rejected. Third, as the old man tries to break off, Hippolytus says, "I have no love for gods worshiped by night" (106); his repression breaks through, as always when we snap or shout in argument; he takes the old man's concern for Aphrodite as meaning "renounce your chastity." So, finally, he himself now breaks off, and his final words—"Your Aphrodite? No! To me she is nothing at all!"—are theological blasphemy and psychological disaster. They will be accompanied by an effective gesture of contumely toward the statue at the door; the old retainer tries to compensate for this in a short act of homage.

The chorus of local women enters, and with them the Phaedra theme for the moment replaces the Hippolytus theme. The contrast is emphasized by their entry from stage-left; the huntsmen came and left by the other entry. Their first word recalls the sea motif, Aphrodite's element, yet reveals that place beyond to which they will seek escape (732). They turn to the queen's illness: the mood is almost one of gossip, but there are subtle undertones that have been carefully analyzed by Grube. Is she possessed by Pan or the Corybants, they ask? (She is possessed, but not by them.) Has she neglected sacrifices to Artemis? (No, Hippolytus has to Aphrodite.) Is Theseus unfaithful? (No, his wife is.) Has she had bad news from Crete? (Not exactly news, but hereditary unnatural love is the curse of Crete.) Is it some woman's disease or woman's madness? (Yes, but not what they think.) The reminder of the Cretan curse brings in a subtle psychological point. Phaedra is what she is, or thinks she is, because of an inherited taint. But what of Hippolytus? He too is the product of lust, Theseus's lust, but he has reacted in the opposite way and has accepted his mother's Amazonian chastity.

Phaedra is now carried out, near to death from weakness. But her weakness is subtly conceived. Hazel Barnes has written provocatively but legitimately:

> Phaedra's conflict is waged in bad faith. First of all, she will not admit to herself that fear of betrayal is balanced by a hope of what betrayal might win. Secondly, she plays the game in such a way that she can persuade herself that she has never willingly confessed her love but was compelled by extreme forces. From the beginning her conduct and words are calculated to make further inquiry inevitable. Her resolve to die by fasting (in itself an overreaction) is certain to attract attention. It enables Phaedra to think that she has chosen death in preference to wrongdoing; yet it keeps her alive in case the situation should change. In other words she is not so much ill as the result of her repressed love as she is making herself ill as a way of expressing her love and in order to be forced to speak it openly. (p. 86)

She is Hippolytus's stepmother, but she is not, of course, old enough to be his mother; she would have married as a young girl, and is younger than Hippolytus or of like age. With her is her nurse, gruff, roughly affectionate, puzzled, and ready to do anything to save Phaedra. She is of the earth, earthy, with a taste for homely philosophy. She intones as Phaedra's couch is set, no doubt close to Aphrodite's statue, and Euripides characteristically gives her powerful words:

> Man's life is filled with sorrow;
>   there's no relief from trouble.
> Is there anything dearer than life?
> If so, it's veiled in dark clouds.
> Clearly we are blind in our passion
> for any glint of light on earth.
> We know no other life.
> We have no proof of what lies underground.
>   We rely on empty tales. (189)

Phaedra is half-delirious. Falstaff, if we accept the emendation, "babbled o' green fields," and Phaedra babbles of mountains, because, as we recognize, her mind is on Hippolytus. It is over-subtle of one critic to suggest that she babbles of Hippolytus because her mind is on mountains. Then she realizes the danger of saying too much and relapses into silence. A puzzled interchange between the nurse and the chorus follows. The nurse turns back to Phaedra, and the sea image returns as she pleads with the girl to be moistened or softened by her words, not stubborn like the sea (303). She happens to mention Hippolytus. Phaedra exclaims at the name, and realizes that she has given herself away, though the nurse has not in fact discerned the truth. But the nurse is on the scent. Phaedra alludes to her mother's love for a bull and her sister Ariadne's desertion of Dionysus for Theseus (a less-familiar version of the myth); she is deserting Theseus for Hippolytus. She is reluctant to mention the name of Hippolytus and speaks as if she cannot remember it; the nurse prompts her, and the truth comes out without her uttering the word. And the nurse says, "That there Cypris never was a god, but something on a higher plane than gods, and she's done for her, me, and house after house" (359). Even she collapses into silence as the chorus sings sympathetically, bringing back the Cretan theme. Now that the thing is out, Phaedra is calm and collected. Her opening words merit close attention. Evil, she says, comes from will, not ignorance; from here Ovid took his *video meliora proboque, deteriora sequor*. It is Paul's insight against that of Socrates and Plato, who claimed that virtue and knowledge are one. We are distracted from right, says Phaedra, by indolence or pleasure; her ideas of distracting pleasures seem odd—conversation and leisure—and are but another reminder of the limited life of respectable Athenian women in the fifth century.

And there is shame, *aidos*. Shame is of two kinds. One is a dream-escape, harmless, but too easy. The other is the open recognition of her complex and mastery of it; this she has found too hard. So the sense of shame that seemed to save her destroys her. In fact Phaedra does violence to her sense of shame in the name of that sense of shame, as Hippolytus does violence to that virtuous moderation, which is self-discipline in the name of that same saving grace of *sophrosune*. Phaedra tells how she has tried to conquer her passion by self-control. She does not believe in free sex and double-faced lives of deceit. As she says this, she invokes Lady Cypris of the Sea (415), turning to the statue at her side. If she cannot control herself, she would rather die for her husband and children.

Euripides throws in a tribute to Athens. The word "freedom" today is enough to win a cheer, whether in Russia, America, Britain, or emergent Africa; Euripides genuinely believed in it, knew how war erodes it, and makes his witness. The chorus comments on the beauty of self-discipline (*sophrosune*); they use the adjective, as the noun is intractable in iambic verse (431). The nurse now stages a comeback. Second thoughts are wisest; this is a Euripidean twist, for Hippolytus and Theseus need this advice and Phaedra does not. Phaedra is in love. It has happened to others before, and will happen to others again. Then follows a key passage. When Cypris is in full surge there is no resisting her (443).

> Cypris strides across the sky, she is found
> in the sea's swelling wave. All things are born from her.
> She sows the seed. She grants the desire
> from which all creatures on earth take their being. (447)

Here we glimpse Power, creative, amoral, ineluctable. The sensible thing, says the nurse, is to give way. "You've fallen in; how do you expect to swim out?" (470). She is not being cynical, she is a woman of the world and cares intensely for Phaedra. The chorus, which has just approved chastity, says that this is good, sound, practical advice;

the contradiction is so glaring that one suspects satirical intent in the poet. This destroys house after house, protests Pheadra, in echo of the nurse's words. What Pheadra needs, adds the nurse devastatingly, is not fine words, but the man. She uses the word for the pride (*semnon*), which has earlier been seen as detestable in man and fearful in a god (490, cf. 93, 99). It destroys Hippolytus, but the nurse's abandonment of it destroys Phaedra. It's no use moralizing, she goes on; morals or not, Phaedra is feeling the passion, and it has become a matter of life and death. The nurse begins to speak of love philters. Phaedra half-suspects that she may betray her to Hippolytus. "Leave that to me," says the nurse (521), and goes out with a prayer to Lady Cypris of the Sea, the very title Phaedra used earlier (522, cf. 415), honoring Aphrodite's statue as she goes in.

The scene has been instinct with the power of Sex, and there follows a mighty choral ode to Love, mightier than the one in *Medea*, standing alongside those in *Antigone* and *The Women of Troy*. The ode is carefully patterned; *hiesin* (533) matches *hienta* (543), *bacchan* (550) *bacchou* (560), *phonioisi* (552) *phonioi* (562); most powerful is the matching of "Love Love" (*eros eros*) at the beginning of the first stanza (525) by "Vain Vain" (*allos allos*) in the corresponding place in the antistrophe (535). The song is of the power of Love, here compared with fire, for Euripides is too skilled to overplay the sea image. This ode places Aphrodite at the center of the play, as we have the visual image of her statue towering over the couch where Phaedra weakly lies. Artemis does not stir, except in a conventional oath, and Hippolytus's words as he leaves for exile, till she appears in person at the end; but her statue is also there. For the moment the triumph is Aphrodite's.

Across their song bursts an agonized cry from Phaedra. As the chorus hushes, the angry voices of Hippolytus and the nurse are heard within the house. The chorus breaks into excited dochmiacs. Phaedra is panic-stricken; she knows she has been betrayed. She is an invalid, half-dead with weakness. She sits up on her couch, then perhaps struggles to her feet to sink and shrink back again. It is too late. The scene that follows is one of the most brilliant even Euripides conceived. Hippolytus storms past her—without a word *to her*. He says all he thinks of her, but to her not a word, as she cowers away from the lash of his tongue. The scene contains Euripides's most notorious line: "My tongue swore—but not my mind" (612). It is dramatically superb, and an odd weapon to use against Euripides, since Hippolytus does not break his oath. As well condemn the author of Job for encouraging his readers to curse.

In this scene the sea image reasserts itself when Hippolytus says, "I'll flush your filthy words from my ears with floods of water" (653). He intends the pure inland streams, but the intensity of his passionate revulsion from passion leads him to the language of a storm at sea. The revulsion *is* passionate, the purity pathological. He cannot bear to be touched even by an old woman (606). Deep down he is not chaste but frightened of sex; hence the obsessive need for cleansing. He dismisses all women, with a special attack on bluestockings; in his eyes the only virtuous women are the helpless sort who have not the brains to be anything else. Like Jason he wishes that propagation had been organized without sex and without women (618). Many Athenians would sympathize with the superior attitude to women. But Hippolytus, like Jason, is wrong, the more wrong because he is not a contemptible villain but a self-righteous prig. Here the last interchange between Hippolytus and the nurse is telling. "No one crooked is my friend," cries Hippolytus, and the nurse answers, "Be charitable, lad; to err is human." The immoral nurse is right; the moral Hippolytus is wrong. Woe to you churchgoers; the quislings and prostitutes go into the kingdom of God before you!

Hippolytus sweeps out threatening to bring his father, and Phaedra breaks her silence in a song of despair. It is brilliantly contrived by Euripides, for it corresponds with the brief song three hundred lines earlier (362) with which the chorus greeted the revelation of her love for Hippolytus; the effect is unique in tragedy. Then Phaedra turns on the nurse, who is impenitent and philosophical; like any doctor's prescription her scheme would have been approved if it had worked. Her high-flown language creates a mild effect of relief, if not fully comic relief: "Expatiating. Not disciplined—that's me" (704). She does indeed lack the self-discipline that is *sophrosune*, but so, for all his professions, does Hippolytus. Phaedra silences her, swears the chorus to a secrecy that they observe, and shows a strength and dignity of purpose that overcomes her weakness of body. She leaves with the haunting words:

> I cannot win. Love is ruthless.
> But in my death I shall become someone else's
> curse. He will learn not to glory
> in my doom. He will catch the same
> disease as me, and learn to avoid excess. (727)

Hippolytus thought, and still thinks that he has nothing to learn (79).

At this moment of high tragedy, what can the chorus sing that is not bathos? Euripides's answer is sheer inspiration, and he produces what some have claimed as the most beautiful of all the verbal music of Greek tragedy:

> O to find some beetling refuge!
> For a god to turn me to a winged bird
> among the flying flocks. (732)

"It is just the emotion that was in our own hearts," wrote Gilbert Murray, "the cry for escape to some place, however sad, that is still beautiful: to the poplar grove by the Adriatic where his sisters weep for Phaethon; or, at least, as the song continues and grows bolder, to some place that has happiness as well as beauty."

> O to reach that headland with its apples,
> where the daughters of the West sing, and where
> the sea-going sailor finds
> no path through the purple waters. (742)

The very song, the thought, the dream, the danced mime of flight, is itself an escape. It is one form of Phaedra's *aidos*. The reassertion here of the sea image is itself momentarily reassuring. For we must not think of the Western Sea as belonging to the stormy realm of Aphrodite. This is the river that encircles the earth in Greek mythology; this is the place of escape for those who can rise on wings above the sea. Here the proud frontiers of the sky (*semnon*, cf. 93, 99) are not menacing in their pride. Then the real world asserts itself. For the thought of the sea leads to the thought of Phaedra's ship from Crete; they landed at Athens and the sailors knotted the ends of their ropes to tie up the ship—knotted the ends of their ropes? A ghastly prophetic vision comes of what is happening within the palace.

The music has scarcely died away when a voice is heard from within the house, the voice of the actor who played the nurse, whether still in character hardly matters. The voice screams that their vision is true. There is a tremendous cry of women within—and Theseus enters from stage-right with a garland on his head. The chorus tells him the news and, true to their oath, no more. Theseus throws away his garland, ill-omened and inappropriate, and our eyes are riveted on Hippolytus's garland, which still adorns the statue of Artemis. The body is wheeled out and Theseus sings a song of death. The chorus longed to fly over the sea like a bird (732); Phaedra's ship had come like a bird but an unhappy bird (759); now Phaedra has escaped like a bird (828), and a sea of troubles is bursting about Theseus (822). He values her companionship (838). The word is unexpected; Hippolytus and most Athenians did not so think of women, and it is hard to imagine that this Theseus did, but it reminds us of the companionship between Hippolytus and Artemis (19). Theseus has been too busy being a king to enjoy much companionship with Phaedra or Hippolytus. "Your death has destroyed much more than yourself," he cries, and his self-pitying words are truer than he knows (839). Then Theseus espies a message in Phaedra's hands; the chorus suspects and fears. It is a false accusation that Hippolytus has raped her. Theseus bursts into a great cry of rage and invokes on his son the first of three curses given him by Poseidon. It is typical of Euripides's dramatic power that he here alters the myth. In the old story it was the third that was here used, but Euripides makes it the first so that Theseus does not know whether it will work, and the change from wishes to curses heightens the drama. The curse of Poseidon is the curse of the sea. Theseus is not a mere adjunct to the plot, and he is far from being the idealized democratic sovereign that he sometimes appears. We may not forget that Hippolytus and Phaedra (a war-captive) are, in different ways, the victims of Theseus's aggressiveness.

Onto this scene, with his hunt, swings Hippolytus, virginal, innocent, self-satisfied. He greets his father without warmth. We must remember throughout—we are reminded of it enough—that he is a bastard, the Amazon's son. We must imagine him, as Grube says, abandoned by his father and ashamed of his mother; there are parallels with Edmund in *King Lear*. Artemis is for him a mother-substitute, and Phaedra, who has usurped his mother's place, brings in an added resentment and no doubt her approaches add a revulsion from incest to the morbid fear of sex. He raises a metaphorical eyebrow at the corpse, but his calmness is unshaken; we can almost see him congratulating himself that he need not break his oath. His self-righteousness has no pity for Phaedra. Theseus is taken aback. Only when the direct word of accusation comes is Hippolytus's self-sufficiency shaken, and he covers his head, horrified not by the account of crime but by the thought of sex crime. Theseus makes it clear that he will not listen to protestations of innocence. This is another reason why Hippolytus keeps his oath; it is no use breaking it. Principle and expediency walk hand in hand. Euripides wants to make it clear that the most pharisaically upright of us act from mixed motives.

Theseus's attack extends to the self-righteousness of Orphics. Hippolytus is not an Orphic; he is a huntsman and they vegetarians, but it is a powerful gibe. Further, Euripides cannot resist putting into Theseus's mouth a rejection of the twofold standard of morality by which a man sows his wild oats, while a woman becomes culpably damaged goods:

> Young men I know
> are no steadier than women. (967)

Theseus ends by banishing Hippolytus. He has already put the curse of death on him, but he does not know that it will work.

The scene is a typical Euripidean debate, and Hippolytus's reply follows the formal structure of rhetoric, from the proemium, with narration omitted as unnecessary, through the confirmatory and refutatory evidence to the conclusion. It is a masterpiece of characterization. He addresses Theseus as if he were a public meeting and actually says, "Unaccustomed as I am to public speaking . . ." (968). He tells how virtuous, moderate, self-disciplined, *sophron,* he is—the quality Phaedra has rightly told us he does not possess. There is a familiar anecdote of the husband who claimed, "I have an utterly virtuous wife: I keep her locked up." Hippolytus keeps his sex locked up. He is intemperately temperate; as Grube puts it, he "mistakes prohibition for 'moderation' and asceticism for self-control." His body is pure of sexual intercourse; he knows nothing about the act except what he has heard people say or seen in pictures: there is a slight suggestion of prurience. He is not keen to see, he says; he has a virgin soul; but his eyes evidently strayed. He protests his innocence, but keeps his oath. He prays that if he is guilty, neither sea nor land may receive his body (1030), and ends with the pregnant words:

> Without the virtue of self-control she kept her virtue.
> I have the virtue: much good it has done me!

The word is *sophronein*. Phaedra could not keep her passion continuously under control, so she crushed it by killing herself. Hippolytus had kept his emotions under control (by crushing them) but the excess of his response drove her to retaliate. Here endeth the first lesson.

In what follows we realize Theseus's uncertainty. Hippolytus says that if he had been in Theseus's position he would have killed the offender himself, and Theseus's answer is a shade too slick: "Death's too swift" (1045). Hippolytus is to be banished beyond the sea, even beyond the chorus's western refuge. Hippolytus says, "Submit the matter to augury," and Theseus shows a Euripidean rationalism about augury. His words against omens are those of Hippolytus against Aphrodite earlier, and Euripides takes a Shavian pleasure in making his own views dramatic *hybris*. The curse is not mentioned, for it is dramatically important to have a scene in which Theseus may change, though we, the spectators, have the knowledge of the gods that he not merely will not but cannot. The sentence of banishment is reiterated and Hippolytus pauses before Artemis's statue to say good-by. We may imagine, if we will, some business before the statute of Aphrodite; his last word is of his own virtuous moderation (*sophrosune*).

The choral ode that follows offers a curious problem. The strophes are sung by men and the antistrophes by women. This is unique in tragedy, but Euripides is willing to be unique. It raises interesting problems of choreography. The contrast is in fact effective as the drawing together of what we may call Phaedra's chorus and Hippolytus's chorus.

One of Hippolytus's attendants now comes in with the news of his death or near-death; the news, by a characteristic Euripidean touch, is momentarily held up. "Poseidon, you were really my father!" exclaims Theseus (1169). The words are pointed, for Theseus also is Hippolytus's father with the same destructive onesidedness. The account of the disaster is magnificent, and Sophocles in *Electra* paid it the tribute of imitation. It is vivid; persuasive even in its supernatural element; frightening; and with a clear symbolism. The bull is the symbol of male sexual aggressiveness. The foam of the sea is the foam that surrounds the semen, the *aphro* of Aphrodite.

The most powerful image is Hippolytus's own horses. They too are a sex symbol, the power he has kept under control, which escapes control. But it is an ambiguous image, for the horse is also a symbol of virginity, and Artemis or Dictynna patronized horse racing, and Phaedra scornfully spoke of the love of horses shown by Hippolytus's Amazon mother (581). Hippolytus's very name means "releaser of horses"; yet he does not, till they escape disastrously from his control. Perhaps from here Plato took his image of the human soul, or perhaps his is an independent expression of the same archetype. Picasso has made splendid use of the confrontation of bull and horse. And behind all is the dominant, triumphant image of the sea. At the end the messenger asserts his belief in Hippolytus's innocence, and Theseus steels himself to a certain ambivalence. He is neither rejoiced nor grieved, and orders the dying Hippolytus to be brought before him.

So we wait for Hippolytus, all our sympathy now with him—and the chorus sings to the glory of Aphrodite, who has destroyed him. We see why, for the rest of the play will belong to Hippolytus and Artemis; yet in a sense it is Aphrodite's play, and we see her in this song not as destructive but as the eternal ruler of youth. Further, at the start of the play Aphrodite appeared, and her appearance was followed by a hymn to Artemis. At the end of the play Artemis is to appear, and her appearance is preceded by a hymn to Aphrodite.

Our eyes rove to the entrance to our left (stage-right) where we expect Hippolytus to appear, when the master dramatist surprises us again. Instead of Hippolytus a figure is speaking from the top of the palace. It is Artemis, as we know from her bow and arrows before she speaks. She addresses Theseus peremptorily: "You there" (1283). The final scene, as S. M. Adams has shown, falls into three movements. The first deals with Theseus. Artemis breaks down his *hybris*, tells him the truth, rebukes him for acting on unconfirmed rumor, and reduces him to pity. In the second, Hippolytus is carried in, broken in body, unchanged in character, full of self-pity, boasting his piety and virtue, still boasting his disciplined moderation, the quality he does not possess; if he had possessed it the tragedy would not have happened. As he lies on the stretcher he is the reflection of Phaedra on the couch, brought to the same pass by the same power. In the third movement Hippolytus comes to enlightenment and a gentle death. Hippolytus has never thought of anyone but himself. He complains of his treatment by "my own horses, whom I fed" (1240, 1355) and protests to Zeus, "I was the most pious of mortals and you killed me. Why?" (1363). He cared nothing for Phaedra. Now he cares something for Theseus. As *The Iliad* is the story of how Achilles learned to pity, so *Hippolytus* is the story of how Hippolytus learned to pity. But this is not the conversion familiar in Restoration comedy; Euripides is far too profound a student of human nature for that. Hippolytus remains a self-satisfied prig. He complains that Artemis leaves their companionship too early (1441). He tells his father to pray for other sons like himself (1453). He breaks through his self-righteousness self-righteously. But something has stirred within him. S. M. Adams wrote:

What Artemis does for Hippolytus she does also for the play. Pain and resentment rather than fear are, I think, the emotions aroused by the body of the play, and the emphasis laid on the other element in the tragic catharsis is vital to the success of the piece as tragedy. It is not enough that a poet should profoundly understand and sympathise with his characters; he must make his audience do so; and when he makes his action turn on human weakness rather than on human strength, his task is much more difficult— until he secures an audience more interested in weakness than strength.

The scene between Hippolytus and Artemis has been variously interpreted; I cannot accept the note of cynicism that has come into some modern accounts. It is a scene of surpassing beauty, and is itself the justification of the *deus ex machina*. For Artemis is not needed to unravel the plot; she is there for her own sake. Hippolytus cannot see her, for she is hidden by the building, but he senses her presence and hears her. What ensues is the nearest thing to a love scene in Greek tragedy, but it is between goddess and mortal; it is not inappropriate to think of those mystic women who have taken Christ as their bridegroom. Then:

ARTEMIS: I charge you: do not hate your father,
            Hippolytus. You have your destiny in death.
            Good-by. I may not look upon the dead.
            I may not pollute my eyes with the last gasps of the dying.
HIPPOLYTUS: Good-by. Go in peace, blest virgin.
            It is easy for you to end our long companionship.
            At your request I drop all bitterness against my father.
            In the past I have always followed your commands. (1435)

It is unspeakably beautiful. All the pain and pride, the striving and suffering are seen in a cosmic context, and death is swallowed up in eternity. For this is the peaceful close of Greek tragedy, and the goddess heightens its effect, and because our tears flow—yes, our tears are meant to flow—we are not far from the realm where all tears are wiped away.

22. *HECABE*

Hecabe, more familiarly known in English by its Latinized name *Hecuba*, is a somewhat neglected play, though occasionally performed by schools with a taste for the grimmer aspects of drama. It was immensely popular in the Middle Ages, when it formed with *The Women of Phoenicia* and *Orestes* a triad of plays for prescribed reading in the Byzantine schools. It made a vivid impact on Dante:

> Ecuba trista, misera e cattiva,
> > poscia che vide Polissena morta,
> > e del suo Polidoro in su la riva
> del mar si fu la dolorosa accorta,
> > forsennata latrò sì come cane:
> > tanto il dolor le fe' la mente torta. (*Inf.* 30.16–21)

Stiblinus accounted it the greatest of all Euripides's plays. Erasmus translated it into Latin, and it became almost the canon of classical propriety for the French seventeenth-century dramatists. We would be

unlikely to elevate it so high today; but its rejection was largely due
to the limitations of nineteenth-century criticism, and the play may
eventually be restored to the favor it once enjoyed. Recent criticism, for
example, has examined the play in the light of the ethical values inherent in the plot and its treatment: the whole theme of *charis* (favor
granted and consequent gratitude) in the interrelations between Hecabe, Odysseus, Agamemnon, and Polymestor.

The exact date of the play is uncertain. Some lines were parodied
by Aristophanes in *The Clouds.* This comedy was produced, unsuccessfully, in 423, and this in itself strongly suggests a date of 424 for
Hecabe. But Aristophanes revised *The Clouds,* though the revised version was not produced at the time, and we cannot be sure that the
parodies were not introduced at the time of revision, which would
make possible a date of 423 or 422 for *Hecabe.* Certainly a date in the
late 420s accords reasonably with stylistic and metrical evaluation. It
also reminds us that the background to the play is war, and that the
war had already lasted about twice as long as the World War of 1914–
1918. We do not know what other plays were presented with it, though
The Cyclops might have been.

The opening is splendid theater. Ghosts were not unfamiliar in
Greek tragedy; Aeschylus used them in two of his surviving plays.
Still, for a ghost to speak the prologue was a decided innovation, and
one imagines that Euripides made the most of it. How the ghost was
dressed we do not know; one guesses at a pallid mask and either dark
or grey wraith-like robes with black wings. He seems to appear on the
crane, rising from behind the stage building and hovering over the
scene, or possibly emerging from a trap door in the stage building onto
the upper roof (1,30). His figure is slight, a boy too young to bear
arms. He speaks in somber words of his passage from the dark world
of the dead, and then identifies himself as Polydorus, son of Hecabe and
Priam, smuggled away for safety to Thrace, and murdered and thrown
into the sea by his father's guest-friend Polymestor out of greed for
gold. In his supernatural state he knows some but not all of the future.

The spirit of Achilles has checked the departure of the Greeks from
the fallen city of Troy, demanding the sacrifice of the boy's sister
Polyxene at his tomb. This, the spirit knows, will be granted. He knows

too that he will be washed ashore to his mother's presence for burial: the two children will lie side by side. But of the fate of Polymestor, or Hecabe—nothing. The speech is effectively unemotional till Hecabe stirs in the tent, which the stage building represents, and the ghost breaks into sobbing at her enslaved state, but behind it is the repudiation of all the violence of men, of which war is a part.

Hecabe, yesterday a queen, today a slave, limps out from the tent with the help of some other women; she chants in anapaests as she comes, and her perturbation is represented by an unusual succession of short syllables (62). When she cries "O lightning-flash of Zeus, O darkness of night" (68), we feel that she is invoking not two powers but one, that the brilliant power of Zeus is darkness for her, and she is living in a blackness of storm and night illuminated only by destruction. She calls on Earth "mother of dark-winged dreams" (71); this is dramatically superb, for the dead rest in earth, and she too is the mother of dark-winged dreams, for man in his ephemerality is, as Pindar puts it, but a dream of a shadow. She has dreamed of her children Polyxene and Polydorus ("the only anchor left to my house" 80); she has seen a fawn dragged from her lap by a wolf, and Achilles's ghost demanding some honor from the women of Troy. Our knowledge of the dream's meaning reinforces the pathos of her uncertainty.

One half of the meaning is swiftly revealed. The chorus of more captive women escape from their own tents and file in. They bring her the news that the Greeks, under guidance from Odysseus, have in full assembly resolved to sacrifice Polyxene to Achilles, though Agamemnon in his love for her sister Cassandra opposed the motion. To plead with Agamemnon is her only chance; they compare Polyxene with a foal (142). This choral entry is unusual and among surviving plays unique in providing information that is normally derived from a messenger or one of the characters in that rôle. Like Hecabe they are excited and disturbed, and their chant contains a unique rhythmic effect in a dactyl and anapaest successively (♩♪♪♪♪♩) giving a rare succession of short notes breathless to sing and complex to dance. Hecabe bursts into an incoherent torrent of grief, and calls Polyxene out from the tent. She joins in the song:

> Oh!
> Mother, mother, what was that cry? What news
> that you start me from within
>   like a bird from a covert? (177)

She receives the news, and her first thought is for her mother. The animal image returns with rare complexity as she compares herself seemingly with a lion cub from the mountains but then changes it to a lamb or calf bred in upland pastures (205). The mood of the song is shown by the occurrence of the word "piteous" four times in as many short lines. But for herself she chooses death above a life of misery.

Hecabe does not have the chance to plead with Agamemnon, as Odysseus arrives to fetch the girl. He speaks bluntly and in formal language of the Greeks' decision, and advises the queen to submit; of his own part in the decision he says nothing. Hecabe asks to speak; she reminds Odysseus that he once owed his life to her, but he is self-satisfied with his own glib inventions and blind to any claims of gratitude; this is the theme of *charis,* favor and gratitude. She speaks powerfully, but her emotion is stronger than her reason. Biting *t* and *d* sounds snap from her (249, 269–272). Her attack on demagogy is not likely to win Odysseus. She suggests as an alternative a bull (Polyxene has called herself a calf)—or Helen. And here the spirit of vengeance that dominates her later in the play shows itself. She falls before him in an excellent tableau, as he once fell before her. Polyxene thought of her mother, but Hecabe thinks of herself. Yet her words have power.

> There are dead enough.
> In her I find joy, forget sorrow,
> know comfort for all that was mine—
> my city, my nurse, my staff, my guide. (278)

She knows that Odysseus can sway the Assembly "even with false arguments" (293)—if he will. She is on Odysseus's own ground now, but she does not persuade.

Odysseus is reasonable; he will save a life for a life, for his own, Hecabe's but not Polyxene's. If the dead are not honored, men will have no motive inducing them to face death in battle. There are women

in Greece no better off than Hecabe. The logic is impeccable, granted
the premises. But, the premises removed, we are left with the propo-
sitions that war hurts victors and vanquished alike, and that if we
eliminate the spurious glory there is nothing left. Hecabe makes no
further plea. She turns to Polyxene and implores her to pour out her
supplication as does the nightingale's throat (377); but the nightingale's song is a song of mourning not of supplication. And now
Odysseus is stirred, not by pity but by policy. He expects Polyxene to
fall at his feet and reach up as a suppliant to touch his hand and beard,
as Hecabe has done; her supplication might blind him. So in a second
tableau, doubly effective because it does not mirror the first, he puts
his hand firmly under his cloak and turns his head away and up—and
she does not move, but leaves him looking foolish. Polyxene is beautifully drawn; she stands alongside Alcestis, Macaria, and Iphigeneia
(in *Iphigeneia at Aulis*) as redemptive women, gentle, firm, attractive,
courageous. Jean Anouilh, seeking the person in mythology who becomes what she becomes by her own free choice, selected Antigone. Yet
Polyxene is really more apposite:

> I will follow you because I must, and because
> I want to die. (346)

She is an existentialist heroine—

> No. My eyes are free. I freely renounce
> the light of day. (367)

—and bears the seal of nobility on her. Hecabe offers her own life,
which Odysseus has expressly spared, but he will have none of it. He
is not inhumane, but policy prevails (375). She pleads furiously:

> HECABE: I'll die with my daughter. I insist.
> ODYSSEUS: I hadn't realized I was the slave, you the masters.
> HECABE: I'll cling to her like ivy to an oak tree. (396)

The image is free from triteness; usually the young ivy clings to the
old oak. Polyxene is not free from normal human emotions, which she
expresses. A bitter little pun follows:

POLYXENE: Farewell, mother. Farewell to Cassandra from me.
HECABE: Others fare well. It is not for a mother. (426)

She makes reference to their hopes in Polydorus, invokes the daylight
for the last time, and goes with Odysseus, leaving Hecabe prostrate
and desolate. But vengeance breaks through grief and the scene ends
with an appalling outburst of hatred against Helen.

The choral song that follows is the finest in the play, and is worthy
to stand alongside all but a very few others in Euripides. The captives
call on the winds and wonder where the winds will carry them. It is
part of Euripides's genius not to refer to Polyxene or even to Hecabe.
This is a tragedy of a total situation, not of an individual.

Now comes Talthybius, the Greek herald, elderly, bluff, sympathetic,
and excellently characterized. He brings the news of Polyxene's death
and an account of the way of it, and an invitation from Agamemnon
to the mother to share in the burial. Again he uses of the girl the word
that naturally means a calf (526, cf. 206). He describes the scene as
Neoptolemus prepares to sacrifice her, and her reassertion of freedom:

> "You Greeks who have laid waste my city,
> I go to my death freely. No one is to touch
> my body. I will bare my neck with a good heart.
> I die in freedom. Let me be free,
> in the name of the gods, as you kill me. I am a princess.
> I scorn to earn the name of slave by my death." (547)

So she prepared freely for the sword, taking care even in death to
fall modestly—a sentiment that duly impressed Ovid and Pliny later.
What is important in this powerful narration is not so much the picture
of Polyxene, for we have seen the girl herself, as the approval of the
Greek GIs. William Arrowsmith puts it well: "And just as Thucydides, by setting his Melian Dialogue on the strategically unimportant
island of Melos, undercuts the Athenian generals' justification of necessity, so Euripides, by introducing Talthybius to pity Hecabe and to
describe the soldiers' admiration of Polyxene's courage, undercuts the
whole force of Odysseus's and Agamemnon's arguments, all based on

the mistaken premise of the insensitivity of the mass to moral considerations."

"Dreadful suffering has spurted out on the house of Priam," comments the chorus with the vision of the blood before their eyes (583).
Hecabe's response is reflective and intellectual:

> It's strange. Poor soil,
> granted good conditions from heaven, bears a fine harvest,
> and good soil, lacking all that it needs to have,
> can produce a poor crop. With men it's different.
> The scoundrel is never anything but rotten,
> the saint a saint. Misfortune never
> corrupts his character. He's consistently good.
> What varies? Heredity? Environment?
> Goodness can be taught by decent
> education. Anyone who learns that lesson
> can recognize evil, using the standard of good.
> My mind's firing arrows at random. (592)

Some have ridiculed these words as sophistic and out of character.
Yet she is a queen; she has a mind and a trained mind; and the reflections are appropriate enough. Above all Euripides is showing that in-
tellectualism is no proof against the bestialization that finally wins.
The German intellectuals of the 1930s are not without responsibility
for Nazism; the sophists did not save Athens from moral degradation.
Now Hecabe's authority asserts itself. She, a slave, commands Talthybius to tell the Greeks to leave the body untouched, while she sends
one of her older women to fetch sea water for the ritual bathing. We
recall Diogenes, to be sold as a slave, calling, "Anyone want to buy a
master?" Hecabe goes into the tent for some gewgaws for the burial.

The choral song is one of the shortest, with less than a hundred
words. Again there is no mention of Polyxene or Hecabe; the tragedy
is seen in its wider setting. Their own calamities are traced to Paris,
and the immeasurable extent of human responsibility receives full emphasis; one man's folly can destroy a whole nation. So comes the wonderful conclusion:

> Yes, and by Eurotas's splendid stream
> some Spartan woman sits at home in tears,

> and a grey-haired mother
> whose children have died
> beats her head and tears her cheeks,
> rends till her nails drip with blood. (650)

This before an audience that has been at war with Sparta for almost a decade.

The old attendant had taken some younger women with her to the shore. They now return with a small body wrapped in a cloak, which they lay in the orchestra as the chorus crowds around. Her opening words contain an extended image:

> Women, where is Hecabe, tried in so many contests,
> victorious over every man and woman
> in sufferings? No one shall deprive her of that prize. (657)

Hecabe comes out; her thoughts fly to Cassandra; the body is uncovered, and she recognizes Polydorus. She bursts into a lament in which the cooler rhythms of speech are mingled with frenzied dochmiacs. Now she recognizes the fulfillment of her dream. She cannot fail to blame Polymestor for the crime, as he should have been the boy's protector, and she guesses at the motive of greed for gold. Agamemnon now arrives in person to see why Hecabe has not come to bury Polyxene. Hecabe is standing by Polydorus with her back to him; she does not turn. He sees the body and exclaims. Still she deliberates and does not turn. She speaks to herself, addresses herself; of Agamemnon she speaks in the third person. He comes round to her side to see more clearly. Then, with a decisive movement, she wheels on him, drops before him, and reaches out to his knees, his hands, his beard. She unfolds her story in a swift line-for-line exchange. "Ah," says Agamemnon tritely, "what woman born was ever so unfortunate?" "None," she cries, "unless Fortune herself" (785). And now she breaks into a great plea, far more powerful than the words she addressed to Odysseus:

> I may be a slave and weak.
> The gods are strong. Their sovereign, Law,
> is strong. Through Law we acknowledge the gods.
> We live by Law, define right and wrong by Law.

> If Law stands before you and is flouted,
> if there is no penalty for those who murder
> their guests, or ransack temples,
> then there is no equity among mankind. (798)

There is reference here to a great argument of the day. The word for law (*nomos*) means also custom or convention. Right or wrong, it is suggested, and religion too, are matters of conventions. But, unlike those who said that therefore the conventions might be broken with impunity, Hecabe insists that the conventions are the foundations of society. Agamemnon turns away, and she calls on Persuasion, man's only dictator (816). She appeals to Agamemnon's love for Cassandra. She demands vengeance. Agamemnon is as polite as Odysseus, but indecisive where Odysseus was decisive. Polymestor, Priam's guest-friend, is, it turns out, an ally of the Greeks; he is in short playing a double game. Agamemnon is not his own master. The comment of Hecabe, herself a slave, is again reflective and again relevant to its context:

> A free man? There is no such person.
> One is a slave to money, one to fortune.
> Public opinion and fear of the law
> force men to act out of character. (864)

Twenty years later Euripides's admirer Socrates asserted his fredom.

Half scornfully, in the language of a queen, Hecabe says to her owner, "I will set you free" (869). If he will let her act, he need do no more. Agamemnon does not see how women can master men, but Hecabe knows the power of vengeance. Still a queen, she sends an attendant to Polymestor with the message:

> Hecabe, formerly queen of Troy, requires your presence
> on business concerning you as well as her,
> together with your sons; they too must hear
> what she has to say. (891)

Agamemnon will delay the burial of Polyxene so that the children may be cremated together. He goes out. Hecabe motions her attendants into the tent and stands waiting.

Another brilliant choral song follows, only a little inferior to the first, and again masterly in its integration with the whole. The chorus broods over the fallen city, hidden behind a storm cloud of Greeks, shorn of its garland of towers. They recall the night when they thought the Greeks had departed as their husbands lay peaceably and they fixed their hair before a mirror; suddenly the battle cry, and distraught flight to Artemis's altar, and the husband lying dead, and a journey across the sea, glancing hopelessly back to Troy. Then in the final stanza an explosion of hatred against Helen. Euripides uses the song with some skill to convey a movement of thought and theme from Troy to Thrace. The song itself is powerful and offers itself to mimetic dance. There are evocative details: the arrangement of the hair under a netted cap, the flight in a single shift "like some girl from Sparta." The final outburst against Helen echoes the earlier words of Hecabe (265) and prepares us for the ghastly vengeance to come.

No words anticipate Polymestor's arrival. Suddenly he is there, with spears in his hand, and children and bodyguard in attendance. His opening words reveal him for the hypocrite that he is: "Oh my dear Priam! Oh my dear Hecabe!" (953). Hecabe wishes to speak to him privately; seeing only women he readily dismisses his guards. He continues to play on the theme of friendship. She asks after Polydorus, and receives reassurances of his well-being; there is irony in her "My dear friend, your words are in character" (990). He also assures her that the gold is safe (995). The vocabularies of safety and friendship recur through this scene. She arouses his covetousness by telling him of another store of gold and of treasure concealed in her tent. The children are there to know the secret, should anything happen to their father. For a moment he suspects that there may be men inside, but there are only women. "So," says Hecabe,

> when your business here is done you may go
> and take your children where you left my son. (1021)

They go into the tent, where the women attendant on Hecabe can be seen receiving them before the flap closes behind them.

The chorus sings a brief song as they wait; the text is uncertain, but they seem to use an image of Polymestor drowning in a flood of water far from harbor. Suddenly the air rings with a terrible series of screams from Polymestor, lamenting his own blindness and his sons' murder, threatening his tormentors. Hecabe comes out exultant, followed by Polymestor on all fours like an animal, with a new mask representing his blindness; behind him comes the moving platform with the bodies of the children and Hecabe's attendants standing over them; the attendants scatter and engage in a grotesque kind of blindman's buff. Polymestor's language is full of animal imagery; he moves like a beast from the mountains; the Trojans are savage bitches. Then he mixes his images fantastically; he wants to make for his lair like a ship making for harbor. He screams to the Greeks for help, and his mind ranges high to where the baleful constellations sit in the sky, and deep to the rivers of the underworld.

His cries bring Agamemnon, and the smooth tongue of hypocrisy takes over as he calls him "my dearest friend"; it is the very word he used of Priam. But when Agamemnon addresses Hecabe, Polymestor's own desire for revenge on the avenger is uppermost, and he snarls like a wild animal. Agamemnon is cool; he has been preparing himself without quite knowing what was coming; it is the speed and thoroughness that have surprised him rather than the vengeance itself.

The scene that follows is somewhat odd, but it is consummately handled by Euripides. Only a year or two before Sophocles had presented *King Oedipus*. There a messenger's speech preceded and opened the way for the startling appearance of Oedipus blind. Euripides could not reproduce the effect. So the blind man crawls out before he is expected, and then acts, so to say, as his own messenger. Moreover, the "messenger's speech" does not stand on its own; it is the first part of a courtroom scene, one of those debates of which Euripides was supreme master. Polymestor, ever the hypocrite, implies that he killed Polydorus as an enemy to the Greeks. He tells how he was enticed inside the tent, how the women admired his cloak, hampering him, his spears, disarming him, his sons, separating them from him; then suddenly drew daggers and killed the boys, and holding him down put out his eyes with their brooches. The animal imagery returns:

> I sprang
> like a wildcat in pursuit of those murderous bitches. (1172)

This is his reward for killing an enemy of the Greeks, an act that he claims as a *charis* or favor. Women are monsters. Hecabe's response lacks the eloquence of her earlier plea; it does not need it. She has her vengeance, she has Agamemnon's protection, and she has only to point to Polymestor's greed and duplicity, which she does effectively enough. Agamemnon accepts his guilt and the justice of the vengeance. But now Polymestor, with a blind prophet's vision, foresees the transformation of Hecabe into a kind of hellhound and raises consternation in her by prophesying Cassandra's death at Clytemnestra's hands; when he foretells Agamemnon's own death the king orders him to be gagged and deported to some desert island. Hecabe goes to bury her children, the chorus to their slavery. The ending is forceful, but oddly abrupt.

The structure of the play has troubled some critics. Euripides was experimenting with structure, and in *Andromache* and *Heracles*, as in Sophocles's much earlier *Ajax*, we have a similar kind of diptych. The play is not necessarily the worse for that, except on *a priori* views of structure, and some kind of episodic treatment was inevitable. For this play is about the bestialization that violence produces. The animal imagery is not incidental but essential. Violence treats Polyxene as a sacrificial victim; it brings Polymestor to crawling like an animal; it turns the women to savagery and the queen to a hellhound. Agamemnon, Cassandra, and Polyxene are all victims of violence. Only Polyxene rises above the violence, and, as Arrowsmith has put it, "her death, futile in itself, exposes, by the quality of its commitment, the dense ambiguity of the moral atmosphere for those who cannot die." Even she cannot arrest the escalation of violence; but once she is removed the degeneracy and degradation steep the scene like some foully increasing fallout and poison all they touch. It was happening in the Greece that Euripides knew, and his play was a warning and a protest.

23. THE SUPPLIANT WOMEN

The Suppliant Women is one of those plays that had a high reputation in antiquity, which it has never recovered. In the fourth century B.C. there are allusions to it in orators, philosophers, and historians, and four hundred years later the Roman poets Ovid and Statius show a continuing awareness of it. Few moderns outside the world of scholarship have such awareness. Even among scholars Del Grande is altogether exceptional in his praise of the play; Van Hook thought it the worst of all Euripides's plays.

It is a puzzling play in many ways. Its general theme is the refusal of the Thebans to allow the burial of the dead after the attack of the Seven, and the Athenian enforcement of that burial. The story had been treated by Aeschylus in *The Eleusinians*, and Euripides's play has an unusual number of reminiscences of Aeschylus, one at least critical. It is hard not to think that the play is in some way tied up with contemporary Athenian politics, even if we do not, with Giles, identify the characters in the funeral eulogy with Nicias, Lamachus, Demosthenes, Laches, and Alcibiades; others have seen Alcibiades in Theseus. Most scholars agree that the Theban refusal of burial after Delium in 424 is a firm point of reference; some pursue the Argive alliance of the years following the peace of Nicias. Zuntz has offered a *caveat* that merits full citation:

Every one of the allusions supposed to afford a clue to the purpose of the play can be countered by instances to the contrary. If the battle of Delion is taken to be re-enacted on the stage, Aeschylus, in the *Eleusinians*, had managed to visualise the same situation nearly fifty years before it became reality. If, on the basis of v. 240, the play is taken to be directed against Kleon and his party, their opponents fare at least as badly immediately before (v. 238). If the quietest policy of the conservative ἀπράγμονες should be discerned in the pacifist sections, Aithra (v. 321) and Theseus (v. 567) answer it in the Periclean vein: and they act upon their words. If the closing scene is supposed to reveal the purport of *The Suppliant Women* in advocating an alliance with Argos, the presumptive ally is poorly recommended by what has been seen of him throughout the play. And, finally, if the stressing, by Adrastus (v. 190), of the usefulness of a youthful leader is interpreted as a recommendation of Alcibiades and his politics, there are numerous passages (v. 160, 232, 250, etc.) urging the perniciousness of the influence of the νέοι. Besides who would honestly find Alcibiades, of all men, impersonated by the Euripidean Theseus, the type also of the more domestic virtues?

Still, it seems certain that there is some political relevance, even if we cannot discern it precisely. There are other problems. Why, in a play that three times attacks war, does he vary Aeschylus's plot so that the issue is decided by force not persuasion? Why is Capaneus idealized by Adrastus to hold a character that runs counter to his image in the rest of this play, let alone tradition? There are a number of problems of staging. Finally, there is the problem of the loose structure of the play; the Evadne scene in particular is not obviously integrated with what has gone before. Hence Norwood's view that the play is a hodge-podge with genuine Euripides jostling the work of Moschion a century or more later. It is not clear that such drastic surgery is needed.

The opening is excellent, but in itself creates three production problems. The scene, we know, is Eleusis; the first line tells us so. We are in fact in the sanctuary, where two altars to Demeter and Kore stood in front of the Telesterion or Building of the Mysteries, and it is interesting that Adrastus and the women from Argos who form the chorus were allowed to penetrate so far. The first question is how precisely the scene was envisaged. At this point in the play there is no difficulty in assuming a considerable measure of realism; the stage building will have represented the Telesterion and the two altars would have been standing in front of it. But Evadne's rock, as we shall see, creates a difficulty; there were plenty of rocks at Eleusis, but none just here. The second problem relates to the opening of the play. Aethra, Theseus's mother, is discovered, with the chorus pleading with her, and Adrastus, standing apart, in the shadow of the great building itself. Without a curtain it is not easy to stage an opening tableau. It is possible that convention permitted the actors to take up their positions before the play began, but such a convention could apply to only two or three of the surviving plays, and this makes it less likely. If the musical score survived it might help; I suggest an opening ballet without words but with miming; it would be unusual but effective.

Finally, there is the problem of chorus numbers. The chorus are the mothers of the dead soldiers, and they apparently identify themselves as seven (963), one for each of the seven warriors. There are however two objections to this; a chorus of seven will hardly do, and a chorus of fourteen, each of the seven with an attendant is not really likely either. Further, of the seven mothers, one was Iocaste and another the goddess Atalanta; and there would be only five bodies, Amphiaraus, who was swallowed-up by the earth (500) and Polyneices, who was interred at Thebes, being omitted. The normal chorus number at this period was 15, and their basis formation 5x3. Probably then we have the five remaining mothers, each with two attendant mothers from the rest of the host. The words of the chorus are not determinative; they do not say "We are seven" but "We were seven," and it is natural for others to speak of them as "those who have lost seven sons" (12,102).

The opening is good. The scene is steeped in religious awe. The setting was inherited from Aeschylus, but Euripides would not have accepted it unless it had served his purpose. It establishes the atmosphere of the opening scene, for suppliants might pollute the sanctuary, and we know from Andocides (1.110) that even a suppliant bough might give offense. Demeter, however, was the type of *mater dolorosa,* and thus we expect the suppliants to be received with sympathy. In addition, the scene gives us the image of the harvest (31), which prepares us for the obvious but powerful thought of the harvest of death; this is also linked with the legendary origin of the Thebans from the dragon's teeth, "the sown men" (712). Here, as occasionally in Greek tragedy, a distant echo of some original fertility ritual peers through. Finally, there is a movement in the play, and a decidedly curious one, from Demeter the mother, goddess of peace, to the motherless unwed warrior Athene.

Aethra, Theseus's mother, is interrupted in her prayer to Demeter by the presence of the mothers from Argos. As a mother she sympathizes with them, and sends for Theseus. Her last words are barbed:

> Intelligent women
> reasonably do everything through men. (40)

It is the women who take the initiative; the men, who think that they are being decisive, are really following the women's lead. The prologue is short for Euripides, and the chorus cut across it with their agonized pleading; there would have been effective use of gesture, outstretched empty hands recurring throughout the play till they receive the bodies of the dead. They speak of their lacerated cheeks as an adornment (*kosmos,* 78); there is perhaps a pun on the Greek for "lament" (*kommos*). There is a spectacular sense of wearing the blood as a robe, but there is an important meaning of "order," a note sounded later in the play. They end with a death wish, a dramatic anticipation of the Evadne scene.

Theseus comes in, young, brash, self-confident. He turns first to his mother, then to Adrastus, who has been hovering, unspeaking, in the background. The scholiast who regarded the interchange that follows as so much padding was hasty in his criticism. The scene reveals both men. Theseus exposes Adrastus's impudence. But what of Theseus himself? Is there not some arrogance in the young man's assault on his elder? Theseus shows himself a clever young man without consistency. At times he shows an almost pedantic precision (129,143), at times a preacher's wordy moralizing (226). At times he is sarcastic (127). His religiosity passes into superstition (211).

> When God gives these preparations for life
> are we not fickle to be unsatisfied? (214)

These key words are taken up later. Adrastus, unsatisfied by his progress, makes a longer emotional appeal, by his own gray hairs and the grayhaired childlessness of the mothers; he is sniffling and sententious. Theseus counters with a mood of optimism. The good things in life outweigh the bad. He attributes the revelations of Prometheus, or the achievements of man in *Antigone*—ordered society, understanding, speech, agriculture, clothes, ships, and divination—to some god. He preaches at Adrastus, a sermon against violence, and puts forward a defense of the middle class as a stabilizing factor in the state. He rejects Adrastus's appeal. It is a sermon against *hybris* delivered in a spirit of *hybris*, and the chorus comments, with unusual decisiveness, "He's wrong; typical of young men and excusable" (250). Adrastus adds with some spirit that he asked for help not moralizing. He turns to the chorus with poetical language doubly linked to the Demeter theme:

> You old women, come along, abandon here
> the rank green, in the dropping of your leaves
> call on gods, earth, goddess of life and light
> Demeter, and the sun's rays, to witness
> that prayers to the gods have not served us. (257)

There is triple meaning here. Theseus is young and in the green of life; the old suppliants are at their fall. They are to drop their suppliant boughs. And Demeter is the goddess who brings the vegetation to life again, and her title here, *purphoros,* means "torchbearer" from her ritual, but suggests the meaning "producer of wheat."

The chorus addresses Theseus, breaking into a song in the dactylic rhythm, and falling at his feet, clutching his knees, and reaching up to his beard in an effective tableau. He is unmoved till he sees his mother's tears. In a good speech she pleads for his intervention. Her argument is *ad hominem;* she appeals to his ambition, pride, and sense of national glory. A fine phrase speaks of Athens as "opening a gorgon's eye on those who mock her." She makes an appeal to religion, but her view of religion is different from that of Theseus. Where Theseus sees a cosmos she sees chance; all stands on the throw of the dice, and God turns things topsy-turvy (320). She knows her son; Theseus is moved and agrees to act. His words, with their assertion of democracy, the right to meddle in other people's affairs, and courage before danger, sound like a satirical summary of Pericles's Funeral Speech. The note of satire is sure when Theseus says that the city must agree to the course "and will if I want it" (350) or when he proposes to negotiate, sitting with arms in hand (357). There is considerable irony in the scene. Aethra, who has seemed peripheral to the action, is pivotal, and the careful arguments of Theseus and Adrastus are swept aside, not by new convictions but by a woman who understands how to handle her menfolk.

Theseus's last words were of children and parents, and the brief choral song of gratitude that follows makes a special point of their motherhood. Theseus returns; his entrance is unusual in that he is engaged in conversation with one of his own heralds, whom he is sending with a polite request to bury the dead, but with the big battalions in the background. He is interrupted by a herald from Thebes, who calls abruptly: "Who's dictator here?" (399). There follows a debate, brilliant even for Euripides, on the merits and demerits of democracy. It has been called a flagrant irrelevancy. Such a view depends on some *a priori* notion of the theme of the play and what is relevant to it. The familiar debate is in fact quite short. The herald is a bit of a philosopher; he has an epigram about time bringing learning (419), as later about hope being unreliable (479), and his indictment of democracy is not without point: the workers are ignorant, and too busy to give due attention to the commonwealth, so that power passes to scoundrels with the gift of the gab (420).

Theseus defends democracy on grounds of equity (441). He "javelins" his answer (456), which reminds us that to him, persuasion must be backed by arms. His attack on dictatorship,

> However could a city be secure
> when a man cuts out enterprise and cuts down the young
> like the harvest of a meadow in the spring? (447)

recalls the famous story of the dictator lopping off the heads of the
tallest plants; it returns us to the Demeter theme. It also reminds us that
this is exactly what happens when Theseus elects war. The herald
moves to the immediate situation. Theseus is heading his ship of state
for the surge of war (473). The herald makes the second antiwar
statement, powerfully and eloquently:

> If death stood before our eyes as we gave our votes,
> Greece would not now be perishing of war-madness. (484)

Peace has many blessings and rejoices in good children. The chorus had
spoken of the *hybris* of the Thebans (464); the herald speaks of the
hybris of Capaneus and those others who attacked Thebes (495). The
chorus reechoes the word (512), and Adrastus is bursting into angry
retort, when Theseus cuts across him and silences him, another unusual
effect in the conventions of Greek tragedy.

Theseus replies at length, too great length. There is a bit of mild
Euripidean philosophy—"body to earth, spirit to the upper air" (533)
—and the thought of children is kept before us when he says, "Are
you afraid the dead may breed children in the depths of the earth?"
(545). His plea is first that of injured pride and national assertion;
Creon shall not dictate to him, nor Thebes to Athens. Second, his plea
is religious, but it is an odd sort of religion imbued with Aethra's
sceptical supernaturalism. "God is fickle," he says (552), using the
very word he has used of man's fickle refusal to be satisfied with what
God brings. In the bitter interchange that follows, Theseus accuses the
Thebans of *hybris* (575), the herald accuses Theseus of being an in-
terfering busybody (576), the image is used of the Thebans as born
from the dragon's sown teeth (578), and Theseus issues a call to arms
in Aeschylean language and a warning to Adrastus not to interfere;
this is now his quarrel and he will lead his own army under his own
divine guide (591).

The chorus sings of the war, again stressing their rôle as mothers,
and ending on the note of *hybris* (633). Their song covers the course

of the war; Greek tragedy did not in fact observe the pseudo-classical
unities, though this is an unusually long interval. A messenger arrives;
he was servant to the dead Capaneus, and reminds us again of the
latter's *hybris* (640). He describes the rejection of Theseus's demand
for the burial, and the battle, won by Theseus's intelligent generalship
and gallantry. "This is the sort of commander to choose, brave in
danger, and a hater of *hybris*" (726). The account of battle is realistic,
but it is not one of Euripides's best compositions. Perhaps the war was
too near; perhaps he did not want to overpower what follows. For
the chorus expresses joy and relief, but Adrastus indulges in self-
recrimination, an assault on *hybris* and a third attack on war:

> You states, when you have the power to turn evil aside by negotiation,
> you destroy your substance by rejecting negotiation for war. (748)

The rest of the dead have been buried; the chiefs for whom the war
was fought are being brought back separately.

The dirge that follows is intense and powerful. The mother-child
relationship rings out from the chorus; Adrastus in his new enlightenment continues his self-renunciation, and wishes to be blasted (like
Capaneus) or engulfed (like Amphiaraus); he holds himself responsible for the deaths. The chorus again ends strongly, on the word
"Avenging Fury" (836); this itself is a deliberate reminder of Aeschylus, who ends a chorus similarly in *Seven against Thebes* (791).
Theseus now enters, again in mid-conversation; Euripides is evidently
trying out a new dramatic effect, but perhaps he also wants to represent
Theseus as the man who never had a minute to spare. He speaks in
commendation of the men of stout heart whose bodies he is bringing
back (841); he has earlier condemned Adrastus for preferring stout-
heartaches to good advice (101). The blunt fact is that Theseus has
taken on the role of Adrastus. There is direct criticism of Aeschylus,
when Theseus refuses full details of the battle array, which occupy
three hundred lines of *Seven against Thebes*.

Adrastus is invited to produce the funeral eulogy of the dead chiefs,
and he does so in words so unctuously false that they must be satirical
on the part of Euripides. Five heroes only are praised, for Polyneices
and Amphiaraus are elsewhere, but it is enough to hear the hybristic

Capaneus (as we have been reminded often enough in this play) praised for his moderation and gentle speech, or Tydeus, who, as Wesley Smith put it, was noted in legend for "bribery, assassination, cannibalism and suspected fratricide," whitewashed as a democrat with a notable sense of honor. Adrastus's conclusion (an important one) is, "Educate your children carefully" (917), and it is of their children that the chorus naturally sings. Adrastus now asks to bury Capaneus, who was killed by a thunderbolt from Zeus, apart, and turns again to his sentiments against war and against interference with others (949).

Again the chorus sings, and again it is of their children; they are bereft and childless in their old age. Suddenly they see and describe a sight that creates a major problem of staging. They see the tomb prepared for Capaneus, and, outside the halls, the offerings of Theseus, and on a rock that towers above the building, Evadne, daughter of Iphis, widow of Capaneus, wearing, as we learn (1054), festal clothes in authentic emulation of Indian *suttee*; there is a parallel with Jennifer Dubedat's brilliant appearance after her husband's death. The scene is superb spectacle and powerful drama, "a sudden shaft of horror" (says Fitton), a tragedy within the tragedy making the general particular and immediate. High on the rock Evadne dances precariously and sings deliriously of her marriage to Capaneus, and proclaims her purpose to leap into his pyre. In a series of vivid images she appears as a Maenad (1001), the bride of death (1022), and a bird tossing in the wind (1046). Her father tries vainly to dissuade her. Her excellence—virtue, *arete*—is to die with her husband (1063).

She throws herself down on the pyre, as Iphis and the chorus shrink away. Iphis, who was father of the dead Eteoclus as well as of Evadne, has joined the chorus in their childlessness. The scene creates grave problems of staging. If I am right in postulating that a backcloth was dropped over the upper part of the stage building, the likeliest explanation is that the rock was painted on this, as rising behind the temple. Evadne would then appear at the appropriate point on top of the stage building, a bold enough effect, if so, seeing that this was in general reserved for gods. It looks as if the pyre was constructed on stage, presumably to one side, and if it were elevated sufficiently high with soft padding in the middle, and shrouded in smoke (it would not be possible to burn the pyre without endangering the stage building, but there *is* smoke without fire), an athletic actor could safely and reasonably convincingly drop down into it; the slave in *Orestes* falls safely from the first floor to the stage, and we know that athletic feats were expected of the actors. It would provide vigorous, unexpected, and rather frightening spectacle.

Now the play moves to its close. The grandchildren of the chorus bring in their father's ashes. Their songs intermingle with those of the chorus; the sevenfold pattern of the lamentations is worth note. They are patterned with Euripides's characteristic repetitions of single words, and filled with his bitter and pellucid clarity:

> Father, don't you hear your children's cries?
> Am I ever to stand, shield on arm, to avenge
> your death. God grant it! (1143)

There are also echoes of Aeschylus (1130, cf. *Ag.* 434; 1139, cf. *Pers.* 1002; 1142, cf. *Choeph.* 319). The reason is obvious. The theme is trilogic; it ends, like *Agamemnon,* with the promise of vengeance in a future generation. This promise is provided by the sudden appearance of Athene on the top of the stage building, just as Adrastus is taking a grateful leave of Theseus. She is less generous than Adrastus or Theseus, insistent on an oath of nonaggression from Argos, ratified by animals killed and buried beside the Seven. She stirs up future generations of Argives to war with Thebes, and caps the bestialism that turns men to animals by saying that they will come as lion cubs. It is an astounding conclusion.

What then is this play about? I suggest that the episode of Delium put into Euripides's mind the possibility of reworking Aeschylus's *The Eleusinians.* But he elected to do it in a very different way. For Aeschylus's play showed rationality winning through: Euripides shows the opposite; at the same time he rejected the heroism of *Seven against Thebes.* On the divine level, Demeter is ousted by Athene; on the human, war escalates. We see men and women in the grip of a war situation, cold or hot, and this said, the play, so far from sprawling, as some have suggested, is tightly knit. As often with Euripides the women control the action. In the suffering of the mothers we see what war means, yet they are not averse from more war; this is human. Aethra and Evadne are consistent, Aethra in compassion, Evadne in partnership with her husband, yet in Theseus's actions Aethra's compassion turns to military power, and Evadne's *suttee* is empty nobility. By comparison the men are weak. Adrastus learns a lesson, and changes from war to peace, but, like some pacifists, becomes a sentimental idealist in the funeral speeches. Theseus at the same time turns from peace to war. He is in no sense idealized; he is putty in his mother's hands—or Athene's; he has in him elements of the anti-hero.

The political debate is another part of the war situation. The points are made cogently, but they contain much insincerity; we are reminded of the way Thucydides shows truth—and the middle class that Theseus upholds—as the victims of party strife. *Hybris* is the common theme, and the common disease. The attack on war comes three times from different people; it is strongly made and seriously meant. But was not Theseus's war just? Possibly. The majority of the audience would think so, and Euripides knew it. Yet even this carries the seeds of future strife in generations to come. So comes Athene, "the Conscienceless Voice of State Power." What is she? Yet another force in human affairs, like Aphrodite and Artemis in *Hippolytus*. She is Patriotism; she is harsh but real. We have to come to terms with her, but there is no peace while she rules, and the Evadne episode is designed to highlight what that means. Demeter is her antithesis, and we must remember that we are visually reminded of her throughout the play by the Eleusis setting.

So seen *The Suppliant Women* is not a patriotic play. It presents problems not answers; it is a realistic play. It is not a great play, perhaps because we do not become sufficiently involved with any one character. It is a good play, better in the theater than in the study, because it is gloriously theatrical both in the spectacular and in more subtle senses.

24. *ANDROMACHE*

The war between Athens and Sparta dragged out with spasmodic explosions for ten years, and in 421 came to a shuddering and temporary halt. The principal hawks, Cleon and Brasidas, had fallen before Amphipolis. There was a deal of war weariness. Pleistoanax, the Spartan king, and Nicias, the leading figure at Athens in military and civil affairs, were both doves, and they patched up a peace. Their plans were shattered by Alcibiades, the brilliant, brazen young aristocrat who had been Pericles's ward and now emerged as leader of the radicals at Athens. Despite Alcibiades's flagrant imperialism, Euripides was at first attracted to him. Although the Spartans gave women a more prestigious position, Euripides was bitterly opposed to them, and Alcibiades perhaps appeared for a time as an apostle of containment without war. He was elected general in 420 and pursued a policy of alliance with Argos, the main democratic power in the Peloponnese; this is referred to by the Spartan Menelaus when he speaks of "a city not far from Sparta, formerly friendly, but now acting hostile" (733).

In this same year Alcibiades succeeded in getting the Spartans excluded from the Olympic games for an alleged violation of the truce; he himself won the race for four-horse chariots, and, we are told by Plutarch (*Vit. Alc.* 11), an ode to celebrate the victory was attributed to Euripides.

The dramatist's *Andromache* must have been written about this time; passages are strongly, even violently anti-Spartan. The argument prefixed to the play informs us that it was not produced in Athens. It seems that the man responsible for its presentation was called Democrates. Euripides had a friend from Argos named Timocrates. It has been argued that the play was produced in Argos. This seems unlikely; after all, the villains of the first part, Menelaus and Hermione, are Spartans, but the villain of the second part, Orestes, is an Argive, and his portrayal would hardly improve relations. It is perhaps more likely that during the jockeying for position there were probings to the north, and that the play was produced either in Thessaly or Molossia. But we cannot be certain.

It may be right to relate Euripides's play not merely to a political situation but also to a dramatic situation. Sophocles wrote a play, *Hermione,* which appears to have been on the same myth. We do not know much of the play; only two citations survive, one of a line, one of a single word. Eustathius (*Od.* 11.1479) tells us the plot. While Menelaus was at Troy his daughter Hermione was given in marriage to Orestes. Meantime her father promised her to Neoptolemus, and on his return fulfilled the promise. But Neoptolemus was murdered at Delphi by Machaereus, and Hermione returned to Orestes and bore him a son Tisamenos. A scholiast to Euripides's *Orestes* (1655) tells us that Sophocles treated the death of Neoptolemus at Delphi, presumably in *Hermione.* We may reasonably deduce that Sophocles set the scene at Delphi, that there was a debate between Orestes and Neoptolemus over their right to Hermione, and that Neoptolemus was arrogantly challenging the Oracle over the death of Achilles, and that thus our sympathies are engaged for Orestes and Apollo whose loyal servant he appears.

We can see something of the reversal that Euripides has produced. There is no mention of Andromache in association with Sophocles's play, and we can assume that her introduction is an innovation. More, Euripides's play is named after her and centers on her; the first half must be presented so that she dominates the second part even in her absence. Neoptolemus does not appear. The scene is set in Phthia; the problems of time involved are no greater than those in *The Men of Persia* or *Agamemnon,* and far less than those in *Rhesus.* Euripides is thus able to make his central *agon* between two women instead of two men, a feature he exploits with extreme brilliance. He is also able to attack Orestes and Delphi as bitterly as he attacks Menelaus and Sparta.

Andromache is there from the start. She opens the play as in a sense she ends it. She is a foreigner, no doubt exotically dressed, and her first word is of Asia (1). She is a slave, and this is stressed throughout the first part of the play (11, 30). Neoptolemus is her owner, and he has not treated her particularly well (26), though she has borne him a son. Andromache at no point shows any sense of love for Neoptolemus; her love was lavished on Hector and remains his. She is now a suppliant in sanctuary at Thetis's shrine. In a little over fifty lines she tells the whole story: the fall of Troy, her transport as a slave to Phthia, the old tale of Peleus and Thetis and the continuing authority of Peleus, the boy she bore Neoptolemus, and then his decision to marry the Sparta princess Hermione, Hermione's childlessness and her attribution of this to Andromache's magic, Neoptolemus's absence at Delphi on a holy pilgrimage of contrition, Hermione and Menelaus conspiring against her life, and her own decision to send her child away to safety and take refuge in the shrine. This type of monologue establishing the plot is admittedly artificial, but, given the convention, it could hardly be better done, and the ancient argument comments on its clarity and construction. It establishes the theme with economical concision, and introduces us to Andromache, a slave and foreigner, but with her own dignity and loyalty.

She is joined by one of her former servants, who accompanied her from Troy. The woman, who has come to warn her that Hermione and Menelaus are plotting to secure the boy, addresses her "My lady" (56), to which Andromache responds, not without grace, "My dearest fellow-slave" (64). With her news an important theme enters. This is the theme of wisdom. Menelaus and Hermione lack it; their thoughts are wicked (62). Andromache calls them "a pair of vultures" (75). Her hope is in Peleus. ("Too old," says the servant.) She has sent messengers. The theme of wisdom returns. "Do you imagine they thought about you?" comments the servant. But Andromache persists and sends the woman with another message. This is an effective scene; it gives dramatic dimension to the situation verbalized in Andromache's monologue.

Alone again, Andromache chants her sorrow in a passage of elegiacs unique in Greek tragedy. This is a musical recapitulation of what has gone before: the doom of Troy, her love for Hector (killed by the son of the very goddess whose statue she is clutching), her fear of Hermione, and slavery, always slavery. At the last she compares herself with Niobe, turned to stone (she feels herself almost one with the statue) and weeping.

Why did Euripides introduce these elegiacs? It is hard to say. D. L. Page, believing that the play was performed at Argos, thought it a compliment to Peloponnesian elegists like Echembrotus, Sacadas and Clonas. It is perhaps more likely that it is intended as a kind of epitaph. This was a usage found as early as the eighth century, and perfected by Simonides; since then a fifth-century audience's instinctive reaction to elegiacs would be "Death." His use here enables Euripides to make a smooth transition to the entry of the chorus.

In their song dactylic hexameters are interspersed with the meter known as ithyphallic (♩♩♩♩♩♩) and other rhythms. Presumably it was as easy to process to dactyls as to anapaests, but the intermediate lines must represent the procession breaking into a dance. The dactylic hexameters in Andromache's solo and in the chorus that follows form a link with Homeric epic. They remind us of that which has been before us since the first mention of Priam and Hector, that this, as much as *Hecabe* or *The Women of Troy* is a play about war and its result; war that leaves the contemptible Menelaus as victor and enslaves the noble Andromache. Euripides enhances this point by making his chorus not slaves from Troy but free women of Phthia, who nonetheless side with Andromache. Their song is notable for its compassion toward one who has become their social inferior. They are obviously frightened of Hermione, and, though she is their queen, they have no love for her. They plead with Andromache in her state of slavery and as a foreigner not to provoke retaliation. Again the insistence on knowledge comes through. She must recognize her fate, calculate her plight (126), recognize her position as a foreign slave (136); the word used is the familiar word for knowledge in "know yourself" (*gnothi*). Their thoughts toward her are kindly, but they would not have Hermione know them (146).

Suddenly Hermione is there, decked in royal finery. The debate that ensues between the women is as skillful as anything Euripides ever wrote: perhaps it comes too early for the play's good. Hermione may be Neoptolemus's queen, but she retains a Spartan independence. She blames Andromache for her own barrenness, taunts her with her slavery and Hector's death.

> Realize where you are. There's no Hector here,
> no Priam, no gold. This is a Greek city-state.
> You simply will not learn. (168)

She accuses Andromache of a failure in self-knowledge, which she herself displays, for a moment before she has been vaunting the gold she herself is wearing. She goes on in the same vein:

> Foreigners are all alike.
> Fathers sleep with daughters, sons with mothers,
> brothers with sisters. Murder splits a family
> apart, and there's no law to prevent it.
> Don't introduce that sort of thing here. (173)

It is Orestes, not Andromache, who introduces that sort of thing. Verrall commented well: "One wonders, not without a shudder, whether the wife of Orestes remembered these words of nights." She takes a metaphor from chariot driving.

> It doesn't work
> for one man to drive two women. (177)

Andromache's reply is brilliant, because it is devastatingly true and utterly unpersuasive. She is a slave, so she cannot win. Hermione is young; the implication is that she has much to learn and is not willing to learn it. Then comes a series of annihilating rhetorical questions. How can she, Andromache, displace Hermione in Neoptolemus's regard? Because Troy is greater than Sparta? Because she is blessed by fortune and free? For her swelling youth? (The word she uses is natural for the swelling breasts of puberty, but can denote swollen pride and anger, 196.) Her political influence? Her friends? The children she bears to be slaves, dinghies towed wretchedly behind her? (This is biting, for Hermione can acknowledge this reason in these terms.) No, if Neoptolemus hates Hermione, it is not Andromache's magic; it is because Hermione is hateful.

> It's character, my girl,
> not looks, that holds a husband. (207)

She breaks into a cry of love for Hector, which shows us, and should show Hermione, where her heart is. She did not grudge his other loves; for love of him, she gave her breast to his bastards. Hermione is frightened to let a drop of rain fall on her husband. This last is a magnificent touch, for the sex image is inverted, as the rain is usually the image of the semen; Hermione is domineering and masculine. Andromache ends strongly:

> My girl, don't try to outdo your mother
> in passion for men. When a mother's warped,
> her children should not follow her, if they've any sense. (229)

Hermione, like Helen, has sex on the brain, which is not the healthiest place to have it. The last word brings back the note of wisdom, which Hermione conspicuously lacks. This note recurs in the bitter exchange that follows:

HERMIONE: Why do you put on airs and challenge me to debate, as if
              you thought high thoughts, and my thoughts were low?
ANDROMACHE: But it's true, from your recent arguments.
HERMIONE: May I never be cursed with a mind like yours, woman!
ANDROMACHE: You're young to be talking of such delicate matters.
              (234)

A moment later Hermione bursts out: "Oh, you're clever, clever, but it won't save you from death" (245). She taunts Andromache again and again with her foreign blood, and threatens to burn her out, even though she were fixed to Thetis's statue by molten lead (a vivid recollection of the stone mason's method of fixing two blocks together) before Neoptolemus can return. As she storms out Andromache meditates on the venom in women.

The choral lyrics, which are generally brief in this play, are dominated by the Trojan War, and this is important to our understanding of the play. This first stasimon is a song of the Judgment of Paris. Hermione spoke of the danger of a husband driving two wives. The chorus sings of Hermes driving a team of three goddesses. It was equally disastrous, and the disaster came from the goddess of love, though all the goddesses brought evil-minded words (288, the theme again). For the yoke that linked that team together (278) was a yoke of slavery for Troy (301). Had Paris not lived,

> No yoke of slavery would have come
>   on Troy, and, woman, you
> would have kept your throne in a royal palace.
> Greece would have been released from anguish
>   when for ten years her lads
>   wandered with spears before Troy.
> Wives would never have become widowed,
>   never orphaned of young the old. (301)

It is concise and powerful.

The chorus has sung of Troy. Enter Menelaus, hero of Troy. He comes in with an escort who hold as prisoner Andromache's son. Menelaus is brutal and cock-a-hoop. The theme of wisdom returns.

> Woman,
> You've turned out less intelligent than Menelaus,
> Leave this spot. Strip it of your presence,
> or the boy here will be—sacrificed—in your place.
> Make that the object of your calculations. (312)

Andromache's reply is a series of general reflections. She begins by invoking Reputation, which gives so many the illusion of greatness.

> I can't believe that those whose glory
> is spurious have anything but an accidental reputation for
> intelligence. (322)

The conqueror of Troy enters the lists against a slave woman!

> I can no longer believe
> that you deserved Troy or Troy you.
> Men with a reputation for intelligence wear their brilliance
> on the outside; inside they're like the rest of us—
> apart perhaps from wealth; there's real power. (328)

The last words are bitterly sarcastic, as we realize when we reflect what wealth does to a man inside, when we reflect on the emptiness behind Hermione's spectacular façade. Andromache turns to a reasoned plea. Her death will merely bring blood-guiltiness on Menelaus and Hermione. She is willing to stand trial for witchcraft before Neoptolemus, but not to succumb to lynch law. She offers a skillful argument, which, based on the double standard of morality, tells against it.

> Grant that we women are a curse and a menace,
> men ought not to imitate our characters. (353)

It is a wedge fractionally inserted between Menelaus and Hermione, but her last words undo the effect.

> I fear one fact
> about your mind. It was also a quarrel over a woman
> which led you to sack and desolate the city of Troy. (361)

This is too much for the chorus, who show themselves fifth-century Athenian women.

> You've said too much for a woman addressing men.
> You too—your mind's control has outshot itself. (364)

Her feminity, not her slavery, is in their minds. She is behaving like Hermione.

Menelaus's reply is brief and tart. Neoptolemus and he are friends, and friends hold all things in common, a piece of proverbial lore picked up by the Pythagoreans and others. He can act in his friend's absence, and the slave Andromache and her slave-son are only "things." There is no wisdom in waiting. He promises that if she gives herself up to die, the boy lives. Andromache reveals her inner thoughts in a staccato pathetic speech. Her love for and loss of Hector come back, and her slavery; she has been forced to lie with her masters (the plural is hardly significant, 371). There is nothing in life for her; her hope is in the child. She leaves the protecting altar with a flood of love for her child, ending with a colossal oxymoron that those without children enjoy a bitter bliss, which will hardly endear her to Hermione or the father who is under Hermione's thumb. Menelaus sets his men on her and promptly boasts his duplicity; she must know her state (the knowledge theme again, 430). He will save himself from technical perjury by handing the boy over to Hermione to dispose of as she will. Andromache utters one cry for her fledgling, snatched from her protecting wing (441) and bursts into a denunciation of Sparta and all things Spartan, ending in a hissing fury of thirty-two *s* sounds in eight lines, as she is dragged off.

The choral song that follows is, on the face of it, slight. It is brief, and it does not link up with any of the great mythological themes, even the Trojan War. In sum, their theme is that bigamy means strife; they sustain it with examples drawn from politics (a covert hit in context at the two kings of Sparta), poetical composition (an odd illustration, especially from the women of Phthia; there must be some contemporary reference we have lost), and the captaincy of a ship (in which a crowd of clever men carry less weight than a single mind, even though inferior, with authority). This last instance shows the theme of the chorus to be wisdom, and as Andromache and her son are led out, bound, to execution, they describe the murder as "godless, lawless, graceless" (491). The two victims join in a song in glyconics and pherecrateans, and Menelaus cuts across their dirge with his own chant of the folly of leaving enemies alive (519). It is an interesting scene, for with Peleus joining them four actors are involved, but the boy sings only and does not speak, and the part may have been taken by a boy; on either score the effect, though exceptional, might be permissible. The boy, who has earlier been snatched from her wing, seeks to go to death under her wing (504). Andromache bursts into a cry for Hector.

> Husband, husband, if only I had
> your strong right arm, your spear to save,
> Priam's son. (523)

The opening words would fit Neoptolemus, but to Andromache Hector is the only husband, and she has no longer any hope in the living. In a splendid image, which recalls Niobe, she sings:

> My eyes are wet with tears.
> I let them fall as water tumbles
> down a sheer cliff out of the sun. (532)

She will not plead for herself, but she directs the boy to plead. "No use," says Menelaus, taking up Andromache's image, "no more than to a rock in the sea or a wave." We think of Canute or Mrs. Partington, but though a wave may not respond to entreaty, it ebbs, it breaks, it vanishes. Menelaus is no rock; he is a wave who ebbs, breaks, vanishes.

Enter, in the nick of time, with all Euripides's melodramatic power, Peleus, escorted by the servant whom Andromache sent out (now of course played by an extra without speaking). Something is rotten in the state of Phthia, and he will set it right. The theme of age returns; he wishes he could recover his youth. He is delightfully characterized, mixing his metaphors as he breathes a following wind to swell the sails of the lamb and ewe led to the slaughter (554). Andromache, still a princess in slavery, rebukes the old man for his tardiness in coming, then in an excellent tableau, bound as she is, drops to her knees before him, not as slave to master but as friend to friend. Peleus orders her release. Menelaus begins to bluster. Peleus raises his stick, and the great commander finds discretion the better part of valor. Then the old man gives him an unmitigated verbal lashing. Menelaus is a villain and coward with no place in the catalogue of men. Sparta cannot breed women with the saving wisdom of chastity (*sophron*, 594, 596, 601), and Helen is the worst of all, and Hermione, her filly, takes after her dam (621). Menelaus came back from Troy without a scratch; he had not even the pluck to kill off his treacherous bitch of a wife, but went soft at the sight of her breasts and dropped his sword. Better a bastard of good stock, like this boy, than a Spartan; sometimes poor soil bears a better harvest than rich. Then the crowning insult:

Take your daughter away. It's better for men
to accept in friendship and family the poor and honest
rather than the wealthy and wicked. You—you're nothing at all. (639)

The chorus sees a quarrel flaring up and suggests that clever men will
avoid it. The comment is brushed away. The insults glance off Menelaus's hide.

Why do they say that old men are clever,
the men whom the Greeks gave a reputation for intelligence? (645)

Menelaus cannot understand Peleus's defense of Hector's wife, a
foreigner and an enemy. He does not actually taunt her with slavery,
but Aristotle can hardly have been the first to say that a foreigner was
a born slave. Menelaus claims that his providential forethought was to
check her influence. If Peleus is not careful, there will be foreigners
ruling in Phthia. He speaks with spluttering scorn of Peleus's age
(678). Helen's defection was involuntary, the work of the gods (he
is evidently under her thumb again, as Peleus said). But at least it
taught the Greeks to fight. Then, with a proverb on the theme of learning: "Partnership is man's universal teacher" (683). It is mordantly
ironical, since the word for "partnership" can mean "sex." He showed
his wisdom in not killing Helen, claims to show it in taunting Peleus
with the death of his brother Phocus (a scandal from the distant past),
and advertises thinking ahead.

Peleus is unmoved. Menelaus has lauded the Trojan War. To Peleus
war means the glory of the generals and the suffering of the privates,
and he says so.

The command sit proudly in office, and think big,
put airs on over the commons; they are nothing.
The commons are a thousand times their betters in mind;
they lack the will to power and the crookedness to get there. (699)

Then, with a cruel taunt, he tells Menelaus to take his "sterile
heifer" away (711). The animal image continues as he sets himself
to untie Andromache; they have trussed her like an ox or lion (770).
The chorus shows a healthy respect for Peleus's age, and Menelaus
flounces out. He remembers a convenient engagement on the battle-

field with a nearby city. He does not even stop to take Hermione; his vaunted forethought seems nonexistent. He promises to come back and deal with Neoptolemus, whom he hopes to find more reasonable, and feebly calls Peleus a shadow with a voice, incapable of anything but words (745). Peleus has in fact achieved the rescue, and by his stick not his words. Now he returns to the first part of his mixed metaphor and remixes it. Andromache has come into a calm harbor out of a bestial storm (749). She is still fearful, scarcely believing her escape, but he chides her with womanly fears. The assault is to come from an unexpected quarter. Peleus takes Andromache out and we do not see her again, but her nobility is not lost to the play.

This is the turning point of the play. The choral song that marks it is again brief. It is a song in praise of Peleus. The chorus sings that it would be better never to have been born except to a house that combines resources and good character. Power without virtue is a burden and reproach; it withers with the passage of time. This is clearly Menelaus. Then they sing directly of Peleus and his exploits, in the battle between Lapiths and Centaurs, the voyage of the Argo, and with Heracles at Troy. The unconscious irony of their praise is revealed later, but anyone who has been caught up into the temper of the play will feel something sinister in the culminating reference to Troy.

The mood of optimism that has supervened on the chorus's opening words ("Better not to have been born," 766) is rapidly shattered. Hermione's nurse pants out of the house to announce that the girl in remorse for her unsuccessful crime against Andromache is hysterically seeking suicide. She has been abandoned by Menelaus and is terrified of Neoptolemus. The nurse speaks high-flown, almost Aeschylean language, as Euripides's nurses sometimes do—one line has only three words (813)—but there is no doubting her concern. She asks the chorus to go in to the girl, but Hermione rushes out, scratching at her cheeks, tearing her hair and clothes. The nurse rebukes her for immodesty; there is a side blow at the freedom of Spartan women. Hermione is represented as emotionally disturbed beyond anything the situation calls for. Neither the chorus nor the nurse joins in her lyrical outbursts; the nurse tries to calm her down in prosaic iambics and the chorus remains silent. She is not lightly silenced:

> Whose statue shall I, suppliant, approach?
> Shall I fall at her knees, a slave to slave?
> O to be a blue-winged bird
> flying far from Phthia's soil!
> O to be a pine-built boat,
> passing through the Dark Blue cliffs,
> first of ships to sail the sea. (859)

The imagery of dark blue is of some interest. It is a somber color, and Homer uses it of the darkness of mist or cloud (*Il.* 5.345), of the terrible brow of Zeus (*Il.* 1.528), and, significantly, of the mourning veil that Thetis wears in anticipation of Achilles's death (*Il.* 24.94).

Suddenly a stranger is there. He introduces himself as "Orestes, son of Agamemnon and Clytemnestra"; they are benumbing words. He is on his way to Zeus's oracle at Dodona. Why? Has not Apollo's oracle done enough damage? Orestes has, one might almost say, dropped in to see Hermione, as young men will do with those they have loved and lost. Hermione, still hysterical, but using the rhythms of dialogue, extravagantly, flings herself at his feet and embraces his knees, calling him a harbor for storm-tossed sailors and her arms suppliant garlands. A mixed metaphor may be a sign of a vivid and proleptic imagination, but Euripides permits his characters some Irish bulls in this play. She is the daughter of a murderess, she introduces herself as Helen's daughter, and Euripides, here as elsewhere, is asserting against Aeschylus that character descends through the mother. Orestes's response is "Phoebus, god of healing, give release from trouble" (900). We know how Euripides regards the release that comes from Phoebus. The story is dragged tendentiously from her. Andromache is "Hector's wife" (908). Orestes shows his character when he says, "Did you kill them, or did some mischance stop you?" (913). Even he expresses surprise that Menelaus gave in to Peleus; "out of respect," says Hermione (918). Hermione is telling untruths, but she at least may be self-deceived. Orestes, we find, has been lying. He was not making for Dodona. He had been in correspondence with Hermione; she had tried to put him off, but he had come, knowing of her quarrel with Andromache, to abduct her when occasion permitted. She was given him for wife, but through the Trojan War she was

promised to Neoptolemus. He tried to get her back, but Neoptolemus
flung his mother-murder in his face.

> I had no pride, because of what had happened at home.
> I was hurt, hurt, but put up with it all
> And went away reluctantly, deprived of marriage with you. (979)

Orestes knows how to get at a girl's heart; and there is a deeper implication, that no one but Menelaus's family (to which he was related),
would have him. As for Neoptolemus, she need not fear.

> He will die horribly through Apollo, and my
> false charges. He will recognize my enmity. (1005)

The language of knowledge again, as Orestes has used with favor
the word for "clever," which even Hermione applied to crooked talk
(*sophos*, 937, 957). Once a man has killed, it is easy to kill again.
Orestes's first murder was justified by some, though not by Euripides,
the second is for petty spite. He takes Hermione out stage-right.

And what does the chorus now sing? They sing again of Troy, and
their first word is of Phoebus who built and abandoned it. Gone is
Atreus's son by the wiles of his wife. (1027) This is Agamemnon, not
Menelaus, but the language conceals a double truth, for Helen has
undone Menelaus. The conqueror was conquered, and from this came
another chain of slaughter through Orestes, set alongside the slaughter
of war. "Holy Phoebus, how am I to believe?" (1036). The last
stanza sums it up in grim but glorious poetry.

> In the city-squares of Greece many women raise a wail
> for the fate of their unhappy sons.
> And women leave their homes to share another's bed.
> Not on you alone, not on your folk alone
> have the sorrows come which spring from wisdom's lack.
> Disease gripped Greece, yes, disease,
> and there crossed to Troy and to Troy's fertile fields
> a thunderstorm dripping conscienceless murder. (1037)

This chorus, although its language is less masterly than Euripides
at his best, is in its way a masterpiece. Knit into the previous scene by
the name of Orestes, it drives home the disaster of the fall of Troy,

ties the two together alike by the name of Apollo, and the sense that a plague of violence has overtaken Greece, and puts the blame for violence squarely on the Greeks. We must suppose that after 421, the Greek world experienced the ineluctable consequence of ten years of war, a rash of violent crimes. This ode joins with the messenger's speech to form the play's climax.

Peleus has heard of Hermione's departure and comes in to confirm it. The chorus tells him of Orestes's threats against Neoptolemus, and Peleus is about to send to the rescue when a messenger comes to tell him that it is too late, and the old man collapses under the news. There is here a small problem. Delphi is sixty miles from Phthia; in the real world, therefore, the choral ode has covered a lapse of some days. There is no difficulty about this; it happens in *Agamemnon*; but it is made harder in that Peleus seems to be operating on a different time scale.

There are three possible explanations. One is that Euripides was indifferent to realism of time, and concerned solely with dramatic effect; this is the usual explanation and may well be right. But it is equally possible that he is indifferent to and possibly ignorant of the realisms of geography, like the Englishman who invited a Canadian friend to meet his daughter on her arrival in Canada and received the answer, "Why don't you meet her yourself? You're nearer." There is a third possibility, which Verrall proposed, and which, like many of Verrall's views, has been too hastily dismissed, that Orestes was lying and the murder had already taken place. It is to be noted that the messenger's speech contains no mention of Hermione, and it may well be that Euripides wants to intensify the impression of violence combined with deceit.

The messenger's speech, though not among the very greatest, is excellent, skillful in evoking excitement by variations of pace. He tells of the way Orestes spread slanders against Neoptolemus, and then attacked him with a gang of armed hoods while he was actually at his prayers. The messenger says ominously that "Clytemnestra's son" was one of the gang and had stitched the plot together. Neoptolemus took refuge on the altar. They pelted him from a safe distance with stones like hail, and Neoptolemus dodged as if he were dancing a war dance.

Then "with a Trojan leap" (apparently associated with Achilles as he landed at Troy, and introduced by Euripides to reinforce the link) he jumped down, scattering them as doves before a hawk. Many were killed or crushed trying to escape. Then the god took a hand. A great voice from the shrine compelled the aggressors; they regrouped, and Achilles's son fell before them. The gang then added atrocity to murder by mutilating the body.

> This is what the lord who offers oracles to others,
> this is what the arbiter of justice to mankind
> did to Neoptolemus who came to make amends,
> bore old grudges in his mind like any crook on earth.
> How can he be wise? (1161)

The body of Neoptolemus is carried in, and an extended dirge follows. Suddenly the chorus becomes aware of a movement in the sky. It is Thetis, carried down on the crane. It is a natural and easy epiphany. Thetis was married to Peleus, mother to Achilles, grandmother to Neoptolemus. Further, she became blurred and blended with Themis as power of justice. She speaks to the point, and as briefly as she may. Peleus must not grieve too much; bereavement comes to all, as she herself knows in losing Achilles. Neoptolemus is to be buried at Delphi, as a lasting indictment of Orestes and the Delphians; this is etiological, since the tomb was shown there. Andromache will go to Molossia and marry Hector's brother Helenus; her son by Neoptolemus will found an enduring dynasty there, perpetuating the stock of Peleus, Thetis—and Troy. Peleus will find immortality. She closes with the reminder that sorrow is idle, for all men must die. Peleus finds consolation in her words, and takes good counsel (1280), and the chorus closes the play with the familiar formula that Euripides had already used in *Alcestis* and *Medea*, and applied whimsically to *Helen*.

Andromache is not in the first flight of Euripides's plays, and the ancient argument says as much. But it is good theater. In structure it is a diptych, and this has hampered its interpretation. Euripides is feeling toward the form he is to use with such brilliant success in *Heracles*. The play is not an anti-Spartan tract. There are anti-Spartan passages, but they are incidental, not central, like the attacks on Apollo and

Delphi; it is a mistake to treat Orestes as a Spartan. What Euripides does is to spotlight Spartan wickedness in the first part, and gradually to spread the light till it falls on all the Greeks. It is not the tragedy of Hermione, or even of Peleus. These two figures are dramatically important in holding the play together, but the play is not primarily about them.

The play declares itself to be, and is, about Andromache. Its theme is seen in the extraordinary concatenation of words relating to wisdom and knowledge, often at dramatically significant points, such as the last word of the choral introit (146), the first word of Orestes's one long speech (957), or the last word of the messenger's speech (1165). And there is the continual stress, especially in the choral lyrics, on Troy and the Trojan War.

Where is wisdom to be found? Not in Apollo and Delphi. Not in Menelaus, Hermione and the Spartans. Not in Orestes. Not in Peleus's family, for Achilles and Neoptolemus alike were involved in the war with Troy, which is rejected as one of the follies of violence. It is to be found in two people. One is Peleus. But Peleus too is a Greek, and is not exempt from the general indictment of the Greeks. He has been a man of violence. He killed Phocus; the reference is incidental but deliberate. He took part in an earlier sacking of Troy. But Peleus has learned wisdom; he has learned wisdom through the age that stands in contrast to Hermione's headweak and heartstrong youth. He shows his wisdom in the very defense of a foreign woman, which Menelaus regards as folly (645). He shows it in his indictment of the war of the generals (699). And at the last he shows it when in obedience to the voice of Thetis he understands what good counsel means (1280). But Peleus has only learned wisdom, Andromache possesses it, and that is why this is her play. And she is a woman, a foreigner, and a slave.

Euripides is tearing down our conventional judgments, and he uses this gracious, courageous woman to do so. And what is wisdom? It is perhaps the object of the prayer "Lord, grant that I may change those things which need to be changed, accept those things which cannot be changed, and know the difference between them." It is this which unites with righteousness and with a warmth of love in Andromache to make wisdom. Peleus has to work this out through suffering. Only Andromache's importunacy leads Peleus to change what needs to be changed; only Thetis brings him to accept what cannot be changed. Andromache has this wisdom from the first, though she too has to exercise it through suffering. She is the norm to which Peleus aspires. This is why she, a foreigner, is brought back in Thetis's speech to found a line of Greek kings. For not merely Spartan treachery and brutality, but the violence of the whole of Greece denies this wisdom.

25. THE WOMEN OF TROY

In the Aegean stands an island, Melos, world-famed for a statue of
Aphrodite discovered there, familiarly known as the Venus de Milo;
to archaeologists Melos stands as the main source of obsidian in the
eastern Mediterranean. The island was colonized by Dorians, and in
the power struggles of the fifth century the islands sympathized with
Sparta rather than Athens but managed for a period to maintain neu-
trality. They fought against the Persians at Salamis but kept out of the
Confederacy of Delos.

As an ally they were no asset, as an enemy no danger, but their independence was an insult to Athenian naval pride. In 426 Nicias as-
sailed them, unsuccessfully. Ten years later an Athenian force descended on the island. They alleged no justification, but demanded by *force
majeure* that the Melians submit to them. When the Melians protested
that the gods would protect them against injustice, the Athenians
smiled pityingly. When they invoked the support of Sparta, the
Athenians smiled more pityingly still. When they said that if all else

failed they would defend themselves, the Athenians shrugged their shoulders, and prepared a siege. When their defense proved tougher than expected, the Athenians sent out reinforcements, sacked the city, killed the men, and sold the women and children into slavery. The act was not unique; Socrates took it for granted (Xen. *Mem.* 4.2.15). The Spartans executed the men of Platea in 427 and of Hysiae in 417–416. The Athenians had proposed similar treatment of Mitylene in 427, but wiser counsels prevailed; by 421 the brutalizing effect of war was six years stronger, and Scione received the treatment Melos was to receive. But those, however evil, were in hot blood, this was in cold; they were in a hot war, this was in a cold; and the Athenians had contrived the situation themselves.

When Thucydides wrote his history of the conflict he saw this apparently minor episode as the turning point. Here was the *hybris* that led to the *nemesis* of Sicily. Athens trampled Melos as Agamemnon trampled the red carpet, and the result was the same. So Thucydides ends his account of the subjugation of Melos, which is disproportionately long by conventional standards, with the Athenians preparing to conquer Sicily. It is the key moment of his tragic story; in the medical terms with which he was familiar, it is the *crisis*. And Euripides, brooding on his country's crime, wrote a play in which he took as his theme the most glorious feat of Greek arms, the conquest of Troy, but portrayed it, not in terms of the glory of the victors but with a deep compassion for the sufferings of the vanquished, so that we see, in Gilbert Murray's words "not glory at all, but shame, and blindness, and a world swallowed up in night."

The play was put on in 415. We happen to know the whole tetralogy, which, astonishingly, received second prize; it is a remarkable tribute to freedom of speech at Athens that it was accepted for performance. The plays were *Alexander, Palamedes, The Women of Troy, Sisyphus*. We know so little of trilogies and tetralogies after the time of Aeschylus that it is of particular interest to reconstruct this one. *Alexander* told the story of Paris. We know the background to the story from other sources. Hecabe, queen of Troy and wife of Priam, while pregnant, dreamed that she gave birth to a firebrand. The seers took this as an evil omen and decreed that the child should be put to death. Like Oedipus, he was rescued by shepherds and brought up among them as a slave with the name of Paris. The boy grew to be a young man, and had in his possessions a pet bull. Hecabe decided to hold funeral games for the child dead long before; the palace officials impounded the bull as a prize. The slave followed his pet and competed in his own funeral games, defeating all his competitors including his brothers. Deiphobus then tried to kill him, Paris took refuge at an altar, Cassandra identified him and prophesied unavailingly all the disasters he would bring, the firebrand who would burn Troy, and Priam welcomed him back with the name Alexander, "Defender-against-men."

This provides on the face of it an exciting melodrama with a last-minute rescue and happy ending, and this is how it may have appeared to the audience during the interval between the first and second plays. But there are somber overtones. We know little of the detailed treatment, but can single out two points. In the first place, a scholiast on *Hippolytus* compares the secondary chorus of huntsmen there with Euripides's use of a chorus of herdsmen here. This suggests an *agon* between the free men and the slaves; the few fragments we possess point to this theme. Deiphobus or some other attacks slaves and says that there is nothing worse than a slave with ideas above his station. "All slaves are abominable; they are all for their bellies, all for the present moment." Yet a slave has beaten Priam's sons, and the sons seek injustice in revenge. So the chorus sings that quality is a gift of the gods and does not come from wealth or family, and one speaker claims that wealth debilitates while poverty makes men tough; more, wealth makes men think that they are above morality. Elsewhere, Euripides questions the presuppositions that underlie the institution of slavery. The old man in *Ion* says:

> One thing, one only, brings disgrace to slaves—
> the word "Slave." In all else a slave
> is as good as free men, if he's honest. (854)

And Aristophanes in *The Frogs* (948) jibes at the freedom Euripides allows women and slaves. It certainly seems that the artificiality of slavery was a theme, perhaps *the* theme of *Alexander*; in one sense it is a pity that the slave-hero turns out to be a prince, yet in the Near East, as in Africa later, many princes must have been enslaved, and in another sense this merely underlines the stupidity of the assumption that slaves are generically different from free men.

The other major theme that we can trace is the theme of Time. Hecabe is at the start of the play still grieving for her lost child. "Time paces onward," they say to her. "Your grief is old; your tears should not be new." "Surely sorrow should relax as time passes." The theme of time recurs at the end of the play.

> Time will reveal you. I accept his decision
> to know whether you come as curse or blessing. (fr. 61)

Gilbert Murray has stressed this aspect of *Alexander*. Mythology is full of wonder-children; he sees them as spirits of the New Year. Sometimes they bring blessing, sometimes a curse.

Oedipus is the best example of a pure curse-child. Many of the curse-children bring a curse to the generation before (in Murray's view the Old Year), but thereafter blessing; such are Perseus, Theseus, or Zeus himself. Alexander is a curse-child who is treated as a blessing-child; he does not destroy Priam as Oedipus destroys Laius. But in the fullness of time he is revealed, as Hecabe's dream and Cassandra's revelation foreshadowed, as a curse-child as bitter as Oedipus bringing down himself and the whole house. There are years like that. In the fullness of time; the end of *Alexander* is pregnant with the future.

And now Euripides passes from the Trojans to the Greeks. The second play, *Palamedes,* was one of his most famous. Its theme was the good man suffering. Palamedes was a polymath, the inventor of writing. Before the Trojan War Odysseus had attempted to evade service by feigning insanity; Palamedes had exposed him. Now at Troy, Odysseus was set on revenge. He buried a sum of gold in Palamedes's tent, wrote a letter purporting to be from Palamedes to Priam accepting a bribe for treason, and gave it to a prisoner of war to take. He then killed the prisoner, discovered the letter, had Palamedes's tent searched and the gold discovered. Palamedes was executed despite the defense of his brother Oeax, who was imprisoned for his pains. But Oeax, in a cell overlooking the sea, carved the story on oar blades, which he threw into the water; the scene is delightfully parodied by Aristophanes in *The Thesmophoriazusae*. According to the myth that this play clearly foreshadowed, the message reached their father Nauplius, who lit false beacons on the coast of Euboea, rather as the Cornish wreckers did centuries later, causing disaster to the returning Greeks. We do not know how Euripides rounded off the play. It is a drama of strong irony. The writing that Palamedes invented is used to destroy him, but it also destroys his destroyers.

How the satyr play *Sisyphus* fitted in, we do not know, for we know nothing about it except that Heracles was a character; it may have dealt with the episode where Heracles, having killed Lycurgus and secured his man-eating horses, had them stolen from him by the cunning Sisyphus. Any link here with the other plays is speculative, but the *agon* over the horses may have parodied the *agon* over the bull in *Alexander*. The fact that Sisyphus was in some stories Odysseus's father provides an obvious connection, and, as Murray has said, a play in which disillusion is treated ludicrously may well be the climax to a series of plays of disillusion, and Sisyphus, the archdeceiver, is well fitted to provide this.

The connection between the three tragedies is clear. It is not as taut as in *The Oresteia*, but it is firm. In the first we see the tragic error of the Trojans, and it is an error arising from the compassionate humanity that let first a child and then a hero live, but at the same time corrupted him by removing him from the manly life of the shepherds to the decadent and unscrupulous life of the court. In the second we see the tragic error of the Greeks, and it is a crime. In the third the two come together and bring disaster upon the Trojans in their comparative innocence and the Greeks in their comparative guilt alike. For what gives the play its peculiar poignancy is the fact that the victors and victims are caught up in the same nexus. The Greeks destroy Troy and are destroyed off Euboea; the Athenians destroy Melos and are destroyed in Sicily. For underlying the skillful weaving together of the three plays is their inner unity. In each we see life through the eyes of those whom life has bruised. In the first, it is the slave; in the second, the victim of political power and intrigue; in the third, the defeated in war.

The Women of Troy begins startlingly. High on the platform above the stage building stands a figure; his trident and his words identify him as the god Poseidon, defender of Troy, taking his leave of the now-shattered city to avoid its pollution and emptiness. His opening words speak of the dances of the sea nymphs (2), a recurring theme of bitter contrast with the fallen, broken, immobile city. But the sea and his account of the Greek ships (19) sound another theme, for those ships will be wrecked. And the smoke that immolated Troy (8) is there at the end as the play comes full circle. He draws the audience's attention to a gray figure lying in the doorway underneath. It is Hecabe, the queen, her husband and sons dead, her daughter Polyxene, though she does not know it, dead at Achilles's grave as a sacrifice. How did she get there? Perhaps she took up position before the play, as Greek convention allowed; perhaps, as Poseidon speaks, the doors open to reveal her; perhaps the moving platform brings her out, though probably not; or perhaps the doors are open from the first and she takes up position while our attention is distracted by Poseidon. Poseidon ends:

> Good-by, my city! You've had your day of blessing.
> Good-by, well-hewn masonry! If Zeus's daughter Pallas
> had not destroyed you, you would be standing firm. (45)

He turns to go, and this same Athene confronts him. She now rejects her Greeks, who have sinned. Together they plan the punishment of the Greeks; they shall be shipwrecked on the voyage home. Mention of Euboea provides the essential link with *Palamedes*. Poseidon's parting words have a fearful intensity.

> Blind is the man who sacks cities
> with temples and tombs, shrines of those whose work is done.
> He brings desolation, himself so soon to die. (95)

"He brings desolation, himself so soon to die." The audience to whom those words were spoken was the very assembly that had voted the massacre at Melos; it contained the very men who had performed the massacre, and were preparing to sail for Sicily, themselves so soon to die.

This prologue is essential to the play. Norwood puts it well. "All the cruelties of the play are committed by the Greeks under the shadow of the calamity denounced against them by the deities of the prologue, whereof we are again and again reminded by sentences casually dropped by Talthybius and others, that the great host is ready to embark. And this when the great Athenian armament was itself thronging the Piraeus in preparation for the voyage to Sicily." Whether or not Euripides takes the gods seriously—and Hecabe's prayer (884) strongly suggests that he does not—he takes the divine dimension seriously. Whatever men say, the Greek behavior at Troy and the Athenian behavior at Melos alike run counter to the laws of the universe.

The gods go, and the gray figure below stirs. In frantic anapaests and wonderful poetry the slave, still a queen, sings the sorrows of Troy. Still a queen—but of what? "Troy is no longer here—and we are sovereigns of Troy" (99), that is, of nothing. In the words that follow her mind is on the ships that will carry them overseas. They are full of metaphors from sailing.

> The tide of fate has turned: bear with it.
> Sail with the ebb, sail with the tide of fate.
> Don't set the prow of life and sail
> against the waves when disaster blows. (101)

Her ancestry has had to lower its sails (108).

Then comes a passage of great daring. As she laments, she sways from side to side and compares herself to a ship rocking as she lets her body keel over in either direction to the rhythm of her song of sorrow (118), a song that allows of no dance (121). She recalls the armada of the Greeks as it descended on Troy, and reverts to the metaphor when she accuses Helen, whom she does not name but calls "that damned wife of Menelaus, Castor's doom, Sparta's shame" (131), of shipwrecking her (137).

The contemptuous hatred of this prepares us for Helen's eventual entry. Like a mother hen with her chicks, she calls in the other slaves, some young, some old, all noble. The rushing anapaests continue as they file in, but there is a difference; they are thinking of themselves, she of herself but also of the woeful widows of Troy's warriors, of the virgin brides of violence, of frenzied Cassandra, of Troy, hapless Troy.

The Argive crews are already gripping their oars. The chorus speculates on their fate and expresses a preference for Athens rather than Sparta. In dramatic context this is reasonable, as Sparta is Helen's country, but Euripides is making clear that a rejection of Athenian brutality at Melos is not a rejection of Athens; to love one's country when she goes wrong is not the same as to support one's country when she goes wrong.

Talthybius, the Greek sergeant major, honest, bluff, unimaginative, sympathetic, but with his job to do, enters. The allocation has been made; they are to go to different masters. Hecabe characteristically asks first about others and only then about herself. The first crime is that Agamemnon is to take Cassandra as his concubine. But she is vowed to virginity; this is the rape of a nun. Talthybius, good old sergeant major that he is, comments that "she's inspired and he's smitten" (255) and thinks her lucky to have a king for a bedfellow.

The second crime relates to Polyxene. We know of her sacrifice at Achilles's tomb, for Poseidon has told us. Talthybius, gruff and kindly, does not say this.

> Appointed attendant at Achilles's tomb. . . .
> Be happy for your daughter; she's all right. (264)

Shakespeare uses the same device with Macduff in *Macbeth*; Ross is his Talthybius. "How does my wife?" "Why, well." "And all my children?" "Well too." "The tyrant has not batter'd at their peace?" "No, they were well at peace when I did leave 'em."

The third crime relates to Andromache, wife to the dead Hector. She has been assigned to the son of the man who killed her husband. Her own son Astyanax is not here mentioned; he is to be killed. Finally Hecabe herself is assigned to Odysseus,

> doomed to serve a dishonest villain,
> an enemy to right, a lawless beast,
> who with his double-talk turns the world
> upside down and downside up,
> till all we love grows sour. (282)

Talthybius gives the order to fetch Cassandra. Suddenly he is startled by a gleam of fire in the gloom of the stage building: are the captives burning themselves to death? In a wonderfully spectacular moment out comes Cassandra, wearing her prophetic garland and emblems, just as we left her at the end of *Alexander* giving her unheeded prophecy of the fall of Troy, but now with bridal torch in hand, ready for marriage, singing and dancing. There is careful planning here by Euripides. Cassandra, Agamemnon's bride, balances the later appearance of Helen, Menelaus's bride. She is dedicated to virginity, Helen to love. She speaks the truth and is not believed, Helen wins credence by lies. She bears a torch; Helen (893) is a torch.

> Wave it high! Bring it here!
> Let me have light. I am a priestess, bearing the flame—See! See!—
> lighting the shrine.
> Lord of the marriage rite,
>   blessed is the husband,
> blessed am I in the bed of a king,
>   bride of Argos,
> Lord of the marriage rite! (308)

The themes of dancing and fire come together in superb poetry with swift short syllables representing pattering dance steps. But for all her wildness her words are sane. The fire of the marriage torch is the same fire that has kindled the towers of Troy. She knows she will be a more disastrous bride to Agamemnon than Helen is to Paris: the theme of Helen's destructive beauty recurs through her words. There follows a bitter attack on aggressive war. A man will avoid war altogether if he is wise. But the Trojans at least died in their own land in defense of their own land, the Greeks far from home, leaving widows, orphans, helpless parents. It is frighteningly contemporary, and the Athenians who were setting out to die far from home in Sicily learned the hard way what he meant. She ends in a great peal of laughter.

Talthybius does not like her words, but recognizes that she is a bit touched. With a fine piece of humor he wishes Agamemnon well of her:

> I'm a poor man myself
> but I wouldn't marry her, not as a free gift. (415)

He tries to push Cassandra out, but she is not done. He is a servant
(424); she is Apollo's servant (450); they are in fact all servants. She
prophesies that Hecabe will die in Troy and that Odysseus will suffer
the familiar long hardships before his return. Then, changing the
rhythm of her speech, she makes ready for her bridegroom's bed—of
death. With a splendid dramatic gesture she enacts the desecration that
is to take place by snatching off Apollo's emblems and hurling them
away. And she is gone. Hecabe collapses on the ground. Her sons have
fallen in battle; she saw her husband butchered in sanctuary; she is to
be a slave; Cassandra is to be violated; she has only her other daughter,
Polyxene—and we know that she has not.

As she lies there the chorus tries to raise her, but she will not. Now
they turn away from her in a solemn dance, and a superb song of the
fall of Troy. They tell of the Trojan horse (the ship image peers darkly
through as it is dragged in, 537), of their joy at the apparent disappearance of the Greeks, of their dancing, and the single beam of light
in the darkness—then disaster, and, in an incredible phrase, "headless
desolation in the beds brought a glory of girls breeding sons for
Greece, sorrow for the Phrygians' fatherland" (564).

And now again spectacle. A chariot enters with Hector's widow
Andromache and young Astyanax on her knee, among the spoils of
Troy. She sits as a slave; she is a part of the spoils. It is a powerful
visual effect; we think of the chariot in *Agamemnon*, but here it is a
sign of degradation not triumph. As the chorus watches their entry
they use another bold expression from the sea: Andromache is ferried
in the chariot and Astyanax is close to the oarage of her breasts (568).
The phrase is daring and difficult; Andromache must be striking her
breasts in rhythmic lamentation, moving her elbows as oarsmen move
rhythmically in striking the water. Hecabe and Andromache join in an
exquisite antiphony of grief, and Andromache now brings the news
of Polyxene's death. There is a significant exchange:

ANDROMACHE: Death is death. But I am left
             alive. Death was a happier fate.
HECABE: No, my child. The gulf between death and light is great.
             The one is nothing, the other leaves hope. (630)

Elsewhere Euripides wonders whether that which we call life is really death; and that which we call death really life. Andromache is puzzled. She won a blameless reputation as Hector's wife, and this is why Neoptolemus chose her. Yet her position is ambiguous: how can she at once maintain her reputation as a good wife, and as a good wife to Hector? Hecabe comforts her by an excellent analogy with sailors who fight a storm when they can and run before it when they can fight no longer; so she should run before this storm. And all the time Astyanax is with her, the doomed hope of the future.

In comes Talthybius, with an armed guard, reluctantly. Cassandra has associated him with them under the name of servitude. Now he speaks of the Greeks not as "we" but "they" (719). Astyanax is to be killed, thrown from the city wall; this on a motion from Odysseus, whom we have seen framing Palamedes. Hurriedly Talthybius warns Andromache not to resist or the boy may remain unburied. The boy senses his mother's distress and starts crying and clinging to her. She fondles him, breathes the scent of his body; we inevitably think of Othello bending over Desdemona. Then she fiercely spits out words against the un-Greek Greeks, and a bitter curse on Helen, child of Vengeance, Envy, Murder, and Death. "Damn you!" (772). Then, in words which in the Greek tumble over one another: "Take him! Carry him off! Dash him to death—if your verdict is 'Death'! Feast on his flesh:" (774).

Said Murray: "This scene, with the parting between Andromache and the child which follows, seems to me perhaps the most absolutely heart-rending in all the tragic literature of the world. After rising from it one understands Aristotle's judgment of Euripides as 'the most tragic of the poets.' " Talthybius is deeply moved; it is he who breaks from the iambics of conversation into the more excited chanted anapaests; at the same time, the change represents the marching measure for the escort to leave with the boy. He has no stomach for his job, but has to do it. Hecabe bursts into sorrow; Andromache is speechless.

The chorus now sings one of Euripides's most beautiful songs, telling of an earlier sacking of Troy by Telamon of Salamis and Heracles. Laomedon was king of Troy; he had three sons, Priam, the last king, Tithonus, who became husband of Dawn, and Ganymede, a boy whom

Zeus loved and made his cupbearer. But when Laomedon cozened the
god, Ganymede and Tithonus could not save Troy. We are reminded
that the gods have again abandoned Troy. We are reminded that they
have abandoned the Greeks. The ode contains a lovely evocation of
the beauty of Salamis:

> with its swarms of bees,
> island circled with waves,
> leaning towards the holy hill where first
> Athene revealed the olive's grey-green branch,
> a blessing from heaven to give Athens a shimmering glory. (799)

and a striking invocation of Love.

Love has abandoned Troy. Enter Menelaus. He has come for Helen.
He is self-centered, pompous, and weak. He assures us that love has
abandoned him too; he wants Helen only to kill her. Poor, self-deluded
fool! Hecabe now offers a novel prayer.

> Sustainer of the earth, throned on the earth,
> whoever you are, hard to discern,
> Zeus, whether natural law or human intellect,
> I call on you; for moving on a noiseless path
> you guide all things human along ways of justice. (884)

There is here a remote but deliberate echo of the first *Agamemnon*
chorus. But, this apart, the prayer is so startlingly out of context and
character that it must reveal Euripides's own view. This makes it of
peculiar interest. There is a principle or power behind the universe,
and, we may say, a single power, discernible alike in nature and in
men, immanent, and giving moral meaning to life.

Hecabe follows her prayer with a bitter pun on Helen's name; again
there is an echo of *Agamemnon*; again the motif of fire appears.

> Don't look at her; she'll put your heart in hell.
> She is hell to men's eyes, double hell to cities,
> she brings homes to ashes. (891)

It is too late. Helen is there, dragged out by her hair, exquisitely
dressed, and making the most of her disarray.

A sweet disorder in the dress
Kindles in hearts a wantonness.

What is to become of her? Menelaus gives himself away. No final
decision has yet been taken. A strange scene of debate follows. Helen
defends herself. Why is no one blamed but her for all that happened?
Blame rather Hecabe for producing Paris; Priam for not killing Paris
at birth despite prophecies that he would prove a firebrand (922; the
image again); Aphrodite for promising her to Paris (if Hera had won,
Greece would have been conquered by the Asiatics); Paris for seduc-
ing her; Menelaus for leaving them alone together. Aphrodite holds
even Zeus under her thumb. Even so, she claims, once Paris was dead,
she tried unsuccessfully to escape. She is the victim of others and of
divine powers. It is a consummate performance, but it is play acting;
these are the artifices of rhetoric.

Hecabe in answer dismisses the story of the Judgment of Paris. She
rejects the plea of Aphrodite; Aphrodite is *Aphrosyne*, lewdness and
folly. It was Helen who was attracted to Paris; she did not resist him;
she never tried to escape; she enjoyed the luxury of the eastern court.
Now she dares to flaunt her fine clothes instead of pleading in rags.
Hecabe calls on Menelaus to kill her.

The interesting feature of this prosecution is that it contains little
of any weight. Helen has propounded a cool, rational case; Hecabe's
is an emotional onslaught without legal substance. But Menelaus is
momentarily moved by the plea, and Helen momentarily breaks and
clasps his knees. But when Hecabe tells him to be firm he snaps at her,
"I don't give her a thought" (1046). No? When she tells him not to
have Helen on his own ship, he passes it off with a weak joke. As
Helen is dragged out, Menelaus's words disown her, but his eyes
follow her. We know, and the chorus who sing of her preening herself before golden mirrors know, that Helen will beat Menelaus. Yet
strangely she does not beat Hecabe.

The point of this apparently anomalous scene is threefold. In the
first place a scene that is not one of suffering, and a long scene at that,
is dramatically vital to throw the final scene into sharper relief. Second,
Euripides was master of scenes of rhetorical debate, and his audience,

delighting in the verbal battles of the assembly and law courts, had come to expect them. Third, the scene, as it were, takes the spotlight off Hecabe and focuses it upon Helen. The visual impact of the scene is itself important: the old queen with her grey hair and torn clothes contrasts with the brilliant beauty of Helen in all her splendor. Euripides is far too subtle to give Hecabe an easy victory. Whatever Menelaus says, Helen wins the debate as she will win its aftermath. Hecabe is governed by unreasoning, unrelenting hatred. She is not a sweet old lady suffering patiently. She is a mass of prejudice. Yet when the scene is over our sympathies are still with her not because she has persuaded us intellectually, or because she is nice to know, but because Hecabe is solid and real, and we have seen the shallowness of Helen with her mask of beauty.

The chorus reverts to the theme that the gods have abandoned Troy; then they turn to their own farewells, and to a prayer that Menelaus may be shipwrecked, the theme of brooding doom for the Greeks. And now Talthybius returns with the broken body of Astyanax and Hector's shield for the burial. His opening words remind us of the ships. Of Neoptolemus's fleet "one single rhythmic rowing of a ship is left" (1123). Decent, kindly man that he is, he has already washed the body in the waters of Scamander. Again there is marvelous spectacle as the tiny body is laid in the huge shield. Hecabe is left to arrange the body for burial, and her lament, spoken not sung, is one of the most wonderful passages that even Euripides ever wrote. It is a great vehicle for a tragic actor, as those who have seen Sybil Thorndike in the rôle will know. She recalls the boy's childish promises to do for her, his grandmother, the office she is now performing for him. She time and again speaks of the cowardice of the Greeks in killing children; she imagines an epitaph in which all the emphasis is on the cowardice:

> This child was once killed by the Greeks
> through fear. (1190)

She broods over the shield and imagines the print of Hector's palm on the handle, and the sweat of his face running over the rim. Then they cover the body, and as they do she draws a lesson of life.

> The man is blind who thinks he's well established
> with solid satisfaction. Fortune's a dervish,
> leaping now one way now the other.
> No one controls his own happiness. (1203)

Fortune's a dervish. So Macbeth on life:

> It is a tale
> Told by an idiot, full of sound and fury,
> Signifying nothing.

So Tennyson:

> Time's a maniac scattering dust
> And Life a Fury slinging flame.

But there is more to it than that. These last words of Hecabe are Euripides's masterstroke. For "the man is blind" takes us straight back to Poseidon:

> Blind is the man who sacks cities
> with temples and tombs, shrines of those whose work is done.
> He brings desolation, himself so soon to die. (95)

Fortune's a dervish, and the Greeks are so soon to die. So are the Athenians in Sicily.

Hecabe and the chorus burst into wild lamentation, a cataclysm of grief. Yet Hecabe retains control as she hands the body in the shield over to the soldiers for burial. Talthybius comes back. The final burning of Troy is at hand. Hecabe tries to fling herself into the flames, but Talthybius will not let her. Odysseus must have her—but we know, for Cassandra has told us, that he will not. Now the songs become more and more excited as short syllables tumble over one another (1312, cf. 1329). The language is vivid. Great-citied Troy is uncitied (1291). The land is dissolving before the spear like a puff of smoke in the sky before a wing (1298). And then the dust *like smoke* blots out the sight of the buildings *with its wing* (1320), a striking combination of simile and metaphor. The smoke brings us back full circle to the opening words of Poseidon (8) and again we recall that disaster is waiting for the Greeks. To the sound of collapsing buildings, the waving of torches and clouds of smoke the prisoners drag themselves off, Hecabe to the uncertain mercy of fate, the chorus to the ships. Hecabe uses a natural phrase "the day of servitude" (1330), but it is literally and ironically true; her servitude lasts one day. The chorus sings:

> Weep for the city, then—needs must—
> direct your steps to the ships of the Greeks. (1331)

Ships of Greece—the last words take up the central doom-laden image.

So ends the greatest antiwar play ever written. As F. L. Lucas wrote, "To initiate a war of senseless conquest the girl Iphigeneia is murdered at Aulis; to secure its sterile fruits the boy Astyanax is flung from the shattered towers of Troy."

26. ION

Ion is in many ways the most puzzling of all Euripides's plays. On stylistic grounds it is reasonable to assign it to the year 414, and the political allusions are not clear enough to make an earlier date cogent: military and political activities round Rhium in 429 and 419 (cf. 1529), problems with those of foreign birth in 424, demagogy and ostracism in 417 (cf. 603). If we are right in assigning a late date to *Heracles*, then it becomes highly probable that they were performed together, and have a common link in the ambiguity of divine paternity. It is tempting to think that *Alope* was the third play; this dealt with a child of Poseidon (cf. 446) and the plot is derived from one of the legends associated with Attica.

   Ion starts with a typically Euripidean prologue of the type that offered itself to Aristophanes's addition of "lost his little oil bottle"; the prologue is spoken by Hermes, who does not reappear. He identifies the scene as Delphi, and tells a story of Athens ("a well-known city," 8). Creusa, daughter of king Erechtheus, was ravished in a cave by

Phoebus Apollo; a child was born, and she left him in the cave to die, with a necklace of golden snakes traditional in the royal house and a shawl she had woven herself. Hermes was sent by Apollo to fetch him to Delphi; the priestess brought him up, and he is now one of the temple servants. Creusa meantime married a non-Athenian ally of Athens named Xuthus. The marriage is childless, and they have come to the oracle because of this. When Xuthus comes to the oracle Apollo will give him the boy so that he may come to his mother's house without any exposure of her union with Apollo. He will be called Ion, father-founder of the Ionians.

It seems straightforward enough, but it is in fact seething with problems. For the plot that Hermes outlines is not the plot that takes place; Creusa's union with Apollo is revealed. The contradiction is flagrant; if the god is unreliable here, can he be trusted elsewhere? Immediately after his outline of the plot he says:

> I'll make my way into this laurel-grove
> to learn what destiny has in store for the boy. (76)

It has become clear that Hermes has no knowledge of himself; all he knows is what he has been told by Apollo, whether of the past or the future. Apollo in fact sent him to pick up a baby from Athens, saying, "By the way, he's mine" (35); and even then the words are ambiguous between "my son" and "my servant" (*pais*). But Apollo himself is characterized as giving oracles about "what is and what is to be" (7); nothing is said about his reliability on the past. Furthermore, in the plot of the play as it unfolds on stage, he is revealed as ignorant about the future. Apollo is an operator, skillful but not impeccable, with no high standards of morality. He is in fact the Delphic Oracle.

Ion comes out (seeing him, Hermes mutters his new name Ion, which means "coming"), and the scene bursts into light as in warm poetical song, which contrasts with the prosy exposition of the god; he greets the dawn. Ion, the teenage boy, is delightfully drawn, naive, open and impulsive, occasionally wise beyond his years and a little proud of it, always warm and attractive. Neither Aeschylus nor Sophocles had the imaginative self-identification with youth that Euripides shows here and in *Iphigeneia at Aulis*. As the boy sweeps the steps and sings to his broom we can hardly fail to think of George Herbert's words:

> A servant with this clause
> Makes drudgerie divine
> Who sweeps a room as to thy laws
> Makes that and th' action fine.

Then in splendid poetry he takes a bow and arrows and in an excellent scene scares the birds away from the shrine: "If you don't listen," he calls to the eagle, "you'll find an arrow in you!" (168). His life is one of joyful duty marred only by his orphan-state, motherless, fatherless (109). But the sonorous words of a perhaps familiar hymn ring from him in repeated refrain (125, 141), as he assigns to Phoebus the place of his father (136).

He retires to put away his tools, and the chorus moves lightly in; the effect is slightly unexpected in that they enter from stage-right. They are Creusa's attendants and have never been out of Athens before; they are making the most of their opportunities of sightseeing. It is not clear whether the sights at which they marvel are actually there to see; a painted backcloth, painted flats, and statues on the stage are all possible, but the precision of their descriptions suggests that they are creating an unseen image for the audience. Ion comes out and watches them, but they are not allowed in. But now Creusa arrives. There is immediate rapport between Ion and the gracious, troubled lady, who addresses hims as "stranger," weeps at memories which the shrine calls up, and speaks of the wickedness of the gods and the wrongs of women (252); "I have shot my arrow," she says (256). Euripides handles the scene with exquisite delicacy. Ion learns that she is Creusa of Athens, and asks whether her ancestor was born from the earth (267); it was a familiar claim that the Athenians were in origin autochthonous, sprung from the soil. Creusa's answer is ambiguous: "Yes, Erichthonius. My birth has not helped me" (268). Birth, *genos*, may refer to her ancestry, or to the child she bore and the process of labor through which she passed. There follows another ambiguity. Ion asks, "Do you know a place there called The Long Rocks?" (283). This was the scene of the rape, and Creusa replies, "Why do you ask that? You reminded me of——" and the word can mean "something" or "someone." She tells of her marriage to the foreigner Xuthus, who has paused to consult the oracle of Trophonius on his way to Delphi. More irony follows.

ION: You've never had a child at all? You're childless?
CREUSA: Apollo knows how childless I am.
ION: Poor woman. Unhappy for all your happiness!
CREUSA: Who are you? Your mother is a lucky woman.
ION: The name I bear, my lady, is Apollo's servant.
CREUSA: Were you an offering from a city, or bought from some owner?
ION: I don't know. All I know is that I am called Apollo's.
CREUSA: Then, sir, it is my turn to pity you. (305)

Every line is loaded. Creusa tells him of a woman who suffered as his own mother suffered, one whom Apollo took as his lover. This draws from the prudishly devout adolescent a startling assertion that she is covering up for some man. She wants to know about the child of the union. The interchange, charged with irony, continues till:

ION: Do you realize your argument is weak in one point?
CREUSA: Everything goes wrong for her, poor woman.
ION: How will Apollo reveal the mystery he wants to hide?
CREUSA: The chair he sits in is open to all Greece.
ION: But his honor . . . Don't press him.
CREUSA: What of her suffering, her misfortune, her grief? (363)

Ion's answer (365) is a breathless outburst of short syllables. Ion sees that her question would bring disrepute on Apollo, but Creusa hisses (386) her denunciation of the god. She breaks off, seeing Xuthus coming, and warns Ion to be silent about her enquiries. Xuthus, gruff, blunt, extrovert, self-satisfied, but not unkindly, greets Creusa and ignores Ion until he wants to use him. He tells Creusa that Trophonius promised "neither you nor I will leave for home without a child" (408); he will press his enquiry with Apollo today. He goes into the sanctuary, Creusa goes out to find laurels to offer at the altars, and they leave Ion agitated in mind. He talks to himself with delightful abruptness; Euripides has blended his own rationalistic spirit with his understanding of the adolescent mind:

> I really must speak severely
> to Apollo. What is he up to? Raping girls
> and abandoning them. Fathering children secretly
> and leaving them to die. It won't do. You have power.
> How about some justice? If a man shows
> a crooked nature, the gods prescribe punishments.
> Here are you, enacting laws for humans, and guilty
> of breaking them yourself. Where's the justice in that?
> Just suppose—impossible, but suppose it for argument—
> you, Apollo, Poseidon, and Almighty Zeus,
> had to give account to men for all your sex crimes,
> you'd strip your temples bare in paying the fines!
> You go all out for pleasure, and think afterwards.
> It's wrong! There's no justice in blaming
> men for copying the glorious actions
> of the gods. Rather blame their instructors. (436)

He is so disturbed that he does not return into the temple but goes out to think by himself.

The choral song that follows is as tightly knit into the plot as any Sophocles wrote. It is a prayer to Athene and Artemis to grant children to the house of Erechtheus. The singers sound like the Hebrew psalmist as they set the blessing of children above riches. Then they sing of the caves, which Pan haunts, where the girl was taken and the child left, the crowning insult (*hybris*, by a god! 506) of a bitter union.

> Never in yarns or in stories
> have I heard tell of happiness
> for the children of mortals and gods. (506)

Ion returns to find whether Xuthus has had his answer. He has indeed; he comes out and tries to kiss Ion. The encounter must be seen against the background of Athenian homosexuality; Ion, chaste and puritanical, misunderstands his advances and tries to hold him off; the scene is as amusing as the encounter between Achilles and Clytemnestra in *Iphigeneia at Aulis*. Xuthus has been told that the first person he meets is his son, a gift of the god, but his by birth. Ion is reluctant to believe. Who was his mother? Xuthus has no idea. "Another child of Earth!" says Ion with some bitterness, and Xuthus comments, "The earth doesn't bear children" (542).

Ion presses for details. Had Xuthus had any love affairs? He confesses to sowing his wild oats, but he has gone steady since marriage. But then Ion must have been brought to Delphi from a distance; this puzzles Xuthus, who plainly has in mind something that did not take place at Delphi. Ion drags from him that he had visited Delphi, that he had been in the company of some Maenads, and drunk, and Ion is satisfied that that was the occasion of his begetting. Reluctantly he calls Xuthus, who is after all descended from Zeus, father. Xuthus wants him to come to Athens as a prince and live in wealth. In a long speech he disclaims such ambitions. Athens does not welcome aliens; her citizens claim to be autochthonous. In addition he is a bastard. With a tender insight he recognizes the pain his presence would cause Creusa; because he understands motherlessness he understands childlessness. It might even drive her to murder. Besides, he has no impulse toward autocracy (*turannis*, 621), "a life of torment behind a pleasant façade." He is content at Delphi and asks nothing more.

Some critics have seen an unnatural precocity in Ion's speech, but it is wholly in character, and much what a conservative adolescent, brought up in a sheltered life and fearing change, might be expected to say. The chorus, identified with Creusa, supports his wish, but Xuthus brushes his arguments impatiently aside. There will be a feast; the boy is to be called Ion, because of their meeting; his identity is to be, for the time being, concealed. Ion assents. But unless he finds his mother, there is no life for him; the words are ironical, since she seeks and nearly causes his death. He would like an Athenian mother; it would give him the right to speak out; Euripides is girding at the comparatively recent innovation limiting citizenship to those of Athenian parentage on both sides.

Again the choral song is closely linked to the action; the exact text is uncertain, but the general sense clear. They are sympathetic to Creusa —the thought of childlessness recurs—and hostile to Ion:

> Let that boy never come to my city!
> Let him leave his new daylight for death!
> A city in hardship with justice

may welcome an alien invasion.
Erechtheus our lord and first ruler
brought *us* together in one. (719)

Creusa enters with an elderly servant, who makes heavy weather of
the steps up to the stage. She is eager for news. The chorus, at first
reluctantly, then impulsively, tells all that they know, and more. As
often in Euripides, they play a significant part in the action. They
betray Xuthus's secret against his orders, and preface it gratuitously
and misleadingly by telling Creusa then she will never have children
of her own at her breast or in her arms (761). Creusa's reply to the
news about Ion is a great cry:

Ottotottoi. A childless childless life
did he then promise me? Shall I have
an empty desolate house to live in? (789)

The old servant, a brooding mixture of bitterness and loyalty, suggests
that the oracle is invented and Xuthus is using cunning to introduce
his own bastard; her best plan is to kill them both.

And now we see why Euripides has played down his choral odes;
he does not wish to detract from the great solo he now gives to Creusa.
For this is one of the great things in all dramatic lyric. It is anapaestic
in rhythm, and its pulsating beat hammers home its insistent point:
Apollo is a criminal betrayer.

You give a voice to the seven-stringed
lyre, a voice which sounds
in the lifeless horns of shepherds
with the Muses' sweet-sounding songs,
yet I denounce you, Apollo,
in the blazing light of day.
You came with the gleam of gold
in your hair, as I picked yellow flowers,
set them in the fold of my cloak,
rivaling your gold with their bloom.
You gripped my wrists till the blood went
from them, and dragged me to lie
in the cave, as I called for my mother's help,
you, a god, a lover,

a shameless ravisher,
Aphrodite's devotee! (881)

She calls him "vile seducer" (912) and "fool" (916), and expresses the loathing his very birthplace and sacred tree must feel for one so callous. It is deeply affecting, a powerful but controlled denunciation. All Creusa's long-dammed resentment pours out, not spreading ineffectually, but channeled with maximum force. Everything is felt, nothing overstated. To one point of the indictment Apollo has an answer: Ion lives. We know this, yet, as we listen, it does not affect our judgment of the violence, the betrayal, and the years of desolation. When Aeschylus wrestled with the story of Io he found consolation that suffering might be the condition of bliss, and Euripides is at pains to keep the two apart. The bliss does not depend upon the prior desolation, and if it did the god who so ordained would be a devil-god; the desolation was wholly evil. This song is the emotional high point of the play, and demonstrates alike Euripides's understanding of the mind of a woman and his superb gifts as a writer of lyric.

The truth, or half-truth, is out, and the startled old man drags the story from her in cold dialogue

I had just used my mind to bale out one wave of disasters
when another caught me astern as I listened to your words. (927)

He joins in the denunciation of Apollo (952). Their exchange is long, nearly as long as her earlier exchange with Ion, which it balances. Both reveal the story; in the first she moves toward Ion, in the second away from him. The old man is eager for action, but his suggestions are not very practical. To set fire to the temple does not appeal to Creusa, who has suffered enough at Apollo's hands, and it is not likely to succeed. To kill Xuthus offends against Creusa's respect for a faithful husband. To kill Ion. . . . Here the appeal is stronger, for her hatred has begun to concentrate on Ion, both as identified with Apollo and as usurping the place of her son. But how? Creusa has two drops of the Gorgon's blood; one gives life, the other destroys it. The Gorgon, like the Athenians, is a child of Earth (989).

In slow narrative with plenary detail, she gives the mythological background to the poison and the way she came by it. The effect is to divert the sense that she is a coldblooded murderess, and to raise the whole story to the level of myth and divine involvement. It prevents too drastic a diversion of sympathy from Creusa. She gives her servant the vial to take to the feast and pour into Ion's cup. The old man recovers an almost fiendish energy by contrast with the senility of his first appearance, and shows himself without scruple in dealing with enemies.

The chorus, still identified with Creusa, has a fine song, praying to Persephone, queen of the dead, for the success of Creusa's plot. They do not want to see an alien prince in Athens. There is an excellent evocation of the dances to Iacchus. They then turn and in the final stanza of the climactic ode denounce male lust. Euripides is again making his witness against the double standard of morality. But there is another point; their preoccupation is with men not gods

> All you poets who sing
> in harsh verses of women's desire,
>   of love-matches
> flouting sacred right, see how
>   in duty we surpass
>   the godless crop of men.
>   The song must change its tune,
> the poetry turn harsh against
>   the male for all his lust. (1090)

Suddenly an attendant of Creusa's is there. "Noble ladies," he greets the chorus, oddly, seeing that they are his fellow-slaves (1106). Perhaps it is Euripides's way of picking up the end of the song; perhaps it means "women of glorious Athens"; perhaps the messenger, who has scoured the town for Creusa, in his haste does not realize who they are, and their leader's "fellow-servant" brings him to himself; or perhaps we should emend so that the word applies to Creusa. As usual with Euripides's messengers, his full narrative is held up for a few lines, but we learn immediately that the plot has failed and the citizens are seeking to stone Creusa.

The attendant tells his story well; he has done his best to find Creusa, and for the moment the chorus distracts him. His narrative begins with a leisurely description of the awning with mythological motifs and embroidered tapestries that adorned the feast, leisurely in one sense, for repeated short syllables sound a note of urgency (1143). The people of Delphi were invited to the feast; the old man appeared and made himself the life and soul of the party. He prepared a special cup of wine for Ion, but as the boy was about to drink a slave spoke a word of ill omen. The cups were poured out and refilled; one of the sacred doves sipped the wine from Ion's cup and died in contorted agony. Ion, swift to realize the truth, leapt at the old man. The vial was found; the poisoner was put to torture and confessed. Then Ion raised the authorities to condemn Creusa.

> She came with a view to desire for children from Phoebus;
> she has lost her life and children together. (1227)

On these ironic words the attendant finishes abruptly and goes.

The chorus again identifies with Creusa in the death that hangs over her. When she bursts in, having heard the news, presumably from the attendant, they persuade her to take refuge at the altar. There she confronts Ion and the crowd of Delphians with him. Ion piles on images from animals.

> Father Cephisus, in form like a ball,
> what is this viper you have spawned, this snake
> with fire of murder flashing from its eyes? (1261)

He hisses at her (1276) that the altar will not save her. She stays in sanctuary but stands up to his attack with a kind of passionate dignity. The whole encounter is heavily charged with irony, and that at two levels, for sometimes Creusa realizes the irony of her words and Ion does not.

ION: What have you to do with Phoebus? What's between you?
CREUSA: I give my body to him to possess in holiness. (1284)

To Ion she means the sanctuary; in her own mind she is giving to Apollo what he has already taken, but ravaged now and useless. Again

ION: Why do you choose to die among the god's garlands?
CREUSA: Because I shall injure one who has injured me. (1310)

She means Apollo; Ion thinks of himself. But sometimes the irony is unconscious:

> CREUSA: You were no longer Apollo's; you were your father's.
> ION: I did *become* my father's; I mean what I really *am*. (1287)

The language is the language of religious mysticism. Again, though more obviously,

> ION: Leave that altar! Leave the holy place!
> CREUSA: Preach at your own mother, wherever she is. (1306)

Ion, young, impetuous, inclined to put his sense of moral rectitude above religious tradition, is almost inclined to break the sanctuary, when the priestess comes from the temple to intervene; her appearance is spectacular. He drives a knife more firmly into Creusa's heart as he calls the priestess "Mother, though not my physical mother" (1324). The priestess has done something rare in emerging; she tells him that to kill Creusa will make him unclean, and he must go to Athens as a blessing. She gives him the cradle and baby clothes in which he was found, and gives him a parting kiss "as if I were really your mother" (1363). He broods over the tokens of his birth, noting that they are fresh and new (1392) when an exclamation from Creusa distracts him. She leaves her sanctuary in her eagerness to see. She is his mother.

> ION: Stop your fabrications; I'll catch you out.
> CREUSA: Let me come to the point, my son; I'm aiming at that. (1410)

The cloth is her "fabrication," and we met him first aiming at the birds. She describes the cloth and its embroidery, the golden snakes, and the branch of Athene's olive tree, which had not lost its freshness. Now he is persuaded and she breaks into a song and dance of joy "No longer sonless, no longer childless" (1463), while he keeps to the rhythms of dialogue. He wants to know his father. She tells him that he is Apollo's child; nothing could bring him more joy. Creusa comments on the change:

> Ah! Fate pressed hard in the past.
> Fate pressed hard just now. We are tossed
> from side to side, from misery to bliss.

The winds are always changing.
Let them hold. Enough of sorrow. Let there be now
    a fair wind out of disaster, o my son. (1502)

And the chorus adds, "After today, nothing can ever again seem strange or unexpected," and Ion invokes the goddess of change, blind Chance, somewhat oddly for one whose life is so wrapped up with Apollo. But Ion is still troubled, not so much about Xuthus, as about Apollo's statements about him:

Are Apollo's oracles true or false?
Mother, it racks my heart, and well it may. (1537)

Ion is not satisfied with her attempts to explain; he is determined to challenge Apollo.

Suddenly, high in the air, swung by the crane, appears Athene. She is acting for Apollo. He did not want to appear because of the reproaches he might incur. He had intended to keep the secret longer, but things had not worked out that way (the god of prophecy!). However, Apollo has done all things well (1595). He, not Xuthus, is Ion's father, but it will be good to keep the secret and leave Xuthus to his delusion. Meantime they will go to Athens; Creusa and Xuthus will have sons from whom the Dorians and Achaeans will spring, and Ion will have four sons, who will give their names to the Ionian tribes. This is typical Euripidean etiology. Creusa turns her curses of Apollo into blessings. Athene goes to some trouble to watch them off stage and follows them to their glory in Athens.

No analysis of the problems that underlie the action should divert attention from the fact that it is a lively and exciting play in its own right. The characters are interestingly conceived and finely drawn: the virginal, naive boy; the frustrated woman with her single-minded obsession that leads her to poison at one moment and a smothering flood of mother love at another; the honest complacent man; the crooked, simple-minded old servant. There is good theater in Ion's opening monody, in the scene between Ion and Xuthus, in Ion's confrontation of Creusa as she takes sanctuary, and in the dramatic appearance of the priestess. Apart from Creusa's great solo, and, to a lesser extent, the messenger's speech, there is not much outstanding writing, but there is always Euripides's lucidity in dialogue and liquid lyricism in song, and Creusa's monody is one of the great things in Euripidean tragedy. Irony there is in plenty, sometimes obvious, sometimes subtle. The sequence of events is gripping, and Euripides has given his play something of the mood of a whodunit by letting the plot move away from the predicted lines and the control of the allegedly divine sponsors. It is as in *Berkeley Square*, where the hero projects himself back in time and appears likely to falsify history by falling in love with the wrong girl.

A whodunit the play remains, it being Ion. It is important to see that Euripides does not give an unequivocal answer to the question "Who are Ion's parents?" For Hermes and Athene alike do not speak for themselves. Both say what Apollo tells them to say, and Apollo, however Creusa may forgive him, is discredited. He is discredited not so much because of his treatment of Creusa as because he, the god of prophecy, fails to foresee the course of events. We may reflect that this was the very thing that happened in the Persian Wars, when Delphi, to put it crudely, backed the wrong horse.

There are three candidates for the position of Ion's mother. The first is an unknown Bacchant. This possibility we can dismiss. Xuthus never admits such an affair; he admits intoxication. It is Ion who jumps to conclusions. The second is the priestess. This was Verrall's view, and it is by no means a foolish one. Her maternal relationship to Ion is stressed in the dialogue. Over and above this is the problem of the tokens. Euripides goes out of his way to stress that they are as good as new, and that the olive branch is still fresh and green. It certainly does look as if the tokens are somehow contrived by Delphian officials; at the very least the gratuitous emphasis upon their apparent newness must be intended by the dramatist to arouse our suspicions in exactly the same way that a writer of detective stories strews false clues and red herrings across the trail. Nonetheless it is not easy to believe that the priestess is the real mother. For though the tokens may be contrived by Delphi, this tells us nothing about the parentage, and the mother relationship with Ion is partly designed dramatically for

Creusa's despair, and partly to show that Ion is indeed spiritually the child of Apollo through the upbringing of his priestess. We are left with Creusa as the mother.

What then of Ion's father? Hermes and Athene answer "Apollo." But they have only Apollo's word for it. And, to Euripides's rationalizing mind, who is Apollo? He is the power of the Delphic Oracle. He does not appear. He does not appear because he does not exist. The Delphic Oracle and its staff exist; they are, in the current jargon, "operators," and on this occasion, as Athene points out, everything works out all right in the end. The whole plot suggests not the controlling power of a god, but a plot from Plautus, Goldoni, or P. G. Wodehouse, in which each operation leads to new complications, until the operator pulls his final rabbit out of the hat. No doubt Athene, goddess of Athens, is pleased to have the son of an Athenian princess as future ruler, giving Athens the eponymous leadership of the Ionians; but there is too much said discrediting the myths of divine seducers to leave us with Apollo as father.

Who is left? "Some man," says Ion (341). But who? The answer is in fact simple. It is the obvious answer; it is the answer of New Comedy, as in Menander's *The Arbitrators*; it is Xuthus, and Euripides goes as far as he can to tell us so directly without removing all ambiguity and spoiling the excitement. First, the oracle of Trophonius, which is not a subsidiary of Delphi, says quite explicitly that neither Xuthus nor Creusa will return home from the oracle without a son (408). There is no qualification; the words can only mean that the son who is found is the son of Xuthus and Creusa. There are two other clues. Xuthus means "red" and suggests that its bearer is red-headed. "Apollo," as he appeared to Creusa, had the gleam of gold in his hair (887). We do not know at what time the incident took place, but as there was no one about and Creusa was picking flowers, we may suppose the half-light of morning. The denunciation in the light of day (886) suggests that she has not known him in that light. Euripides is at pains to establish Creusa's impressionable and superstitious nature: a figure with gleaming hair at dawn would be for her the sun god.

The third clue lies in the conversation between Xuthus and Ion.

ION:	Did you ever have a love-affair?
XUTHUS:	Yes. I was young and foolish.
ION:	Before you took Erechtheus's daughter?
XUTHUS:	Yes. Never since then.
ION:	Then that was when you fathered me?
XUTHUS:	Yes. The time fits.
ION:	And how did I come here?
XUTHUS:	I can't imagine. (545)

The arm of Delphi is long. The point is, first, that Ion's age corresponds to the time shortly before Xuthus's marriage; second, that Xuthus has clearly in mind some actual episode that took place away from Delphi at about that time. It is Ion, not Xuthus, who sheers off to the Bacchant at Delphi. Xuthus has no memory of a love affair there; it is elsewhere that he is thinking of. Where was he at an appropriate interval before his marriage? The answer is "Athens." For Xuthus was an ally of Athens against Euboea, and no doubt was in Athens for a period before the campaign. The child would be born during the campaign, and he would return to a bride, older and matured from the girl he had seen only in the dawn light without knowing who she was. Here we have added point to the jibes at Athenian autochthony and their insistence on citizens having Athenian parents on both sides; the national hero had a non-Athenian father; but that father himself, as Euripides carefully preserves, was descended from Zeus.

Divine parentage in this play is treated differently from that of Heracles in *Heracles*. In both, the human parentage is left open. Here the rationalizing element is stronger, the spiritual aspect of divinity weaker, precisely because Euripides does believe in some kind of life force, which he can name Zeus, and hardly believes in Apollo in the same way. Yet is it so much weaker? For Ion, in being the servant of Apollo, has been the child of Apollo (*pais*), and, growing up with the façade of piety, still shows himself, like the oracle, something of an operator who will set aside the laws of sanctuary at convenience; his joy in believing himself to be Apollo's son is part of his spiritual nature. In fact Ion says this himself, and gives us the key to this aspect of the play. "I did become my father's; I mean what I really *am*"

(1287). Here Euripides is being genuinely philosophical. For what this means, in cold terms, is that it does not matter that Ion is physically Xuthus's son; what matters is that he is spiritually bound up with Apollo. We can extend this. He does not need to be physically Apollo's son, any more than Heracles needs to be physically Zeus's son. What counts is what they really are. And here Euripides drives his point home, and we see why in this play the putative father is Apollo.

For the two focal characters are human in their frailties, Creusa with her warmth, her romanticism, her loving heart, is ready to connive at murder, Ion with his attractive openness, his sympathy, his piety, is ready to kill a woman in sanctuary. Euripides does not idolize or idealize. Yet each is of stronger moral fiber than the god in whom they both believe. It is what we really are that makes life, and it is an irony of life that they agree out of kindness to deceive Xuthus into believing—the truth.

27. HERACLES

August Strindberg, faced with the bitter criticism aroused by the un-orthodox character of *A Dream Play*, wrote: "As far as the loose incoherence of the form is concerned, it is only apparent. For study will reveal that the composition is very tight—symphonic, polyphonic, fugal here and there with the main themes continually recurring, re-peated and varied. The orchestration is strictly controlled." Euripides's *Heracles* is a puzzling play. Like *Ajax* it is a diptych, but the break is even more clearly marked; the play almost seems to end and begin afresh. Partly this is due to the fact that the single play remained occa-sionally cramping, partly to the fact that Euripides had a new concept of drama, not to be measured on the Procrustean bed of Aeschylus, Sophocles, or Aristotle; Svendsen compares Strindberg's expres-sionism.

Our capacity to interpret *Heracles* is further hampered by our in-capacity to date it. Grace Macurdy argued on political grounds for 420–418, but stylistic considerations point rather to a later date, possibly as late as 414. We cannot be certain of its political or dramatic context, but I am inclined to think that 414 may be right, and Ion may have been presented at the same festival.

The play begins powerfully. There is an altar and by it a statue of Zeus the Deliverer, a powerful visual symbol throughout the play. Perhaps by convention the actors could take their place in the sight of the audience before the play began; in a modern production they would be "discovered." A woman and three boys, with an elderly man, group themselves round the altar. The elderly man speaks:

> All men know me—the man who shared his marriage with Zeus,
> Amphitryon of Argos, son of Alcaeus,
> grandson of Perseus, and father of Heracles. (1)

From the first comes ambiguity: who is Heracles's father—Zeus or Amphitryon? The woman is Heracles's wife Megara. The place is Thebes; Amphitryon was exiled from Argos; Heracles offered the reigning king Eurystheus to cleanse the earth of violence as the price of his return, a task imposed by Hera or in accordance with destiny. Rationalism here breaks through, significantly, as we shall see. His last "labor" (a key word, 22) is to bring the three-headed hound Cerberus from Hades up into the light; light-dark is one of the basic themes of the play. The Cerberus story is traditional, but it is hard to see how this is cleansing the earth of violence. Thebes was diseased with civil strife (34); one Lycus had seized his moment and with it the throne and is now threatening to kill Heracles's family, resolving "to extinguish murder by murder" (40). Amphitryon in his age is impotent; his son in the vigor of youth has passed to the black night of the lower world. So the intended victims have taken refuge at the altar of Zeus the Savior, built by Heracles "my well-born son" (50). But they are without food and drink. Another important theme enters at the end of his speech:

> Friends? Some I see blurred and faint.
> Our true friends are genuinely powerless to help.
> This is what misfortune does to men.
> If anyone thinks kindly of me at all, may he never
> face this, the infallible test of friends. (55)

Megara, wife of Heracles and daughter of the murdered Creon, answers. Her opening words recall Amphitryon's past record as a soldier and the impotence of age. Creon had wealth and political power (*tyrannis*, 65); it has all gone. An important image comes as she describes herself as a mother bird with her nestlings protected beneath her wings (71). Escape seems impossible; yet they love light (90). Megara is near despair; Amphitryon still hopes for a fair wind after the storm; while there is life there is hope.

The chorus of Theban elders joins them. Like Amphitryon, they are in the impotence of old age, and their words bring out this theme, in sound as well as meaning, for there is a curiously intense alliteration of ending, which may represent a kind of stammering repetitiousness (107 *a*; 120ff. *s, on*; 134ff. *s*). They compare themselves to gray birds (110), or, as they move in effective spectacle, each leaning on his neighbor for support, to a horse and wagon straining uphill. Their faltering entry contrasts with the dynamic pride of Lycus as he strides in from stage-left. He scorns Amphitryon's claim to be co-partner with Zeus, rationalizes the Labors, mentioning only animals, the hydra, and the lion, which, he suggests, Heracles did not strangle but trapped, and dismisses Heracles's archery as cowardice.

Amphitryon defends his son in careful legal language. The Giants and Centaurs know Heracles's heroism. There follows a defense of the bowman; the debate seems oddly irrelevant, and may have political connotations, for the light-armed troops won Sphacteria, the absence of them lost Delium, and Demosthenes, their main proponent, had not in 414 been sent to Syracuse. Irony is strong when the bowman's attack is said to be invisible (199), but the word is ambiguous and means "blind," and Heracles is to give this second meaning tragic power. We note too that the arrows are winged (179). Amphitryon pleads for exile, pleads for the fledglings (224), and bursts out into the contrast between the impotence of age and the strength of youth. It is a long speech, and the sense of holding up the action is deliberate. Lycus points the contrast.

> Words! Build a fortress of words against me.
> I shall act—and you'll pay for those words. (238)

He sends attendants for logs to burn out the suppliants. He is a man
of action; he speaks fourteen lines, then is silent for a hundred before
speaking four more. The chorus, huddled perhaps round their own
altar, speak at unusual length. Lycus has called them slaves of his
autocracy (*tyrannis,* 251); they are stung to reply, for Thebans were
sprung from the dragon's teeth; but again the impotence of old age
prevents them from action. Megara, in a speech of some nobility, calls
the elders true friends and (using the same word) speaks of her own
love for her children. But better to die nobly than ignominiously.
There is no hope of Heracles's return. The chorus and Amphitryon
reassert the impotence of age, Amphitryon saying with terrible irony,

> I want to save
> these children for my son. (317)

The suppliants surrender and are permitted to dress for the execution.
The statue and altar of the Deliverer who has not saved stand bare, and
Amphitryon cries bitterly:

> Zeus, you shared my marriage; does that count for nothing?
> For nothing that I called you partner in my son?
> You professed to be our friend; you were not really so.
> You are god almighty, I'm a mortal, but I put you to shame.
> I didn't abandon Heracles's children.
> You knew how to creep secretly into my bed,
> to take another's wife without permission—
> but not how to rescue your friends.
> For a god you're ignorant—or else naturally crooked. (339)

The great choral ode that follows sings the praises

> of one who passed into the darkness
> of earth and the dead (shall I call him
>   Zeus's son?
>   Amphitryon's offspring?) (352)

They proceed to outline the Labors: the lion of Nemea; the Centaurs killed with winged arrows; the stag of Artemis; the man-eating
horses of Diomedes; the killing of Cycnus, who used to murder his
guests; the fruit and dragon of the Hesperides; the clearing of pirates

from the sea; the sustaining of the sky at the hands of Atlas; the acquisition of the girdle of Hippolyte with the aid of friends; the many-headed hydra, here described as a hound; Geryon (coupled closely with the hydra); and finally the assault on Hades, which is ironically described as "the end of labors" (427). The list is not the most familiar; it is slanted toward the service of mankind, at least in the inclusion of the elimination of piracy; there is no mention of the bull of Marathon, which is remembered before the play's end (1327), or the Stymphalian birds, though it should be remembered that Cycnus bears a bird name, nor the Erymanthian boar nor the Augean stables; perhaps the pirates take the place of the last; in general there seems a tendency to rationalization. At the end the chorus returns to the themes of friendship ("His house is stripped of friends" [430]), and of light ("Your home looks to your hands" [435]), and of age and impotence ("If only I were young and strong" [436]). The contrast between the Labors, with allies, brilliant and ablaze, young and powerful, and the situation at Thebes, friendless, dark and powerless, is marked.

Megara, Amphitryon, and the boys appear, dressed for death (an effective spectacle), "in the traces," says the chorus (445), "under the yoke," says Megara (454). She speaks movingly to the children. "I reared you for enemies," she says bitterly, using three bold abstractions, "an (object of) insult, delight, and destruction" (459). She speaks of Heracles's hopes for them, with marriage alliances so that

> anchored with cables
> from the stern, you might ride out your lives in prosperity. (478)

Instead, their brides are powers of death. She continues in almost lyrical strain:

> If only, like a yellow-winged
> bee, I could gather sorrow from every side,
> bring it to a single store, and distil one tear. (487)

She calls to Heracles, even as a ghost, with the fearful words, "Evil to you are those who kill your children" (496).

Amphitryon takes up her prayer with the familiar imagery. "My labor is vain," he says (501), and advises the chorus "from day to night to avoid sorrow" (505). Time flies (507, the metaphor is not yet a cliché), and fortune has snatched away—his words become ambiguous—"me" or "my glory from me" as the wind snatches a feather to the sky (509).

Suddenly in strides Heracles. The victims think they are dreaming, then Megara sends the children to greet him, for he is no less to them than Zeus the Savior (521). They explain the situation, with repeated references to their friendlessness: "To be luckless is to be friendless" (561). Heracles asks if the land has been diseased (542); he will himself suffer from a worse disease. Heracles cheers them in a rousing speech. Now they have light for darkness; he will throw Lycus's head to the dogs and use his club and feathered shafts to eliminate his enemies.

Good-bye to his labors; they were all vain. The hydra and lion were nothing. Then, with terrible ambiguity: "Shall not my final labor be over the death of my children?" (580). We are now in the presence, it seems, not of impotence but action. Amphitryon warns him to be cautious; Lycus is backed by the poorer classes. But Heracles, warned by a bird omen, has arrived in secret. Still, Amphitryon has spoken sensibly, Heracles will act sensibly: the contrast again. He has emerged from the sunless caves. Before going down he had been initiated into the Mysteries (613); this seemingly incidental reference is part of Euripides's campaign against Athenian exclusiveness, and a typical example of his delight in etiological myth, for according to the story Heracles as an alien was not eligible for initiation, and Theseus inaugurated the lesser Eleusinia to remedy this. The reference forms an easy introduction to the mention of Theseus, whom Heracles rescued. He goes in, protesting that he won't fly away, as the children clutch him, and taking them in tow like little ships (631); the image, as we shall see, is structurally vital to the whole play. "The whole of mankind," he says, "love children" (636).

"Youth is what I love," responds the chorus in their next song, which is full of the contrast between age, more burdensome than Etna, and the vigor of youth, and between vigor and wealth or political power. Age brings darkness; away with it on the wings of the air.

> If only the gods had understanding,
> had wisdom as men know wisdom

sing the chorus, echoing the apparent blasphemy of Amphitryon (655, cf. 347). The virtuous would have a second youth, rising after death into the sun's beams. Bad breed would drop out, and in this way it would be possible to distinguish good men from bad, as sailors discern stars through a rift in the clouds. But the gods make no such distinctions, and the passage of years brings wealth and nothing else. Even in old age, however, they can sing, sing like an aged swan—but the name of the bird is that Cycnus whom Heracles killed (692). Their theme is Heracles, son of Zeus, who, by destroying the terror of the wild beasts, won for men a wave-free life (698). Ah, but has the terror gone? For Heracles himself wears the lion skin; Heracles himself is to behave like the bull he has killed (869). This choral ode is masterly in its interweaving of the play's themes; here at least Euripides's handling of the choral lyric is beyond cavil.

The end for Lycus comes quickly. He enters, impatient for the sacrifice, Amphitryon meets him and persuades him in, a sacrifice himself. The situation is ironical, and the verbal irony intense for Euripides. This is deliberate, for the irony is reduplicated; the primary irony relates to Lycus, the secondary to Heracles, who is ambiguously called Alcmene's son. Lycus thinks Megara's prayers in vain—so at the last they are (716). He calls his own efforts "labors" (725); they too are in vain, but so are those of Heracles. He goes in, and the chorus comments on the change of misfortune (735). Under the power of the gods fate is running backward in its course. They speak truer than they know.

Across their song and movement rings the death cry of Lycus. It comes in the middle of a stanza, and cannot interrupt words or dance; the chorus comments on the death agony as fluently as they have sung of justice. Their song is of the victory of their friends, of the change of fortune that has given birth to songs; but in fact the change of fortune and the nature of the songs are as ambiguous as the parentage and character of Heracles (766). The new king is gone (768); but Heracles himself is an alien immigrant, and the word for "new" (*kainos*) bears a sinister resemblance to the word for "kill" (865), the theme of another grim pun later. Wealth leads to pride and unscrupulous power; these are overthrown. (But what of the force that overthrew them?) The chorus sees light breaking over Thebes in the succession of children's children; that light will be darkness. So they speak of the double parentage. Once they did not believe in Zeus as father of Heracles; now for some time Heracles's strength and exploits have made them believe; and we ask ourselves what they will believe next.

The light becomes darkness more swiftly than they expect. We are waiting for the messenger who will tell us how Lycus died. He does not come. The crane swings over the top of the palace with a car, and in it Iris, the Rainbow, the gods' messenger, spectacularly dressed, and a grim black figure with snakes in her hair and a terrifying mask, identified as Madness, daughter of Night and Heaven; she proclaims her high birth. The chorus sees them, hears them, and cowers away. They are sent by Hera to drive Heracles mad and make him kill his children.

> The gods are nowhere,
> might is with mortals, if he escapes punishment. (841)

We are not told, punishment for what. Madness holds back in pity: "I call the sun to witness that I'm acting against my will" (858). But Hera and Iris are implacable: "The wife of Zeus did not send you here to show moderation" (857).

The car swings right down to the front of the palace, and Madness, with a description of the madness she will inflict so that Heracles behaves like a bull (869), passes into the palace, as Iris swings back into the sky in a flash of color. It is an astonishing scene, this second prologue, as we may call it; even Aeschylus, the master of bizarre effects, never devised anything quite so bizarre.

The choral song—if it is right so to call it—that follows is of an almost equally bizarre brilliance, and matches anything Euripides wrote in this field. It is written in a medium that Euripides made peculiarly his own, especially at this stage in his career, and which he uses at moments of high emotional tension. It is best explained by saying that speech rhythms keep breaking through the elaborate pattern of song, and this is no doubt what happened. In musical terms we might speak of a quasi-recitative in which lyrical snatches are linked with passages parlando. Their song is a cry of grief.

> Ototototottoi! Mourn! Cut
> is the flower of your city, the son of Zeus.
> Unhappy Greece, to lose
> your benefactor. (875)

Vivid imagery piles up: the joyless music of Madness, the Gorgon of Night, with her snakes around her, lashing on her chariot; the flesh-eating judgments descending on Heracles; Madness revelling like a Bacchant, but without gladness, and seeking not wine but blood; it is a hunt and the children are the prey. An incessant pulsing rhythm sets up in the flute, louder and louder, till a great whirlwind seems to sweep across the stage and an earthquake to shake the palace. The opportunity for choral mime conveying this is superb. Then, suddenly, stillness, and across the stillness the messenger we have been awaiting, not now with news of Lycus's death. He staggers out, and in broken tones announces that the children are dead.

The speech describing the killing is a tour de force even by Euripidean standards. Perhaps it savors too much of Grand Guignol; yet the Greek theater did not espouse violence for its own sake as did the Roman. What is remarkable is the accurate, almost clinical description of mental delusion combined with gripping narrative—the silence, rolling eyeballs, frothing mouth, unnatural laughter, exaggerated sense of the size of the house, swift movement from one delusion to another till the killing of the children as if they were the children of his enemy Eurystheus, and the final insensible collapse. Euripides has added some masterful touches. Heracles describes the imagined walls of Mycenae as fitted together with a ruddled line (945); but the word for "ruddled" is the color of blood, and the word for "line" (*kanon*) contains a double pun, on the word for sacrificial basket (*kanoun*, 926, 941) and the word for killer (also *kanon*, 865). Grim too are Heracles's words, when he was about to offer cleansing sacrifice for the killing of Lycus in the house; he asks why he is sacrificing before killing Eurystheus, and having his labors all over again. The house has to

be cleansed, not from the killing of Eurystheus but the killing of his
children; but also Hera could not afflict him until his labors were finished. Now he is indeed having his labors all over again. The bird
image is pitifully used: one of the children cowers behind the altar
like a bird (974), Heracles shoots him and cries, "One of Eurystheus's
fledglings lies dead" (982). He himself is compared to a Gorgon
(990). Eventually, the carnage over, with only Amphitryon left alive,
Heracles collapsed—to the watchers it seemed that the figure of
Athene thrust him down with a rock—and the servants and Amphitryon bound him to a pillar and left him sleeping.

The chorus breaks into their chant again; the rhythms are complex
and very free; we know that Euripides was a daring musical innovator.
They sing of Procne, who likewise killed her son; we remember that
she and Philomela and Tereus were turned into birds. Then the palace
doors open, and the moving platform displays a tableau in which all
visual reticence is gone—the towering figure of Heracles slumped to
the ground and fastened to a pillar, blood-bespattered; the bow and
arrows lying scattered on the ground; the dead bodies of Megara and
the three children, one with an ugly mess instead of a head, one pierced
with an arrow, and the third in his mother's arms with an arrow trans-
fixing both; above them broods Amphitryon "like a bird mourning her
unfledged young" (1039). His thoughts are now for his son "who
killed with the bowstring's song" (1063). As Heracles stirs and awakens, the chorus cower away. But he is now in his right mind, oblivious
of all that he has done. He feels that he has passed through a storm,
and, finding himself tied, compares himself to a moored ship (1024).
He speaks of his youth; he sees the feathered arrows, and the dead
bodies, but does not recognize them. He calls for a friend who will
cure his ignorance (1106). His ignorance can be cured, but it will take
a real friend to cure his plight. Amphitryon is weeping, and says significantly, "Even a god would groan to hear the story" (1115). He
reveals to his son the "non-war war" that he has fought (1133).
Heracles, released now that he is not a danger to others, threatens his
own life.

Suddenly he sees Theseus approaching, "my friend" (1154). He
who told his sons that he would not fly away (628) now wishes for

wings (1158). To avoid polluting his friend he covers his head, presumably in his lion's skin, creating a striking picture alike in itself and in its symbolism. The scene that follows is a wonderful demonstration of the meaning of friendship:

> All right. You are sitting in sorrow.
> Listen. Show your friends your face.
> No darkness contains a cloud so black
> as to hide the bitterness of your suffering. (1214)

Theseus cares nothing for possible pollution. Heracles brought him from darkness to light; he will now share his friend's affliction; he will "sail with his friends through disaster" (1225). So he speaks with authority in his voice, and slowly Heracles rises to his feet and uncovers his head. It is a tremendous moment; we may remember that in *King Oedipus* Creon rebukes Oedipus for not veiling his head after the pollution he has incurred. It is an entirely visual affirmation of light breaking into darkness and life victorious over the death wish.

Heracles declares that God is an inflexible thing (1243); he compares himself to a ship with a cargo of trouble (1245); he is still set on death. Theseus reminds him of his benefactions and friendship to mankind. A long, characteristically Euripidean debate follows; the Athenians with their passion for political and forensic dialectic loved them. We love them less, but they are effective drama, and here the interplay of argument is theatrically necessary to lead us to a more tranquil close, and dramatically necessary to give Heracles time to accept life. Heracles speaks of the reasons pointing him to death. There was a curse on his father.

> Then Zeus—whoever Zeus is—fathered me for hate
> from Hera—do not be distressed, Amphitryon;
> I count you my father, not Zeus. (1263)

He tells of the perils he has faced from wild animals and monsters, snakes in his cradle, lions, giants, centaurs, the hydra (again described as a hound), Cerberus. Now he has killed his children. He must leave Thebes; he cannot return to Argos. Wherever he goes people will point and say, "Isn't that Zeus's son, the one who killed his wife and children?" (1289). Earth and Sea will alike reject him; he will be tossed round like Ixion on his wheel. He has nothing left to live for. Hera can exult.

Theseus is calm and reasonable. He sympathizes with the desire to die; but better to live. Even the gods offend against morality, yet they live on.

> You were born to die. How dare you
> grumble at your fate when gods do not! (1320)

This is an astonishing piece of humanism. Man must show himself as good as or better than the gods. Theseus goes on to say that Athens will receive him and purify him; Euripides, as so often, links his drama with the origin of an Attic cult. Heracles saved Theseus; now he himself needs friends. And now Euripides produces a touch of delicacy and understanding. Heracles heard Theseus's opening words and expresses his rejection of any story of crime committed by gods: "A god, if he is genuinely a god, needs nothing" (1345). For the rest he has hardly been listening. But while Theseus has been speaking he has been rapt in his own thoughts, and from those has come the will to live. To leave the light would be the coward's way. He will go to Athens. He had been through his labors without shedding a tear. Now the tears flow. Why? He does not say. The words that follow are of misfortune and exile, but the words that precede are of the generosity of Theseus. He kisses the dead bodies, picks up the fatal bow, makes to break it or throw it away, then resolves to keep it. It has been his power in the past for good and evil, and it will be his power for the future.

Euripides has not quite done with us. As they make to go, Heracles is rooted to the ground; he wishes that he could become an unfeeling rock. And now Theseus reaches out and takes him by the hand, touches the polluted Heracles, and when Heracles protests that the touch is pollution, says, "Wipe off on me all your uncleanness" (1400). It is in some ways the most awesome moment in Greek tragedy, the visual expression of friendship. Heracles puts his arm round Theseus's neck —a yoke of friends—and goes out like a boat in tow (1424); it is a magical touch, for it is the word that he has used earlier of the children clutching him (631), and it binds the two halves of the play together.

It is by any standards a mighty play. The sharp break in the middle is disconcerting to those who judge by *a priori* theories of dramatic structure. It is undoubtedly daring, but it is also vital to the play that Euripides chose to write, and its justification lies in the outcome. The break is further pointed. The first half is full of the contrast between words and action. First Lycus and then Heracles declare themselves men of action not words. But in the second half Heracles destroys by actions and Theseus, though his words are sealed by an act, saves by words.

But Euripides has modeled his play with an exceedingly subtle structure. On top of the diptych structure he has superimposed a triptych. In the first third of the play the action is controlled by Lycus; he stands, as we are often enough reminded, for wealth and political power, and his wealth and politics cannot save him. The center of the action, overlapping the break, is controlled, humanly speaking, by Heracles. He stands for strength, and in the first half his youth and strength are powerfully contrasted with the age and impotence of Amphitryon and the elders. But the strength that saves is also the strength that destroys, and it is demonstrated in all its ambivalence. The third part of the action is controlled by Theseus, who stands for friendship. It is notable that the chorus, whose dramatic function is to provide a contrast with Heracles's youthful vigor, now falls away; there is no choral ode in this last section. The power of Lycus is used solely for evil, that of Heracles first for good then for evil, that of Theseus solely for good. Seen like this, the play is almost a hymn to friendship.

The imagery of the play is controlled by the Labors. The word itself recurs, often in association with the idea of frustration and emptiness ("in vain"). The lion's skin and the bow and arrows are visual reminders of the Labors, and most of the characters refer to them. They are sometimes depicted as the triumph of humanity over bestiality; yet Heracles has not overcome the bestiality in himself and can behave like an animal after its prey, a bull, a Gorgon. In struggling with monsters, he has forgotten the monstrosity that is man. The three principal fields of imagery are birds, sailing, and light and darkness; we remember the Stymphalian birds and Cycnus with his bird name, the cleansing the sea of pirates and the journey to Hades. There are others too, snakes and bulls and hounds, which recall some aspect of the legends, and few images that do not form a link of some sort with the Labors.

Finally there is Heracles's relation to Zeus and Hera. The ambiguity of his parentage runs through the play. Is he son of Zeus or Amphitryon? The statue and altar of Zeus confront us throughout the play. The first characterization of Zeus is as Savior (48, cf. 521), and Heracles does indeed save before he destroys. Perhaps, though only perhaps, at the end of the play with its stress on friendship, we should remember the cult title of Zeus, God of Friendship. But Heracles's name means "Glory of Hera," and Hera is a part of him as is Zeus. What is Hera? We learn three things about her: Amphitryon thinks of her as necessity or destiny (*chreon,* 21); Iris describes her as having no truck with moderation and saving wisdom (*sophronein,* 857); Heracles says that the disasters have come from a single unlucky hit from Hera (*tyche,* 1393).

The play is full of rationalization about the gods. Improper myths are rejected, and there is agnosticism about the ultimate power. With *Hippolytus* behind us we may suspect that Euripides means by the gods forces that are inherent in man himself, which sometimes seem too powerful for him to control. Can we apply this here? I think that we can. Zeus is the life-affirming element in man, and Hera the life-denying. Both are in us. Zeus, detached from man, symbolized in the statue and altar, does not save; Zeus in Heracles does, till Hera takes over. We cannot escape from Hera; we may not deny Zeus. Heracles tries to in declaring Amphitryon his father, but he accepts the rôle of benefactor. He is indeed the child of Amphritryon and Alcmene; but Zeus is also his father and Hera part of his inheritance. The life force is in him, and the power of death and destruction.

There is a continuing parable here for the generation of men that holds the secret of atomic power. For Euripides makes it clear that our salvation lies in our own hands. There may or may not be an ultimate god, but we men must learn to behave better than the gods of legend. At the last it is by man, by a man who denies supernatural pollution and shows human friendship, that the conflict is resolved and salvation comes. We have been reminded of Zeus the Savior; we recall Zeus God of Friendship. But Theseus is the friend who saves.

28. ELECTRA

Neither the date of Euripides's *Electra* nor its relationship to Sophocles's play of the same title is completely certain. Right at the end of the play the Dioscuri say that they will speed westward to the waters of Sicily to protect the ships. It is hard to think that this does not refer to the ships that, under Demosthenes in 413, went on a fruitless attempt to salvage the Athenian expeditionary force. Stylistic tests suggest a slightly earlier date, after *Andromache* but before *The Women of Troy* or *Heracles*, presumably therefore to the years 419–416. It is doubtful whether the stylistic test is quite so fine an instrument of dating, but it is possible that Euripides wrote the bulk of the play earlier, but did not complete it, perhaps because it did not fit with the trilogic groupings he was writing at the time. Certainly it fitted well with *Iphigeneia among the Taurians*; it is tempting to date *Helen* a year earlier than usual to form a third play in the sequence. On the whole, 413 remains the most likely date of performance. On the whole, too, it is likely that Sophocles's play was the earlier, though Wilamowitz argued vigorously to the contrary, and if it were really pro-satyric, Sophocles might have been demonstrating to Euripides how to write his own sort of melodrama without being quite so nasty. Probably Sophocles wrote in the early 410s, and if the stylistic tests are valid, Euripides may have written his first draft as a counterblast.

The theme is set. It is the killing of the mother and her lover by the son and daughter. To Aeschylus it was a problem, to Sophocles a drama, to Euripides a crime. Hence Clytemnestra is brought back into the center and she is made pitiable, while Electra is a pathological harridan. Aegisthus welcomes his murderers warmly and they stab him in the back at a religious act: contrast *Hamlet*. In Euripides's critique there are four elements. First, there is the attack on the blood feud, mother murder, the doctrine of an eye for an eye, and the escalation of violence. It is bitter and pellucid, and in the context of a world at war peculiarly powerful.

Second, there is the attack on the god who orders this, pointed by the rationalism of the chorus when they suggest that legends were invented to bolster up religion (737), intensified by the impiety of killing Aegisthus while at sacrifice after avoiding technical impurity by refusing the ritual washing that would have made them participants, and driven home in the finale by the Dioscuri, who give divine sanction for the rejection of divinity.

Third, there is the defense of women. Aeschylus makes determinative the superior function of man. Euripides makes Clytemnestra ask, "If Menelaus had been kidnapped would I have had to kill Orestes so as to save my sister's husband?" (1041). This is a denial of a twofold standard. It is true that Electra twice says that the man not the woman should rule (932, 1052); but Electra suffers from a father fixation, and denies her own professions by her dominance over Orestes. The authority of Electra, for good or ill, strides across this play as assuredly as the authority of Clytemnestra bestrides *Agamemnon*.

Finally there are dramatic and technical criticisms of Euripides's predecessors. This is particularly strong in the recognition scene. Euripides rejects the lock of hair (men's and women's hair is not identical), the footprint (Aeschylus's most fatuous suggestion, since the sizes would obviously be different), the cloth (Orestes would hardly still be wearing his baby clothes), and accepts the evidence of a scar. It has been suggested, not wholly implausibly, that the tottering, ragged, ghoulish, slightly ridiculous old man who produces the rejected clues might have been given a mask suggesting in caricature the features of Aeschylus. Another ground of criticism is the ease with which, alike in Aeschylus and Sophocles, the murderers enter the palace. Euripides twice adverts to the impossibility of this (94, 615), and sets his own murders elsewhere.

The scene in fact is surprising. The stage building does not represent a palace or temple, but a cottage, and some kind of backdrop over it or flats in front of it would have represented this; we may also imagine straw on the stage. The opening speakers in *Alcestis, Hippolytus, The Women of Troy, Ion,* and *The Bacchants* are gods, in other surviving plays from the 410s heroic figures such as Aethra, Amphitryon, Iphigeneia, or Helen. Enter from the cottage a peasant, seemingly some country bumpkin, though he turns out to have rare character and good sense. He sets the scene, Argos. Agamemnon is dead, killed by Clytemnestra and Aegisthus. Aegisthus is married to Clytemnestra and is king. Orestes has been smuggled off to Phocis by an old slave. Aegisthus kept Electra a prisoner, refusing her marriage for fear of her children. He thought to kill her, but Clytemnestra protected her. So then he thought to marry her to a nobody—and, with a start, we realize that this is Electra's husband (34). He is poor but honest, and he has not taken advantage of the situation; she is still virgin.

> If anyone calls me a fool for taking
> a young girl in my house and leaving her virgin,
> he's using a crooked ruler to measure in his mind
> decency—and he's the fool himself. (50)

This is exactly what many of the audience were thinking, and they stand rebuked by the man's innate dignity.

He moves to one side out of the way, and a woman dressed in rags emerges from the cottage with a jar on her matted hair. It is Electra. Her opening words are brilliantly conceived:

> Black night, nurse to the golden stars,
> in your blackness I bear this bucket on my head,

and fetch water from the river,
not driven to this by any compulsion,
but exposing Aegisthus's brutality to the gods.
I pour out my grief to the open sky, to my father.
That damned daughter of Tyndareus, my mother,
has banished me from home, to oblige her husband.
She's born Aegisthus other children
and treats Orestes and me as bastards in our own home .(54)

The image of the nurse immediately suggests her yearning for the baby she has not had: the name Electra means "unmarried." From the first her sexual obsession is stressed. Then comes her masochism; she tortures herself so that she can feel self-pity. Besides, she deceives herself, for there is no one else to deceive; the peasant has already told us that it was Aegisthus not Clytemnestra who turned her out, but her hatred of her mother warps her sense of truth, and that hatred, as we shall see, arises from her own fear of sex and jealousy of her mother's sexual freedom. Then again the yearning for children, as she speaks bitterly of the children her mother has born to Aegisthus. The peasant has been watching her, and tells her that there is no need for her to work. Her answer is smoother than butter, but war is in her heart; she patronizes him; she says that she wants to help him, but we know she does not, for she has told us her motives. He humors her tolerantly, but his

Idle hands and calling on the gods
butter no parsnips without hard work. (80)

is a little more biting than it seems.

They go out stage-left (they are not going far) as two men with an attendant enter from stage-right, as does the old man who passes Agamemnon's tomb on his way from the country later. The first addresses the other as Pylades, and we know him to be Orestes. He speaks of Aegisthus, who murdered his father—and, after a pause, of his abominable mother as associate. Orestes is trying to eliminate the matricide by not thinking of it: Electra will not let him escape so easily. He has offered sacrifice and a lock of hair at his father's tomb, and now has retreated near the frontier, so as to escape easily and (secondarily) to consult his sister. Dawn breaks, and he speaks of its bright glance (102); the phrase is ambiguous, somewhat as if we said "the red letters spell day in the sky," and points to a day of blessing. He sees Electra approaching and takes her for a slave; the valiant hero promptly hides.

Electra has a long and lovely song in anapaests: it is enhanced by Euripides's familiar device of the repeated word. The rhythm is processional, yet she is surely doing more than walking as she enters, and one suspects a simple but powerfully effective rhythmic movement with the water pot balanced on the head; an African actor could carry it off well. She calls for a servant (a servant!) to take the jar, so that she may indulge more freely in self-pity. She is known as "poor Electra." She invokes her murdered father, then calls on her absent brother to save her from misery, and, as second thought, to avenge her father. And her brother, who is not absent, does not show his face. The song is of special interest because there is an interlude between each pair of stanzas, presumably mimed in movement on the spot before the pattern is unwound.

She is joined by the chorus of unmarried girls. The power of the song they sing was stronger than the printed page suggests; through accidentally hearing it, the victorious Peloponnesians were led to pity Athens and spare her from annihilation (Plut. *Lys.* 15); the music must have had rare pathos. The chorus invites Electra to share in their coming festival, but she refuses. Their dance of joy and hers of sorrow form a marvellous contrast. She is filled with self-pity and points to her matted hair and rags of clothes (184). In the end her sexual obsession cannot be repressed:

> And I am living in a shack,
> driven from my father's palace,
> eating out my heart
>   among craggy rocks,
> while my mother sleeps with a stranger
>   in her butcher's bed. (207)

Orestes and Pylades emerge: Electra panics and tells the chorus to run away. Pylades blocks the chorus's escape with his sword while

Orestes intercepts Electra as she tries to slip into the cottage. There is a little mild irony:

> ELECTRA: Go away! What right have you to touch me?
> ORESTES: There is no one I have more right to touch. (223)

Orestes knows who Electra is, but still does not reveal himself; the bold assassin is frightened of the women of the chorus. Even when they are identified as friendly he will not come out into the open, though we may agree with England that "even the boldest of us, if we had an Electra as our sister, and were not quite sure whether we wanted to do what she wished or not, would probably prefer that she should remain ignorant of our identity." For the moment he represents himself a friend of Orestes. Electra promptly indulges in self-pity and points to her withered body (239) and shorn hair. There is unbelievable bitterness when she speaks of Clytemnestra: "Sir, women love their men, not their children" (265). She seeks revenge, and her resolution contrasts powerfully with his indecision. Then more irony:

> ORESTES: I wish Orestes were at hand to hear this!
> ELECTRA: Sir, I should not recognize him if I saw him. (282)

Then the exaggeration that her father's body was thrown out of doors and left where it lay. The line-for-line exchange has lasted for seventy lines, punctuated only by sighing pauses from the irresolute Orestes. Now Electra bursts out, first in self-pity:

> Tell Orestes my troubles, and his.
> Tell him the robes I wear, the court where I'm installed,

There is some ambiguity of language here, none in what follows:

> the filth that bears heavy on me, the hut
> which shelters me, who once knew royal halls.
> I labor at the loom to make my own clothes,
> or I should go naked, stripped of everything.
> *I* have to carry water from the spring.
> Never a festival. Never a share in dancing. (303)

It is largely her own doing: we have just seen her refuse the feast on holy days. From this she turns to a contrast between her father, and

Clytemnestra and Aegisthus: Clytemnestra served by her father's captives, Aegisthus holding her father's scepter and drunkenly throwing stones at her father's tomb—the tomb whose existence she has just denied. These are pathological imaginings and not to be trusted. She harps on Orestes's absence and ends:

> It's a scandal. His father destroyed the Trojans,
> and he, younger and better-born,
> can't, man for man, kill one enemy. (336)

The honest peasant returns and rebukes Electra for not inviting the visitors in, and Orestes comments sententiously that you cannot judge inward worth by outward appearance; birth and wealth are no standards. There is irony too when he says, "I've seen a man, born from a noble father, turn out to be nothing" (369); so have we. When they have gone in, Electra, disregarding the chorus, turns furiously on her husband, and shows her own snobbery:

> You lout, you know your cupboard's bare.
> These gentlemen are your betters. How dare you ask them in?
> (404)

Shades of Philemon and Baucis! He replies sanely:

> Why not? If they're as noble as they look, they'll be
> equally at home in a cottage or anywhere else. (406)

She sends him off to find her father's old tutor, the man who smuggled Orestes away, and goes into the cottage.

The choral song that follows is of considerable interest. It is a romance of the legendary war against Troy; but woven into its fabric are monsters—Gorgon, Sphinx, Chimaera—and even the stars dancing on Achilles's shield appear as an object of terror. The result is a deliberate ugliness, and the miming and dance patterns accompanying the song would have expressed this ugliness visibly up to the climactic vision of the mother lying with her throat cut.

Four themes in this song are of special importance. The first is Achilles, who is made the center of the ode; he is the type of the athlete, and the athletic theme is here introduced (439). The second is the theme of light. The play has opened with the dawning of a new

day, and this is at first sight an obvious symbol of the new light dawning for Argos with the arrival of Orestes. The song reminds us that
light is ambivalent. Achilles is brought up to be a light for Hellas
(449). Fire illuminates but it also destroys; the Chimaera breathed
fire; the sun and the stars terrified Hector; and the light of Hellas
carried a bloodstained sword (476). The third is the Trojan War.
Euripides leads us subtly: the chorus starts from glory; the final stanza
passes from the soldier with the bloodstained sword to his commander
killed by his adulterous wife and so to the hope that she will lie bloodstained; the glory of the assassination is parallel to the glory of war.
But the assassination will turn out inglorious and ignoble, and the
parallelism stands. If Achilles is a type of Orestes, Orestes is a type of
Achilles. The political context of war, cold or hot, is inescapable.
Electra is in its way as much of an antiwar play as *Helen*. Finally, there
is the image of the Gorgon. This is a reminder that Aeschylus (*Ch.*
832) used Perseus as an analogue of Orestes; the final picture of
Clytemnestra with her throat cut intensifies this, and Euripides will
pick it up later. This in turn is linked with the Furies, for they, like
the Gorgon, had snakes in their hair. So, in place of hope, we are left
with terror.

The old man for whom Electra has sent limps in from stage-right
with a lamb, garlands of flowers, and some provisions; he grumbles
about the climb up to the house, his words being a small piece of internal evidence that there really was a raised stage as well as a neat
device to allow him to stop and catch his breath instead of speaking
with his back to the audience. Electra greets him. He is emotionally
excited. He has seen the offerings at the tomb; they must be from
Orestes; he suggests that she compare locks of hair. Electra demurs:
Orestes's is an athlete's hair, hers a woman's, softened with combing.
The athletic image is important; so is the revelation that Electra is car-
ing for her hair and matting it only for public consumption. In any
event, she says, Orestes would not come fearfully and in secret, though
this is precisely what he has done.

The evidence of footprints and cloth is similarly rebutted, and the
old man gives up and asks to meet the strangers. Orestes is visibly dis-
concerted to be told that the old man is the very person who is liable

to recognize him, and there is some amusing stage business as the old man circles round him scrutinizing him like the mint mark on a coin, while he himself still hopes to conceal his identity. The mint mark is in fact a telltale scar, the matter is clinched, brother and sister embrace, and the chorus sings a brief paean of joy for the day that has dawned and the beacon that has blazed. Perhaps.

Now they set their plans. The old man is bloodthirsty, Orestes cautious, Electra silent and brooding. The old man has seen Aegisthus away from his protective walls, sacrificing to the Nymphs, for children expected or received. But what of Clytemnestra? Electra has been silent for fifty lines, though she would have visibly represented by a violent movement her response to the sacrifice for children. Now she bursts in: "I shall look after my mother's killing" (647). The old man is to take the news that she bore a son ten days before; the invention is typical of the girl's bitter brooding. Clytemnestra will come to shed tears over the child's rank (658). The words are ambiguous and ironical. Are the tears because the child has a peasant for a father and is degraded or a princess for a mother and is dangerous? The conspirators invoke religion in their cause. They pray to Zeus, and Electra reverts to self-pity (672); to Hera, with Orestes significantly crying, "Grant us victory, if our prayers are just" (675); to Agamemnon and to Earth; and they pray for the hosts of the dead (including Thyestes and Iphigeneia?) and the heroes from Troy (the war theme) to join them. If they fail, Electra resolves to take the sword to herself. The men go out stage-right, Electra into the cottage.

Now comes another remarkable song. Again it starts innocently as it tells of the golden-fleeced lamb that Pan brought to Atreus. But this time, by the second stanza, corruption sets in, and we are in the tale of Thyestes, Aerope, and Atreus, a tale of adultery, deceit, and theft, and beyond it, as we know, of murder and cannibalism. And as in the previous song the blessing of light turns to a curse, and the sun and the stars are fearful and punitive. As in the previous song also they turn at the last to Clytemnestra, though here they do not even name her by her patronymic. Why did she not remember these stories when she killed her husband? So the chorus; but we cannot evade the further question, "Why does Orestes not remember these stories as he prepares to kill his mother?" These two choral odes—the only two in the whole play—are a surprising and masterly invention, the deliberate brutalizing of beauty; we wish here more than almost anywhere that we had the music and choreography.

A distant cry is heard; the chorus calls Electra out. She panics, fearing the worst in the match (751 *agon*, an athletic term, but appropriate to tragedy), and makes to die. Then comes a messenger to proclaim Orestes's victory. Electra still doubts; then she recognizes the man as Orestes's attendant. Then and only then does he embark on his narrative; the holding-up of the speech is a characteristic device of Euripides. The narrative is vivid and vigorous. Aegisthus's welcoming courtesy contrasts with the treachery and impiety of Orestes, who is strong enough to carve up a bull but stabs his host in the back while examining the entrails of sacrifice. The death is powerfully told:

> As he stooped,
> your brother stood on tiptoe,
> smashed down on his backbone, shattered
> his spine.. His body jerked
> up and down and screamed in death-agony. (839)

The themes return: athletics when Orestes

> flayed the carcass more swiftly than a runner
> could complete two lengths of a half-mile track (824)

the Gorgon's head, when the messenger cries,

> He's on his way.
> The head he brings to show you is no Gorgon's,
> but your enemy Aegisthus's. (855)

The killing of the Gorgon is yet to come; light, in Electra's cry of joy in response to the news (866); athletics again, as she fetches out the flowers the old man brought her and garlands the returning victors with them. It is a splendid visual effect; we know that the gaiety will fade more swiftly than the flowers.

Now comes the sheerly ugliest passage of the play. For fifty lines Electra exults with sadistic brutality over the dead body of Aegisthus, pouring out all the ugly accumulation of poison that fear had pushed down and intensified. Her obsession with sex dominates the speech, though there is a moment when the inhibitions come out:

> Your dealings with women—a girl like me can't decently
> put them in words. I say nothing—hint what I know. (945)

Her obsession with Clytemnestra is also clear; he was always "Clytemnestra's husband," she was not "Aegisthus's wife." Electra, totally involved with Agamemnon, may rule men in practice, but she talks of the virtue of submission in women. At the end the athletic image recurs:

> No crook,
> however good his initial start,
> should think he's beaten justice, till he's reached
> the final straight and life's finishing-post. (953)

Electra asserts her authority; the body is unceremoniously carried into the cottage. Suddenly Clytemnestra is seen approaching, and Orestes awakens from his self-preening to stark reality. The exchange that follows is superb in its characterization:

ELECTRA: Splendid. She's coming straight into the net—
all dolled up with chariots and escort.
ORESTES: What are we going to do? Murder our mother?
ELECTRA: Does sight of your mother's body start you snivelling?
ORESTES: Oh!
How can I kill her? She brought me up. She bore me.
ELECTRA: You can kill her as she killed our father.
ORESTES: Phoebus, your oracle was sheer folly.
ELECTRA: If Apollo is foolish who is wise?
ORESTES: You bade me kill my mother. It is forbidden.
ELECTRA: What harm can it do you to avenge your father?
ORESTES: I was once pure. I shall be guilty of matricide.
ELECTRA: Not taking your father's cause, you will show yourself irreligious.
ORESTES: But I shall meet judgment for my mother's murder.
ELECTRA: You'll meet judgment for failing to avenge your father.
ORESTES: The oracle came from some fiend disguised as a god.
ELECTRA: On Apollo's holy tripod? I do not think so.
ORESTES: I can't believe this prophecy is good.
ELECTRA: No cowardice! Don't lose your nerve! (965)

Orestes has been rooted to the spot. He marks his stride forward by the word (reading *probematos*, 985); it is full of fear. Yet "if the gods will it, so be it." It is not so easy to push one's decision onto the gods; the hands will not be clean again. He and Pylades go in.

Clytemnestra arrives spectacularly in a carriage attended by exotically clothed Trojan slaves. She is middle-aged, unhappy, gentle, seeking only peace. Electra greets her bitterly; as the slaves help Clytemnestra down, she sees herself as a slave, prisoner of the sword without even their privileges—and fatherless. This leads Clytemnestra to a strong and persuasive defense. Agamemnon killed Iphigeneia and sought to foist Cassandra and a second wife on the home. "The men are at fault—but no one attacks them" (1040).

Her brilliant inversion of the situation drives the point home: Agamemnon killed Iphigeneia for Helen; if Menelaus had been abducted should she have killed Orestes? Electra, or perhaps the leader of the chorus, comments, "Your words are just but their justice is shameful" (1050); it is an ironical preparation for the shameful justice to be inflicted by Electra and Orestes. Electra's answer is paltry; she has no answer except that once Agamemnon had gone Clytemnestra spent too long before the mirror. For the rest self-pity wells up as she claims that her living death is a worse fate than Iphigeneia's. She boldly asserts the principle that if Iphigeneia's death demanded the murder of Agamemnon by Clytemnestra, Agamemnon's death demands the murder of Clytemnestra by Orestes and herself. Clytemnestra's reply is sad and tolerant: "My child, you were naturally inclined to love your father" (1102); the word "love" (*stergein*) has overtones of "be indulgent to." In Sophocles's play Clytemnestra says, "I have no misgivings at what has passed" (549); in Euripides she says "I am not so very happy about the things I have done, my child" (1105). There follows a passage of strong irony:

> ELECTRA: I am stubborn because I am hurt; I will stop being angry (1118).

Clytemnestra thinks that this is an act of will; Electra knows that Aegisthus cannot hurt her now; in fact her anger will be exposed as criminal.

> CLYTEMNESTRA: Then he won't oppress you any more.

Of course not; he is dead.

> ELECTRA: He's too proud; he's staying in my house.

He has usurped her palace; his body is in the cottage.

> CLYTEMNESTRA: You see? You are bringing to life new quarrels.

To bring to life is what she cannot do.

> ELECTRA: I say no more. I fear him as I fear him.

That is, not at all. But retribution will catch up. Electra invites her mother in to conduct the customary tenth-day sacrifice after a birth. There is more bitterness and more irony.

> Come in to our humble house. Please take care
> not to dirty your dress with the soot on the wall.

It is not the soot on the *wall* that will soil the dress.

> You shall offer the gods your own due sacrifice. (1139)

The words are ambiguous between "the sacrifice due from you" and "the due sacrifice—yourself."

She follows her in, exultant. The chorus recalls the death cry of Agamemnon when Clytemnestra was like a mountain lioness; not so have we seen her. Suddenly her own death cry rings out. After Aegisthus's murder there were ceremonial rejoicings. Now there is only pity and horror. The murderers stagger out, at last aware of what they have done, and we learn that Orestes lowered the sword before his mother's pleas and covered his face with his cloak, as did Perseus in killing the Gorgon, while Electra placed her hand on his and helped drive the sword home.

And now above the house appear two shining figures. They reveal themselves as Castor and Polydeuces, the Dioscuri, brothers to Helen and Clytemnestra, and Castor resolves the plot: Electra is to marry Pylades; Orestes is to go into exile, and be pursued by the Furies with their snakes—the final reference to the Gorgon motif—till he finds acquittal at Athens and peace in Arcadia. And Helen never saw Troy:

Zeus sent a phantom to stir up strife. Euripides's use of the *deus ex machina* has often been criticized. Here it is of great beauty. As Orestes and Electra embrace before they part they give a great sobbing sigh, and the gods echo it:

> Ah! That cry is fearful
> even for gods to hear.
> I and the powers of heaven
>   feel pity for men's troubles. (1327)

The dramatic element in this epiphany is richly handled: the spectacle; the three-level tableau; the delightful characterization, to which Norwood has drawn attention, "the bluff naval character of these minor deities, who are clear on morals but out of depth in theology"; the way they preside over the parting of brother and sister, and their own departure on an errand of salvation (1348). But their dramatic function extends beyond this. In Aeschylus the divinity produces a solution to a moral problem. In Euripides he does the same but in a very different way. Here the god produces the element of judgment.

> Her doom was just, your act was not.
> Phoebus . . . Phoebus . . . Well, he is my sovereign.
> No more. Wise as he is, his words to you were not wise. (1244)

Later, the condemnation of Apollo is explicit (1296, 1302). This is a condemnation of Delphi. But the murderers are not allowed to slough off their human responsibility, for Electra was not under Apollo's orders (1303), though both were involved in the solidarity of human destiny. And this is the other element provided by the epiphany, the solution that is no solution. Gods do not so appear, as Euripides makes as clear as he can when the chorus asks why the Dioscuri did not intervene to save their sister, and they have no real answer (1298); nor is there any Supreme Court for the warring states of Greece. This is a thirteenth hour solution, and it involves the suspension of belief, the reversal of nature, events running counter to their own logic. It is an effect he is to employ with even greater power in *Orestes*.

The play has been variously estimated. In the nineteenth century there was a tendency to denigrate it. Paley called it "skimble-skamble stuff, whose only merit is that it is easy Greek and eminently suitable for schoolboys," and Schlegel, "perhaps of all Euripides's plays the very vilest." Yet Murray saw it as "a close-knit, powerful, well-constructed play," and Grube wrote, "In its own genre this is undoubtedly Euripides' masterpiece." The late twentieth century, with its own mood of "sickness" and its own violence and revolt against violence, is better able to understand it. Clearly it is written by a master of the theater. It makes its point with rare pungency.

Its greatest dramatic strength lies in the characterization. Electra, a brilliant pathological study, fascinated and repelled by sex, with her masochism and sadism, her fixation on her father and hatred of her mother, her obsessive hopes and fears, her dominating personality. And alongside her, Orestes, a weak and cowardly poltroon, marked by fatal irresolution. Between the two there is a kind of Medea-Jason situation; she is powerful, he is empty. In all there is only one decent character, the peasant "the only gentleman present" (says England ironically), a breath of sanity in a world of explosive and destructive madness.

For behind all the dramatic skill of Euripides lies the strength of moral indignation. There is a better way than violence. Peasants like Electra's husband appear in the theater of Aristophanes, and they too are a breath of sanity in a world of explosive and destructive madness. They are men like Dicaeopolis and Trygaeus, and they stand for peace. The solution of *Electra* is no solution. Euripides does not believe in gods who will intervene to save the ships. But man, if he will heed, may still save himself—and others.

29. *IPHIGENEIA AMONG THE TAURIANS*

Stephen Stanton, in his analysis of the "well-made play," *pièce bien faite*, associated with Augustin-Eugène Scribe and his nineteenth-century successors, of whom Victorian Sardou was chief, picks out seven structural features:

1. A plot based on a secret known to the audience but withheld from certain characters until its revelation in the climactic scene

2. A pattern of increasingly intense action and suspense (assisted by contrived entrances and exits, letters, and other devices)

3. A series of ups and downs in the hero's fortunes, caused by his conflict with an adversary

4. The counterpunch of *peripeteia* and *scène à faire* marking, respectively, the lowest and highest point in the hero's adventures (Stanton means by *peripeteia* something like "culminating mishap")

5. A central misunderstanding or *quiproquo*, made obvious to the spectator but withheld from the participants

6. A logical and credible dénouement

7. The reproduction of the overall action pattern in the individual acts

Scribe was not original and inventive in this. He was logically and systematically applying the canons of light drama that had been introduced in a tragic context by Euripides and had governed the construction of the central tradition of comedy thereafter.

Something in Euripides drove him toward melodrama. The word is not derogatory: melodrama is drama, and Euripides practised it with extraordinary skill. As it excited his imagination, melodrama had two principal elements. The first we may call romantic. The remark of Sophocles—"I portray men as they ought to be, Euripides portrays them as they are"—has been taken to apply to his pathological studies of Jason or Electra; yet it belongs far more justly to the characters in his romantic melodramas. For though Jason or Electra is cut down from the superhuman world of heroic legend to life size, there is no element of self-identification with them on the part of the spectator. In *Iphigeneia among the Taurians* we are involved in and share the hopes and fears of the characters. The second element is the release of tension in escape from danger: these are adventure stories with a happy ending. In both they point to New Comedy, which stands in the line of Euripidean tragedy rather than Aristophanic comedy; in this way they have some claim to be accounted the most influential, though not inherently the greatest Greek plays.

Euripides had essayed romantic melodrama early in his career in *Alcestis*. This tragicomedy took the place of a satyr play, and was evidently a failure; the play, exquisite in itself, did not satisfy an audience that was expecting an altogether cruder burlesque. It looks as if Euripides bided his time till he felt able to make the new experiment of substituting melodrama for tragedy. For there is nothing here of the conventional accompaniment of tragedy. Death does not strike; Iphigeneia broods on her death, but after all it never took place; Orestes is threatened with a death he does not meet. If there is a tragic theme it is exile rather than death, but that too is brought to an end. Thoas loses his image and his priestess, but accepts the loss with tranquility, like the gentleman that he is.

Four *leitmotifs* are scattered through the play and give it point. The first is *xenia*. It is exceedingly difficult to translate. In the Greek world the stranger was under the special protection of Zeus Xenios. There is some indication that Zeus the god of strangers was originally Zeus the stranger himself. Some have entertained angels unawares, and an old Phrygian legend told how Philemon and Baucis made Zeus and Hermes welcome in their poor cottage while others rejected them and received their reward; this was why the inhabitants of Lystra treated Barnabas and Paul as Zeus and Hermes.

From the Homeric poems onward hospitality is a sacred duty. Charondas, the Sicilian lawgiver, lays it down in the proem to his code. Pindar more than once couples Themis, the goddess of Right, and Zeus, the god of Strangers. The stranger thus becomes a guest, and the word *xenos* means stranger, guest, or host impartially. The Taurians live on the Black Sea, which was called A-xeine, "hostile to strangers," or, with hopeful flattery, Eu-xeine, "kindly to strangers." The Taurians themselves behave in this way. But Iphigeneia is not called stranger by the Taurian herdsman, or, in the first scene, by Thoas; she *has* received hospitality, and her theft of the statue is treacherous, though she refuses to kill Thoas.

On the other side is *philia*. Conventionally this means "friendship," but it is in fact the tie that binds members of a family. It binds Orestes and Iphigeneia as brother and sister. It binds Orestes and Pylades as cousins. In the context of the extended family it binds all three to the chorus who are also Greeks, and its use between Iphigeneia and the chorus deserves scrutiny. Some of the poignancy of the play is emphasized because Iphigeneia and Orestes appear at first as strangers without the honoring of the tie of hospitality, and it is only when the bond of *philia* is revealed that rescue can take place.

The play is thus written verbally to bring out the paradox in the plot. This is intensified by the third leitmotif, which is the oxymoron, the putting together in a single phrase of two notions which are formally contradictory. This is, as we shall see, an effective device, and the turning point of the play is marked when the expected oxymoron is replaced by an intensive repetitive tautology.

Finally, there is the note of *barbaros*. This means literally one who

makes unintelligible noises, "bar-bar-bar" instead of speaking a pellucid language like Greek. It becomes the generic term for a non-
Greek, and it is typical of Greek arrogance that the English word we
derive from it is "barbarian." But *Medea* has long ago warned us that
Euripides does not take the assertion of Greek superiority lightly, and
we do well to be on our guard when the word appears.

Alongside these leitmotifs there is one parallel on which the structure of the play depends. Agamemnon sacrificed Iphigeneia; Iphigeneia
prepares to sacrifice Orestes; in between, Clytemnestra has murdered
Agamemnon and Orestes has murdered Clytemnestra. The wheel
comes full circle:

But in fact the act between Agamemnon and Iphigeneia was unfulfilled, and the act between Iphigeneia and Orestes will remain
unfulfilled. Yet there is something deeper still. The relation of love
between Agamemnon and Iphigeneia was broken and not restored;
the relation of love between Iphigeneia and Orestes is established, and
we are left with the feeling that this has restored what was lost at Aulis.

The material Euripides had to work on suggested but in no sense
dictated the plot to him. The name Iphigeneia means "strong in birth,"
and it was a cult title of Artemis at Brauron (Paus. 1.33.1) in Attica
and at Trozen (2.35.1); at Brauron there are traces of an original
ritual of human sacrifice. In the Black Sea area we have the testimony
of Herodotus to a goddess called the Maiden, to whom Greeks and
other sailors were sacrificed; Herodotus (4.103) says that the Taurians
call this goddess "Iphigeneia, daughter of Agamemnon." But in the
earliest traditions Iphigeneia was not Agamemnon's daughter, but the
child of Helen and Theseus, who was sent to Mycenae to be brought
up. Later she becomes child of Agamemnon and Clytemnestra.

The legend of her sacrifice by her father attaches orginially to Brauron not Aulis, linking with the goddess and sacrificial customs there.

But as early as 700 B.C., in Stasinus's *Cypria*, the goddess rescues the girl, sends her to the Taurians and makes her immortal. Euripides's treatment, so far as we can see, contains two innovations. He frees Artemis of all responsibility for the original sacrifice; this enables him to put all the blame upon Apollo's priest Calchas. More important, he appears to have invented the idea of Orestes's visit to the Black Sea. As this is the whole plot of the play we can say that we are here for the first time dealing with a play in which the dramatist invents rather than selects his plot.

The play is set not in the familiar surroundings of Greece, but in the wild lands of the Black Sea; but the stage building is a solidly built temple. We know too little about the resources of scene painting; we do not even know how far it was possible to change the scenery from one play to another of a given tetralogy. We may imagine a suggestion of rocks and wilderness, and perhaps a tastelessly megalomaniac parody of a Greek temple. But nothing is certain.

The play begins in characteristically Euripidean fashion. Iphigeneia appears from the temple and introduces herself: the opening words lend themselves to the Aristophanic addition "lost his little oil bottle." She tells the story of her sacrifice at Aulis, putting the blame on Calchas, and of her rescue by the goddess. She identifies the scene as the land of the Taurians,

> where Thoas rules over barbarous men,
> barbarous himself (3)

—a line to bring a laugh from the unwary. She hints, but no more, at her dreadful duties (for we must excise those lines that elaborate too closely).

There follows the theme of loneliness and exile; she has been dreaming of her homeland Argos, and in her dream she saw the palace totter and tumble till only one pillar is left standing. The dream is skillfully contrived; she thinks that it means that Orestes is dead, whereas in fact it points to his survival. As she tells the dream she lets slip her true office, and in doing so introduces another of the themes: she "kills strangers." She goes to look for her Greek attendants, a slightly contrived exit, and two dark figures slip on the stage; they are soon identified as Pylades and Orestes; they have only just missed hearing her soliloquizing. The scene between them calls for little comment; it is a second half to the prologue, explaining their presence. Orestes is also an exile and refugee, pursued by relays of Furies because he shed his mother's blood, driven by bouts of madness. Phoebus has told him that release lies in securing the image of Artemis from the Taurians and bringing it to Attica. So he has come to an unfamiliar, unfriendly (*a-xenos*) land (94). Orestes is not in the heroic mold. He knows that the Taurians sacrifice foreigners. He looks at the height of the walls and the formidable locks, and promptly gets cold feet; his cowardice is more than a little comic. Pylades is made of stronger stuff. For once a dramatist has given him a fair deal; this is no mere walk-on part. His answer is that of the storybook hero:

Run away? Intolerable! We don't do things like that. (104)

He suggests hiding in a cave while it is light, and his eye is already scanning possible ways of breaking into the temple after dark. Orestes is encouraged, and they go to earth.

The chorus of captive Greek girls now enters to solemn spondaic measures. Their function is to intensify the sense of yearning, and our compassion for the homeless refugees. As Iphigeneia comes to meet them they burst into anapaests, and use Euripides's favorite lyric device of a repeated word:

Why have you called, have you called me to the temple? (138)

Iphigeneia in her reply uses the same device:

I am ruined, ruined. (153)

Her song is a song of mourning for Orestes, and right at the outset she establishes the mood of paradox and contradiction.

Servants,
I am plunging in grief which is hard to grieve. (143)

The chorus joins in sorrow for the house of Atreus and the monarchy at Argos; they sing antiphonally (179) but the rhythms do not correspond, and Iphigeneia's dance would have been independent of the choreography of the chorus. They claim to be singing in a foreign idiom, and the key word *barbaron* returns (180); it is likely that Euripides produced some exotic effect in the music and dancing, which would be spectacularly effective and would help to drive home the alienation of the chorus. Iphigeneia's final song is beautifully conceived. The chorus ends on the note of contradiction:

> Fate desires
> things undesirable for you. (201–202)

Iphigeneia takes up the theme in her initial reference to "ill-fated Fate" (203–204), and then couples the theme of contradiction with the theme of her marriage at Aulis, "bride in a sorry bridal" (216), and then with the theme of hospitality, as she is now "guest of the Inhospitable Sea" (218). In tumbling short syllables she describes herself as "husbandless, childless, cityless, friendless" (220). Her very gloom hides an immense, unfulfilled capacity for joy. Then she turns back to Orestes, and echoes the rhythm of the description of herself and she tells how she left him "baby yet, young yet, tender yet" (232). The irony is bitter as she pictures him at his mother's breasts. She does not know it, but he has killed that mother; she does not know it but he is near. The name is climactically held up to the very end of her song (235).

A herdsman enters with news of the apprehension of two Greek strangers. He is down to earth and the whole effect is exciting but slightly comic. He caught the name of one, Pylades (a name that means nothing to Iphigeneia, as he was not born at the time of the Aulis episode). Iphigeneia asks in a line of strange assonances the name of the other (250), but they did not catch it. She says, "It was time they came"—the words have double meaning—

> the goddess's altar
> has not yet been crimsoned with Greek blood. (258)

Euripides is not consistent about this; elsewhere it is categorically stated that there have been such sacrifices. The herdsman tells his story with a parody of Aeschylean magniloquence,

> ferrying his tread on the tips of his toes. (266)

They saw the Greeks in a cave: one took them for gods, but a rationalist—Euripides laughs at himself—decided that they were shipwrecked strangers. As they watched, Orestes raised a hunter's cry (an ironical contradiction since he was the quarry) with a vision of the Furies in the herds and hounds. He drew his sword and set about them. The herdsmen were circumspect.

> We didn't think cowherds good enough to fight
> Against fine young foreigners. (304)

They maintained a reluctance to fight, another comical touch, but threw things from a safe distance. Meantime Orestes had collapsed in a fit, but Pylades was protecting him.

> It was quite incredible. Out of tens of thousands of hands
> no one had the luck to hit the goddess's victims. (328–329)

We are not told what the rationalist's comment was on this. At the end the herdsman brings together the theme of the sacrifice of strangers and the sacrifice at Aulis.

Iphigeneia's speech as they go to fetch the strangers is of great importance for our understanding of her. She used to be gentle and pitiful to her own people; now she is bitter. She shows that she was her father's daughter; her mind was centered on him. When he betrayed her, she transferred all her emotions to Orestes. She speaks of her mother without emotion, and her sister not at all, of Helen with extreme bitterness, and of Menelaus as an afterthought to Helen. She also shows an element of self-dramatization; her language is vivid— she speaks of "javelining words" (362) and of Agamemnon dangling a husband in front of her exactly as a carter dangles a carrot before a donkey (370)—but it is also incongruous. She also shows a spirit of rationalizing about a goddess who demands ritual purity but delights in ritual murder. Her last words are:

> I think that those here, who delight in killing,
> attribute their pettiness to the goddess.
> I do not believe that any of the gods is wicked. (389)

"Those here." The language is subtle. Dramatically it means "amongst

the Taurians." But the words are spoken at Athens in the middle of a
war of which Euripides was critical; in any case the expression is
familiar for "men on earth."

The chorus now sings, with characteristic Euripidean repetitions, of
the dangerous journey to the Black Sea and of what men will risk for
wealth, turning to share in Iphigeneia's curse on Helen, and sounding
again the note of escape from exile, if only in dream and fantasy. There
is point here, for Iphigeneia has in a sense taken her dream too seriously, and they, in a sense, do not take theirs seriously enough. Their
mention of a white promontory covered with birds opens a theme that
is for them important (435).

Orestes and Pylades are brought in bound, and Iphigeneia gives
orders for their release. She addresses them as "unhappy strangers"
and (with perhaps too obvious irony) sheds a tear for the sister who
will lose them. A new theme, that of Chance, springs from her words,
but, except that it gives Orestes room to call himself Child of Mischance, it is not taken up. She ends with a grim jest:

> You've been on a long voyage to this land
> and you'll be a long time away from home, underground for
>   ever (480)

Pylades's name is established; that of Orestes is evaded:

> You will offer up my body, not my name. (504)

His country is at first evaded, then the news that he comes from Argos
draws a startled exclamation from Iphigeneia. He is a kind of a refugee,
both voluntary and involuntary (512). They skirt round the subject
of Helen, hateful to both of them, and Iphigeneia exults pitilessly in
the news of Calchas's death. Then,

> IPHIGENEIA: Is Thetis the Nereid's son still alive?
> ORESTES: No. His marriage at Aulis came to nothing.
> IPHIGENEIA: Exactly. It was crooked, as those who had anything
>   to do with it know.
> ORESTES: Who are you? You are well up in Greek history.
> IPHIGENEIA: I come from there. I was lost as a child. (537)

Next comes news of Agamemnon's death, which visibly affects her, followed by two brilliant lines:

> ORESTES: He passed on in a terrible way. He was murdered by
>   a woman.
> IPHIGENEIA: How pitiable the woman who killed . . . and the man
>   who killed! (552)

She does not yet know that the woman was Clytemnestra. Her thoughts pass to Agamemnon's sacrifice of her. But her words can refer to Orestes who also killed, and to herself who has been ready to kill Greeks in revenge. She hears with grim approval of Orestes's act, and, without interest, of Electra's survival. They turn back to Iphigeneia and Agamemnon, and the *motif* of contradiction appears:

> His death was an ill-favored favor to an evil woman. (566)

And now she learns that Orestes is alive, though wretched, nowhere and everywhere. They indulge in rationalism at the expense of dreams and, significantly, oracles.

The chorus puts in a desire for news of home. Iphigeneia ignores this. She has an idea. She will release Orestes if he takes a letter home for her, and sacrifice Pylades alone. Orestes reverses their rôles. Iphigeneia's words are charged with irony. She could wish for a brother like that; she has none, or none in sight. She accepts in Orestes a combination of nobility of character and the death wish. Orestes realizes that there will be no sister to perform the obsequies. Iphigeneia answers,

> Vain hope, poor man, whoever you are;
> she lives far from this barbarous land. (628)

Then, with still obvious irony, she promises to fulfill the office herself. And now she will send to Argos to one of her loved ones (*philon*) unexpected news. Her letter will tell him that those whom he thinks dead are alive. Only, as we know, unless something happens he will be dead.

Iphigeneia goes to fetch the letter; again we learn something of her psychology, a brooding obsession combined with readiness for any contingency. The chorus sings a short dirge over Orestes. In the conversation between Orestes and Pylades that follows, the theme of *philia* is strong. They are puzzled by Iphigeneia, whom they call, meaningfully, "stranger." Pylades honorably seeks to die with Orestes, who will not let him; Orestes calls him "fellow-huntsman" (709) and attacks Apollo, as Euripides could not resist doing. Now Iphigeneia returns, and the greatest of all recognition scenes follows. There is one clever exchange

> IPHIGENEIA: You must say "I will give this to your friends."
> PYLADES: I will give these letters to your friends. (744)

Pylades does not take the document but the girl to Argos, and her words, unwittingly, could mean exactly that; his answer could not. Iphigeneia in turn prays that if she does not rescue Pylades she may never set foot in Argos alive. Then a thought strikes Pylades. Suppose the letter is lost in a shipwreck; he should have an escape clause. This gives Iphigeneia the idea of getting him to memorize the letter as well.

> IPHIGENEIA: Tell Orestes, Agamemnon's son
>   "This is a message from your sister who was sacrificed
>   at Aulis,
>   Iphigeneia; she is alive, though dead as far as they
>   are concerned. . . ."
> ORESTES: Where is she? Has she come back from the dead?
> IPHIGENEIA: Standing before your eyes. Don't interrupt. . . . (769)

The last touch is brilliant. The dagger of irony drives deeper; she reads on, oblivious, and tells of her charge to sacrifice strangers, repeating the name Orestes for fear that Pylades should forget. Then comes an exquisite touch. Pylades says that she has enfolded him with oaths easy to keep (788) and in her presence hands the letter to Orestes, addressing him by name. And now Orestes uses the language of *philia* to her, while the chorus, not understanding, calls him "Stranger" and protests against his enfolding (Pylades's word) their priestess in his arms. Iphigeneia cannot believe it. She has overdramatized Orestes.

> You my brother! Stop saying such things!
> His presence fills Argos and Nauplia. (803)

But she is convinced by details that Orestes has learned from Electra.

The Aulis theme returns (818–819), and the brother and sister join in a great song of joy, in which the chorus is brought within the web of *philia* (842) and Iphigeneia dreams of home. The somber note of Aulis breaks through, then the countervailing sacrifice she had so nearly performed, then their present dangers, barbarous tribes and trackless tracks (889). Her fertile mind ranges swiftly over the situation; but without help their resources are resourceless (897); there is no escape for—she has utterly forgotten Electra—the two last of the house of Atreus.

They come back to the sober language of dialogue; the chorus uses an idea that was not yet stale from excessive exposure, that it's like something on the stage (900–901). Pylades, sounding the note of friendship, gets down to planning. Now Iphigeneia is unbusinesslike. She wants news. She remembers that she has forgotten Electra, but her words are strange and harsh: "You are all loved things (*phila*) to me." Electra has married Pylades, and we pass on to the next topic. We are learning more about Iphigeneia. We may add that there is much in a Greek name, and Euripides means it to be pointed that Electra ("unwed") is wed, and Iphigeneia ("strong in birth") is not. In Orestes's long speech the theme of hospitality to strangers comes right to the front (947–949) as he tells his story. Euripides likes to introduce the etiology of Athenian ritual, and the speech has this purpose, as well as introducing the theft of Artemis's statue. They plan. Iphigeneia refuses the idea of killing Thoas,

> A terrible thought, that guests should murder their host! (1021)

even though he would sacrifice them. She devises a scheme of purification for victims and image that will enable them to get away. Orestes is alliteratively excited at the prospect (1046), and Iphigeneia turns to invite the chorus's help in a speech full of *philia*; she is now slightly gushing about Electra (1059). The chorus speaks of her as *phile* (1075); they are all Greeks together, all in the plot. Before she goes out Iphigeneia prays to Artemis; she is still thinking of Aulis (1082), and her scorn of the barbarous land of the Taurians must have given Athenian patriotism a delusive warmth.

The choral ode that follows ranks with any Euripides wrote. He is at his best when his theme is birds; perhaps that tells us something of his psychology. The chorus is wholly relevant. They compare themselves, wingless birds, with the kingfisher, whose song is easy for the understanding to understand. The conceit of contradiction has turned to the conceit of agreement. The plot has turned. The heroes are not out of the wood, but they are on their way out. The chorus sings of Artemis, goddess of childbirth, and of their own captivity in barbary, where the goddess is leaving them and the gracious home she will enjoy in Athens instead of the impious altars of the Taurians.

Now Thoas appears—the chorus has anticipated his entry in a daring pun (1142). He is courteous, superstitious, trusting, and Iphigeneia takes him in without difficulty. She tells of a miraculous movement of the goddess's statue; Thoas with gentle rationalism suggests an earthquake (1166). There is one powerful exchange:

IPHIGENEIA: They dealt with their mother with a common sword.
THOAS: Apollo! Even among barbarians no one would have the
            nerve for that (1173)

Apollo ordained the murder. Thoas calls his own people barbarians; there may be an innuendo about the Hellenizing, culture-conscious court of Macedon. Thoas admires Iphigeneia's skill and decisiveness in coping with the crisis, but he sees the wrong crisis. The situation is delicate:

IPHIGENEIA: They offered my mind attractive bait.

Irony!

THOAS: Did they bring you a love charm of news from Argos?
IPHIGENEIA: Yes, that my only brother Orestes is well.
THOAS: In the hope that you'd save them in delight at the news?

This is too near the bone, and she covers up with a hurried lie.

IPHIGENEIA: And that my father is alive and well.
THOAS: Of course you've made all your decisions for the best
            interests of the goddess.
IPHIGENEIA: Rather in hatred of the whole of Greece, which de-
            stroyed me. (1181–1187)

Methinks the lady doth protest too much! A little later she speaks in a famous line of taking them to the sea for purification.

IPHIGENEIA: The sea washes away all men's evil.

Presently we shall learn that the sea spews them back to land.

THOAS: They would thus fall before the goddess more holily as victims.
IPHIGENEIA: And my interests would be better served. (1193–1195)

The scene is filled with obvious but telling irony. Thoas again commands her piety and forethought. They break into trochaic tetrameters, breathlessly exchanging half-lines. Iphigeneia comments that Greece cannot be trusted (1205), in the mood that clients described a later nation of shopkeepers as "perfidious Albion." *Timeo Danaos, et dona ferentes.* Thoas says that she cares well for the city (1212); ah, but which city? "And my loved ones," she adds, "to whom I owe the duty." She brilliantly calls for all citizens, including the king, to keep out of sight during the ritual of purification, and she goes out with a prayer to Artemis.

The chorus now sings of Artemis's brother Apollo, when a messenger bursts in with news of the attempted escape. Euripides is sometimes accused of a chorus that is no part of the action. Here, as in *Medea*, the chorus intervenes. They lie to the messenger in the hope of delaying his report to the king. But the king comes out and receives the report; he is familiar with Orestes from Iphigeneia, which saves needless explanation. The messenger's speech is brilliantly exciting. He tells how they were sent apart, how Iphigeneia started chanting in a barbarous foreign tongue (presumably Greek!), how they took the Greeks for slaves, kidnapping their priestess, and how Orestes revealed himself as Agamemnon's son come to fetch his sister whom—and the word is subtly ambiguous—"he killed" or "I lost" (1363). Then there was a scuffle, and the Greeks got away with the object of their "inhospitable voyage" (1388). Inhospitable: they were not received as guests, but they did not behave as guests.

And now, just as we think the thing is over, Euripides gives his play a double twist. For the Greeks do not escape. The waves sweep them back, and they are cornered. Thoas, swift by name, and swift to act when aroused, moves to the roundup.

> Hurry, and with the goddess's help
> you'll hunt down these wicked men. (1425–1426)

The goddess. He means Artemis, but he hasn't reckoned with Athene. He threatens throwing over a precipice, which was a Greek practice, and piercing with stakes, which was not (1430). In his dynamic excitement he speaks of sending cavalry by sea and land (1428) and his last words tumble over one another in a stammering medley of recurrent sounds (1434).

And Euripides produces his second twist. The goddess Athene stands on the temple roof and calls to the king to desist. Euripides has been accused of dragging in a *deus ex machina* because he could not otherwise unravel his plot. Nothing could be further from the truth; it might be truer to say that he ravels his plot so as to drag in a *deus ex machina*. For the last-minute failure of escape was his own invention, and the goddess does not appear merely to rescue the chorus.

We should not underestimate the spectacular power of this ending, and the effect of using different levels of the set. But in addition it gave Euripides two other advantages. The *deus*, with the gift of foresight, could engage in those etiological explanations that he and his audience seemed to love. And it amused his whimsical rationalism to put the criticism of one divinity in the mouth of another. Athene checks Thoas, and with a side glance at his confused command (1428) tells him to check the flood of his army (1437). Then with a simple but splendid visual effect she turns to call to Orestes. The prophecies follow about Artemis Tauropolos and the ritual at Brauron. Thoas is told to release the chorus, and assents.

> Lady Athene, if anyone hears the words of the gods
> and does not trust them, he is wrong in his mind. (1475)

What are we to say? It is dangerous to extrapolate from one play to another. But in Electra Euripides is sweeping in his condemnation of Apollo's oracular command to kill Clytemnestra. Orestes has trusted this, and we have seen him wrong in his mind; it follows that these were not words of a true god, and Euripides is having his usual fling at Apollo. And Euripidean rationalism has the last word, or the next to last word, when Athene tells us gratuitously that necessity rules men and gods alike (1486).

One final feature of this play deserves comment. This is its relation to *Electra* and to *Helen*. There is a reasonable probability that *Electra* and *Iphigeneia among the Taurians* were both presented in 413. If so, we have plays dealing with two members of the house of Atreus. *Helen* clearly bears a close resemblance to *Iphigeneia*. The evidence points to its production in 412, but it is just possible that the evidence is misleading and it formed the third member of this trilogy. In any case the two plays are related. *Helen,* as we shall see, is certainly an attack on the illusion of war. *Iphigeneia* was written under the shadow of Melos and the expedition to Sicily. In *Electra* those who take the law violently into their own hands were condemned; what is war but taking the law violently into one's own hands? In *Iphigeneia* a sister dedicates her brother to death by the sword, and recognizes his true identity in time. What is war but blood sacrifice? Why should Greeks kill Greeks? When will men learn to see our victims as our brothers? At the end of the play Athene establishes in Attica a cult of Artemis, civilized, with an end to human sacrifice. Is Euripides not, by analogy, praying for an end to war?

30. HELEN

Helen is an entertaining but elusive play, which is why some critics say that we should enjoy rather than analyze it. This will not do; the questions press too urgently and cannot be silenced; they sent Verrall off on a wild-goose chase; yet Verrall saw real problems. The simple thing is to call the play a "tragicomedy" and classify it with *Alcestis* and *Iphigeneia among the Taurians*. *Alcestis* is a much earlier play, a substitute for a satyr play, and not to be interpreted as a tragedy. Yet there is a genuinely tragic situation in *Alcestis*; there is none in *Helen*. With *Iphigeneia* there is a closer relationship in time and theme. But *Iphigeneia*, as we have seen, is a serious play seriously handled. Until the very end *Helen* is handled with the lightest of touches, and there is nothing serious. It is tempting to think that *Helen*, like *Alcestis*, took the place of the satyr play, but there is no evidence of this as there is with *Orestes*.

The date is apparently fixed by the scholiasts to Aristophanes. From *The Thesmophoriazusae* and *The Frogs* we learn that *Helen* and *An-*

dromeda were presented on the same occasion, and that that occasion was the year before *The Thesmophoriazusae* and seven years before *The Frogs*. The evidence is probably decisive, and it should make us cautious about our interpretation of *Andromeda*. From Aristophanes and elsewhere we know of the striking opening of this play with Andromeda chained to a rock and singing a lament, and Echo answering her song. But we do not know how the play ended beyond the fact that Perseus rescued the girl, and we should hesitate before we assume that it was a simple romantic story. The two stories are not mythologically related, but bear an affinity of theme, since both deal with a rescue. We do not know what other plays completed the tetralogy. *Iphigeneia* might have been one, since that is another rescue story, but it is perhaps more likely that *Iphigeneia* was presented with *Electra* in the previous year. *Helen* is, however, not to be wholly dissociated from those plays, and it is just possible that the scholiast was making a wrong deduction from the text of *The Thesmophoriazusae* and that *Helen* was performed with the other plays in 413; Aristophanes only says that *Andromeda* was "last year" and *Helen* "recent." *Iphigeneia* and *Helen* are, in different ways, debunkings of the myths which surround the Trojan War; *Helen* debunks the war itself. Here too it must be seen in its political context. If we accept the more probable date of 412, this was the first festival since the news of the Sicilian debacle. The whole of Greece, said Thucydides, promptly turned against Athens. Euboea, Lesbos, Chios and Erythrae were negotiating with Sparta revolt from Athens. Sparta and her allies were building a large fleet. Persian gold was ready to back the Spartans. Athens pared her other expenditures, and put all her resources into a renewed war effort. And Euripides wrote a play whose theme was that the Trojan War was fought over an illusion.

A strong note of irony is struck from the first. A figure of a woman stands, apparently in sanctuary, by a tomb. She is very beautiful. She tells us that we are in Egypt, where the old king Proteus had left a son Theoclymenus, and a daughter of prophetic vision Theonoe. In her first line she speaks of the streams of Nile "virgin-beautiful" (1). The word is meaningful. The sky was mythically believed to impregnate the earth through rain; but the Nile found its water not from rain

but melted snow. The theme of virginity recurs (6, 10, 25). Euripides's opening characters usually reveal themselves in their first words.
This woman does not speak her name for twenty lines, and it is with
a shock that we learn that this obsession with virginity is coming from
the lips of Helen. She alludes with amusing scepticism to the legend
that she was fathered by Zeus in the form of a swan, a swan that was
hiding from an eagle, if you please! She tells of the rivalry of the goddesses, and the judgment of Paris, allured by the bribe of her beauty.
And now she turns to a story that we know derives from the famous
Recantation of Stesichorus:

> It's all a lie:
> You never sailed in the well-benched ships,
> never trod the towers of Troy.

Hera, resentful at losing the prize, baulked Paris of his bribe and
substituted a breathing likeness fashioned from the upper air. Helen
was not consulted, and is noncommittal; she does not say that it was a
disappointment or a relief. She was bundled through the air by Hermes,
and Proteus protected her chastity against the arrival of Menelaus. But
Proteus is dead, Theoclymenus suing for her love, and she herself a
suppliant at Proteus's tomb. Meantime the Greeks and Trojans have
been fighting over a phantom, and she is cursed as the cause of a pes-
tilential war.

Suddenly a figure bursts in, wearing Greek clothes, bow in hand.
He looks at the walls of the palace with admiration, and thinks that
they might belong to the god of Wealth. Then he spots Helen—or, as
he must believe, her double, the likeness so great that he would shoot
if he were not in a foreign country He too holds up his name for some
twenty lines; it is Teucer. He tells of the fall of Troy, a victory that
was defeat for him!

> HELEN: Poor Helen! The Trojans have perished through you.
> TEUCER: *And* Greeks. It's all been a great disaster. (109)

Helen's sympathy is pointed. A little later, irony links with illusion.
Teucer saw Helen dragged off:

TEUCER: I saw her with my own eyes—just as I see you now.
HELEN: Suppose it was a fancy sent by the gods?
TEUCER: Enough of her. Talk about something else.
HELEN: Then you fancy your fancy was infallible?
TEUCER: I saw her with these eyes. What the eye sees the mind
      sees. (118)

He reports Menelaus lost and Leda dead through suicide at Helen's disgrace, and two different stories of her brothers, one that they were deified as stars, the other that they too took their own lives. Teucer has come to consult Theonoe about settling in Cyprus. Helen packs him off. Cyprus is plain sailing; no need of a seer. But Theoclymenus will kill any Greek he finds, for no reason that Helen is prepared to give. The point is clear; Theoclymenus's irrationality is no worse than the irrationality that is war. More, where Helen is, wraith or reality, there is destruction. Teucer blesses her, and curses the Helen he knows; but they are tarred with the same brush. The Teucer scene is contrived, but skillfully contrived. It was essential to have some other arrival before Menelaus, and the scene gives Euripides space to maneuver, establishing motifs, irony, and anticipation.

Now Helen sings and is joined by the chorus of Spartan women. Their song is rhythmically fascinating; Euripides makes full use of a device called syncopation, by which a shorter unit is the metrical balance of a longer one, and one suspects that this represents a musical effect of a rest or break, sometimes in the middle of a word. Helen invokes the Sirens, winged, half-birds, half-women; they link the theme of bird, which in its truth is associated with escape (1479, 1516) and with Helen, born of an egg, and the theme of woman. But the Sirens are also spirits of death, and this anticipates the nightingale ode (1107), and in the mention of Persephone prepares for the Demeter ode (1301), reminding us that the ultimate theme of this play is not life but death. Furthermore, in *The Odyssey*, familiar to the audience, the Sirens sang to Odysseus "all that the Greeks and Trojans suffered on the plains of Troy" (Hom. *Od.* 12.189–190). She invokes the Sirens, and the chorus enters. Spartan women were notoriously sturdy—"Lampito, darling," says Lysistrata in Aristophanes's comedy, "how well you're looking; just as if you could strangle an ox!" (Ar. *Lys.* 78)—and it may be that the debunking of supernatural myth, which is a marked feature of the play, was pointed by the choral entrance. The first words of the chorus are almost self-parody, based as they are on the corresponding ode in *Hippolytus* (*Hipp.* 121–130). There the waters in which they were washing their clothes become the flood that sweeps away Hippolytus; there is ambiguity here too. They speak of "spiraling greenness" (180); both words recur in the Demeter ode (1331, 1360), but they have darkened and become somber. They have heard Helen's song, and use of it a word that is not found elsewhere in tragedy and generally implies the shouting of soldiers (*homadon*, 184). They compare it to the cry of a nymph raped by Pan, and this recalls to us the seduction that started the war. Between them they sing of disaster, and Helen tells how

> Treacherous,
> murderous Aphrodite
> brought death to Greeks, to Trojans. (238)

Then (but when? where?) Hera sent Hermes to sweep her off to Egypt. Hermes found her gathering flowers; and the implicit comparison with Persephone is of major importance.

Helen feels that life has become insupportable. That we are not to take this seriously is suggested by her opening petulance:

> Women, in Greece or abroad,
> don't produce fledglings in white shells. (257)

She laments her birth, her reputation, her exile, the apparent death of her husband, her mother's death, her daughter's aging virginity (the theme again!), and "the two so-called Dioscuri, sons of Zeus, do not exist" (84), a fine rationalizing ambiguity. She will seek suicide. But a touch of comedy supervenes. A real aristocrat, she says, prefers the knife to the rope—only it does hurt. The chorus persuades her first to consult Theonoe, and, singing and dancing, they all go in. The absence of the chorus is rare, except to represent a change of scene, and their passage into the palace reminds us that there is no rigid separation of chorus and actors. Theoclymenus is admittedly out hunting, but the freedom with which Helen moves away from her sanctuary makes us wonder whether she is really as imperilled as she implies.

The exit of the chorus leaves the scene free. On it appears, stealthily, a figure in rags, an effect for which Euripides was famed. His words belie his state; after a pompous exordium he reveals himself as Menelaus. He shows his character, first in his claim that he (not Agamemnon) was commander-in-chief of the Greek forces at Troy, then in his embarrassed avoidance of people because of his dirty old clothes. He explains, talking to himself, that he did possess some decent clothes, but they were lost in a storm. He and Helen escaped—Helen, the source of all his sufferings, whom he has left under guard in a cave. He, like Teucer, is impressed by the signs of wealth. We have the sense that Euripides is jibing at Greek parochialism; they do not know what real wealth means. Menelaus calls out the old crone who answers the door; the Greeks move in fear of their lives, but the defense system is scarcely formidable. The deflation continues as she pushes him away and he does not resist.

OLD WOMAN: You're a nuisance. I'll have you thrown out.
MENELAUS: Ow! What's happened to my magnificent army? (452)

He begins to blubber. He learns that he is in Egypt, that they are hostile to Greeks—and that Zeus's daughter Helen is inside. The old woman gives him a kindly warning in an oxymoron "If my master catches you, you'll have death for a welcome" (479), and the door shuts behind her, leaving Menelaus puzzled. Can there, he wonders rationalistically, be a man called Zeus? His complacency gets the better of him and irony again supervenes, as he says "No one could have such an uncivilized mind as to refuse me a meal, once he knew my name" (501). In fact he survives only by concealing his name. He ends with a cliché— "Nothing is stronger than necessity"—carefully explaining that he did not coin the phrase (513), then hurriedly retreats as the chorus and Helen return.

Theonoe has said that Menelaus is still alive. Helen apostrophizes him romantically:

Oh, when will you come? I long for your arrival.
Oh! who's that? (540)

She sees him, looking like some wild man from Borneo, and makes a dash "like a racehorse or a Maenad" for her sanctuary, which she grips tight. Menelaus, who had no intention of intercepting her, is somewhat surprised. But he has seen her face; he tries to pull her round to look at him, and a comical tug-of-war ensues. Suddenly, she sees, and in famous words cries, "Gods! To recognize a loved one is god" (560). The phrase is extraordinary; the parallels alleged are not precise; it is in fact another touch of rationalism, reverent rationalism but rationalism nonetheless. And now it is she who presses forward and he who holds back. She tries to embrace him, and as he pulls away, grasps only his rags, and he says petulantly, "Leave my clothes alone" (567). She shows a mole or birthmark (578), and one wonders on what part of her body the producer should choose to locate it. Menelaus finds two Helens too many; one suspects that one was too many for him. He cannot believe in the ether-formed phantom. He is about to go—"The weight of hard experience at Troy is more convincing than you" (593)—leaving her in despair, when one of Menelaus's men, a fellow of amiable and ingenuous sententiousness, comes in. In this land, so strongly guarded against the Greeks, he has been wandering all over the place in search of Menelaus. Helen, Helen of Troy, Helen in the cave, has vanished into thin air, gone up into the sky; how she achieved this feat inside a cave is anybody's guess. Before she went she spoke words of pity for Greeks and Trojans who had been suffering for an illusion. Then, as the messenger reports this, delightfully he spots Helen:

> Hallo, daughter of Leda. Were you here all along?
> I was announcing that you'd passed to the recesses
> of the stars. I didn't realize that your body
> was winged. I shan't let you fool us
> again like this. In Troy you gave enough
> trouble to your husband and his allies. (616)

A dance-song of recognition and reunion follows. It is written in the strange mixture of speech rhythm and song that Euripides sometimes affects; the implication is a lyrical duet interjected with spoken phrases. The whole thing is grotesquely overwritten, and this must be deliberate. Some reads almost like self-parody:

> Friends, friends, the past has lost its sting.
> No more grief.
> The man I'm holding—holding—is mine—mine.
> I've waited, waited years for him to come from Troy. (648)

On their reunion the shadow of disaster hangs.

MENELAUS: Paris, you ravaged my whole house from top to bottom,

—this is quite unjust—

> but the act brought death to you and thousands
>   of bronze-armed Greeks.
> HELEN: And I under doom, under curse, was exiled
>   by god from my country, my city and you,
>   forced to leave my palace, my marriage, but not
>   for a shameful love. (691)

There is a lack of proportion somewhere! The messenger has been watching these interchanges with puzzlement—plenty of opportunities for comedy there!—and asks to have it explained. Menelaus does so, and his reply is, "Do you mean we went through all that for a shadow?" (707). He makes a sententious speech about the ups and downs of life, with an affecting memory of Helen's wedding to Menelaus, and a proud assertion that slave in body does not mean slave in spirit (730), and, as Menelaus sends him off to report back to the others, another speech against seers and prophets: "The best oracle is thought and common sense" (757). Yet another rationalizing touch, which the chorus echoes.

The messenger's exit leaves Helen and Menelaus together to work out their plans. The ensuing scene, which includes over sixty lines of swift interchange in strict *stichomythia*, is exceedingly funny. Helen asks about his journey, and Menelaus answers pompously, making it sound as if he had been halfway round the world. Helen changes the subject and almost casually reveals that in Egypt he is liable to death. "What are you saying? What will you say next? You've already killed me, woman," says Menelaus (779), jumping out of his skin. Menelaus now understands what the old woman whom he encountered said.

HELEN: Begging for bread? I'm ashamed.
MENELAUS: Well, that's what it was, but I didn't call it that. (791)

Helen, revealing that importunity of the king, assures Menelaus of her chastity. She suggests that he escape without her; if he can, it is not clear why he should not escape with her. However, he sacked Troy for her, and puts on a typical braggart soldier act; here as elsewhere Euripides anticipates New Comedy. Helen, shrewder, seeks a device; the word is ambiguous, for it is used of the crane from which divinities appeared. But they must win Theonoe's support, or she, omniscient, will reveal his presence. They seal a suicide compact if they should fail; but it is noteworthy that Menelaus first puts the words into Helen's mouth, then makes her swear, and finally says that he will kill her first anyway.

Suddenly there is a noise within the palace; the great gates clang open, and a torch procession emerges with Theonoe; it is good spectacle. She gives her attendants ritual instructions; then, without emotion or change of mood, she tells Helen that Menelaus has arrived, and then, to his discomfiture, pointing to him in his rags, "obviously there he is" (874). Then, "Voyage home? Or remain here? You don't know" (877). Still quite casual, she tells of a dispute among the gods; the word *eris* (878) takes us back to the dispute that Paris had to adjudge.

Hera wants Menelaus's return, Aphrodite opposes it. Theonoe has been asked to give the casting vote. It is an extraordinary passage. There is clear rationalism, a human called in because the gods cannot agree; for even if we accept the view that Theonoe, whose name means "Divine Intellect," and who is addressed by Helen as "Maiden" (894), in some sense stands for or takes the place of Athene, it is as a human being that she is presented. Besides this, Hera's switched favor is suspicious; can we really believe that it is for the good of Greece that Menelaus and Helen should return? Theonoe pauses and tests Helen and Menelaus by a suggestion of calling her brother. The words are not out of her mouth before Helen is clinging to her knees in supplication. Her plea is eloquent, tinged with philosophy, and self-centered. "God hates violence," she says, meaning that Theonoe should not expose them to Theoclymenus (903); yet how will they eventually escape? She speaks of the sky and earth as common to all, and attacks the pursuit of riches. The lines are slightly irrelevant in immediate context, but the play is about war, and Euripides is repudiating the economic motive for war that led the Athenians to Sicily. She goes on:

> Shameful for you to have deep knowledge of divine love,
> of all that is and all that is not, and none of justice. (922)

All that is and all that is not: present and future no doubt, but Euripides, if not Helen, implies that Theonoe has solved the dilemma of Parmenides. Helen does not plead for Menelaus; she pleads that she shall not lose him again, that she shall see her daughter and rehabilitate her own reputation.

Menelaus follows. "Menelaus is wonderful," says Kitto, "the Rev. Mr. Collins himself could have done no better." Not for him to kneel or weep. He is asking his just due, his own wife. He turns from Theonoe and in excellent pageantry, no doubt with the help of the chorus, invokes first Proteus, then Hades. Through the parody the bitterness of Euripides flashes out; Hades has had his pay, many bodies from Menelaus's sword. Menelaus is a man of blood; he will not hesitate to kill Theoclymenus, or Helen and himself. He dramatizes himself, his voice breaks, and the tear that he has disowned drops.

Theonoe is quite unmoved by Menelaus's piling horror on horror. Aphrodite does not interest her; her brother's reputation and her father's promise to protect and restore Helen do. Here again a little philosophy, relevantly and not unmovingly, obtrudes itself. "Dead men's minds have no life, but have deathless understanding as they mingle with the deathless principle above" (1014). With a prayer to her father she promises them protection and stalks out. A small part, but whimsically and delightfully sketched.

A dialogue in units of two lines follows. Menelaus makes a series of ridiculous suggestions; it is the women, Theonoe and Helen, and perhaps even the chorus, who control the action. Helen suggests inventing a story that Menelaus is dead. Menelaus does not like it; it seems a hoary device, but he is prepared to die—in fiction. They will then ask for a ship to perform burial rites at sea. Menelaus can appear the sole survivor of the wreck; he looks the part, and he has the sanctuary of the tomb. Helen must change her white for the black of mourning. She goes in, praying for success to both Hera and Aphrodite. Menelaus remains.

Up to this point in the play there has been no formal choral song in 1,100 lines; in the next four hundred lines there are three. This is so odd that it must be deliberate. Euripides has been giving us a kind of comedy-thriller. He has intensified this because his fundamental purpose is serious. His object is to strike home the more effectively because we are off our guard. But the seriousness of the final messenger's speech would not hit us unless there were something implanted in our minds already. The choral odes link the theme of the play with mythology; they set it *sub speciem aeternitatis*. They are put close together because they reinforce one another; the later are to be seen in the light of the earlier. And their theme is death.

The first starts exquisitely from the nightingale, a stock tragic image because of its song of grief and its association with loss; here we remember too rape and violence and death. They pass to the theme of Troy, and they, Greeks, sing of the sorrows of the Trojans as well as of the Greeks. At one moment the rhythm and words pick up Helen's earlier lament (1117, cf. 194). Suddenly, momentarily, the mood changes to the reverent scepticism that presses behind laughter and preaching:

> Pressing enquiry to the utmost limit,
> watching divine decrees tossed up and down
> in history's dialectic
> and the unexpected twist,
> who dares to claim to find
> where God is, God is not, what lies between? (1137)

The shade of Parmenides stirs again; to say that it is and is not, this is altogether intractable. If Zeus's daughter is cursed, "crook, traitress, fruitless, godless," then nothing is certain. The conclusion might be

that she is not Zeus's daughter, but we are left to make the deduction
if we will. The chorus returns to their theme.

> You who win honor in war
> at the point of your sturdy spears,
> ignorantly trying to halt
> the trouble of the world—you're all mad.
> If bloodshed is to settle
> the issue, violence will never
> abandon the cities of men. (1151)

The end of the verse is uncertain in reading, but it is an application
of the general assertion to the Trojans. Why destruction rather than
negotiation? It is a powerful indictment even of the just war; the more
powerful because we have waited so long for the chorus to sing, and
their words burst out with pent-up impetus.

Theoclymenus comes with an escort of hunters and hounds; the
effect is repeated from *Hippolytus*, but nonetheless vivid. He greets
Proteus's tomb with piety. Menelaus is in sanctuary there; as Theoclymenus does not see him, it follows that the gallant hero has ducked
out of sight behind. The king has heard that some Greek is about and
threatens death for him if caught. Then he notices Helen's absence.
He is about to send out a search party when she appears in mourning.
"Menelaus—oh, how can I say it?—is, for me, dead," she says. "For
me," lighter in Greek than in English, is an exquisite touch. She tells
her cock-and-bull story and implicates Theonoe in it. She produces her
eyewitness—"He's sitting there, cowering by the tomb" (1203). "My
husband's in rags like him" (1205); "the scum sometimes is luckier
than the noble" (1213). It is all very amusing.

Theoclymenus asks after the wraith, and hearing of its disappearance, jolts us back to earth: "Then Priam and his people perished for
nothing" (1220). Irony continues throughout the scene, especially
when Helen tells Theoclymenus that he can prepare for her marriage
(1231). He renounces his anger; "let it take wings," a familiar motif
(1236), and she takes advantage of a gentleness that we gradually see
to be his real nature to clasp his knees and seek her boon. Menelaus is

drawn in, and, speaking no doubt with a coarsened accent that would
add to the humor, gives instructions for his own burial. Theoclymenus
is gracious to them both; he forgets the destruction he has vowed to
any Greek and promises them a Phoenician bark. "That is well," says
the supposed sailor, "you are generous to Menelaus" (1273), and the
king offers him a change of clothes, food, and a safe return. Menelaus
tells Helen to accept the husband who stands before her, and Helen
promises him his reward undeferred.

There follows the crux of the play. The chorus sings a mighty song
in honor of Demeter, who seems partly identified with Cybele. The
apparent irrelevance struck A. W. Verrall so strongly that it set him
off on a chain of theory, implausible no doubt, which lesser men have
rejected without approaching his grasp of the problem. Aristotle accused Euripides of irrelevance in his songs. The truth is that this is the
sole ode against which the charge can be leveled; it is intrinsically one
of the greatest of the songs, as we can discern through the uncertainties of reading, and it stands centrally to a block of choral odes that
give every impression of being carefully planned. It is exceedingly
unlikely that it is discrete, and if we do not discern the connecting links
we must realize that with all the apparatus of scholarship we remain
ignorant of many things the Greeks took for granted. We may however notice that Euripides has prepared our minds for this chorus with
some care, by the reference to Persephone in Helen's first song (175),
by the implicit comparison of herself with Persephone later in that
song (244), perhaps also by the mention of the common fruits of the
earth (907). The theme of the song is death; not just the death of
Persephone, but blight on the earth.

> The plains of earth, parched brown,
> offered no harvest in the furrows.
> A whole generation washed away.
> For the flocks no fattening food
> emerged from curling leaves.
> Life in the cities ceased. (1327)

Even the gods suffered. But this is what war does. The theme is not
irrelevant; it is central. We see now why Demeter is equated with the

Great Mother and yet called by the old Greek name Deo (1343). Demeter is a Greek goddess, the Great Mother is universal. We are here dealing with a universal law of life that Theoclymenus honors; yet at the same time it is particularized so that those at Athens with their special cult of Demeter at Eleusis cannot miss the implications for them. Demeter relented—and then (though the text is uncertain) found that her daughter herself had offended and stirred her anger again. Anyone, no matter who he may be, offends against the laws of the goddess of life at his peril.

So comes Helen, telling the chorus that all is going well. As Theoclymenus follows with Menelaus, dressed in fresh clothes and every inch a king, she drops her voice to a whisper: there are five *s*'s in eight letters (1389). A moment later she has a most extraordinary sequence of sounds.

> *theoi de soi te doien hoi egô-ô thelô-ô*
> *kai tô-ô(i) xenô-ô(i) tô-ô(i)d'*

where *kai* was no doubt in pronunciation close to *ke*. It is hard to be sure quite what this denotes, perhaps a stammering nervousness for fear the last deceit of Theoclymenus go astray, perhaps an overconscious rhetoric; certainly the jingle is comic. Irony is laid on thick.

> May the gods give you all that I desire,
> you and this foreigner for his co-operation.
> You will find in me a wife for your home after
> your own deserts, for your goodness to Menelaus and
> to me. (1405)

So Helen to the king. A few lines later Theoclymenus calls for her heart, and she replies, "I shall need no lesson in loving my beloved" (1426). So they go, Theoclymenus with courtesy and gentleness returning to the palace, Helen spectacular in procession with the attendants carrying offerings out stage-right, followed by Menelaus after a brief prayer to Zeus.

Now the chorus sings and dances of their voyage. The language is exquisite, and no doubt the dance was vivid and mimetic, first representing the boats and the dolphins, then the birds, which the chorus would wish to be in order to join them, the symbol of escape. But underneath not all is light and gay. For Helen is going to Sparta, and Sparta is characterized as the place of Hyacinthus's death. Sparta meant death to more than Hyacinthus; the Spartan Gylippus was the decisive factor in crushing the Athenians at Syracuse, and Spartan troops were occupying the fort of Decelea on the borders of Attica. So at the end they sing of lifting the reproach of the Trojan War from Helen. Perhaps, but the Trojan War did take place.

Comes a messenger with news of the escape. In vivid narrative he recounts the launching of the ships, the arrival of Menelaus's men, the bloody slaughter of the Egyptian sailors, and Helen, lovely-footed Helen, beautiful, innocent Helen, who had no part in the Trojan War, calling on the Greeks to show the reputation they won at Troy to these "wogs" (1604). It is a magnificent evocation in somber colors, and it is surely erroneous to say that we, the audience, have our sympathies with the escaping Greeks. We expect it to be there, but if the messenger does his work properly, we will be one with him in his sense of desolation: "their bodies flew hurtling overboard till he had cleared the benches of your sailors" (1609). This was murder, and the messenger so calls it (1613).

Theoclymenus, far from being the buffoon some interpreters make of him, has a swift mind and is swift to act. He realizes that Theonoe has been an accessory, draws his sword, and makes for the palace. Someone—our manuscripts say the chorus, which would give a powerful visual effect, but there is an awkward masculine in Theoclymenus's words (1630), and it may be the messenger or one of the king's attendants—someone flings himself in the king's path and will die before he passes. Across a spirited exchange in broken trochaic tetrameters breaks a voice from above. It is the Dioscuri, Castor and Polydeuces, Helen's divine brothers. They check the king's hand and his anger; then they call far away to Helen to promise her worship and an island bearing her name, the sort of link with current practice that Euripides liked to forge. Theoclymenus's true self is peaceable, and he is glad to make his peace. He turns, it seems, to the chorus, and greets them for Helen's inborn intelligence, of a quality rarely found in women. The words of the chorus that end this, as other of the plays, are here more than usually apposite:

> Divine powers appear in many shapes.
> The gods bring many an unexpected ending.
> The probable does not come to pass.
> The improbable happens by grace of god.
>   And so it was in these events. (1688)

Norwood wrote a well-known comparison of Euripides with Shaw. In no play does Euripides appear more Shavian than in *Helen*. The wit sparkles throughout, in word and situation. The comparison is apt; Menelaus continually recalls Sergius Saranoff in *Arms and the Man*. But there is another comparison. Shaw was an Irishman, and the Irish produced in the early years of this century other dramatists who worked in the medium of tragedy. Yet their plays are tragicomedy, and in *Juno and the Paycock*, for example, the robust, exhilarating humor of Joxer and Boyle prefaces the flickering out of the light before the Virgin's statue and the shooting of Johnnie. Synge and O'Casey, like Euripides, saw life as a complex tapestry:

> Joy & Woe are woven fine,
> A Clothing for the Soul divine.

Man is infinitely comic and infinitely tragic, and the one sets off the other. To see *Helen* as a romantic comedy is a mistake; it is a mistake too to deny the lightness of touch that pervades most of it. That lightness of touch prepares us for the grim darkness of the messenger's speech and makes it grimmer, and the gentle peaceableness of the "barbarian" contrasts more powerfully with the slaphappy slaughter that the Greeks leave in their train, and that had been bloodying Greece for nearly twenty years when Euripides wrote.

For this play is about war. The great war was fought for an illusion. But the real Helen is no jot better than the wraith, and destruction walks at her side. We may not forget, once Aeschylus had made the point, that her very name bears destruction in it. Why does Hera, the archenemy of the Greeks, let her home? Because, real or imaginary, she is the spirit of destruction, and her seeming innocence is the front that the powers of destruction often wear, alike before the world, and when they look at their own faces in the mirror. Helen came out dressed to celebrate death, and death attended the celebration; in their three great songs the chorus pointed the reference. Yet there is a power of life, and to turn the mind to Demeter in her mercy is not unlike beating the sword into a ploughshare.

31. *THE WOMEN OF PHOENICIA*

The Women of Phoenicia was one of the most popular of Euripides's plays in earlier times, ranking for the Byzantines with *Hecabe* and *Orestes*. It has not since regained that popularity, and the fact that there are few opportunities to see it staged does not help to dissipate the prejudice. For the play has obvious theatrical merits, as the Byzantine commentators well knew. It is, apart from anything else, a magnificent pageant of Theban mythology, spectacular and rich in characters, though it is surely a counsel of despair to see this as its prime purpose and main merit. Besides this, it contains powerful epigrammatic rhetoric. The Victorian lady complained that *Hamlet* was not original because it was full of quotations; the Byzantines might have felt similarly about *The Women of Phoenicia.*

Its very richness is, however, puzzling. It is the longest of Euripides's plays, though less than 75 lines longer than *Helen* and *Orestes*, which belong to the same quinquennium. It has clearly suffered some interpolation in later performance; in one or two places the manuscripts or early commentators indicate this (e.g., 1225, 1346); in one or two we can guess at insertions by producers to clarify a situation on the stage (e.g., 11, 141–144). In one or two there may have been expansion to integrate this play, already rich, with Aeschylus's *Seven against Thebes*, Euripides's own *Heracles's Children*, and Sophocles's *Antigone* and *Oedipus at Colonus* (in 1104–1140, 1221–1258, 1582–1709). But though there are insertions and adjustments it is unwise to exaggerate this, and those critics who excise whole scenes and whole characters carry academic logic too far. Probably the interpolations do not amount in sum to more than twenty or thirty lines, and the only point where they seriously affect our understanding of Euripides's dramatic purpose is the final scene. The Byzantine commentator complained that the play suffered from padding and (if we accept an easy but ingenious emendation) episodic treatment. His comment was on Euripides, and we must suspect a dramatic purpose that did not allow a narrow concept of dramatic unity.

It happens that we have external evidence about the date and dramatic context of the play. An ancient commentator on Aristophanes (*Frogs* 53) is surprised at a reference to *Andromeda* rather than the more recent *Hypsipyle*, *The Women of Phoenicia*, or *Antigone*. *Andromeda* is dated by the same source to 412. A mutilated note by the other Aristophanes, the scholar and literary critic, shows that Euripides won second prize with a tetralogy that comprised *Oenomaus*, *Chrysippus*, *The Women of Phoenicia* and a satyric or pro-satyric play. Metrical analysis of the scanty fragments of the other plays cannot tell against this. Various dates from 411 to 406 have been propounded. Of these 411 or even 410 would scarcely seem to justify the remark of the commentator. 409 is possible and is the date most favored by critics, because *Orestes* is firmly dated to 408, and Euripides left Athens for Macedon shortly after, though it is not impossible to suppose that he submitted plays for performance *in absentia*. But if, as the evidence suggests, *Orestes* is a pro-satyric play, then there is much to be said for the date 408, for *Chrysippus* draws together the house of Laius and the house of Atreus in a common criminality, and *Orestes* would provide a devastating conclusion to the tetralogy, though we may sympathize with an audience that sat through two plays as long as *The Women of Phoenicia* and *Orestes* consecutively.

One problem remains. We know that Glaucippus was presiding magistrate in 409, Diocles in 408; Aristophanes gives Nausicrates as the presiding magistrate. No Nausicrates appears in the lists of magistrates, and as the text hereabouts is clearly faulty it is best to assume that Nausicrates was the man who put up the money for the production. There is one curious story relative to the date. At the battle of Arginusae in 406, Thrasyllus, one of the commanders, dreamed that he and six colleagues were acting in *The Women of Phoenicia* while the enemy officers were acting in *The Suppliant Women* (D.S. 13. 97). They won, but perished. Whatever the exact date, the political context is the renewal of open fighting with Sparta, the remarkable resilience of Athens after the disaster in Sicily, intervention by Persia, and political intrigue at home with constitutional changes and criticisms and reassertions of democracy.

Oenomaus was the story of how Pelops won his wife Hippodameia from her father Oenomaus, who challenged all suitors to a chariot-race. According to the most familiar version of the myth, Pelops bribed Oenomaus's charioteer to substitute defective lynch pins in the wheels of the chariot. Oenomaus crashed and died cursing his murderer and son-in-law to be. *Hippolytus* and Sophocles's *Electra* suggest that we have lost a stirring messenger's speech, but the fragments are insufficient to allow us to evaluate the play and its treatment, and we cannot tell whether vase paintings represent scenes from Sophocles, Euripides, or neither.

Chrysippus carries the story into the next generation. Pelops had two sons by Hippodameia, Atreus and Thyestes, and one, his favorite, Chrysippus, by a nymph. The story now becomes raveled. Laius of Thebes tried to kidnap Chrysippus but was foiled. In one version Hippodameia stole Laius's sword and tried to kill the boy out of jealousy. Laius was suspected but Chrysippus before his death told the truth and Hippodameia was banished. In another the boy was killed by his stepbrothers; in yet another he committed suicide. We cannot be certain which of these Euripides followed or how much he included in his play, but we may reasonably deduce that Pelops cursed Laius, and a collateral curse on Hippodameia's house is also likely.

The third play then takes up the succession of curses with Oedipus's curse on his sons, which is explicitly said to be the transmission of a curse (1611). We are thus confronted with a highly Aeschylean theme, yet with a highly Euripidean treatment. For, if this interpretation is right, the curse is renewed from one generation to the next; it does not stand immutable; further, it is transferred from one house to another. Euripides in short emphasizes the continuing element of human responsibility; in this he is not in contrast with Aeschylus, save in emphasis.

The plays are all violent, and there is much unnatural violence, if the phrase be allowed: incestuous love (Oenomaus with Hippodameia as well as Oedipus with Iocaste), rape (Laius with Chrysippus), fratricide (Atreus and Thyestes with Chrysippus, as well as Eteocles and Polyneices), apart altogether from the original murder by Pelops and the lust and parricide in the story unfolded by Iocaste. Such violence is nearly always to be seen as a commentary on war and on the crimes of violence that war brings in its train, and in *The Women of Phoenicia* our consciousness of the background of war is particularly strong.

The opening is unexpected. The stage building represents a palace; from it emerges a queen, but darkly and somberly clad, and with her hair cut short like a mourner's (cf. 322). She sets the scene in familiar Euripidean fashion, somewhat over-discursively. She invokes the sun in fine rhetoric, imitated later by the Roman Accius, and later still by Milton at the start of *Paradise Lost* Book 4:

> You cut your path among the stars in the sky,
> you ride upon a chariot forged of gold,
> Sun, the swirl of your swift mares produces light;

And then the image darkens:

> it was an ill-fortuned beam you directed on Thebes
> on that day when Cadmus came to this land,
> leaving the sea-swept shore of Phoenicia. (1)

The place is identified, but not yet the speaker; and we have been prepared for the chorus of women from Phoenicia. Her comprehensive sweep recounts the full background of Theban history. The note of *tyche* "fortune" sounds time and again (4, 49, 64, 66, 87), and we have the first mention of the sinister, monstrous Sphinx, half-human, half-beast(46). Euripides holds up the name of the speaker enough but not too long (12), and we learn that it is Iocaste, mother and wife of Oedipus, but it is not till much later that we gradually realize that Euripides has repudiated Sophocles's treatment, and Iocaste is alive to witness the conflict of her sons Eteocles and Polyneices. Her reference to them suggests a preference for Polyneices (56); she speaks with an oxymoron and a play on words of "Eteocles"—the name means "glorious in truth"; Polyneices means "versed in strife" —"and the glorious violence of Polyneices." The tone of her narrative is grim, as we hear of Laius's drunken incontinence, and Oedipus's propensity to violence, and the curses which in his sickness he directs against his sons (66). She closes with a prayer, which recalls at two points her opening invocation.

> O Zeus, dwelling in the brilliant recesses
> of the sky, save us and reconcile my children.
> If you are really wise you must not allow
> the same mortal to live forever ill-fortuned. (84)

"The same mortal" is Oedipus, who appears only at the end, but is never far from the center of the play.

As she goes in, on the balcony above a figure appears. The change of eye level is curiously infrequent in the tragedians; in a play as long as this it is well taken. The newcomer is a slave, but one with a position of trust, tutor to the princesses. He gazes round to make sure that there are no onlookers, then helps the princess Antigone up at his side. The careful observance of the proprieties and the naive excitement of Antigone, who sings almost all of her part in the scene, are delightful, and form an effective dramatic contrast with her later attitude. As they look out they identify the leaders of the army of Polyneices who are even now encamped before the city; the scene is an exciting and skillful blend of the scene on the walls in *The Iliad* and the description of the champions of *Seven against Thebes,* but the poet has made something original and individual out of his sources.

The order of identification is interesting: Hippomedon, who appears as a giant, impious and doomed to fall; Tydeus, half-foreign; Parthenopaeus with his brilliant, monstrous gaze. So far the scene has been dominated by the fearful. But the slave reminds Antigone that the attackers have justice on their side. This leads her to ask about Polyneices. The slave points him out near Adrastus (the king of Argos), and her warm love spills over:

> O could I speed with my feet on the course of a wind-swift cloud
>> through the sky
> to my own dear brother and throw my arms
> at last around his darling neck.
>> Poor refugee! How
> brilliant he is in his golden armor,
>> flashing like the first arrows of dawn. (163)

The tutor tells her that her brother is coming, under a truce. Next they see Amphiaraus, calm and self-controlled. He is too close a reminder of the virtue of the attackers, and she passes again to the note of insolvent aggression represented by Capaneus. The identifications end as they have begun, on this note, though only six of the aggressors are seen, unless Adrastus (159) is the seventh. The scene is bathed in baleful light, which recalls Iocaste's opening words. Antigone sees the bronze weapons flashing like lightning (110). Hippomedon is brilliant as a star (129). Polyneices is "flashing like the first arrows of dawn" (169). The sight of Amphiaraus leads Antigone to invoke Selene, daughter of the gleaming-belted Sun, with her rounded golden light; and at Capaneus she calls on Nemesis, the deep-rumbling thunder of Zeus and the blazing flame of the lightning. Suddenly the flute strikes up; the tutor hears the chorus approaching and hustles the girl back into the palace.

The processional song is well written. The chorus reveal themselves as girls from Phoenicia on their way to offer temple service at Delphi. No doubt they are wearing unfamiliar clothes (278), though they sing in familiar rhythms. It seems however that Euripides made them use a foreign accent (301; so also the scholiast). Iocaste has prepared us for their declaration of kinship through Cadmus; yet the remarkable nature of this chorus has hardly been recognized. For the Phoenicians were an integral part of the Persian Empire, which was at the very time conspiring against Athens. Yet the chorus is sympathetically handled. A disastrous civil strife among Greeks in which Persians are sharing as kin; it is a startling commentary on contemporary events. An idealized picture of Delphi contrasts with the reality of war. The ambivalent nature of fire gleams through their song, on the one hand the Dionysiac torches flashing from the Phaedriades at Delphi (226), on the other the blaze of bloodshed lit by the god of war (241) and the cloud of shields around the city kindling the shape of death (205), a bold phrase.

The long scene that follows is dramatically admirable. During it the poet deliberately darkens his imagery (276, 309, 324–326, 336, 346). We have seen Polyneices through the eyes of his sister, brilliant in his armor in the distance. Now he appears under a safe-conduct, but nervous, with sword drawn, starting at every noise, trusting and untrusting, like a wild animal entering a glade ringed with nets. The chorus calls Iocaste out and an affecting reunion takes place between the queen and her son-grandson. Her excitement shows as she chants in dochmiacs, she tries to calm herself into iambics, but the emotion of the moment is too great, and the rest of the song is almost entirely in cretics and dochmiacs, the rhythms of unrestrained emotionalism. We must fill out the printed word here with mime as well as music. As she sings we are not allowed to forget in the background the brooding presence of Oedipus and the curse.

> The old man within, sightless,
>   grips fast his tearful yearning
>   for the team of birds of a feather
>   unyoked from their home,
>   darts to his sword
>   for self-inflicted death,
>   or ropes across the beam,
> bemoaning his curse on his sons. (327)

The mixed metaphor is startling. The ambiguity of the fire image returns as Iocaste sings of Polyneices's wedding to Adrastus's daughter; she did not light the torch of marriage for him, and his wedding is doom laden. She ends with fearful words: a curse on the cause of sufferings, whether steel or strife, Oedipus or a divine power. The last is blasphemy. Polyneices bears the equivalent of strife in his name, and it is not fanciful to see in "steel" an equivalence of the glory (in a military sense) of Eteocles. She does not mean it, but unwittingly she is cursing her sons.

Euripides shows his usual sensitivity in the comment of the chorus:

> Women have a grim time in childbirth;
> that is why women always tend to love their children. (355)

Polyneices speaks more calmly. His position is paradoxical; he comes in wisdom and unwisdom (357, cf. 272) and it echoes his father's paradox who "sees darkness" (377). Something of Euripides's self shines through Polyneices, a patriot even in his disaffection; the poet went abroad with his eyes open, knowing that a stranger in a foreign court must learn to keep his mouth shut and suffer fools with apparent gladness (a line which it cost Mamercus Scaurus his life to quote under Tiberius: D.C. 58, 24), and he put these into the picture of the exile. As for hopes, they look with eyes that charm but do nothing; the image reminds us that in the palace is Oedipus with no eyes to charm but a curse of mighty effect. The sense of divine doom is joined with animal imagery; Apollo told Adrastus to marry his daughters to a boar and lion.

> IOCASTE: What have you to do with the names of animals, son?
> POLYNEICES: I don't know. The power was calling me to my destined
>   fortune.
> IOCASTE: Yes, the god is wise. How did you come to your marriage?
> POLYNEICES: It was night; I reached Adrastus's porch. (412)

It was night; there is rich irony and depth of meaning there. He and Tydeus married the girls.

Eteocles comes to the parley and checks his step with a fixed glare as if he had seen the Gorgon. "Stop," cries Iocaste; "there is no justice in haste" (452). A brief scene of debate follows with Iocaste "in the chair." The brothers speak at equal length. Polyneices bases his claim on justice, repeating the words several times for emphasis, and his case is in fact just; an echo of Aeschylus (489) helps us to think of the high moralism of that poet. Eteocles sweeps it aside with a brilliant tirade of sophistry in defense of dictatorship and the pursuit of power at all costs; it is the mood of Plato's Callicles or Thrasymachus; he starts indeed from the sophistic argument that right and wrong are matters of convention. His justification of autocracy was constantly on Caesar's lips centuries later (Cic. *Off.* 3.21.82), and his ambition for power is echoed by Shakespeare's Hotspur in his ardor for honor (2 *H. IV* 1.3.201). The difference between the brothers is well expressed in their final words. Polyneices closes with "I feel," Eteocles with "must." Iocaste's speech is longer than the two put together. In the brothers' brevity we discern their closed minds; in her abstract prolixity we sense her failure to persuade.

Iocaste offers the voice of experience. To Eteocles she speaks in indictment of the false god Ambition, and asserts the principle of Equality; this is in fact a brilliant touch, for Equality was a democratic catchword against oligarchy and dictatorship alike, yet it has its obvious application in the undemocratic situation of the play to the two brothers. To Polyneices she argues, much more briefly, that it is wrong to right wrongs by violence. As she speaks, there are overtones of sinister irony; she exemplifies equality by the partnership between the lightless eye of night and the light of the sun (543); we are back to the ambivalence of the play's opening with the image of Oedipus superimposed; the image of fire returns as she pictures Polyneices firing the city (575).

Now the scene explodes in violence. Eteocles bursts into impatient trochaics; Polyneices takes him up, but Eteocles remains the more brutal, impatiently interrupting as the lines become broken between the brothers. The divisions are handled with Euripides's customary skill in producing a varied pattern. One line of Polyneices on the "better safe than sorry" theme was taken as a motto by the emperor Augustus (Suet. *Aug.* 25). Toward the end of the scene Euripides does a very interesting thing. Real *scènes à trois* in dialogue are very

rare in Greek; the dramatists prefer a series of confrontations with the
third character a significant background. Here Euripides brings all
three together, and as Polyneices turns away from his brother to take
his leave of his mother, the succession of speakers is Polyneices–Iocaste–Polyneices, Iocaste–Polyneices–Eteocles, Polyneices–Eteocles–
Polyneices, Eteocles–Iocaste–Polyneices, and Iocaste–Eteocles–Polyneices. At the end we come back to the curse.

> IOCASTE: Won't you try to escape your father's Avenging Spirits?
> ETEOCLES: Let the whole house go down to destruction! (624)

We have seen the curse, but it is worked out by free agents. Polyneices, with words of some dignity, goes to prepare the attack, as his
brother taunts him with living up to the strife in his name.

The chorus now sings the first *stasimon*; the text is in a sad state,
and there are grave problems about it, but the general sense is clear.
They tell allusively how Cadmus drove a heifer (marked with a crescent moon on either flank) till it collapsed, and there he founded
Thebes; the first stanza is full of joy, as they recall the fertility of the
land and the youth of Bacchus. Then the screen darkens, and there
appears the snake of the war god, which Cadmus crushed, and from
whose sown teeth armed men arose in mutual slaughter, which

> soaked with blood the land which exposed them
> to the sunny winds of the sky. (674)

The recurrence of the sun image is noteworthy.

Finally, they turn to the present and pray to Epaphus, child of Io
and Zeus, and to Persephone and Demeter to protect the land. But
their words are doubtful, for the land is the very land that spawned
the armed men to mutual destruction, and the goddesses "carry fire"
in the torches of Eleusis, and we know that Polyneices is engaged in
carrying fire against Thebes (687, cf. 575).

The scene that follows is short and strange, a tactical discussion
between Eteocles and his uncle Creon. The brevity is readily explained; it is in fact the absence of a scene. Aeschylus in *Seven against
Thebes* centered his play on the organized matching of champion with
champion. The scene was spectacular but static, dominated by words.

Euripides shows a deliberate realism. Eteocles impetuously aims to act without forethought; Creon cautiously diverts him from one disastrous action after another, and it is Creon who proposes the scheme of seven defenders, one for each gate, to oppose the seven attackers. Eteocles accepts this, and his refusal to discuss details is in character as a man of action not words; it is also an implicit criticism of Aeschylus (751). The contrast between action and word or thought, the familiar antithesis of *ergon* and *logos*, is strong throughout the scene. There are other important elements. The presence of Oedipus inside broods over the scene; Eteocles at the first sees Creon approaching "my house" (696); but is it really his? There is an important exchange:

ETEOCLES: Night grants equality but favors the bold.
CREON: The dark of night is fearful for ill fortune. (726)

The mention of equality is an ironic reference to his mother's creed. The imagery of light and dark have come together with the curse. Yet Eteocles remains a free agent, moving against his brother of his own will (754). Then he reverts to his father, blinded by self-folly, and to the curse, charging Creon with care of Antigone and enjoining him to refuse Polyneices burial: the two charges are incompatible. Finally he sends for the seer Teiresias, and with dramatic economy uses Creon's son Menoeceus as messenger. Suddenly the mood changes. He calls for his armor, and, as he buckles it on, claims to march out with justice that brings victory (not at all his plea in the debate) and prays to Discretion; this was an issue in contemporary politics at Athens, but Euripides means us to see Eteocles having second thoughts. Eteocles goes out, and Creon is left brooding.

Another choral song follows; the text is again corrupt and difficult. Dactylic rhythms establish a mood of epic heroism, but there is a somber note. The opening invocation is to Ares, god of war and full of troubles, and contrasts his love of blood and death with the music and dancing of Bacchus; he inspires armies to blood and leads a reveling dance with no music; this contrast will prove vital to our understanding of Antigone. Strife is a dread goddess (798); the phrase links the Oedipus saga with the Agamemnon saga, since in the myth Strife set in motion the wheels that led to the Trojan War. She devised these woes for the rulers of the land, the house of Labdacus, full of troubles.

The repetition of the epithet from the god of war is brilliant. Ares inflicts troubles. To the chorus, the rulers suffer them, but the active meaning persists: Laius, Oedipus, and Eteocles were all free agents, and all made trouble. Now they sing of Cithaeron as the "eye," or favorite of Artemis, rich in the wild beasts she loves; but we remember that an eye may be blinded and that the "boar" and the "lion" are closing in on Thebes. The theme of the monster takes over as they recall the Sphinx, and speak yet again of the brood grown from the teeth of the savage, crimson-crested snake, the brood that was Thebes's glorious shame; at the last they return to the god of war, and the warlike repute of Thebes.

Teiresias arrives, his hand on a girl's shoulder:

> Lead on, my daughter; you are an eye
> to my blind foot, like a star to sailors. (834)

Creon's young son Menoeceus is with him. Teiresias is strong in will, weak in physique. Creon transmutes the simile to a metaphor, assuring him he has come to harbor, and tells Menoeceus to give him a hand, such as carriages and the feet of old men need. Teiresias has received a golden crown for helping Athens to victory. Thebes, as Creon puts it, is still out in the waves (859). Teiresias, who would have withheld the oracles from Eteocles, uses the image of disease; the land is sick. Laius defied the gods in producing Oedipus to be a husband to his mother, and the bloody destruction of Oedipus's eyes is an example to Greece of the cleverness of the gods; the phrase is ironical, since the cleverness of Oedipus has been a central theme of Sophocles's *King Oedipus*. Teiresias goes on to tell how by their behavior to him the sons made their father wild in his ill fortune, and in his sickness and in the fact of their dishonorable treatment he cursed them.

Here many of the themes come together: the combination of destiny and freewill; blindness, disease, and wild animals. Teiresias knows the remedy, but is reluctant to speak in face of (with marvelous ambiguity) "those who have prosperity" or "those who have in their hands the destiny of the city" or "those who have misfortune" (*tyche*, 892). In revealing that he has a secret he reveals a readiness to have it wrested from him. He turns to go, but Creon cries, "Stop"— the very word Iocaste used to Eteocles (896, cf. 452). But it is fortune not Teiresias that is deserting Creon. Teiresias reminds us of his blindness by asking where Menoeceus is, and suggests that he move out of earshot. Creon sees no need for this and so unwittingly makes possible the boy's self-sacrifice. The safety of Thebes demands the death of Menoeceus. "I didn't hear; I wasn't listening. Damn the city," cries Creon, much as Eteocles cried before (919, cf. 624). "Is truth dead because your fortune is harsh?" rejoins the prophet. In a pathetic tableau the one old man drops on his knees before the other and pleads with him to keep quiet. "Unjust!" says Teiresias. "What then will you do to me? Are you going to kill my child?" asks Creon, and the *logos-ergon* contrast comes strangely forward as the prophet says that he deals in words not actions.

Teiresias takes the doom back to Cadmus's offense in killing Ares's snake. A pure virginal child of the snake's teeth must be offered, blood for blood; Haemon's engagement to Antigone saves him and there is no other. This "colt" will serve and save, bringing dark death on the eyes of the Argives and glory to Thebes. (Perhaps Menoeceus seeks a truer glory than Eteocles, who bears the name.) Teiresias is led out by the girl, grumbling that those who study the science associated with fire (he means burnt offerings, but the phrase picks up the ambiguous imagery already established) have a bitter reception; Phoebus should give his own oracles.

It is a curious scene, and it is not yet over. Teiresias's final reference to Phoebus should give us pause. It is dangerous to extrapolate from one play to another, but Euripides was no friend of Delphi, and the association of Apollo with the sun reminds us that the sun in this play is an ambiguous image. Teiresias would have refused to tell Eteocles; what sort of prophet is that? Yet he tells Creon, whom it hurts, and plays cruelly with him. If Oedipus's bloodstained eyes are the cleverness of the gods, what sort of gods are they? Euripides treats destiny and free will ambivalently throughout; we see the curse freely renewed in each generation. What are we suddenly to make of a demand for atonement that goes back to Cadmus? Creon does not doubt. He echoes for men the chorus's comment on Iocaste: "For all men their lifeblood is to love their children" (965, cf. 356), and tries to hustle the boy away.

Rather to our surprise, Menoeceus speaks. He appears to acquiesce in his father's plans, but when Creon goes, he confides in the chorus that he intends to go willingly to death. The boy has real nobility, like Macaria, Polyxene, and Iphigeneia; yet one feels the wastage alongside the nobility. He may call on Zeus among the stars (1006), but he is going to the black depths of the snake's den (1010). For his sacrifice has no discernible effect upon the result, which Euripides expounds in purely military terms. Menoeceus is yet another victim to the god of war, and after nearly a quarter century Euripides had not tired of attacking that particular Moloch and the political religion behind it.

The chorus that follows is superb; it is one of the finest lyrics Euripides ever wrote. In this play of all plays the choral songs are vital because they set the tone; the ancient commentator who complained that where they should have sung a dirge over Menoeceus they go over the old business of Oedipus and the Sphinx, misses the whole point, apart from the glory of the poetry:

> You came, you came,
> winged creature, spawn of Earth,
>   of monster underground,
>   to ravage the children of Cadmus,
>   bringing biers, bringing tears,
>   half-woman
>   portent of death
>   with roving wings
>   and flesh-hungry claws. (1018)

The chorus sets up the theme of monstrous animal imagery. Then follows the see-saw of history. The Sphinx terrorized the land. Oedipus overcame her and brought first joy and then sorrow. He cursed his children. Now they praise Menoeceus, but return again to Cadmus killing the snake, an act of salvation that brings a curse. Where does it end?

From this point, problems increase. The new scene brings a messenger. Iocaste comes out, and after the usual preparation for the speech, in the course of which we learn that the defense stands firm and the brothers are both alive, Iocaste asks for detailed news:

> Tell me; I will go and bring joy to the blind
> old man indoors, at the preservation of the city. (1088)

Again we feel the unseen presence of Oedipus.

The messenger's speech uniquely falls into two sections. The first is much longer than the second, and some have seen here the hand of the interpolator, though it is not easy to identify the interpolations. After a brief reference to Menoeceus's death we hear how Eteocles covered the "diseased" point of the walls; the disease did not lie there. The descriptions of the attackers is an expansion of the scene on the walls; it is the picture that Euripides refused to draw in the hurly-burly of organizing the defense. But it is appropriate here, and the blazons on the shields are apt to Euripides's purposes: Atalanta killing a boar, the blank on Amphiaraus's shield, Argus the All-Seer with spangled eyes, Prometheus with a torch on a shield of lion skin, the wild mares of Glaucus on Polyneices's shield, a giant with a town on his shoulders for Capaneus, and the hundred snakes of the Lernaean hydra for Adrastus. Every one of these fits in with the themes Euripides has already established.

The description of the battle is overwritten, and, if authentic, is intended as a parody of Aeschylus. Fortune seems fair, and the chorus, Iocaste, and the messenger all say it, but now the messenger goes on to tell of the brothers' challenge to single combat. Iocaste no longer thinks of Oedipus; she calls out Antigone to help her intervene. Enough of words; they go to act.

The choral song is slighter than any of the others, but there is power in the four rising and falling cries that open the second stanza, and the mood of the previous choruses is reinforced in the description of the brothers as "twin beasts" (1296). Furthermore, Euripides pays Aeschylus a notable compliment in reminding the audience of the song his predecessor wrote at the corresponding point of *Seven against Thebes* (720–791). That song began, "I tremble," and ended "Fury." Euripides has the word "trembling" in his first line and ends with "Furies."

Creon comes in with his son's body, looking for Iocaste. But now another messenger arrives with news of the combat: both sons are dead, and so is their mother. The story is well told. First the prayers, Polyneices's to Hera of Argos, Eteocles's to Pallas Onca of Thebes, both a blasphemous desire for fratricide, causing tears at fortune and meaningful glances among the crowd. Then the encounter, like boars. Then the stealthy seeking of an opening—at the other's eye, a dreadful touch. Then Eteocles slipped, and his brother drew first blood on the leg, but in doing so exposed his own shoulder. Ares was on equal terms: another dreadful mockery of Iocaste's preachment. They took to their swords. Eteocles by a skillful swordman's trick struck the decisive blow—his clever device is the same word as the cleverness of the gods in Teiresias's account of Oedipus's blindness (1408, cf. 871); then with characteristic impetuosity went in too early and too carelessly and received a mortal wound himself. "They did not divide their power,"

> Oedipus, I grieve for your troubles.
> Some god, it seems, has fulfilled your curses. (1425)

cries the chorus. The messenger then tells of the arrival of Iocaste and Antigone; the line "with speed of foot and daughter" is comparable to Dickens's "in a flood of tears and a sedan-chair," and there is good reason for expunging it (1430, cf. 1435).

Eteocles was still breathing, incapable of speech, but tears from his eyes showed his love; the motif of the eyes is vital in this scene. Polyneices spoke in gentleness and pity of his "beloved enemy," pleaded for burial in his fatherland (the phrase, repeated, calls Oedipus to mind as we listen), and placed Iocaste's hand on his eyes to close them as he felt darkness coming. Iocaste saw, and having seen acted, seizing one of the swords and killing herself. She acted; the people turned to words, but strife still ruled in a quarrel about who had won the victory. Antigone slipped away, the soldiers made for arms; the Thebans had kept theirs close, and put the others to rout in an inglorious victory. Fortune good and ill mingled together on that day.

Antigone is left to lament. She comes in with the bodies; the ill fortune of the house can now be *seen* (1481). Her shyness is laid aside; she is a bacchant of death (a significant phrase, 1489), as she dances her grief and the flood of words pours out. She sings of the strife, inherent in Polyneices's name, of the Fury, of the savage Sphinx, and once and again the name of Oedipus rings from her song. Then suddenly, startlingly:

> Otototoi, leave your house,
>> with your darkened eye,
>> old father Oedipus,
>> show your wretched years. (1530)

The palace door creaks open, and there, white, halting on a stick, shuffling like Teiresias with blind foot, exposed to the ambiguous light of day, a gray ghost, a corpse from the underworld, a winged dream, is the being whose presence we have felt throughout. It is a theatrical master stroke. He hears of the death of his wife and sons, and the fatal success of the curse. "You have passed through grief," she says.

> If only you could see the chariot of the sun,
> if only observe with radiance of eye
> these bodies of the dead. (1561)

He joins in her lamentation, and she sings of the sons lying among the meadow flowers like lions in their lair (1573), of the mother in sorrow for her sons falling with her sons, of the god who has brought these accumulated sorrows to fulfillment.

Quieter speech rhythms follow: a prayer from the chorus for better fortune in the future, and the arrival of Creon, who proclaims his succession and Haemon's marriage to Antigone. He also uses some words of Teiresias as grounds for banishing Oedipus. "Teiresias clearly stated. . . ." (1590). He did nothing of the sort and Creon's dogmatic implementation of an ambiguous statement contrasts with his refusal of an unambiguous one when it affected his own son. This may reflect not so much political opportunism as the too literal learning of a lesson. Oedipus receives his verdict with some dignity. He blames Apollo. He received the curses from Laius and passed them on to his sons:

I am not by nature so lacking in understanding
to contrive such acts against my own eyes,
against my sons' lives, without some god. (1612)

He sees no future, but is too proud to cringe and plead before Creon. This is another fine touch; we remember Creon cringing to plead before another blind man. Creon now decrees the refusal of burial to Polyneices. Antigone protests both against this and against her father's exile. Sixty lines of *stichomythia* follow, first with Creon, then with Oedipus. She is no longer the shy retiring girl of the balcony scene; she has grown up in an hour or two of crisis. Yet this is not unnatural; it is human nature to respond to challenges; and Euripides wants us to recall *Antigone*. She defies Creon and he her.

CREON: Don't let your grief bring disaster on your marriage.
ANTIGONE: Do you think I'll marry your son this side of the grave?
CREON: You'll have to. How can you avoid it?
ANTIGONE: My wedding night will turn me into a single daughter of
            Danaus.
CREON: Do you see? Her impudence! Her insolence!
ANTIGONE: Let the steel hear, the sword by which I swear. (1672)

This is excellent drama, with its ironical allusions to *Antigone*, the mythological reference forming a link with Io and the chorus but showing Antigone ready to commit a damnable act, Creon's ironical "Do you see?" to Oedipus, and Antigone picking up Polyneices's sword (and Creon no doubt retreating hastily). Antigone resolves to go with her father, and Creon expresses a grudging admiration of her as he leaves. The old man tries to dissuade her, then in another marvellous scene lets her lead him over to feel with blind fingers the faces of the three dead. Antigone says nothing of Eteocles but cries, "Polyneices, dearest name to me" (1702). Some editors find this frigid, and emend "name" (*onoma*) to "eye" (*omma*), with a double meaning of "face" and "treasure" combined with the eye imagery; yet the manuscript reading has powerful irony, since Antigone is to be involved in much strife. Oedipus tells of his final resting place at Colonus; this need not be a later interpolation, since the tradition was there before Sophocles. Plainly, however, there are contradictions in the scene; Antigone cannot both be involved in the burial of Polyneices and its consequences, and accompany Oedipus into exile. There may be interpolation; but it is possible that the contradiction originates with Euripides, who wants to leave the play pointing to an open future.

The scene breaks into song, and we may imagine an effective dance with Antigone active and Oedipus passive while the chorus, which does not sing till the very end, weaves sympathetic dance patterns to the music. Antigone offers her help as the wind helps a ship (1712), a strained simile, as she leads whereas the wind follows. Oedipus keens over his misfortune, and Antigone bitterly comments that Justice fails to see the wicked (1726). The Sphinx, the key image of the piece, returns (1752). Then Antigone reverts to her determination to bury her brother under cover of darkness, the last appearance of the light-dark imagery (1746). Oedipus tells her to go to the Bacchic dances. "Wearing a fawn skin?" she cries, and the animal imagery peers through again. "An ungracious grace I should be offering." This is the climax, for it represents Antigone's choice. For the chorus has continualy alluded to the worship of Bacchus, in their entry (228), and in the first stasimon (649), and in the great second stasimon has expressly contrasted the musicless revel of Ares with the joyful dance of Bacchus (784). Suddenly, in our text as it stands, as the old man hobbles out he stops, turns round, and calls:

> Citizens of this great city, open your eyes. Here is Oedipus.
> I was a man of might; I understood notable riddles.
> On my own I suppressed the power of the murderous Sphinx.
> Now I am dishonored, pitiable, banished from the land.
> Why lament at this? Why shed vain tears?
> Every mortal must accept the inevitable from the gods. (1758)

It is of course based on Sophocles. Yet (apart from a brief prayer for victory from the chorus) it may be Euripides's conclusion. If it is not, we do not know the note on which he ended.

For here is no *deus ex machina* to bring the thing to a spuriously happy conclusion. The contrast with *Orestes*, whether or not that play belongs to the same sequence, is marked and obvious. For we have seen spurious religion decreeing crime; we have seen a curse indeed, but that curse renewed from generation to generation by a free choice; we have seen the curse finding its outlet in fratricidal war, such as was still raging in the Greek world; we have seen the spirit of violence turning men to beasts, wisdom degenerating into cleverness, light that brightens yet consumes as fire, and all the ambiguity of our human condition; and at the last we see Antigone poised at a choice between escorting her father to his place of rest, and acts (like the threatened murder of Haemon) which, springing from a warm and sympathetic nature and a hatred of injustice, nonetheless renew the cycle of violence: if we prefer it, a choice between Bacchus and Ares. It was this choice Euripides laid before his people.

32. *IPHIGENEIA AT AULIS*

Euripides continued to evoke conflicting judgments by his writings to the end of his life. Whereas *The Bacchants* is an acknowledged masterpiece, *Iphigeneia at Aulis* has been variously evaluated. The normally judicious Kitto called it "thoroughly second-rate." By contrast Patin termed it "one of the masterworks of the Greek stage, its author's most perfect piece," Rivier saw it as a key play, and Croiset claimed that in no play did Euripides show himself a finer interpreter of the world around him. The fact is that if we seek to apply to *Iphigeneia* the critical yardsticks apposite to *The Oresteia, King Oedipus,* or even *The Bacchants,* we shall be disappointed. The critic who called it the favorite Greek tragedy of those who do not appreciate Greek tragedy had some truth behind his epigram.

Iphigeneia at Aulis is a creative play of a new type. In structure it is melodrama, and exciting beyond any other Greek play. In earlier melodramatic essays, *Helen* and *Iphigeneia among the Taurians,* the play is built on the blueprint of other tragedies, with recognition scene and messenger's speech at the climactic points of a raising graph of excitement. Here the excitement is present from the first; episode follows episode on the same level. But whereas in most melodramas the concentration on action and event turns the characters into puppets, here they are people in their own right. And whereas in most melodramas the need for fast movement leads to the playing down of language, which becomes hackneyed and bathetic, here the poetry is glorious. It is a modern play with modern appeal, as the New York revival of 1967 showed; in the context of the late fifth century it must seem highly original.

It was however unfinished by Euripides at his death; of this there is no doubt. We are told by a scholiast to Aristophanes that it was presented after his death by his son, also called Euripides. Parts of the play show signs of reworking, and we may deduce that the young man patched it and to some extent botched it.

The problems begin with the opening scene. Lines 1–48 are a dialogue in anapaests between Agamemnon and an old slave; lines 49–114 are a monologue by Agamemnon; at line 115 the anapaests resume. This is almost impossible. The last ten lines of Agamemnon's monologue are addressed to the slave, who therefore must be on stage; yet, in the succeeding anapaests he asks questions that are otiose if he has heard the monologue. Further, the interruption of the anapaestic dialogue is awkward and without parallel. No solution of rearrangement or deletion solves all the problems. The probable explanation is that Euripides originally wrote a typical prologue setting the scene, followed by a scene in anapaests between Agamemnon and his old slave. He then thought that it would be exciting, as he had done in *Andromeda*, to begin the play with anapaests—and indeed it is—and wrote an alternative beginning. He had not chosen between these alternatives, or even fully fashioned them, when he died. His executors were confronted with both; both were from the master hand; both must go on.

If this is right, the original monologue set the scene in the characteristic deliberation of a Euripidean prologue. Helen had many suitors; they all swore to defend the man who won her. Menelaus won her. Paris arrived with his eastern finery (a mild political reference, for the Persians had come back into Greek politics, and Athenians and

Spartans alike were feeling the magnetic temptations of Persian gold).
Helen and Paris fell in love, and he abducted her. Menelaus behaved
like someone stung by a swarm of bees. The army assembled at Aulis,
and Agamemnon was made commander-in-chief; then, for want of
sailing weather, Calchas the seer told him to sacrifice his daughter
Iphigeneia. Agamemnon gave orders to cancel the expedition, but
Menelaus pleaded with him. He wrote a letter to his wife, telling her
to send Iphigeneia to marry Achilles, laying on the latter's charms so
thickly that Euripides has to invent a word for the process (*ekgaurou-
menos*, 101). Now he is regretting his action and has decided to send
a second letter canceling the first. This is good, honest, straightforward, craftsmanlike prologue. It sets the scene clearly. It contains
an amusing picture of Menelaus. It reveals Agamemnon as inclined
to blow hot and cold, and Achilles as a man whose virtues are capable
of exaggeration. Early comes the key word of the whole play, *tyche*
"fortune" (56). Helen's father Tyndareus was at a loss how to handle
the tricky situation (*tyches*) without stumbling or breaking anything.

There is nothing wrong with this till we look at the alternative. In
place of the leisurely iambics we have scurrying anapaests. There is a
sense of urgency, of excitement. There is a beautiful evocation of the
night scene, with Sirius and the Pleiades overhead, and the winds'
silences (an unparalleled plural, 10); the tranquillity contrasts powerfully with the tortured anxiety of the king, as Vergil saw, and borrowed the device in depicting his Dido (*Aen.* 4.522).

There is fine character drawing: the blunt vigor of the old slave, the
wearied emptiness of the king as he seals and unseals his letter. The
difficulties of a king, some from men, some from gods are gloomily
retailed by Agamemnon. There is no explicit reference to an offense
against Artemis; this aspect of the traditional myth is not contained in
Euripides's play. But the gods are holding up the fleet, and men will
not let Agamemnon spare his daughter. The old man's rebuke to the
king is full of irony: "Atreus did not father you to enjoy unmixed
happiness, Agamemnon" (29). No, indeed; we are being reminded of
the traditional curse on the house of Atreus. It is established that the
old man is one of Clytemnestra's servants: this is to be important later.
We lack a few lines in which Agamemnon must have told the

servant of the summons to Iphigeneia as Achilles's bride. He now gives him the countermanding letter. The old man's surprise that Achilles's name is so lightly taken is easy preparation for what follows later. Agamemnon urges him in fine language to haste, and tells him what to do if he meets Iphigeneia. Neither of them dreams that Clytemnestra will come with her; so little do they understand women in general and Clytemnestra in particular. As the old man goes, Agamemnon speaks sententiously to the effect that no man is happy all through life and no bliss unmixed with pain. The words became proverbial and are quoted centuries later (161).

Enter the chorus of young married women (for they sing of their husbands) from Chalcis, to—no other word is possible—rubberneck at the soldiers. As it stands, without music and choreography, their song is good but not brilliant. The scene at Aulis is graphically depicted, and characters individually sketched; they have watched, among others, Palamedes at draughts, Diomedes throwing the discus, and Achilles racing his four-horse chariot; the chorus blushed attractively to see them.

There follows a catalogue of ships, based on Homer, and intended to remind us of Homer. This is overlong to read, but we must remember that it was sung and danced, and there may have been musical and choric reasons for its length. Certainly a long chorus here helps the dramatic structure by increasing our sense of expectation. Besides, the effect of the length is to emphasize the sheer magnitude of the host. As Achilles was the last-mentioned of the generals, his ships are the first-mentioned of the fleet; the effect is to create a significant centrality.

Across the song comes the sound of quarreling voices. Menelaus has been eagerly watching for Iphigeneia's arrival and has seen the old servant sneaking away in the opposite direction; he intercepted him and snatched away the letter. He opens and reads it; the old man fails to snatch it back and calls for Agamemnon. Agamemnon confronts his brother, and the meter breaks into trochaic tetrameters, still speech rhythm rather than song, but swifter moving and less common in tragedy. The brothers pile line upon line till Menelaus bursts through with accusations. He accuses Agamemnon of shiftiness and backs his indictment with examples. In fact he offers an amusing description of the canvassing of a political candidate, subservient, shaking hands with everyone he meets, holding open house, and greeting everyone whether they want it or not, but who, once elected, closes his doors, puts on airs and greets no one.

In Menelaus's picture, Agamemnon, once the expedition was assembled, was much put out by the failure of the wind, a stroke of misfortune (*tyche*, 351) coming from the gods. He was happy to do anything to keep his command and win glory; he willingly sent for Iphigeneia. Now he is chopping and changing to find a way out. There follows an almost Lucretian generalization about the ups and downs of politics. Men put all their energies into public affairs, and then fall, some by the ignorance of popular judgment, some deservedly because they show themselves incompetent. "I," says Menelaus (the text is slightly uncertain), "would not choose a commander-in-chief for some other quality, only for his brains" (473). The implication is that Agamemnon has not much else to commend him, and no brains.

The chorus produces a typically sententious anticipation of Isaac Watts:

> But 'tis a shameful sight,
> When children of one family
> Fall out and chide and fight.

Euripides's version became something of a proverb. Agamemnon now charges into the attack. Menelaus is dominated by lust; all he cares for is to bed a beautiful woman. He made a bad mistake over Helen; the gods gave him a second chance (*tyche*, 390), and instead of taking it he started chasing her with an expedition. Agamemnon himself had made a mistake in sending for Iphigeneia, but he had the sense to admit that he was wrong and undo it. In a remarkable passage he describes himself wearing himself out night and day with tears at the thought of the wrong he was doing his children. His words contain a strong element of self-pity, but they are not insincere.

Agamemnon is the weak man who wants to do right, but lacks the courage to behave consistently. Such men are constantly found in politics; they are pathetic; they are also dangerous. But what has he in mind? Iphigeneia of course, but more than Iphigeneia. Perhaps his leaving his children, not looking after them as they grow up—an almost Epicurean sense that he is wrong to put public responsibility before private life. Perhaps an Aeschylean sense that the whole expedition is ill-omened and will bring disaster on his house. For the rest, we may note the identification of Hope as a goddess (392), which goes back to Theognis (1135): "Hope is the only noble goddess among mortals."

The quarrel flares up. Menelaus complains that Agamemnon is not acting as a friend, and Agamemnon steals a thought from Antigone in an expression unique in harsh elision, when he says that he is prepared to join Menelaus in health not fever (407). As they fling words at one another, suddenly, unprecedentedly breaking into mid-line, arrives a messenger with news of Iphigeneia's coming. Not merely so, but—an unexpected twist—Clytemnestra is with her. The news of the arrival has spread through the army; it is impossible to keep it dark. The messenger, blindly blithe, prances out, and Agamemnon comments grimly (441): "Everything will turn out well as *tyche* takes her course."

And now Agamemnon's self-pity gets the better of him. He forgets his quarrel in his own problems. There are advantages in low birth; a man can let his feelings come out. What can he, Agamemnon, say to his wife? What to the virgin who will soon be violated by Death? His grief stirs even the self-centered Menelaus who comes for a moment to self-knowledge; Kitto unkindly says that he "changes what we have to call his mind." Kitto is very critical of this scene, but he underestimates the strength of family feeling. Menelaus is not "converted"; within a minute he is proposing the elimination of Calchas. What happens is that whereas a mixture of lust and injured pride was dominating him, family feeling now comes out on top. He is still unscrupulous, but for the family, not for himself. It is in fact excellent psychology; it is also splendid drama. For now it is Agamemnon who hangs back; he realizes that the army will not let him send Iphigeneia away again; Odysseus will rouse the rabble. The scene contains an attack on the breed of prophets, and on Odysseus, who is depicted as a demagogic politician of the Cleophon brand. Agamemnon steels himself to go through with the sacrifice and asks Menelaus and the chorus to keep it from Clytemnestra until it is over and done with.

A good choral song follows. It starts from the power of love—to bring happiness or to destroy. Human beings have different characters, but true goodness is always clear. Education too helps toward excellence; wisdom and morality go hand in hand, a Socratic thought. It is a great thing to pursue excellence: for a woman it resides in married love in purdah, for a man there are many forms of public honor. This of course has to be seen in context and character. It is the conventional Athenian view, and Euripides certainly did not hold it himself; indeed the play contradicts it, for the diverse ambitions of the men are disastrous, whereas Iphigeneia offers herself for her country. But we see why Euripides had to make his chorus consist of married women; it drives the point home more forcibly and effectively. The last stanza of the song deals with the fatal love of Paris for Helen. It is pointed with a grim pun. He sowed *eros*, love, and reaped *eris*, strife (585).

Suddenly, as in *Hippolytus*, a secondary chorus enters, of men from Argos escorting Clytemnestra, Iphigeneia, and the baby Orestes in a carriage: there is an excellent tableau as the two choruses confront one another, greet the carriage, and help Clytemnestra and the children down. Clytemnestra says a few royal words, and suddenly Agamemnon is there. What follows is marvellously beautiful. Iphigeneia, who has a special love for her father, flings herself into his arms. A poignant exchange follows.

IPHIGENEIA: Father, I joy to see you after so long.
AGAMEMNON: And I—your father—you. Your words hold good for us both.
IPHIGENEIA: Hello! You did well to bring me to you, father.
AGAMEMNON: I can't say yes and I can't say no, my child.
IPHIGENEIA: Oh!
             You're glad to see me—but you don't look happy.
AGAMEMNON: Kings and generals have a lot to worry them.
IPHIGENEIA: Stick to me now, don't bother with things which worry.

AGAMEMNON: Right, I'm completely wrapped up in you—nothing else at all.
IPHIGENEIA: Then stop frowning and let's have a twinkle in your eye.
AGAMEMNON: There you are, my child; I joy in seeing you, as I may.
IPHIGENEIA: And at that moment you start crying?
AGAMEMNON: We're going to be away from one another for a long time.
IPHIGENEIA: I don't understand what you mean, father dear. I don't.
AGAMEMNON: It's true, and it makes me sadder still.
IPHIGENEIA: I'll talk nonsense, if it'll cheer you up.
AGAMEMNON: Oh! I haven't the strength to say nothing. Thank you.
IPHIGENEIA: Father, stay home with your children.
AGAMEMNON: I want to. But I can't do what I want, and it hurts.
IPHIGENEIA: Blast the war—and Menelaus's grievances.
AGAMEMNON: There are things blasting me; they'll blast others first.
IPHIGENEIA: You've been a long time away in the gulf of Aulis.
AGAMEMNON: And there's still something stopping my sailing with the army.
IPHIGENEIA: Father, where do they say the Phrygians live?
AGAMEMNON: Where Priam's son Paris should never have lived.
IPHIGENEIA: Are you going on a long voyage and leaving me behind, father?
AGAMEMNON: The same is true of you, my daughter.
IPHIGENEIA: Oh!
               I'd love you to take me on board with you.
AGAMEMNON: You've a voyage to take, and you'll be thinking of me.
IPHIGENEIA: With mother or on my own?
AGAMEMNON: On your own, on your own without father or mother.
IPHIGENEIA: Have you found me a new home, father?
AGAMEMNON: Let be. Young girls oughtn't to know that sort of thing.
IPHIGENEIA: Settle everything in that other place, and hurry back from the Phrygians for me, father.
AGAMEMNON: I must first offer sacrifice here.
IPHIGENEIA: Yes, it's good to observe religion with ritual.
AGAMEMNON: You'll see this. You'll stand right by the front.
IPHIGENEIA: Father, shall I lead dances round the altar?
AGAMEMNON: I envy your lack of understanding more than mine.
               Go inside. I know young girls hate
               being seen. Give me your hand. Give me a kiss.
               You're going to be long away from your father. (640)

The irony is Sophoclean in its intensity. At two points it breaks in with special strength. When Iphigeneia says "settle everything in that other place" (672), her words overtly refer to Troy, but it is the normal idiom in speaking of the afterlife. When Agamemnon speaks of "lack of understanding" (677), his words have powerful double meaning. The interchange with Clytemnestra that follows is bound to be stilted by comparison. But Agamemnon finds it hard to lie. There is an important passage where the theme of *tyche* blends with the irony:

CLYTEMNESTRA: Will Achilles take your daughter and mine to Phthia?
AGAMEMNON: He who claims her will see to that.
CLYTEMNESTRA: May they have good *tyche*. On what day is the marriage
              to be?
AGAMEMNON: Full moon—that is good *tyche*.
CLYTEMNESTRA: Have you offered preliminary sacrifice to the goddess?
AGAMEMNON: I am going to. We are engaged on that *tyche*. (713)

Agamemnon tries to persuade Clytemnestra back to Argos. But Clytemnestra—thirty or less, as we must remember—shows the will power that becomes the Clytemnestra of Aeschylus, and stays. Agamemnon goes out, muttering to himself that he has a good wife—if only he'd trained her to stay at home. It is again the typical Athenian view, which Iphigeneia is to shatter.

The choral song that follows is also good, a prediction of the victorious expedition, and of Helen weeping for the dead Paris; the chorus has no illusions about Helen or Menelaus. They picture the women of Asia, wondering, brooding, dreading—"What man will tighten his grasp on my richly-flowing hair, and pluck me, weeping, as a flower is plucked, from my country as it perishes?"—hauntingly lovely words. All for Helen, the swan's daughter—and then rationalism triumphs even over poetry—"or, on the poet's page, are these brought us by fictions, without point, idly?"

And now comes Achilles, a little self-important. There is no contrary wind, no wind at all. Why have they not put to sea? Euripides deliberately abjures the contrary winds of Aeschylus's account: to sail is not impossible, only—according to Calchas—irreligious. Achilles calls for Agamemnon, and out comes Clytemnestra, still in her twenties, Helen's sister, and embarrassingly beautiful. The interchange that follows is very amusing. Clytemnestra is full of the marriage and warm toward Achilles. Achilles knows nothing of it and misinterprets her advances. They are parting in mutual embarrassment when the old servant comes out and spills the beans; he was, it is to be remembered, part of Clytemnestra's dowry and wishes them all well. Through the dialogue, which is long, the note of *tyche* rings. The old man says he is a slave and may not be fastidious about it: *tyche* will not let him (858). He prays to *tyche* and his own foresight to save those whom he wants saved (864). He uses a cliché that when Agamemnon tried to send the countermanding letter he was by *tyche* in his right mind (893). Now the story is out, and Clytemnestra in another excellent tableau falls at Achilles's feet, clasps his knees, reaches for his boyish beard, his right hand.

And how does Achilles respond? Euripides can still surprise us. Writes Gilbert Norwood:

"Perhaps nothing even in the deadly Euripides is quite so fatal to the traditional halo than the incredible speech wherewith Achilles comforts Clytemnestra. Of vast length, full of spurious, jerky rhetoric and contradictory comments on the situation—which, however frightful, appeals to him mostly as an atmosphere in which he can pose—this oration reveals him as a sham. Fortunately for him, he is never undeceived. This man is not the Achilles of tradition; he is a spiritual brother to the mad prince in the *Orestes* and a forefather of Shaw's Sergius Saranoff."

The comment, except for being gratuitously insulting to Sergius Saranoff, is just. Achilles starts with his personal pride. He has one brief word of pity for Clytemnestra and none for Iphigeneia. It is his injured pride that fills his mind, the insult to the purity of his body that Iphigeneia should die on the pretext of a marriage with him. He is not interested in brides; there are ten thousand girls lying in wait for him. It's the insult. As for prophets—a trickle of truth and a stream of lies when *tyche* is with them, and when *tyche* is not with them they are done for. "I wouldn't have minded lending my name to get Iphigeneia here for the sacrifice if they had asked me first; but they didn't,

so they shan't have her. I looked like a god to you; I wasn't, but I'm
going to become one." It is masterly. Achilles with ruthless uninten-
tion dissects himself. But—he is going to save Iphigeneia. The pendulum has swung again.

Clytemnestra offers to bring Iphigeneia out to say thank you, but
Achilles, conscious as ever of his reputation, is afraid of gossip. But
he reassures her, slightly oddly:

> If I'm telling lies in your despite, may I be struck
> dead, and not struck dead if I save the girl. (1006)

We know that Achilles is not immortal, nearly but not quite; it follows
that he is not going to save the girl. But Clytemnestra does not know
this, and responds "Bless you for helping those whose *tyche* is bad"
(1008). She adds the word "continuously." It has been placed by the
poet with masterly ambiguity. Achilles will not have continuous blessing, nor will he go through with his help. The one thing that will be
continuous is the one thing Clytemnestra does not mean, the ill fortune.
When it comes to practicalities Achilles backs down slightly from his
brave show. Perhaps it might be better if Clytemnestra spoke to Agamemnon first. Clytemnestra says, "He's a coward who's afraid of the
army" (1012). We shall find another. And of course, says Achilles,
she must not go dashing through the army looking for him, forgetting
her reputation. Forgetting whose reputation?

The chorus that follows is of incredible loveliness: Markland
thought it the most beautiful Euripides ever wrote. Throughout this
play each choral ode is a song in its own right, yet completely relevant
to the play. Here the marriage of Peleus and Thetis is eloquently contrasted with the non-marriage of their son and Iphigeneia.

And now Agamemnon and Clytemnestra come face to face for the
second time, and this time there is no unfounded emotion for Clytemnestra, and Agamemnon's mask is stripped from him. The moment
is superb. Agamemnon is confronted with Iphigeneia; he does not
know that his secret is out. Clytemnestra asks him one question, and
holds up the key word to the end:

> This child, yours and mine, are you going to—kill her? (1131)

And Agamemnon gives himself away by a gasp of horror outside the metrical scheme. He invokes (1136) Destiny, *tyche*, and his guardian genius. He is horrified that the truth is out, but glad to be done with lies.

And now all the past resentments flood out, as they do in marriage when a breaking point is reached—"Euripide était excellent observateur," said Weil—and we hear of Agamemnon killing a previous husband and child to get Clytemnestra, a story Homer and Aeschylus never knew. But she has been a good wife and given him a son—and now he wants to kill one of the daughters so that Menelaus can have Helen. Her words tumble over one another in indignation as she says it (1168). Why not Menelaus's daughter? Iphigeneia too joins her plea to her mother's. She doesn't want to die before her time.

> It's good to look upon
> the light; don't force me to a sight of the world below. (1218)

She was the first to call him father, she was the first he called child. Her last word is that it is better to live in sorrow than to die in glory. Its effect is reinforced by the echo of Homer's Achilles: "I would rather *live* as steward to a poor man than be emperor of the dead" (*Od.* 11.488). The pleas, backed by the presence of Orestes, are moving. But Agamemnon is now unmoved. This has passed beyond a personal matter. Not Helen, but the reputation of Greece is now in the balance. Agamemnon is the type of imperialist who thinks in terms of wogs and dagos. Western culture is at stake. We shall see how this prepares us for Iphigeneia's last speech.

He goes ("runs away," says Clytemnestra scornfully, 1278), and all depends on Achilles. And now Iphigeneia sings and no doubt dances a great monody of grief on which Euripides must have lavished all his musical skill. He uses his characteristic device of repetition redoubled:

> child of Ida,
> child of Ida was he called was he called. (1289)

And again:

> My father has passed on,
> oh mother, oh mother,

> betrayed me, and helpless and wretched I am;
>   unhappy in seeing that
>   bitter bitter helenhound.
>   butchered, destroyed
> slaughtered godlessly by my godless father. (1312)

"Passed on" is just. Iphigeneia will die, but Agamemnon is spiritually dead, and perhaps already dead in Clytemnestra's mind.

Suddenly a crowd is approaching. It is Achilles and his bodyguard. Iphigeneia falls back, ashamed for the *tyche* of her marriage (1342). Achilles has been driven away by mob violence, the whole army, including his own troops, threatening to stone him. He has been forced away. Yet the legendary Achilles shines through. He *will* defend Iphigeneia to the last.

There is a long, swift, skillfully patterned interchange between Achilles and Clytemnestra in trochaic tetrameters catalectic. That is to say that each line has basically fifteen syllables, and the speakers divide each line between them as follows (a number in parentheses means that the line has been given more pace by the use of two short syllables in place of one long): 10 (11), 5; 8, 7(8); 5, 10; 6, 9; 11(12), 4; 8, 7; 4, 11; 5, 10; 8, 7(8); 10(11), 5(6); 11, 4; 8, 7; 8, 7(8); 8, 7; 9, 6; 6, 9; 6, 9; 8, 7; 4, 11(12); 5, 10; 6, 9; 8, 7(8); 6, 9; 8.

Then at the last it is Iphigeneia who breaks through. In a speech of great nobility she is willing to sacrifice her life for Greece. The change in Iphigeneia has exercised the commentators. I do not see their problem. They treat her as if she were twenty-five and incapable of making up her mind. She is in fact half that age; why should she not shrink from death? It is only natural in her youth, and it makes her a true heroine not a plaster saint. The real problem is the nature of the arguments she adduces, that one man is worthier to look on the light than ten thousand women, and that Greeks are naturally rulers and Asiatics naturally slaves. To this we must return. Her avowal creates universal relief. The chorus says, "You play your part nobly; *tyche* is at fault" (1402). Achilles says, "I would be lucky to marry you, if *tyche* permitted" (1404).

The rest we can pass over quickly. Euripides had not completed the writing of the play, let alone the polishing, and his son did the best he could with it. What is authentic shows Iphigeneia growing in certainty and courage, blessed by *tyche* (1446), and gives us hints of Clytemnestra's coming revenge. Iphigeneia has some two-edged words to her mother: "You shall be glorious because of me" (1440). She tells her mother not to hate her father (1454) and receives a bitter reply. The scene breaks into song and dance in which the chorus prays for an outcome blessed by *tyche* (1523). Then a messenger comes in with news of the sacrifice. It is possible that the messenger's speech is authentic at the beginning, as he tells how Iphigeneia prays that the people may be blessed by *tyche* (1557), but the last part with the sacrifice of the substitute deer and the favorable treatment of Calchas is plainly not by Euripides, and a quotation preserved, which does not appear in our text, suggests that Euripides planned a rather different ending. What this was, it is hard to be sure, but it almost certainly contained an appearance of a divinity (here Artemis) in judgment, as in *Electra*, possibly a more devastating judgment than we can imagine.

The sheer theatricality of the play is superb. It has a splendid opening with the urgent message by night. It thus opens on the note of hope, and thereafter fluctuates between hope and despair. As Menelaus intercepts the message hope fades. Then in the quarrel between the brothers we have continually the hope that Agamemnon may persuade Menelaus. With the arrival of the messenger hope goes, and it is a brilliant stroke of drama to give it an illusory flicker as Menelaus is persuaded, too late.

Now comes the scene between Iphigeneia and her father, and hope soars as we see the love between them and sags as we find it to be ineffectual. The most that Agamemnon can do is to try to spare Clytemnestra—or himself—by sending her back to Argos. In this latter half of the scene hope, but now in Agamemnon, directed to this limited end, rises again and falls. But hope is not extinguished on the deeper issue. From the confrontation of Achilles and Clytemnestra comes hope. Clytemnestra is to challenge Agamemnon. With Iphigeneia she does so, Agamemnon is inflexible, and hope changes to despair. Still there is Achilles; he will face the assembly; and again hope rises, and again it is dashed to the ground. Yet Achilles will fight. Hope staggers manfully up till Iphigeneia by her sacrifice puts the matter beyond hope and despair.

Iphigeneia then provides the solution, and in so doing she reasons in a way counter to everything Euripides stood for. He did not believe that one man is worthier than ten thousand women or that Asiatics are naturally slaves. Shades of Medea! This is no deathbed recantation of his life's work. It is tempting to suppose irony in view of the pretentious Hellenism of the Macedonian court. Yet Iphigeneia is no tongue-in-cheek creation. She goes on:

> I say this with no—NO—reservations.
> Helen has done enough by her beauty to cause
> quarrels and bloodshed among men. Stranger—

she is addressing Achilles—

> do not die for me or put others to death.
> Let me save Greece if I may. (1416)

There is no irony there. Of course it is true that Iphigeneia is Agamemnon's child, physically and spiritually, and we may expect her to share his prejudices, and Euripides has prepared us for this. But there is more to it than that. What Euripides is doing is showing that a girl with all the prejudices of Athenian womanhood can still be a heroine. His most dominant women, Medea, Phaedra, Hecabe, all except the pathological Electra, have been non-Greek. Here is a typical Athenian woman, and she still dominates the scene. This is not Pericles's injunction to the women of Athens that their greatest glory was "to be least talked about by men for praise or blame" (Thuc. 2.44). On the contrary, the note of glory in fame is sounded by the chorus (1504). But it is Periclean woman attaining a glory that prejudiced males arrogated to themselves.

Behind all stands *tyche*. It is highly probable that Thucydides was in Macedon when Euripides was writing the play; his name is linked with that of Archelaus, and in one traditon he wrote the poet's epitaph. Resemblances between the thought of Euripides and the thought of Thucydides are extensive, and many of them may be attributed to a common stock of thought on which both were drawing. This suffices to explain some of the parallels even in this play. Thus Agamemnon's words in praise of the sheltered life and the general sense of the dangers that surround power (16–27) resemble the Athenian defense of their empire (Thuc. 1.72).

The contrast between the honest man's worth and the unscrupulous malaise of the average politician (527) recalls some words of Pericles (Thuc. 2.65). The justification of an apparently irreligious action in terms of military necessity (394–395) is used by the Athenians in favor of their fortifying Apollo's precinct at Delium (Thuc. 4.97–98). The importance of training to the achievement of excellence, *arete*, (558–572) is a commonplace that Thucydides set in Spartan mouths (e.g. 1.84.4).

But there is more to it than this. It is not too much to say that Thucydides's total analysis of history is in terms of the interaction between the constant factor of human nature and the variable factor represented by *tyche*. This is the precise theme of *Iphigeneia at Aulis*, and we may legitimately infer that it was suggested to Euripides by his contact with Thucydides. For *tyche* controls the action of the play, in Menelaus's interception of the old man, in the arrival of the messenger just before Menelaus is persuaded, and in the accidental encounter between Achilles and Clytemnestra, just as *tyche* dominates the speech.

As for human nature, we meet, says Norwood, "five ordinary characters under the strain of extraordinary circumstances." Agamemnon is an ordinary, very ordinary, man, put into a position where he has to make decisions too big for him. Menelaus is an ordinary man, with the ordinary man's compromises, selfishness, and family interests. Clytemnestra is an ordinary woman, full, when unruffled, of a dignity that she sheds when ruffled. Achilles is an ordinary man, vain, self-centered, and courageous in defense of his own reputation. And Iphigeneia is an ordinary girl; this is the point. The others set off Iphigeneia. Euripides seems to be saying: "Here is human nature—you—the one constant factor in human affairs. Look at the compromising self-centered mess we make of human nature. If only we could keep the child's view." "Except you become as little children, you shall not enter even the kingdoms of this world."

33. THE BACCHANTS

"The *Bacchae*," wrote Macaulay "is a most glorious play. It is often very obscure; and I am not sure that I understand its general scope. But, as a piece of language, it is hardly equalled in the world. And, whether it was intended to encourage or to discourage fanaticism, the picture of fanatical excitement which it exhibits has never been rivalled." "Intoxicatingly beautiful," wrote Norwood, "coldly sordid, at one moment baffling the brain, at the next thrilling us with the mystic charm of wood and hillside, this drama stands unique among Euripides' works."

The poet was now an old man in Macedon. His own country was a war criminal brought almost to her knees. He, the greatest dramatist of his time, had been writing plays for nearly fifty years and had won the prize only four times. Yet in this his last and in some ways his greatest play, there is no trace of old age, faltering, bitterness, or grumbling. On the contrary, Euripides seems to have experienced a strange liberation of spirit in the wild mountain scenery of the north. Here ecstatic religion could be known and experienced. Here men might be torn to pieces by animals, and perhaps animals by women. Here no doubt there were secret societies corresponding to the leopard men of Africa. Here he wrote *The Bacchants*.

There is some evidence that the play was designed to serve a dual purpose. In the course of his policy of Hellenization, Archelaus, the Macedon king, introduced dramatic competition at Aegae in Pieria; the evidence about this is uncertain over the details but unequivocal over the fact (Arr. 1.11; D.S. 17.16.3). It would have been for this festival that Euripides wrote his lost *Archelaus,* a play dealing with the mythical founder of the royal house. It is a reasonable deduction that he also intended *The Bacchants* for performance at this festival; the chorus in praise of Pieria (408) would be particularly apposite in that context.

But *The Bacchants* was in fact performed at Athens in a trilogy with *Iphigeneia at Aulis* and *Alcmaeon at Corinth.* The production was posthumous, directed by the poet's son, the younger Euripides. Some critics have supposed that the three plays were designed to be shown together. They belong to different cycles of myth, but we can pick out certain points of contact. For one, each concerns a family killing: Agamemnon kills his daughter, Alcmaeon his mother, Agave her son. For another, a god, Artemis, Apollo, or Dionysus, plays the crucial rôle in each decision. But the handling is very different. In *Alcmaeon* the killing lies in the past; the attitude of the victims, Iphigeneia and Pentheus, is very different; and the divinities involved are equally diverse.

The scene is the palace of Pentheus at Thebes; at some point is a precinct sacred to Semele, mother of Dionysus; it is attractive to think that this is the center of the orchestra, where Dionysus has his own altar. Semele has her own altar too, and on this a low flame is visibly burning. A figure enters. It is hard to know whether he comes on from stage-right (from the country), stage-left (suggesting that he has already been active in the town) or swing down in the crane, which would detract from his final epiphany in glory. He is young, almost effeminate, with long hair. He wears a fawn skin. He carries a staff in his hand whose tip is concealed in ivy leaves, wears ivy in his hair, and carries strands of ivy, which he lays ceremoniously on Semele's tomb.

Then he speaks, identifying himself as Dionysus, come among men in the form of a man. In sixty-three lines he sets the scene. He has recently arrived from Asia. Thebes is the place of his introduction into Greece, because Semele's sisters have suggested that Semele was not brought with child by Zeus at all, but by some mortal. So he has driven them to ecstasy. But old Cadmus has handed over the royal power to his grandson Pentheus, who is opposing Dionysus. "So to him—to all Thebes—I shall reveal myself a god" (46).

This initial appearance of Dionysus is marked by power. Underlying his words and breaking through there is a cruelty, or rather a ruthlessness that terrifies. Twice he insists upon his divine epiphany (22, 42), twice upon his disguise as a man (4, 54); the theme of metamorphosis is an important one. There are others too. Dionysus is a power of nature. It is noteworthy that the first line ends with "earth," the third with "fire," and the fifth with "water," and that these elements recur in the same position (8, 15, 17). Fire, which is also light, is of special import, fire that blasted Semele and delivered Dionysus (3, 8). For this is the nature of fire; it may give light and warmth, and it may destroy. The same ambiguity attaches to the thyrsus, which Dionysus carries, and has given to his followers (25). The thyrsus was a staff topped with a pine cone and wreathed in ivy. The pine cone is a phallic symbol, and represents creative power, but Dionysus describes the thyrsus as a spear. He speaks of putting it in their hands; the hand too, the instrument of good or evil, takes on some importance in the course of the play.

Dionysus summons his followers and leaves for Cithaeron. Unless he is swept up by the crane, this must be to stage-right. This suggests that his original entry was from stage-left, and the chorus follows from there, but it is possible that he watches their entry from stage-right before leaving in that direction himself. The choral entry is marvellous; there is nothing quite like it elsewhere in tragedy. Aeschylus had called his play on this theme *Pentheus*. Euripides gives the title to his chorus. He does this in only three other of the extant plays and in only six of fifty-five others of which we know anything. This is in a real sense the chorus's play, because it is about the followers of Dionysus. They wear spectacular costumes and engage in spectacular dances. The rhythms belong to authentic Bacchic ritual and are based upon the ionicus a minore(♪♪♩♩); it will be noticed that this is in three-time and suggests a swirling dance. Throughout the play the lyrical element, which means dancing, is long and pronounced.

Before Dionysus has finished speaking the flute is heard, and the chorus dances in with tambourines; this is the only example of a percussive accompaniment. The first line consists of two anapaests (♪♪♩); this is the ordinary processional rhythm, but instead of continuing they expand into the breathless, pulsating rhythm of the dance. Erwin Rohde wrote in *Psyche* (English translation, p. 257): "These dances were something very different from the measured movement of the dance-step in which Homer's Greeks advanced and turned about in the *Paian*. It was in frantic, whirling, headlong eddies and dance-circles that these inspired companies danced over the mountain slopes." Rohde notes that complete revolution around one's own axis was not a normal feature of Greek dancing; it was confined to religious ecstasy and it must have been sensational in the theater.

The first choral ode is designed to present, powerfully and purely, the pattern of Bacchic worship. Their ecstatic song is filled with the wonders of nature. Where Dionysus rules,

> The ground streams with milk, streams with wine,
> streams with nectar of bees. (142)

The animals too share in this; Dionysus is "the bull-horned god" and wears a crown of snakes (100). His followers catch animals (102) and wear fawn skins and ornaments of wool (111) and feast on the flesh of goats (139); they compare themselves with young foals at pasture (166). That they come from Asia is stressed in their first word (64); the point is that nature is not different in Asia and Europe; at the same time it enables Euripides to produce exotic effects. In an important phrase they describe how the women of Thebes have left their looms (118); this is a typical expression of the domestic subjection of women, from which the god frees them; under his power they wear skins not woven clothes.

The note of fire is there too in the destruction of Semele (90) and in the lighting of the thyrsus to provide a torch (146). The ambiguity is strong, and it is reinforced by the phrase "be devout when carrying the hybristic thyrsus" (113), which is almost an oxymoron. There are sinister overtones, but the general sense is:

> O
> the happiness, the blessing,
> of knowing the gods' mysteries,
> of a life held holy,
> of a soul in fellowship,
> of mystic mountain dances,
> of solemn ritual. (72)

As the chorus end, singing of skipping like a colt and suiting the action to the words, a strange figure enters from stage-left. This is a man, old, blind, as his mask shows, yet wearing exactly the same costume as the girls of the chorus, using the thyrsus to feel his way forward, and perhaps essaying a step or two to the last bars of the music. He goes to the palace door, knocks, and calls for Cadmus, identifying himself as Teiresias. The door opens and Cadmus appears, another old man, similarly dressed. The effect is of course comic. It is a mistake to play the scene for broad humor and to make the old men galumph and cavort around the stage. But there *is* humor as well as powerful irony. Pentheus calls them—the phrase is now archaic but precise—"a laughingstock" (250); and, unless we chuckle as we see them, the remark is pointless. We have had the god himself. We have had a choral song and dance of unsurpassed beauty, telling audibly and visibly of the power of the god. Now we have prosaic expression of the god's power in two old men wearing women's costume. The very sight of them is enough to provoke a laugh. Is this a miracle of rejuvenation? After all, Teiresias has come without a boy to lead him.

CADMUS: Where are we to dance? Where to take our positions,
whirling our gray hair round. Lead on,
Teiresias. We're both old, but you have understanding.
No, I shan't grow tired. I could go on all night, all day,
beating the ground with my thyrsus. It's lovely to forget
our age.

TEIRESIAS: I feel just the same.
                    I'm young again. I'll try some steps.
CADMUS: Had we better take a carriage to the mountains? (184)

There is no miracle of rejuvenation because there is no faith. Cadmus has adopted Dionysus out of family pride and nothing else (181, 336); he tries to persuade Pentheus to do so as an honorable lie in the family interest. There is really grim irony in the way in which he harps on the theme of his other grandson Actaeon, who was torn to pieces by hounds (337, 1227, 1291). "His part . . . ," says Verrall, "before the catastrophe, is ridiculous; after the catastrophe, his very weakness, his extreme misery, and the irony of his suicidal success, add a poignant touch to the bacchic triumph." Cadmus is in fact to be punished; Dionysus will include him among those who have never recognized him; those who play safe usually get the worst of both worlds.

But what of Teiresias? Is he not sincere? Not wholly, though he is tarred with a different brush than Pentheus. Teiresias stands for Delphi; he foretells the acceptance of Dionysus by Delphi, and the chorus congratulates him on the mental gymnastics that can accept both Apollo and Dionysus (328). Euripides spent much of his dramatic life attacking Delphi, and we cannot suppose him to have much sympathy for Teiresias. Teiresias says, "No do not rationalize about the gods" (200); Euripides did. Teiresias is a very subtle study, the type of the religious establishment. His little sermon to Pentheus includes, as Grube says, the most extraordinary theological acrobatics; Tyrrell compared him with a Broad Church Dean; the speech is surely a parody of a priestly address. Teiresias is wiser than Pentheus. He sees the strength of religious enthusiasm; instead of meeting it with a head-on collision he will accept it, provided it leaves the rest of the religious system unaltered; this is in fact exactly how Delphi handled Dionysus. Cadmus accepts Dionysus for the sake of his own family, Teiresias for the sake of the ecclesiastical hierarchy. Teiresias is subtler than Cadmus, but not sincerer.

While the two old men are conversing at the palace gate, Pentheus comes in from stage-right. He has been away from Thebes. He is only a boy, as we learn later; the down is hardly on his cheeks (1186). He shows his character from the first. He is, says Verrall, "prejudiced, rash, violent, deaf to advice." Worse, he is a Puritan with a prurient mind, a Hippolytus without the worship of another goddess to redeem him. His obsession with sex is revealed from the first. He imagines the women creeping off to serve the beds of men, under the guise of maenads, more interested in Aphrodite than Bacchus (222). He has heard of the arrival of a stranger from Lydia with the vinous charms of Aphrodite in his eyes (233). He does not at first see the other two; when he turns to go in, he bursts into angry laughter at the spectacle. They try to persuade him that he is wrong to try to suppress the worship; the scene is full of the language of wisdom, prudence, and good sense (179, 196, 203, 266, 268–269, 287, 312, 314, 332); a secondary image of some importance is that of disease (283, 311, 326–327).

Pentheus is adamant. The hand theme recurs as he cries, "Take your hands off!" (343). Their wisdom is to him folly. He gives orders to break down Teiresias's place of augury (a tyrannical act of which we hear no more), and gives orders to arrest "this effeminate foreigner, infecting our women with a new plague, the plague of whoredom" (352). He strides into the palace. As the old men go out stage-right to their revels, Teiresias speaks words of warning. Pentheus means grief, and his own actions seem likely to end in grief. The theme of the scene has been good sense. Teiresias's last words are, "He is a fool and talks like a fool" (369).

The chorale ode that follows evokes in exquisite language the spirit of Reverence, and its keynote is the gladness that comes from Bacchus. But there is a warning note, clearly directed to Pentheus, against folly, *hybris,* and over-busyness:

> Unbridled speech,
> short-sighted lawlessness,
> end in trouble . . .
> Our wisdom is folly,
> our high-flying dreams.
> Life passes; those are our terms.
> We aim high, and miss
> the things within our reach.

> I call it madness,
> criminal guilt
> for men. (387)

There is one problem in this ode. It contains an escape verse in which the chorus dreams of the joys of Cyprus, Aphrodite's isle. The connection of the Bacchants with Aphrodite is precisely what Pentheus seeks to establish, and it seems odd to introduce it here. The explanation is precisely that this is a dream, an escape. Those who are living in an excess of sex indulgence do not dream of escape to a world of sex indulgence. They dream of escape to a world in which there are no members of the opposite sex—or else they are too busy to dream. The point of this verse is that the Bacchants are chaste, and its innocence is shown in that Cyprus is coupled with Pieria, home of the Muses, a delicate compliment to Archelaus.

A brief but powerful and important scene ensues. One of the guards who was sent to arrest the foreigner from Lydia comes, bringing him in handcuffs. He addresses the king as "Pentheus." It is abrupt and disrespectful, perhaps because of the king's youth; no one so addresses Creon in *Antigone*; it also reminds us of the sound of grief. He speaks of the man he has arrested as an animal, a quarry. Yet he did not resist arrest; he laughed out loud. The guard also brings news that the women whom Pentheus had imprisoned have escaped miraculously and taken to the mountains.

Who is the prisoner? Most people assume that he is the god Dionysus incarnate. He never in fact says so; his language is ironic and ambiguous. He left us for Cithaeron, yet he is arrested in Thebes, and on the face of it he was in Thebes when the herdsmen saw the women on Cithaeron and commented, "A god was with them" (764). It is possible to construct a timetable fluid enough to permit this; the chorus do not recognize him, and he always appears as the god's servant. These ambiguities are of course deliberate, but it is important to observe that Verrall and Norwood (in his earlier views) in their wilder flights of fancy were giving irrelevant answers, but they were not asking irrelevant questions. To put it bluntly, the same actor played the two rôles; did he change his mask? The answer is probably no. Dionysus in the prologue emphasizes his human form and mentions his arrival from Lydie, but it is at least possible that the answer is wrong.

Pentheus is still obsessed with sex and sees darkness only as a cover for sex; he stresses this more than once (458, 487). The theme of Asia also returns. Pentheus takes a characteristically and arrogantly Greek view of foreign practices; Dionysus remarks drily that in this they are superior. The prisoner's answers are marked by a mixture of ambiguity and candor. He says that Dionysus the son of Zeus instructed him (466), that he saw him face to face and that he gives (present tense) mysteries (470), and that his appearance was what he wished it to be ("I had no say in that," 478). Then:

PENTHEUS: First I'll crop these charming curls.
DIONYSUS: My hair is holy: it is dedicated to my god.
PENTHEUS: Next, let go that thyrsus. Hand it over.
DIONYSUS: Take it from me yourself. I am holding it for Dionysus.
PENTHEUS: I shall incarcerate you securely.
DIONYSUS: My god will release me when I wish.
PENTHEUS: Oh yes!—when you stand among your women and pray.
DIONYSUS: This minute he's close by, seeing all that I suffer.
PENTHEUS: Where? There is no epiphany to my eyes.
DIONYSUS: With me. You are godless; it makes you blind. (493)

Even Teiresias in his blindness has seen something; not so Pentheus. Pentheus is supposed to be investigating Dionysus, but as with the attorney general and Whistler, one feels that it is the witness who is calling the tune. Pentheus at the beginning of the scene orders Dionysus to be freed; at the end he orders him to be fettered again. This incoherence of purpose draws from the divine prisoner the key line, "You know nothing of your life, your actions—even who you are" (506). Pentheus's reply is charged with irony: "Who I am? Pentheus, son of Agave and Echion." It is a prosaic answer, but its underlying meaning is "Grief, son of Glory and the Snake." The grim pun will return (1244); it underlies every mention of the name. In this *gnothi sauton,* this failure of self-*anagnorisis,* lies the key to the drama.

Pentheus, like Oedipus in *King Oedipus,* is a know-it-all, but because he does not know himself, he knows nothing and does not discern the divine pattern till it is too late. Pentheus orders the guard to incarcerate the foreigner in the royal stables, like a horse, and threatens the women of the chorus with the slave market or loom (514, cf. 118). The escort marches the prisoner into the palace, and as he goes he warns that Dionysus will take revenge. "In treating me violently, you are imprisoning *him*" (518).

The Bacchants return to their wild dancing. They invoke the spring of Dirce, then they turn to Pentheus, and the animal imagery is now applied to him, the son of a snake (539), a portent with the looks of a wild beast. They describe the prisoner as their comrade (548), and call on Dionysus to come to the rescue. Then they imagine him in the wild mountains of Olympus or Pieria, and finally, with consummate irony, picture him in a place of fine horses (574). At that moment a great shout is heard; it is the voice of Dionysus calling on his followers. He calls for an earthquake; the chorus sees the pillars and the roof falling. He calls for fire to consume the palace, and the chorus sees the flame leap up on Semele's tomb. Then the doors open, and the prisoner walks out free. The chorus greets him as "Light" (608), and he immediately comments that Pentheus threw him into a dark dungeon. But Pentheus was deluded, he hobbled a bull in place of the prisoner. Then Bacchus shook the palace and kindled the flame on Semele's tomb, and he imagined the palace on fire, and was darting here and there, calling on servants to bring water, and was himself a complete slave to an imaginary task. Then he started pursuing a phantom with drawn sword. Then Bacchus (or a follower of Bacchus; the word is ambiguous) broke his house down to the ground. The prisoner left him and walked out free.

What has happened? And what is supposed to have happened? There are two elements—fire and earthquake. The first is straightforward. A voice calls for fire to burn the palace. The chorus sees the flame flare up on Semele's tomb, and we must see this: it would be an easy effect to produce either through one of the chorus tossing on something inflammable or through a concealed stagehand. Dionysus (as we will continue to call him) says that this happened, and the rest was illusion.

The earthquake is harder. The voice calls for an earthquake and the chorus says that they see its effect. Further Dionysus says—though the order of events is different in his speech—that Bacchus brought the house to the ground. Yet when Pentheus comes out he does not say, "This is a disaster; my palace is ruined"; he says, "This is outrageous; the foreigner has escaped"—and at the very least he is supposed to have a delusion of destruction. No one else, herdsman, Cadmus, or messenger, comments on any devastation. There are three possibilities: the palace has been destroyed; the stables only have been destroyed (some interpreters even write this illegitimately into the translation); or nothing has happened. It is possible that at Aegae Euripides devised some spectacular effect, but at Athens we can discount any collapse of the stage building. We are left with the problem whether to provide "noises off"; in the orchestra the chorus would provide effective mime of response to an earthquake, real or illusory.

The simple fact is that Euripides has deliberately created an ambiguous miracle. Even the apparently explicit statement that Bacchus broke his house down to the ground may carry a spiritual and symbolic meaning. That Dionysus has the power to create hypnotic illusion in Pentheus is already clear, and becomes clearer in the scene that follows; and his power to create mass hysteria is unquestioned. But the whole point of the play is that illusion is a form of reality. When Pentheus sees Dionysus as a wild animal, he *is*, for Pentheus, a wild animal. When the Maenads see Pentheus as their prey, he is their prey.

The enemies confront one another, Pentheus angry, Dionysus calm.

PENTHEUS: You're clever, clever, except where you need to be clever.
DIONYSUS: On the contrary, I'm clever where it is needed. (655)

A herdsman bursts in excitedly on the scene, coming from stage-right. He too addresses the king abruptly as "Pentheus." He has seen the Theban women on the mountainside with Pentheus's mother, Agave, one of their leaders. The scene was one of modest chastity. It is a kind of Garden-of-Eden vision, a prophetic evocation of the Messianic kingdom. All nature flows with milk and honey and wine. The division between humans and animals is done away; the women nurse gazelles, wolves, and snakes, and when they dance the animals dance with them, and the whole mountain joins in the revel.

But then the herdsmen unwisely attack them, and the other face of nature appears. Agave calls on the women as on hounds; they fall on the herdsmen's cattle and rend them limb from limb. Then they fly like a flock of birds to the village and ransack it. They carry fire on their heads without being burned. They remain unharmed in a fight with the villagers, using the thyrsus as a spear. Then they return and the snakes lick the stains from their cheeks. This is a magnificent narrative, from the exquisite picture of nature at peace to the horrific scene that follows. The only weapons of the Bacchants are their hands—and the thyrsus—and the use of their bare hands in rending the animals is mentioned three times (736, 738, 745). The tearing of the animals, the *sparagmos*, is the first step toward the *sparagmos* of Pentheus. The herdsman concludes that whatever this god is, he is powerful, and that the wine he brings is the only thing that gives pleasure to love or life.

The reference to love is not calculated to appease Pentheus. He gives orders for the guards to be called out; their weapons, shields, and bows stand in marked contrast to the bare hands of the Bacchants. The fanaticism is spreading like fire (778). Yes, indeed. Dionysus intervenes and Pentheus splutters with rage in reply (792–793). Dionysus is, it seems, genuinely giving Pentheus a chance to save himself; indeed he specifically offers to save him (806). Pentheus is adamant; he calls for his armor, and the contrast with the bare hands of the Bacchants becomes more pointed and grim. This is the pivotal moment of the play, and it is marked by an extra-metrical cry of "Ah!" from Dionysus.

At this point the mood changes, and whether or not we play the rest of the scene for hypnotic suggestion in the narrower sense, the god in some way asserts his spiritual power over the mortal. The result is the same: the power of salvation has become the power of destruction. The god is now as pitiless as any other power of nature, a forest fire, tornado, or earthquake. Dionysus offers to take Pentheus to see the Bacchants, and Pentheus's voyeurism cannot refuse. He must be dressed in the robes of the Bacchic women. He goes into the palace. "Women," says the god, "the man is standing within the trap" (848), and then, "Dionysus, the task is now yours; you are not far away." He follows Pentheus in.

The choral ode that follows stands, alongside one in *Hippolytus* and one in *The Women of Troy*, among the finest Euripides wrote. The last words of the scene described Dionysus, "who though most gentle to mankind, can prove a god of terror irresistible" (860). In the song that follows a verse of exquisite beauty evokes the joy of the long nights of worship, playing in the fields like a fawn. But a sinister refrain follows:

> What is wisdom? Or what gift
> of the gods is lovelier for men
> than to hold a hand of victory
> over our enemies' head?
> What is lovely is always welcome. (877)

The introduction of the hand motif is especially noteworthy. The somber note continues into the echo of the opening dance, as they sing in condemnation of those who deny the gods. The unbeliever (terrible words in context) is the prey of heaven. It is not extravagant to believe in the strength of the divine, of that which is established by long tradition, and that which is naturally and permanently true; the phrase is an interesting coupling of *physis* (nature) and *nomos* (convention). The refrain rings out again in all its exaltation of vengeance. Then gladness returns, joy in escape from storm, joy in catching the moment as it flies.

The god returns, followed by Pentheus. Pentheus is drunk, probably physically; if we accept the manuscript evidence (913, cf. 924), they have pledged one another in wine. Certainly the god has produced the same symptoms in him by some means; he sees two suns, two cities of Thebes, and fourteen gates. Dodds has expressed the scene brilliantly:

Re-enter the stranger from the castle, followed at 917 by Pentheus dressed as a maenad, wearing wig, μίτρα, and long linen χίτων, and carrying a thyrsus. Both antagonists are now transformed into something other than human. . . . The stranger reveals himself as more than man: he no longer tempts, but commands; his tones are those which Athena uses in the *Ajax* (71ff) when she summons the mad hero to be mocked. And what follows him on to the stage is less than man: it is a giggling, leering creature, more helpless than a child, nastier than an idiot, yet a creature filled with the Dionysiac sense of power, and capable of perceiving the god in his true shape, because the god has entered into his victim. The scene between these two is as gruesome as anything in literature, and its gruesomeness is enhanced by a bizarre and terrible humour. The situation of scene 2 is now reversed: the stage business with Pentheus' costume (925–44) is the counterpart of the stage business with the stranger's costume at 493–7; for the outrage then done to his person the stranger now takes a fantastic revenge on the pretext of playing the valet (θεραπεύειν, 932). Such a situation might easily be exploited as pure farce: cf. the very funny scene in the *Thesmophoriazusae* (213–68) where Mnesilochus is dressed up as a woman. But here the effect of the farcical by-play is to intensify the underlying horror which peeps out in lines like 922 and 934. As Hermann said, the groundlings will laugh, and are meant to laugh; but for the sensitive spectator amusement is transmuted into pity and terror.

Pentheus now sees the wild animal nature of Dionysus in the form of a bull. "The god is with us," says Dionysus. "Now you are seeing what you ought to be seeing." This sinister "ought" returns: "Before, your attitude was unhealthy; now it is as it ought to be" (948). Pentheus's imagination is still prurient; he looks forward to seeing the Maenads "like birds in the bushes, limed in love's welcome grip" (957). "Yes," answers Dionysus, "perhaps you will catch them—if you are not first caught yourself." The scene ends with these fearful words:

DIONYSUS: Alone you are facing these trials for your city—alone.
             The ordeal which faces you is worthy of you.
             Follow me. I shall be your Escort and Savior.

—a superb touch, since these are divine titles, and Hermes the Escort was guide to the dead—

               Someone else will bring you home.
PENTHEUS: You mean my mother?
DIONYSUS: A cynosure for all eyes.
PENTHEUS: That is my object in going.
DIONYSUS: You shall be carried home . . .
PENTHEUS: What luxury!
DIONYSUS: In your mother's hands.
PENTHEUS: You will spoil me.
DIONYSUS: I mean to spoil you.
PENTHEUS: I am getting my due.
                       (963; "spoil" comes from Arrowsmith's version)

Even Sophocles never essayed irony so grim. And at this moment something begins to crack. As he follows Pentheus out, Dionysus throws out another reference to the tragic *agon* at the hands of Agave (973). In so doing he refers to Pentheus as "a young man" (*neanian*); the word has all the overtones of "impulsive," "headstrong." This is the moment at which we begin to experience a shift of sympathy toward Pentheus, which is extended into the messenger's speech.

This feeling is intensified by the next choral ode. We expect, perhaps a brooding anxiety, perhaps an affirmation that in the divine order *hybris* is followed by *nemesis*, perhaps a song of escape. What we get is a brutal song of vengeance, without parallel in Greek tragedy. The rhythm is dochmiac (♪♩♩♪♩ and its variant ♪♪♪♩♪♩); it is the most frenzied of all the rhythms to Greek ears. Animal language predominates. They call on the hounds of Madness to speed to the Theban Bacchants and sting them like gadflies against Pentheus. They describe Pentheus as born of a lioness or a Gorgon. They sing of their own joy in the hunt. Then, excitedly, they call on Bacchus to appear as bull or snake or fire-breathing lion, to pounce on the hunter of the Bacchants and let him fall beneath the stampeding herd of the Maenads.

At that moment there comes the messenger, one of Pentheus's attendants. With his usual flair for the dramatic Euripides momentarily holds up his narrative. His opening words with their reference to the "once glorious house" prepare us but hold us in suspense. Then the direct statement "Pentheus, the son of Echion, is dead." Then a brief interchange with the chorus. Then, and only then, the full narrative. The messenger's speech is one of the great things in Greek tragedy. He tells how they came near the Maenads and found them "their hands engaged in tasks they loved" (1053), like foals loosed from the yoke. Pentheus wanted to climb a tree to see properly,

> And then I saw the stranger perform a miracle.
> He grasped the towering topmost branch of a fir
> and heaved it down, down, down to the black earth. (1063)

The last line is without parallel in tragedy. Pentheus mounted and was swept into the heights—and suddenly the foreigner had disappeared, and a great voice ("I suppose it was Dionysus") pealed out, calling on the women to punish the blasphemer, and a flash of unearthly fire stretched between the sky and the ground. What follows is magical in its beauty:

> Silence in the air. Silence among the leaves
> of the forest-glades. No sound of animals to hear. (1084)

Then comes a second word of command, and the whole scene vibrates into life—and death—as the Maenads dart with the speed of doves to surround the "climbing beast" and, failing to dislodge him with missiles or to lever up the tree with branches, they tear the tree down with their bare hands (1109), rend the fallen body limb from limb, and toss the remains from hand to hand like Nausicaa and her girls playing ball (1136). Agave is left holding in her hands the head, fixing it on her thyrsus point, as the head of a lion. The messenger hurries away to avoid seeing her, with some properly sententious words about honoring the gods.

The chorus has a brief song of exultation; there is no pity here. They see Pentheus as the snake's child, and Dionysus as the bull who led man to the slaughter. The *agon* has been glorious.

So comes Agave, and pity now begins to move the chorus. She carries Pentheus's head on her staff; the effect is far more realistic than it is, say, in *Macbeth*, for it is the very mask we have been watching. Her first words, "Women of Asia," recall the original entry of the chorus (1168, cf. 64). She sings and dances her pride in her prey, the lion cub: at one point there is a metaphor within the animal illusion as she calls him by a word naturally rendered "bullock" (1185), thus creating another link with the god. With fearful irony she sings that Pentheus will praise her hunting. Then the fervor begins to recede, and she talks in speech rhythms, still boasting the lion she has killed with her hands (1209). Cadmus enters with the remains of Pentheus's body, and Agave eagerly tells him that she has forsaken the loom to hunt animals with her hands (1236); she gives him the head as a trophy. Cadmus responds in his son's name, and goes on, "You have used your unhappy hands to shed blood!" (1245). Gradually he leads Agave back to sanity and the truth. The psychology of the scene is superbly handled. And now in Cadmus's words we see another Pentheus, who showed tenderness toward his mother's father, and who will never again stroke his grandfather's chin with his hand.

> If there be any man who slights divinity,
> let him look at Pentheus's death—and believe in gods. (1325)

These words again draw words of pity from the chorus.

The end of the play has fallen into fragments, with gaps that we can conjecturally fill from the Christian adaptation, *The Suffering of Christ* (*Christus Patiens*). We have lost what was evidently a magnificent speech in which Agave handled her son's mangled body and blamed herself, and yet at the same time called on him to forgive her, for it was the god's doing and not hers, and on the god to give her a cup to pour a libation of her son's blood, and to make her mad again so that she might forget what she had done. She will bury him and inscribe a stone over him. Suddenly, on the top of the palace, there is an epiphany of Dionysus in his glory. We have lost part of his speech also; he must have exulted over Pentheus and decreed banishment to Agave. Cadmus and his wife are to be changed into snakes, and will be cult spirits. Cadmus, weak as ever, pleads for mercy. There is one curious exchange.

> CADMUS: Gods should not show anger like men.
> DIONYSUS: My father Zeus decreed this long ago. (1348)

This is an implicit rejection of anthropomorphic gods for natural law.

Dionysus disappears, and Agave throws her arms round Cadmus and strokes his white hair—and again the animal imagery becomes mixed—as a cygnet cares for its old drone. They part with a sad but effective pun as she bids him farewell, and he responds "Farewell—if you can ever find welfare" (1379). The familiar words with which the chorus ends are more than usually relevant: "Divine powers appear in many shapes..." (1388).

The play is a masterpiece of construction. We may represent it schematically as follows:

> The god in power
> Cadmus with Teiresias
> Pentheus and the stranger: Pentheus dominant

> The earthquake
>> First messenger
>> The stranger and Pentheus: the stranger dominant
>> Second messenger
>> Cadmus with Agave
>> The god in power

The structure is thus basically symmetrical around the palace miracle, but the two messengers' speeches frame the episodes that represent the stranger's dominance over Pentheus, and it is on the first of these that the play pivots. Further, the two scenes that introduce the ludicrous appear toward the beginning, but not right at the beginning, of each half. The imagery, as we have seen, holds the whole play together.

It remains a puzzling play. It is closer to the basic pattern of the year drama than any other. The killing of the god is actually mentioned (138). The characters, as Murray has said, might be called the God, the Prophet, the Old King, the Young King, and the manuscripts actually tend to call Agave "Woman." Murray speaks of the essential elements of the year drama: "the Contest, the Tearing Asunder, the Messenger, the Lamentation mixed with Joy-cries, the Discovery of the scattered members, and the Epiphany of the Daemon in glory." The word *agon* is repeatedly used. But is it so easy? For it is not the Old King who is dismembered, but the Young King, and he brings the Old King down with him. It is not the god who is dismembered but the god who presides over the dismemberment. As Toynbee put it in a rare moment of flippancy,

> The god recovered from the bite,
> The man it was that died.

Substitutes and doubles are common enough in these rituals; it has been argued that Becket was a surrogate for Henry II; but there is a twist somewhere. We have noted the ambiguities that attach to the person of the stranger and to the palace miracle.

Some older critics have seen in *The Bacchants* a recantation of all Euripides's attacks on religion. Lobeck in *Aglaophamus* called it an attack on rationalism, and K. O. Müller commented, "In this play Euripides appears, as it were, converted into a positive believer." Even

Murray, with qualifications, described the play as "a heartfelt glorification of 'Dionysus.' " Others, like Glover, have seen the play as a
warning. " 'Beauty is good,' we cry, with passionate insistence. And
as in the old tale of the sirens, 'there lie close at hand the rotting bones
of men.' " Neither view can be sustained; in this sense, we must not
moralize.

Dionysus is seen as a natural power; we might almost say as *the*
power of nature. Hence the reference to the elements at the beginning,
the repeated introduction of the theme of fire, and the animal imagery.
Nature is amoral: the rainstorm fertilizes and ravages, fire means light
and warmth but also destruction, the animal kingdom is red in tooth
and claw and filled with mother love, the power of the atom can be
used to build or to annihilate, and the human hand can tear Pentheus
apart or smooth Cadmus's hair.

"We are shown," wrote S. H. Mellone in *The Bearings of Psychology on Religion* (p. 42), "a kindly God, a comfort to the afflicted,
a redeemer from care, implacably practising a cruelty that surpasses
even the cruelty of mankind. We are shown the spirit of joy remorse-
lessly bringing to pass the most overwhelming of griefs. We are shown
a new and exhilarating life of freedom leading to a wretchedness more
hideous than the old slavery." Winnington-Ingram, who has written
more sense on this play than most other interpreters put together, expressed it with his customary lucidity: "Euripides saw Dionysus clearly and whole, both in his beauty and in his great danger, and . . . so
shaped the play as to focus attention upon the cruelty and to demon-
strate the inexorable interdependence of the cruelty and the beauty."
This is the god who "though most gentle to mankind, can prove a god
of terror irresistible" (860).

One aspect of Dionysus on which Euripides focuses his spotlight is
the power of ecstatic religion, but it is one aspect only. Of course
Euripides did not believe in an anthropomorphic Dionysus; he, to all
intents and purposes, says as much. Yet there is such a power, operating within us and upon us, and we seek to repress it at our peril.
Pentheus is not wrong to associate it with the *libido*; he is wrong to
isolate its sexual aspect. He has of course externalized a repressed part
of himself.

Euripides is aware of this externalization; hence the ambiguities that attend his portrayal of Dionysus. Dionysus is power, *mana*, *orenda*, and that power can save or it can destroy. Grube sums the matter up well:

It is Dionysus' power, and therefore his divinity which is vindicated. Nor need the poet turn theologian and define the exact nature and significance of those forces of which Dionysus is the religious expression. The general meaning of Dionysiac worship is quite clear. Wine is the god's symbol, and wine destroys purely external brakes on conduct, it releases the elemental emotional urges of the human heart, the deep passions of men, Eros and Desires in the widest sense. These include the sexual, but—and this Pentheus failed to understand—they spread far beyond the realm of sex. Passions must be recognized as the essence of life and then they become the source of all loveliness and joy. But if man fights against them, instead of with them, if he tries to deny them altogether, they will conquer him in the end, and tear him limb from limb, themselves becoming ugly and fiendish in the process. For them Dionysus becomes a fiend as he does in this play, as the chorus do to some extent when they reflect the change in him, as do the Theban Bacchants on Cithaeron when, but only when, attacked by unbelievers. It is this god, and this worship, that Euripides has dramatized in all its aspects, its beauty and its joy, its ugliness and terror; he has even included the disgusting and the merely silly. Few will deny that it is from the very completeness of the picture that the play derives its power and its greatness.

V

AN ANONYMOUS TRAGEDY

34. RHESUS

Rhesus is of considerable interest because it is the only surviving Greek tragedy not written by one of the three great dramatists. The statement is contentious. The play has come down to us with the works of Euripides and was believed by Aristophanes of Byzantium to have been authentic, as the second Argument to the play indicates. Ritchie has recently restated the case for authenticity in a carefully argued volume. Nonetheless, the case is not easy to accept.

It is not appropriate here to argue the matter in detail, but we may note seven points. First, there was doubt about its authenticity already in ancient times, and the first Argument alludes to these doubts. Second, it is exceedingly difficult to believe that Euripides could at any time in his career have written a play which, while not without dramatic skill, was so barren of ideas. Third, the play appears to need four actors. Fourth, *Rhesus* is by far the shortest extant Greek tragedy, and even if, as some have suggested, a prologue has been lost—there is no manuscript evidence of this, but the first Argument alludes to more than one prologue in circulation, which seems excessive—the play would still be short. Fifth, the proponents of authenticity build on the authority of the Aristotelian Dicaearchus. The name of Dicae-archus has been restored to a passage in the first Argument by con-jectural emendation alone, and is a hazardous foundation for any dogmatic view. Sixth, Ritchie offers some percentage tables for vo-cabulary, using as controls three dated plays *Medea, The Women of Troy* and *The Bacchants.* Contrary to his deductions, these tables make it almost certain that the play cannot be authentic. For, unless a play contains some necessary peculiarity of theme, and consequent vocabu-lary, such tables make it possible to place a play within the pattern of an author's development. The figures for *Rhesus,* though none in iso-lation is incompatible with Euripidean authorship, do not fit any period of his life; some suggest a date before *Medea,* some a date after *The Bacchants.* This makes it probable that we are dealing with an imitator who knows Euripides's work well. Seventh, the play is in fact a curious amalgam. There are phrases borrowed directly from Aeschylus; Eu-ripides too did this, but usually with a critical point in view. The first Argument sees Sophoclean traits in the play; we find these less obvious, though there are again verbal echoes. In addition there are verbal echoes of Euripides himself. Ritchie collects and presents these with scrupulous fairness and says, "The phrases are often not merely similar but identical, and the language has been seen to possess a typically Euripidean stamp. These resemblances are too many to be coinci-dental." Ritchie takes these as evidence of identity of authorship. The overall picture looks far more like that of a fourth-century imitator.

Rhesus has another point of general interest. It is the only surviving Greek tragedy in which the plot is taken directly from *The Iliad* or *The Odyssey*; *Cyclops* is of course a satyr play. No known play of Euripides was derived from *The Iliad* (another argument against au-thenticity), only one of Sophocles, *The Phrygians* (and there can be no certainty about that), and four by Aeschylus, *The Ransoming of Hector* or *The Phrygians, Europa* or *The Carians, The Myrmidons,* and *The Nereids.* We have in this way an unusual opportunity of observing a dramatist at work on epic material.

The first 150 lines are largely the dramatist's own invention, though he has drawn on other parts of Homer than the lay of Dolon. The brief appearance of Dolon is of course modeled on *The Iliad*, though here again the dramatist has modified and expanded. In Homer, Rhesus arrives before Dolon leaves, and it is Dolon who betrays his presence. The change here creates a certain dramatic suspense, but it also necessitates the rather clumsy introduction of Athene. The Rhesus scenes are largely added, though hints from Homer about the godlike appearance of Rhesus, the whiteness of his horses, and the segregation of his camp are taken up and given dramatic significance.

The Odysseus-Diomedes scene, including the supporting presence of Athene, is modeled closely on *The Iliad*, even to details of language, but the interception of the Greeks by the chorus and their use of the password is an invention of the dramatist. The charioteer is substituted for a noble named Hippocoon, presumably so as to stress the theme of the horses; the dream has been transferred from Rhesus to him. Finally the appearance of the Muse has no counterpart in Homer, and is an effect borrowed from Aeschylus's lost play *The Weighing of Souls*. We know that Pindar (*fr.* 277 B) used a version in which Rhesus was the Muse's son, and it is possible that some of the details that do not correspond with *The Iliad* come either from him or from some other writer whose work is lost.

One other curious feature of the play is that it takes place at night. A number of surviving plays, *Agamemnon*, *Antigone*, and *Iphigeneia at Aulis* for example, open with or before dawn; we may suppose them to have been the first of their sequence, so that the words greeting dawn would come not inappropriately. No other known play has a night scene throughout, unless we may assume this for Sophocles's *The Women of Sparta*, which had as its theme the theft of the Palladium. It has been argued that this may mean that the play was written for reading rather than performance, but the argument is not cogent. The merits of the play lie in its action not its language. It is more likely that it is an experimental effect. The use of torches would have conveyed the situation, as well as adding to the spectacle, and the entry of Odysseus and Diomedes, as if in the dark, could be skillfully mimed; such an effect was employed for comic purposes in *Black Comedy* and could be adapted to serious ends.

The play opens strikingly with the chorus entering to an anapaestic march with news for Hector; they are Trojan soldiers on the night watch and make it clear by their words that the scene takes place at night; there are repeated reminders of this throughout the play. There is no reason to suppose a lost prologue if the work is not by Euripides; the entry would be less effective if it were not the very start of the play, and it is a variation on the opening of *Iphigeneia at Aulis*. Hector comes out from the stage building that represents his tent, and immediately we see the play's curious unevenness. He demands the password. This is an important motif later in the play, and it was ingenious to introduce it here. Only the watch does not give the password, and Hector does not seem to care or even to notice. Yet the central scene depends for its effect upon the contrast between the military efficiency of the Trojans and laxity of the Thracians. It would have been good drama to give the password without more ado, differently good for Hector to rebuke their laxity in such a way as to increase their efficiency later. Neither happens. The exchange continues in anapaests. Hector demands to know why they have left their posts.

Now their chant bursts into song and their march into a war dance, and they sing of rousing the leaders without answering his question. Their words introduce obliquely another motif. Sarpedon is commander of the Lycians, the wolfmen, and the wolf is to play a significant and sinister rôle in the drama. Hector, still in anapaests, accuses the chorus of panic, and then and only then do they sing their news of unusual activity among the Greeks. The general effect is borrowed from the scene between Creon and the Guard in *Antigone*, but the dramatist has made it his own.

Hector now changes to speech rhythm. He takes the activity to mean that the Greeks are seeking to escape. He, the lion, will be robbed of his prey. He speaks of the lights in the Greek camp as "wagging their tail" at him (55). If the seers had let him have his way he would have overwhelmed the enemy already; similar attacks on seers are found in Sophocles as well as Euripides. Aeneas comes in, and his reasoned calmness contrasts with the impetuous militarism of Hector:

> I wish your wisdom matched your power in action.
> It is not given to one man to possess
> every skill. Different people, different gifts.
> You're a fighter, others take decisions best. (105)

The words anticipate Odysseus's dominance of the plot. He advises Hector to send a spy into the Greek camp; the guard, still singing, agrees, and Hector gives way. The guard produces an odd little pun, using a word for enemy (*daios*), which recalls the blazing of the fires (135). It is a curious scene altogether, for Aeneas is favorably portrayed, yet his plan leads to disaster. Hector now calls for a volunteer to go as spy. He has to ask three times "Who . . .? Who . . .? Who . . .?" and his words "to go to the Greek fleet" are repeated insistently in this scene and later (150, 155, 221, 589, cf. 203, and slighter echoes at 297, 502, 602, 843). It is not easy to see any major purpose in this; it is rather a sign of unimaginative writing. There is a further clumsiness in Dolon's appearance; it is not clear whether he has entered with the guard originally or with Hector, or with Aeneas, or whether he comes from offstage at the third call.

The rest of the scene is Dolon's. In less than a hundred lines he is nicely sketched, devious, arrogant, too clever by half. He volunteers— on one condition. "You've earned your name," says Hector; the name is roughly our Crook or Wiles. Hector means that he has earned it by his willingness to spy, but the deviousness is in fact shown in the condition. Dolon secures from Hector a promise of reward, any except Hector's autocracy (*tyrannis*, 165). Dolon says drily that he has no urge for that, a remark that would win amused cheers from an Athenian audience.

For a minute or two they spar verbally, as Dolon makes sure of his promise. Then it is out. Dolon wants Achilles's horses. So does Hector. For a moment he seems explosive; then he pulls himself together and reaffirms the promise. There is no thought from either that Hector may never have the horses to give. The chorus sings that they would have chosen a princess to marry. They are of the earth, earthy, and the effect is of a music-hall ditty when we are expecting a Schubert *lied*.

There is an interesting ambiguity in the scene. Hector speaks of

Dolon's reward as an honor (*geras*, 169, 181), but Dolon sees it as the stake for which he is gambling (155, 183). This reveals, as is intended, a difference of character between the two men. Here Dolon is right. He is gambling, he knows it, and he loses. But had he won through, Hector by the standards of war would not be wrong. It is not clear whether Hector goes out at this point, or whether silently, broodingly, he watches Dolon's disguise; it is a feature of the play that exits and entrances are not clearly marked.

In *The Iliad* Dolon wraps himself in a wolf skin and places a fur cap on his head. A fine kylix fragment from Munich, painted by Euphronius and datable to somewhere about 500 B.C., depicts him wearing the wolf skin, complete to tail, as a disguise, though he walks upright and wears a helmet. Here he goes further, framing his head in the wolf's, as Heracles in the lion's, and going on all fours. A similar ruse was used by messengers breaking through the Roman lines at Jotopata in the Jewish War (Jos. *B.J.* 3. 7. 14), but they did not disguise themselves as wolves. The disguise is not really a happy one; a soldier, seeing a wolf, would be likely to shoot. Dolon's account of his disguise is framed in the words "wolf" and "wile" (*dolos*, 215).

The chorus blesses his enterprise as he no doubt demonstrates his four-footed gait, and he goes out with the ironical boast that he will bring back the head of Odysseus or Diomedes. He is getting above himself; the object of his expedition is information not assassination. At least he will not return with hand unstained with blood. True.

The chorus sings, appropriately enough, a hymn and prayer to Apollo. He is the power behind Troy, and "wolf god" was one of his titles; they address him as lord of Lycia or wolf land. Throughout the play there is thought of the Greek ships; Hector's assault on them is one of the great battle scenes in Homer. Here it is the Trojan ship of state they see tossing, and Dolon as the sort of hero that Ajax proved for the Greeks; they are bitterly wrong. They pray for his success, so that when Hector has won in battle (a significant condition) he may have Achilles's horses. They wonder whether he will kill Menelaus or Agamemnon and lay his head in Helen's hands, a revoltingly gory thought not helped by a slight pun on Helen's name (258). They have forgotten that Dolon has been sent to spy not to kill, and they do not even think of Odysseus or Diomedes. They have also forgotten that they are supposed to be on guard duty, not singing hymns to Apollo.

A messenger arrives; he is a shepherd from the hills, who announces the arrival of Rhesus. The scene is clumsy in a number of ways. There is no particular point in the characterization of the messenger as a shepherd, and one suspects that it is an echo of *King Oedipus*; a courier from Rhesus or a guard from an outpost would have been more rational. However, it allows, a little heavily, light relief as Hector, assuming that he has come to report a happy event in his flock, tries to dismiss him. More serious is the fact that a stranger arrives in the dark without being challenged by the guard. How the shepherd finds Hector is not clear. His first word is "Sir"; it is possible that this calls Hector out of the tent. The other possibilities, that Hector has been on stage all along or comes out for no particular reason, are intolerably clumsy.

This is a remarkable shepherd. He reports what he has seen with Aeschylean magniloquence; four- and five-syllable words ripple from his tongue, and one line consists of three words only (297); the bombast suits the scene but not the speaker. Further, he tells how he listened to Rhesus's soldiers conversing, discovered that they were not speaking Greek, so addressed them in Thracian. His detailed description is singularly inappropriate; how could he discern the frontlets of the horses at a distance in the night? The important part of his narrative is the description of Rhesus in his glory, "like a god" (301), and his horses, whiter than snow (304). He will prove a counter to Achilles (316).

This last remark understandably incenses Hector, who echoes the chorus's picture of the ship of state tossing in a storm. Rhesus was not there then; he is arriving for the feast without having been at the hunt. The chorus warns him against being too certain of victory; the shepherd adds, "The very sight of him should make the enemy panic" (338); and Hector, with a biting allusion to Rhesus's gold armor, agrees to receive him.

He presumably remains on stage during the choral song. This is addressed to Adrasteia, a Trojan goddess associated with Nemesis; there are somber overtones. It is a song in praise of Rhesus, who is ad-

dressed as Zeus the Light-bringer or Deliverer incarnate; the title is
hybris and *nemesis* will follow. Rhesus's horses gallop through the ode
(356, 374), and again the guard sings of his challenge to Achilles
(371). And now Rhesus is there, and again they hail him as a god,
this time Ares, god of war, a colt of the Muse come to inspire Troy
(387). His entry, with the white horses in full view, and the part his
single scene plays in the whole structure recall *Agamemnon*.

Hector stands silent, and it is Rhesus who breaks the silence. His
boastful introduction leads Hector to a blunt rebuke of Rhesus's failure to come before. There is some implicit wordplay on Rhesus's name;
it is akin to the words for "speech" (*rhesis*) and "smashing" (*rhexis*).
When Rhesus was in need, Hector came and smashed his enemies
(410); Rhesus has kicked his services away as a horse kicks (411).
The implication is that Rhesus is words without action. Rhesus, a typical braggart-soldier, tells of his wars and hardships. But he has come
in time. Hector has for ten years been gambling ineffectually with war
for stake.

> One single day's light will be enough for me
> to tear down their towers, fall upon their fleet,
> and wipe out the Greeks. Next day I shall go home
> from Troy; I shall have cut your troubles short. (447)

O! never shall sun that morrow see! The home he will find will not be
Thrace, and it is not Hector's troubles that are cut short.

The chorus is a little shocked; they sing a verse to which the answer,
significantly, does not come till after Rhesus's death (454, cf. 820).
They have sung of Rhesus as Zeus; now they call him "sent from Zeus,"
and pray that Zeus will not grudge his boastfulness. Achilles and Ajax
will hardly withstand him. Hector says nothing. Rhesus soars higher.
Once Troy is liberated he and Hector will descend on Greece and make
them suffer. Hector now treats Rhesus as Aeneas treated him, with a
cold douche, and Hector is again right, for Rhesus is looking too far
ahead. There is an oddly pointless wordplay, something like: "This
way of yours is suffering without action. This sway of mine is quite
wide enough as it is" (483). They turn to battle dispositions. Rhesus

wants to finish the war without help; however he graciously permits the commander-in-chief some share. There follows a dry exchange:

RHESUS: Post me opposite Achilles and his regiment.
HECTOR: You can't point your angry spear at him.
RHESUS: But rumor ran that he sailed for Troy.
HECTOR: He sailed and arrived. But he is angry
      with the High Command, and refuses to join battle. (491)

They speak of other Greek heroes, Ajax, Diomedes, and Odysseus, and Hector outlines Odysseus's exploits. Rhesus, like Dolon, asserts that he will capture and kill Odysseus. Hector escorts Rhesus to his place in the camp, apart from the others, and gives him the password, "Phoebus." It is, as he says, night; but the euphemism he uses, "the kindly time," *euphrone*, proves ironical. He sets the chorus to watch for Dolon.

There follows the only lyric of real merit in the play; it is a song welcoming the coming dawn, with the signs that Euripides had used in *Phaethon*, the setting of the stars, the nightingale's lament, and the shepherd's pipe. There is a certain ironic appropriateness about the song, but otherwise it is wildly irrelevant, for the rest of the play, as we are constantly reminded, takes place in continuing darkness, and Odysseus and Diomedes would never risk their venture if dawn were near. The chorus is anxious about Dolon, and go to wake the next watch, the Lycians or wolfmen.

Dolon went out wearing a wolf skin, and a figure wearing a wolf skin returns, walking delicately in the dark, starting at a sound, which turns out to be the clank of horses' harness. He has a companion, who is immediately identified as Diomedes; Odysseus is not actually named for some sixteen lines. They have evidently caught Dolon and wrung from him the password "Phoebus" and the position of Hector's tent. Of Rhesus they naturally know nothing. They have come to kill Hector, but the tent is empty; to seek Aeneas or Paris in the dark is impracticable. They are about to return when the figure of Athene appears. Since she appears to them as Athene and to Paris as Aphrodite, and since it is her voice that Odysseus recognizes (an echo of *Ajax*), we must suppose that she speaks from the stage building or the crane rather than that she appears on stage, blocking their departure. She tells them that they are not fated to kill Hector or Paris, but that if they do not kill Rhesus, no one, not even Ajax or Achilles, will withstand him; in addition, his horses are a prize worth having. This is quite extraordinary.

Rhesus has appeared as the braggart-soldier who boasts enterprises he cannot fulfill. Now we learn that his vaunts are justified, and if he reaches the battlefield he will succeed where Hector is doomed to failure. Athene remains to direct operations from the sky. Pearson called her "a mischievous stage-puppet," but she is really a mischievous stage-puppeteer. By a peculiarly clumsy device to cover the killing of Rhesus, Paris is brought on and dismissed by Athene pretending to be Aphrodite; no doubt there was play with a cool femininity of voice contrasting with Athene's own martial decisiveness.

We may accept the fiction that a choral song and dance covers an indefinite period of time, but it is difficult to accept that an ordinary stage scene lasting less than three minutes allows Odysseus and Diomedes to go to the Thracian camp, which is at a distance from the Trojan, kill Rhesus, and return. Further, no indication is given of how they found their way; they did not know it and Athene did not escort them. Again, they have explicitly arranged that Diomedes will do the killing and Odysseus will manage the horses. Yet it is Odysseus who comes on pursued by the guard, and he evidently has not the horses with him; whether he has Diomedes with him is not wholly clear.

Athene is completely identified with the Greek cause; which she speaks of as "us" (670). As usual there is no indication of when she leaves; probably we are to suppose that she watches Odysseus fool the chorus and leaves with him. Athene is introduced partly because she is in the Homeric tradition, partly because she gives information about Rhesus that Dolon did not possess (though a more skillful dramatist might have allowed Dolon the knowledge of his imminent arrival and prospective camping place), partly perhaps to give supernatural sanction to the plot. The whole scene is dramatically inept; further, the appearance of Athene detracts from the dramatic force of the appearance of the Muse at the end.

By contrast, the confrontation of Odysseus and the chorus is good theater. Odysseus comes on, now, we must suppose, having discarded the wolf skin and wearing Thracian armor. The chorus rushes after him, crying:

> Hey! Hey!
> Hit him, hit him, hit him, hit him,
> stab him, stab him. Who is he? (675)

There is a similar passage in Aristophanes's *The Acharnians* (280), but the language is natural (Xen. *Anab.* 5.7.21,28) and if it is parody, both Aristophanes and *Rhesus* may be drawing on a similar scene in Euripides's lost *Telephus*. In the excited interchange the exact allocation of lines is uncertain, but it appears that one of the guard demands the password, and Odysseus counters with, "Was it you who assassinated Rhesus?" (685). This is almost too clever. The password is held up just long enough for dramatic excitement; Odysseus gives it and is allowed to escape. It is ironical that the god who supports Troy and, according to one story, came from Thrace is the god whose name allows the Greeks to escape. The chorus still thinks that there are spies about; they suspect that Odysseus has slipped through and that Hector will hold them responsible.

Suddenly a cry is heard offstage. The chorus lays an ambush, but it turns out to be Rhesus's charioteer; it is noteworthy that they do not ask him for the password. He chants the news that Rhesus is dead, then, in a typical messenger's speech, tells the story. The Thracians were tired and posted no guard. After a brief sleep he himself had got up to feed the horses. He saw two men prowling around, shouted at them, thinking they were Trojans thieving, and went to sleep again. As he slept, he dreamed of wolves riding his master's horses; he awoke from his dream to hear Rhesus's death cry, and to sense a sword through his own ribs, and the horses being ridden away.

The story has come full circle: Dolon, the man of wiles in name, set out as a wolf to kill Odysseus and win Achilles's horses; Odysseus, the man of wiles in act, has killed Dolon and come as a wolf to win Rhesus's horses. The charioteer knows nothing of this and suspects his allies. Hector has heard of the disaster and now arrives, though where he has been since leaving Rhesus we are not told. He accuses the guard of negligence. They, rather oddly, sing their answer: it is the second part of their unfinished song. They have not slept. True, but they did neglect their duty while going to find the Lycians; while they were looking for one group of wolfmen, another group was bringing disaster. The charioteer bursts out with an accusation that Hector murdered Rhesus for his horses; we know, though the charioteer does not, that Hector did covet Achilles's horses, and his traditional epithet was "horse-taming." Hector is patient before his accusations; he himself recognizes the hand of Odysseus and has the charioteer taken for medical treatment; the latter is left in ignorance of the truth.

They are making arrangements for the burial when the Muse, Rhesus's mother, appears on the crane with the body of Rhesus in her arms. The scene, as we have said already, was borrowed from a similar scene with Dawn and Memnon in Aeschylus's *The Weighing of Souls.* Her appearance adds a note of pathos. She identifies Odysseus and Diomedes as the killers, with Athene behind them. There is a curious dissociation of Athene from Athens, with implications of a political concord between Athens and Thrace; the suggestion is almost that the play was written by an Athenian for performance in Thrace or perhaps Macedon. If so we can speculate, provided we realize that we are only speculating, that the younger Euripides, flushed with his success in adapting *Iphigeneia at Aulis* for presentation, tried his hand at drama for himself in Archelaus's court, and this is the result. The Muse ends with the prophecy of the heroizing of Rhesus; she compares him with "Bacchus's prophet" (972). Exactly who this is is not clear, and perhaps is not meant to be clear; it is interesting for our knowledge of ancient religion, but it does not affect our understanding of the play. The Muse goes with her son's body as dawn breaks, and Hector prepares his assault on the ships. It is a surprising finish, for it points to an unfinished future, as the chorus marches off with a song on their lips.

Rhesus is a second-rate play. The scene with Athene is badly conceived and clumsily contrived. The language is highly repetitive and contains little that is memorable. Both language and dramatic effects are derivative. The theme is not truly tragic; as Aristotle saw, there is no tragedy in the killing of an enemy by an enemy. Further, Rhesus cannot bear the weight of being a tragic hero on the strength of his one appearance. Aeschylus achieved this by sheer genius with *Agamemnon,* but the author of *Rhesus* conspicuously lacks genius. When we hear from Athene of all that Rhesus will achieve if allowed to live, we raise our eyebrows: surely this is not the man we have met. There are other clumsinesses, in the exits and entrances, for example, and in the handling of the password, which could have been made much more powerful.

But *Rhesus* is a good second-rate play. Pearson said well, "The curious thing about the *Rhesus* is that, when all this has been said, the play is not nearly so bad as it ought to be." The characters lack depth, but each gives scope for a good character actor. The author has a vigorous sense of theater, which he applies miscellaneously with mime (Dolon as the wolf and Odysseus in the dark), two-level acting (Athene and the Muse), vocal effects (Athene as Aphrodite), spectacle (the general use of torches and the entry of Rhesus), and pace and tension (the chorus with Odysseus). It is a play to see, to enjoy, and to forget.

VI

SATYRIC AND PRO-SATYRIC PLAYS

35. THE SATYR PLAY

The satyr play forms to our way of thinking a strange adjunct to the lofty themes of tragedy. The Greeks themselves came to feel this, and in later revivals either omitted it or placed it at the beginning of the performance. Here we find ourselves back in the origins of tragedy; the connection with Dionysus and the spring fertility festival is explicit and clear, and the bawdy and cheerful obscenity of performance must have been a relief after the tensions of the earlier plays. Horace wrote:

> The bard who strove of yore in tragic strains
> To win the goat, poor guerdon of his pains,
> Anon brought woodland satyrs in, and tried,
> If gay with grave might somehow be allied.
> For only by the lure of things like these,
> That by their novelty were sure to please
> Could audiences be kept, who were, no doubt,
> By the religious service half tired-out,
> And, being flushed with wine, could scarce restrain
> The lawless humour of their madcap vein. (*A.P.* 220, tr. Martin)

It is important to remember that the authors of these plays were tragedians, not comedians. The plays are in fact a part of the picture of man that the tragedians seek to convey—"the glory, jest and riddle of the world."

The relationship of these plays to the preceding trilogy remains uncertain, and it is possible that there was no standard pattern. Aeschylus seems to have liked to treat some part of the myth in a different spirit. Thus the Oedipus trilogy was completed by a play called *The Sphinx*, the Lycurgus trilogy by a play called *Lycurgus*, in which there was some discussion of the power of beer, by contrast no doubt with the lofty treatment of wine earlier in the trilogy. It is hard to fit all the known satyr plays into this pattern, and it is an attractive suggestion that the satyr play, not necessarily belonging to the same cycle of myth as the tragedies, hinges on a parodic treatment of some key theme or scene. The plays were short, because, as Croiset says, pure fantasy is hard to sustain for any length of time, and because in general after three tragedies a long postlude would be inappropriate.

The range of characters in the satyr plays seems to have been limited. Typical characters are Hermes, the god of thieves (in Sophocles's *Inachus* he wore a cap of invisibility, a fact that raises some interesting questions about staging); Odysseus, the trickster; Autolycus, the snapper-up of unconsidered trifles; Sisyphus, who cheated death; and all the Coyotes and Ananses of East European myth. These were linked in some way with the satyrs, the lewd ithyphallic rout of Dionysus, usually horse-tailed (though affinities with other animals have been argued for some plays), and their leader Silenus. Part of the challenge to the poet lay in the need for a plausible ingenuity in forging this link. In an anonymous innominate play, possibly by Sophocles, possibly called *Oeneus*, the chorus introduce themselves:

> You shall learn it all. We come as potential bridegrooms.
> Our mothers were nymphs, our master is Bacchus,
> we live in the suburbs of heaven. Every scientific skill
> is our stock-in-trade, provided it's proper: fighting with
> spears, wrestling, riding, running,
> boxing, biting, hitting below the belt,

(a beautiful catalogue of *double entendres*)

> musical serenades, a complete understanding
> of oracles without cheating,
> medical-exposure, astronomical measurements,
> dancing, all the language they use in hell.
> What class degree do you think we'll get?

Aeschylus had the highest reputation in antiquity as a writer of satyr plays. A fragment or two of *The Fishermen* survive; it was a treatment of the Danaë-Perseus story. A fragment from the opening shows a fisherman thinking what a wonderful catch he has; a later fragment shows Silenus making up to the baby Perseus in order to sleep with his mother Danaë. There is not enough for us to make a firsthand appraisal. Next to Aeschylus was ranked, at least in the judgment of the philosopher Menedemus, the otherwise minor figure of Achaeus (D.L. 2.133); as Menedemus came from the same town of Eretria his judgment may not have been objective.

But one can imagine that Sophocles and Euripides found the genre irksome, and it is not surprising to find Euripides experimenting with a very different type of drama in place of the satyr play. This is seen most clearly in *Alcestis*, which we know to have been the fourth of the plays presented in 438. The shortage of satyr plays in the catalogue of Euripides's plays leads us to think that even if this experiment proved a disappointment to an audience expecting something more boisterous and bawdy (as we may readily imagine), he nonetheless repeated it.

We are told in an anonymous pamphlet *On Comedy* (published conveniently by Cramer in the nineteenth century in his *Anecdota Graeca*) and by the Byzantine critic Tzetzes in his work *On the Distinctive Quality of the Poets* that the dramatists sometimes substituted for the satyr play a drama of a different kind, lacking the satyrs, but with much more of the mood of comedy than tragedy; they offer three examples: *Alcestis*, *Orestes*, and Sophocles's *Electra*. This evidence has been strangely neglected, or rejected on *a priori* grounds (such as the fact that *Orestes* uses three actors: so does *The Cyclops*). We know it to be true of *Alcestis*, we know that it must have been true of some other of Euripides's plays; yet had we been merely guessing, among the surviving plays we should probably have thought of *Iphigeneia among the Taurians* or *Helen*. Further, we know that Sophocles was a great enough man to learn from the brilliant younger man, and the last two surviving plays, *Philoctetes* and *Oedipus at Colonus,* contain Euripidean elements. There is no reason to doubt that Sophocles emulated this further device of Euripides or that he did so in *Electra*; it would help to justify the rather odd mood of that play.

It is important that the satyric and pro-satyric drama should neither be evaluated as tragedy nor apart from tragedy. Demetrius of Phalerum called it "tragedy on holiday" (*De interpret.* 169). On the one hand then we have the *holiday*, the parodic element, which seems to have formed a link between the satyric and pro-satyric plays. If it is right to associate *The Women of Phoenicia* and *Orestes*, the ending of the latter is a mockery of the ending of the former, and there are certainly plenty of points at which we can reasonably suppose *Alcestis* to be parodying one of the earlier plays; the distortions, gigantesque figures like Cyllene, Heracles, and the Cyclops; the dénouement of joy. On the other hand it is *tragedy* on holiday; the vision that is distorted in the tragic vision. The parody is the parody of tragedy; the plays do not exalt comic values but toy with tragic ones, and the backcloth of the preceding tragedies is not to be ignored or forgotten (we tend to treat the plays in isolation).

The audience was awaiting relief from tension, and we do well to watch the plays with a readiness to laugh and indeed to imagine "business" designed to promote laughter. But we must not forget the tension. There is a seriousness of dramatic purpose in the satyric *The Trackers* and the pro-satyric *Alcestis* and *Orestes*. They are none of them tragedies, and they must not be so analyzed. But they remain with the tragic vision.

36. SOPHOCLES: *THE TRACKERS*

Euripides's *The Cyclops* is the only complete satyr play to survive. The discovery in 1907 of a papyrus containing in a fragmentary form the first four hundred lines of a satyr play by Sophocles was thus a major event. It is likely that these lines constitute well over half the play, and this enables us to make some kind of judgment of Sophocles as a writer in this genre.

The story of *The Trackers* is based upon the Homeric *Hymn to Hermes*, which is no doubt also the origin of the scene on a Caeretan hydria in the Louvre. The hymn sings of Maia's precocious son Hermes. Hermes was originally the spirit of the cairn, which marks the path in wild mountain country. Because of this he was associated with shepherds, brigands, and travelers, and naturally also with traders. A friendly, popular god, he became something of a trickster, and folk tales accumulated round him. He would appear a helpless infant in his cradle and then creep out on adventures, first killing a tortoise, making the first lyre from its shell, and then stealing Apollo's cattle in such a way as to reverse and confuse their tracks and conceal his own footprints. Eventually he was found out and gave Apollo the lyre in compensation for the cattle he had taken. Such is the basis of Sophocles's play, but he did not hesitate to innovate: his Hermes is in the care of Cyllene not Maia and at Mt. Cyllene not Pylos; the theft of the cattle precedes the invention of the lyre and provides the young inventor with the necessary oxhide, which also betrays him, and the satyr chorus is inevitably introduced.

We have the start of the play; on the manuscript line 94 is marked as line 100, but such attributions are not always accurate, and a cast list may account for the remaining lines. The scene is set on Mt. Cyllene in Arcadia. Apollo appears and makes a formal proclamation of reward for his cattle, like some towncrier; it seems that he is carrying a herald's staff, and this is no doubt used for "business" throughout the play. His busy anxiety is mildly amusing. He has chased halfway round the world looking for them; he is full of self-importance. Silenus, aging, potbellied, leader of the satyrs, comes panting in. He is eager to help —at a price; the word he uses is appropriate to a hound on the trail. Apollo promises them money and freedom, though freedom from whom or what is not wholly clear. Apollo goes out, perhaps giving Silenus the herald's staff, with which he in turn makes a formal proclamation.

Silenus calls the satyr chorus, which dances in, and sets them on the trail. It has been suggested that the chorus is dressed as hounds; this is not very likely, but they certainly mime hounds with their noses to the trail. The scene is spectacular and amusing. The satyrs get highly excited: "A god, a god, a god, a god! Hallo! Hallo!" (92). They are thrilled to have Apollo in charge of their expedition. They find with ludicrous ease the hoofmarks that Apollo has been round the world to seek, but find them confused and puzzling.

A lyre sounds offstage. It is an unfamiliar noise. At first they think that it must be the indistinct lowing of cattle. But it sounds again; they panic and fall writhing on the ground—like hedgehogs in the bush or apes in heat rather than hounds on the trail, says Silenus scornfully. Sophocles certainly gives them curious exclamations: "Whew! whew! whew! ps! ps! aaa! aaa!" Silenus indulges in the vocabulary of abuse, which is always good for a laugh, and in some boastful reminiscences about his glorious victories in his youth—over nymphs. A game of tag follows as the old man blunders round trying to catch them; they evade him, but he catches one and gives him a good spanking. Suddenly the lyre rings out so clearly that Silenus hears it too. It is now his turn to panic. He has to go to an appointment.

> SILENUS: Must be off.
> CHORUS: Don't go!
> SILENUS: Must. You look here there and everywhere.
> Get on the trail. Get rich quick. Get
> the cows and the reward. I don't really think
> I can waste my time hanging about here. (199)

The boot is now on the other foot; he is trying to get away, and they try to stop him. But they are too many for him. They hold him back, shout to whoever is within, and stamp on the ground.

What emerges from the cave is a gigantic, towering female figure, such as might be expected to portray a mountain deity. Before her the satyrs quail, and this makes more amusing her words:

> I heard some shouting, crazy, out of tune.
> I thought there must be something seriously wrong
> with you. What do you want with a poor innocent girl? (234)

She greets them as "Animals" and suggests that their present behavior as hunters is very different from the innocence of the Dionysiac rout.

The chorus cover their nervousness by singing their answer in a basically cretic rhythm, pleading to know what was the "voice" they heard. This, says Cyllene (they know who she is without her introducing herself; 250), is better than attacking the virtue of a poor girl. She tells them, as a secret, under the threat of dire punishment if they disclose it (there is room for amusing byplay here) that Zeus had found Atlas's daughter Maia in that cave and ravished her without Hera's knowledge. From this union Hermes was born; Maia is weak and Cyllene is nursing him, and he is growing at an alarming rate. The noise came from an invention of the baby, and was made from a dead animal.

An excellent exchange follows in the rare iambic tetrameter between Silenus and Cyllene. The ancient Greek, like the modern African, loved riddles, and the scene is really a variant on the game of riddles:

SILENUS: No dead animal could produce a strain like that.

CYLLENE: It's true. I'm a goddess, and my words greet you with truth.

SILENUS: How *do* you expect me to believe that booming voice comes from beyond the grave?

CYLLENE: Because I tell you. It's a wild animal, silent in life, vocal in death.

SILENUS: What shape? Long? Humped? Short?

CYLLENE: Short, like a pot, shrivelled up, with spotty skin.

SILENUS: I've got it! Like a cat? ... No? ... Like a leopard?

CYLLENE: You've got it all wrong; it's round with short legs.

SILENUS: Yes ... It sounds just like a tracker ... or a crab.

CYLLENE: Still wrong: try, try, try again.

SILENUS: Ah! Like a horned beetle, the sort found on Etna?

CYLLENE: *Now* you're getting somewhere near the likeness.

SILENUS: Which part produces the sound—inside or outside? Do tell me.

CYLLENE: It's the crust which sounds the changes; it's rather like a shell.

SILENUS: What name do you give it? Come along, if you've anything more to say.

CYLLENE: The baby calls the animal "tortoise" and the part which sounds "lyre." (289)

The "tracker" is a kind of weasel, but it is a delightful joke at the expense of Silenus himself, with his potbelly, pimply face (spotted skin), and short, fat legs. As Cyllene goes on she reveals that the shell rings because Hermes has stretched an oxhide over it, and the chorus is quick to make the deduction, and sings in excited cretics that they have found the thief. Cyllene becomes indignant. What an accusation against a six-day-old baby! And there are no thieves in *his* family. Silenus and the satyrs are behaving like children—and like amorous goats as well. Again we can imagine byplay. The chorus will not let her off the hook, and insists that "crooked is as crooked does" (372). They continue to press her to bring out the cattle, and she replies, "You and your cattle will be the death of me" (391).

At this point the fragments become impossibly disconnected. The satyrs evidently revealed their discovery to Apollo and claimed their reward, and Apollo seems to have acknowledged that they merit it. We may reasonably suppose that Apollo recovered most of his cattle but remained indignant about those which had already been killed, that there was a confrontation between Hermes and Apollo over the gift of the lyre, that the herald's staff was received as part of the bargain, and that the play ended in general celebration with lyre accompaniment. It is not clear whether the later scenes required two actors or three.

The Trackers is frankly not a particularly good play. We do not know enough about the treatment of satyr plays to use the style as an instrument for dating the play, nor do we know anything for sure about the relationship of the satyr play to the rest of the tetralogy. If we are right to think that the satyr play may have been built round a parody of some episode in one of the other plays, it is possible that *The Trackers* may have been performed with *Ajax*, and this would accord with the view of some scholars that it is early.

The language is closer to that of tragedy than to that of comedy, but it lacks the exaltation of Sophocles's tragic diction; it is in fact somewhat undistinguished. The vocabulary is however not without interest, and Walker claimed no less than forty-three words as unique to this play, and nearly a hundred more not found elsewhere in tragedy. The text, as it stands, has nothing to shock the most inhibited maiden aunt, though the Cyllene scenes offer some scope for obscene byplay. What is more, the text is not at all funny, and humor must have depended on the antics of the satyrs and perhaps later on the incongruity of the appearance of the "baby" Hermes.

The solid merit of the play is as a detective story. Dorothy Sayers once wrote an article, "Aristotle and Detective-Fiction," in which she suggests that the modern genre that fulfills the canons of the *Poetics* is the detective story. Of this Sophocles was the master; Euripides preferred the thriller to the whodunit. Here the master stroke lies in turning the plot so that the use of the oxhide in creating the lyre provides the essential clue to the thief. Sophocles may not be the antecedent of Plautus or Molière, but he does foreshadow Agatha Christie.

37. EURIPIDES: *ALCESTIS*

Alcestis is a puzzling play. It is the first known example of a non-satyric drama in place of a satyr play. It is hard to know what the audience would expect of such a play or how far Euripides would feel able to give them something different. We may suppose that the presence of Heracles made the transition easier; of Euripides's few known satyr plays, *Busiris*, *Eurystheus*, and *Syleus* certainly centered on his adventures, and a good case can be made for his appearance in *Autolycus*. But it certainly seems risky to interpret the play, as is so often done, as tragedy with some slight buffoonery in the person of Heracles as a sop to the audience. The ironic structure, as some critics have rightly seen, would hardly be enough to satisfy an audience waiting to relax into altogether broader effects. Much would have depended upon the presentation, and it would be tempting to produce it in parodic, exaggerated style throughout, except for the actual passing of Alcestis.

Our understanding would be enhanced if we knew more of Phrynichus's *Alcestis*. Neither Aeschylus nor Sophocles treated the theme; so Phrynichus is the only precursor we know. The sole surviving fragments, five words and one of those corrupt, suggest a wrestling match between Heracles and Death. In *The Kindly Goddesses* (723) the Furies refer to Apollo making the Fates drunk so that they let Admetus off death. It sounds suited to a satyr play. If Phrynichus's was a satyr play, we must suppose that Euripides endowed a burlesque with genuine emotion. But it remains primarily burlesque.

It was performed in 438 after *The Women of Crete, Alcmaeon at Psophis,* and *Telephus.* Of these the first is obscure, but it seems to have dealt with the loose sex life of Aerope, wife of Atreus. She was doomed to execution by drowning, but the sentence was commuted. Euripides wrote her some wonderful love lyrics; his sympathetic understanding of her emotions caused some scandal. *Alcmaeon at Psophis* had an involved plot. Alcmaeon, like Orestes, had murdered his mother, whose name was Eriphyle. The rest of the adventures deal with Alcmaeon's chastisement by the Furies, his marriage to Alphesiboea and then to Callirrhoe, the trickery he uses to secure for Callirrhoe the fabulous necklace he had given to Alphesiboea, and his murder by Alphesiboea's father Phegeus. *Telephus* was a more famous play altogether. Telephus, king of Mysia, had been wounded by a Greek reconnoitring expedition in the preliminaries to the Trojan War. He was told that he could be healed only by the spear that wounded him ("the hair of the dog that caused the bite"). In a beggar's disguise, he went to the Greeks assembled at Argos and pleaded his own cause, the cause of a public enemy. He was exposed by Odysseus and used the infant Orestes as a hostage for his own safety. It was fine melodrama, yet lacking the sense of unreality that goes with melodrama, a play of disillusionary realism with no escape clause.

It is not easy to discern a common theme between these plays or between these and *Alcestis,* though Dale is unkind when she writes, "Only excess of zeal has enabled scholars to discern in these four plays some common underlying theme, or specially significant correspondences and contrasts; any four plays of Euripides taken at random could with a little goodwill be made into as significant a group." The last sentence may be true; nonetheless Euripides did group these plays together and, we may suspect, not at random. We may admit agnosticism without scepticism.

It is not hard to discern a reason for rounding the tetralogy with *Alcestis*. Two of the plays deal with people who are snatched away from death in different circumstances; after this the actual appearance of Death must have been horrific-comic in effect. Further, in the middle play it seems that Alphesiboea retained her love for Alcmaeon, but that that love could not save him. In fact all the plays contained interesting studies of women, the loose Aerope, the passionate Alphesiboea, and in *Telephus,* Clytemnestra, who befriended Telephus. Whatever the connection between the other plays, *Alcestis* was well suited to take them up in such a way as to release tension.

The play begins with Apollo coming out of the house with his bow and quiver. He addresses the house; he has lived here as serf to Admetus in punishment for an offense against Zeus after Zeus had killed Asclepius. He speaks of Admetus's hospitality (8) and his religiosity, and tells how he himself tricked the Fates into sparing Admetus if he could find a substitute. Admetus's father and mother refused; his wife agreed. Now she is dying, and Apollo must leave; he is the god of light and may not encounter the darkness of the underworld, just as his temples were preserved from the taint of death. Apollo's words are brief, factual, and, apart from his obvious affection for Admetus and the house where he has been surprisingly happy, contain no element of judgment.

So far there has been nothing out of the ordinary. Suddenly, from the same underground chamber that admitted the ghosts of Darius and Clytemnestra, appears a dark, winged figure with a sword. It is Death, eager, bourgeois in his punctuality. He stands with his back to the audience and checks as he sees the great golden god in his path. It is a splendid tableau. Then he gives two wolf howls (*a-a-a! a-a-a!* or ♪♩♪♩♪♩). He addresses Apollo in chanted anapaests. They are overdone; they are as near to rhyme as a Greek poet came. The half-line endings are:

-ois	*-eis*
-eis	*-o-ôn*
-os	*-o-ôn*
-oi	*-ou*
-ai	*-o-ôi*
-e-ei	*-au*
-e-e	*-as*
-e-e	*-as* (29)

The effect is exaggerated melodrama; the result is, and is meant to be, comic without losing its sinister note. Death is, so to say, twirling his mustachios. The comic element remains in the ensuing dialogue. Death is snarling, Apollo self-consciously calm. But Apollo's "I did not use force to rob you of your prey" (44) is chicanery; his swift following of a criticism of Admetus's parents, who cling on to the old age (50), with the suggestion that Alcestis might be allowed to reach that same corrupting old age is ludicrous. His attempt to bribe Death with the rich gifts that accompany the old is met with "Phoebus, you make your rules to favor the haves" (57), which is as direct a criticism of Delphi as the plays contain. Apollo's reply—"Clever, aren't you? Why has nobody noticed it before?"—is a schoolboy retort of the crudest kind.

Apollo is a caricatured aristocrat, Death a caricatured democrat. Apollo prophesies, in words that Death is bound to regard as empty, the coming of a man who will receive hospitality in the house and wrest Alcestis from his grip, and goes his way; one suspects that he snaps his fingers and a golden chariot sweeps down to pick him up. Death, still growling, gives some practice slashes with his sword and slips into the house.

As the door closes the chorus of old men from the neighborhood enter from stage-left in two lines and chant antiphonally. Their entry is startling; the audience is expecting satyrs. But though the obscenity of the satyr chorus is missing, the comic element is there, the fervor of their singing contrasting with the hush of which they speak. It is an effect that Gilbert espoused in *H.M.S. Pinafore* and *The Pirates of Penzance* ("with catlike tread"). Their first words are questions. They are expecting Alcestis's death but see no signs of mourning. Then (as also happens in Gilbert and Sullivan) comedy is transmuted into poetry as they sing of the dead Asclepius, who might have saved her.

They see a girl coming out of the house in tears; Euripides makes a point of the love the servants hold for Alcestis. The chorus asks whether she is alive or dead, and the girl's first words contain the play's central paradox: "What shall I tell you? Alive? Yes. Dead? I can say that too" (141). The chorus thinks of Admetus: "Poor man! What a man! What a wife you're losing" (144). "Yes," says the girl, "and Master doesn't realize it till he suffers." This is a foretaste of the outcome. The chorus and the girl use of Alcestis the simple superlative "best of women," and the girl gives an affecting description of Alcestis's preparations for death; the description is a skillful preparation for Alcestis's entry.

Like Agamemnon in his play, Alcestis is on stage for only a fragment of the whole, but it is emphatically her play. We see her gentle but strong, dutiful and pious, through the servant's eyes, praying for her children, honoring the altars, long impassive till she reaches the marriage bed when she breaks into tears, and seems incapable of leaving it; she will not betray it (180). She thinks of Admetus taking another wife and cries in a memorable line, too easy to parody, "She may be happier; she could not be more virtuous" (182). Then she kisses the children and greets all the servants individually. It is exquisite, and we must take it seriously, but not too seriously, for in the middle of it Euripides gives this simple girl a wicked parody of Aeschylean magniloquence:

> She knelt beside the bed and kissed it till all the coverlet's by
> eye-welling springtide bedewed. (184)

The chorus thinks again of Admetus, who is to lose such a good wife. He is with her, pleading with her not to betray him (202), and will shortly be bringing her out to look her last on the light.

The choral song that follows is short, but it is prolonged by Alcestis, who is carried in on a couch, attended by her young son and daughter and her prosaic husband, who continues to interject iambic speech rhythms into the lyrical outbursts. The scene is marvelously conveyed.

Alcestis is sometimes described as delirious; but it is all appallingly real; she has the double vision of which Blake speaks. Her eye lights on the powers of nature:

> Sun! Daylight!
> You sky-borne whirlpools of scudding clouds! (244)

Admetus again calls on her not to betray him (250). Soon with her inward eye she is seeing Charon and the Styx. Invisible hands tug at her:

Pulling me, someone's pulling, someone's pulling me; can't you see? (258)

There follows a delightful touch. Alcestis quietens herself, and her unimaginative husband chooses this moment to burst into a chant. His words are ludicrously exaggerated. For the third time he speaks of betrayal.

> In God's name—not betrayal, not cruelty—
> in the name of the children you leave motherless—

Who has asked her to do so? It is not a betrayal.

> Up! Take heart!
> If you are dead I should no longer exist.
> I depend on you—my life, present, absent, depends on you.
> Your love is my god. (275)

The meaning of the last line is obscure. Alcestis's return to speech rhythms is a douche of cold water on his self-centered pseudo-emotionalism. Browning speaks of his empty protestations; Alcestis makes a last effort to try to induce him to understand. She is giving up everything for him; she rebukes his parents for their failure; they did betray him (290). She asks him to remember, and she asks him not to marry again; this is important for the final scene; her description of a stepmother as a viper serves to lighten the tension again. She accepts the appellation the chorus has given her, "best of wives" (324), simply, factually, without boasting, and says "Farewell!" The speech is not melting and tender, and it is an error to play it so; it is hard, almost harsh. Alcestis is not "the little woman." She is strong; it is Admetus who is the little man. Admetus's reply is not to be taken seriously; it is grotesquely over-played and should be delivered with an extravagant rhetoric that contrasts with her simple directness. She will be his only wife; he will mourn her all through life; his parents are his enemies. A sculptor will carve her likeness, which he will embrace, "cold comfort, I realize, but I should be bailing out a weight from my soul" (353); the comic element is there inescapable, as the marble will be decidedly cold and weighty, and the language is ambiguous between the statue "stretched out" for love or in death. If he had Orpheus's gift he would bring her back from the dead. Heracles, without Orpheus's gift, is to do just that. But Admetus lets her die. There is a brief exchange of greetings ("Time will cure," says Alcestis; 381); at the very end the verse pattern is broken between husband and wife. Then she dies. The moment is touched by a monody of grief from her son, who bursts directly into song (he never speaks), while his sister weeps at his side. Admetus does not keen; he organizes the funeral.

There follows a fine choral ode in praise of Alcestis, who again is given her title "best of women" (442). They accept her vision of the journey across the Styx. The song contains the first recorded use of the prayer "Let the earth lie lightly," the Latin *sit tibi terra levis*, the theme of many subsequent epitaphs. It concludes with a masterly ambiguity, which reminds us that even this is not to be taken too seriously. The chorus prays for a wife like Alcestis; "she would be through life my companion, free from trouble" (474). The ambiguity is deliberate; *alupos* can mean "without causing pain" and "without suffering pain"; one half means that she would be a wonderful wife, the other that, unlike Admetus, they would not let her die.

In bursts Heracles from stage-right, recognizable by club and lion skin, noisy, extravert, abrupt. He is played by the same actor who has played Alcestis. He addresses them as "friends"—the word (*xenoi*) is a key word, with its meaning of host and guest—and as "countrymen," with a punning meaning in the direction of "revelers," inappropriate to the moment but appropriate to his own behavior. He is on his way to fetch the man-eating horses of Diomedes; Euripides introduces a touch of rationalism while establishing the hero's prowess— and boastfulness. The exaggeration is decidedly humorous. Admetus joins them, his hair short in mourning. Heracles asks why, enquiring first for his children, then his parents. Then:

HERACLES: It's not your wife Alcestis who is dead?
ADMETUS: I can answer about her in two ways.
HERACLES: Do your words mean that she is dead or alive?
ADMETUS: She lives—and does not live. Hence my distress.
HERACLES: I don't understand. Your words convey no sense.
ADMETUS: You know the fate which she is bound to meet?
HERACLES: I do—volunteering to die in your place.
ADMETUS: How can we say she lives, since she agreed to that?
HERACLES: Hey, don't anticipate the mourning. Hold it for the proper
           time.
ADMETUS: The will to death is death. The dead are not alive.
HERACLES: Most people distinguish between what is and what is not.
ADMETUS: That's your view, Heracles, not mine.
HERACLES: But why the grief? Who's dead? Someone you love?
ADMETUS: A woman. We were just speaking of a woman.
HERACLES: Was she a blood relation to you or not?
ADMETUS: She was not, but in all else an integral part of my home.
HERACLES: How did she come to end her life in your house?
ADMETUS: She came here as an orphan when her father died. (518)

It is brilliant. The stichomythia covers a deception that evades an actual lie but that comes near to a terminological inexactitude. The paradox of Alcestis's state is reinforced (521, cf. 141). When Admetus says that he was speaking of a woman (531), the Greek could equally mean "my wife," who is not in the strict sense a blood relative. Heracles is for going elsewhere, but, says Admetus "the dead are dead" (541); only they are not.

The note of hospitality rings out clear (540, 542, 543, 547, 550, 552, 554, 556, 558, 559, 567). It is a merit in Admetus, but an equivocal one. Hospitality is for him an abstract ideal and a source of self-pride, almost self-righteousness. The chorus speaks of Heracles as a friend of Admetus (562), but Admetus does not; his hospitality is impersonal. But he describes Heracles as "best of men" (559), which links him with Alcestis.

Admetus ends with the word "guests," and the chorus sings of his guest-full house, passing to the time when Apollo was his guest; Apollo has in gratitude already foretold the coming of Heracles. It is a hymn to hospitality.

And now comes the funeral cortège from the palace, a splendid pageant, which is met by Admetus's father, Pheres, who has come with his own offerings. He joins in praise of Alcestis, to be roughly rebuffed by his son. The rebuff strikes home, but at the same time it reveals an ugliness in Admetus.

> Were you not my physical father in fact?
> Did not the woman who claimed to bear me, whom I called
> mother, give me birth? Was I slave-born,
> secret and suppositious at your wife's breast? (636)

He takes up the very words Alcestis has used (651, cf. 295). Alcestis is his father and his mother; for all he cares Pheres can go unburied. Pheres's reply is a bluster, without substance. He is utterly selfish and unloving. "Don't talk to me like a slave!" he cries. "You enjoy life; do you think I don't?" (691), words that Aristophanes enjoyed taking up. But the ruthless old man, with no real defense for himself, shows up Admetus for what he is:

> You had no shame; you fought to the end to avoid death.
> You are alive—you've bypassed your destiny
> by murdering her. You talk of my cowardice,
> you blackguard. You've been beaten hollow by a woman
> dying for her glorious young hero. (694)

The scene breaks into petty altercation, with some startling assonance (722–724) and Pheres storms out—and we realize that the coffin is still standing there. It is a scene of sick humor, very sick but clearly humor, and the contrast between the turbulent quarrel and the resumption of the solemn procession takes the edge off the solemnity; it is the contrast of moods used in "In a Contemplative Fashion" in *The Gondoliers*. The chorus resumes its praise of "the best of women" (742) and follows out behind the cortège.

And now there is a sound of banging and clattering and raucous singing within the palace, and a servant comes out. He has served many guests but never a worse one than this. The scene that follows is well in the tradition of satyric drama. The servant describes Heracles's uninhibited behavior (his singing is like a dog's howling and bears no relation to the Muse; 760) and stresses the canons of hospitality (748,

749, 754, 763, 766, 771). Heracles emerges, thick of speech, tipsy, maudlin, and moralizing, laying down the philosophy that, since we are all mortal, we may as well pursue wine, women, and song, and eat, drink and be merry for tomorrow we die; the familiar phrases were commonplaces already but not yet clichés.

In the exchange that follows, the truth emerges about Alcestis; the moment of truth is pointed by a verse divided between the two speakers (819). Heracles's discomfiture has its comical side, as does the soliloquy in which the tough he-man flexes his muscles to wrestle with Death, and, if he misses him there, resolves to go down to the underworld. With Admetus it has been an idle dream, but it will be Heracles's final labor. The rescue of Alcestis is his reward for the hospitality of Admetus. Heracles goes, and his exit is awkward, since he must not meet Admetus; perhaps he hides till the procession passes, and then slips out.

A more serious scene must follow between this and the lightness of the finale. Admetus and the chorus return, chanting a song of sorrow as they process in; it looks as if there is a long procession, perhaps all round the orchestra, with a song interspersed with interjections from Admetus, followed by a dance of sorrow in two parts. There is momentary irony when the chorus cries, "You cannot wrestle with Fortune" (889) or when Admetus recalls the marriage that "linked the best of families in one" (921): hers perhaps, but in light of all that has been said, his? But now Admetus, who has never known suffering before, begins to realize what it means to suffer, and accepts for himself the taunts that his father laid upon him. As Alcestis passed from song to speech, so now does he. He has "bypassed his fate" (939, cf. 695). Her state *is* happier than his; hers is glorious, his ignominious. It is serious; it is indeed the turning point of the play, but even here Euripides warns us not to take the play too seriously by giving him a piece of Aeschylean bombast (952).

The song that follows is serious, almost too serious, but again it is needed to set off the light-hearted ending. It too is somewhat Aeschylean, though rather in thought than language, but one wonders if there was not a parody of familiar Aeschylean music. Dale summarizes it brilliantly:

An ode on the inexorable power of Necessity: poetry, science, philosophy, all agree in this lesson; even the skills revealed by Orpheus, and by Apollo to his descendants can avail nothing against her, nor can prayer and sacrifice; even Zeus must harmonize his will with her, and the hardest matter is bent to her shaping. One of her laws is that the dead are dead and weeping will not restore them; Admetus must then cease pining for Alcestis and take comfort in her renown among men, who will pay her divine honours. Thus the chorus emphasizes the irrevocability of it all, and rounds it off with a devout and chastened reflection on the only kind of survival which mortals can achieve.

The effect is pseudo-tragic, and Heracles (whom they thought to be inside the palace) restores the comic balance as he appears with a veiled, unspeaking woman. He addresses Admetus as a friend, where Admetus treated him as a guest, and rebukes Admetus for not sharing his sorrow. He asks him to look after the woman, whom he has won in wrestling. Admetus is frightened, uncertain of himself, fearful of temptation, startled because he seems to see Alcestis through the veil; to an audience in the mood to laugh his words are irresistably comic. "What will people say?" he asks (1051). He addresses her with the same ambiguity, "Woman" or "Wife" (1060, cf. 531), and for all his alleged indifference is swift to sum up her vital statistics (1063).

Heracles plays with him, uses irony, suggests that Admetus will want to marry again (a thought he repudiates too strongly), presses him till he agrees to look after the woman, and insists that he take her in himself: "I would never entrust the woman/your wife to servants" (1111). "Pluck up courage, stretch out your hand, touch your guest," says Heracles (1117), and Admetus does so, looking the other way, as if he were cutting off a Gorgon's head. It is another echo of Aeschylus; so was Orestes enjoined to smite his mother.

Euripides again points the climactic moment by a verse divided between two speakers (1119). As he stands looking the other way, at a sign from Heracles, she withdraws her veil. It is of course Alcestis, and it is glorious comedy as he stands with his back to her, and she waits silently till at Heracles's insistence he reluctantly turns round. "There," says Heracles with marked irony, "you will say that Zeus's son is an appreciative guest" (1120). The play ends with relief, but not without a lesson. Heracles says to Admetus

> In future, Admetus,
> show your justice by a proper respect for your guests. (1148)

And Admetus acknowledges the change that has taken place.

> I am reforming my life to make it better
> than before. I cannot deny that I'm a lucky man. (1157)

The words the chorus use at the close are found elsewhere.

> Divine powers appear in many shapes.
> The gods bring many an unexpected ending.
> The probable does not come to pass.
> The improbable happens by grace of god.
> And so it was in these events. (1159)

This is perhaps their first and certainly their most appropriate appearance.

The comparison has been made with *A Winter's Tale*. But that play has an underlying seriousness of treatment in the study of the sin, pain, and active will of Leontes. To this theme of reconciliation time is essential. To Euripides time is of the vaguest. The appointed day has come for Alcestis, but time is not for Admetus what it is for Leontes, for this is comedy with a serious touch, not tragedy with a light touch, and it is Greek not Christian drama; details of time are nonexistent because they are irrelevant. We cannot take Admetus seriously; he may be a study for Jason, but he is not Jason; and this is why the critics who write about the play as if it ought to be called *Admetus* are wrong.

Alcestis is an experiment, revolutionary in its way but historically not an unqualified success, an attempt to diversify the last play of the tetralogy by freeing it from the constraint of a narrow satyric element while retaining whimsicality, parody, and buffoonery. It remains in its own way brilliant, a unique blend, touching and amusing.

38. EURIPIDES: *THE CYCLOPS*

The theme of *The Cyclops* was familiar from the ninth book of *The Odyssey*, and *The Cyclops* and *Rhesus* are the only plays that treat dramatically a subject narrated in the two surviving Homeric epics, though *The Trackers* came from a Homeric hymn. Odysseus and his companions land on an island inhabited by Cyclopes, a race of lawless one-eyed giants. They are trapped by one of these monsters, who shuts them in the cave where he pens his sheep and proceeds to eat them two by two. Odysseus gives him wine and pretends that his name is Nobody. The Cyclops, who has never had wine, is enchanted with the drink and promises to eat Nobody last. The Cyclops relapses into a drunken sleep and Odysseus puts out his eye with a sharp stake heated in the fire. The Cyclops screams. His screams arouse the neighbors who ask, "Who's hurting you?" "Nobody." So they go away again. He has to let the sheep out to pasture, and Odysseus and the other survivors escape by clinging on the underneath of the sheep.

This is a typical folktale. The myth of the one-eyed blinded monster is not uncommon; it appears, for instance, in the Sindbad stories in *The*

Arabian Nights, and altogether well over a hundred versions of the tale have been traced. It represents the sun in eclipse or covered by a storm cloud. Elsewhere in mythology the Cyclopes appear as semi-divine smiths. One legend from Sicily told of the love of the Cyclops for the nymph Galatea, a variant of the Beauty and the Beast myth. This was presumably the theme of a lost satyr play by Philoxenus entitled *The Loves of the Cyclops.*

What matters here is not origins but drama. Euripides set his scene outside the Cyclops's cave. Silenus, the aging potbellied sot, representing the older generation of satyrs, enters carrying a rake; he evidently prefers leaning on it to using it. His first words call on Dionysus. Dionysus was kidnapped by pirates, and Silenus tells, with plenty of nautical color, how he and the satyrs went in search of him, were shipwrecked on the coast of Sicily, and were captured and enslaved by the cannibal Cyclops Polyphemus. The chorus of satyrs, whom he calls "my sons," now enters with real or (more likely) imaginary sheep and dances the Sicinnis. We are ignorant about this; the evidence is conflicting. It was probably a dance of swift movement with some parody of tragic dancing involving animal and bird imitations. Then they sing a song of folding the flocks and mime the actions as they sing, returning again to a song to Dionysus.

Suddenly Silenus tells them to shut up and shift the sheep (his alliteration is on *p*). He has spotted a Greek ship drawn up on the beach and the sailors climbing up for food and drink. Poor mutts! They won't find much hospitality here! Odysseus, short and foxy, comes in with a group of sailors. He addresses the satyrs politely, as "Friends" or "Strangers" (the word is double in meaning and invokes the laws of hospitality), evidently without looking at them. Then, with a start, he realizes that they are satyrs. He turns to Silenus as the senior and a long passage of stichomythia follows:

SILENUS: Good-morning, sir, tell me your name and country—

always the first question in Greece, even today.

ODYSSEUS: Odysseus from Ithaca, king of the Cephallenians—

as if he were speaking of a third party.

SILENUS: Ah yes, the snare drum, one of the sharp sons of Sisyphus.
ODYSSEUS: Don't be so rude; it's me you're talking to. (102)

The Greeks too have been blown off course. Odysseus elicits that
the Cyclopes live here; they have no cities, no rulers, no democracy;
it is "each for himself and the devil take the hindmost." Reduplicated
negatives in Greek intensify instead of canceling, and these are very
intense: "Nobody obeys nobody in nothing" (120).

ODYSSEUS: Do they honor Demeter and sow corn? What do they
           live on?
SILENUS: Milk, cheese, and mutton.
ODYSSEUS: Do they honor Bacchus and enjoy the drink that flows from
           the vine?
SILENUS: No fear. No dancing in this land.
ODYSSEUS: Do they show respect to foreigners? Do they welcome
           them?
SILENUS: They claim that foreigners provide the tastiest joints.
ODYSSEUS: What's that? Cannibals?
SILENUS: All visitors are consumed. (121)

However the Cyclops is at the moment away. Odysseus wants meat
and cheese: he offers in payment not money but wine. Silenus is de-
lighted. He uses the language of the bonds of friendship (*philia*, 140).
He plays oneupmanship with Odysseus. Maron gave Odysseus the
wine; Silenus knew him when he was "so high." The wine is poured
gurglingly out; it has a rich feminine bouquet.

ODYSSEUS: There.
SILENUS: Whew! What a *beautiful* bouquet!
ODYSSEUS: Can you *see* it?
SILENUS: No, by Zeus, but I can scent it! (153)

Odysseus tells him to taste it, so that his testimonial is not merely
theoretical. He offers money as well. "To hell with the money," says
Silenus. "Open the wineskin," and he goes into the cave to get the
provisions.
     During the scene there would have been a deal of business with the
chorus jealous of Silenus and trying to intercept the wine. Now that
he has gone, they crowd around Odysseus, a little nervously. They have

a question. "Did you really capture Troy—and Helen?" (177). Odysseus answers pompously: "Assuredly; we destroyed—root and branch —the halls of the Priamidae." The chorus plunges in. "Did you all screw her, one after another? She seems to like changing husbands!" Their mood is "damn all women—but leave one or two for me." Silenus interrupts this interesting theme, but as he comes out with the provisions we may imagine a "Fee Fi Fo Fum" offstage, and, petrified, they see the Cyclops approaching. There is no time to escape. Silenus cunningly tries to lure the Greeks into the cave; they decide to face it out, so Silenus slips into the cave, and no doubt tries to take the wine with him.

The Cyclops, a colossal figure with a monstrous one-eyed mask, enters with a parody of the words of a wedding hymn; a modern equivalent might be to have a record playing the Bridal March from *Lohengrin*. Why are the satyrs idle? He has not noticed Odysseus and the Greeks. "Come on," he says, as their eyes are guiltily downcast, "look up not down." With an exaggerated movement they all stare straight up at the sky. "Is breakfast ready?" They nudge one another and point at Odysseus. "Yes!" "How's the milk?" "All poured out." Then (218), in a parody of Aeschylus, "Ovine or bovine or a synthesis." Suddenly he espies the Greeks. "Ha! Pirates?"

Silenus rolls out, his head hastily bandaged, his clothes torn, his gait genuinely unsteady. He claims that he has been beaten up by the Greeks while trying to defend the Cyclops's possessions. He tells the Cyclops that the Greeks were going to tie up the Cyclops himself, disembowel him, flay him, and take what was left to sell as a slave for hard labor. The Cyclops towers over the puny men and coolly says "Really?" Then "Sharpen the axe and light the fire. I'm tired of venison and lion's meat. I've not had a good man for ages." Odysseus calls Silenus a liar. Silenus protests:

> By your father Poseidon, Cyclops,
> by Triton in his power, by Nereus,
> by Calypso, by Nereus's daughters,
> by the sacred seamen—

There is an abscene pun here, which I have adapted—

> by every sort of fish,
> I solemnly swear, dear, beautiful Cyclops,
> my pretty little master, I am not engaged in selling
> your property to strangers. (262)

Christopher Fry uses the same device of humor in *A Phoenix Too Frequent*:

TEGEUS: I swear. I swear by Horkos and the Styx,
             I swear by the nine acres of Tityos,
             I swear by the Hypnotic oath, by all the Titans—
             By Koeos, Krios, Iapetos, Kronos, and so on—
             By the three Hekatoncheires, by the insomnia
             Of Tisiphone, by Jove, by jove.
DYNAMENE: You needn't
             Labour to prove your secondary education.

"If I'm lying," says Silenus, "may hell take—my sons." The sons promptly repudiate their father and add a plea for hospitality to strangers. But the Cyclops accepts Silenus's version of events. He fires the stock questions at Odysseus: "Who are you? Where do you come from?" Odysseus answers cautiously, but alludes to the Trojan War; the Cyclops does not accept the sense of a war over a woman. Odysseus, a born talker, tries to talk his way out of the situation with an appeal to religion. His speech is carefully constructed in the best professional debating style: Euripides is parodying himself. It cuts no ice. He ends with an aphorism: "Many have found ill-gotten gains bring disaster with them." Silenus cuts in:

> I warn you straight. Don't leave a morsel
> of meat from him. Get your teeth into his tongue,
> Cyclops, and you'll talk the hindlegs off a donkey. (313)

"Look, Shorty," says the giant, "sensible men have one god—Wealth. All the rest is hot air. I'm not afraid of Zeus's thunderbolts. I'm as strong a god as he is. I don't care, because when it rains I go into my cave, and when I've had a good meal, my noises rival his. My belly's my god. What more does anyone want than food and drink and no troubles. This is Zeus. It's legislation that causes all the trouble.

Here's your guest-gift: a nice cauldron—on the fire. C'mon in, brother,
and be eaten." Odysseus cries:

> Zeus, god of hospitality, look at this! If you don't look at it,
> Zeus, you're no god and it's no use worshiping you. (354)

And they go in.

The passage of time and the gory events within are covered by a song
about them with a dance from the chorus. The exact meaning of their
words is uncertain, but we may represent it approximately and with
appropriate economy of language as "Lovely, tasty meal, Cyclops. . . .
No need to leave me any. . . . He's a real tough guy." The point is that
normally in the Greek world meat was eaten on sacrificial occasions
only, and shared. This is sick humor, of the type of Roald Dahl, or
Evelyn Waugh's *Black Mischief.*

Odysseus comes out from the cave. This is dramatically necessary.
We ask, if he can come out why does he not escape? Euripides provides the answer with a piece of old-school-tie morality about not letting the side down (478), though he teases us by holding it up to the
end of the scene. The truth is, as we realize when we reflect a moment,
that he cannot escape without his companions, since he needs them to
man the ship. As he emerges he staggers with horror; the movement
would have been grotesquely and melodramatically exaggerated by the
actor. It's more like a play than real life, he says. The satyrs ask in-
terestedly,

> What's up, Odysseus? Did that Cyclops make
> a meal of your dear friends? How disrespectful! (377)

Odysseus gives a parody of a messenger's speech, a skillful piece of
crime reporting with verbal photographs of the scene of the crime. Two
of his men had been cooked and eaten; the precise recipe is given. Then
Odysseus had a bright idea. He got the Cyclops drunk with wine (till
the Cyclops combined the themes of *xenia* and *philia*, the guest-friend
and the personal friend in speaking to him, 418) and has now left him
happily singing, the wails of the others providing a cacophonous discord. In telling of this, Euripides puts into Odysseus's mouth a splendid

parody of Aeschylus. Aeschylus had written, "I made his inmost self hot with the news." Odysseus says, "I made his inmost self hot with the—booze" (*kotoi* and *potoi*, 424). The chorus is on *philia* terms with Odysseus, who encourages them to leave the unmixed man (the man who is a bad mixer and is full of unmixed wine) and go for the girls (429).

Odysseus now unfolds a plan; he is like the Yvonne Arnaud character who was forever saying, "Aubrey, I've got an idea." At the moment the Cyclops is at the merry stage of tipsiness; he will want to go and find his pals. "Excellent," says one of the chorus, "so you're going to push him over a precipice." "No, you fool," answers Odysseus, who is not big enough to push Silenus over a precipice, let alone the Cyclops. "I use my brains." The Cyclops must be persuaded to keep the drink to himself, drink enough to become drowsy, and then they can put out his eye with a sharpened olive stake heated in the fire. The satyrs are overjoyed and offer to help lift up the stake. They will provide a burnt offering after the libation the Cyclops has poured down his throat (469). They start a rollicking riotous dance, then break into bibulous anacreontics, dividing into two groups, as the Cyclops is heard singing inside. He comes out with Silenus, and joins in, hiccuping as he sings and galumphing elephantinely as he dances.

The next scene is mainly dialogue between Odysseus and the Cyclops. The plot advances: the Cyclops is persuaded to keep the wine to himself and drink himself drowsy. As a reward he promises to eat Odysseus last; this is his hospitality gift (551). There is some Euripidean rationalism. Bacchus is a god, and the Cyclops likes belching up Bacchus, but wonders why a god should have a wineskin for a palace (525). There is some verbal humor, as when Odysseus says, "Drinking deep you must die with the cup" (571); the expression is proverbial and it is tempting in translation to use our "blind-drunk." Again, the Cyclops, who has been himself described as unmixed (429), says, "My pleasure's undiluted" (577), and Odysseus presently prays for "undiluted Sleep" to fall on him (602).

In particular, the Nobody episode is brought in. It does not play the important part in Euripides's plot that it does in *The Odyssey*. But

Euripides could hardly omit it, and he handles it well. At 535 the Cyclops says, "I'm getting drunk. Nobody's going to lay a hand on me." This is where Odysseus gets his idea, and his reaction at this moment must be visible to the audience. Then when the Cyclops asks his name, he replies "Nobody" (549). In addition to the verbal humor there is good foolery as Silenus drinks behind the Cyclops's back, and the chorus tries, we may assume, unsuccessfully, to steal a swig or two. There is a particularly good moment when Silenus achieves a long drink on the pretext of giving the Cyclops a demonstration lesson in drinking (564).

The humor becomes broader. The climax is an excellent drunk scene where the Cyclops sees sky and earth mixed, Zeus's throne and gods everywhere. He imagines the Graces trying to kiss him; there is plenty of scope for business with the chorus. The scene ends in rollicking obscenity when the Cyclops, now quite drunk, takes Silenus, the elderly, gross Silenus, for Ganymede, Zeus's cupbearer and Nancy-boy, and drags him into the cave for a fate worse than death.

Now the moment is near. Odysseus strengthens the chorus, and, with a mock-tragic prayer to the God of Fire and the God of Sleep, offspring of black Night, follows them:

> after all our glorious work at Troy,
> do not doom to death Odysseus and his crew
> at the hands of a being who cares not for god or man.
> Or I am bound to think Chance a god
> and the power of the gods subject to Chance. (603)

The chorus sings a brief song of triumph. The moment has come. Odysseus tiptoes out: "Stop this noise, creatures; you'll wake the Cyclops." So they all start standing stockstill, whispering and holding their breath. The sudden contrast is admirably comic. "Come in and we'll do the deed." But now the chorus show cold feet and make lame excuses: "I'm too far away; I've got a limp; I've sprained my ankle, standing still; I've got some dust in my eye." They decide not to join in actively, they'll help by singing a spell, and let the Carian (i.e., a cheap hired substitute—so much for Odysseus) face the danger.

> Yo-ho! Heave with a will!
> Thrust! Haste! Burn out the eye
> of the cannibal monster!
> Smoke out, burn out
> the shepherd of Etna!
> Twist! Turn! See that in pain
> he does you no harm! (656)

It is an excellent scene, with a spectacular, and perhaps spectacularly obscene, dance.

There is a scream from inside. The Cyclops comes into the cave entrance, his mask now changed to show the eye seared and bloody. "Who has hurt you?" ask the satyrs. "Nobody." "Then you aren't hurt. . . . Who has blinded you?" "Nobody!" "Then you're not blind." "I wish *you* were. Where is Nobody?" "Nowhere." The Cyclops blunders grotesquely round the stage banging his head as Odysseus and his men slip out; Euripides is too wise to attempt the scene with the sheep. Odysseus reveals himself and takes Silenus and the chorus with him in his getaway, as the Cyclops, with a curse on Odysseus that suggests that the latter is not wholly in the right, stumbles up an inner tunnel to throw rocks Homerically and hopefully at the departing ship; it is just possible that Euripides staged a final appearance of the blind monster on the *distegia*.

The play has been unwarrantably dismissed. Norwood writes, "Considered in itself it is of small value, though it must have formed an agreeable light entertainment." Grube assigns to it half a page in a book of 450 pages on *The Drama of Euripides*: "It is a competent piece of fooling, neither tragedy nor comedy but rather burlesque, with the wine-bibbing Silenus, the cowardly satyrs, the coarse, boastful, drunken Cyclops, as the butts. Tragic emotions are nowhere aroused, there is no subtlety, tragic or comic. It is all good, though not too clean fun, and contains little or no trace of Euripidean techniques and skills. It therefore has no real place in a study of Euripides's dramatic art, beyond being a further proof of his versatility." Murray more fairly calls it "gay and grotesque" and speaks of its "farcical and fantastic note"; but he too says that it is without any *arrière-pensée*. There is more to it than this.

In the first place it is very funny. It wins laughs more readily from a modern audience than even Aristophanes. Its humor is obvious, knockabout, and none the worse for that. It is good theater. Silenus pretending to work is good theater. The satyrs' Sicinnis dance and their mime of folding flocks are good theater. The Cyclops's entry to a wedding song is good theater; so is the visible, physical contrast between the colossal giant and puny Odysseus. The fooling as Silenus drinks behind the Cyclops's back is good theater. The scene with the Cyclops drunk is good theater. The rollicking obscenity over Silenus-Ganymede is good theater. The satyrs' spell-dance is good theater. The final scene and the blinded Cyclops blundering over the stage is good theater. We have spent too long in theaters waiting for something to happen, waiting in fact for Godot. Drama means action; theater means spectacle. It is not the function of the theater to express thoughts except through action. If the action has thought behind it, a play is more likely to have lasting qualities. But action comes first, and this is a play of action.

Second, there *is* thought behind the action. The play is compact of the New Learning and the new rationalism. Patterson is right when he says, "The tragic characters of Polyphemus and of Odysseus appear sometimes to be used to give occasion to Euripides to launch, mostly for veiled purposes of humor, scoffing sentiments without absolute conviction of blasphemy, to make innuendo at heroes and hero-worship, to emphasize for amusement the knavery and the semi-bestial nature of the satyrs and the satyr-chief Silenus. The play seems also occasionally intended to appeal to that restrained element of human nature which loves sometimes to relax and find almost barbaric amusement in moral revolt." This is true and well said. The whole of the Cyclops's speech—"Wealth is god for men of sense. . . . What do I care for Zeus's thunderbolt. . . . My god's my belly. . . . As for those who have complicated life by making laws they can go to hell. . . ." (316)—is designed to provide an intellectual shock, and there are many comparable passages.

Third, we must remember that the play had a context, even if we cannot now identify it, and that that context would have affected the response of the audience. There is no external evidence of the play's date. Scholars have tended to place it early, but on tenuous grounds. Stylistic consideration hardly applies, as we do not know enough about the style of satyr plays. If we are right in supposing that the satyr plays may have parodied an episode or theme in the earlier tragedies, then we may have a clue. The obvious episode is the putting out of the eye; this would suggest a link with *Hecabe*. But there is another possibility. There are certain parallels with *Iphigeneia among the Taurians,* notably in the theme of hospitality, and the whole interplay between *xenia* and *philia*. If this play belongs to 413, then the Sicilian setting takes on a fresh significance and seriousness. The Athenian expedition has been mauled; can it escape without being annihilated?

This leads to a final point, more difficult, more controversial. Euripides was notoriously a rationalist. The rationalism here is put into the mouth of the Cyclops. Is Odysseus any better? He talks too much; he is utterly unscrupulous; he is the very type of the Athenians as seen through the eyes of Thucydides. He is certainly here a comic figure, and scarcely sympathetic. There is an *agon* between a colossal monster and a puny Greek, and our first instinct is to go with the Greek.

But there is a subtler instinct. Which of us does not—at times—find himself on Goliath's side, wishing that just for once the little runt will not swing his way to the top? Which of us has not experienced a deep and intense loathing for 007 because, whatever stupid things he does, he always gets away with it in the end? To put it differently, in an *agon* between the monstrous giant and the puny Greek with technical knowhow, if we side with the underdog, where are our sympathies? Euripides sided with Medea against Jason—and with the Cyclops against Odysseus. It is important not to misunderstand this. The final scene is ludicrous. We cannot help laughing, but, if we are sensitive, our laughter has an echo that is grim. The majority left the theater roaring with laughter. A few, as they laughed, went away feeling a little uncomfortable. It was ultimately for those few that Euripides wrote.

39. SOPHOCLES: *ELECTRA*

The date of Sophocles's *Electra* is not wholly certain. Stylistic considerations place it after *King Oedipus* and before *Philoctetes* or *Oedipus
at Colonus*, but Sophocles's life was so long and the surviving plays so
few that this does not greatly help. The relationship of the play to that
of Euripides on the same theme is a matter of controversy. Probably,
though Wilamowitz argued weightily to the contrary, that of Sophocles
came first, but probably not by many years, and it may have been
Sophocles's play that suggested to Euripides a very different treatment.
If Euripides's *Electra* is rightly dated to 413, that of Sophocles will be
some time in the preceding five years.

The play is said, as we have seen, to be pro-satyric, and this goes far
to explaining its peculiar mood. The killing of Aegisthus and Clytemnestra by Orestes was to Aeschylus a problem, to Euripides a crime;
to Sophocles it was a drama. Hence its lack of clear moral comment.
Moses Hadas said, "A play which represents a man killing his mother
and her husband starts with birds singing and finishes with congratu-

lations on a good day's work." Another critic characterized the play as a "mixture of matricide and good spirits."

The comments are wrongly emphasized, for the matricide is hardly an issue. In Sophocles alone is Clytemnestra killed first; the climax is the killing of Aegisthus; this is, so to say, the taste in the mouth at the play's end. This is important, for some interpreters, including Kitto, go astray. It is not true that if Sophocles "abdicates his moral sense here he abdicates his title as poet." Nor is it true that we are intended to see Electra as Clytemnestra's daughter, tarred with her mother's brush, and to make the same moral judgment of them both. A man with a moral message and strong dramatic sense, like Euripides or Shaw, may frame his message in dramatic form and write a powerful play of lasting value; but there are also powerful plays of lasting value which do not depend upon any moral message at all, but upon theatrical and verbal effectiveness. A noncontroversial example in the lighter vein is *The Importance of Being Earnest*. This is the sort of play that Sophocles chooses to write, a play of theatrical and verbal effectiveness.

Three things follow. First, Sophocles centers his play on Electra. After Aeschylus, to make Orestes central would be inescapably to raise the moral issues. This is one reason for thinking that Sophocles antedates Euripides in treating the theme. He takes Electra as central so as to divert attention from the problem inextricably associated with Orestes; Euripides restores the problem while leaving Electra at the center. It is a remarkable rôle, one of the longest in Greek tragedy. She is in full view nine-tenths of the time; she plumbs the depths and climbs the heights of emotion; she has more lyric singing than any other protagonist in Sophocles. But secondly, Electra has to be seen against a backcloth. It is the merit of Thomas Woodard to have identified that backcloth in the interplay of *logos*, theory or speech, and *ergon*, actuality or action. Electra's movement between these two is her drama. Third, because of the concentration upon drama and the particular importance of Electra, the chorus tends to fall into insignificance. There are only three choral odes, comprising less than one-tenth of the whole and, unless their musical setting was something exceptional, they are of no great merit. This accords with its pro-satyric nature.

A further explanation is that the theme is developed through action, potential and actual, rather than reflection; that the typical choral theme of *sophrosune*, self-discipline, might be inappropriate here and lead to the sort of moral questions that Sophocles wishes to avoid; that such drama depends on the characters rather than the chorus, and the play is hence entitled *Electra* by contrast with Aeschylus's *The Libation Bearers*; that Electra provides the musical arias; and that Sophocles's drama takes its strength from its characters and, whatever Aristotle implies, he was not a sustainedly great writer of choral lyric as Aeschylus and Euripides were.

The scene is set before the palace at Mycenae, the comparatively recent art of scene painting in perspective provided—somewhere—a distant view of Argos. The time is established as dawn, symbolically and actually. Enter three figures, one old, two young. One of the latter is identified in the first line as Orestes; his unspeaking companion is Pylades. The old man is Orestes's tutor, the slave who supervised his boyhood upbringing. He is a curious figure. J. T. Sheppard has seen him as a master criminal, the archvillain of the piece; to others he appears slightly comic, like the guard in *Antigone* or the shepherd in *King Oedipus*. Perhaps rather he is a kind of personification of Apollo's oracular power, a human with a superhuman tinge, a controller of destiny. Yet he is a slave, and in another context we think of the tricky servant of New Comedy, Plautus, Goldoni, or P. G. Wodehouse. In the context of a pro-satyric play it is probably right to make him grotesque and to play for the laughs that would come without much encouragement.

From their conversation it is established that they are there by command of the oracle. The tutor is to be sent inside to spy out the land with a story of Orestes's death in a smash at a chariot rally; this prepares the way for one of the great things in Greek drama. Orestes and Pylades will meantime go and offer libations and a lock of hair at Agamemnon's tomb; we recall the recognition device of Aeschylus and wonder how Sophocles will use it. Through the prologue comes the *logos-ergon* contrast, the word *logos* occurs five times in Orestes's speech: once the contrast is explicit—"a *fictitious* death brings me *actual* security and glory" (59). Orestes is a man of *erga,* as his speech shows, soldier, sportsman, adventurer, man of action. There is another key word, *kairos,* time in the sense of opportunity; the word comes three times (22, 39, 75), and is in the last line of each of the speeches, as when Orestes says, "The opportunity has come, and opportunity presides over all human activity" (75).

Suddenly Electra's voice is heard, keening within. She is at this stage the embodiment of *logos,* thought and word without action. It is significant that her voice is heard within, for this is the way she is orientated. By contrast, they do not stay to listen; they leave to act. The scene of song and dance that follows lasts nearly two hundred lines as the chorus of local women joins Electra, and it offers the finest lyric writing in the play. After ten years Electra has still nothing to do but mourn Agamemnon. She is living in the past; yet at the same time she brings Agamemnon's murder into the present.

> Pure, holy light,
> and air, light's partner over earth,
> often my songs of sorrow,
> often the sound has reached you
> as I strike my breasts till the blood flows,
> when black night fails.
> Night through night the bed
> I loathe in this house of disaster
> shares all my tears for my lost
> father. (86)

The note of dawn has again sounded, but for Electra even dawn is dark. As Woodard says, "Whether mourning becomes Electra or not, it has become her life." She is all *logos*—words, words, words. She has two interesting and important comparisons of herself. The first is with the nightingale crying "Itys, Itys"; the chorus accepts this and much later in the play (1077) calls her "nightingale." The nightingale is inconsolable because it is faithful, and it is used in *The Odyssey* as a similitude of the faithful Penelope. Here Electra stands on contrast with the gay birds we have already heard. The second is with Niobe, who even when turned to stone continued to lament her children, another image from the Homeric poems. Her fate was not enviable, yet Electra envies her, and sees her as a goddess because her grief is eternal.

Early in her song, before the chorus enters, Electra calls upon the Furies (112). In Aeschylus they are for Clytemnestra, in Sophocles against her. Clytemnestra is not mentioned by name. Electra sings of "my mother and her lover Aegisthus" (97), the chorus of a "mother doomed to disaster" (121). When she is seen no longer as mother, she is doomed to death.

There is another important aspect to Electra's lament. Her name means "unwedded." In Euripides this will become a pathological disorder. But even in Sophocles there are strong sexual overtones in her words. She has no child, no husband; she says this more than once in different language. At the same time the chorus declares explicitly that lust murdered Agamemnon (198). In fact Electra's whole hope is projected on Orestes. All her sex energy is focused on him: "I pace up and down, without child, without husband, tirelessly waiting for Orestes" (164). The chorus's answer is, "Time is a god of healing" (179). But this is the answer of *logos*, for the word for time is *chronos*, mere transience, that which is measured by a chronometer and studied by chronology. Orestes has already given the answer of *kairos*, Lloyd George as opposed to Asquith, not "wait and see" but "act at the right moment." The song ends with Electra's desperate faith:

> For if *he* is to lie in the misery of death,
> dust, nothingness,
> and *they* not make
> just requital of blood for blood,
> there is an end to faith
> and piety in all mankind. (244)

The song and dance cease, and Electra reveals the true position to the chorus. There is a kind of verbal recognition scene, in which Clytemnestra is seen not as Electra's mother but as Aegisthus's mistress, living "unafraid of the Fury" (276). Aegisthus, "utterly feeble, utterly villainous, who uses women to fight his battles for him" (301), is identified as *the* murderer. Both are seen in a most unfavorable light, and in this we do not feel that Electra is misleading us, as we do in Euripides.

Sophocles now follows a device he has already used in *Antigone*; he brings on a sister of different character and caliber for purposes of contrast. This is Chrysothemis, a nice girl, but weak, who has already made her compromises. Her compromising mood—she knows and admits her weakness and Electra's rightness, and she cares for Electra—provokes Electra to quarrel. Electra is by no means the spotless heroine. We learn that when Aegisthus, who is away, returns, Electra is to be imprisoned away from the light of day and the sight of men; the purpose of this invention is partly to eliminate any residual sympathy for Clytemnestra and Aegisthus, partly to throw light on Electra, who welcomes the solitary confinement as a means of escape from life.

Then the temper of the scene changes. Chrysothemis is carrying libations from Clytemnestra to Agamemnon's tomb. The queen has had a frightening dream: Agamemnon, restored to life, seizing his scepter from Aegisthus and planting it so that it takes root and grows. Electra is encouraged by the dream and persuades Chrysothemis to throw away Clytemnestra's tributes and take offerings of their own instead; to this Chrysothemis agrees. The dream is full of peculiar interest. Sophocles eliminates the dream of the snake that Aeschylus used; on the one hand the meaning was too clear, on the other there was, as Aeschylus knew and intended, something not wholly healthy about the comparison of Orestes to a viper, and this effect was alien to Sophocles's purpose. This dream owes a debt to a dream of Xerxes in Herodotus. It is ambiguous: to see the dead is ill-omened, but a growing tree is a good omen, and there is nothing clearly to make Clytemnestra think of Orestes. The gods have sent a warning dream, and Clytemnestra, though disturbed enough to offer sacrifice, at the last, like Xerxes, does not heed the warning.

This scene is also full of *logos* and *ergon*. Chrysothemis challenges Electra as futile. Electra claims that she is active in help of her father, while,

> You say you hate, as I do. Hate in theory!
> In practice you side with our father's murderers. (357)

But Chrysothemis tells the chorus that she is used to Electra's stories (*mythoi,* 373; words without truth). After all, what does Electra do? Nothing. And she welcomes the prospect of being shut up where she will be able to do nothing. At the end it is Chrysothemis who both calls for silence, that is, fewer words, and also acts.

> I will do it. Right is not a matter for words
> or debate; it demands to be done, promptly.
> I will attempt this act.
> But O my friends, for god's sake keep your counsel. (466)

She goes, and the chorus sings, briefly, relevantly, and on the whole unmemorably. Justice *will* come; the Fury *will* come; there will be an end of the suffering of the house. Their song is compact of Aeschylean themes.

A long scene follows, three hundred lines without a break, and, taking in the lament (*kommos*), which does not technically constitute a break, five hundred and forty. The scene falls into four sections. In the first Clytemnestra confronts Electra. She tries to justify her killing of Agamemnon by reference to his killing of Iphigeneia; she claims that justice was on her side. Electra's answer is that Artemis called for the sacrifice of Iphigeneia, that Clytemnestra was motivated by lust, that she is no mother, but a jailer, and that her admission that she killed Agamemnon is enough.

> It was not for Menelaus.
> But let me take your view. If he had done the act
> desiring to help his brother, was it right for him
> to die at your hands? What sort of law is that?
> Bring in that law among mankind, and watch out:
> you're bringing on your own head troubles you'll regret.
> If the law is to stand "Life for life," your life
> is forfeit first, if justice is to be done. (576)

It is true, at least on the face of it, as Kitto says, that this would expose Electra to the same condemnation at the play's end; true also that she ends her speech in a way that could link her to Clytemnestra:

> For this
> denounce me publicly, call me vile,
> call me foul-mouthed, call me criminal.
> If my nature is familiar with these actions,
> it's a close tribute to yours. (605)

But the point is dramatic not moral. Electra does not think that she is like that, and the chorus says that she is moved more by anger than by justice. She is not like Clytemnestra, precisely because she does not act; her world is the world of words. The interchange that follows picks up this antithesis.

ELECTRA: Atrocity learns from atrocities.
CLYTEMNESTRA: You shameless creature! you talk far too much
                       of what I am and what I say and what I do. (622)

When Orestes leads Electra across the boundary between word and deed, Clytemnestra dies.

ELECTRA: You say it, not I; for you do
                       the act, and acts find words for themselves.
CLYTEMNESTRA: Now by queen Artemis, you shall not go unpunished
                       for this insult, once Aegisthus returns. (624)

How dare she appeal to Artemis! She has more offerings to counter her dream and prepares to go out with them, with a prayer to Apollo.

But now follows the second part of the scene. The tutor enters with the feigned news of Orestes's death. He says it bluntly, and the word breaks Electra. The *logos* is, for her, *ergon,* the fiction an experienced reality. Clytemnestra has no pity: "Mind your own business. Speak to me sir, tell me the whole story. How did he die?" (678). The speech that follows is one of the most brilliant things in Greek literature, in all literature. Who in our day ever reported the death of poor Donald Campbell with a fraction of comparable power? It is brilliant, accurate, exciting, persuasive, delusive. It stands right athwart the middle of the play. There is an interesting and deliberate debt to Euripides's *Hippolytus.* There the news that seems to fulfill Theseus's desire is in fact disastrous. Here the news, which seems to frustrate Electra's desire, is in fact the prelude to success. Again we remember that this is pro-satyric, not full tragedy. Clytemnestra's response to it is now ambiguous:

O Zeus, what shall I say? Is this triumph?
Or tragedy, from which I am the gainer? It's a sorry state
if I can only keep my life at my own loss. (766)

To suffer is the opposite, the passive of action. Clytemnestra feels as a mother. Waldock comments: "Clytemnestra drops a tear—and notes her emotion with surprise. It is only a passing pang, a reaction of some nerve of motherhood, not quite atrophied even in her." The tutor says that his errand has been thankless; he means in part that if her sorrow is genuine then there is no room for the vengeance. Clytemnestra, however, shows that relief is her dominant emotion, and so condemns herself. Dreadful is the exchange:

ELECTRA: Show your *hybris*; you're landed in success.
CLYTEMNESTRA: Will you and Orestes stop me?
ELECTRA: We've been stopped ourselves; we can't stop you. (794)

But they can.

The third part of the scene is the *kommos,* a broken and often single-word lamentation in song between Electra and the chorus, deeply and genuinely affecting. Its very opening is pointed; for the chorus the sun has grown dark. Then onto the scene comes Chrysothemis, running in joy. She has seen new libations and a lock of hair at Agamemnon's tomb. It must be Orestes; who else can it be? Electra disillusions, or rather, illusions her. Orestes is dead, and the messenger who brought the news has received a royal welcome. But who has brought the offerings? Electra dismisses the question: someone in memory of Orestes. And now we see a change in Electra. Now she seeks to change from *logos* to *ergon*. She proposes that they, the two girls, should kill Aegisthus; there is no mention of Clytemnestra. These are women of the heroic age, but the suggestion is to be seen against the background of Athenian society; we have the counterpart of *Lysistrata* or *The Parliament of Women.* To the chorus and Chrysothemis this is still *logos*: it is not a practical possibility. Electra presses on; she will go it alone. Chrysothemis comments meaningfully:

If only you had shown the same determination on the day
our father died. You could have done anything. (1021)

An extra-metrical exclamation picks out the couplet. The bill is true.

ELECTRA: I had the same nature but a different judgment.

CHRYSOTHEMIS: Stick to that judgment.

She means that wishful thinking is better than rash action.

ELECTRA: Yes, you give that advice in refusing to act with
                  me. (1023)

A little later:

ELECTRA: Don't you agree my *words* are just?
CHRYSOTHEMIS: Justice can be dangerous.
ELECTRA: I don't want to live by that principle.
CHRYSOTHEMIS: If you do *act*, you'll see that I was right. (1041)

In fact Chrysothemis is wrong; it is the words without the actions
that are dangerous. The long scene is over, and the chorus sings to
Electra of her courage and faithfulness. It is interesting that they call
Clytemnestra and Aegisthus "a double Fury" (1081). They end on the
note of "the mighty laws of Zeus" (1095).

There follows another very great scene. Up to this point we are two-
thirds of the way through the play, and not appreciably nearer the
dénouement. Now Orestes and Pylades return, carrying an urn that
is almost a character: we see it on an exquisite vase painting in Vienna,
dominating the scene. They have brought the suppositious ashes of
Orestes to Aegisthus. Electra asks to hold the urn, and Orestes, not
knowing who she is, passes it to her. The speech that follows is of the
utmost beauty, yet we must remind ourselves that she is sorrowing
over an illusory death.

> I hold a memory, all that is left of the dearest
> of all men to me. O Orestes, this is not the welcome
> I hoped to give you when I saw you go.
> I saw you go in the brilliance of boyhood,
> and now I clasp—a handful of nothingness.
> Better that I had looked my last on life
> than that I should have seen you go to a foreign land,
> smuggling you out to keep you safe from murder.
> You would have fallen in death that very day
> and shared the inheritance of our father's grave.
> Now, away from home, a refugee in a foreign land,
> you have met your death in misery, without your sister near.

Grief on grief! I was not there with loving hands
to perform the rites of washing or to lay
the sad burden, as my duty called, upon the pyre.
Strange hands decked out your body for burial,
and here you are, a little dust in a little urn. (1126)

She ends:

Brother, dear brother, you have brought me to my death.
Welcome me into this shelter of yours,
nothing to nothing, that I may be with you
below forever. While you were here above,
we shared and shared alike. Now I long
to die and share your grave.
I do not see trouble afflicting the dead. (1164)

She has, as Robert Corrigan put it in an acute analysis, "given up
to time." Orestes now knows who she is, and is much moved—more
when she speaks of her affliction at the hands of a mother who is no
mother (1194). Sophocles's handling of the scene deserves close attention. Thirty-three lines of *stichomythia* end when Orestes tells her
to give back the urn. She begs him by his chin, reaching out one hand
to touch. He now has an abrupt half-line: "I tell you I can't let you"
(1209). She, in one and a half lines, "O Orestes, I shall be in utter
misery if your tomb is taken from me." The *stichomythia* returns:

ORESTES: Speak words of good omen. You are not right to weep.
ELECTRA: Not right to weep for my dead brother?
ORESTES: Don't say that word.
ELECTRA: Have I no rights in my dead brother?
ORESTES: You have no rights in—nothing. This is nothing to do with you.
ELECTRA: Nothing—in that I'm holding Orestes's body here?
ORESTES: That is not Orestes, except in *logos*.

She still does not understand. "Then where is his tomb?" "Nowhere: a living man has no tomb." A silence; then in breathless half-
lines: "What did you say?" "The truth." "He's alive?" "As I am
alive." This time there is no mistake. "Is it really you?" Then in a line
and a half, "Look: father's signet, do you believe me now?" Then
surely another pause, and she flings herself into his arms. All her sis-

terhood, all her stifled daughterhood, all her pent-up bridal love, all her unleashed motherliness flood out.

For the next fifty lines Electra sings her joy, and Orestes tries to instill action in the language of conversation. She is still *logos*, he *ergon*. She, appropriately, invokes the virgin huntress Artemis. He reminds her that Ares, the war god, is sometimes found in women, as she has good cause to know. The key word *kairos* returns. Orestes says, "No long *talk* when it is not *timely*" (1259). Electra calms herself, and Orestes looks for action: "*Words* would hinder the *timeliness* of the moment" (*kairon chronou* 1292). Electra, calmer but still excited, reveals her hatred for her mother and her lingering love for her father: if he were to appear, she would believe him alive again (1316); there is a sinister reminder of Clytemnestra's dream.

She steels herself to act a part, and is about to usher them in when the tutor, their guardian deity, comes out. Every word was audible in the palace; the words are an incidental reminder of the ebullience of natural Greek behavior and the degree of projection the actors must have brought to their parts. Fortunately he was seeing that no one else heard. Electra almost panics at his appearance, then, being told who he is, bursts into hysterical joy, and calls him "father." There is a lightness hereabouts that reminds us that the play is pro-satyric. The tutor brings them up short with a douche of cold common sense. Words can be left to the future. Now is the time (*kairos*) to act; now Clytemnestra's alone; now there is no male inside (1368). The insistent "now" is compelling. Orestes uses a striking phrase, "There's no action in words" (1372), and as they go in Electra offers a prayer to Apollo, bitingly echoing Clytemnestra's earlier words (1376, cf. 655) and follows them in: this is the only moment when she acknowledges Apollo.

The chorus sings a very brief song (another indication of pro-satyric drama)—barely fifty words—when Electra bursts out. It has taken us fourteen hundred lines to reach this point: the rest follows with unparalleled swiftness and is over in a hundred lines. The swift onset of bliss seems to have been characteristic of the pro-satyric plays. Electra has been sent out to watch for Aegisthus. Suddenly there is a cry from within. Electra is now deadly calm: "There is someone shouting inside the house. Do you hear, my friends?" (1406). The chorus shrinks away. Clytemnestra's voice is heard again. Electra is still calm. "Another scream." Clytemnestra's voice rings out: "My son, be gentle with your mother." Then Electra shouts at the closed doors: "You weren't gentle with him—or his father." Another scream from inside—and another shout: "Hit him back—if you can." Then the death shriek, and another shout: "I wish Aegisthus were with you." Then silence.

Orestes and Pylades come out with dripping hands. Electra, conversationally: "All right?" Orestes: "All right . . . if Apollo was right." Orestes's words do not represent doubt, but a difference between Electra and Orestes. Orestes acts in response to Apollo; Electra is governed by her own emotions arising from her own experience. But Aegisthus is approaching. The young men slip back into the palace, and there follows Sophocles's final master stroke. In fifty lines he sketches a man of brutal but dominant authority. The dramatic irony is startling, even for Sophocles. A volatile audience will laugh, but not in a comic mood.

AEGISTHUS: Where are the visitors?
ELECTRA: Inside: they have found a way to their hostess's heart.

The words are terrible, two-edged.

AEGISTHUS: Did they genuinely tell of Orestes's death.
ELECTRA: No—they offered practical proof, not words.
AEGISTHUS: Can I see with my own eyes?
ELECTRA: You can. You won't like the sight.
AEGISTHUS: You don't usually bid me "fare well!"

—another terrifying ambiguity.

ELECTRA: Fare well, if it serves your welfare. (1450)

The shrouded body, which he believes to be that of Orestes and is in fact Clytemnestra, is pushed out on the moving platform, with Orestes and Pylades standing over it.

AEGISTHUS: O Zeus, I have seen a semblance of divine jealousy
            in action. If those are guilty words, count them unsaid.
            Release the veil from the face. The body
            was close to me and should have my tears.

ORESTES: Stretch out your hand yourself. What is here is yours not
              mine—yours to look on this sight with loving words.
AEGISTHUS: Well said, I will comply. [The word could mean "suffer."]
                                      You, Electra,
              call Clytemnestra, if she's at home.
ORESTES: She's right by you. No need to look for her elsewhere.
AEGISTHUS: God, what I am seeing?
ORESTES: Of whom are you afraid? Whom don't you
                                                  recognize? (1466)

Aegisthus tries to talk, but Electra cuts across with the determination
to kill. She has passed from word to act.

ORESTES: Inside with you. Hurry. The issue is not
              now of *words*. Your life is at stake.
AEGISTHUS: Why force me indoors? If the *deed* is good,
              what need of darkness? (1941)

But they edge him in and the play abruptly ends with three anapaestic
lines from the chorus:

              Race of Atreus, you have suffered much,
              won perilously through to freedom,
              found fulfillment in this enterprise. (1508)

There are no Furies, no problem, only the end of tension and the certainty of right.

By making Clytemnestra and Aegisthus unadulterated villains Sophocles has created a melodrama rather than a tragedy. The analysis
of the play confirms it as pro-satyric. Its lasting qualities depend upon
two factors. First there is the character and personality of Electra.
She has been much misunderstood. She is certainly not the blue-
eyed innocent whom Letters saw as "a clear-eyed, conscientious
heroine whose very hatred is rooted in love and justice." Kitto was
closer in calling her "a woman of heroic qualities, capable of great
natural affection, loyalty and self-sacrifice, but warped by circumstances
into something terrible: a woman as capable as Antigone of self-ab-
negation before an ideal, only that ideal is murder." But the portrait is
subtler than that. Electra has a fundamental integrity of purpose. But

all her sex energy is focused upon Orestes and has no outlet; she remains a dreamer and talker, and only when her libido is released does she become a doer.

Alongside the character of Electra stands the sheer dramatic and theatrical skill of the play, especially in the first lyrical sequence, the messenger's speech, Electra's speech over the urn, the recognition scene, and the manipulation of dramatic irony after Aegisthus's arrival.

The structure is in fact brilliantly conceived. At the start of the play Orestes establishes the plot; at the end he fulfills it. The center of the play is the tutor's description of the chariot race; Chrysothemis with her two scenes frames this. The false death in the center balances the real deaths at the end. The deceit at the center is important; one aspect of the structure is that each scene after the opening has two or three people, at least one of whom is blind to the truth. The pattern, as Segal has shown, is enhanced by the interplay of life and death. On the one hand, Hades "is a vivid and insistent presence" (110, 137, 463, 542, 833, 939, 1342); on the other, "the play is full of the language of growth, birth, fertility." As he points out, the play, in plot and imagery, moves from death to life.

Yet it is from a faded, half-forgotten death, from the spiritual death of a house, from a fictitious death, to a life that is found through two new deaths, and this is marked by a regress from the light of dawn in which the play opens to the darkness in which the killing of Aegisthus is consummated. The patterns are subtle and elaborate. Waldock summed up the play well:

> Sophocles did not bring the moral problem into focus; the moral problem was what he suppressed. It is not that he could not see it (that might have been the case with Pindar). He was not inclined to make it his theme. That was perhaps reprehensible of him, but who are we to repine? He has given us a remarkable play. It is stronger in some ways than the *Antigone*. Electra is an extraordinary study. Sophocles is *closer* to feelings than before. And the skill with which our curiosities are whetted, the superb drawing out of the material, the absolute command of the timing—all these are things to be prized. Sophocles aims lower than he could: but how much occasion for our thanks! The *Electra* is not a great tragedy, is not even (in a deep way) a tragedy; it is still a play by a very great dramatist. And in what other play of the seven can we so observe the sleights of the Master?

40. EURIPIDES: *ORESTES*

Orestes was presented in 408; it is a harsh, bitter play, one of the last Euripides wrote before leaving Athens for Macedon. In the light of all that has gone before it is reasonable to see the harshness and bitterness as arising out of the renewal and by now long-drawn continuation of the war with Sparta. The theme "madness leads to violence" does not have as its logical correlative "violence arises from madness," but it is easy to pass from the one to the other. The play is related to *Electra*; it is in fact a reenactment of the murder there, with Helen playing the part of her sister Clytemnestra, and Orestes and Electra reversing roles. It is also related to *Helen*. There the Trojan War was fought over a phantom Helen. Here a murder plot is carried out against a phantom Helen. The result might almost be, anachronistically, an Epicurean parable of the vanity of violence.

There is a further problem about *Orestes*. We have already noticed evidence from the Byzantine period suggesting that *Orestes*, like *Alcestis*, was pro-satyric. It is hard to see why this view should survive if it were not true. Additional evidence is provided by the introductions, one of which describes *Alcestis* as satyric in manner because it moves to a dénouement of joy and delight, and links *Alcestis* and *Orestes* as plays that are not at home in tragedy, having strong affinities with comedy. One of the introductions to *Orestes* comments that the dénouement is close to comedy. But this is not just a matter of the happy ending: *Iphigeneia among the Taurians* and *Helen* have that. The scene with the Phrygian slave is undoubtedly comic, as the scholiasts saw and commented. But there is a mood of fantasy as well; one is tempted to say that whether or not *The Women of Phoenicia* and *Orestes* belong to the same cycle they cannot belong to the same *genre* of drama. The length of *Orestes* is somewhat against the authenticity of the tradition; yet we know of so few satyr plays in proportion to Euripides's total output that there must have been other pro-satyric plays beside *Alcestis*, and this disposes us to place *Orestes* in that category. If so, it may have completed the trilogy *Oenomaus, Chrysippus, The Women of Phoenicia*.

The play contains no prologue of the sort Euripides made familiar. Electra is discovered watching over a bundle of rags that turns out to be Orestes; in this play, as in a few others, we feel a convention that the actors may take up their positions before the play begins. Her opening words are curiously philosophical:

> There is scarcely anything so terrible,
> no human suffering, no disaster brought by gods,
> that human nature may not have to bear the burden of it. (1)

She goes straight on to speak of the blood feud in her own family, and in this way passes from the general to the particular. As she leads up to the killing of Clytemnestra, she begins to wallow in her own emotions, with a deal of self-deception. Uncertainties peer through: "glorious Agamemnon, if he really is glorious" (17), or (of the murder) "not to all bringing glory" (30). She shows a curious coyness that will not allow her to speak of Clytemnestra's behavior (26) and plays down her own part in the murder (32); this is not the Electra of *Electra*. Responsibility for the murder she lays squarely on Apollo (30, cf. 76). Then she turns to the prostrate figure of Orestes. She describes his disease (34), an important theme, and another important theme appears in her description of it as savage; presently she describes him as behaving like a colt (45).

Orestes is the quarry of the Furies, and the development of the play will show the hunted becoming the hunter. Meantime, for five days he has been lying unwashed and fasting. The Argive assembly has decreed that no one shall welcome the matricides, and will that very day determine whether they should suffer death by stoning. Their one hope lies in Menelaus; he had left his daughter Hermione with Clytemnestra during his absence at Troy, and on his return had smuggled Helen up by night for fear that those who had lost sons at Troy might stone her. So Euripides establishes the theme of war.

He establishes also a novelty of plot. The opening leads us to expect *The Kindly Goddesses* rehashed, and the decision of the Assembly at Argos is an almost parodic parallel to the trial before the Areopagus; what we find is something startlingly different. Electra is well characterized, with some tenderness to her brother, but otherwise unstable and excited; her speech has numerous resolutions of long syllables into short, and two lines (20, 65) have no fewer than three examples.

Her references to Helen prepare us for Helen's entry. It is important that we establish the link between Helen and Clytemnestra, and this is enforced by the mention of her sister twice in her opening words. Helen is present to our eyes only for this short scene of little over fifty lines, but she is brilliantly portrayed, beautiful of course, self-satisfied, and without thought for or understanding of anyone but herself. There is the same visual contrast that Euripides used in *The Women of Troy*, between her elegance and the rags of the rest. Her opening words are tactless enough

> Child of Clytemnestra and Agamemnon,
> Electra, marriage has passed you by for long years. . . . (71)

Helen will not allow Electra to make Apollo responsible for the murder (76) but claims that her own acts were divinely directed (79); Electra will not allow Helen the justification she claims for herself

(99); they are in fact tarred with the same brush. Helen is afraid to move around for fear of the parents of the dead soldiers (102), another reminder of this theme. With incredible tactlessness she wants Electra to carry offerings for her to Clytemnestra's tomb. Electra suggests that she might send Hermione, and Helen, who has just been taunting Electra on her unmarried state, counters by saying that unmarried girls should not appear in public. However she changes her mind, calls Hermione out and sends her with the offering of a lock of hair. Helen goes in and Electra explodes in vehement hatred.

The chorus makes a spectacular entrance, tiptoeing in and singing *pianissimo* so that they will not wake Orestes. Electra sings to them in breathless short syllables. Her words are of the grace of sleep, and she invokes Night in beautiful poetry to spread her sheltering wings over Agamemnon's house (174). Apollo's justice, she cries, was unjust and he himself unjust (162); she reverts to the theme of Apollo's responsibility for the bloodshed. "With justice," sings the chorus, employing the particle *men*, which anticipates a contrasting rejoinder, and Electra supplies this "But not with righteousness" (194).

Orestes wakes; his first words are of sleep, the ally against disease (211). The word "ally" anticipates the arrival of Menelaus, who proves a vain ally. The scene that follows is justly famed. On the one hand we have the *treue Geschwisterliebe* of Electra as she holds her brother up from the ground and wipes the foam from his lips, and her care and love for him all through the scene to her final resolve:

> No. My choice is firm: to live or die
> with you. (307)

On the other hand we have Orestes, awakening to weakness, bursting out in mad fury. Electra tells him that Menelaus has arrived, and the proof is Helen. Here we may think that Helen has come out on the balcony at first-floor level to watch the scene. Her appearance is Electra's evidence; she points up. Orestes scorns Helen; Electra recalls that Helen and Clytemnestra were both children of Tyndareus; Orestes bursts out telling her not to behave like that, but his words are ambiguous and ironical: "Be different from those crooks" or "Outdo those

crooks" (251). "Don't just talk, but set your mind on these things,"
he goes on; she sees his eyes rolling and cries in horror. Then the climax is marked as, in an interchange of two lines each, he extends his
words to three lines, whirling around, seeing Helen in her sister's
image, and crying "Please, mother, don't . . ." (255). Now madness is
upon him in what Mullens called "the most horrific moment in Greek
tragedy"; the unrestricted portrayal owes something to Sophocles's example in *Philoctetes*. He sees his mother's Furies with their hound faces
and Gorgon eyes. Electra tries to hold him down, but he throws her
off.

> Let me go. You are one of my Furies.
> You're holding me by the waist to throw me into Hell. (264)

She is indeed one of his Furies. Now he calls for the horn-tipped
bow that Apollo gave him. Later actors mimed the archery, but there
is nothing in the language to suggest that the bow is imaginary, and it
might be more effective with a real bow and arrows shot at empty air,
with perhaps one fired up toward Helen as she hastily retires. Then
sanity returns as swiftly as it had departed. After the stormy waves
he sees a calm: a line notorious for its mispronunciation by an actor
who turned into a weasel (279). Electra's head is in her hands. He
now tries to comfort her. The guilt is his; no, not his but Apollo's; and
the murder of Clytemnestra did Agamemnon no good. She must not
break down; she is his only ally (305). So Electra goes in to rest, de-
pendent on him as he on her, leaving him lying on his stretcher, either
ill or with the delusion of illness (314). Euripides is suggesting that
Orestes's illness is psychologically self-induced. This scene is in fact
brilliantly contrived. For the moment our sympathy is with Orestes in
his sickness, but the last words sound a warning; what will he do in his
sanity? For the moment Electra is tender and seemingly lovable, but
she will be ready to outdo her mother's crimes.

The chorus takes Electra's task of watching over Orestes as they sing,
pleading first with the Furies and then with Zeus to release him; again
we recall Aeschylus. Their song is strengthened by powerful repetitions of long words (324, 339), and by the continued imagery of the
storm at sea.

> Some power has torn at the sail
> of their scudding boat, plunged her
> in tossing death-dealing waves
> of commotion, of ocean. (340)

The assonance points the imagery. We have a short fragment of the music of this song, but it is impossible to build much on it.

Menelaus enters with pomp and circumstance, from stage-right, and the chorus breaks into anapaests to greet him. The scene that follows is very long, lasting all of 450 lines, more than a quarter of the whole play. It is Shavian, a "talky" scene with little action. But it is skillfully organized. The main part of the scene is, so to say, in sonata form ABA, the dialogue with Menelaus being interrupted by the arrival of Tyndareus. The scene seems over and we expect a choral ode, when we find a coda in the arrival of Pylades and his conversation with Orestes. The apparent inconsequence is meticulously planned. Throughout the major part of the scene Menelaus stands for good sense, cleverness, opportunism, political adroitness (*sophia*), Orestes for love, affection, friendship (*philia*). The scene with Pylades is packed with friendship. We have seen the compromises of cleverness; we have yet to see the criminalities of friendship.

Menelaus appears—home at last. He has heard from the sea god Glaucus of Agamemnon's death in "the last bath his wife will ever give him"; the words have a ludicrous element covering their grimness. He was looking forward to greeting Orestes and his mother; the not-very-bright Menelaus had not realized what the god was saying. Then he heard from a sailor of the shocking murder of Tyndareus's daughter. Now he is looking for Orestes; we have the impression of a man who takes a moral situation as he finds it. Orestes identifies himself, and Menelaus is horrified at his appearance; he finds it hard to look below the surface physically or spiritually.

ORESTES: Here I am, my poor mother's murderer.
MENELAUS: So I have heard: you can leave off. With horror, least said soonest mended.
ORESTES: I will leave off—but fate has been generous with horrors for me.

MENELAUS: What's wrong with you? What's your disease?
ORESTES: Conscience; I know my guilt.
MENELAUS: I don't understand; good sense lies in clarity not obscurity.

(392)

Orestes sees one hope. Menelaus thinks he means suicide: most unwise (*sophon*, 415). This was not in Orestes's mind. Apollo commanded: Apollo must save. "We are slaves of the gods, whatever the
gods may be" (418). Only he is taking his time, as gods always do.
Orestes asks Menelaus for help: "I am not clever but I love my friends"
(424). Argos is against him, especially Palamedes's son Oeax (432).
This particularity serves a treble purpose. First, there is irony: Orestes
is to suffer for what his father did to another man's father. Second,
there is allusion: according to one story Oeax had falsely told Clytemnestra that Agamemnon was unfaithful to her, and for this reason she
took Aegisthus as her lover. The allusion complicates our sympathies;
we favor Orestes in face of prejudice, but also move to Clytemnestra
and therefore away from Orestes. Third, there is a political point: if
in the Assembly one man's motive is vengeance rather than justice, may
this not be more widely true? How can such decisions be trusted? Orestes used a metaphor from wrestling to express his utter humiliation;
he has been thrown three times (434). Menelaus, stupid in his as-
tuteness, does not understand: "Who else besides Oeax?" The city will
vote on Orestes's case that very day. Orestes again appeals to Menelaus:

> Friends who are not friends in time of misfortune
> bear the name of friendship without the substance. (454)

We expect Menelaus's answer, but the dialogue is interrupted by
the arrival of Orestes's maternal grandfather Tyndareus, mourning
his daughter, come to greet Menelaus. There is an interesting point
of staging here. Tyndareus enters from stage-left. Orestes crouches
down at the far side of Menelaus to evade notice. But Tyndareus crosses
to give Menelaus a well-omened greeting from the right, and in so
doing sees the lad. Tyndareus refuses to address him; he speaks of
him as a snake with disease blazing from his eyes (479). Menelaus

shows tolerance; Tyndareus says that he has been abroad too long. Menelaus still talks about good sense (*sophia*). Tyndareus stands for law.

Where Aeschylus uses the saga to establish the rule of law and oust the blood feud, Euripides makes the murder a crime in which the murderers have refused to appeal to a law that is already established. Those interpreters who suggest that Tyndareus is sophistic and Clytemnestra and Aegisthus are above the law are clearly wrong, since Orestes does not make the point in reply. To Euripides, Apollo's command to kill was a flagrant breach of the ordered society that, in Aeschylus, was established by Zeus. But to Tyndareus the law stood for banishment not death, and Euripides is establishing the further point that the political Assembly, which condemned Orestes to die by stoning, was going beyond the bounds of law: it is almost as if he foresaw the mass condemnation of the Athenian generals after the battle of Arginusae two years later. Tyndareus makes his point with great reasonableness. He does not defend Clytemnestra—or Helen. He defends the rule of law against the unending assertion of private vengeance. Then suddenly, unexpectedly, for the first time he turns to Orestes; his anger overcomes his fear of pollution—and his rationality. Orestes is to be stoned; his madness is the sign of his guilt.

Orestes's reply is in its way as brilliant as anything Euripides ever wrote, because it is so bad. It is charged with a kind of adolescent eloquence. It is clever in an opportunist, Menelaan way. It contains no trace of the love Orestes has boasted. It evades the central charge as effectively as Demosthenes or Cicero was ever to do, and deals with inessentials. It is brash; in speaking of Clytemnestra's adultery he says, "Your daughter—I blush to call her my mother" (557). It is inconsistent in argument, but consistent with Orestes's character.

He begins by admitting his guilt; he then defends his crime, on the Aeschylean grounds that the father provides the seed, the mother only the furrow. His action was a service to the whole of Greece, a discouragement to adultery by the wives of serving soldiers (this argument had its appeal to a wartime audience!). He puts an end to the practice (but the word is the same as "law," *nomon*, 571) of wives murdering husbands; he points his words by a startling rhyme (567–568).

Then he bursts out, "I hated my mother and was right to kill her." She murdered Agamemnon to save herself. The gods are divided: his father's Furies on one side, his mother's on the other. Penelope was no Clytemnestra; why should not Clytemnestra have been a Penelope? Apollo commanded the murder; if anyone, he should be executed for it. Life is like marriage, a lottery; you may be lucky and you may not. This callow speech is in character: we note the suggestion at the end that Orestes's violence is linked with sexual abnormality and the love-hate relationship with his mother; we notice too the urge to relive his crime through a confession of guilt.

The chorus makes an ambiguous comment:

> Women were born always to stand in the way
> of their husband's fate in looking toward disaster. (605)

This is usually interpreted to mean "an impediment to their husband's good fortune," but the more natural meaning is the other, and the chorus are after all women. Even if the unfavorable meaning be taken it is a wry interpretation of the men's attitude. Probably the words have a double meaning. Orestes's speech suffers the most serious condemnation of oratory: it is ineffectual. Tyndareus will advocate the stoning of Electra as well as Orestes, and he warns Menelaus not to stand in his way.

Orestes and Menelaus are left. Orestes renews his plea at some length. Again he admits his crime—and asks Menelaus for another crime to support him. Agamemnon acted for Menelaus, even unjustly. He gave him ten years; Orestes asks for one day in return. He gave him Iphigeneia; Orestes asks for help not Hermione (but there is irony here). Orestes even invokes Helen—though not by name—before Menelaus. His pleas are vain; his hunt bootless. Menelaus urges expediency, practicality, resourcelessness; he will use persuasion but no more. A democracy in a fury is like a raging fire to quench (697). Menelaus's language is tortuous and full of similitudes. Bide your time; slacken your bow when they draw theirs; the fire burns itself out;

the wind shifts. It's like a ship; you need to slacken your sails. Menelaus will use cleverness. He hurries off, as Verrall puts it, "pursued by the taunts, prayers, and curses of the unhappy Orestes."

Orestes's order of thought is interesting: abuse of Menelaus, self-pity, thought for Agamemnon abandoned by his friends, extended self-pity. But as we expect the chorus to sing, in comes Pylades, and again Orestes sees a moment of calm (728). The scene between them is in trochaic tetrameters. First Pylades has five lines; his entrance, a key moment in the play, is marked by the rhyme in this passage. There follows extended line-for-line dialogue (*stichomythia*) breaking more excitedly into divided lines (*antilabe*), and ending with a few lines from each. Pylades has been banished from Phocis for his part in the murder; it will be remembered that this was the legal penalty that Tyndareus justified. They resolve to go and defend Orestes before the Assembly. There is abuse of Menelaus as a coward and a womanizer (754). There is an extraordinary pun, when Orestes calls on Pylades to be his tiller (*oiax*, 795, the very name of his chief opponent). Electra for the moment is left in the dark.

Orestes and Pylades are political caricatures of the young aristocrats, common enough in Athens, who think that democracy is all right with the right leaders. The scene is redolent of friendship. Orestes greets his dearest friend (725); Pylades quotes the famous "Friends hold all things in common" (735), which was, it is important to remember, a right-wing rather than a left-wing sentiment in antiquity. He continually reasserts his friendship (794, 795, 802), and the scene ends on the word "friend." Yet Orestes's last speech speaks of "comrades," and that, in its day, was a right-wing political term too.

The choral song that at last follows is finely written; its theme is obvious and relevant: the collapse of the house of Atreus, first the legendary strife, then the murder of the mother by the son, and finally his diseased, haunted madness. There is startling wordplay in the first stanza betwen *palin* "again," *palai* "formerly," and *palaios* "former"; it is almost "Past is the past glory of the past" (810). This paves the way for the paradox of "inglorious glory" that opens the second stanza (819), and in its turn leads to the "fire-born implement," a vivid and unexpected phrase linking the sword that killed Clytemnestra with the important motif of fire. Though fine, the song is brief; the brevity and scantiness of the choral songs is another indication of pro-satyric drama.

Electra comes out. She left Orestes with strict injunctions not to stir from his pallet, and she is startled to find him gone. A messenger from the Assembly comes, a peasant and a devoted supporter of Agamemnon and his house. He brings the news that Orestes and Electra have been condemned to death by stoning, with a day's grace to allow them suicide. Euripides's audience expected debate, and the dramatist has given the debate scene a different twist by inserting it in the messenger's speech; a skilled actor would have rich opportunities to show his versatility.

The first speaker was Talthybius, the herald, who is sympathetically portrayed in *The Women of Troy*. Here he is unsympathetic, climbing on the bandwagon of power, licking the boots of the moment, and speaking for condemnation. Next Diomedes spoke for banishment and received a mixed response. Then an unnamed blustering speaker backed by Tyndareus called for stoning. Now at last came a speaker on the other side, a peasant farmer of the type that appears in *Electra,* who defended Orestes for killing a wicked godless woman, who herself was preventing men from going to war for fear of their wives' behavior. He seemed to be persuading the decent citizens (though the word might mean "upper classes," 930). Now there was silence. Then Orestes spoke. He claimed to be a public benefactor, and to be defending the law that he had in fact flouted. It was at best a foolish speech: it gave the demagogue his opportunity, and he secured their condemnation.

This is a strange and fascinating speech. It is deliberately written badly. It is tight-packed with rhyme and similar effects: a single example may point an important moment, like the end of a Shakespearean speech, but their accumulated impact upon an audience used to blank verse must have seemed jingling and trivial. Yet we have, 871ff.:-*an* . . . *-as* . . . *-as* . . . *-o-on* . . . *-a* . . . *-in* . . . *-as* . . . *-on* . . . *-on*; 891–892, *-ous* . . . *-ous*; 901ff., *-oi* . . . *-ai* . . . *-ei* . . . *-os* . . . *-a-ai* . . . *-i*; 915–916, *logous* . . . *legein*; 919–922, *-on* . . . *-e-en* . . . *-o-on* . . . *-on*; 926–929, *-a* . . . *-a* . . . *-menoi* . . . *-menoi*; 937–938, *chreo-on* . . .

chreo-òn; 943–946, *legein* . . . *lego-òn* . . . *ktanein* . . . *thanein*; 951–952, *-oi* . . . *oi*; and these are only the more striking instances.

It follows that the account of the Assembly is not detached and objective. Insofar as we identify ourselves with the speaker our sympathies are with Orestes. But before the play is over our sympathies are alienated from Orestes because of his violence, and we note here that the one speaker who defends Orestes is militarily a hawk, not a dove. There are other problems. Where is Menelaus? And where Oeax? Menelaus, we later learn, "did not show his face," though the exact meaning of the words is obscure (1058, cf. 894). Oeax seems to be replaced by the demagogue who is described in a word not found elsewhere: "with-ùngated-tongue" (*athuroglossos*, 903), strong through impudence, a non-Argive Argive, pressed into service, persuasive through volume of sound and his combination of ignorance and confident speech, and able to use his persuasive powers to invoke them in crime. This is a hit at Cleophon, the contemporary Athenian demagogue, who was twitted on his Thracian blood.

As for Orestes's speech, one wonders whether Socrates, a keen admirer of Euripides, did not have it in mind at his own trial, when, instead of admitting guilt and pleading for banishment, he too claimed to be a public benefactor with the same result. The messenger's last words are rationalist, ominous, ironic: "Apollo has destroyed you" (956). They could apply to Socrates also.

Electra sings and dances her grief in a marvellous solo. She calls on Persephone, the lovely girl-goddess of the dead, and invokes pity on "those who are about to die who were once the fighters of Hellas" (968). This self-identification of the girl with Agamemnon is remarkable. The house of Pelops is broken by democratic vote and the envy of the gods.

> O generations of mortals, steeped in tears,
> deep in trouble, see how Destiny
> moves contrary to hope. (976)

She recalls, no doubt with powerful mime, the past disasters of the house. Orestes and Pylades come in waving goodbye to their weeping friends. Electra has sung of the horses of Argos and of Dawn driving a solitary horse: Pylades is supporting Orestes, and the chorus compares them to race horses.

The scene that follows is the most frightening in all Euripides; it is worse than the earlier mad scene, for Electra and Pylades are not mad, and Orestes is no different from them; it shows the depravity of human nature naked and exposed. Belsen and Büchenwald would not surprise Euripides. Electra at first panics before death; yet her thoughts are still more for Orestes than herself. She asks Orestes to kill her, but his mother's blood is—for the moment—enough for him. Their thoughts turn to Menelaus, whom Orestes accuses of coveting power at Argos. Pylades joins the suicide pact: "What is life for me without your comradeship?" He claims to have planned the original crime; he will die with his comrade, and with his promised wife. But first he has a suggestion. A foolish scholiast says that Pylades is the only noncriminal character in the play: on the contrary, it is he who proposes vengeance on Menelaus by murdering Helen.

The old Greek definition of justice involved doing good to your friends and harm to your enemies. Orestes and Pylades have asserted the claims of friendship, but for them harming enemies replaces benefit to friends. Orestes, who has just said that his mother's blood is enough, becomes more bloodthirsty than his friend. He is for killing all the slaves and treats "Death to Helen" as a kind of battle cry (1130). Pylades now starts rationalizing the revenge on Menelaus into an execution of a vicious woman; when men hear the news they will light bonfires (1137). This is an ironic introduction of the fire motif, for he goes on to say that if they fail they will set the palace on fire and die in it (1150). Orestes reverts to the praise of friendship, but his mind is fixed on revenge.

But now Electra takes a hand, and we see what underlies her tender sisterly love. She suggests kidnapping Hermione and holding her hostage against Menelaus's support for their escape. If Menelaus raises a hand, Hermione is to be killed without compunction. "A woman with a man's mind!" cries Orestes; it is a damning indictment of men; it also makes us think of Aeschylus's Clytemnestra. More, it was Orestes who scorned his mother for using murder to save herself; yet he is doing it. Orestes now speaks of Hermione contemptuously as a cub (1713), a familiar Spartan image. There ensues the most ghastly moment of the scene, a horrible, blasphemous prayer to Agamemnon, parodying *The Libation Bearers*, for success in their crime.

ORESTES: I killed my mother!
ELECTRA:　　　　　I held the sword!
PYLADES: I laid the plans! I stopped them from holding back! (1235)

They are a teen-age gang, and one imagines that after years of war similar delinquency was familiar at Athens.

The men go in. Electra is left outside with the chorus. She disposes of them to keep guard at the two approaches, and they sing as they dance their way to their stations. Electra panics at the false alarm of a peasant approaching, panics again at the silence within. Then come Helen's screams, and Electra half-sings, half-shouts:

> Cut her down, wipe her out
> kill her, use your twofold two-edged swords,
> 　　be rid of
> the woman who abandoned father and marriage. . . . (1302)

It is horrible; it also revealing of the frustrated father-fixated spinster. On top of this Hermione arrives, "a glorious prey." Electra, exulting as she is, drops into an attitude of despondency. Hermione heard Helen's cries; Electra quickly improvises the explanation that it was Orestes weeping before Helen. Her inner tendencies to violence and deceit are coming out, and we realize that she resents Hermione for being what she might be, and enjoying the mother love she never knew. Hermione is full of good will, willing to plead for them. Electra hustles her within, where Orestes is waiting. Electra follows and pulls the doors to. Incoherent sounds and cries come from behind, which the chorus drowns with singing.

And now at this tense moment the play as tragedy falls apart, and is meant to do so. A slave dressed in foreign costume squeezes himself out onto the balcony (where Helen was seen earlier) and drops to the ground where Orestes's paillasse is still lying. He chants fantastically of his escape in a breathless flood (1444), with incoherent stammering and presumably exotic eastern melodies. He mixes his images and calls Helen the swan's cub. He raises the old dirge cry *Ailinos! Ailinos!* in grotesque parody of the chorus in *Agamemnon*. Two lions (another echo) burst into the palace, one had the general for a father and the other was Strophius's son. The second was a kind of Odysseus and turned out to be a snake. So he sings of the scene inside with Helen spinning, Orestes pleading, Pylades locking up the servants, the drawn sword—and the chorus interrupts. He goes on to the attempted rescue, the death of one slave, another wounded, all finding dark corners to hide, dead bodies falling, or about to fall, or already stretched out, Hermione's arrival, the men seizing her like Bacchants with a cub, turning to finish off Helen—and Zeus! Earth! Light! Dark! She was vanished. And we suddenly realize that this barbaric chant has been the second messenger's speech.

The scene is not over. Orestes emerges with drawn sword in pursuit of the refugee. Whether or not we laugh at the slave earlier we can hardly fail to do so now.

ORESTES: Where's that fellow who rushed from the house to escape my
           sword.
PHRYGIAN: Salaam, master, I prostrate; we easterners do.
ORESTES: You're not in Troy now, you're in the land of Argos.
PHRYGIAN: Wherever you are if you've sense, life is better than death.
ORESTES: Weren't you raising a shout for Menelaus to come to the rescue?
PHRYGIAN: Oh, no sir, for help for you; you needed it more.
ORESTES: The death of Tyndareus's daughter—was it just?
PHRYGIAN: Oh, yes sir, if she had her throat cut three times over. (1506)

Orestes brings his sword close to the quivering creature and asks if he's frightened of some Gorgon's head. The Phrygian does not understand him, but we do; Clytemnestra's Furies have Gorgon eyes (261). Orestes contemptuously lets him go and returns inside. There is a brilliant analysis of this whole scene by A. W. Verrall, but he takes it too seriously; his comparison with the porter scene in *Macbeth* is just; his analysis false. For he treats the porter scene as a kind of challenge to show that the tragedy has so gripped us that we cannot even smile at that which in other contexts is undeniably funny. Nothing is more certain than that the groundlings, whether at *Macbeth* or *Orestes*, laughed, or that the dramatist intended them to do so. If we are right in accepting the evidence that *Orestes* is pro-satyric, they have been waiting a long, long time to laugh and will laugh in good measure when given the opening.

Not that Euripides has done. He gives his play a double twist. The tension returns. The chorus realizes at what they are conniving. They see the smoke from torches ready for the conflagration Pylades has promised; the theme of fire now comes uppermost, visibly and symbolically. Menelaus arrives; he has met the slave and heard a garbled story of two lions and Helen's disappearance. As he gives orders to his men to break in, Orestes drags Hermione at sword's point onto the balcony; Pylades and Electra stand by with torches. A swift interchange, first in lines, and then in broken lines, follows between Menelaus and Orestes. Helen has somehow escaped; all Orestes's murderous thoughts are directed to Hermione and the destruction of the palace by fire. Menelaus has one chance—if Orestes is spared.

MENELAUS: Can you in justice live?
ORESTES: Yes, and rule a nation.
MENELAUS: What nation?
ORESTES: Pelasgus's land of Argos.
MENELAUS: You? Touching the ritual libations?
ORESTES: Why not?
MENELAUS: Sacrificing for war?
ORESTES: As much as you.
MENELAUS: My hands are clean.
ORESTES: Your heart isn't. (1600)

Of course Orestes is fit to sacrifice for war; war is fostered by people like Orestes. "You've caught me," says Menelaus, and Orestes answers, "In your crookedness you've caught yourself" (1617). He is just telling Electra and Pylades to set fire to the palace when the crane swings into the air above them, the radiant figure of Apollo with Helen, demurely divine, with her own nimbus, at his side. With its three or—if Menelaus is on stage—four levels it is an unusually impressive tableau.

Among the cheers of the volatile audience Apollo solves all the problems. Helen is a star, protecting sailors. Menelaus must marry again,

> since the gods used her beauty to bring
> Greeks and Trojans together in one

—the words are highly ambiguous—

> and decreed deaths to bail out from earth
> the excess of man's overpopulation. (1639)

(This was hardly the human motive for the Peloponnesian War.)

Orestes is to go into exile, receive his acquittal from the Areopagus,
and marry Hermione. Electra is to marry Pylades—lucky man. Orestes
will rule Argos, Menelaus will rule Sparta, and Apollo will deal with
the Assemby. "Oh," says Orestes, "I thought your oracles fiendish, but
they have turned out all right in the end." For whom? Clytemnestra?
The dead slaves? Orestes is so compliant that he asks Menelaus for
Hermione's hand, Menelaus gives it, the lovers embrace, Pylades and
Electra turn their torches into marriage torches, Apollo takes Helen
off to see Zeus, and the chorus prays for victory. And they all lived
happily ever after.

The ending is ludicrous—intentionally. Humanly speaking, Helen is
dead, and since Menelaus cannot possibly touch the decision of the
Assembly, Hermione's throat will be cut, and the palace will go up in
flames, forming a pyre for the three warped adolescents on the roof.
The solution is a miracle, and being a miracle is no solution. If *Orestes*
is really pro-satyric and belongs to the same cycle as *The Women of
Phoenicia*, the juxtaposition of realism and unrealism makes the point
still more effectively. As Arrowsmith puts it, "If the experience of the
play is a real one, what remains after Apollo leaves is not the taste of a
happy ending, but the image of total disaster: the burning palace, the
dead girl, the screaming mob, and the degenerate heirs dying in the
arson of their own hatred." The logic of violence is such that not even
a god can halt it.

So we return to the inescapable political context. For this is a play
with direct political reference. Any Athenian would see in the demagogue of the Argive Assembly a picture of their own Cleophon. This

was the period of Alcibiades's comeback as a political force in the country he had betrayed; his triumphal return to Athens lay within a month or two of the presentation of the play. Alcibiades was the symbol of the imperialism Euripides detested, and he had betrayed his country once. A play suggesting that a young man who has committed one crime will commit others of the same sort may well appear a warning. Aristophanes in *The Frogs* associated Euripides with views of this temper. Further, Alcibiades was playing with a Persian alliance; the contemptible cowardice of the Asiatic slave, involving as it did the (to the Athenians) typically Persian prostration, must appear a commentary on the help the Athenians might expect from such an alliance.

There is rejection alike of left-wing demagogy and right-wing conspiracy. But above all there is explicit reference to and implicit concern with the war. Arrowsmith's final words in his introduction to his translation are masterful:

The political climate of the play itself graphically represents the state of affairs in Athens, and, presumptuous or not, I am tempted to see in the play Euripides' prophetic image of the final destruction of Athens and Hellas, or that Hellas to which a civilized man could still give his full commitment. It is a simple and a common symbolism: the great old house, cursed by a long history of fratricidal blood and war, brought down in destruction by its degenerate heirs. The final tableau is the direct prophecy of disaster, complete, awful, and inevitable, while Apollo intervenes only as an impossible wish, a futile hope, or a simple change of scene from a vision that cannot be brooked, or seen for long because it is the direct vision of dispair, the hopeless future.

GREEK VOCABULARY

AGON. a contest

AGORA. city center, associated with the market area

AIDOS. a sense of honor, and especially modesty

AISCHUNE. a sense of shame

ANAGNORISIS. recognition

ANAPAEST. a foot or bar in 4/4 time ♩♩♩ used for processional movement and sometimes to express excitement

ANTILABE. the division of a line between two speakers

ANTISTROPHE. lit. an unwinding, the second stanza of a pair, in which the chorus executed a dancing movement counterclockwise

ARCHON. a general term for a magistrate

ARETE. excellence of any kind, later especially of moral virtue

BARBAROS. a foreigner who does not speak Greek but goes "bar-bar-bar"; hence barbarian

BEMA. a speaker's platform

CHARIS. favor, gratitude, reciprocal to one another; grace

CHOEPHORI. libation bearers; title of a play by Aeschylus

CHOREGOS. a wealthy citizen who paid for the training of the chorus

CHRONOS. time, as duration

CORYPHAEUS. leader of the chorus

CRETIC. a foot or bar in 5/4 time ♩♩♩ used to express excitement

DACTYL. a foot or bar in 4/4 time ♩♩♩

DAIMON. god, especially in relation to man; sometimes almost a man's destiny

DEIXIS. interpretation through dance and mime

DIKE. right

DISTEGIA. a balcony at the first floor level representing the roof of the house

DOCHMIAC. a strongly syncopated rhythm in 4/2 time ♩♩♩♩♩ used to express wild excitement

EKKUKLEMA. a moving platform rolled out from the stage building with a tableau, often of dead bodies

EPODE. the concluding stanza of a choral lyric

ERGON. work, action, practice, often contrasted with *logos*

ERINYS. a Fury

EROS. love, passion

EUMENIDES. the Kindly Goddesses, euphemism for the Furies; title of a play by Aeschylus

EXODOS. the exit of the chorus

GENOS. birth, ancestry, child

GLYCONIC. a line of verse in which the first foot may be ♩♩/ or 𝅗𝅥♩/ or ♩𝅗𝅥/, followed by ♩♩♩♩♩♩

GNOTHI SAUTON. know yourself

HYBRIS. an overweening arrogance or violence

HYPOCRITES. an actor, lit. an answerer

IAMBIC. a foot or bar in 3/4 time ♩♩♩, the basic rhythm of verse dialogue

IONICUS A MINORE. a foot or bar in 3/2 time ♩♩𝅗𝅥

KAIROS. time, as opportunity

KOMMOS. a lament or threnody with the actors still on stage

KOSMOS. order, an ordered universe

LOGOS. word, reason, theory, often contrasted with *ergon*

MECHANE. a crane for introducing characters, especially divinities, in mid-air

NOMOS. law or convention, often in contrast with *physis*

ORCHESTRA. a dancing-floor; the large circle which was the center of spectacle and used for the main choral dances

PAEAN. a foot or bar in 5/4 time, most commonly ♩♩♩𝅗𝅥 or 𝅗𝅥♩♩♩, metrically equivalent to a cretic

PAIS. boy, son, servant

PARODOS. the processional entry of the chorus, accompanied by an anapaestic chant in 4/4 time

PERIAKTOS. a triangular structure used in the later theater to represent the scene, a fresh scene being turned to the audience for a fresh play

PERIPETEIA. a reversal of fortune when a course of action designed for one result leads to its opposite

PHERECRATEAN. a glyconic lacking the final syllable

PHILANTHROPIA. love of mankind

PHILIA. friendship, affection, reciprocated love

PHORA. movement and step

PHYSIS. nature, often contrasted with *nomos*

PROBEMA. step forward

SCHEMA. pose and gesture

SEMNON, SEMNOTES. the sublime or exalted; sometimes the pompous

SOPHIA, SOPHON. wisdom, cleverness

SOPHRONEIN, SOPHROSUNE. saving wisdom, moderation, self-control

SPARAGMOS. a rending apart

SPONDEE. a foot or bar in 4/4 time ♩♩, a slower and heavier rhythmic equivalent of anapaest or dactyl

STASIMON. a song of the chorus once they have reached their stand in the orchestra, but by no means sung standing still

STICHOMYTHIA. an extended dialogue in which the characters match line with line

STRATEGOS. a military general, but also responsible for leadership in civil administration

STROPHE. lit. a winding, the first stanza of a pair, in which the chorus executed a dancing movement clockwise

TETRALOGY. a set of four plays by one dramatist, presented on a single day, a trilogy of tragedies, followed by a satyr-play or pro-satyric play

TETRAMETER. a line of verse consisting of eight double units; each unit often being based on the trochee

THEOLOGEION. a platform on the top of the stage building for the appearance of gods

TRIBRACH. a foot or bar in 3/4 time ♪♪♪, a freer or a more excited equivalent of an iambic

TRILOGY. the first three plays of a tetralogy

TRIMETER. the basic line of dialogue, consisting of three double units, based on the iambic

TROCHEE. a foot or bar in 3/4 time ♩♪

TURANNOS (TYRANNOS). dictator, autocrat

TYCHE. fortune, sometimes tending to chance, sometimes to destiny

XENOS. guest, host (a reciprocal relation), stranger, but also friend

BIBLIOGRAPHY

General Works on the Greek Theater
and the Origins of Tragedy

Anti, C. *Teatri Greci Arcaici*. Padua, 1947.

Arnott, P. D. *An Introduction to the Greek Theatre*. London, 1959.

————. *Greek Scenic Conventions in the Fifth Century B.C.* Oxford, 1962.

Bieber, M. *The History of the Greek and Roman Theater*. Princeton, 1961.

Bülle, H., and Wirsing, H. *Szenbilder zum griechischen Theater des 5. Jahrhunderts v. Chr.* Berlin, 1950.

Dieterich, A. *Kleine Schriften*. Leipzig, 1911.

Dinsmoor, W. B. "The Athenian Theater of the Fifth Century." In *Studies Presented to D. M. Robinson*. St. Louis, 1951–1953.

Dörpfeld, W., and Reisch, E. *Das griechische Theater*. Athens, 1896.

Dugit, E. "Oreste et Hamlet." *Annales de l'enseignement supérieur de Grenoble*, 1889, pp. 143ff.

Else, G. F. *The Origin and Early Form of Greek Tragedy*. Cambridge, Mass., 1965.

Exon, C. "A New Theory of the Ekkyklema." *Hermathena* 26 (1900): 132ff.

Ferguson, J. "From Ilissus to Niger." Unpublished MS in author's collection.

Flickinger, R. C. *The Greek Theater and Its Drama*. 7th ed. Chicago, 1936.

Gow, A. S. F. "On the Meaning of the Word Thymele." *Journal of the Hellenic Society* 32 (1912): 213–238.

Haigh, A. E. *The Attic Theatre*. 3rd ed. rev. by A. W. Pickard-Cambridge. Oxford, 1907.

Jevons, F. B. "Masks and the Origin of Greek Drama." *Folk Lore* 27 (1916): 171–192.

Lawler, L. B. *The Dance of the Ancient Greek Theater*. Iowa City, 1964.

Mahr, A. C. *The Origin of the Greek Tragic Form: A Study of the Early Theater in Attica.* New York, 1938.

Murray, G. "Excursus on the Ritual Forms Preserved in Greek Tragedy." In *Themis* by J. E. Harrison. London, 1963.

———. "Hamlet and Orestes." In *The Classical Tradition in English Poetry.* Oxford, 1930.

Navarre, O. *Le théâtre grec.* Paris, 1925.

Nietzsche, F. *The Birth of Tragedy.* Translated by F. Golffing. New York, 1956.

Nilsson, M. P. "Totenklage und Tragödie." *Archiv für Religionswissenschaft* 9 (1906): 281ff.

Page, D. L. *Actors' Interpolations in Greek Tragedy.* Oxford, 1934.

Pickard-Cambridge, A. W. *Dithyramb, Tragedy and Comedy.* 2nd ed. Oxford, 1962.

———. *The Dramatic Festivals of Athens.* 2nd ed. rev. by D. M. Lewis and J. P. Gould. Oxford, 1967.

———. *The Theatre of Dionysus at Athens.* Oxford, 1947.

Ridgeway, Sir W. *The Dramas and Dramatic Dances of Non-European Races.* Cambridge, 1915.

———. *The Origin of Tragedy.* Cambridge, 1910.

Rumpf, A. "Classical and Post-Classical Greek Painting." *Journal of the Hellenic Society* 67 (1947): 10–21.

Schuré, E. *The Genesis of Tragedy and the Sacred Drama of Eleusis.* Translated by F. Rothwell. London, 1936.

Stuart, D. C. "The Origin of Greek Tragedy in the Light of Dramatic Technique." *Transactions and Proceedings of the American Philological Association* 47 (1916): 173–204.

Untersteiner, M. *Le Origini della Tragedia.* Milan, 1942.

Webster T. B. L. *Greek Theatre Production.* 2nd ed. London, 1970.

———. "Staging and Scenery in the Ancient Greek Theatre." *John Rylands Library Bulletin* 52 (1960): 493–509.

GENERAL WORKS ON GREEK TRAGEDY

Arrowsmith, W. "The Criticism of Greek Tragedy." *Tulane Drama Review* 3, no. 3 (1959): 31–56.

Aylen, L. *Greek Tragedy and the Modern World.* London, 1964.

Buchwald, W. *Studien zur Chronologie der attischen Tragödie.* Dissertation. Köningsberg, 1939.

Carrière, J. "Sur l'essence et l'évolution du tragique chez les Grecs." *Revue des Etudes Grecques* 79 (1966) : 6–37.

Dale, A. M. *The Lyric Metres of Greek Drama.* Cambridge, 1948.

Duchemin, J. *L'Agon dans la tragédie grecque.* Paris, 1945.

Fritz, K. von. *Antike und moderne Tragödie.* Berlin, 1962.

Greene, W. C. *Moira: Fate, Good, and Evil in Greek Thought.* Cambridge, Mass., 1964.

Howald, E. *Die griechische Tragödie.* Munich, 1930.

Jones, J. *On Aristotle and Greek Tragedy.* London, 1962.

Kitto, H. D. F. *Greek Tragedy.* 3rd ed. London, 1961.

Kranz, W. *Stasimon Untersuchungen zu Form und Gehalt der griechischen Tragödie.* Berlin, 1933.

Lattimore, R. *The Poetry of Greek Tragedy.* Baltimore, 1958.

———. *Story Patterns in Greek Tragedy.* Ann Arbor, 1964.

Lesky, A. *Greek Tragedy.* Translated by H. A. Frankfort. London, 1965.

Lucas. D. W. *The Greek Tragic Poets.* London, 1959.

Matthaei, L. E. *Studies in Greek Tragedy.* Cambridge, 1918.

Mayerhoefer, F. *Über die Schlüsse der erhaltenen griechischen Tragödien.* Erlangen, 1908.

Norwood, G. *Greek Tragedy.* 4th ed. London, 1948.

Patin, M. *Etudes sur les tragiques grecs.* 7th ed. 4 vols. Paris, 1904.

Pohlenz, M. *Die griechische Tragödie.* 2nd ed. Göttingen, 1954.

Ronnet, G. "Le sentiment du tragique chez les Grecs." *Revue des Etudes Grecques* 76 (1963) : 327–336.

Séchan, L. *Etudes sur la tragédie grecque dans ses rapports avec la céramique.* Paris, 1926.

Sheppard, J. T. *Greek Tragedy.* Cambridge, 1920.

Spira, A. *Untersuchungen zum Deus Ex Machina bei Sophocles und Euripides.* Munich, 1957.

Weil, H. *Etudes sur le drame antique.* Paris, 1897.

Weiss, A. "L'ésprit de la tragédie." *Revue d'Esthetique* 16 (1963): 371–387.

Wilamowitz-Moellendorff, U. von. *Griechische Tragödien.* 4 vols. Berlin, 1899–1923.

Zielinski, T. *Tragodoumenon libri tres.* Cracow, 1925.

COLLECTED TRANSLATIONS

Cooper, L. *Fifteen Greek Plays.* New York, 1943.

Grene, D., and Lattimore, R. *The Complete Greek Tragedies.* 4 vols. Chicago, 1959–1960.

Lind, L. R. *Ten Greek Plays in Contemporary Translations.* Boston, 1956.

Oates, W. J., and O'Neill, E. *The Complete Greek Drama.* 2 vols. New York, 1938.

Wilamowitz-Moellendorff, U. von. *Griechische Tragödien.* 4 vols. Berlin, 1899–1923.

AESCHYLUS
Texts and Commentaries

Mazon, P. *Eschyle* 2 vols. vol. 1 Paris, 1958, 7th ed.; vol. 2 Paris 1955, 6th ed.

Murray, G. *Aeschyli Septem Quae Supersunt Tragoediae.* 2nd ed. Oxford, 1955.

Paley, F. A. *Aeschyleus.* 4th ed. London, 1879.

Rose, H. J. *A Commentary on the Surviving Plays of Aeschylus.* 2 vols. Amsterdam, 1957.

Sidgwick, A. *Aeschylus.* 7 vols. Oxford, 1903–1927.

Wecklein, N. *Aeschyli Fabulae.* Berlin, 1885.

Weil, H. *Aeschylus Tragoediae.* Leipzig, 1903.

Wilamowitz-Moellendorff, U. von. *Aeschylus Tragoediae.* 2nd ed. Berlin, 1958.

Translations

Macneice, L. *The "Agamemnon" of Aeschylus.* London, 1936.

Murray, G. *The Complete Plays of Aeschylus.* London, 1952.

Vellacott, P. *Aeschylus: The Orestes Trilogy.* 2nd ed. Harmondsworth, 1959.

———. *Aeschylus: "Prometheus" and Other Plays.* Harmondsworth, 1961.

General Works

Cantarella, R. *Eschilo.* Florence, 1941.

Croiset, M. *Eschyle: Etudes sur l'invention dramatique dans son théâtre.* Paris, 1928.

De Romilly, J. *La Crainte et l'angoisse dans le théâtre d'Eschyle.* Paris, 1958.

Dumortier, J. *Les images dans la poèsie d'Eschyle.* Paris, 1935.

———. *Le vocabulaire médical d'Eschyle et les écrits hippocratiques.* Paris, 1935.

Earp, F. R. *The Style of Aeschylus*. Cambridge, 1948.

Finley, J. H. *Pindar and Aeschylus*. Cambridge, Mass., 1955.

Gladigow, B. "Aeschylus und Heraklit." *Archiv fuer Geschichte der Philosophie*, n.s. 44 (1962) : 225–239.

Golden, L. *In Praise of Prometheus*. Chapel Hill, 1966.

Hughes, B. L. "The Dramatic Use of Imagery in Aeschylus." Ph.D. dissertation, Bryn Mawr, 1955. Ann Arbor: University Microfilms, 1956.

Italie, G. *Index Aeschylus*. 2nd ed. Leiden, 1964.

Kaufmann-Buhler, G. *Begriff und Funktion der Dike in den Tragödien des Aischylos*. Bonn, 1955.

Kent, R. G. "The Aeschylean Universe." *Journal of the Hellenic Society* 63 (1943) : 15–20.

Kitto, H. D. F. *Poiesis*, pp. 33–116. Berkeley, 1966.

———. "The Idea of God in Aeschylus and Sophocles." In *La Notion du Divin depuis Homère jusqu'à Platon*, pp. 69–89. Geneva, 1954.

Lloyd-Jones, H. "Zeus in Aeschylus." *Journal of the Hellenic Society* 76 (1956) : 55–67.

Maddalena, A. *Interpretazioni Eschilee*. Turin, 1953.

Méautis, G. *Eschyle et la Trilogie*. Paris, 1936.

Mostopoulos, E. "Une philosophie de la musique chez Eschyle." *Revue des Etudes Grecques* 72 (1959) : 18–56.

Murray, G. *Aeschylus: The Creator of Tragedy*. Oxford, 1940.

Owen, E. T. *The Harmony of Aeschylus*. Toronto, 1952.

Patin, M. *Etudes sur les tragiques grecs: Eschyle*. Paris, 1890.

Pearson, L. *Popular Ethics in Ancient Greece*, pp. 90–135. Stanford, 1962.

Podlecki, A. J. *The Political Background of Aeschylean Tragedy*. Ann Arbor, 1966.

Porzig, W. *Die attische Tragödie des Aischylos*. Leipzig, 1926.

Post, C. R. "The Dramatic Art of Aeschylus." *Harvard Studies in Classical Philology* 16 (1905) : 15–61.

Reinhardt, K. *Aischylos als Regisseur und Theologe*. Bern, 1949.

Robertson, H. G. "Legal Expressions and Ideas of Justice in Aeschylus." *Classical Philology* 34 (1939) : 209–219.

Sheppard, J. T. *Aeschylus and Sophocles: Their Work and Influence*. London, 1927.

Smyth, H. W. *Aeschylean Tragedy*. Berkeley, 1924.

Snell, B. *Aischylos und das Handeln im Drama*. Leipzig, 1928.

Solmsen, F. *Hesiod and Aeschylus*. Ithaca, N.Y., 1949.

Stanford, W. B. *Aeschylus in His Style*. Dublin, 1942.

Stoessl, F. "Aeschylus as a Political Thinker." *American Journal of Philology* 73 (1952): 113–139.

Thomson, G. *Aeschylus and Athens*. 2nd ed. London, 1946.

Wiliamowitz-Moellendorff, U. von. *Aischylos: Interpretationen*. Berlin, 1914.

Yorke, E. C. "Trisyllabic Feet in the Dialogue of Aeschylus." *Classical Quarterly* 30 (1936): 116–119.

Individual Plays

The Persians

Alexanderson, B. "Darius in the *Persians*." *Eranos* 65 (1967): 1–11.

Broadhead, H. D. *The "Persae" of Aeschylus*. Cambridge, 1960.

Craig, J. D. "The Interpretation of Aeschylus' *Persae*." *Classical Review* 38 (1924): 98–101.

Driver, T. F. *The Sense of History in Greek and Shakespearian Drama*. New York, 1960.

Groeneboom, P. *Aischylos' "Perser."* Göttingen, 1960.

Headlam, W. "Ghost-raising, Magic, and the Underworld." *Classical Review* 16 (1902): 52–61.

Lattimore, R. "Aeschylus on the Defeat of Xerxes." In *Classical Studies in Honor of W. A. Oldfather*, pp. 83–93. Urbana, 1943.

Verrall, A. W. *The "Bacchants" of Euripides and Other Essays*, pp. 223–308. Cambridge, 1910.

Seven against Thebes

Bacon, H. H. "The Shield of Eteocles." *Arion* 3 (1964): 27–38.

Dawe, R. D. "The End of *Seven against Thebes*." *Classical Quarterly*, n.s. 17 (1967): 16–28.

Fraenkel, E. "Zum Schluss der *Sieben gegen Theben*." *Museum Helveticum* 21 (1964): 58–64.

Groeneboom, P. *Aeschylus' Seven tegen Thebe*. Groningen, 1938.

Klotz, O. "Zu Aischylos' thebanischer Tetralogie." *Rheinisches Museum fuer Philologie* 72 (1917–1918): 616–625.

Lesky, A. "Eteokles in den *Sieben gegen Theben*." *Wiener Studien* 74 (1961): 5–17.

Lloyd-Jones, H. "The End of the *Seven against Thebes*." *Classical Quarterly*, n.s. 9 (1959): 80–115.

Otis, B. "The Unity of the *Seven against Thebes.*" *Greek, Roman and Byzantine Studies* 3 (1960): 153–174.

Patzel, H. "Die dramatische Handlung der *Sieben gegen Theben.*" *Harvard Studies in Classical Philology* 63 (1958): 97–119.

Podlecki, A. J. "The Character of Eteocles in Aeschylus' *Septem.*" *Transactions and Proceedings of the American Philological Association* 95 (1964): 283–299.

Post, L. A. "The *Seven against Thebes* as Propaganda for Pericles." *Classical Weekly* 44 (1940): 49–57.

Regenbogen, O. "Bemerkungen zu dem *Sieben* des Aischylos." *Hermes* 68 (1933): 51–69.

Rosenmeyer, T. G. *The Masks of Tragedy*, pp. 7–48. Austin, 1963.

Sheppard, J. T. "The Plot of the *Septem contra Thebas.*" *Classical Quarterly* 7 (1913): 73–82.

Solmsen, F. "The Erinys in Aischylos' *Septem.*" *Transactions and Proceedings of the American Philological Association* 68 (1937): 197–211.

Tucker, T. G. *The "Seven against Thebes" of Aeschylus.* Cambridge, 1908.

Verrall, A. W. *The "Seven against Thebes" of Aeschylus.* Cambridge, 1887.

Wolff, E. "Die Entscheidung des Eteokles in den *Sieben gegen Theben.*" *Harvard Studies in Classical Philology* 63 (1958): 89–95.

The Suppliant Women

Diamantopoulos, A. "The Danaid Tetralogy of Aeschylus." *Journal of the Hellenic Society* 77 (1957): 220–229.

Earp, F. R. "The Date of the *Supplices* of Aeschylus." *Greece and Rome* 22 (1953): 118–123.

Garvie, A. F. *Aeschylus' "Supplices": Play and Trilogy.* Cambridge, 1969.

Golden, L. "Zeus the Protector and Zeus the Destroyer." *Classical Philology* 57 (1962): 20–26.

Korte, A. "Die Entstehungszeit der Hiketiden des Aischylos." In *Mélanges Nicole*, pp. 289–300. Geneva, 1905.

Macurdy, G. "Had the Danaid Trilogy a Social Problem?" *Classical Philology* 39 (1944): 95–100.

Murray, R. D. *The Motif of Io in Aeschylus' "Suppliants."* Princeton, 1958.

Robertson, D. S. "The End of the *Supplices* Trilogy of Aeschylus." *Classical Review* 38 (1924): 51–53.

Robertson, H. G. "Δίκη and ὕβρις in Aeschylus' *Suppliants.*" *Classical Review* 50 (1936): 104–109.

Sheppard, J. T. "The First Scene of the *Suppliants* of Aeschylus." *Classical Quarterly* 5 (1911): 220–229.

Tucker, T. G. *The "Supplices" of Aeschylus*. London, 1889.

Von Fritz, K. "Die Danaiden Trilogie des Aeschylus." *Philologus* 91 (1936): 12–36, 249–269.

Winnington-Ingram, R. P. "The Danaid-Trilogy of Aeschylus." *Journal of the Hellenic Society* 81 (1961): 141–152.

Wolff, E. A. "The Date of Aeschylus' Danaid Trilogy." *Eranos* 56 (1958): 112–139; 57 (1959): 6–34.

The Oresteia

Arrowsmith, W. "The Criticism of Greek Tragedy." *Tulane Drama Review* 3, no. 3 (1959): 31–56.

Bergson, L. "The Hymn to Zeus in Aeschylus' *Agamemnon*." *Eranos* 65 (1967): 12–24.

Burke, K. "Form and Persecution in the *Oresteia*." *Sewanee Review* 60 (1952): 377–396.

Cunningham, M. P. "Didactic Purpose in the *Oresteia*." *Classical Philology* 45 (1950): 183–185.

Denniston, J. D., and Page, D. L. *Aeschylus: "Agamemnon."* Oxford, 1957.

Dodds, E. R. "Morals and Politics in the *Oresteia*." *Proceedings of the Cambridge Philological Society*, n.s. 6 (1960): 19–31.

Dover, K. J. "The Political Aspects of Aeschylus' *Eumenides*." *Journal of the Hellenic Society* 77 (1957): 230–237.

Driver, T. F. *The Sense of History in Greek and Shakespearian Tragedy*. New York, 1960.

Fraenkel, E. *Aeschylus: "Agamemnon."* 3 vols. Oxford, 1950.

Friedman, J., and Gassel, S. "Orestes." *Psycho-Analytic Quarterly* 20 (1951): 423–433.

Goheen, R. F. "Aspects of Dramatic Symbolism: Three Studies in the *Oresteia*." *American Journal of Philology* 76 (1955): 113–137.

Golden, L. "Zeus, whoever he is. . . ." *Transactions and Proceedings of the American Philological Association* 92 (1961): 156–167.

Greene, W. C. "Dramatic and Ethical Motives in the *Agamemnon*." *Harvard Studies in Classical Philology* 54 (1943): 25–34.

Hammond, N. G. L. "Personal Freedom and its Limits in the *Oresteia*." *Journal of the Hellenic Society* 85 (1965): 42–55.

Headlam, W. *The "Oresteia" of Aeschylus*. Cambridge, 1938.

Jones, J. *On Aristotle and Greek Tragedy*, pp. 65–137. London, 1962.

Kitto, H. D. F. *Form and Meaning in Drama*, pp. 1–86. London, 1956.

Knox, B. M. W. "The Lion in the House." *Classical Philology* 47 (1952): 17–25.

Lloyd-Jones, H. "The Guilt of Agamemnon." *Classical Quarterly* 12 (1962): 187–199.

Peradotto, J. J. "Some Patterns of Nature Imagery in the *Oresteia*." *American Journal of Philology* 85 (1964): 378–393.

Reeves, C. H. "The Parodos of the *Agamemnon*." *Classical Journal* 55 (1960): 165–171.

Scott, W. C. "Wind-Imagery in the *Oresteia*." *Transactions and Proceedings of the American Philological Association* 97 (1967): 459–471.

Stanford, W. B. *Ambiguity in Greek Literature*, pp. 137–162. Oxford, 1939.

Stewart, S. J. "*Agamemnon*: A Play of Distortion." Unpublished MS.

Thomson, J. A. K. *Irony*, pp. 39–53. London, 1926.

Verrall, A. W. *Aeschylus: "Agamemnon."* London, 1889.

Wainwright, P. *The Burning Fountain*, pp. 232–267. Bloomington, 1954.

Whallon, W. "The Serpent at the Breast." *Transactions and Proceedings of the American Philological Association* 89 (1958): 271–275.

Wills, G. "*Agamemnon* 1346–71, 1649–53." *Harvard Studies in Classical Philology* 67 (1963): 255–267.

Winnington-Ingram, R. P. "Clytemnestra and the Vote of Athens." *Journal of the Hellenic Society* 68 (1948): 130–147.

Zeitlin, F. I. "The Motif of the Corrupted Sacrifice in Aeschylus' *Oresteia*." *Transactions and Proceedings of the American Philological Association* 96 (1965): 463–508.

Prometheus Bound

Bacon, J. R. "Three Notes on Aeschylus' *Prometheus Vinctus*." *Classical Philology* 46 (1951): 237–239.

Cole, S. "Prometheia." Unpublished MS.

Dawson, C. M. "Notes on the Final Scene of *Prometheus Vinctus*." *Classical Philology* 46 (1951): 237–239.

Farnell, L. R. "The Paradox of the *Prometheus Vinctus*." *Journal of the Hellenic Society* 53 (1933): 40–50.

Fitton-Brown, A. D. "Prometheia." *Journal of the Hellenic Society* 79 (1959): 52–60.

Fowler, B. H. "The Imagery of the *Prometheus Bound*." *American Journal of Philology* 77 (1957): 173–184.

Golden, L. "Zeus the Protector and Zeus the Destroyer." *Classical Philology* 57 (1962): 20–26.

Harry, J. E. *Aeschylus: "Prometheus."* New York, 1905.

Havelock, E. A. *The Crucifixion of Intellectual Man.* Boston, 1951.

———. *The Liberal Temper in Greek Politics.* New Haven, 1957.

Herington, C. J. "Aeschylus: *Prometheus Bound,* fr. 193." *Transactions and Proceedings of the American Philological Association* 92 (1961): 239–250.

———. "Some Evidence for a Late Dating of the *Prometheus Vinctus.*" *Classical Review,* n.s. 14 (1964): 239–240.

———. "A Study in the Prometheia." *Phoenix* 17 (1963): 180–197, 236–243.

———. "A Unique Technical Feature of the *Prometheus Bound.*" *Classical Review,* n.s. 13 (1963): 5–7.

Matthaei, L. E. *Studies in Greek Tragedy.* Cambridge, 1918.

Mullens, H. G. "Date and Stage Arrangements of the Prometheia." *Greece and Rome* 8 (1938–1939): 160–171.

Murray, R. D. *The Motif of Io in Aeschylus' "Suppliants."* Princeton, 1958.

Rosenmeyer, T. G. *The Masks of Tragedy,* pp. 51–102. Austin, 1963.

Séchan, L. *Le mythe de Prométhée.* Paris, 1951.

Thomson, G. *Aeschylus: The "Prometheus Bound."* Cambridge, 1932.

Yorke, E. C. "The Date of the *Prometheus Vinctus.*" *Classical Quarterly* 30 (1936): 153–154.

SOPHOCLES
Texts and Commentaries

Campbell, L. *Sophocles: The Plays and Fragments.* 2 vols. London, 1879–1881.

Dain, A., and Maxon, P. *Sophocle.* 2 vols. Paris, 1955–1958.

Jebb, R. C. *Sophocles: The Plays.* 7 vols. Cambridge, 1883–1908.

Pearson, A. C. *Sophoclis Fabulae.* Oxford, 1924.

Pearson, A. C., and Jebb, R. C. *The Fragments of Sophocles.* 3 vols. Cambridge, 1917.

Schneidewin, F. W., and Nauck, A. *Sophokles.* 7 vols. Berlin, 1909–1914.

Wunderus, E., and Wecklein, N. *Sophokles.* 7 vols. Leipzig, 1875–1890.

Translations

Green, R. L. *Two Satyr-Plays.* Harmondsworth, 1957.

Murray, G. *Antigone.* Oxford, 1941.

———. *Oedipus at Colonus.* Oxford, 1948.

———. *Oedipus King of Thebes.* Oxford, 1938.

———. *The Wife of Heracles.* Oxford, 1947.

Watling, E. F. *Sophocles: The Theban Plays.* Harmondsworth, 1947.

———. *Sophocles: "Electra" and Other Plays.* Harmondsworth, 1953.

Yeats, W. B. *Sophocles' "King Oedipus."* London, 1928.

General Works

Allègre, F. *Sophocle.* Lyon, 1905.

Bates, W. N. *Sophocles: Poet and Dramatist.* New York, 1961.

Blumenthal, A. von. *Sophokles.* Stuttgart, 1936.

Bowra, C. M. *Sophoclean Tragedy.* Oxford, 1944.

———. "Sophocles on His Own Development." *American Journal of Philology* 61 (1940): 385–401.

Earp, F. R. *The Style of Sophocles.* Cambridge, 1944.

Ehrenberg, V. *Sophocles and Pericles.* Oxford, 1954.

Ellendt, F. *Lexicon Sophocleum.* Rev. by H. Genthe. Hildesheim, 1958.

Helmreich, F., *Der Chor des Sophokles und Euripides nach seinem ἦθος betrachtet.* Erlangen, 1905.

Kamerbeek, J. C. *Studien over Sophocles. Utrecht,* 1934.

Kirkwood, G. M. *A Study of Sophoclean Drama.* Ithaca, 1958.

Kitto, H. D. F. *Sophocles: Dramatist and Philosopher.* London, 1958.

———. "The Idea of God in Aeschylus and Sophocles." In *La Notion du Divin depuis Homère jusqu'à Platon* (Fondation Hardt), pp. 69–89. Geneva, 1954.

Knox, B. M. W. *The Heroic Temper: Studies in Sophoclean Tragedy.* Berkeley, 1964.

Letters, F. J. H. *The Life and Work of Sophocles.* London, 1953.

Long, A. A. *Language and Thought in Sophocles.* London, 1967.

Maddelena, A. *Sofocle.* Turin, 1959.

Méautis, G. *Sophocle: Essai sur l'héros tragique.* Paris, 1957.

Muff, C. *Die chörische Technik des Sophokles.* Halle, 1877.

Opstelten, J. C. *Sophocles and Greek Pessimism.* Translated by J. A. Ross. Amsterdam, 1952.

Owen, E. T. "Sophocles the Dramatist." *University of Toronto Quarterly* 5 (1936): 228–250.

Perrotta, G. *Sofocle.* Messina, 1935.

Post, C. R. "The Dramatic Art of Sophocles." *Harvard Studies in Classical Philology* 23 (1912): 71–127.

————. "The Dramatic Art of Sophocles as Revealed by the Fragments of the Lost Plays." *Harvard Studies in Classical Philology* 33 (1922): 1–63.

Reinhardt, K. *Sophokles.* 3rd ed. Frankfurt, 1947.

Sheppard, J. T. *Aeschylus and Sophocles: Their Work and Influence.* London, 1927.

————. *The Wisdom of Sophocles.* London, 1947.

Siess, H. "Chronologische Untersuchungen zu den Tragödien des Sophokles." *Wiener Studien* 36 (1914): 244–298; 37 (1915): 27–62.

Tournaud, R. "Essai sur Sophocle." *Bulletin de l'Association Guillaume Budé: Lettres d'humanité,* 1942, pp. 1–137.

Untersteiner, M. *Sofocle.* Florence, 1935.

Waldock, A. J. A. *Sophocles the Dramatist.* Cambridge, 1951.

Webster, T. B. L. *An Introduction to Sophocles.* Oxford, 1936.

Weinstock, H. *Sophokles.* 3rd ed. Wuppertal, 1948.

Whitman, C. H. *Sophocles: A Study of Heroic Humanism.* Cambridge, Mass., 1951.

Wilamowitz-Moellendorff, T. von. *Die dramatische Technik des Sophokles.* Berlin, 1917.

Woodard, T. *Sophocles: A Collection of Critical Essays.* Englewood Cliffs, 1966.

Individual Plays

Ajax

Adams, S. M. "The *Ajax* of Sophocles." *Phoenix* 9 (1955): 93–110.

Calder, W. M., III. "The Entrance of Athena in *Ajax.*" *Classical Philology* 60 (1965): 114–116.

Dalmeyda, G. "Sophocle *Ajax.*" *Revue des Etudes Grecques* 46 (1933): 1–14.

Dalcourt, M. "La Suicide par vengeance dans la Grèce ancienne." *Revue de l'Histoire des Religions* 119 (1939): 154–171.

Ebeling, R. "Missverständnisse um den Aias des Sophokles." *Hermes* 76 (1941): 283–314.

Ferguson, J. "Ambiguity in *Ajax.*" *Dioniso* 44 (1970): 12–29.

Guthrie, W. K. C. "Odysseus in the *Ajax.*" *Greece and Rome* 16 (1947): 115–119.

Jones, J. *On Aristotle and Greek Tragedy,* pp. 177–192. London, 1962.

Kamerbeek, J. C. *The Plays of Sophocles: Part I, The "Ajax."* Leiden, 1953.

Kitto, H. D. F. *Form and Meaning in Drama,* pp. 179–198. London, 1956.

Knox, B. M. W. "The *Ajax* of Sophocles." *Harvard Studies in Classical Philology* 65 (1961): 1–37.

Linforth, I. M. "Three Scenes in Sophocles' *Ajax*." *University of California Publications in Classical Philology* 15 (1954): 1–28.

Lobeck, C. A. *Sophocles "Ajax."* Leipzig, 1866.

Platt, A. "The Burial of Ajax." *Classical Review* 25 (1912): 101–104.

Positano, L. M. *L'unita dell' Aiace di Sofocle.* Naples, 1946.

Rosenmeyer, T. G. *The Masks of Tragedy*, pp. 155–198. Austin, 1963.

Seidenberg, R. and Papathomoulos, E. "Sophocles' *Ajax*: A Morality for Madness." *Psychoanalytic Quarterly* 30 (1961): 410.

Untersteiner, M. *Sofocle: "Aiace."* Milan, 1934.

Wigodsky, M. M. "The 'Salvation' of Ajax." *Hermes* 90 (1962): 149–158.

Antigone

Agard, W. R. "Antigone 904–920." *Classical Philology* 32 (1937): 263–265.

Arrowsmith, W. "The Criticism of Greek Tragedy." *Tulane Drama Review* 3, no. 3 (1959): 31–56.

Drachmann, A. B. "Zur Composition der Sophokleischen *Antigone.*" *Hermes* 43 (1908): 67–76. Translated by H. A. Siepmann in *Classical Review* 23 (1910): 212–216.

Goheen, R. F. *The Imagery of Sophocles' "Antigone."* Princeton, 1951.

Havelock, E. *The Liberal Temper in Greek Politics.* New Haven, 1957.

Heidegger, M. *An Introduction to Metaphysics.* New Haven, 1959.

Jones, J. *On Aristotle and Greek Tragedy*, pp. 192–213. London, 1962.

Kitto, H. D. F. *Form and Meaning in Drama*, pp. 138–178. London, 1956.

Linforth, I. M. "Antigone and Creon." *University of California Publications on Classical Philology* 15 (1961): 183–266.

Muller, G. "Überlegungen zum Chor der *Antigone.*" *Hermes* 89 (1961): 398–422.

Rose, H. J. "Antigone and the Bride of Corinth." *Classical Quarterly* 19 (1925): 147–151.

Rouse, W. H. D. "The Two Burials in *Antigone.*" *Classical Review* 35 (1911): 40–42.

Roussel, P. "Les fiançailles d'Haimon et d'Antigone." *Revue des Etudes Grecques* 85 (1922): 63–81.

Segal, C. P. "Sophocles' Praise of Man and the Conflicts of the *Antigone.*" *Arion* 3 (1964): 46–66.

Slade, N. T. "Antigone." Unpublished MS.

The Women of Trachis

Hoey, T. F. "The *Trachiniae* and Unity of Hero." *Arethusa* 3 (1970): 1–22.

Kamerbeek, J. C. *The Plays of Sophocles: Part II, The "Trachiniae."* Leiden, 1959.

Kirkwood, G. M. "The Dramatic Unit of Sophocles' *Trachiniae.*" *Transactions and Proceedings of the American Philological Association* 72 (1941): 203–211.

Kitto, H. D. F. *Poiesis*, pp. 154–200. Berkeley, 1966.

———. "Sophocles, Statistics and the *Trachiniae.*" *American Journal of Philology* 60 (1939): 178–194.

Kranz, W. "Aufbau und Gehalt der *Trachiniai* des Sophokles." *Sokrates* 75 (1921): 39 ff.

Linforth, I. M. "The Pyre on Mount Oeta in Sophocles's *Trachiniae.*" *University of California Publications in Classical Philology* 14 (1952): 255 ff.

Murray, G. *Greek Studies*, pp. 106–126. Oxford, 1946.

Pound, E. *"Women of Trachis": A version.* London, 1958.

Webster, T. B. L. "Sophocles' *Trachiniae.*" In *Greek Poetry and Life: Essays presented to Gilbert Murray*, pp. 164–180. Oxford, 1936.

King Oedipus

Ax, W. "Die Parodos des *Oidipus Tyrannos.*" *Hermes* 67 (1932): 413–437.

Benardete, S. "Sophocles' *Oedipus Tyrannus.*" In *Ancients and Moderns* by J. Cropsey. New York, 1964.

Cameron, A. *The Identity of Oedipus the King.* New York, 1968.

Carroll, J. P. "Some Remarks on the Questions in the *Oedipus Tyrannus.*" *Classical Journal* 32 (1937): 406–416.

Croiset, M. *"Oedipe-Roi" de Sophocle: Etude et analyse.* Paris, n.d.

Deubner, L. "Oedipusprobleme." *Abhandlung der Preussichen Akademie der Wissenschaften*, 1943, pp. 1–43.

Diano, C. "Edipo figlio della Tyche." *Dioniso* 15 (1952): 56–89.

Dodds, E. R. "On Misunderstanding the *Oedipus Rex.*" *Greece and Rome* 13 (1966): 37–49.

Driver, T. F. *The Sense of History in Greek and Shakespearian Tragedy.* New York, 1960.

Errandonea, I. "El estasimo segundo del *Edipo Rey.*" *Textos y Estudios.* La Plata, Argentina, 1952.

Ferguson, F. *The Idea of a Theater.* Princeton, 1949.

Freud, S. *The Interpretation of Dreams.* 2nd ed. Translated by A. A. Brill. London, 1945.

Frierman, J., and Gassel, S. "The Chorus in Sophocles' *Oedipus Tyrannus.*" *Psychoanalytic Quarterly* 19 (1950): 213–226.

Fromm, E. *The Forgotten Language.* New York, 1951.

Helmbold, W. C. "The Paradox of the *Oedipus.*" *American Journal of Philology* 72 (1951): 293–300.

Hug, A. "Der Doppelsinn in Sophokles *Oedipus König.*" *Philologus* 31 (1871): 66–84.

Jones, J. *On Aristotle and Greek Tragedy,* pp. 192–214. London, 1962.

Kallich, M.; MacLeish, A.; and Schoenbohm, G. *Oedipus: Myth and Drama.* New York, 1968.

Kamerbeek, J. C. *The Plays of Sophocles: The "Oedipus Tyrannus."* Leiden, 1967.

Kitto, H. D. F. *Poiesis,* pp. 200–242. Berkeley, 1966.

Knox, B. M. W. *Oedipus at Thebes.* New Haven, 1957.

O'Brien, M. J., ed. *Twentieth Century Interpretations of "Oedipus Rex."* Englewood Cliffs, 1968.

Ostwald, M. "Aristotle on *Humartia* and Sophocles' *Oedipus Tyrannus.*" In *Festschrift Ernst Kupp,* pp. 93–108. Hamburg, 1958.

Owen, E. T. "Drama in Sophocles' *Oedipus Tyrannus.*" *University of Toronto Quarterly* 10 (1940): 46–59.

Reid, S. A. "Teaching *Oedipus Rex.*" *College English* 29 (1968): 615–619.

Robert, C. *Oidipus.* Berlin, 1915.

Sanderson, J. L., and Zimmerman, E. *Oedipus: Myth and Dramatic Form.* Boston, 1968.

Schrade, L. *La Représentation d'Edipo Tirrano au Teatro Olimpico.* Paris, 1960.

Sheppard, J. T. *The "Oedipus Tyrannus."* Cambridge, 1920.

Stanford, W. B. *Ambiguity in Greek Literature,* pp. 163–173. Oxford, 1939.

Thomson, J. A. K. *Irony,* pp. 54–69. London, 1926.

Vellacott, P. "The Guilt of Oedipus." *Greece and Rome* 11 (1964): 137–148.

————. "The Chorus in *Oedipus Tyrannus.*" *Greece and Rome* 14 (1967):
   109–125.

Electra

Calder, W. M., III. "The End of Sophocles' *Electra.*" *Greek, Roman and
   Byzantine Studies* 4 (1963): 213–216.
Corrigan, R. W. "The *Electra* of Sophocles." *Tulane Drama Review* 1
   (1955–1957): 36–66.
Johansen, H. F. "Die *Elektra* des Sophokles: Versuch einer neuen Deu-
   tung." *Classica et Mediaevalia* 25 (1964): 8–32.
Jones, J. *On Aristotle and Greek Tragedy*, pp. 141–159. London, 1962.
Kaibel, G. *Sophokles "Elektra."* Leipzig, 1896.
Kirkwood, G. M. "Two Structural Features of Sophocles' *Electra.*" *Trans-
   actions and Proceedings of the American Philological Association* 73
   (1942): 86–95.
Linforth, I. M. "Electra's Day in the Tragedy of Sophocles." *University of
   California Publications in Classical Philology* 19 (1963): 89–126.
Segal, C. P. "The *Electra* of Sophocles." *Transactions and Proceedings of
   the American Philological Association* 97 (1967): 473–547.
Sheppard, J. T. "The Tragedy of Electra According to Sophocles." *Classical
   Quarterly* 12 (1918): 80–88.
————. "*Electra*: A Defence of Sophocles." *Classical Review* 41 (1927):
   2–9.
————. "*Electra* Again." *Classical Review* 41 (1927): 163–165.
Wilamowitz-Moellendorff, U. von. "Die beiden Elektra." *Hermes* 18
   (1883): 214–263.
Woodward, T. "*Electra* by Sophocles: The Dialectical Design." *Harvard
   Studies in Classical Philology* 68 (1964): 163–205; 70 (1966): 195–
   233.

Philoctetes

Alt, K. "Schicksal und Φύσις im *Philoktetes* des Sophokles." *Hermes* 89
   (1961): 141–174.
Avery, H. C. "Heracles, Philoctetes, Neoptolemus." *Hermes* 93 (1965):
   279–297.
Biggs, P. "The Disease Theme in Sophocles' *Ajax, Philoctetes, Trachiniae.*"
   Classical Philology 61 (1966): 223–236.
Dale, A. M. "Seen and Unseen on the Greek Stage." *Wiener Studien* 59
   (1956): 96–106.

Fedder, L. "The Image of the Desert Island in Sophocles' *Philoctetes*." *Drama Survey* 3 (1963): 33–41.

Harsh, P. W. "The Role of the Bow in Sophocles' *Philoctetes*." *American Journal of Philology* 81 (1960): 408–414.

Hinds, A. E., "The Prophecy of Helenus in Sophocles' *Philoctetes*." *Classical Quarterly*, n.s. 17 (1967): 169–180.

Kieffer, J. P. "Philoctetes and Arete." *Classical Philology* 37 (1942): 38–50.

Kitto, H. D. F. *Form and Meaning in Drama*, pp. 87–137. London, 1956.

Linforth, I. M. "Philoctetes: The Play and the Man." *University of California Publications in Classical Philology* 15 (1956): 95–156.

Robinson, D. R. "Topics in Sophocles' *Philoctetes*." *Classical Quarterly* 19 (1969): 34–66.

Rosenquist, S. L. "*Philoctetes*." Unpublished MS.

Vourveris, K. I. Σοφοκλέους Φιλοκτήτης. Athens, 1963.

Webster, T. B. L. *Sophocles: "Philoctetes*." Cambridge, 1970.

Wilson, E. *The Wound and the Bow*. New York, 1965.

Woodhouse, W. J. "The Scenic Arrangements of the *Philoctetes* of Sophocles." *Journal of the Hellenic Society* 32 (1912): 239–249.

Oedipus at Colonus

Adams, S. M. "Unity of Plot in the *Oedipus Coloneus*." *Phoenix* 7 (1953): 136–147.

Hay, J. "Oedipus Coloneus." Unpublished MS.

Jones, J. *On Aristotle and Greek Tragedy*, pp. 216–235. London, 1962.

Linforth, I. M. "Religion and Drama in *Oedipus at Colonus*." *University of California Studies in Classical Philology* 14 (1951): 75–191.

Méautis, G. *L'Oedipe à Colone et le culte des héros*. Neuchâtel, 1940.

Robert, C. *Oidipus*. Berlin, 1915.

Shields, H. G. "Sight and Blindness Imagery in the *Oedipus Coloneus*." *Phoenix* 15 (1961): 63–73.

The Trackers

Allègre, F. "Les *Limiers*: Drame satyrique de Sophocle." *Revue des Etudes Ancienne* 15 (1913): 237ff.

Ferrante, D. *Sofocle: I "Braccatore*." Naples, 1958.

Harrison, J. E. "Notes on the *Ichneutae*." In *Essays Presented to W. Ridgeway*. Cambridge, 1913.

Page, D. L. *Greek Literary Papyri I: Poetry*, pp. 26–53. London, 1942.

Pearson, A. C., and Jebb, R. C. *The Fragments of Sophocles I*. Cambridge, 1917.

Vollgraff, G. "Ad Sophoclis Indagatores." *Mnemosyne* 42 (1914): 81–90, 165–177.

Walker, R. J. *The "Ichneutae" of Sophocles*. London, 1919.

Walton, F. R. "A Problem of the *Ichneutae* of Sophocles." *Harvard Studies in Classical Philology* 46 (1935): 167–189.

Wilamowitz-Moellendorff, U. von. "Die *Spurhünde* des Sophokles." *Neue Jahrbuch für das klassische Alterthum* 29 (1912): 449–476.

EURIPIDES
Texts and Commentaries

Méridier, L.; Chapouthier, F.; Grégoire, H.; and Parmentier, L. *Euripide*. 6 vols. Paris, 1947–1961.

Murray, G. *Euripides Fabulae*. 3 vols. Oxford, 1935.

Nauck, A. *Euripidis Tragoediae*. 2nd ed. 3 vols. Leipzig, 1880–1881.

Paley, F. A. *Euripides*. 2nd ed. 3 vols. London, 1872–1880.

Prinz, R., and Wecklein, N. *Euripidis Fabulae*. Leipzig, 1878–1902.

Schwartz, E. *Scholia in Euripidem*. 2 vols. Berlin, 1887–1891.

Translations

Green, R. L. *Two Satyr-Plays*. Harmondsworth, 1957.

Murray, G. *The Plays of Euripides for English Readers*. London, various dates.

Vellacott, P. *Euripides: "Alcestis" and Other Plays*. Harmondsworth, 1953.
————. *Euripides: The "Bacchae" and Other Plays*. Harmondsworth, 1954.
————. *Euripides: "Medea" and Other Plays*. Harmondsworth, 1963.

Warner, R. *Euripides: "Medea."* London, 1946.

Way, A. S. *Euripides*. 4 vols. London, 1912.

General Works

Allen, J. T., and Italie, G. *A Concordance to Euripides*. Berkeley, 1954.

Appleton, R. B. *Euripides the Idealist*. London, 1927.

Arrowsmith, W. "A Greek Theater of Ideas." In *Ideas in the Drama* by J. Gassner. New York, 1964.

Barlow, S. *The Imagery of Euripides*. London, 1971.

Bates, W. N. *Euripides: A Student of Human Nature*. New York, 1961.

Berry, E. G. "The History and Development of the Concept of *Theia Moira* and *Theia Tyche* down to and including Plato. Dissertation. Chicago, 1940.

Blaiklock, E. M. *The Male Characters of Euripides.* Wellington, N.Z.

Busch, G. *Untersuchungen zum Wesen der τύχη in den Tragödien des Euripides.* Dissertation. Heidelberg, 1937.

Ceadel, C. B. "Resolved Feet in the Trimeters of Euripides and the Chronology of the Plays." *Classical Quarterly* 35 (1941): 66–89.

Conacher, D. J. *Myth, Theme and Structure in Euripidean Drama.* Toronto, 1967.

Dalymede, G. "Observations sur les prologues d'Euripide." *Revue des Etudes Grecques* 32 (1919): 121–131.

Decharme, P. *Euripides and the Spirit of His Drama.* Translated by J. Loeb. New York, 1906.

Delcourt, M. *La vie d'Euripide.* Paris, 1930.

Delebecque, E. *Euripide et la Guerre du Peloponnèse.* Paris, 1951.

Dodds, E. R. "Euripides the Irrationalist." *Classical Review* 43 (1929): 97–104.

Friedrich, W. H. *Euripides und Diphilos.* Munich, 1953.

Girard, P. "La trilogie chez Euripide." *Revue des Etudes Grecques* 17 (1904): 149–195.

Goossens, R. *Euripide et Athènes.* Brussels, 1962.

Greenwood, L. H. G. *Aspects of Euripidean Drama.* Cambridge, 1953.

Grube, G. M. A. *The Drama of Euripides.* London, 1941.

Harsh, P. W. "Repetition of Lines in Euripides." *Hermes* 72 (1937): 435–450.

Helmreich, P. *Der Chor des Sophokles und Euripides nach seinem ἦθος betrachtet.* Erlangen, 1905.

Howald, E. *Untersuchungen zur Technik der euripideischen Tragödien.* Leipzig, 1914.

Klotsche, E. H. *The Supernatural in the Tragedies of Euripides.* Lincoln, Nebraska, 1918.

Macurdy, G. H. *The Chronology of the Extant Plays of Euripides.* Lancaster, Pa., 1905.

Masqueray, P. *Euripides et ses Idées.* Paris, 1908.

Méridier, L. *La Prologue dans la tragédie d'Euripide.* Bordeaux, 1911.

Mierow, H. E. "Euripides' Artistic Development." *American Journal of Philology* 52 (1931): 339–350.

Murray, G. *Euripides and His Age.* London, 1913.

Nestle, W. *Euripides: Der Dichter der griechischen Aufklärung.* Stuttgart, 1901.

————. "Untersuchungen ueber die philosophischen Quellen des Euripides." *Philologus,* suppl. 8 (1902): 559–656.

Phoutrides, A. E. "The Chorus of Euripides." *Harvard Studies in Classical Philology* 27 (1916): 77–170.

Reverdin, O. *Euripide (Entretiens sur l'antiquité classique 6).* Geneva, 1960.

Ridgeway, W. "Euripides in Macedon." *Classical Quarterly* 20 (1926): 1–20.

Rivier, A. *Essai sur la tragique d'Euripide.* Lausanne, 1944.

Schmidt, J. *Freiwilliger Opfertod bei Euripides.* Vol. 17 of *Religionsgeschichtliche Versuche u. Vorarbeiten.* Giessen, 1921.

Segal, E. *Euripides.* Englewood Cliffs, 1968.

Steiger, H. *Euripides: Seine Dichtung und seine Persönlichkeit.* Leipzig, 1912.

Steinweg, C. *Euripides als Tragiker und Lustspieldichter.* Halle, 1924.

Strohm, H. *Euripides.* Munich, 1957.

Thomson, D. *Euripides and the Attic Orators.* London, 1898.

Van Lennep, D. W. F. *Euripides.* Amsterdam, 1935.

Verrall, A. W. *Euripides the Rationalist.* Cambridge, 1895.

Webster, T. B. L. *The Tragedies of Euripides.* London, 1967.

Wilamowitz-Moellendorff, U. von. *Analecta Euripidea.* Berlin, 1875.

Zielinski, T. "L'évolution religieuse d'Euripide." *Revue des Etudes Grecques* 36 (1923): 459–479.

Zuntz, G. *The Political Plays of Euripides.* Manchester, 1955.

Individual Plays

Alcestis

Beye, G. R. "Alcestis and Her Critics." *Greek, Roman and Byzantine Studies* 2 (1959): 109–127.

Burnett, A. P. "The Virtue of Admetus." *Classical Philology* 60 (1965): 240–255.

Croiset, M. "Observations sur le rôle d'Admète." *Revue des Etudes Grecques* 25 (1912): 1–11.

Dale, A. M. *Euripides: "Alcestis."* Oxford, 1954.

Drew, D. L. "Euripides' *Alcestis.*" *American Journal of Philology* 52 (1931): 295–319.

Driver, T. F. *The Sense of History in Greek and Shakespearian Drama.* New York, 1960.

Ebeling, H. L. "The Admetus of Euripides Viewed in Relation to Admetus of the Tradition." *Transactions and Proceedings of the American Philological Association* 29 (1898) : 65–85.

Jones, I. D. M. "Euripides' *Alcestis.*" *Classical Review* 62 (1948) : 50–55.

Lesky, A. *Alkestis: Der Mythus und das Drama.* Vienna, 1925.

Myres, J. L. "The Plot of the *Alcestis.*" *Journal of the Hellenic Society* 37 (1917) : 195–218.

Paton, J. A. "The Story of Alcestis in Ancient Literature and Art." *American Journal of Archaeology* 4 (1900) : 150–151.

Rosenmeyer, T. G. *The Masks of Tragedy*, pp. 201–248. Austin, 1963.

Séchan, L. *Le Dénouement d'Alceste.* Paris, 1927.

Smith, W. D. "The Ironic Structure in *Alcestis.*" *Phoenix* 14 (1960) : 127–145.

Verrall, A. W. *Euripides the Rationalist*, pp. 1–128. Cambridge, 1895.

Weber, L. *Euripides: "Alkestis."* Leipzig, 1930.

Wilson, J. R., ed. *Twentieth Century Interpretations of Euripides' "Alcestis."* Englewood Cliffs, 1968.

Andromache

Aldrich, K. M. *The "Andromache" of Euripides.* Lincoln, 1961.

Garzya, A. "Interpretazione dell'*Andromaca* di Euripide." *Dioniso* 14 (1951) : 109–138.

———. "Quelques notes sur l'*Andromaque* d'Euripide." *Revue Belge (de Philologie et d'Histoire)* 29 (1951) : 1142–1150.

Hermann, G. *Euripides: "Andromache."* Leipzig, 1938.

Hyslop, A. R. F. *The "Andromache" of Euripides.* London, 1900.

Jarde, A. "Sur la date d'*Andromaque* d'Euripide." *Revue des Etudes Ancienne* 25 (1923) : 209–214.

Johnson, V. "Euripides' *Andromache.*" *Classical Weekly* 48 (1954–1955) : 9–13.

Norwood, G. *The "Andromache" of Euripides.* London, 1906.

Page, D. L. "The Elegiacs in Euripides' *Andromache.*" In *Greek Poetry and Life: Essays Presented to G. Murray on His 70th Birthday*, pp. 206–230. Oxford, 1936.

Robertson, D. S. "Euripides and Tharyps." *Classical Review* 37 (1923) : 58–60.

Verrall, A. W. *Essays on Four Plays of Euripides*, pp. 1–42. Cambridge, 1905.

The Bacchants

Banks, T. "A Pattern of Imagery in *The Bacchae*." Unpublished MS.

Bather, A. G. "The Problem of Euripides' *Bacchae*." *Journal of the Hellenic Society* 14 (1894): 244–263.

Bellinger, A. R. "The *Bacchae* and *Hippolytus*." *Yale Classical Studies* 6 (1939): 15–27.

Deichgraber, K. "Die Kadmos-Teiresiasszene in Euripides' *Bakchen*." *Hermes* 70 (1935): 322–349.

Dodds, E. R. *Euripides: "Bacchae."* 2nd ed. Oxford, 1966.

Grube, G. M. A. "Dionysus in the *Bacchae*." *Transactions and Proceedings of the American Philological Association* 66 (1935): 37–54.

Lejnieks, V. "Interpolations in the *Bacchae*." *American Journal of Philology* 88 (1967): 332–339.

Nihard, R. "Le Problème des *Bacchantes* d'Euripides." *Musées Royaux des Beaux-Arts de Belgique* 16 (1912): 91–120, 297–375.

Norwood, G. *The Riddle of the "Bacchae."* Manchester, 1908.

———. *Essays on Euripidean Drama*, pp. 52–73. Cambridge, 1954.

Rohde, E. *Psyche*, pp. 253–334. Translated by W. B. Hillis. London, 1925.

Rosenmeyer, T. G. *The Masks of Tragedy*, pp. 105–152. Austin, 1963.

Sandys, J. E. *The "Bacchae" of Euripides*. Cambridge, 1880.

Stanford, W. B. *Ambiguity in Greek Literature*, pp. 174–179. Oxford, 1939.

Verrall, A. W. *The "Bacchants" of Euripides and Other Essays*. Cambridge, 1910.

Winnington-Ingram, R. P. *Euripides and Dionysus*. Cambridge, 1948.

Cyclops

Arnott, P. D. "The Overworked Playwright." *Greece and Rome* 8 (1961): 164–169.

Arrowsmith, W. Introduction to *Cyclops*. In Grene, D., and Lattimore, R., eds., *The Complete Greek Tragedies*. Vol. 3, pp. 224–230. Chicago, 1959.

Duchemin, J. *Le "Cyclope" d'Euripide*. Paris, 1945.

Kaibel, G. "Kratinos' Ὀδυσσῆς und Euripides' Κύκλωψ." *Hermes* 30 (1895): 71–87.

Kassel, R. "Bemerkungen zum *Kyklops* des Euripides." *Rheinisches Museum fuer Philologie*, n.f. 98 (1955): 279–286.

Masqueray, P. "Le *Cyclope* d'Euripide et celui d'Homère." *Revue des Etudes Anciennes* 4 (1902): 164–190.

Pathmanathan, R. S. "A Playwright Relaxed or Overworked?" *Greece and Rome* 10 (1963): 123–130.

Simonds, D. M., and Timberlake, R. R. *Euripides' "Cyclops."* Cambridge, 1927.

Electra

Adams, S. M. "Two Plays of Euripides." *Classical Review* 49 (1935): 118–122.

Denniston, J. D. *Euripides: "Electra."* Oxford, 1939.

England, T. "The *Electra* of Euripides." *Classical Review* 40 (1926): 97–104.

Jones, J. *On Aristotle and Greek Tragedy*, pp. 239–245. London, 1962.

Kubo, M. "The Norm of Myth: Euripides' *Electra.*" *Harvard Studies in Classical Philology* 71 (1966): 15–39.

O'Brien, M. J. "Orestes and the Gorgon: Euripides' *Electra.*" *American Journal of Philology* 85 (1964): 13–39.

Sheppard, J. T. "The *Electra* of Euripides." *Classical Review* 32 (1918): 137–141.

Steiger, H. "Warum schrieb Euripides seine *Elektra?*" *Philologus* 56 (1897): 561–600.

Stoessel, F. "Die *Elektra* des Euripides." *Rheinisches Museum fuer Philologie* 99 (1956): 47–92.

Weil, H. *Sept Tragédies d'Euripide.* 2nd ed. Paris, 1879.

Wilamowitz-Moellendorff, U. von. "Die beiden *Elektra.*" *Hermes* 18 (1883): 214–263.

Hecabe

Abrahamson, E. L. "Euripides' Tragedy of *Hecuba.*" *Transactions and Proceedings of the American Philological Association* 83 (1952): 120–129.

Adkins, A. W. H. "Basic Greek Values in Euripides' *Hecuba* and *Hercules Furens.*" *Classical Quarterly*, n.s. 16 (1966): 193–219.

Arrowsmith, W. Introduction to *Hecuba*. In Grene, D., and Lattimore, R., eds., *The Complete Greek Tragedies*. Vol. 3, pp. 488–493. Chicago, 1959.

Matthaei, Louise E. *Studies in Greek Tragedy.* Cambridge, 1918.

Pearson, L. *Popular Ethics in Ancient Greece,* pp. 144–148. Stanford, 1962.

Sheppard, J. T. *Euripides: "Hecuba."* Oxford, 1924.

Spranger, J. A. "The Problems of the *Hecuba.*" *Classical Quarterly* 21 (1927): 155–158.

Vandaele, H. "L'Unité d'*Hécube.*" *Xenia,* 1912, pp. 10–24.

Weil, H. *Sept Tragédies d'Euripide.* 2nd ed. Paris, 1879.

Helen

Alt, K. "Zur Anagnorisis in der *Helena.*" *Hermes* 90 (1962): 6–24.

———. *Euripides: "Helena."* Leipzig, 1964.

Caldwell, R. "The First Stasimon of Euripides' *Helen*" Unpublished MS.

Campbell, A. Y. *Euripides' "Helena."* Liverpool, 1950.

Dale, A. M. *Euripides: "Helen."* Oxford, 1967.

Drew, D. L. "The Political Purpose in Euripides' *Helena.*" *Classical Philology* 25 (1930): 187–189.

Golann, C. P. "The Third Stasimon of Euripides' *Helena.*" *Transactions and Proceedings of the American Philological Association* 76 (1945): 31–46.

Griffiths, J. "Some Thoughts on the *Helena.*" *Journal of the Hellenic Society* 73 (1953): 36–41.

Pearson, A. C. *Euripides' "Helen."* Cambridge, 1903.

Pippin, A. N. "Euripides' *Helen*: A Comedy of Ideas." *Classical Philology* 55 (1960): 151–163.

Solmsen, F. "*Onoma* and *Pragma* in Euripides' *Helen.*" *Classical Review* 48 (1934): 119–121.

Verrall, A. W. *Essays on Four Plays of Euripides,* pp. 43–133. Cambridge, 1905.

Zuntz, G. "On Euripides' *Helena*: Theology and Irony." In *Euripide* (Entretiens sur l'antiquité classique 6) by O. Reverdin. Geneva, 1960.

Heracles

Adkins, A. W. H. "Basic Greek Values in Euripides' *Hecuba* and *Hercules Furens.*" *Classical Quarterly,* n.s. 16 (1966): 193–219.

Arrowsmith, W. *The Conversion of Heracles: An Essay in Euripidean Tragic-Structure.* Dissertation. Princeton, 1954.

———. Introduction to *Heracles.* In Grene, D., and Lattimore, R., eds.,

The Complete Greek Tragedies. Vol. 3, pp. 266–281. Chicago, 1959.

Chalk, H. H. O. "Ἀρετή and βία in Euripides' *Herakles.*" *Journal of the Hellenic Society* 82 (1962): 7–18.

Conacher, D. J. "Theme, Plot and Technique in the *Heracles* of Euripides." *Phoenix* 9 (1955): 139–152.

Greenwood, L. H. G. *Aspects of Euripidean Drama,* pp. 59–91. Cambridge, 1953.

Hendrickson, G. L. "The Heracles Myth and Its Treatment by Euripides." In *Classical Studies in Honor of Charles Forster Smith,* pp. 11–29. Madison, 1919.

Kamerbeek, J. C. "The Unity and Meaning of Euripides' *Heracles.*" *Mnemosyne* 19 (1966): 1–16.

Kroeker, E. *Der "Herakles" des Euripides: Analyse des Dramas.* Dissertation. Leipzig, 1938.

Parry, H. "The Second Stasimon of Euripides' *Heracles.*" *American Journal of Philology* 86 (1965): 362–374.

Sheppard, J. T. "The Formal Beauty of the *Hercules Furens.*" *Classical Quarterly* 10 (1916): 72–79.

Svendsen, J. T. "Dramatic Form and the *Heracles.*" Unpublished MS.

Verrall, A. W. *Essays on Four Plays of Euripides,* pp. 134–198. Cambridge, 1905.

Wilamowitz-Moellendorff, U. von. *Euripides "Herakles."* 2nd ed., 2 vols. Berlin, 1895.

Heracles's Children

Fitton, J. W. "The *Suppliant Women* and the *Heracleidai* of Euripides." *Hermes* 89 (1961): 430–461.

McLean, J. H. "The *Heraclidae* of Euripides." *American Journal of Philology* 55 (1934): 197–224.

Pearson, A. C. *Euripides: The "Heracleidae."* Cambridge, 1907.

Spranger, J. A. "The Political Element in the *Heracleidae* of Euripides." *Classical Quarterly* 19 (1925): 117–164.

Wilamowitz-Moellendorff, U. von "Excurse zu Euripides *Heraklidai.*" *Hermes* 17 (1882): 337–364.

Zuntz, G. "Is the *Heraclidae* Mutilated?" *Classical Quarterly* 41 (1947): 46–52.

———. *The Political Plays of Euripides.* Manchester, 1955.

Hippolytus

Adams, S. M. "Two Plays of Euripides." *Classical Review* 49 (1935): 118–122.

Barnes, H. E. "The Hippolytus of Drama and Myth." In Sutherland, D., and Barnes, H. E. *Hippolytus in Drama and Myth.* Lincoln, Nebraska, 1960.

Baron, J. R. *"Hippolytus*: Some Comments on a Play by Euripides." Unpublished MS.

Barrett, W. S. *Euripides' "Hippolytus."* Oxford, 1964.

Bellinger, A. R. "The *Bacchae* and *Hyppolytus.*" *Yale Classical Studies* 6 (1939): 15–27.

Conacher, D. J. "A Problem in Euripides' *Hippolytus.*" *Transactions and Proceedings of the American Philological Association* 92 (1961): 37–44.

Crocker, L. G. "On Interpreting *Hippolytus.*" *Philologus* 101 (1961): 238–246.

Dodds, E. R. "The Αἰδώς of Phaedra and the Meaning of the *Hippolytus.*" *Classical Review* 39 (1925): 102–104.

Graham, H. F. "The 'Escape-Ode' in *Hippolytus.*" *Classical Journal* 42 (1947): 275–276.

Grene, D. "The Interpretation of the *Hippolytus* of Euripides." *Classical Philology* 34 (1939): 45–58.

Hadley, W. S. *Euripides: "Hippolytus."* Cambridge, 1889.

Herter, H. "Theseus und Hippolytos." *Rheinisches Museum fuer Philologie* 89 (1940): 273–292.

Knox, B. M. W. "The *Hippolytus* of Euripides." *Yale Classical Studies* 13 (1952): 3–31.

Lattimore, R. "Phaedra and Hippolytus." *Arion* 13 (1962): 5–18.

Linforth, I. M. "Hippolytus and Humanism." *Transactions and Proceedings of the American Philological Association* 45 (1914): 5–11.

Lucas, D. W. "Hippolytus." *Classical Quarterly* 40 (1946): 65–69.

Matthaei, L. E. *Studies in Greek Tragedy.* Cambridge, 1918.

Méridier, L. *"Hippolyte" d'Euripide.* Paris, 1931.

Norwood, G. *Essays on Euripidean Drama,* pp. 74–112. Toronto, 1954.

Sanderson, J. C., and Gopnik, I. *Phaedra and Hippolytus: Myth and Dramatic Form.* Boston, 1966.

Séchan, L. "La Légende d'Hippolyte dans l'Antiquité." *Revue des Etudes Grecques* 24 (1911): 105–151.

Segal, C. P. "The Tragedy of the *Hippolytus*: The Waters of Ocean and the Untouched Meadow." *Harvard Studies in Classical Philology* 70 (1965): 117–169.

Smith, W. D. "Staging in the Central Scene in the *Hippolytus*." *Transactions and Proceedings of the American Philological Association* 91 (1960): 162–177.

Snell, B. *Scenes from Greek Drama*. Berkeley, 1964.

Soury, G. "Euripide: Rationaliste et mystique d'après *Hippolyte*." *Revue des Etudes Grecques* 56 (1943): 29–52.

Spranger, J. A. "The Art of Euripides in the *Hippolytus*." *Classical Review* 33 (1919): 9–15.

———. The Meaning of the *Hippolytus* of Euripides." *Classical Quarterly* 21 (1927): 18–19.

Stanford, W. B. "The *Hippolytus* of Euripides." *Hermathena* 63 (1944): 11–17.

Weil, H. *Sept Tragédies d'Euripide*. 2nd ed. Paris, 1879.

Wilamowitz-Moellendorff, U. von. *Euripides: "Hippolytus."* Berlin, 1891.

Willink, C. W. "Some Problems in *Hippolytus*." *Classical Quarterly*, n.s. 18 (1968): 11–43.

Winnington-Ingram, R. P. "*Hippolytus*: A Study in Causation." In *Euripide: Entretiens sur l'antiquité classique*. Vol. 6, pp. 171–197. Geneva, 1960.

Ion

Colardeau, T. "Ion à Delphes." *Revue des Etudes Grecques* 29 (1916): 430–434.

Imhof, M. *Euripides' "Ion."* Bern and Munich, 1966.

Matthaei, L. E. *Studies in Greek Tragedy*. Cambridge, 1918.

Owen, A. S. *Euripides: "Ion."* Oxford, 1939.

Rosenmeyer, T. G. *The Masks of Tragedy*, pp. 105–152. Austin, 1963.

Solmsen, F. "Euripides' *Ion* im Vergleich mit anderen Tragödien." *Hermes* 69 (1934): 390–419.

Verrall, A. W. *The "Ion" of Euripides*. Cambridge, 1890.

———. *Euripides the Rationalist*, pp. 129–165. Cambridge, 1895.

Wassermann, F. M. "Divine Violence and Providence in Euripides' *Ion*." *Transactions and Proceedings of the American Philological Association* 71 (1940): 587–604.

Wilamowitz-Moellendorff, U. von. *Euripides: "Ion."* Berlin, 1926.

Iphigeneia at Aulis

Bonnard, A. "*Iphigénie à Aulis*: Tragique et poésie." *Museum Helvetium* 2 (1945): 87–107.

England, E. B. *The "Iphigeneia at Aulis" of Euripides*. London, 1891.

Ferguson, J. "*Iphigeneia at Aulis*." *Transactions and Proceedings of the American Philological Association* 99 (1968): 157–164.

Friedrich, W. H. "Zur Aulischen Iphigenie." *Hermes* 69 (1934): 73–100.

Meunier, J. "Pour une lecture candide d'*Iphigénie à Aulis*." *Musées Royaux des Beaux-Arts de Belgique* 31 (1927): 21–35.

Page, D. L. *Actors' Interpolations in Greek Tragedy*. Oxford, 1934.

Parmentier, L. "L'*Iphigénie à Aulis* d'Euripide." *Académie Royale de Belgique, Bulletin de la Classe des Lettres*, 5th ser. 12 (1926): 266–273.

Roussel, P. "Le rôle d'Achille dans l'*Iphigénie à Aulis*." *Revue des Etudes Grecques* 28 (1915): 234–250.

Wassermann, F. M. "Agamemnon in the *Iphigeneia at Aulis*." *Transactions and Proceedings of the American Philological Association* 80 (1949): 174–186.

Weil, H. *Sept Tragédies d'Euripide*. 2nd ed. Paris 1879.

Iphigeneia among the Taurians

Platnauer, M. *Euripides: "Iphigenia in Tauris."* Oxford, 1938.

Verrall, A. W. *Euripides the Rationalist*, pp. 166–230. Cambridge, 1895.

Weil, H. *Sept Tragédies d'Euripide*. 2nd ed. Paris, 1879.

Medea

Blaiklock, E. M. "The Nautical Imagery of Euripides' *Medea*." *Classical Philology* 50 (1955): 233–237.

Buttrey, T. V. "Accident and Design in Euripides' *Medea*." *American Journal of Philology* 79 (1958): 1–17.

Cunningham, M. P. "Medea ἀπὸ μηχανῆς." *Classical Philology* 49 (1954): 151–160.

Mead, L. M. "A Study in the *Medea*." *Greece and Rome* 12 (1943): 15–20.

Page, D. L. *Euripides: "Medea."* Oxford, 1938.

Palmer, R. B. "An Apology for Jason: A Study of Euripides' *Medea*." *Classical Journal* 53 (1957): 49–55.

Reckford, K. J. "Medea's First Exit." *Transactions and Proceedings of the American Philological Association* 99 (1968): 329–359.

Sanderson, J. L., and Zimmerman, E. *Medea: Myth and Dramatic Form*. Boston, 1967.

Schlesinger, E. "Zu Euripides' *Medea.*" *Hermes* 94 (1966): 26–53.

Snell, B. *Scenes from Greek Drama.* Berkeley, 1964.

Tanagras, A. *Medea.* Athens, 1910.

Tarditi, G. "Euripide e il dramma di *Medea.*" *Rivista di Filologia e di Istruzione Classica* 25 (1957): 354–371.

Thompson, E. A. "Neophron and Euripides' *Medea.*" *Classical Quarterly* 38 (1944): 10–14.

Usscher, R. G. "Notes on Euripides' *Medea.*" *Eranos* 59 (1961): 1–7.

Weil, H. *Sept Tragédies d'Euripide.* 2nd ed. Paris, 1879.

Orestes

Arrowsmith, W. Introduction to *Orestes.* In Grene, D., and Lattimore, R., eds., *The Complete Greek Tragedies.* Vol. 4, pp. 186–191. Chicago, 1959.

Biehl, W. *Euripides: "Orestes."* Berlin, 1965.

Boulter, P. N. "The Theme of ἄγρια in Euripides' *Orestes.*" *Phoenix* 16 (1962): 102ff.

Di Benedetto, V. *Euripides: "Orestes."* Florence, 1965.

Feaver, D. D. "The Musical Setting of Euripides's *Orestes.*" *American Journal of Philology* 81 (1960): 1–15.

Greenberg, N. A. "Euripides' *Orestes*: An Interpretation." *Harvard Studies in Classical Philology* 66 (1962): 157–192.

Krieg, W. *De Euripides Oreste.* Halle, 1934.

Lesky, A. "Zum *Orestes* des Euripides." *Wiener Studien* 53 (1935): 37–47.

Mullens, H. G. "The Meaning of Euripides' *Orestes.*" *Classical Quarterly* 34 (1940): 153–158.

Peprotta, G. "Studi Euripidei." *Stud. H. di Fil. Class.*, n.s. 6 (1928): 117ff.

Verrall, A. W. *Essays on Four Plays of Euripides,* pp. 199–264. Cambridge, 1905.

Wedd, N. *The Orestes of Euripides.* Cambridge, 1895.

Weil, H. *Sept Tragédies d'Euripide.* 2nd ed. Paris, 1879.

Wolff, C. "Orestes." In *Euripides* by E. Segal, pp. 132–149. Englewood Cliffs, 1968.

The Women of Phoenicia

Conacher, D. J. "Themes in the *Exodus* of Euripides' *Phoenissae.*" *Phoenix* 21 (1967): 92–101.

Meredith, H. O. "The End of the *Phoenissae.*" *Classical Review* 51 (1937): 97–103.

Pearson, A. C. *Euripides: The "Phoenissae."* Cambridge, 1909.

Podlecki, A. J. "Some Themes in Euripides' *Phoenissae*." *Transactions and Proceedings of the American Philological Association* 93 (1967): 355–373.

Powell, J. U. *Euripides: "Phoenissae."* London, 1911.

Treves, P. "Le *Fenicie* di Euripide." *Atene e Roma* (1930): 171–195.

Verrall, A. W. *Euripides the Rationalist*, pp. 231–261. Cambridge, 1895.

Webster, T. B. L. "Three Plays by Euripides." In *The Classical Tradition* by L. Wallach, pp. 83–97. Ithaca, 1966.

The Suppliant Women

Colord, C. "Notes on Euripides' *Supplices*." *Classical Quarterly*, n.s. 13 (1963): 178–187.

Conacher, D. J. "Religious and Ethical Attitudes in Euripides' *Suppliants*." *Transactions and Proceedings of the American Philological Association* 87 (1956): 8–26.

Erasmi, G. "The Suppliant Women of Euripides." Unpublished MS.

Fitton, J. W. "The *Suppliant Women* and the *Heracleidai* of Euripides." *Hermes* 89 (1961): 430–461.

Giles, P. "Political Allusions in the *Suppliants* of Euripides." *Classical Review* 4 (1890): 95–98.

Goossens, R. "Périclès et Thésée: A propos des *Suppliantes* d'Euripide." *Bulletin de l'Association Guillaume Budé* 35 (1932): 9–40.

Greenwood, L. H. G. *Aspects of Euripidean Tragedy*, pp. 92–120. Cambridge, 1953.

Hermann, G. *Euripides: "Supplices."* Leipzig, 1811.

Koster, W. J. W. "De Euripidis *Supplicibus*." *Mnemosyne*, 3rd ser. 10 (1942): 161–203.

Kuiper, G. "De Euripidis *Supplicibus*." *Mnemosyne*, n.s. 51 (1923): 102–128.

Longman, G. A. "Prof. Norwood and the *Supplices* of Euripides." *Durham University Journal* 21 (1959–1960): 29–32.

Nicklin, T. *Euripides: "The Suppliant Women."* Oxford, 1936.

Norwood, G. *Essays in Euripidean Tragedy*, pp. 112–181. Toronto, 1954.

Smith, W. D. "Dramatic Structure and Technique in Euripides' *Suppliants*." *Harvard Studies in Classical Philology* 62 (1957): 152–154.

———. "Expressive Form in Euripides' *Suppliants*." *Harvard Studies in Classical Philology* 71 (1966): 151–170.

Zuntz, G. "Ueber Euripides *Hiketiden*." *Museum Helveticum* 12 (1955): 20–34.

————. *The Political Plays of Euripides*. Manchester, 1955.

The Women of Troy

Hanson, J. O. de G. "Reconstruction of Euripides' Alexandros." *Hermes* 92 (1964): 171–181.

Havelock, E. A. "Watching the *Trojan Women*." In *Euripides* by E. Segal, pp. 115–127. Englewood Cliffs, 1968.

Murray, G. "The Trojan Trilogy of Euripides." *Melanges Glotz* 2 Paris (1932): 645–656.

Steiger, H. "Warum schrieb Euripides seine *Troerinnen?*" *Philologus* 59, n.f. 13 (1900): 363–366.

Tyrrell, R. Y. *The "Troades" of Euripides*. London, 1897.

Rhesus

Barlow, C. W. "Rhetorical Elements in the *Rhesus*." *Transactions and Proceedings of the American Philological Association* 72 (1941): xxvii.

Bates, W. N. "Notes on the *Rhesus*." *Transactions and Proceedings of the American Philological Association* 47 (1916): 5–11.

Bjork, G. "The Authenticity of *Rhesus*." *Eranos* 55 (1957): 7–17.

Elderkin, G. W. "Dolon's Disguise in the *Rhesus*." *Classical Philology* 30 (1935): 349–350.

Goossens, R. "La date du *Rhesos*." *Archaeologia Classica* 1 (1932): 93–134.

Grégoire, H. "L'Authenticité du *Rhesos* d'Euripide." *Archaeologia Classica* 2 (1933): 91–133.

Grégoire, H., and Goossens, R. "Sitalkes et Athènes dans le *Rhesos* d'Euripide." *Archaeologia Classica* 3 (1934): 431–446.

Keyes, C. W. "Apollo and Athena in the *Rhesus*." *Transactions and Proceedings of the American Philological Association* 59 (1928): xxviii.

Leaf, W. "Rhesus of Thrace." *Journal of the Hellenic Society* 35 (1915): 1ff.

Macurdy, G. "The Dawn Songs in *Rhesus* (527–556) and in the Parodos of *Phaethon*." *American Journal of Philology* 64 (1943): 408–416.

Mierow, H. E. "The Sophoclean Character of the *Rhesus*." *American Journal of Philology* 49 (1928): 375–378.

Nock, A. D. "The End of the *Rhesus*." *Classical Review* 40 (1926): 184–186.

————. "The *Rhesus*." *Classical Review* 44 (1930): 173–174.

Parry, H. "The Approach of Dawn in the *Rhesus.*" *Phoenix* 18 (1964): 283–293.

Pearson, A. C. "The *Rhesus.*" *Classical Quarterly* 20 (1926): 80–81.

Porter, W. H. *Euripides: "Rhesus."* 2nd ed. Cambridge, 1929.

———. "The Euripidean *Rhesus* in the Light of Recent Criticism." *Hermathena* 17 (1913): 348–380.

Richards. G. C. "The Problems of the *Rhesus.*" *Classical Quarterly* 10 (1916): 192–197.

Ridgeway, W. "Euripides in Macedon." *Classical Quarterly* 20 (1926): 1–19.

Ritchie, W. *The Authenticity of the "Rhesus" of Euripides.* Cambridge, 1964.

Rolfe, J. C. "The Tragedy of *Rhesus.*" *Harvard Studies in Classical Philology* 4 (1893): 61–97.

Steadman, S. H. "A Note on the *Rhesus.*" *Classical Review* 59 (1945): 6–8.

Strohm, H. "Beobachtungen zum *Rhesos.*" *Hermes* 87 (1959): 257–274.

INDEX